CARNAL KNOWLE

C000121704

How was the law used to control sex in Tudor England? And what were the differences between secular and religious practice? This major study reveals that – contrary to what historians have often supposed – in pre-Reformation England, both ecclesiastical and secular (especially urban) courts were already highly active in regulating sex. They not only enforced clerical celibacy and sought to combat prostitution but also restrained the pre- and extra-marital sexual activities of laypeople more generally. Initially destabilizing, the religious and institutional changes of 1530–60 eventually led to important new developments that tightened the regime further. There were striking innovations in the use of shaming punishments in provincial towns and experiments in the practice of public penance in the church courts, while Bridewell transformed the situation in London. Allowing the clergy to marry was a milestone of a different sort. Together these changes contributed to a marked shift in the moral climate by 1600.

MARTIN INGRAM is an Emeritus Fellow in History at Brasenose College, University of Oxford. His publications include *Church Courts, Sex and Marriage in England, 1570–1640* (1987) as well as numerous articles on sex and marriage, crime and the law, slander and defamation, scolding women, 'rough music' and related topics.

CAMBRIDGE STUDIES IN EARLY MODERN BRITISH HISTORY

Edited by

JOHN MORRILL, *Emeritus Professor of British and Irish History, University of Cambridge, and Fellow of Selwyn College*
ETHAN SHAGAN, *Professor of History, University of California, Berkeley*
ALEXANDRA SHEPARD, *Professor of Gender History, University of Glasgow*
ALEXANDRA WALSHAM, *Professor of Modern History, University of Cambridge, and Fellow of Trinity College*

This is a series of monographs and studies covering many aspects of the history of the British Isles between the late fifteenth century and the early eighteenth century. It includes the work of established scholars and pioneering work by a new generation of scholars. It includes both reviews and revisions of major topics and books which open up new historical terrain or which reveal startling new perspectives on familiar subjects. All the volumes set detailed research within broader perspectives, and the books are intended for the use of students as well as of their teachers.

For a list of titles in the series, go to www.cambridge.org/earlymodernbritishhistory.

CARNAL KNOWLEDGE

Regulating Sex in England, 1470–1600

MARTIN INGRAM

Brasenose College, University of Oxford

CAMBRIDGE
UNIVERSITY PRESS

CAMBRIDGE
UNIVERSITY PRESS

University Printing House, Cambridge CB2 8BS, United Kingdom

One Liberty Plaza, 20th Floor, New York, NY 10006, USA

477 Williamstown Road, Port Melbourne, VIC 3207, Australia

4843/24, 2nd Floor, Ansari Road, Daryaganj, Delhi – 110002, India

79 Anson Road, #06–04/06, Singapore 079906

Cambridge University Press is part of the University of Cambridge.

It furthers the University's mission by disseminating knowledge in the pursuit of education, learning and research at the highest international levels of excellence.

www.cambridge.org
Information on this title: www.cambridge.org/9781107179875
10.1017/9781316841150

© Martin Ingram 2017

First published 2017

Printed in the United Kingdom by Clays, St Ives plc

A catalogue record for this publication is available from the British Library.

ISBN 978-1-107-17987-5 Hardback
ISBN 978-1-316-63173-7 Paperback

For Keith Thomas

Contents

Tables

Maps

Preface

This book is in many ways a companion to my *Church Courts, Sex and Marriage in England, 1570–1640* (Cambridge, 1987). When I wrote that work, the prevailing orthodoxy among early modern English historians was that the legal regulation of sexual transgressors was essentially a post-Reformation phenomenon. I already knew enough about earlier periods to dissent from this view, as did others, such as Marjorie McIntosh and the late Margaret Spufford, around that time. But a detailed study was lacking, and I decided to fill the gap. Since then, others have published much that bears on the issue – their contributions are gratefully acknowledged throughout my text and footnotes – but I believe that this book is the first to examine the issues systematically and in depth, whether for England or for anywhere else in Western Europe. The time-scale, focusing on the late fifteenth and sixteenth centuries and spanning the period of the Reformation, has affinities with the approach of Marjorie McIntosh, as also with the work in the political sphere of my first Oxford tutor, the late Cliff Davies. It contrasts with the work of many later medievalists writing in this field, who characteristically draw examples from a long period from 1350 to 1500, and with that of early modern historians, whose detailed evidence often dates from the mid-sixteenth century or even later.

But the form and content of this book – examining the legal regulation of sexual behaviour over a lengthy time-span, paying attention not only to rural areas but also to urban centres including London, recognizing the great importance of jurisdictional issues and accepting that while the work of the church courts was important in this sphere, so also were the activities of city and borough tribunals and some other secular courts – owe most to Keith Thomas's 'The Puritans and Adultery: The Act of 1650 Reconsidered', which appeared in Donald Pennington and Keith Thomas (eds.), *Puritans and Revolutionaries: Essays in Seventeenth-Century History Presented to Christopher Hill* (Oxford, 1978). Indeed the present work may be considered a meditative expansion on a few characteristically penetrating paragraphs in that remarkably seminal article. Keith Thomas was the inspiration for my choosing to become a social historian in the first place and was the supervisor of my doctoral thesis. I owe him a great deal in very many ways, so this book is dedicated to him.

During the long period of the book's gestation, I have incurred many obligations. Some of the initial spadework for the project was funded by the Queen's University of Belfast in my last year there in 1988–9. During the 1990s, I was mostly otherwise engaged, and this particular project was hardly more than an aspiration. But work began in earnest in the winter of 2002–3, and since then, the bulk of the research has been generously funded by Brasenose College – endlessly supportive in many other ways too – supplemented by grants from the History Faculty of the University of Oxford. With regard to practicalities, I owe a special debt of thanks to the staff of the many archives and libraries that I have had occasion to use. Many of them have been quite extraordinarily helpful – not least in the closing stages as I rushed round checking references and chasing up elusive items. But closer to home I would especially like to thank Liz Kay, the librarian of Brasenose College, and her assistant, Lianne Smith.

I have carried out most of the research and all the analysis myself, but I must thank Ian Warren, who created for me a database of the bishop of London's visitation of the city in 1589; Eleanor Fox, who abstracted the Bridewell Hospital Register for 1600; and Jonathan Healey, who did similar work on material for the archdeaconry of Chichester in 1574. Individuals who have generously brought specific items of interest to my attention are mentioned in the references. Shannon McSheffrey very kindly made available to me before publication the manuscript of her book, *Marriage, Sex, and Civic Culture in Late Medieval London* (Philadelphia, 2006). This not only gave me advance knowledge of her ideas but also helped me to shape my own research so as not to duplicate her work unduly. Generations of Oxford research students, particularly those attending the Early Modern Britain seminar, have also been helpful and stimulating, as have been my colleagues in Brasenose, in the History Faculty, in other Oxford faculties and indeed in many other universities. Some of them are particular experts in the field or closely related areas, and among those I must single out both for stimulating discussions and for many kindnesses Rowena Archer, Joanne Bailey, Caroline Barron, Eric Bramhall, Bernard Capp, Faramerz Dabhoiwala, Ellie Fox, Loreen Giese, Laura Gowing, Paul Griffiths, Ralph Houlbrooke, Tom Johnson, Satu Lidman, Marjorie McIntosh, Julia Merritt, Stuart Minson, Rebecca Probert, Jim Sharpe,

Tiffany Shumaker, Pieter Spierenburg, Mark Stoyle, Stephanie Tarbin, David Turner, Robert von Friedeburg, Tim Wales and Dinah Winch.

I have not yet mentioned people who have generously given of their valuable time to read the manuscript while it was in preparation and offer me critical feedback. Three of the Cambridge University Press series editors provided anonymous detailed comments on an unfinished draft, while a fourth did the same for the near-final version. Steve Gunn gave me invaluable advice and encouragement on the basis of an intermediate version. More recently, the book has been read by Ian Archer, Paul Cavill, Jonathan Healey, Paul Slack and Keith Thomas. Their comments have greatly improved the text and saved me from many errors. Any misconceptions, omissions and mistakes that remain are my own.

My personal friends and family have always been very supportive, but I will mention only one by name. My wife, Gill Ingram, is an endlessly creative psychodynamic counsellor who in a long, busy and still continuing career has touched many, many lives for the good. It is a great privilege to be married to such a person – especially as she is also a wonderful cook. My greatest debt is to her.

Conventions and Abbreviations

Many of the ecclesiastical and other court records used in this study are in Latin. Quotations from them are my own translations into modern English; occasionally, the Latin words are given if the terminology is of interest or the meaning is uncertain. English words and phrases embedded in Latin texts have been put into italic. Not least in order to differentiate them from the translations, quotations from materials in English and the titles of printed books follow contemporary spelling – but a completely faithful transcription would be extremely cumbersome, even if feasible, so I have tried to strike a balance between readability and scholarly accuracy. Thus *i*/*j* and *u*/*v* have been regularized according to modern usage (except that *j* has been retained in roman numerals), obsolete letter forms (including *y* for *th*) have been replaced by modern equivalents, standard contractions and abbreviations (including '&' for 'and' or 'et') have been silently extended, while missing characters (whether lost by damage, omitted by the scribe in error, or required for clarity of meaning) have been supplied in square brackets. Minor duplications have been ignored, and contemporary corrections and interpolations are noted as such only if they appear to be of some significance. Arbitrary word divisions have mostly been regularized according to modern usage (e.g. 'avoyde' for 'a voyde' and 'together' for 'to gether'). Except within quotations, forenames have been standardized in conformity with modern usage; variant spellings of surnames have been ignored. No attempt has been made to reproduce contemporary punctuation and capitalization, which are erratic at best. Following established usage, the 'Journals' and 'Repertories' of (respectively) the Court of Common Council and the Court of Aldermen of the City of London are cited simply by volume number. Full archival references for these and other manuscript sources are given in the Bibliography. Some of the manuscripts consulted have been foliated more than once. In citing them, modern archival foliation numbers have generally been preferred, but in certain cases, dual foliation numbers – e.g. fo. 394(400)v – have been supplied.

Readers should be aware that it is sometimes difficult to trace folio or page numbers when the original manuscripts are available to researchers only as microfilms or imperfect copies. Dates are Old Style, but the year is taken to begin on 1 January.

BCB	Bridewell Hospital Court Book
BL	British Library, Department of Manuscripts
BR	Borough Records
d.	old penny (12 old pence = 1 shilling)
DHC	Devon Heritage Centre, Exeter
LA	Lincolnshire Archives, Lincoln
LMA	London Metropolitan Archives, Clerkenwell
m., mm.	membrane, membranes
NA	Nottinghamshire Archives, Nottingham
ODNB	*Oxford Dictionary of National Biography*, online version
RO	Record Office
ROLLR	Record Office for Leicestershire, Leicester and Rutland, Leicester
s.	shilling(s) (20 shillings = £1)
TNA	The National Archives, Kew
WAC	Westminster Archives Centre
WAM	Westminster Abbey Muniments
WSA	Wiltshire and Swindon Archives, Chippenham
WSRO	West Sussex Record Office, Chichester

Prologue

In August 1556, the borough court of Devizes (Wiltshire) heard a case of adultery leading to assault. Apart from the actual content, the vivid and informal nature of the record itself, including an element of irony, is very striking. Firstly, a marginal entry announced 'Alyce Stephens punished for adultrie her husband takyng her with the maner [that is, in the act] in hys kychyn upon a hepe of strawe'. Then the main account followed:

> At thys court Robert Stephens and Alyce hys wyff were examyned upon the cryme of adultery … The foreseyd Robert wente to Rangebornes mylne with hys gryste, and when he came home he was shut out att hys wyket, and he called very lowde and in a fume broke up the seyd wyket and went in and founde John [*blank*] hys jurneyman upon hys wyfe in hys kychyn, and [in] a sodeyne fume to[ok] a theshold and furiously ranne at the seyde John. Then John ranne into the entrye with hys hosen hangynge about hys legges and the seyde Robert gave hym suche strokes that he defyled the place and then gett out into the streat and ranne awey holdyng hys hosen up with hys handes, his neyghbowres marveylyng at that sodayne aventure, and so went into the grene. But after he had hys rayment conveyed to hym owt of the seyde Robertes howse but how the seyde Robert seyethe that he knowethe not.

The fact that Stephens would not explain how his journeyman had managed to secure the clothes left behind 'at such an honest departyng' raised the suspicions of the court, whereupon the mayor and burgesses concluded 'that for the punishement of the seyde adultery, and for the example of others, the seyde Robert and Alys hys wyfe should sytt in the open stockes all that whole day and to avoyde the towne within xx[ti] dayes then next foloeng.'[1]

To take another case, in 1567, the churchwardens of the country parish of Thurmaston in Leicestershire reported a certain Joan Squire

[1] WSA, G20/1/10, fo. 5r–v.

I

to have comitted adulterye with Harrolde Byddel of Onelyppe [Wanlip]
beinge taken suspyciouslye with the said Johanne in the howse of William
Squyre her husband not koninge thereof and when the said Harrolde harde
the cunstable knocke at the dore he ranne and hyd hymselfe behynd
a chymnye in the kytchen and theire was he taken by Richard Peper
churchewarden, Thomas Ducket, Thomas Kylbane cunstable, John
Raynoldes, Thomas Jenkynson, William the weaver, Christofer Alsope
and William Parker, and he left behynde hym in her parlure his dagger
and gerdell and his shoes and this was done when the said Johanne dyd lye in
chyldebed.[2]

This book is about attempts to regulate sexual behaviour and to punish
what was conceived to be misconduct by legal procedures in courts of law.
Its focus is on England, especially the south, from the late fifteenth to the
late sixteenth century – corresponding to the rule of the Yorkist and Tudor
monarchs and spanning periods before, during and after the Reformation.
The cases just quoted have not been chosen for their typicality but rather
as pointers to the problematic nature of this subject and a reminder of how
much remains to be understood. The second case is actually the more
representative in being taken from the records of the church courts. These
were institutions so closely associated with prosecuting sexual misdeeds in
this period that colloquially they went by the name of 'bawdy courts' or
'bum courts'. But it will be noticed that in this particular case the church-
warden – an elected church officer charged with reporting offences to the
authorities – and ordinary parishioners were assisted by the village constable, an officer acting in the name of the queen. As will be seen, secular
tribunals of various kinds, ranging from tiny borough courts and the
meetings of local justices to King's Bench, the most exalted common-law
court in the land, had an important part to play in sexual regulation.

Most historians would locate the high noon of legal restrictions on
sexual behaviour in the so-called puritan reformation of manners of the
late sixteenth and early seventeenth centuries, or in the short-lived
Commonwealth experiment that in 1650 made adultery a felony punishable by death. Yet, as this book will show, the century before 1570 was also
of crucial importance. When Edward IV and Henry VII were on the
throne, the courts were already policing a wide range of sexual transgressions on the basis of long-established ideas of 'reformation of manners'.
If these efforts to change behaviour were a shade less draconian than some
of those that followed, they were in their own terms serious, their effects by

[2] ROLLR, 1 D 41/13/4, loose paper.

no means negligible and overall represented a firm basis for later developments. The ideas and events of the Reformation, halting and complex though the process was, inevitably brought changes that by no means worked consistently in one direction. Some were institutionally disruptive and legally restrictive; they undermined the church courts (at least in the short term) and made the participation of secular courts in this area of 'reformation of manners' more difficult. However, the Protestants who gained the ascendant in the reign of Edward VI, and their Elizabethan successors, presented themselves as fierce opponents of sexual transgression and, indeed, proved remarkably successful in appropriating the rhetoric of moral reform. They were responsible for some remarkable innovations in what they saw as a war on sexual sin. Overall, in line with broader trends in penal practice, there was a tendency to ratchet up the severity of punishments. Whether because the system worked or as a result of wider social and cultural changes, shifts in the pattern of people's actual behaviour are visible by the end of the period.

The cases of Robert and Alice Stephens and of Joan Squire and Harold Byddel point to some of the complexities of motive and morality that underlay legal action at the grass roots. It may come as no surprise that the cases are inscribed, in the first instance, as ones of female transgression, though there is little indication of the women's motives or agency. Yet, as the fate of Byddel suggests, men were also the target of prosecution – indeed, in many cases, the prime target. This was a society in which a double standard of sexual morality was not absolute but a matter of degree. The fact that these illustrative cases featured adultery is also significant. To be sure, there were many prosecutions of men and women who, at the time of the alleged transgression, had no marital ties. But, as will be seen, married people did feature very prominently during much of the period that is the focus of this book. It was only in the late sixteenth century that single people became the main target of prosecutions. Some cases of sexual transgression between unmarried people were complicated by the fact of illicit pregnancy, which, it may be surmised, gave added urgency to (even if it was not the sole motive for) prosecution. But, while this was the characteristic motive for action by the early seventeenth century, this was by no means true in the century before 1570.

Both quotations illustrate how deeply prosecutions were embedded in local social relations, to the extent that informal, unofficial action by ordinary people, whether spouses, other family members, friends or neighbours, guild members or the like, supplemented or supplanted legal processes. This interpenetration of the official and unofficial, formal and informal, is very characteristic of all legal proceedings in the period and raises important questions. Was this a 'top down' pattern of sexual regulation, by which the authorities sought to impose standards of behaviour on a more or less unwilling populace? Or was it rather a 'bottom up' enterprise, whereby ordinary people looked to the courts to support local surveillance? No doubt it was both, but the balance between the two varied from time to time, place to place, and court to court. In so far as the impetus came from below, was the aim to impose condign punishment on notorious transgressors; to help to resolve disputes between neighbours or marital conflicts and restore local harmony; to enable one section of local society to control another (a village elite as against the poor, for example, or the older generation facing what they saw as disorderly youth); or perhaps to exploit the courts to pursue personal enmities? Again, all these elements can be found, but the pattern varied from place to place and time to time.

At least superficially, informal activity seems to amount to a kind of neighbourhood watch. Yet the behaviour of Robert Stephens and what happened to him defy such simple interpretation. He appears first in the guise of a punisher of sexual transgression, if an intemperate one, but the fact that the adulterer somehow got his clothes back eventually brought the husband under suspicion for having connived at his wife's adultery. The upshot is that both husband and wife were 'set by the heels' in the stocks and so exposed to public shame and abuse. More drastically, they were given summary notice to quit the town. But what of journeyman John, who seems to have escaped formal censure? Most probably, having pulled up his hose and retrieved his other garments, he had already made a strategic withdrawal. It is not clear whether, amid the rain of blows from the outraged husband, he had 'defiled the place' by vomiting, wetting himself or suffering some more substantial personal accident. Contemporary usage of the word 'defile' suggests the worst, in which case he was probably so much a laughing stock that further censure was hardly necessary.

In exploring these and other complexities, successive chapters will constantly return to the houses, streets and market squares of numerous villages and small towns, as well as visiting such larger, more crowded and imposing places as London and Westminster. But the subject is by no means of merely parochial or antiquarian significance. At the outset, therefore, it is important to establish contexts and offer some wider perspectives.

CHAPTER I

Contexts and Perspectives

All societies regulate sexual behaviour and sexual expression, though how they do so, and to what degree, varies enormously. The reasons are not far to seek. Sex is a powerful human instinct, and its expression is intimately bound up with personal and social identity. The fruit of sexual congress is not only essential for the reproduction of society but also closely linked, often via the transmission of property and power, with the aspirations of families and individuals. At the same time, many religions embody some form of sexual proscription. Regulation of this area of human life is therefore an essential skein in the tangled web of social discipline.

Much of this regulation is implicit, fashioned from an early age by socially conditioned feelings of shame and embarrassment that channel expectations, shape emotions and restrain behaviour. These deeply engrained ideas and beliefs are closely associated with gender roles that constrain, if they do not dictate, socially determined patterns of 'appropriate' conduct and sentiment for boys and girls as they grow into men and women. Historians nowadays accept that sexuality cannot be understood in essentialist terms; it is to a great extent culturally and socially constructed. Yet, in most societies, sexual identities are shaped in such a way that they seem to the inhabitants 'natural' and 'decent', while alternatives appear disgusting or unnatural, if not actually unthinkable. But there are tensions inherent in these cultural constructs, revealed by the embarrassed laughter, sometimes escalating into hostile derision, which is often released by sexual 'matter out of place'. At a lighter level of human interaction, the relish that many societies display – especially in relatively uninhibited situations such as relaxed, same-sex gatherings of people who know each other well – for bawdy stories, dirty jokes and salacious gossip demonstrates the perennial power of sexual instincts, the difficulty, if not impossibility, of keeping them in rein – even supposing that it is desirable to do so – and the capacity of the human mind to find creative displacements.

5

Although any society's inherent ideas about male and female, right and wrong, natural and unnatural, decent and indecent exert a powerful force, they are invariably complemented by institutions and social arrangements that in more overt ways constrain liberty of action. Some, such as conventional restrictions on dress, personal movement and the freedom of the sexes to meet and interact, themselves may appear part of the natural order of things, the unspoken assumptions of the society, though today's debates about the hijab, niqab and burqa show how easily such matters, far from being taken for granted, may become politicized. Others may be more palpable demonstrations of social power and hence more open to questioning, negotiation or challenge. The role of families or of particular family members, such as a right claimed by fathers to arrange the marriages of sons or daughters and, more fundamentally, to restrain their sexual activities, is particularly important. But the range of kin or affines who may be involved in such matters and the nature and scope of family intervention vary greatly. In many societies the wider community of friends, neighbours and more distant connections also has a role to play in sexual regulation, though usually one which is ill-defined and subject to contest. Other social entities, from trade associations such as guilds to the youth groups that exist in some cultures, may also play a part.

Global Perspectives

Much of this is commonplace and either easily related to our own everyday experience or common knowledge. But using the law to regulate sexual behaviour and punish misconduct is a more arresting phenomenon. In present-day Britain we are familiar with the panoply of institutions – from the former Child Support Agency to the Family Division of the High Court – that deal with the divorces that are such a remarkable feature of contemporary Western society and the financial and other issues associated with them. It is also a familiar fact that some sexual acts are subject to the criminal law, but only those which the legislature reckons to be outside the extreme limits of acceptable behaviour – in England comprising rape (only quite recently extended to include marital rape), underage sex (including child sexual abuse) and certain forms of incest. Far more contentiously, until the 1960s, same-sex activities between men were also criminalized. But other forms of sexual behaviour, unless conducted in public places, have long been regarded as private matters and not subject to legal regulation, far less criminal sanctions. Thus, the Street Offences Committee that reported in 1928 took for granted that the English common law 'has never taken upon itself the prohibition by criminal sanctions of voluntary illicit intercourse between the sexes'.[1] Yet, not all societies and legal systems are like this, Islam offering the most famous contrast. Shari'a law, a set of traditions based on the Quran, prescribes that sexual intercourse between unmarried persons is punishable by flogging, while adultery renders the guilty person liable to death by stoning. Less well known is the fact that over many centuries the Chinese imperial codes identified illicit sexual relations as a public crime and prescribed draconian punishments.[2]

In fact, there have been numerous societies, from ancient times to the present, in which sexual misconduct has been subject to criminal sanctions. Yet, the subject has not attracted as much attention as one might suppose. The concentration of sociologists on Western industrialized societies has meant that the legal regulation of ordinary consensual sexual relations has not much presented itself as an object of study, except with regard to prostitution. Sexual regulation was of some interest to the social anthropologists of the early and mid-twentieth century but rarely top of their agendas unless in relation to the study of incest. In any case, the kinds of small-scale societies they tended to study, in which legal proceedings were usually unwritten and barely distinguishable from communal action, did not usually lend themselves to much emphasis on legal codes and legal institutions. Lawyers have a more fundamental interest in the subject, not least as a result of recurrent efforts to redefine, or justify the limits of, legal intrusion into personal life.[3] This is true not only in the West. For example, Islamic fundamentalism and the problems of applying Shari'a law in societies such as modern Pakistan and Nigeria have raised urgent issues and hence stimulated some important empirical, as well as theoretical, research.[4]

Among historians, one major area of interest has been ancient Greece and Rome, the latter being of particular significance because Roman law was to have such a major influence in medieval and modern Europe. The problem faced by ancient historians, however, is the paucity or at least fragmentary nature of the sources. While high-quality work has been

---

[1] Quoted in Jeffrey Weeks, *Sex, Politics and Society: The Regulation of Sexuality since 1800*, 3rd edn. (Harlow, 2012), p. 277.

[2] Joseph Schacht, *An Introduction to Islamic Law* (Oxford, 1964), pp. 175, 178; Majid Khadduri (ed.), *Islamic Jurisprudence: Shāfi'ī's Risāla* (Baltimore, 1961), pp. 105, 137; Geoffrey MacCormack, *Traditional Chinese Penal Law* (Edinburgh, 1990), p. 202; William C. Jones with Tianquan Cheng and Yongling Jiang (trans.), *The Great Qing Code* (Oxford, 1994), p. 347.

[3] A classic study is Patrick Devlin, *The Enforcement of Morals* (London, 1965).

[4] Noel J. Coulson, *A History of Islamic Law* (Edinburgh, 1964), pp. 156–8; S. H. Amin, *Islamic Law in the Contemporary World* (Glasgow and Tehran, 1985), chap. 2.

done on, for example, the Athenian adultery laws and Roman prostitution, the actual impact of the law on ordinary people's sexual lives on an everyday basis is little understood.[5] Only for later periods and for certain locations is it possible to study sexual regulation not only from law codes and legal commentaries but also on the basis of detailed examination of records of actual court proceedings and with a sound knowledge of the cultural and social contexts in which those proceedings occurred. By no means are all of these confined to Europe and Europeanized America; areas such as Ottoman Syria and Palestine and early Qing China have also been the subject of detailed studies.[6]

Late Medieval and Early Modern Europe

But it is Europe from the late fifteenth century to the early eighteenth century that has seen the greatest concentration of recent historical work on sexual regulation and related topics such as marriage formation and divorce. This is so for a number of reasons. Late medieval and early modern Europe was one area – perhaps it will eventually emerge, the pre-eminent location – where systematic attempts were made to regulate sexual and other forms of personal behaviour by legal means. The precise arrangements varied considerably from region to region. The late medieval church and its successor churches in Catholic and Protestant areas after the upheaval of the Reformation played an important part, as also did a multitude of municipal and state courts. Moreover, many of these courts and analogous institutions kept more or less detailed records, some of which have survived – often in bulk. Further, the major developments of the period reinforced contemporary interest in, and debate about, moral (including sexual) regulation and among modern historians have generated a multitude of theories and controversies, including some broad conceptualizations of political, social and cultural change under such labels as 'the civilizing process', 'the reform of popular culture' and 'social disciplining'.

[5] David Cohen, *Law, Sexuality, and Society: The Enforcement of Morals in Classical Athens* (Cambridge, 1991); Catharine Edwards, *The Politics of Immorality in Ancient Rome* (Cambridge, 1993); Rebecca Flemming, '*Quae corpore quaestum facit*: The Sexual Economy of Female Prostitution in the Roman Empire', *Journal of Roman Studies*, 89 (1999), 38–61; Rebecca Langlands, *Sexual Morality in Ancient Rome* (Cambridge, 2006); Sara Forsdyke, 'Street Theatre and Popular Justice in Ancient Greece: Shaming, Stoning and Starving Offenders Inside and Outside the Courts', *Past and Present*, 201 (November 2008), 3–50.
[6] Judith E. Tucker, *In the House of the Law: Gender and Islamic Law in Ottoman Syria and Palestine* (Berkeley, CA, 1998); Matthew H. Sommer, *Sex, Law and Society in Late Imperial China* (Stanford, CA, 2000).

The dominant line of argument sees the Reformation as a watershed. It takes as axiomatic, often on the basis of limited evidence, that around 1500 the church courts were virtually moribund as agents of sexual regulation and that other tribunals were likewise of limited efficacy. The shock of Reformation changes stimulated the overhaul of old procedures and the search for new arrangements. More basically, the reformers rejected the ideal of celibacy, except in special cases, and jettisoned the idea that matrimony was a sacrament while at the same time exalting marriage, household and family as a set of institutions blessed by God and fundamental to church and commonwealth – a set of changes that inevitably stimulated a reappraisal of many aspects of the inherited pattern of sexual regulation. These new initiatives, already a feature of the Lutheran and Zwinglian churches, became in the developing Calvinist tradition part of a broader project of 'reformation of life' (*reformatio vitae*) to complement the *reformatio doctrinae* of the early Reformation. Among other things the period witnessed, in many areas that became Protestant, a rejection of ideas and institutions conducive to prostitution, redefinitions of the law of divorce and stronger measures against adultery and, indeed, any sexual activity outside marriage. These developments were accompanied by important institutional changes. In many Protestant cities and principalities, the existing church courts were drastically remodelled or replaced by new 'marriage courts', 'discipline lords' and the like; often, in the process, the boundaries between the secular and spiritual authorities were redrawn.[7] The Counter-Reformation Catholic church responded by reviving, revising or simply reinforcing its own disciplinary institutions, which in southern Europe included varieties of Inquisition court. More broadly, the religious and political culture shifted in ways that greatly tightened sexual

---

[7] E. William Monter, *Enforcing Morality in Early Modern Europe* (London, 1987), chaps. 2 and 3; Lyndal Roper, *The Holy Household: Women and Morals in Reformation Augsburg* (Oxford, 1989); Heinz Schilling, *Civic Calvinism in Northwestern Germany and the Netherlands: Sixteenth to Nineteenth Centuries* (Kirksville, MO, 1991), chap. 2; Raymond A. Mentzer (ed.), *Sin and the Calvinists: Morals Control and the Consistory in the Reformed Tradition* (Kirksville, MO, 1994); Robert M. Kingdon, *Adultery and Divorce in Calvin's Geneva* (Cambridge, MA, and London, 1995); Heinrich R. Schmidt, *Dorf und Religion: Reformierte Sittenzucht in Berner Landgemeinden der Frühen Neuzeit* (Stuttgart, 1995); Margo Todd, *The Culture of Protestantism in Early Modern Scotland* (New Haven and London, 2002); Graeme Murdock, *Beyond Calvin: The Intellectual, Political and Cultural World of Europe's Reformed Churches, c.1540–1620* (Basingstoke, 2004), chap. 4; Terence McIntosh, 'Confessionalization and the Campaign against Prenuptial Coitus in Sixteenth-Century Germany', in John M. Headley, Hans J. Hillerbrand and Anthony J. Papalas (eds.), *Confessionalization in Europe, 1555–1700: Essays in Honour and Memory of Bodo Nischan* (Aldershot, 2004), pp. 155–74; but cf. Joel F. Harrington, *Reordering Marriage and Society in Reformation Germany* (Cambridge, 1995), chap. 3, which stresses complexities and continuities.

regulation in Catholic states and regions as diverse as Bavaria, France and Catalonia.[8]

Work on sexual regulation in post-Reformation Europe is now extensive and often of high quality. However, it does have its limitations. Its relation to broader themes of social and moral discipline and of religious and cultural change mean that in many cases the specifically sexual aspects of the subject are not treated in much depth and detail. Often marriage and divorce are the real centre of interest.[9] Moreover, many studies focus on a particular court or tribunal, to the relative neglect of other agencies that may have shared jurisdiction or otherwise had an impact on similar areas of people's lives. As a research strategy, this is understandable, especially when records are analysed over lengthy periods to reveal not just short-term fluctuations but also long-term trends, with a view to charting major social, religious or other cultural changes. In any case, the records of complementary jurisdictions often do not survive. But the dangers are obvious, in particular, the likelihood of underestimating the intensity of regulation and the possibility of receiving a distorted picture of major patterns.[10]

Another limitation of this corpus of work on continental Europe is its chronological scope and, in particular, the fact that the period before the Reformation remains relatively neglected. There have been interesting studies of late medieval prostitution, emphasizing public tolerance to the extent that in some areas municipally licensed brothels were allowed to trade. This fact is sometimes used to underpin the notion of a Reformation watershed, a marked increase in the scope and intensity of sexual regulation from the mid-sixteenth century, a model that derives added plausibility from the fact that in the generations following the Reformation, a wider

---

[8] E.g. Henry Kamen, *Inquisition and Society in Spain in the Sixteenth and Seventeenth Centuries* (London, 1985); Henry Kamen, *The Phoenix and the Flame: Catalonia and the Counter Reformation* (New Haven and London, 1993), esp. chap. 6; Stephen Haliczer (ed.), *Inquisition and Society in Early Modern Europe* (London, 1987); Stephen Haliczer, *Inquisition and Society in the Kingdom of Valencia, 1478–1834* (Berkeley, CA, 1990); James R. Farr, *Authority and Sexuality in Early Modern Burgundy (1550–1730)* (Oxford and New York, 1995); Ulrike Strasser, *State of Virginity: Gender, Religion and Politics in an Early Modern Catholic State* (Ann Arbor, MI, 2004); Satu Lidman, *Zum Spektakel und Abscheu. Schand- und Ehrenstrafen als Mittel öffentlicher Disziplinierung in München um 1600* (Frankfurt am Main, 2008).

[9] Thomas Max Safley, *Let No Man Put Asunder. The Control of Marriage in the German Southwest: A Comparative Study, 1550–1600* (Kirksville, MO, 1984); Jeffrey R. Watt, *The Making of Modern Marriage: Matrimonial Control and the Rise of Sentiment in Neuchâtel, 1550–1800* (Ithaca and London, 1992). This is not, of course, to criticize the actual content of these studies.

[10] Martin Ingram, 'History of Sin or History of Crime? The Regulation of Personal Morality in England, 1450–1750', in Heinz Schilling (ed.), *Institutionen, Instrumente und Akteure sozialer Kontrolle und Disziplinierung im frühneuzeitlichen Europa: Institutions, Instruments and Agents of Social Control and Discipline in Early Modern Europe* (Frankfurt am Main, 1999), pp. 94–5.

range of behaviour – from tippling and drunkenness to mixed dancing – was deemed to be morally transgressive and subjected to discipline, while all over Europe Catholic and Protestant authorities alike made great efforts to improve the quality of the clergy and to instil higher standards of religious belief, knowledge and commitment among the lay population.[11]

However, it is also widely recognized that already in the later fifteenth century many cities and states in Europe were issuing ordinances or taking other action to restrain sexual behaviour more firmly. Depending on emphasis, this trend may be presented either as the precursor of the major shift associated with the Reformation or in support of an alternative model that sees post-Reformation moral discipline merely as an intensification (even in some respects simply a continuation) of already well-established patterns of public policy.[12] Either interpretation is consistent with the fact that, to judge by recent research, in some areas ecclesiastical courts were more active and effective in the fifteenth century than has often been supposed.[13] But, in any event, it is only for a few areas that sexual regulation in its entirety has been studied in detail. Among other reasons for this lack is a paucity of records, so many having disappeared either through the lapse of time or as a result of deliberate destruction in Protestant areas of pre-Reformation church records. Given that many of the arguments about post-Reformation changes assume knowledge of what

---

[11] Leah Lydia Otis, *Prostitution in Medieval Society: The History of an Urban Institution in Languedoc* (Chicago, 1985); Jacques Rossiaud, *Medieval Prostitution*, trans. Lydia G. Cochrane (Oxford, 1988); Roper, *Holy Household*, esp. chap. 3; Beate Schuster, *Die unendlichen Frauen: Prostitution und städtische Ordnung in Konstanz in 15. und 16. Jahrhundert* (Constance, 1996); Kathryn Norberg, 'Prostitutes', in Natalie Zemon Davis and Arlette Farge (eds.), *A History of Women in the West*, Vol. III: *Renaissance and Enlightenment Paradoxes* (Cambridge, MA and London, 1993), pp. 458–74, 540.

[12] James A. Brundage, *Law, Sex and Christian Society in Medieval Europe* (Chicago and London, 1987), chap. 10; Nick Davidson, 'Theology, Nature and the Law: Sexual Sin and Sexual Crime in Italy from the Fourteenth to the Seventeenth Century', in Trevor Dean and K. J. P. Lowe (eds.), *Crime, Society and the Law in Renaissance Italy* (Cambridge, 1994), pp. 74–98; Merry E. Wiesner-Hanks, *Christianity and Sexuality in the Early Modern World: Regulating Desire, Reforming Practice* (London and New York, 2000); Susanna Burghartz, 'Ordering Discourse and Society: Moral Politics, Marriage, and Fornication during the Reformation and the Confessionalization Process in Germany and Switzerland', in Herman Roodenburg and Pieter Spierenburg (eds.), *Social Control in Europe*, Vol. I: *1500–1800* (Columbus, OH, 2004), pp. 78–98.

[13] Thomas D. Albert, *Der gemeine Mann vor dem geistlichen Richter: Kirchliche Rechtsprechung in den Diözesen Basel, Chur und Konstanz vor der Reformation* (Stuttgart, 1998); Sara McDougall, 'The Prosecution of Sex in Late Medieval Troyes', in Albrecht Classen (ed.), *Sexuality in the Middle Ages and the Early Modern Times: New Approaches to a Fundamental Cultural-Historical and Literary-Anthropological Theme* (Berlin, 2008), pp. 691–713; Ruth Mazo Karras, 'The Regulation of Sexuality in the Late Middle Ages: England and France', *Speculum*, 86 (2011), 1010–39; Véronique Beaulande-Barraud and Martine Charageat (eds.), *Les Officialités dans l'Europe médiévale et moderne. Des tribunaux pour une société chrétienne* (Turnhout, 2014).

went before, the lacuna is a severe handicap to understanding what happened before and after the Reformation watershed.

Reformation of Manners in Yorkist, Tudor and Stuart England

Enough work has already been done to locate the English experience firmly in this wider European context. Indeed, for the period after about 1570, England is among the best-studied areas from this point of view.[14] Some of this work relates directly to changes in marriage law and to the operation of the ecclesiastical and secular courts and will be referred to extensively in following chapters. The broader theme that has most relevance to English society is captured in the phrase 'reformation of manners', a contemporary concept that has been appropriated by modern historians and may usefully be explored here to set the scene for what follows. In Tudor and Stuart England, the term 'manners' was ambiguous. It could carry its modern sense of polite behaviour and deportment. But its more usual meaning approximated more closely to what we would call 'morals', albeit with the emphasis on externals of behaviour rather than on an inward state of mind. In brief, it was the stock translation of the Latin word *mores*. Discourse often centred on 'ill', 'evil' or 'corrupt' manners, but this was balanced by a strong ideal sense of 'good' or 'sound' manners which were thought to be fundamental to a well-ordered society. The word 'reformation', further- more, did not in this period necessarily bear the associations with religious upheaval that it does today. Rather it meant 'improvement' or 'reform', whether a major overhaul or a relatively minor correction or amendment. The word did, however, connote decisive action, as like as not by legal means. So 'reformation of manners' could embrace both routine regulation and more radical efforts, often taking the form of 'drives' or campaigns, to alter people's behaviour.

   Writers on the subject of 'reformation of manners' sometimes had in mind an educational setting and the behaviour of children and adolescents. In this context, fathers and mothers, schoolmasters and tutors, masters and mistresses were the agents of discipline. In the wider world and among adults, the task of correction lay with the public authorities. They had the duty not only to pass and enforce sound laws to inculcate good 'manners' but also to repress bad behaviour. Sometimes such ill 'manners' were conceived in terms of the organic and medical imagery of disease and hence seen as 'infirmities', 'imposthumes' and 'ulcers' that required 'salves',

---

[14] For periods later than those reviewed here, see Weeks, *Sex, Politics and Society.*

'remedies' or (sometimes sharp) 'medicine', lest they spread their deadly corruption. Alternatively – sometimes in conjunction with the medicinal metaphors – they were thought of more legalistically and expressed in a series of overlapping concepts: 'faults', 'sins', 'vices', 'crimes' and 'enormities', the repression and punishment of which lay with the public authorities or, in default of effective action on their part, with God.[15]

The public regulation of morals (including sexual behaviour) through legal institutions, which could administer condign punishment, was thus crucial to the idea of 'reformation of manners'. By the end of the middle ages, this framework was well established. The church's jurisdiction over 'religion and manners' had been a reality at the grassroots level at least from the thirteenth century.[16] Sin was primarily a matter between the individual and God, and in pre-Reformation times (and even afterwards to some extent), hidden sins were dealt with in the secrecy of the confessional. But when offences became a matter of scandal and an affront to the Christian community, they were punishable in the 'external forum' of the spiritual courts. These were supposed to operate both *pro salute animæ* and *pro correctione* (or *reformatione*) *morum* – for the health of the soul and for the reformation of manners.

These courts, and the corpus of 'canon' – that is, ecclesiastical – law that governed their activities, had developed in the high middle ages. Patchily surviving records show that in some areas they were already in vigorous operation in the fourteenth century.[17] By the late fifteenth century – from

---

[15] Martin Ingram, 'Reformation of Manners in Early Modern England', in Paul Griffiths, Adam Fox and Steve Hindle (eds.), *The Experience of Authority in Early Modern England* (Basingstoke, 1996), pp. 47–88; on the broader rhetorical context, see Benjamin Thompson, 'The Polemic of Reform in the Later Medieval English Church', in Almut Suerbaum, George Southcombe and Benjamin Thompson (eds.), *Polemic: Language as Violence in Medieval and Early Modern Discourse* (Farnham, 2015), pp. 183–222.

[16] Ian Forrest, 'The Transformation of Visitation in Thirteenth-Century England', *Past and Present*, 221 (November 2013), 3–38.

[17] In the diocese of York, records of party-and-party suits survive from the late fourteenth century, though pre-Reformation disciplinary proceedings are less extensive; the material relating to sex and marriage has been studied by Frederik Pedersen, *Marriage Disputes in Medieval England* (London, 2000); P. J. P. Goldberg, *Women, Work, and Life Cycle in a Medieval Economy: Women in York and Yorkshire, c.1300–1520* (Oxford, 1992). There are other fourteenth- and early fifteenth-century survivals of matrimonial suits and disciplinary proceedings from Ely, Hereford, Rochester and elsewhere: full references may be found in M. M. Sheehan, 'The Formation and Stability of Marriage in Fourteenth-Century England: Evidence of an Ely Register', *Medieval Studies*, 33 (1971), 228–63; Andrew John Finch, 'Parental Authority and the Problem of Clandestine Marriage in the Later Middle Ages', *Law and History Review*, 8 (1990), 189–204; Andrew John Finch, '*Repulsa uxore sua:* Marital Difficulties and Separation in the Later Middle Ages', *Continuity and Change*, 8 (1993), 11–38; Andrew John Finch, 'Sexual Morality and Canon Law: The Evidence of the Rochester Consistory Court', *Journal of Medieval History*, 20 (1994), 261–75; L. R. Poos (ed.), *Lower*

which point more records begin to survive in more or less continuous series – the spiritual courts formed an omnipresent set of interlocking institutions that were comparable to the royal courts in complexity and probably exceeded them in the scale of their activities. Amid the huge amount of business they conducted, matters concerning marriage and sexual transgressions always loomed large.[18]

But the secular courts also were increasingly concerned with 'reformation of manners', and the theme is reflected in numerous royal proclamations and acts of parliament of the late fifteenth and sixteenth centuries. For William Lambarde, the Elizabethan author of one of the best-known handbooks for justices of the peace, 'corruption of manners' and 'amendment of manners' were key themes, to which he returned time and again in his charges to the juries at quarter sessions.[19] The antecedents of this rhetoric will be traced in later chapters. Suffice to say here that the Yorkist and early Tudor kings, as part of a process whereby the crown appropriated the rhetoric of 'reform' of the 'commonweal' or 'common wealth', took an increasing interest in 'reformation of manners'. Admittedly neither Lambarde nor earlier and later writers on the theme were concerned exclusively – or even primarily – with sexual behaviour. The 'manners' that required reformation included a wide range of what contemporary moralists and social commentators considered to be 'vices' and 'disorders', including concerns as apparently diverse as usury; excesses in apparel; playing cards, dice and other 'unlawful games'; vagabondage; 'picking' or petty theft and, increasingly, drunkenness, tippling and alehouse-haunting. Morally speaking, the main targets were the overlapping

---

Ecclesiastical Jurisdiction in Late-Medieval England: The Courts of the Dean and Chapter of Lincoln, 1336–1349, and the Deanery of Wisbech, 1458–1484 (British Academy Records of Social and Economic History, New Series 32, Oxford, 2001); Lindsay Bryan, 'Marriage and Morals in the Fourteenth Century: The Evidence of Bishop Hamo's Register', *English Historical Review*, 121 (2006), 467–86. Sara M. Butler, *Divorce in Medieval England: From One to Two Persons in Law* (New York and London, 2013), is distinctive in approaching this subject through the records of both ecclesiastical and secular courts. For matrimonial litigation at York and Ely compared with some continental jurisdictions, see Charles Donahue, Jr, *Law, Marriage, and Society in the Later Middle Ages: Arguments about Marriage in Five Courts* (Cambridge, 2007).

[18] R. H. Helmholz, *Roman Canon Law in Reformation England* (Cambridge, 1990), chap. 1; R. B. Outhwaite, *The Rise and Fall of the English Ecclesiastical Courts, 1500–1860* (Cambridge, 2006), chap. 1. For broader contexts, see DeLloyd J. Guth, 'Enforcing Late-Medieval Law: Patterns in Litigation during Henry VII's Reign', in J. H. Baker (ed.), *Legal Records and the Historian: Papers Presented to the Cambridge Legal History Conference, 7–10 July 1975, and in Lincoln's Inn Old Hall on 3 July 1974* (London, 1978), pp. 80–96; John A. F. Thomson, *The Early Tudor Church and Society, 1485–1529* (London, 1993); James A. Brundage, *Medieval Canon Law* (London and New York, 1995).

[19] Conyers Read (ed.), *William Lambarde and Local Government: His 'Ephemeris' and Twenty-Nine Charges to Juries and Commissions* (Ithaca, NY, 1962).

concepts of idleness, waste and excessive consumption. But sexual transgressions and the social ills to which they gave rise were a real target for concern, not least because they were often perceived as being closely related to the other species of disorder.

There were ambiguities, however. The main targets of some of these strictures were labourers, servants and apprentices; their activities were subject to the firmest regulation, while laws were often framed to protect in particular the property and interests of their masters and employers. More broadly, moral reform in the secular courts appears as part of a wider pattern of sumptuary regulation – rationing the good things of life.[20] But this was always understood in hierarchical terms – greater wealth and higher status bestowed the right to consume more goods and of higher quality. Manifestly this logic was at odds with Christian principles that made no distinction of rank in their demand for chastity. Inevitably, this complicated the framing and application of secular laws designed to regulate sex, as proceedings in parliament in the late sixteenth century and early seventeenth century were to demonstrate with particular clarity. However keen they were to decry the sins of the poor, noble and gentry legislators were markedly unwilling to contemplate harsh restrictions and swingeing punishments that might have an impact on their own behaviour and demean their status.[21]

Nonetheless, as succeeding chapters will reveal, secular judges were more active in the sphere of sexual regulation than has often been supposed. Marjorie McIntosh has demonstrated that the jurors and local office holders who assisted in the running of manorial courts leet and borough and city courts also had a part to play.[22] The relationship between the temporal and ecclesiastical courts is of double-sided significance. On the one hand, the two jurisdictions can be seen, especially in the period covered by this book, as in de facto alliance, operating together, albeit sometimes uneasily, as a powerful system of social discipline. These were the antecedents of what English Calvinists were later to prize as the mutual support of 'magistracy and ministry'. On the other hand, partly for reasons already stated, contest and conflict between the temporal and spiritual powers and among the various local and central courts in the secular sphere were also in

---

[20] Alan Hunt, *Governance of the Consuming Passions: A History of Sumptuary Law* (Basingstoke, 1996), esp. chaps. 11 and 12.

[21] Joan R. Kent, 'Attitudes of Members of the House of Commons to the Regulation of "Personal Conduct" in Late Elizabethan and Early Stuart England', *Bulletin of the Institute of Historical Research*, 46 (1973), 41–71.

[22] Marjorie Keniston McIntosh, *Controlling Misbehavior in England, 1370–1600* (Cambridge, 1998).

evidence. In the short run, such tensions made the ideal of 'magistracy and ministry' hard to achieve in the late sixteenth century. In the long run, they were to contribute to a process – recently subjected to penetrating scrutiny by Faramerz Dabhoiwala – by which the public regulation of sexual morality was increasingly contested in the seventeenth century and gradually decayed in the eighteenth.[23]

Historiographically, the theme of 'reformation of manners' was first investigated thoroughly with reference to the Societies for Reformation of Manners – voluntary associations that sprang up in the wake of the Glorious Revolution of 1689 to initiate large-scale prosecutions against prostitution and other forms of 'vice'.[24] But the idea had already received glancing attention in accounts of the moral activism of the 1650s, which Oliver Cromwell himself characterized as 'reformation of manners'.[25] From the 1970s onwards, some of the context and antecedents of these developments came to light as it emerged that in the seventy years or so before the civil wars, church courts, assizes, quarter sessions and city, borough and manor courts had mounted thousands of prosecutions to combat sexual transgressions along with such offences as running unlicensed alehouses, drunkenness and 'tippling', unlawful games, lax religious observances and a variety of other activities that contemporary officials saw as 'vice', 'sin' or 'disorder'.[26] More recent work is gradually establishing the pattern of regulation and moral activism in the fifteenth and early sixteenth centuries – but this has hitherto remained (as on the continent) a relatively neglected period and hence is the particular focus of this book.[27]

State Building and Sexual Regulation

The theme of 'reformation of manners', and within it the issue of sexual regulation, is of interest not only in itself but also for the light it sheds on

[23] Patrick Collinson, *The Religion of Protestants: The Church in English Society, 1559–1625* (Oxford, 1982), chap. 4; Faramerz Dabhoiwala, *The Origins of Sex: A History of the First Sexual Revolution* (London, 2012).

[24] The best introduction is still Dudley W. R. Bahlman, *The Moral Revolution of 1688* (New Haven and London, 1957). For a more recent contribution, with references to the extensive body of previous work, see Faramerz Dabhoiwala, 'Sex and Societies for Moral Reform, 1688–1800', *Journal of British Studies*, 46 (2007), 290–319.

[25] Samuel Rawson Gardiner, *History of the Commonwealth and Protectorate, 1649–1656*, 4 vols. (London, 1897–1903), Vol. III, chap. 42; Bernard Capp, *England's Culture Wars: Puritan Reformation and its Enemies in the Interregnum, 1649–1660* (Oxford, 2012).

[26] The findings of the earlier phases of this work are summarized in Keith Wrightson, *English Society, 1580–1680* (London, 1982), chap. 6.

[27] Ingram, 'Reformation of Manners', esp. pp. 57–64; McIntosh, *Controlling Misbehavior*.

broader developments. The extent to which sexual behaviour was subject to legal sanction; the courts that dealt with it, whether ecclesiastical or secular, royal or local; and the nature and severity of the penalties that they deployed are all matters that bear on the growth of the state in early modern England, itself a complex and contested field. While many of the arguments and assumptions that constituted Sir Geoffrey Elton's notion of a 'Tudor revolution in government' no longer pass muster, this phrase remains of use in capturing the idea of a bundle of important governmental initiatives that occurred in the reign of Henry VIII, the implications of which continued to be played out under his successors in the second half of the century and beyond. Among other things, the pretensions, if not the actual scope, of government were extended to cover an increasingly wide range of religious, social and economic issues, so royal power came to impinge far more directly on the lives of ordinary people. But, as some historians have long recognized, these developments did not come out of nowhere, and their antecedents must be sought in the late fifteenth century, if not earlier. As the recent work of John Watts indicates, this was an important period for the English monarchy, as an increasingly confident body of government officials, whose classical Latin studies imbued them with a strong sense of the pre-eminence due to princes, sought to give substance to a resurgent royal power through the effective exercise of legal and administrative authority. The development already noted – the appropriation of the rhetoric of reform and the association of the crown with 'reformation of manners' – is thus integral to and must be understood as an important element in the development of the Tudor state.[28]

The social and cultural significance of these changes was enhanced by the peculiar relationship between the machinery of English government and the wider social structure. Recent work, particularly that of Steve Hindle, has defined 'the state' to include not merely the crown itself, ministers and crown officers and the institutions of central government, but also local government in the counties, cities, boroughs and parishes of England and the army of minor officers – petty constables, churchwardens, overseers of the poor – who made these institutions work. These were 'ordinary people' in the sense that usually they served for short terms (chosen either on a rota basis or by local election), were unpaid and were

---

[28] John Watts, '"Common Weal" and "Commonwealth": England's Monarchical Republic in the Making, c.1450–c.1530', in Andrea Gamberini, Jean-Philippe Genet and Andrea Zorzi (eds.), *The Languages of Political Society: Western Europe, 14th–17th Centuries* (Rome, 2011), pp. 147–63.

not of particularly high social status. On this view, the English state may be seen as supported by a high degree of popular participation, perhaps even as much a 'bottom up' as a 'top down' phenomenon. Active involvement in 'reformation of manners' was an important element in this dynamic, and this was so as much in the early and mid-Tudor periods as in the decades after 1570 emphasized by Hindle.[29]

Yet, it is equally important to recognize that state development in this period was in a sense an arrested or at least truncated process. A striking feature of the medieval English polity – a variant on patterns found elsewhere in Europe – was a fundamental distinction between temporal and spiritual matters and a corresponding division between legal systems, royal and ecclesiastical. By the late middle ages, many sources of conflict had been resolved, and the two systems worked on the basis of mutual recognition and support. Nonetheless, there remained the potential for serious clashes between the universalist claims of the papacy and the crown's demand for obedience within the realm.[30] Even within England, tensions persisted on such matters as sanctuary and benefit of clergy, while there was piecemeal encroachment on ecclesiastical court jurisdiction. More strikingly, around the turn of the sixteenth century there were some major adjustments of the boundary between the two jurisdictions. Debt suits, formerly handled in the guise of 'breach of faith', were gradually driven out of the church courts. In a parallel development, the royal judges denied the spiritual courts' jurisdiction over slander where the matter at issue was cognizable in the royal courts (particularly cases concerning theft and other felonies), and subsequently, King's Bench and Common Pleas developed their own jurisdiction in these areas. On this basis it has been asserted that 'by the time the "official" Reformation arrived, a jurisdictional reformation . . . had already happened.'[31]

Yet, although successive Acts of Supremacy made the monarch Supreme Head (1534) or Governor (1559) of the Church in England, a fundamental division between the spiritual and temporal powers persisted. In the wake of the breach with Rome, the crown and its advisers did seriously consider dismantling the ecclesiastical jurisdiction and transferring most, if not all,

---

[29] Steve Hindle, *The State and Social Change in Early Modern England, c.1550–1640* (Basingstoke, 2000). See also Michael J. Braddick, *State Formation in Early Modern England, c.1550–1700* (Cambridge, 2000), esp. chap. 4.

[30] Benjamin Thompson, 'Prelates and Politics from Winchelsey to Warham', in Linda Clark and Christine Carpenter (eds.), *The Fifteenth Century*, Vol. IV: *Political Culture in Late Medieval Britain* (Woodbridge, 2004), pp. 69–95.

[31] Helmholz, *Roman Canon Law*, pp. 25–7, 30–4 (quotation p. 33).

of the business of the church courts to their secular counterparts. This could have radically altered the nature of the English state and would certainly have transformed the way in which sexual behaviour was publicly regulated.[32] In the event, the spiritual courts survived, and secular court encroachment on jurisdiction over sex and marriage was severely limited. Indeed, in most respects the inherited division between secular and ecclesiastical jurisdiction in this sphere was in the reign of Queen Elizabeth powerfully reaffirmed.

It is in fact one of the major themes of this book that over the period there occurred an important process of jurisdictional winnowing. In the late fifteenth century, a wide range of secular tribunals – especially borough and city courts – worked in tandem with the church courts to restrain sexual behaviour outside marriage. In these areas, as in the spheres of debt and defamation, the boundaries between ecclesiastical and secular jurisdictions were sometimes quite blurred. By the beginning of the seventeenth century, as a result of changes that had begun earlier but were stimulated by issues arising from the breach with Rome and the establishment of the Royal Supremacy, the divisions were much more clear-cut. Sexual regulation was recognized to be primarily a matter for the spiritual courts.

Deviations from this principle did exist but were limited. On the one hand, civic authorities in London and some larger provincial towns were able to claim some jurisdiction over sexual matters on the basis of local custom backed by royal charters. The work of the London Bridewell was by far the most striking example – to the extent that some contemporaries denounced it as an unjustifiable anomaly – and it is notable that Bridewell's handling of sexual offenders diminished sharply from about 1620. On the other hand, acts of parliament brought certain matters within the jurisdiction of secular courts or the justices of the peace, namely, bigamy (made a felony in 1604) and bastard-bearing when the illegitimate child was likely to charge the poor rates (acts of 1576 and 1610). Before the passage of the notorious and short-lived Adultery Act of 1650, other parliamentary attempts to extend secular jurisdiction in this sphere made little headway.

Sexual Regulation and Religious Reformation

Another major topic to which 'reformation of manners' relates is the nature of the English Reformation or, as Christopher Haigh would have

---

[32] See Chapter 9.

it, 'reformations'. Since the 1980s, Haigh, J. J. Scarisbrick, Eamon Duffy and others have established a new orthodoxy that stresses the strength (by and large) of the eve-of-the-Reformation church; the absence of any strong popular demand for religious change; the limited, if not minimal, significance of Lollardy (the native English heresy) and the restricted penetration of Lutheran or other continental Protestant ideas before the late 1520s at the earliest. George Bernard's study of areas of 'vitality and vulnerability' in the late medieval church subjects the issues to detailed scrutiny but is essentially congruent with this vision.[33] On this view, the so-called Henrician Reformation was instigated by the crown for its own purposes. Admittedly, the Royal Supremacy and the dissolution of the monasteries massively altered the ecclesiastical landscape, while royal sponsorship of the vernacular Bible, half-hearted though it turned out to be at first, was another notable break with the past. But doctrinally and liturgically, the changes were incoherent and never constituted a Protestant church.

The boy-king Edward VI and his advisers did establish the framework of a Protestant church, while their iconoclastic policies were highly destructive of the apparatus and institutions of Catholic doctrine and worship. Nonetheless, it is argued, their rule was too brief to have a deep impact on the real beliefs of most ordinary people. Hence, the efforts of Mary I not merely to restore Catholicism, including the obedience to Rome, but also in some measure to reform it had the potential for success and were frustrated only by the queen's early death without offspring and the decision of her successor to reverse her policies. But Elizabeth was in some respects an equivocal supporter of Reformation; the advance of Protestantism was hampered by a groundswell of religious conservatism and even hostility, and it took decades, if not generations, for England to become in any sense a Protestant nation, let alone a nation of Protestants.[34]

The slant of this set of arguments depicts Protestantism in terms of 'a difficult labour and a sickly child'. But without doubt it did eventually

---

[33] J. J. Scarisbrick, *The Reformation and the English People* (Oxford, 1984); Christopher Haigh (ed.), *The English Reformation Revised* (Cambridge, 1987); Christopher Haigh, *English Reformations: Religion, Politics and Society under the Tudors* (Oxford, 1993); Eamon Duffy, *The Stripping of the Altars: Traditional Religion in England, c.1400–c.1580* (New Haven and London, 1992); G. W. Bernard, *The Late Medieval English Church: Vitality and Vulnerability before the Break with Rome* (New Haven and London, 2012).

[34] G. W. Bernard, *The King's Reformation: Henry VIII and the Remaking of the English Church* (New Haven and London, 2005); Scarisbrick, *Reformation and the English People*, chaps. 3–8; Haigh (ed.), *English Reformation Revised*; Haigh, *English Reformations*; Duffy, *Stripping of the Altars*, chaps. 11–17.

become a powerful force, generating a rich variety of forms of spirituality and religious behaviour. Diarmaid MacCulloch has gone so far as to describe it as 'a howling success', and even Haigh, in his more recent work, has acknowledged some of the achievements of those who built a Protestant church under Elizabeth and the early Stuart kings.[35] As has long been recognized, the work of the ecclesiastical courts, and more broadly a campaign of 'reformation of manners' espoused by urban magistrates, justices of the peace and local officers such as churchwardens and petty constables, were integral to this development.[36] In this sense, sexual regulation is recognized to have been a major element in the 'long Reformation'. Its role in the decisive period of policy changes in the mid-Tudor decades needs to be explored further. Ian Archer has drawn attention to the role of Protestant reformers from the 1540s in appropriating the rhetoric of sexual reformation by spearheading an attack on vice, especially in the city of London, but there is more to be said on this topic.[37] Even less attention has been paid to the creative efforts of churchmen and some provincial city and borough authorities, to an extent in the reign of Edward VI and then in the first two decades of the Elizabethan regime, to establish a framework of institutions capable of carrying out far-reaching reform in sexual 'manners'. Among other things, this involved a rethinking of the practice of judicial penance to bring it in line with Protestant doctrine, together with debate on and experimentation in the use of secular punishments to combat sexual transgression – both developments occurring in the broader context of a penal regime that increasingly favoured the use of corporal punishment. These are major themes of the closing sections of this book.

Sexual regulation also impinges on the prehistory of the Reformation – the word 'origins' begs too many questions – opening up lines of interpretation that either complement or bring into question recent approaches. As against those historians who insist that in the decades around 1500 there was not much wrong with the church, R. N. Swanson and others stress that – as might be expected in continental perspective – at the end of the

---

[35] Christopher Haigh, 'The English Reformation: A Premature Birth, a Difficult Labour and a Sickly Child', *Historical Journal*, 33 (1990), 449–59; cf. Christopher Haigh, *The Plain Man's Pathways to Heaven: Kinds of Christianity in Post-Reformation England, 1570–1640* (Oxford, 2007); Diarmaid MacCulloch, 'The Impact of the English Reformation', *Historical Journal*, 38 (1995), 152.

[36] Martin Ingram, *Church Courts, Sex and Marriage in England, 1570–1640* (Cambridge, 1987); Keith Wrightson and David Levine, *Poverty and Piety in an English Village: Terling, 1525–1700*, 2nd edn. (Oxford, 1995).

[37] Ian W. Archer, *The Pursuit of Stability: Social Relations in Elizabethan London* (Cambridge, 1991), pp. 251–3.

fifteenth century and in the early decades of the sixteenth there existed powerful currents of questioning and reform within the church, in part in response to lay criticism. The fact that in the 1530s these initiatives were to be swamped by an entirely different and extremely powerful current of 'reformation', emanating from the crown, should not obscure the fact that this was a dynamic, not a static, situation.[38] A related theme is the existence of great diversity of religious belief and pious practice in England well before continental Protestant ideas began to have an impact. The patchy persistence of Lollardy in some areas is merely one dimension of this diversity, which current work is beginning to explore more thoroughly. From another viewpoint, the church's renewed assault on heretics in the decades preceding the Reformation represents a powerful effort to promote orthodoxy, based on belief in the sacrament of the Eucharist as indeed *corpus christi*. Compelling dissidents to recant, if this was at all possible, and burning the relatively small numbers of the obdurate were measures designed both to limit the dangers of 'contagion' and to send a powerful deterrent and, more broadly, educative message to reclaim waverers and rally the faithful.[39]

Plainly, the issue of heresy had a particularly high profile not least because of its associations with sedition and the fact that statutes of 1401 and 1414 enabled the church to hand obdurate and relapsed heretics over to the secular arm to be burnt. But it is the contention of this book that new initiatives towards more intense sexual regulation and tighter control of marriage represent another area that may fruitfully be explored in the contexts of diversity, reform and the imposition of orthodoxy. The extent to which ordinary people were or were not amenable to the Catholic vision of sexual relations and of marriage – the sacramental status of which was reaffirmed at the Council of Florence in 1439 – is an important index of religious commitment and identity. At present, the topic receives scant attention even in the most recent and sophisticated studies of pre-Reformation English piety.[40]

---

[38] R. N. Swanson, 'Problems of the Priesthood in Pre-Reformation England', *English Historical Review*, 105 (1990), 845–69. See also Thompson, 'Prelates and Politics', esp. pp. 91–5.

[39] The literature on Lollardy and the church's response is vast. For a recent review, see Bernard, *Late Medieval English Church*, chap. 9.

[40] Robert Lutton, *Lollardy and Orthodox Religion in Pre-Reformation England: Reconstructing Piety* (Woodbridge, 2006); Robert Lutton and Elisabeth Salter (eds.), *Pieties in Transition: Religious Practices and Experiences, c.1400–1640* (Aldershot, 2007). Neither work says anything of substance about sexual regulation, despite its obvious relevance. But cf. Andrew D. Brown, *Popular Piety in Late Medieval England: The Diocese of Salisbury, 1250–1550* (Oxford, 1995), pp. 15, 79–80, 181, 184, 192, 243–4, 260, 261.

Another theme that demands further attention is 'anticlericalism'. It is widely accepted that this is at best a slippery notion – or perhaps a blunt instrument – and that it would be misleading to think in terms of widespread criticism of, or hostility to, the clergy among the mass of the people on the eve of the Reformation. If there were criticisms, they were usually directed at individuals, and what was demanded was redress of these particular complaints in accordance with the traditional values to which the bulk of the clergy no doubt strove to aspire. The behaviour of sexually immoral clerics, for example, provoked demands for the disciplining and reform of those guilty of such behaviour – not a fundamental rethink of the clerical role and the advocacy of a married clergy according to Protestant doctrine. Nonetheless, there are grounds for thinking that the sexual transgressions of clergymen were a matter of more widespread complaint and graver concern than Haigh and others have been willing to recognize. Moreover, there is evidence that when the time was ripe, some lay people deliberately seized on cases of clerical immorality as a means of bringing the church into disrepute. This, in turn, suggests that there did exist deeper currents of hostility towards church and clergy that cannot be ignored.[41]

Demography

Of course, not all the existing literature bearing on sexual regulation is related directly to 'reformation of manners', far less to state development or religious 'reformation'. The main focus of the work of historical demographers is quite different, yet they have established a demographic framework within which legal sanctions on sexual behaviour may be considered and have generated important ideas about the underlying (and not necessarily conscious) motives for such regulation. Peter Laslett, a pioneer in historical demography, saw the issues in terms of 'personal discipline' to ensure 'social survival': that is to say, he assumed that society generated mechanisms to restrain sexual relations outside marriage to ensure that the scarce resources of the pre-industrial world were not swamped by unbridled procreation. These mechanisms included legal sanctions, but they fitted into a wider pattern of customs, practices, assumptions and prescriptions that together formed a demographic regime that operated to restrain fertility.[42]

---

[41] Christopher Haigh, 'Anticlericalism and the English Reformation', *History*, 68 (1983), 391–407; but cf. Peter Marshall, *The Catholic Priesthood and the English Reformation* (Oxford, 1994), chap. 5.

[42] Peter Laslett, *The World We Have Lost – Further Explored* (London, 1983), chap. 7.

The nature of this regime from the mid-sixteenth century onwards has been explored in detail by E. A. Wrigley and R. S. Schofield.[43] The extent to which it was a truly homeostatic or self-regulating system and the emphasis that Wrigley and Schofield place on fertility rather than mortality factors in explaining the course of population change have been questioned.[44] However, its key features are not in dispute; indeed, some are characteristic not only of England but of north-west Europe generally. The first was a relatively late age of first marriage (on average, the middle to late twenties) for both men and women, the effect of which was to shorten the female reproductive span and so restrict fertility. In the seventeenth century, a complementary feature of the demographic landscape, likewise tending to reduce the number of births, was a relatively high proportion of people who never married; this characteristic also applied to the sixteenth century but was then much less marked.

Associated with both these demographic features were the social institutions of apprenticeship and service. Servants – whether in husbandry or domestic service – were usually engaged for a year at a time, whereas apprentices were legally bound to serve for much longer periods (seven years or more in some cases) while they learned a trade. They were alike, however, in that they usually lived in the households of their masters or mistresses, who legally assumed a position *in loco parentis* and who exercised over them very wide powers, including that of 'lawful correction'. Crucially, the marriage of servants was very strongly disapproved of and usually forbidden to apprentices. Socially, the importance of apprenticeship and service in early modern England can hardly be exaggerated; from a demographic standpoint, the effect was to prolong adolescence for many years beyond physical puberty.

Another factor tending to delay marriage was a widely though flexibly enforced 'rule', or rather deeply engrained assumption at all but the highest social levels,[45] that couples should not live with parents or other relatives but establish a new household. This meant inheriting or otherwise acquiring a house or cottage, or at least some kind of lodging or tenement – not always easy in this period. A complementary belief, widely and strongly

---

[43] E. A. Wrigley and R. S. Schofield, *The Population History of England, 1541–1871: A Reconstruction*, 2nd edn. (Cambridge, 1989); E. A. Wrigley et al., *English Population History from Family Reconstitution, 1580–1837* (Cambridge, 1997).

[44] John Hatcher, 'Understanding the Population History of England, 1450–1750', *Past and Present*, 180 (August 2003), 83–130.

[45] The situation was different among the aristocracy and higher gentry. For dynastic reasons, they often arranged marriages in which one or both partners were very young and provided houseroom for the couple in the early years of the union.

held on both moral and prudential grounds, was that couples intending marriage should accumulate the wherewithal to ensure that they could maintain themselves adequately. As one man stated in a London marriage case in 1488, quoting a contemporary proverb that was still widely cited a century or more later, more was needed in a household than 'four bare legs' in a bed.[46] By the very end of the period covered by this book and onwards into the early seventeenth century, this was a desideratum that for many couples was becoming increasingly difficult to achieve. The under-lying reason was a long phase of demographic growth, particularly marked in the period 1570–1630, which put pressure on resources and increased both the proportion and the absolute numbers of poor people. The social and economic effects were compounded by price inflation – the precise causes of which remain controversial[47] – and a variety of changes in production, distribution and land use. The upshot was a difficult economic climate in which the features of the demographic regime already outlined were intensified.

'The peasants and the craftsmen of Tudor and Stuart times,' Laslett concluded, 'seem on the whole to have been cautious about the procreation of children and the formation of families . . . they were well enough aware that the fund of food and conveniences of life were strictly limited.' Hence, sex outside marriage was the object of strong disapproval.[48] In support of his case, Laslett adduced low rates of illegitimacy. As a generalization, this holds true, though the more recent work of Richard Adair has shown that the matter is not as clear-cut as appeared at first sight. Numbers of bastard births appear much more obtrusive if they are compared with numbers of marriages or first births rather than with all births. Moreover, in some parts of the north and west, particularly Cheshire and Lancashire, even illegi-timacy ratios calculated in the normal way were quite high (more than 5 per cent) in the late sixteenth and early seventeenth centuries. There are other reasons to suppose that a rather different sexual regime operated in the north-west, at least before about 1600, and this is a main reason why this particular study confines itself to the south.

Elsewhere in England, illegitimacy ratios were much lower. It is true that in most areas the proportion of bastard births to all births was rising in the later part of Elizabeth's reign, but numbers peaked around the turn of the century and subsequently declined. Bridal pregnancy was much

---

[46] LMA, DL/C/A/001/MS09065B, fo. 15v; Wrightson, *English Society*, p. 82.
[47] N. J. Mayhew, 'Prices in England, 1170–1750', *Past and Present*, 219 (May 2013), 3–39.
[48] Laslett, *World We Have Lost*, pp. 155–6.

commoner – parish register analysis suggests that perhaps a fifth of all brides were ascertainably pregnant when they got married – though again the figures seem to have declined in the seventeenth century, at least in some parishes in some areas.[49] However, the bridal pregnancy statistics are not fatal to the theory of regulated sexuality. As Keith Wrightson nuanced Laslett's argument, 'restraints upon sexual activity . . . [only] crumbled once marriage was in sight . . . popular attitudes, though far from loose, were simply more flexible than those of society's professional moralists.'[50]

Wrigley and Schofield discuss English demography with scant reference to the effects of legal regulation and other direct social constraints; behaviour is presented as conforming to implicit rules and responding to economic indicators such as wage rates. But unquestionably the late sixteenth- and seventeenth-century demographic regime is better understood in its full legal context. Whatever the limits on enforcement – and they were many – the Statute of Artificers of 1563 reinforced apprenticeship and service and increased the restrictions on young people. The impact of the poor laws was of even more profound and far-reaching significance, already in some areas (particularly major towns) by the late sixteenth century and more generally after the passage of the great codifying statutes of 1598 and 1601. Again, an important effect was to direct many young people, whether they willed it or not, into service or apprenticeship, while local concerns to keep poor rates as low as possible (or at least to use them to best effect) led to restrictions on the movement and other patterns of behaviour of potentially 'chargeable' people. Attitudes towards idleness and waste hardened, as did condemnation of sexual transgressions and what were seen as irresponsible attitudes towards marriage.

These arguments and explanations make most sense in the period of steeply rising population after about 1570. The relationship between sexual regulation and demographic stress in the preceding hundred years is less clearly evident. In the absence of parish registers before the 1540s – indeed survivals are quite sparse until the later part of Elizabeth's reign – the kinds of evidence on which Wrigley and Schofield depended are simply lacking, so the nature of the demographic regime itself remains very uncertain. Virtually nothing is known about specific indicators such as illegitimacy rates before 1538, though such evidence as exists suggests that bastardy was at a relatively high level in the 1540s but had fallen back by the early decades

---

[49] Richard Adair, *Courtship, Illegitimacy and Marriage in Early Modern England* (Manchester, 1996). See also Peter Laslett, Karla Oosterveen and Richard M. Smith (eds.), *Bastardy and Its Comparative History* (London, 1980), chaps. 1–6 and 8.
[50] Wrightson, *English Society*, p. 85.

of Elizabeth's reign.[51] It seems likely that – at least for the middling and lower ranks of society – a pattern of relatively late age at marriage, associated with household or farm service and with apprenticeship, was already in existence in the fifteenth century. However, there are strong indications that high mortality, especially in towns, played a much more important role than it did later. Peaks of mortality occurred at intervals in the 1470s and 1480s, while the decades around 1500 appear to have been especially lethal. The combination of high age at marriage and high mortality kept population levels low, probably under 2.5 million in the country as a whole. There may have been population growth in the 1460s, subsequently arrested, but overall there is little sign of marked demographic upturn before the 1520s, and even then population increases were subject to severe interruption. The years 1556–60 witnessed a severe influenza epidemic: estimates of mortality vary, but the evidence suggests that at least 8 per cent and perhaps as many as 15 or 20 per cent of the population died.[52]

It might be thought that, in contrast to the later situation, attitudes towards sexual transgression in this 'low-pressure' demographic regime would be relatively relaxed. The situation is more complicated. As McIntosh has pointed out, some places did indeed suffer the stress of increasing population, often the result of in-migration, even in the late fifteenth century – in particular, this was true of certain market centres in the orbit of the metropolis.[53] Elsewhere the difficult circumstances that were in many areas the concomitant of low population levels were not necessarily conducive to tolerant attitudes. There were also medical concerns, centring on the plague and – especially after the arrival of syphilis in England in the closing years of the fifteenth century – on sexually transmitted disease, though this issue is far less prominent in the records than might have been expected.[54] However, it is plain that opinions and behaviour were also shaped by religious ideas and ethical concerns, by

[51] Adair, *Courtship, Illegitimacy and Marriage*, pp. 28, 48–61.
[52] Mark Bailey, 'Demographic Decline in Late Medieval England: Some Thoughts on Recent Research', *Economic History Review*, 49 (1996), 1–19; John Hatcher, A. J. Piper and David Stone, 'Monastic Mortality: Durham Priory, 1395–1529', *Economic History Review*, 59 (2006), 667–87; John S. Moore, 'Jack Fisher's "Flu": A Visitation Revisited', *Economic History Review*, 46 (1993), 280–307; John S. Moore, 'Demographic Dimensions of the Mid-Tudor Crisis', *Sixteenth Century Journal*, 41 (2010), 1039–63; Michael Zell, 'Fisher's "Flu" and Moore's Probates: Quantifying the Mortality Crisis of 1556–60', *Economic History Review*, 47 (1994), 354–8.
[53] McIntosh, *Controlling Misbehavior*, p. 141.
[54] Jon Arrizabalaga, John Henderson and Roger French, *The Great Pox: The French Disease in Renaissance Europe* (New Haven and London, 1997).

inherited prejudices and by notions of orderly and disorderly conduct that were not directly related to the demographic regime. As will be seen, in towns and cities and even, to some extent, in the countryside, sexual transgression was viewed more broadly as a threat to the peace and a disruption of neighbourhood and civic values. More positively, city and town councils self-consciously asserted jurisdiction over sexual offenders to claim the moral high ground associated with the Christian moral order. Underpinning these initiatives, in the late fifteenth and early sixteenth centuries the church was – as subsequent chapters will make plain – increasingly insisting that to be legally and socially acceptable, marriage must be solemnized in a church wedding blessed by a priest and followed by a nuptial mass. This striking development inevitably sharpened the distinction between licit and illicit sex.

That said, the marked hostility to fornication, bastard-bearing, bridal pregnancy and even to the marriage of poor people that is visible in the early seventeenth century is much less evident in the late fifteenth and early sixteenth, whether in popular attitudes or those of legal officers. Indeed, this contrast is one of the key findings of this book. It was a dictum of the church courts in this earlier period that they acted 'in favour of marriage', and the fact that a couple planned to marry or were prepared to consider this course of action was grounds for leniency far more often than it was to be later. More fundamentally, sexual relations between young people free to marry were in themselves of limited interest to the authorities. They were far more concerned about *householders* behaving irresponsibly. This might be through their own illicit relationships with individuals within the household (maidservants, for example) or with the wives or husbands of other people; or by allowing or, worse still, promoting illicit sex to take place on their premises. This was indeed a major issue. There is abundant evidence that not only in the environs of London but also in provincial towns and even in some rural areas, sex trade in one form or another was a prominent feature of the social landscape. Neither church nor state authorities publicly condoned this situation, and they made considerable efforts to combat it. But these aspirations were undercut by a variety of institutional obstacles, of which the licensed brothels known as the Southwark 'stews' were the most blatant; by the attitudes and actions of numerous individuals – both clergy and lay people, sometimes of promi-nent social status – who behaved as if the rules did not apply to them; and by the vested interests of many people, women as well as men, for whom the trade in sex was a source of profit, or at least part of the 'economy of makeshifts' that helped the poorer sections of society to make some kind of living. To summarize in a few words, in the century before 1570, 'adultery', 'keeping a whore' and 'promoting bawdry' were of more concern to the authorities, and also to ordinary people, than simple 'fornication' between unmarried youngsters or courting couples, and engaging with the challenge of sexual trade – a cause to which a wide variety of interests could rally – was one of the main stimuli to periodic efforts at moral reform.

Sexuality and Gender

Also crucial to understanding sexual regulation is the study of sexuality and gender. The relationship between the sexes is integral to the latter concept, but in practice, women have tended to remain the main focus of inquiry, albeit more recent studies have given increasing attention to masculinity or 'manhood'.[55] Still influential is Thomas Laqueur's identification of a 'one-sex model' of gender difference, rooted in anatomical and humoral theory, which is supposed to have prevailed from late classical times to around 1700. However, Laqueur has been criticized for basing his work on limited evidence and for oversimplifying and in some degree distorting the ideas he discusses.[56] Moreover, in so far as the idea of the one-sex body existed, its impact and influence outside the pages of medical and anatomical treatises are open to question. Certainly it is not one that features significantly in church and secular court prosecutions for sexual transgressions, either in the form that accusations took or in the responses of defendants to the charges against them.

To an extent the same may be said of the broader framework of contemporary medical and philosophical ideas about male and female, men and women. It was a sixteenth-century truism that the characteristics or 'temperaments' of the two sexes were shaped by the relative balance of the 'four humours' (blood, phlegm, yellow bile and black bile), which were, in turn, related to the 'four elements' (fire, air, earth and water). Men were ruled by the hotter, drier humours, women by those that were cold and moist. As a result, women were conventionally, indeed proverbially, thought to be mentally as well as physically weaker than men. They were

---

[55] Elizabeth A. Foyster, *Manhood in Early Modern England: Honour, Sex and Marriage* (London and New York, 1999); Alexandra Shepard, *Meanings of Manhood in Early Modern England* (Oxford, 2003); Patricia Simons, *The Sex of Men in Premodern Europe: A Cultural History* (Cambridge, 2011).

[56] Thomas Laqueur, *Making Sex: Body and Gender from the Greeks to Freud* (Cambridge, MA and London, 1990); cf. Helen King, *The One-Sex Body on Trial: The Classical and Early Modern Evidence* (Farnham, 2013).

less rational, more subject to their passions and hence susceptible to bodily temptation or even to be sexually voracious.

While such ideas did not monopolize thinking about the sexes, they were certainly an important force, part of the framework of ideas of late fifteenth- and sixteenth-century society. They are reflected in the material used in this book to the extent that men – especially young men and those in the prime of life – were characteristically assumed to be powerfully attracted to women and likely to give vent to their passions if they were not restrained by their own powers of reason and self-control, backed up by the strictures of the law and social pressure. In the act itself, men were conventionally viewed as the prime agents. They had the 'carnal knowledge' or the 'use' of women's bodies; more euphemistically, they 'meddled' or 'lay' with them; in the language of the street, they 'fucked', 'swived' or 'japed' them. Women were characteristically viewed as more passive yet also powerfully inclined to sexual activity in certain circumstances – most obviously if they were of age to marry and had hopes or expectations of marriage; if they were already married but had unfulfilled desires for children; or if they were widows whose sexual desires had been previously aroused but were now frustrated. Some women, generally viewed with disfavour in these sources, were seen as lusty individuals with an insatiable appetite for sex. A much larger group was thought to be willing, either for greed or need, to sell their bodies for money or other benefits. Such straightforward assumptions account for virtually all the cases found in the records. Scarcely ever did defendants in court attempt to explain their behaviour by reference to their 'humours'. Frustratingly for the historian, they rarely offered any other deeper insights into why they had, or had not, done the things of which they were accused. In the records of court proceedings, as also the writings of moralists, legists and theologians that underpinned them, the emphasis was on acts rather than intentions. So, while such sources tell us a great deal about the behaviour of men and women, questions of sexual identity remain elusive, while even issues of agency – especially *female* agency – are only partially open to investigation.[57]

One issue that these sources bear on much more directly is the 'double standard', the idea (as stated by Keith Thomas in a pioneering study) 'that unchastity, in the sense of sexual relations before marriage or outside

---

[57] Useful introductions to ideas about sexuality in this period include Ruth Mazo Karras, *Sexuality in Medieval Europe: Doing unto Others* (New York and London, 2005); Katherine Crawford, *European Sexualities, 1400–1800* (Cambridge, 2007).

marriage, is for a man, if an offense, none the less a mild and pardonable one, but for a woman a matter of the utmost gravity'.[58] Laura Gowing has used the evidence of slander suits in the London church courts to argue that this notion is inadequate and misleading: rather, the way the reputations of the two sexes were constructed was incommensurable. Men, she insists, were rarely made culpable for their sexual transgressions and never defined by them; women, however, 'were at the pivotal centre of the circulation of blame and dishonour for sex: responsibility was channelled entirely through them'.[59]

It is now widely accepted that this is both a simplification and an exaggeration. Gowing relied heavily on church court evidence, but the tight legal restrictions within which these tribunals operated confined them largely to sexual defamation. Study of slander litigation in other courts and of attributes of honour, reputation and 'worth' as they emerge from a variety of other sources very much modifies the picture. In much better accord with the facts is the long-established view that the double standard in England in this period was a matter of degree, not an absolute dichotomy.[60] This argument has been reinforced by Bernard Capp's studies of the possibilities open to resourceful – sometimes opportunistic and unscrupulous – women to exploit men's fear of being disgraced for adulterous behaviour or begetting illegitimate children. As Capp's evidence indicates, it was men in positions of special trust or responsibility, such as clergymen, who had the most to lose from such attacks, but to an extent, other men were vulnerable too. Yet more evidence to support this view will emerge in succeeding chapters.[61]

An interesting feature of much recent work on sexual slander, gender and related issues is that the authors make only passing reference to criminal prosecutions for sexual transgressions. Though obviously aware that the church and, to a lesser extent, the secular courts played an important role in this sphere, they give little sense of the intensity of such regulation, how far its impact varied in different places and how the pattern changed over time. The premise of this book, in contrast, is that

[58] Keith Thomas, 'The Double Standard', *Journal of the History of Ideas*, 20 (1959), 195–216.
[59] Laura Gowing, *Domestic Dangers: Women, Words, and Sex in Early Modern London* (Oxford, 1996), p. 109 and chaps. 3 and 4 *passim*.
[60] Martin Ingram, 'Law, Litigants and the Construction of "Honour": Slander Suits in Early Modern England', in Peter Coss (ed.), *The Moral World of the Law* (Cambridge, 2000), pp. 134–60, which reviews or cites other work relating to slander litigation and related topics.
[61] Bernard Capp, 'The Double Standard Revisited: Plebeian Women and Male Sexual Reputation in Early Modern England', *Past and Present*, 162 (February 1999), 70–100; Bernard Capp, *When Gossips Meet: Women, Family, and Neighbourhood in Early Modern England* (Oxford, 2003), pp. 252–63.

such matters are of crucial importance. It is a disagreeable matter in any circumstances to be defamed as a whore in the open streets or publicly accused of fathering an illegitimate child. But if these events took place in a society in which such matters were regularly the subject of legal prosecution, where people were commonly expected to observe their neighbours' behaviour and to evaluate their sexual 'honesty', and where charges of fornication, adultery, bigamy and the like could lead to humiliating and in some cases extremely painful punishments, social ostracism or ejection from house and home, the jeopardy is all the greater and the social and psychological drama of the confrontation all the more intense. This was above all true in London, where the mesh of sexual regulation was especially fine. In the streets and alleys of the metropolis, especially in the city itself, sexual reputation was of intense and tangible importance. This context needs to be understood if the significance of being denounced as a 'whore', a 'bawd', a 'whoremaster' or the like is to be fully appreciated.

The church had always insisted that adulterous men and women were both guilty in the sight of God; indeed, some theologians argued that men were *more* culpable because they were the more reasonable of the two sexes and hence better able to resist temptation.[62] To what extent the late fifteenth- and early sixteenth-century church courts did hold men to account for their sexual misdeeds and how far secular tribunals followed suit are therefore issues of prime importance. Valuable work on this theme has already been done by Karen Jones and Shannon McSheffrey, among others, but the issues are further explored in the following chapters.[63] It will not be surprising to find that women were indeed often at the sharp end of legal action against sexual transgression. Far more striking is that often the courts rigorously pursued the *menfolk* too. Indeed, in some tribunals, men were the main targets. More basically, it is incontrovertible that legal regulation of sexual behaviour in both men and women was so important as to be a defining feature of late medieval and early modern society. The gradual disintegration of this system of moral surveillance from the later seventeenth century onwards was to represent a big step towards the emergence of a recognizably modern society, but that development was a long way off when Queen Elizabeth died in 1603.[64]

---

[62] Christine Peters, *Patterns of Piety: Women, Gender and Religion in Late Medieval and Reformation England* (Cambridge, 2003), pp. 145–6.

[63] Shannon McSheffrey, *Marriage, Sex, and Civic Culture in Late Medieval London* (Philadelphia, 2006); Karen Jones, *Gender and Petty Crime in Late Medieval England: The Local Courts in Kent, 1460–1560* (Woodbridge, 2006), esp. chap. 5.

[64] This is the main theme of Dabhoiwala, *Origins of Sex*.

Same-Sex Relationships

This book is an attempt to analyse in detail this pattern of sexual regulation and to investigate the course of change down to the end of the sixteenth century. For several reasons, it is confined to sexual transgressions that took place between men and women and were at least notionally consensual in nature. There is no attempt to treat systematically rape, child sexual abuse, bestiality, same-sex relationships (whether between men or women) or masturbation. The last, sometimes referred to as (or subsumed with) 'sodomy', sometimes described as 'voluntary pollution', was denounced by the church as a grave sin. Some cases found their way into the records in monastic contexts, and the issue was to feature quite prominently in the findings of the commissioners investigating the state of the smaller monasteries in 1536, but the practice was not generally regarded as a matter for the courts. Presumably it was dealt with in private confession or, after the Reformation, left to the individual conscience.[65] David Crawford states that a man from Light (Kent) was prosecuted by the court of the bishop of Rochester for masturbation in 1523. In fact, the charge was 'for myslyvyng and abusyng his body as he hath openly sheuyd and confessed', a formula that might refer to virtually any sexual transgression. The fact that a female partner was not specified is not conclusive; the man may have had sex with one or more unnamed prostitutes, and/or the fact of transgression may have been betrayed by venereal disease. The culprit was said to have left the vicinity, suggesting a charge of some gravity. Even if this was a prosecution for masturbation, it was an isolated instance.[66] Equally rare are references to sexual activities between females. In 1555, a Sussex maidservant was accused of reporting that the daughters of two local householders 'did put in theyr ffyngers one into anothers privyties' when they were alone together in a pigsty. While their ages were not stated, they were evidently young and unmarried, and what they were supposed to have done may well have been simply a matter of sexual experimentation.[67]

Most of the other acts and practices listed in the preceding paragraph were, or became, felonies during this period. The sources required to study them are different from those relating to the mass of heterosexual

---

[65] David Knowles, *The Religious Orders in England*, Vol. III: *The Tudor Age* (Cambridge, 1959), pp. 296–7; Bernard, *King's Reformation*, pp. 258–64.

[66] David Crawford, 'The Rule of Law? The Laity, English Archdeacons' Courts and the Reformation to 1558', *Parergon*, New Series 4 (1986), 158; cf. Kent History and Library Centre, DRb/Pa 7, fo. 211v.

[67] WSRO, Ep.II/9/1 (Archdeaconry of Lewes, Detection Book, 1550–7), fo. 105v (I owe this reference to Paul Cavill).

transgressions and demand a separate methodology, if not a longer time scale to make sense of changing patterns.[68] Moreover, some of these offences came before the courts very rarely indeed. In principle, this raises compelling questions about the 'dark figure' between numbers of prosecutions and actual transgressions. In practice, it makes serious analysis impossible. On the basis of modern ideas about the incidence of same-sex inclinations and contemporary denunciations of 'sodomy' as an unnatural crime, it might be expected that homosexual practices would feature prominently in legal records. There were some places in Europe where this was so. An extreme case was Florence, where in the seventy years from 1432 to 1502, the 'Office of the Night' investigated some 17,000 men – in a city of only 40,000 people – for same-sex activities. Bruges – roughly the same size – saw over a hundred convictions for sodomy in the period 1385–1515, including ninety executions.[69] On a more limited scale, sodomy was a target of Catholic Inquisition courts in Spain and Italy, while there were prosecutions in many Protestant towns and cities in Europe, including Geneva – though not all Calvinist cities reflected a similar interest.[70]

In England, apart from a limited number of cases revealed by visitations of monasteries, there is a distinct paucity of cases. An act of 1534, re-enacted in 1563 after repeals in 1547 and 1553, subsumed sodomy and bestiality into the new felony of 'buggery committed with mankind or beast'.[71] In 1541,

---

[68] On child abuse, see Martin Ingram, 'Child Sexual Abuse in Early Modern England', in Michael J. Braddick and John Walter (eds.), *Negotiating Power in Early Modern Society: Order, Hierarchy and Subordination in Britain and Ireland* (Cambridge, 2001), pp. 63–84, 257–62. On the complex law of rape and ravishment, see Henry Ansgar Kelly, 'Statutes of Rapes and Alleged Ravishers of Wives: A Context for the Charges against Thomas Malory, Knight', *Viator*, 28 (1997), 361–419; Caroline Dunn, *Stolen Women in Medieval England: Rape, Abduction, and Adultery, 1100–1500* (Cambridge, 2013). See also Nazife Bashar, 'Rape in England between 1550 and 1700', in The London Feminist History Group, *The Sexual Dynamics of History: Men's Power, Women's Resistance* (London, 1983), pp. 28–42, 209–11; Miranda Chaytor, 'Husband(ry): Narratives of Rape in the Seventeenth Century', *Gender and History*, 7 (1995), 378–407; Garthine Walker, 'Rereading Rape and Sexual Violence in Early Modern England', *Gender and History*, 10 (1998), 1–25; Garthine Walker, 'Everyman or a Monster? The Rapist in Early Modern England, c.1600–1750', *History Workshop Journal*, 76 (Autumn 2013), 5–31. There is no detailed study of bestiality in England for this period.

[69] Michael Rocke, *Forbidden Friendships: Homosexuality and Male Culture in Renaissance Florence* (Oxford and New York, 1996); Marc Boone, 'State Power and Illicit Sexuality: The Persecution of Sodomy in Late Medieval Bruges', *Journal of Medieval History*, 22 (1996), 135–53.

[70] Tom Betteridge (ed.), *Sodomy in Early Modern Europe* (Manchester, 2002); Helmut Puff, *Sodomy in Reformation Germany and Switzerland, 1400–1600* (Chicago, 2003); William G. Naphy, 'Reasonable Doubt: Defences Advanced in Early Modern Sodomy Trials in Geneva', in Maureen Mulholland and Brian Pullan with Anne Pullan (eds.), *Judicial Tribunals in England and Europe, 1200–1700: The Trial in History*, Vol. I (Manchester, 2003), pp. 129–46.

[71] 25 Henry VIII c. 6, repealed by 1 Edward VI c. 12; 2 and 3 Edward VI c. 29, repealed by 1 Mary st.1 c. 1; 5 Elizabeth I c. 17.

Nicholas Udall, headmaster of Eton, was (among other misdeeds) accused of buggery when he appeared before the Privy Council. In Elizabeth's reign, Edward de Vere, earl of Oxford, was smeared with charges of buggery with a number of boys, while Christopher Marlowe was said to have opined that 'all they that love not tobacco and boies were fooles'; both Oxford and Marlowe were at the same time accused of holding views that were sceptical of Christian religion, if not downright blasphemous.[72] But actual prosecutions under the acts of 1534 and 1563 were very few. Problems of evidence and the strictness of the penalty (death by hanging) only partly explain this dearth.[73]

In earlier times, 'buggery' in the sense of bestiality was in principle a matter for the ecclesiastical authorities, but examples are rare. In 1520, a Grinstead (Sussex) man had to clear himself of the slander that more than two years before he had 'committed' 'against nature' with a cow; a neighbour's son had seen him at it and upbraided him with the words 'thou lewde felow what dost thou?', later spreading the story to others. The previous year the holy water clerk of Tingewick (Buckinghamshire) had been reported for unnatural carnal connection with a horse; a local woman had spotted him in the act.[74]

Before 1534, 'buggery' in the sense of sodomy was also primarily a matter for the church courts, but in rare instances and in special circumstances cases did crop up elsewhere. In 1385, the mayor and aldermen of London were perplexed by a transvestite male prostitute who had sexual relations with both men and women.[75] In 1492, a fellow of Merton College, Oxford, was expelled, after careful investigation by the warden, for abusing several youths; the matter was hushed up as far as possible.[76] Throughout the late fifteenth century, Italian galley fleets regularly put into the port of Southampton. Partly to accommodate demand from their crews, the town

---

[72] Sir Harris Nicolas (ed.), *Proceedings and Ordinances of the Privy Council of England*, Vol. VII: *32 Henry VIII. MDXL. to 33 Henry VIII. MDXLII* (London, 1837), p. 153; C. F. Tucker Brooke, *The Life of Marlowe and the Tragedy of Dido Queen of Carthage* (London, 1930), pp. 98–101; Lawrence Stone, *The Crisis of the Aristocracy, 1558–1641* (Oxford, 1965), p. 666. Vaguer charges of same-sex transgression were made against Sir Humphrey Gilbert and Henry Wriothesley, earl of Southampton: see *ODNB*.

[73] Bruce R. Smith, *Homosexual Desire in Shakespeare's England: A Cultural Poetics* (Chicago and London, 1991), pp. 43–51.

[74] A. Hamilton Thompson (ed.), *Visitations in the Diocese of Lincoln, 1517–1531*, 3 vols. (Lincoln Record Society 33, 35 and 37, Hereford, 1940–7), Vol. I, p. 47; WSRO, Ep.I/10/2, fos. 53v–54r, 55r.

[75] David Lorenzo Boyd and Ruth Mazo Karras, 'The Interrogation of a Male Transvestite Prostitute in Fourteenth-Century London', *GLQ*, 1 (1995), 479–85. The possible presence of male prostitutes in fifteenth-century London and Westminster is discussed in Chapter 7.

[76] H. E. Salter (ed.), *Registrum Annalium Collegii Mertonensis, 1483–1521* (Oxford Historical Society 76, Oxford, 1923), pp. 162–4.

had a licensed brothel of the kind common in parts of southern Europe but extremely rare in provincial England. But some of the galleymen had same-sex predilections that occasionally caused trouble. In 1491–2, one of them was fined the substantial sum of £3 6s. 8d. 'by cause he wold a dealed with a boye unlawfully'. Two years later, goods to the value of £20 were seized from another of the visitors who 'shamefully delt with a boye'; the large forfeit may indicate that severe injury had been occasioned.[77]

It is sometimes suggested that sodomy cases must have been more common but that the records are lost or were deliberately destroyed; if so, it is surprising not to find at least some echoes in the quite extensive sources that do survive. The paucity is striking. In her study of the local courts in Kent in the period 1460–1560, Karen Jones encountered 'no accusations of homosexual activity' whatsoever. From another source it is known that in a dispute over the priory of Folkestone in 1463, Brother Thomas Banns was described as 'notoriously excommunicated, and [accused] of a crime most foul ... (for which Almighty Providence has destroyed many cities and towns) ... by him confessed, and he also judicially convicted' or, more pithily, as 'a fals sodomyte' who 'for opene and proved sodomyte stante accursed'. But there is no doubt that cases were extremely uncommon.[78] Likewise, Richard Wunderli found, among more than 21,000 defendants before the court of the bishop of London's commissary in the period 1470–1516, only one man accused of sodomy – or rather with having publicly declared that he had committed sodomy with a named individual – while another possible reference occurs in an obscurely worded defamation case.[79] The paucity of slander suits featuring accusations of buggery or sodomy, in London as elsewhere, is especially telling. Even in the most heated slanging matches in alehouses or on the open streets, it would seem that people did not raise accusations of same-sex acts or predilections.[80]

---

[77] Cheryl Butler (ed.), *The Book of Fines: The Annual Accounts of the Mayors of Southampton*, Vol. I: *1488–1540* (Southampton Records Series 41, Southampton, n.d.), pp. 17, 38. I am grateful to Steven Gunn for drawing my attention to these cases. On brothels licensed and unlicensed, see Chapters 4 and 5.

[78] Jones, *Gender and Petty Crime*, p. 129; *Historical Manuscripts Commission, Fifth Report, Part 1* (London, 1876), Appendix, pp. 590–2.

[79] Richard M. Wunderli, *London Church Courts and Society on the Eve of the Reformation* (Cambridge, MA, 1981), p. 84. For the paucity of cases in other areas of England, see Guth, 'Enforcing Late-Medieval Law', p. 90; R. H. Helmholz, *The Oxford History of the Laws of England*, Vol. I: *The Canon Law and Ecclesiastical Jurisdiction from 597 to the 1640s* (Oxford, 2004), p. 629. The same point is made with reference to church courts in France and the Netherlands by McDougall, 'Prosecution of Sex in Late Medieval Troyes', p. 698.

[80] This issue is addressed in Mario DiGangi, 'How Queer Was the Renaissance?', in Katherine O'Donnell and Michael O'Rourke (eds.), *Love, Sex, Intimacy, and Friendship between Men, 1550–1800* (Basingstoke, 2003), pp. 128–47.

Prosecutions were perhaps more likely to occur in higher ecclesiastical courts, but even so, they were rare. In the bishop of Lincoln's court of audience in 1529, William Baly of Kirby Bellars (Leicestershire), aged forty, confessed that six years before he had twice committed the 'sodomitical sin' with John Jolybrand, a married man living in the same place, and a couple of times the last summer had 'uncleanly' stroked another local man's 'privy members'. Jolybrand admitted the two acts of sodomy, one in bed and the other standing up, and confessed that Baly had also fondled his genitals on several occasions. However, he denied committing sodomy himself and claimed that none of these contacts had led to ejaculation on his part.[81]

A moderately explicit account like this is at odds with another possible explanation for the paucity of cases, namely, that the authorities deliberately avoided references to what was conventionally described as the 'sin not to be named' (*peccatum non nominandum*), a matter thought so detestable that even its perpetrators would be expected to feel a strong sense of shame. Yet, fifteenth-century moralists wrote explicitly of 'sodomy' in the sense of same-sex physical contacts, assuming that either men or women might be subject to this 'sin'. Perhaps, as may be implied in these texts, this was another matter that was characteristically dealt with in private confession rather than the 'external forum' of the courts.

A more basic reason for neglect is that same-sex acts and emotions did not easily mesh with the conceptual framework of procreation, marriage, household and neighbourhood that, as will be seen in Chapter 2, underpinned the authorities' concern with sexual regulation. Writing of late fifteenth-century London, Shannon McSheffrey has further speculated that the city's sexual culture was one 'in which the idea of same-sex relations was deeply repressed'; any such relations would have 'remained outside public discourse, below the documentary radar'. 'Sodomy' was to come to the surface in Reformation polemics, notably in the works of John Bale, but how far this affected the ideas of ordinary people is uncertain. Alan Bray's suggestion, as applicable to the period before the passage of the 1534 buggery act as afterwards, is that in England as a whole there was an extreme disjunction between abhorrence of 'sodomy' in principle and, in practice, a reluctance on the part both of the actors themselves and of neighbours and friends to recognize it in most concrete situations.[82] How

---

[81] LA, DIOC/Cj4, fo. 54v.

[82] McSheffrey, *Marriage, Sex, and Civic Culture*, pp. 149–50; Helen Parish, *Clerical Marriage and the English Reformation: Precedent, Policy, and Practice* (Aldershot, 2000), pp. 121, 126, 130; Alan Bray, *Homosexuality in Renaissance England*, 2nd edn. (New York, 1995), pp. 47, 68–71, 77–80.

common homosexual practices actually were can only be a matter of speculation, while affective aspects and questions of sexual identity are even more elusive. What is quite clear is that the pursuit of same-sex relationships was effectively not part of the normal pattern of legal regulation.[83]

Quantification and Other Methodological Issues

Methodological issues will mostly be discussed as they arise, but one matter needs to be addressed at the outset. The records of the secular and ecclesiastical courts hardly lend themselves to sophisticated statistical analysis; this is particularly true for the period before about 1570 because survivals are mostly extremely patchy, in some cases fragmentary and, as will be seen, often extremely difficult to interpret. Questioning the value of any attempt to quantify the records of Calvinist church discipline, Judith Pollmann has highlighted further problems. Having compared the activities of the Utrecht consistory with the detailed personal journal of one of the church elders for the years 1622–4 and 1626–8, she found that only nineteen of the sixty-eight matters that he noted were recorded in the official record and that this minority of cases was by no means representative of the whole. Underlying the recorded *acta* was a complex of principles and disciplinary processes that shaped what went into the record and what did not in ways that are often inaccessible to the historian.[84]

Pollmann recognizes that selectivity may have been greater in the context of an essentially voluntary system of church discipline such as operated in the Dutch Republic compared with the systems that had a 'judicial character and civic repercussions', as in Scotland and Geneva[85]; clearly, this caveat needs to be applied to English church court materials and other judicial records used in this book. But it would be a mistake to use this to explain away Pollmann's criticisms. On the contrary, the underlying issue cannot be emphasized too strongly. As was said in the Prologue, action against sexual transgressors, whether in the secular or the ecclesiastical courts, was the product of complex interactions between initiatives from the authorities and the participation of ordinary people – of various ranks

---

[83] For a broader approach, see Tom Linkinen, *Same-Sex Sexuality in Later Medieval English Culture* (Amsterdam, 2015).

[84] Judith Pollmann, 'Off the Record: Problems in the Quantification of Calvinist Church Discipline', *Sixteenth Century Journal*, 33 (2002), 423–38.

[85] *Ibid.*, 438.

and conditions and of both genders – in local settings where much (if not most) of what was important to people's lives was done orally, face to face and in exchanges varying in tone from friendly discussion to hard-nosed bargaining and blunt threat. Suspicions of misbehaviour might or might not coalesce into accusations, and even these might well be dealt with by warning and reproof, or – before the Reformation – in the confessional, rather than by denunciation to the authorities. The courts themselves filtered the cases that came to their attention, while recording practices were always flexible and varied greatly from court to court. Undoubtedly not all cases ended up in the formal record. Moreover, the relationship between court records and the complex processes of social discipline to which they relate was not stable and cannot be assumed to have been consistent over time.

It follows that conclusions about the intensity and scope of discipline cannot be simply 'read off' from the numbers of cases. Historians of the drink trade have long been aware that very large numbers of prosecutions, at first sight indicative of intense discipline, may in fact be a disguised form of licensing system.[86] At least to some extent the same principle may apply to some areas of sexual regulation, notably prostitution. Such complexities obviously pose problems of interpretation or, to put the matter more positively, they generate part of the interest of the subject in posing hard questions about the changing relationships between legal institutions and the societies in which they were embedded. But it does not therefore follow that we should not count. At the least, the numbers of recorded cases provide a minimum indication of the incidence of legal regulation and a starting point for discussion of the nature, scope and purpose of what was done.

Preview

This book is based on extensive reading of a wide range of secular and ecclesiastical court records, supplemented by related sources – the works of moralists, legal commentators and contemporary chroniclers, for example – and compared with the findings of other scholars.[87] Sharper focus and detailed analysis are provided by the close examination of surviving

---

[86] Judith M. Bennett, *Ale, Beer and Brewsters in England: Women's Work in a Changing World, 1300–1600* (Oxford and New York, 1996), pp. 158–63.

[87] Preference has been given to moralists whose works (whenever they were first written) were put into print in the decades around 1500 and may therefore be supposed to have had some contemporary relevance.

materials for particular years or groups of years, or occasionally periods shorter than a year when the nature of the sources so dictates.[88] On this basis, ensuing chapters explore both the pattern of prosecutions for sexual transgressions and, where possible, the underlying contours of people's behaviour, which changed considerably over the period in question. Chapter 2 establishes the context by emphasizing the massively important role that marriage, household and reputation played in late fifteenth- and sixteenth-century English society. The next six chapters focus on the fifty years or so before the Reformation. The overall paucity of source materials and the patchy coverage of what does survive make it impossible to do full justice to this complex period. In particular, some of the changes that may have occurred within this half century cannot be fully recovered; hence, the emphasis is not chronological but rather on variations in different social, administrative and political environments (Map 1).

Since England was a predominantly rural society in this period, Chapter 3 concentrates on country areas and on the ecclesiastical courts – far and away the most important agents of sexual regulation in such regions – using samples of material drawn mainly from Leicestershire and from the western part of the county of Sussex (archdeaconry of Chichester). In Chapter 4, urban communities, particularly Exeter, Colchester, Salisbury, Leicester and Nottingham, are investigated, with particular attention to the special arrangements that many cities and boroughs had developed to regulate the sexual behaviour of their inhabitants and the ethos of urban government that underpinned these activities. Albeit in a different religious context, these regimes foreshadowed the moralism that became characteristic of such towns in late Elizabethan and early Stuart times.

In Chapter 5 the spotlight moves to urban and suburban communities close to London, including the borough of Southwark, where there existed the famous London 'stews', a string of licensed brothels within the jurisdiction – to the church's no small embarrassment – of the bishop of Winchester. What this chapter emphasizes is that the rest of Southwark, Westminster and even the adjacent suburbs were by no means areas of sexual lawlessness. On the contrary, they witnessed some major efforts at moral regulation involving secular as well as ecclesiastical courts. The focus then shifts to London itself, and the city's complex and, in many ways, idiosyncratic arrangements for dealing with sexual offenders are

---

[88] For example, the records of particular 'visitations' (explained in Chapter 3) may be the appropriate focus for the study of some church court materials.

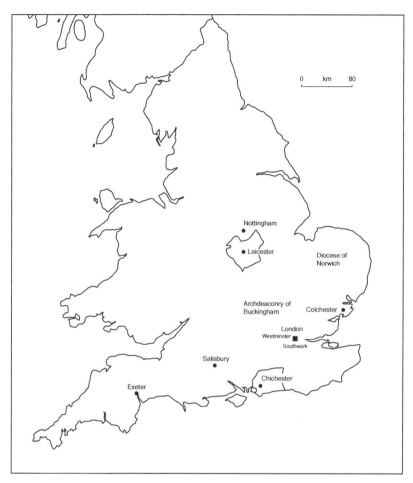

Map 1 England showing the locations of the archdeaconries of Chichester and
Leicester and other principal places discussed in this book

reconstructed in their entirety for the first time. These topics are the subject
of Chapters 6 and 7. Together they reveal that well before the Reformation,
London experienced an extraordinarily intense regime of sexual regulation,
articulated by both the ecclesiastical and secular courts, embedded in a
peculiarly active form of 'neighbourhood watch' and rooted in a powerful
and proud ethos of civic morality. If the ecclesiastical side of this regime
was beginning to slacken in the early decades of the sixteenth century,
secular initiatives were growing in strength, encouraged in part by crown as

well as specifically city pressures and further stimulated by the growth in
the population of London and perceived problems of vagrancy with which
it was associated. Chapter 8 draws together materials from all the jurisdictions previously surveyed to focus on clerical immorality on the eve of the
Reformation. It is argued here that this was quantitatively more important,
and a greater source of lay resentment, than many recent accounts have
suggested.

   In the next three chapters of the book, covering the half century or so
after 1530, the emphasis shifts more decisively to change. Chapter 9 exam-
ines the ways in which the religious and jurisdictional changes of the
Reformation destabilized and temporarily weakened the institutions of
sexual regulation in many areas, yet in London triggered an anti-vice
campaign of great intensity. Reconstructed for the first time, this spectacular campaign of moral activism, persisting for several years around 1550,
was a major event of the English Reformation that deserves more attention
than it has hitherto received from historians. Chapters 10 and 11 investigate
the re-establishment of moral regulation in the early decades of Elizabeth's
reign. This was a period not only of recovery and consolidation but also of
striking innovation. In London, Bridewell Hospital – founded by Edward
VI but under threat in the reign of Mary – developed as a key institution of
social discipline, dealing with numerous cases of sexual transgression as
well as many other forms of disorder and petty crime. Meanwhile, major
efforts, hitherto little noticed, were made in the 1560s and 1570s to revitalize
the church courts. While some of these initiatives faltered or were abandoned, others proved durable, forming the basis of the courts' activities in
the late Elizabethan and early Stuart periods. At the same time, many
provincial towns and cities redoubled their efforts against sexual transgressions, making increasing use of public shame sanctions and sometimes
even harsher means of punishment. Since there were jurisdictional and
other legal obstacles, the outcome in different towns was very varied. Often
the firm alliance of 'magistracy and ministry' to which godly Protestants
aspired was to prove elusive.

   By the 1580s, the world was changing. The beginning of a sustained rise
in the population of England as a whole, with an even more dramatic
increase in the size of London, had social effects that made the task of
sexual regulation seem even more urgent, yet magnified the problems of
pursuing it successfully. The situation was further complicated by the so-
called puritan movement and other ecclesiastical conflicts of the period, by
the increased sensitivity to jurisdictional boundaries that brought some
forms of legal action into question and by the social and political

conditions associated with the long wars with Spain from 1585. This new world of sexual regulation in the closing decades of the reign is the subject of Chapter 12. Many aspects of it have already been well studied, but they can now be seen in a wholly new light by contrasting them with what had gone before.

CHAPTER 2

Marriage, Fame and Shame

William Harrington was a priest and ecclesiastical lawyer in touch with current trends in late medieval piety, including the latest humanist thinking. In this vein, his *Commendacions of matrymony*, first published around 1515 by John Rastell, brother-in-law of Sir Thomas More, at the instigation of the historian Polydore Vergil, presented marriage as very much a positive good for lay people rather than as a second best to celibacy. Indeed, the work was explicitly intended 'for the instruction and informatyon of all such as have chosen or intendeth to chose the way of lyvinge in the laufull and approved state, ordre and holy sacrament of matrimony'.[1] But there was a hard edge to this advice, and Harrington included some notable strictures on sexual relations. From this text, as from others of the late fifteenth century and early sixteenth century, it is clear that at least among the clergy an uncompromising line on sexual ethics based on the idea of the sanctity of marriage long predated the Reformation.

In general, Harrington warned, 'every fleshely medlynge together of man and woman oute of matrimony is dedly synne.' In particular, he was insistent that 'advowtre [adultery] is a grete and grevouse synne and abhominable bothe afore god and man', as was plainly to be seen 'by the grete punysshementes whiche is ordeyned therfore and hathe ben in all lawes and tymes'. He cited approvingly civil law precedents to the effect that the penalty for adultery for a man was death, while a woman was to be beaten naked with rods or scourges and then confined in a nunnery – for two years if she could reconcile herself to her husband; if not, then she was to take the habit of religion and remain in lifelong celibacy. 'In the olde

---

[1] William Harrington, *The commendacions of matrymony* (title page mutilated, ?1515), sig. A2r (there were subsequent editions in ?1517 and 1528). On positive appraisals of marriage in the later middle ages, see David d'Avray, *Medieval Marriage: Symbolism and Society* (Oxford, 2005); Anthony F. D'Elia, *The Renaissance of Marriage in Fifteenth-Century Italy* (Cambridge, MA and London, 2004).

law', noted Harrington ominously – meaning the Old Testament law of Moses – 'the payn was to be stoned to deth.'[2]

Harrington was also strict on the question of prenuptial sex, warning that 'the man maye not possesse the woman as his wyfe, nor the woman the man as her husbonde, nor inhabite, nor fleshely medle togyther as man and wyf, afore suche tyme as that matrimony be approved and solempnysed by oure mother holy chirche; and yf they do indede they synne dedly.' This was true even if, as was common practice, the couple had first entered into a binding marriage contract in advance of the church wedding.[3] Even within marriage, couples were 'to have an honeste temperaunce and moderacion in the desier of the secrete duety of matrimony, wherin wisedome and discretion shulde moderate and rule the sensuale habilite and desier of the fleshe, for that acte may nott be lawfully exercised by man and wife at all seasons, nor of all occasions'. First and foremost, it was forbidden during Lent, as also on rogation and ember days and on all holy days and, Harrington insisted, holy nights. It was also forbidden 'at al such tymes as the wyfe hath a certeyne accostumed and natural diseas and syknesse' and when she is 'with childe and nygh the tyme of the birth and so ... to after that she be puryfyed as the lawe and costume requirith'. Harrington even suggested that couples should abstain from sex for three days, at the least two, or at the *very* least one day and a night, immediately after solemnization of marriage in honour of the sacrament; though this advice, he conceded, was 'gode counsel and no commaundement, and therfore if the[y] do not so thei sinne not; but and they so [do] they shal have gret merite with gode fortunes and gracious fruyte, and the better prospere in al theyr werkes'.[4]

Here, despite Harrington's claims to the commendation of matrimony, may easily be detected a deeply rooted suspicion of sex. His strictures reflected thinking about human nature in general and sexuality in particular that derived from an amalgam of Judaeo-Christian elements and Stoic and other late classical ideas with a strong ascetic component laced with concepts of impurity. Fallen man was corrupt, the higher faculties or reason constantly under threat from the lusts of the flesh. Those who abandoned themselves to habitual lust were guilty of *luxuria* (usually Englished as 'lechery') and, by definition, steeped in deadly sin. Those who were betrayed by mere frailty yet remained aware of the need for restraint and of the sinfulness of their actions were said to have incurred the

---

[2] *Ibid.*, sigs. D1r, D4v.   [3] *Ibid.*, sig. A4v.   [4] *Ibid.*, sigs. A6v, D2r.

somewhat more pardonable sin of 'incontinence'.[5] In the words of another text printed shortly before Harrington's, 'for to synne nature is sone enclyned'.[6]

How far such ideas had purchase on people's actual lives is a key question for this book. In Spain at a slightly later date, some ordinary people were willing to say that sex outside marriage was 'not a sin' – or at least not always. Perhaps the Inquisition was especially inclined to bring such cases to light.[7] In England, such views had occasionally been expressed by the more extreme among Lollard suspects, while a few similar cases have been recovered for the late sixteenth and early seventeenth centuries. But the extreme paucity of expressions of this kind for most of the period covered by this book is very striking. If there were people who consciously dissented from the major tenets of the church's teachings on illicit sex, their voices were extremely muted.[8] This is not to say, of course, that in terms of behaviour the populace always conformed. It seems overwhelmingly likely that Harrington's recommendation that couples should abstain from sex immediately after the wedding was more honoured in the breach than in the observance. There is less certainty about his other strictures on the intimate behaviour of husband and wife within marriage. For the most part, these matters were regulated, if at all, in the secrecy of the confessional and have left little trace in the historical record; we simply do not know how people behaved.[9] It is quite otherwise with transgressions such as adultery and fornication, which could easily become common knowledge and which were often, for reasons that will emerge, matters of great public concern. These were subject to legal regulation for which the evidence, though patchy for the pre-Reformation period, is nonetheless

---

[5] James A. Brundage, *Law, Sex and Christian Society in Medieval Europe* (Chicago and London, 1987), pp. 420–30; Pierre J. Payer, *The Bridling of Desire: Views of Sex in the Later Middle Ages* (Toronto and London, 1993).

[6] Jacques Legrand, *Here begynneth a lytell boke called good maners* (London, 1487 edn.), sig. C3r.

[7] Alain Saint-Saëns, '"It Is Not a Sin!" Making Love According to the Spaniards in Early Modern Spain', in Alain Saint-Saëns (ed.), *Sex and Love in Golden Age Spain* (New Orleans, 1999), pp. 11–26.

[8] John A. F. Thomson, *The Later Lollards, 1414–1520* (London, 1965), pp. 64, 177; Keith Thomas, 'The Puritans and Adultery: The Act of 1650 Reconsidered', in Donald Pennington and Keith Thomas (eds.), *Puritans and Revolutionaries: Essays in Seventeenth-Century History Presented to Christopher Hill* (Oxford, 1978), pp. 260–1; Andrew D. Brown, *Popular Piety in Late Medieval England: The Diocese of Salisbury, 1250–1550* (Oxford, 1995), p. 212; Faramerz Dabhoiwala, *The Origins of Sex: A History of the First Sexual Revolution* (London, 2012), pp. 18–19. But cf. Ruth Mazo Karras, 'Two Models, Two Standards: Moral Teaching and Sexual Mores', in Barbara A. Hanawalt and David Wallace (eds.), *Bodies and Disciplines: Intersections of Literature and History in Fifteenth-Century England* (Minneapolis, 1996), p. 127.

[9] Thomas N. Tentler, *Sin and Confession on the Eve of the Reformation* (Princeton, NJ, 1977), esp. chap. 4.

quite abundant. The implications of this material, in terms of how far people conformed to Christian sexual morality, will be considered in subsequent chapters.

Interestingly, Harrington said very little about this public regime of moral discipline; he took it for granted, and in any case it was tangential to his purpose of giving confidential advice to lay people and the priests whose duty it was to counsel them. What Harrington did linger over was the law concerning the making and breaking of marriage. He knew that a firm sense of the importance of matrimony in the Christian life was fundamental to his moral strictures. Moreover, he was only too aware that this was a complex area in which lay people were apt to go astray. For the same reasons, it is important here to establish contemporary understandings of how marriages were made, and what that meant for the individuals concerned, before exploring in detail the system of moral discipline and legal regulation.

Marriage and Its Social Significance

A marriage, insisted Harrington, restating conventional Christian teaching, must be grounded in 'a gode cause and intent'. There were three 'ends' of marriage. The 'moste principal cause' was to have children. The second was the avoidance of fornication, following St Paul's dictum that it was better to marry than to burn with lust. The third was for mutual support, companionship and consolation. Any one of these three was sufficient to justify entering into marriage. While privileging procreation over the other ends of matrimony, the church did not make it an absolute requirement. Having established all this, Harrington conceded that a person 'may secondarly desyre and wyll rather to marry the ryche than the pore, rather the fayre than the foule, rather the yonger than the olde, rather in noble blode than lowe blode and suche other'. But he warned that if such worldly and fleshly considerations were the main motivation, 'they synne dedly and the devyl hath grete power of them' and 'selden cometh gode fruite of suche matrimony.'[10]

Whether prime causes or not, the aspirations that Harrington briefly outlined were plainly of great concern to most ordinary people. Of course, not everyone got married, and it cannot be assumed that all who were eligible desired to do so. Moreover, as will be seen, the fact of not being married did not stop many people from pursuing sexual liaisons in a variety

---

[10] Harrington, *Commendacions of matrymony*, sigs. A3v–4r.

of circumstances.[11] It is nonetheless incontrovertible that in this period marriage was an institution of central economic, social and indeed political importance. As a personal tie and as the site for procreative sex, it was pre-eminent. The couple were expected to love one another. What this meant is open to question, but certainly the idea of 'love' as a powerful, compelling emotion was a commonplace, taken-for-granted element in many of the courtships revealed by the court records of the period. In a London case in 1531, John Mylward told Agnes Clark, 'I love you so well that I cannot ete, drynk, nor slepe, nor be in rest tyll I know whether ye love me so perfectly as I love yowe.'[12] If unrequited, such feelings could, it was thought, lead to life-threatening sickness, and there are occasional references to suitors who thereby tried to soften the heart of otherwise reluctant young men or women. In another London case in 1487, John Crote, lying sick in bed, told Beatrice Smyth that it was all her fault: 'I have a cause to curse you while I lyve, for the thought I have taken for you is al the cause of my sekenes.' 'I am comme now to make amendes', she replied – or so it was said.[13] However, some people clearly thought that individuals should be able to control their feelings and not pursue hopeless infatuations. In 1492, another woman contemptuously told an unwelcome suitor, 'ye be but a chyld to love ther as ye be not lovyd agayne.'[14] Very commonly the assumption seems to have been that the couple might not actually be 'in love' at the time of marriage but should nonetheless be able to 'find in their heart' to take each other as man and wife. Variations on this formula are commonplace.[15]

There were theological principles to justify these emotions. As Harrington put it, the essence of marriage 'ought to be in both theyr soules by true love so that other shold consent to love other above al the creatures of the world'. Indeed, 'the husbonde ought to love his wife and the wife her husbond above their fader and moder. And this love ought to be contynual and hartely of bothe their partes.'[16] This, in turn, gives important clues to the significance of marriage for social identity. For a man, embarking on

---

[11] Ruth Mazo Karras, *Unmarriages: Women, Men, and Sexual Unions in the Middle Ages* (Philadelphia, 2012). See also Amy M. Froide, *Never Married: Singlewomen in Early Modern England* (Oxford, 2005), though the main focus of this work is the seventeenth and early eighteenth centuries.

[12] LMA, DL/C/208, fo. 190r.

[13] LMA, DL/C/A/002/MS09065, fo. 34(35)r (but in the event it was the woman who sued the man for marriage).

[14] LMA, DL/C/A/002/MS09065, fo. 110(111)r.

[15] E.g. LMA, DL/C/A/002/MS09065, fos. 51(52)r, 137(138)r, 199(200)r; DL/C/A/001/MS09065B, fo. 13v.

[16] Harrington, *Commendacions of matrymony*, sigs. A3v, C6r.

matrimony meant leaving behind the dependence of childhood, service or apprenticeship to become a fully-fledged adult, the master of a household. A woman, it is true, passed from one kind of dependence to legal subjection to her husband. Nonetheless, being mistress of a household or 'family' – these two words were virtually synonymous in Tudor England and implied the fact that both children and servants or apprentices lived under one roof – itself conferred status and authority.

Within the 'family', both husband and wife had a duty to teach – the skills of trade and craft, husbandry and housewifery, perhaps basic literacy, certainly the rudiments of religion and morality, and also the rules of conduct appropriate to the social status of those within the household. In this sense, the family was an educational institution. In the wider sphere it was also of prime political significance. In the course of the sixteenth century, the principle that 'the common wealth doth depend' on the 'good goverment of the houshoulder' was enunciated frequently and with greater and greater insistence, until by 1600 it was a commonplace.[17] But the idea was already current in the fifteenth century; indeed, in so far as the scope of central government was at that time narrower and less certain in its impact, the political importance of householders was, relatively speaking, all the greater. As the anonymous early fifteenth-century Franciscan author of *Dives and Pauper* put it:

> [T]he offys of teching and chastysing longyth nout only to the buschop but to every governour aftir his name and his degre, to the pore man governynge his pore houshold, to the riche man governynge his mene [meinie], to the housebond governynge his wif, to the fadir and the moodir governynge her [i.e. their] childryn, to the justice governynge his contre, to the kyng governynge his peple.[18]

The household, to which a 'shop' (in the sense either of a workshop or a retail outlet) might well be attached or integral, was likewise important economically as the site of craft production, sale of goods, farming activities or even (at higher social levels) the management of estates. A family household was also the centre of a complex and long-drawn-out process whereby if a couple 'prospered', money and property were accumulated and eventually distributed for the benefit of the next generation. The act of

[17] TNA, SP12/276, fo. 104r; Christopher Hill, *Society and Puritanism in Pre-Revolutionary England* (London, 1964), pp. 445–8.
[18] Priscilla Heath Barnum (ed.), *Dives and Pauper*, 2 vols. in 3 parts (Early English Text Society 275, 280, 323, London, 1976, 1980, 2004), Vol. I, part I, p. 328. The work has sometimes been seen as reflecting heretical tendencies, but is now generally regarded as orthodox.

marriage, normally involving the creation of a new household and the amalgamation of property from two pre-existing families, was usually pivotal to such calculations and was hence of great interest not merely to the couple themselves but also to their parents and siblings and perhaps (depending on family circumstances) to other relatives as well. Those of the older generation who had property to pass on – perhaps including not only fathers and mothers but also collateral kin such as aunts and uncles, surviving grandparents, and other 'friends' with some kind of stake or material interest in the transaction – expected to be consulted about marriage plans. It was a universally recognized rule, albeit one that was sometimes flouted, that marriage required the permission of parents, especially if the children concerned were minors.

The Making of Marriage

It might be expected that in a society in which marriage was of such prime social and economic importance, the law concerning marriage formation would be clear and unambiguous, with ample safeguards to protect the interests of parents and other family members. There were indeed some well-established formalities. Certainly by the end of the fifteenth century the church expected people to solemnize their marriage publicly 'in the face of the chirche in the clere day after the sonne be rysen and with honoure and reverence'.[19] The solemnization was presided over by a priest, and it was normal for the wedding ceremony to be followed by a nuptial mass in church. The ceremony began at the church door, instead of in the body of the church, as was the case after the Reformation, and only proceeded into the church during the course of the service, but the core rituals, including the exchange of vows, were very similar to the forms later prescribed in successive versions of the *Book of Common Prayer*.[20] Moreover, the law prescribed that marriages should be announced before-hand by the calling of banns on three successive Sundays or major feast days. In a Whitechapel case in 1523, it was recalled that immediately after a couple had committed themselves to marriage, the parish clerk who was present wrote their names down 'in his book' for publication of the

---

[19] Harrington, *Commendacions of matrymony*, sig. A5v.

[20] Usages varied slightly in different parts of the country; the Sarum use mostly prevailed in southern England. See *Manuale secundum usum insignis ac preclare ecclesie Sarum* (London, 1523), fos. 37r–45v; cf. Brian Cummings (ed.), *The Book of Common Prayer: The Texts of 1549, 1559, and 1662* (Oxford, 2011), pp. 64–71, 157–64.

banns.[21] Failure to observe these rules was subject to penalty. Indeed, ceremonies performed without banns or licence, or in other respects 'clandestine', rendered the couple liable to excommunication, while the priest who married them faced suspension from his priestly function and from receiving the profits of his benefice. Before the Reformation, prosecutions were relatively rare, but when they occurred, they were pursued with rigour.

Irrespective of the penalties, it is likely that for most couples custom and the desire to establish an incontrovertible, socially recognized marriage were sufficient to ensure compliance. It is a commonplace that marriage in late medieval England was a 'process' in the sense that it characteristically involved negotiations – sometimes long drawn out – among the various interests involved.[22] But this is perfectly consistent with the idea that contemporaries understood the *process* to culminate in the *event* of ecclesiastical solemnization. In the decades around 1500 in the Gloucestershire parish of Ashleworth, and no doubt elsewhere, it was the custom that couples 'shulde have their place in going in processyon accord[ing] unto the tyme of theyre mariage in as moche as the yonger brother haithe alweys and yet dothe goe befor his elder brother . . . if so be that . . . [he] be first maryed'. Around 1510, a man 'dyd drawe his dagger' in response to an attempt to transgress this principle.[23]

Weddings were memorable occasions, not least because the ecclesiastical rites of solemnization were usually accompanied by – indeed intertwined with – secular celebrations to mark the event. It is unfortunate that simply because matrimonial contracts entered into before the church ceremony feature so prominently in church court records, they are more familiar to (and have attracted far more attention from) historians than the customs associated with the actual nuptials. The bride was supposed to be properly attired, and many marriage cases refer to lengths of cloth bestowed beforehand for the making of wedding garments, if not also to jewellery or other items of adornment to be worn on the day. In a case in 1523, a man gave his bride a 'cyprys rede' kerchief and three ells of linen to make her 'weddyng smokke', while she ordered the gilding of a pair of silver aglets for the adornment of her 'maryeng rybone'. In the case of a poorer couple in 1521,

[21] LMA, DL/C/207, fo. 225r.
[22] Richard M. Smith, 'Marriage Processes in the English Past: Some Continuities', in Lloyd Bonfield, Richard M. Smith, and Keith Wrightson (eds.), *The World We Have Gained: Histories of Population and Social Structure. Essays Presented to Peter Laslett on His Seventieth Birthday* (Oxford, 1986), pp. 43–99.
[23] Gloucestershire Archives, GDR/1, p. 40.

one of the neighbours lent the bride 'a womans gowne and a womans kyrtyll' to make an appropriate show. On this and other occasions, neighbours followed the couple to church, and a covering called a 'care cloth' was held over them in the church porch. Someone – usually the father or other relative but perhaps a neighbour if the bride was a widow – had to make the response when the priest asked, 'Who gyves me thys woman?' After the nuptial mass, the guests led the couple home from the church, and there invariably followed a breakfast or dinner on a scale appropriate to the purses of the couple, their families or other well-wishers. One man felt able to testify to a wedding, even though he had not attended the actual celebration, because he was present at the subsequent dinner where the woman sat 'lyke a bryde'.[24]

Yet there were uncertainties and complexities deriving from the very law of marriage that Harrington was concerned to publicize. The canon law rules established around 1200 still applied: essentially, marriage was made simply by the free consent of the couple expressed in words of the present tense. As Harrington put it:

> When both the man and the woman dothe consente bothe in one tyme to be husbonde and wyf and that consent doo shewe eyther to other by expresse wordes of the tyme presente as by theise wordes or other lyke, 'I take the to my wyf', or 'I frome this tyme forwarde wyll have the to my wyf'. And yf the woman also incontinently [i.e. immediately] expresse ye same or other lyke wordes then there is contracte matrimony betwixt them.[25]

Of course, it was expected that the marriage would be consummated, but sexual congress was not in itself integral to the act. Witnesses were a practical necessity to prove the marriage if there was any likelihood of dispute, and canon law forbade couples to enter into 'privy' or unwitnessed contracts. Nonetheless, a marriage made without witnesses could be valid. The consent of parents or other kin was expected but was not essential. Nor was the presence of a priest or the religious ceremony. At base, a simple, verbal exchange of consent between the couple could constitute a binding union.

Moreover, it is evident that many couples did enter into such contracts in advance of solemnization, whether as a planned stage in a carefully conducted series of marriage negotiations or, more spontaneously or even precipitately, as an act of personal commitment by courting couples.[26]

---

[24] LMA, DL/C/207, fos. 70v, 71r, 127r, 127v, 143r, 148v, 149r.
[25] Harrington, *Commendacions of matrymony*, sig. A3r.
[26] R. H. Helmholz, *Marriage Litigation in Medieval England* (Cambridge, 1974), pp. 26–31.

Often they were urged to do so by friends and neighbours. For their part, the ecclesiastical authorities in England – unlike some of their continental counterparts – did not in practice regard such contracts as illicit. On the contrary, they took them for granted and happily entertained party and party suits to resolve disputed cases.[27] A man who in 1521 declared, 'Nay, I wyll doo as my father dyd, for I woll never be suer untyll I come to the churche dore', was evidently expressing an idiosyncratic opinion.[28] His remark reflects the fact that people who had contracted themselves in this way were said to be 'sure' or 'handfast'; the more or less informal ceremony that made them so was often referred to as 'spousals' or 'handfasting'.

A situation in which a binding union could be made by a simple declaration but remained illicit unless properly witnessed and solemnized in church inevitably led to ambiguities of attitude and behaviour. As will be seen in subsequent chapters, there is abundant evidence that couples – in defiance of Harrington's strictures – frequently behaved as though spousals, even if unwitnessed, licensed sexual relations; indeed, some courting couples did not even wait that long. But the indications are that the issue was a sensitive one. In a London case in 1513, a man was said to have declared to his betrothed, 'Kateryne, I most nedes be your husbond for I have lyen with yew ij nyghtes.' While apparently not denying it, the woman urged him to be quiet and keep the fact to himself.[29]

Could a marriage contract alone be the basis for a permanent relationship in which the couple cohabited, bore children and were recognized as 'married' by their neighbours and the community at large? Some medievalists assume that it could. Peter Fleming states as a fact that some couples 'made their exchange of vows *per verba de presenti* and never proceeded to the next stage of a church wedding'. Such arrangements, he suggests, 'may have been practised among some of the poorer members of society, who could not afford a proper church service and for whom, perhaps, the familiar domestic environment was more welcoming than the parish church ... Clearly, as late as the fifteenth century, many of the laity persisted in the belief that marriages made without benefit of clergy were ... perfectly acceptable.' Yet Fleming offers no clear examples to support these confident generalizations.[30] Making similar claims, albeit

---

[27] Cf. Shannon McSheffrey, *Marriage, Sex, and Civic Culture in Late Medieval London* (Philadelphia, 2006), pp. 28–9.

[28] LMA, DL/C/207, fo. 117r.   [29] LMA, DL/C/206, fo. 291v.

[30] Peter Fleming, *Family and Household in Medieval England* (Basingstoke, 2001), pp. 48–9. See also Sara M. Butler, *Divorce in Medieval England: From One to Two Persons in Law* (New York and London, 2013), pp. 2–3.

more circumspectly, Richard Smith does cite instances in which manor courts, in contested cases of inheritance, sometimes adjudicated in favour of unsolemnized unions. But most of the examples date from the thirteenth and fourteenth centuries rather than any later period, and none of itself clearly indicates that long-term unsolemnized unions were a commonly accepted social arrangement.[31]

Indeed, it is hard to see how they could have been. Whatever the views of ordinary neighbours, couples cohabiting in this way would surely have excited the attention of the ecclesiastical authorities, particularly since by the fifteenth century the very idea that a church wedding was unnecessary – an opinion that impugned the sacrament of marriage – was regarded as heretical and was among the charges commonly brought against suspected Lollards. Thus, in 1504, a cleric of Great Stanmore (Middlesex) was indicted in King's Bench for expressing the view that a 'weddyng was nothyng elles in effect but the yokyng of a bore and the rynglyng of a sowe'.[32] Fleming and others seem generally to agree that whatever the situation earlier, the solemnization of marriage in church became increasingly widely practised as time went on.[33]

As will be seen in Chapter 3, this is consistent with the pattern of church court disciplinary prosecutions found in the decades around 1500. Contracted couples who delayed solemnization were routinely prosecuted to force them either to regularize their position or to explain why they should not do so.[34] A case of a different nature from Binstead (Sussex) in 1524 reveals how temporary cohabitation might occur – in this case when a master developed a sexual relationship with his servant – but also how

---

[31] Smith, 'Marriage Processes', pp. 52–69. For a discussion of some northern evidence, see P. J. P. Goldberg, *Women, Work, and Life-Cycle in a Medieval Economy: Women in York and Yorkshire, c.1300–1520* (Oxford, 1992), pp. 233–43.

[32] TNA, KB 9/435, m. 78; for other examples, see Norman Tanner (ed.), *Kent Heresy Proceedings, 1511–12* (Kent Records 26, Maidstone, 1997), pp. xii–xiii, xxv, 2, 9, 17, 20, 22, 27, 29, 30, 37, 39, 41, 44, 51, 53, 77. See also J. Patrick Hornbeck II, *What Is a Lollard? Dissent and Belief in Late Medieval England* (Oxford, 2010), chap. 4.

[33] Fleming, *Family and Household*, p. 48; Helmholz, *Marriage Litigation*, pp. 29–30. But cf. the more equivocal findings of Llinos Beverley Smith, 'A View from an Ecclesiastical Court: Mobility and Marriage in a Border Society at the End of the Middle Ages', in R. R. Davies and Geraint H. Jenkins (eds.), *From Medieval to Modern Wales: Historical Essays in Honour of Kenneth O. Morgan and Ralph A. Griffiths* (Cardiff, 2004), pp. 76–80, though the matter is complicated by the possible influence of Welsh marriage customs and that fact that Smith makes no attempt to distinguish between long-term illicit sexual relations – which certainly existed in many parts of England – and consensual unions that were socially accepted locally.

[34] Cf. L. R. Poos, 'The Heavy-Handed Marriage Counsellor: Regulating Marriage in Some Later-Medieval English Local Ecclesiastical-Court Jurisdictions', *American Journal of Legal History*, 39 (1995), 296–8, 309.

fragile such an arrangement was. The parish priest reported that Thomas Coby had promised that he would 'make Alys Hacher my servant as good a woman as I am a man' and on another occasion had admitted that 'I do use Alys Hacher as my wif and I intend to mary hir shortly before harvest or after.' But there are hints that he was under pressure to regularize the union and was by no means enthusiastic. According to another witness, he insisted that he had 'made never no promes to mary with hir except she be with child'. In the event, another women claimed a prior contract, and it was this that the court upheld.[35]

Individuals, Families and Marriage Contracts

This case among others demonstrates how far marriage contracts or spousals, even if it was assumed that they would normally be followed by a church wedding, remained a source of uncertainty and potential conflict. A binding union was created only if the words were themselves in law sufficient to achieve this. But since no set form was prescribed, possible variations were infinite, and there was the danger that words might be employed that failed to do the job. This might simply be the result of ignorance or innocence on either part, or it might derive from fraudulent intent – seduction, for example, or temporary access to land or goods under colour of marriage. A prime source of confusion was the legal distinction between a present-tense declaration to take each other immediately as man and wife and a promise to marry in the sense of a statement of future intent. As Harrington warned: 'But and they use wordes of the tyme to come, as yf the man saye thus "I shall take the to my wyfe", and the woman saye "I shal take the to my husbonde" ... then it is noo matrimony butt promysse to make matrimony.' Yet this was a simplification, since formulae employing the word 'will' could, depending on sense and context, imply either the present or the future tense. Even assuming a degree of legal awareness among the population, if not legal sophistication, the dangers of getting things wrong are manifest. As has often been observed, those impelled by powerful feelings of love or lust are of all people least likely to pay heed to such niceties.[36]

The fact that irrespective of the ages of the couple, a binding union could be entered into without the consent of parents or other kin was a potential threat to family interests. In particular, there was a danger that

[35] WSRO, Ep.I/10/3, fos. 24r, 26r–27r.
[36] Harrington, *Commendacions of matrymony*, sig. A3r; Helmholz, *Marriage Litigation*, pp. 31–47.

youngsters with good prospects would fall victim to rapacious suitors. Well-endowed widows were also vulnerable. The fact that a marriage could be made without witnesses and without the calling of banns or other safeguards of publicity also made it easier in some respects for individuals to defy or ignore the wishes of family and friends. But the formlessness of clandestine unions cut both ways. Unwitnessed contracts were hard to prove, easy to deny. Faced with an unauthorized marriage contract, parents or other relatives often put pressure on the errant family member to disown it; sometimes they went further and swiftly took steps to marry the individual to someone else, more to their liking.

Families' room for manoeuvre was, however, reduced if the couple had already had sexual relations, especially if the woman had become pregnant. Sex was important in other respects too. The law recognized that marriage contracts could be made in conditional form, contingent on the provision of house, lands, goods or money or on the agreement of parents or other relatives. Family consent featured particularly often in this context for two reasons. Not only was it a real issue for many individuals, dependent on gifts or inheritances to set themselves up, but it also served as a plausible and irrefutable reason for avoiding commitment, especially handy for young women who wished to deflect the attentions of importunate suitors. However, all such conditions fell by the wayside if the couple had intercourse. The law stated firmly that sexual relations immediately made a conditional contract fully binding. Sex also gave immediate, *de praesenti* force to a future contract.[37]

Family influence was also limited by its structural weaknesses. Certainly beyond the nuclear core of husband, wife and underage children, families were loose associations, not tightly organized corporations. There were no prescriptive rules about which kin should be involved in marriage strategies or how decisions should be reached. Hence, there might well be disagreement between the parents of a marriageable child and his or her wider kin such as uncles and aunts. A grown-up son, with an eye to his own inheritance, might have views on the marriages of younger siblings at odds with those of his parents. Even the father and mother might differ on occasion. Thus, youngsters intending marriage might find themselves the subject of uncertain or conflicting advice. If they were inclined to exercise their own will, they might be aided by differences of opinion among their relatives.

---

[37] Helmholz, *Marriage Litigation*, pp. 47–57.

Mortality patterns, and the circumstances in which young people found themselves as they matured, were also of importance. In the absence of parish registers, the ages at which young people commonly married remains uncertain. However, most historians now accept that late fifteenth- and early sixteenth-century England already demonstrated the demographic features characteristic of the reign of Elizabeth and her Stuart successors: that is, a pattern of late age at first marriage for both sexes, perhaps already as high, on average, as the middle to late twenties, and a relatively high proportion of people who never married. However, the ravages of diseases such as plague and sweating sickness kept expectation of life quite low. This combination of low nuptiality (and hence low fertility) and high mortality would explain why English population levels remained stagnant at least until the 1520s.[38]

In individual terms, the pattern meant that in the case of many young people, father, mother or both were already dead by the time they came to approach marriage. The ability of parents to exercise influence beyond the grave was limited. Bequests in wills were sometimes made conditional, but this was relatively rare.[39] In the absence of legally binding conditions, parents might propose, but their children disposed. In 1528, the vicar of Slawston (Leicestershire) recounted how he heard one of his parishioners, Henry Nicols, at various times during his sickness state his intention to leave twenty pounds to his servant, Joan Turner, 'to hir mariage'. Nicols also appealed to the vicar to 'counsell my son John Nicols to mary hyr', but the cleric's response was sceptical: 'I wyll give hym suche counsell as I can but I think he wilbe at his libertie.'[40]

Spousals Litigation

As indicated by some of the examples already cited, rich evidence of difficulties over marriage formation can be found in the records of suits over disputed matrimonial contracts brought before the church courts.[41] They were a regular feature of most jurisdictions in the late fifteenth and

---

[38] For discussion of the demographic context, see Chapter 1.

[39] E.g. E. M. Elvey (ed.), *The Courts of the Archdeaconry of Buckingham, 1483–1523* (Buckinghamshire Record Society 19, Welwyn Garden City, 1975), pp. 228, 408 (and for expectations of obedience more generally stated, *ibid.*, pp. 138, 411–12); Jacqueline Murray, 'Kinship and Friendship: The Perception of Family by Clergy and Laity in Late Medieval London', *Albion*, 20 (1983), 380, 382.

[40] LA, DIOC/Cj 4, fo. 7v.

[41] Litigation over marriage contracts is a complex area of study with a very extensive historiography. What follows here is not intended as a full treatment but merely highlights a few key points germane to the main subject of this book.

early sixteenth centuries, as they had been in earlier periods, and took various forms. The simplest was when one individual claimed another as his or her spouse on the grounds that they had entered into a binding marriage contract using words of the present tense. Such petitions accounted for the bulk of litigation, while suits based on conditional contracts were not uncommon. But litigation over mere promises of marriage – words *de futuro* – was very rare because such contracts were hard to enforce and were legally superseded by spousals *de praesenti*. Sometimes two individuals each claimed to be contracted to one person, and two suits were prosecuted more or less simultaneously or combined in a three-cornered action. It was also possible to bring an action for 'impediment of marriage', for example, when a father refused to allow a son or daughter to solemnize a marriage contracted with someone of whom he disapproved. Individuals were sometimes vexed by suitors who made false claims that they had made a binding contract with them. They could bring an action, technically called 'jactitation' (or 'boasting') of marriage, to get such claims dismissed, but if the other party brought evidence that a contract did indeed exist, the cause would proceed much like a normal spousals suit.[42]

It has been suggested that spousals suits were more commonly or more characteristically brought by women – albeit some evidence suggests that this tendency diminished as the fifteenth century progressed, perhaps as the result of increasing economic and social restrictions on women. The reason for the preponderance of female plaintiffs is supposed to have been that marriage was of more central concern for women than for men.[43] The importance of marriage for late medieval women can hardly be doubted. Except for those destined for the religious life, it was the only practicable career opportunity available to most females, the only socially acceptable context for having children, the most likely – though still risky – means of securing support and protection and the accepted route to local prestige and status. Testators with unmarried daughters envisaged that they would, in due course, be wed and tended to refer to marriage, rather than specific ages, as the marker of female adulthood;

[42] Helmholz, *Marriage Litigation*, chap. 2.
[43] Charles Donahue, Jr, 'Female Plaintiffs in Marriage Cases in the Court of York in the Later Middle Ages: What Can We Learn from the Numbers?', in Sue Sheridan Walker (ed.), *Wife and Widow in Medieval England* (Ann Arbor, 1993), pp. 183–213; cf. P. J. P. Goldberg, 'Gender and Matrimonial Litigation in the Church Courts in the Later Middle Ages: The Evidence of the Court of York', *Gender and History*, 19 (2007), 43–59. See also Charles Donahue, Jr, *Law, Marriage, and Society in the Later Middle Ages: Arguments about Marriage in Five Courts* (Cambridge, 2007), esp. chap. 3.

they made provision, if they could, for marriage portions. Benefactors might make a contribution to the dowries of 'poor maidens' as they might make provision for apprenticeship or education of poor boys.

Yet marriage, for the reasons already discussed, was important for men too. The sampling of spousals litigation in the years around 1500 reveals different gender ratios among plaintiffs at different times and in different jurisdictions, and the picture is further complicated by the different kinds of suits on offer. In the Chichester consistory court in 1520, twelve spousals suits were entered, of which ten were initiated by women. In the court of the archdeacon of Leicester, the pattern was different. Between December 1524 and January 1527, there were twenty-six spousals suits, of which fifteen were initiated by women and eleven by men. But there were five other causes concerned with disputed contracts, mostly entered under the heading of 'impediment of marriage', and in each of these the party claiming the existence of a contract or demanding enforcement of it was male. When these cases are taken into account, it emerges that marriage contract litigation in the area was divided almost equally between men and women. If the year 1520 was typical, the officials of the Chichester courts may have had a clear sense that spousals suits were characteristically brought by females. No such certainty would have been possible for their colleagues in Leicestershire.[44] In late fifteenth- and early sixteenth-century London there was a preponderance of male plaintiffs, albeit not a very clear one.[45] The overall conclusion must be that spousals suits were not the prerogative of either sex, and the precise pattern was unstable, influenced by local administrative as well as social factors.

The circumstances underlying suits are often hard to determine, not least because many were very briefly recorded. Most commonly, the plaintiff appeared in court to claim the existence of a marriage contract, only to meet a denial. In the absence of witnesses, there was little that the court could do save to examine the defendants on oath. If they persisted in their denial, the case was dismissed. Sometimes the judge referred the parties 'to their consciences'. In so doing the court recognized that a contract might indeed have been made and that the couple were man

---

[44] WSRO, Ep.I/10/2, *passim*; ROLLR, 1 D 41/11/1, *passim*. Cf. in the archdeaconry of Buckingham between 1483 and 1505, of seventeen identifiable spousals suits for which records survive, ten were brought by men. In a cluster of fifteen suits recorded for the period 1519–21, male plaintiffs outnumbered females in a ratio of 4:1. Elvey (ed.), *Courts of the Archdeaconry of Buckingham*, pp. 240–314 *passim* (including one jactitation case in which the party claiming a contract was male).

[45] Based on McSheffrey, *Marriage, Sex, and Civic Culture*, p. 111, and analysis of cases in LMA, DL/C/207.

and wife in the eyes of God but that the marriage was unenforceable and the parties were free, if their consciences could stand it, to marry elsewhere. Some of these cases may have been collusive or semi-collusive, prosecuted rather to draw a line under a failed courtship than with any real expectation of having the disputed contract confirmed. Even a disappointed suitor stood to gain by a clear legal judgement that he or she was free to marry. In a minority of cases, witnesses were produced, but often the testimony was inadequate or inconclusive, and the lawsuit eventually petered out. Only a few were prosecuted really hard, fewer still fought to a finish. When cases did go to judgement, there were usually strong wills at work, substantial amounts of property at stake and powerful family interests – whether for or against – in the background. Sentences confirming disputed contracts were hard to get, and even when they had been obtained, they were sometimes appealed. Compromise was at a premium.

On the basis of evidence from the diocese of York in the fourteenth and fifteenth centuries, Jeremy Goldberg distinguishes between urban and rural marriage contract cases. The former, he suggests, mostly arose from circumstances in which working women had a good deal of freedom in courtship and marriage making, whereas the latter tended to reflect the parental or kin control characteristic of peasant societies where marriage was very much viewed as a family affair. But the pattern appears to have been changing by the late fifteenth century, and in any case it is doubtful how far this typology applies elsewhere.[46] From the relatively few better-recorded cases reviewed here, it is plain that circumstances were very various. What is clear is that in both town and country many young people – especially men, but to an extent women also – had considerable freedom of movement and scope for independent action which could, depending on circumstances, lead them into morally difficult situations and into conflicts with their own family members. A few cases will illustrate these themes. In the winter and spring of 1528, a Leicestershire man named Richard Bate was evidently conducting two parallel love affairs. Though his father seems to have been dead or absent, his mother was alive and had a keen interest in his matrimonial prospects. But he had a mind of his own. In court, he admitted that on a date in March he had had sex with a certain Alice White of Blaston and that

> on Wednisday in Easter weke [8 April] he and she went to hir ffathers . . . and her ffather dyd aske hym, 'Ar you content to mak a bargayn off mariage with

---

[46] Goldberg, *Women, Work, and Life Cycle*, pp. 251–66; Goldberg, 'Gender and Matrimonial Litigation', 48–9; cf. Donahue, *Law, Marriage, and Society*, pp. 201–15.

my doughter Alice?' and he sayd ye. And . . . he saith when he and she come home togidder his mother wold nott suffre them to come into hir hows, and then Richard said to his mother in the presence off Alice, 'I will have hyr to my wiff, and iff we cannot come into the hows togidder we wyll worke togydder on the daylight.' And he saith that he desiered hys mother to 'Be good unto me for I wyll have hyr to my wiff,' and at his desier his mother went to the churche and desiered the parson to aske them in the churche [i.e. to call the banns of marriage] on the Sonday after and ageyn on the Sonday after that.

Alice, for her part, agreed in court 'that this is truthe and that she was every tyme contented to have hym to hyr husbond, and by hir consent was asked in the churche'. Both Richard and Alice admitted that after the publication of the banns, they had had sexual relations at least a further six times.

However, there were complications. Questioned about another woman, Margaret Treman of Sayton, Richard confessed

that he come ffyrst to hyr abowt the Twelft Day [6 January], and after that he dydd send hyr a pair of gloves and a sylken lace for tokens in that entent to mary with hym. And upon Palmesonday last he come to Sayton hymselff to hyr masters hows, and their he hasked hyr iff she myght fynd hir in hir hart to love hym bifour all other, and she sayd that she myght fynd in hyr hart to love hym bifour all other if he myght get hyr emmys [i.e. her uncle's] goode will; and then they poynted that he myght come to Sayton on the Tuesday in Easter weke that they myght goo togidder to hir uncle to knowe his mynd. But he saith he come nott that day bicause that Alice sayd she was with child with hym and that she wold devoure [i.e. destroy] hyrselff except she hadd hym to hyr husbond.

Although there is no formal record of the outcome of this case, on the basis of this evidence, the presumption was clearly in favour of the marriage with Alice, and it also seems plain that Alice's desperate avowal, when she found herself pregnant, had tipped the balance of Richard's decision in her favour. Not all women who consented to sex in expectation of marriage were so lucky. Eleanor Redyng, a Chichester servant, appealed urgently to Thomas Caplyn: 'Thomas, I am with childe and thou promised me be thy faith and trouthe thou woldst mary with me.' According to her, he reassured her that he would be as good as his word, and a witness reported him as saying, 'Be my faithe and be my cristendome I will never forsake hir.' Instead, he contracted marriage with a certain Joan Borishe in a ceremony, sealed with a kiss, conducted before witnesses in her own house. It was this better attested and, for Caplyn, no doubt financially more advantageous union that the consistory court upheld.[47]

---

[47] LA, DIOC/Cj 4, fos. 9v–10r; WSRO, Ep.I/10/2, fos. 4v, 5v, 6r, 12r, 14r–v, 22v.

Even more openly defiant was Thomas Bartlett, also of Chichester, who had apparently made a promise of some sort to Agnes Martyn and, by his own confession, had sex with her. When his parish priest confronted him about the matter, Bartlett allegedly replied, 'I can not deny but I am sure to Agnes Martyn and promysed hir mariage, but I will never mary with hir.' Agnes herself made a heartfelt appeal to his better nature: 'Thomas Bartlett, if thou be a trew man I take the for my housband, thou cannot say naye, thou promysed me by thy faith in thy body thou woldest never dyshonour me nor disseve me.' 'And suche a worde I saide,' replied Thomas stonily, but nonetheless he refused to marry her, and the court gave sentence against Agnes because there was no direct evidence of a contract in due form. It did punish Thomas for seducing her, however, and occasionally in such circumstances the courts went further and insisted on some kind of financial recompense. In a Leicestershire case in 1525, Margaret Holme's spousals suit against Thomas Galyns foundered on lack of evidence. But the court referred the parties to arbitrators 'for the dowering of the said Margaret, for that he begot her with child, she being before that time of good fame and in no way stained'.[48]

In many of these cases, family influence, if not absent, was very much a background factor. Suits in which it was more prominent often turned on the fact that a young man or young woman had had enough freedom to entangle themselves with a partner whom their families regarded as unsuitable, and were sometimes bold enough to talk big about it, yet lacked the strength and independence to resist family pressure to repudiate the union. Joan Aylmer of West Wittering (Sussex), asked how matters stood between her and William Collwell, answered, 'Be my ffayth it standith thus, that I can never have any other as long as he levith nor he as long as I leve, butt and if my father knowe it I shall not be able to abide it.'[49]

A trio of London cases will serve to illustrate the extent of and limits to parental control over the marriages of their offspring, especially daughters; they also indicate that betrothal customs in the capital were not much different from those in the country.[50] The ideal of all-round consent, based on careful attention to the desires of the daughter but assuming also due

[48] WSRO, Ep.I/10/2, fos. 12v, 14v, 61r–v, 69r; ROLLR, 1 D 41/11/1, fo. 6r.

[49] WSRO, Ep.I/10/2, fo. 37r. For a vividly worded Buckinghamshire case, see Elvey (ed.), *Courts of the Archdeaconry of Buckingham*, pp. 303–4, 308.

[50] For fuller discussion of London matrimonial cases, see Shannon McSheffrey, '"I will never have none ayenst my faders will": Consent and the Making of Marriage in the Late Medieval Diocese of London', in Constance M. Rousseau and Joel T. Rosenthal (eds.), *Women, Marriage, and Family in Medieval Christendom: Essays in Memory of Michael M. Sheehan* (Kalamazoo, MI, 1998), pp. 153–74.

deference on her part, is reflected in a case of 1521. The father – or rather stepfather in this case – was a citizen of some substance, Rowland Herbert, while the suitor was the well-connected William Monoux. (George Monoux, referred to in the depositions, was sheriff of London in 1509 and mayor in 1514). Herbert challenged the suitor: 'William, for what intent come yow to my howse, whether for love of my doughter or otherwyse?', receiving the conventional reply, 'I come to your howse for thentent to make your doughter my wif.' Thereupon Herbert questioned his stepdaughter: 'Mary, canst thow fynde in thy hert for to love William ... as a woman owte to love hir husbond and for him all other to forsake?' With becoming deference, Mary replied, 'Father, if it please yow that I have hyme to my husband I ame content.' The stepfather interjected, 'It shall nott be as it please me but as it shall please yow bothe.' He went on to question William in similar vein, who answered, 'If so be that I may have your good wyll and hirs together I ame content to mary hyr to my wife and to love hyr as a man ought to love his wyf.' Thus assured of their mutual consent, Herbert ordered them to complete the contract by joining hands, afterwards sealing it with a kiss and by drinking together. In fact, this account simplifies events, since it is clear that before-hand there had been considerable discussion about the terms of the marriage. All seemed to be plain. But before the marriage was solemnized, Monoux travelled abroad, where he decided to become a friar; in any case, it appears that Mary's mother was not in favour of the match.[51]

A more complex situation, in terms of the young woman's wishes, is revealed in a case from 1488. A citizen of substance, Henry Heed, had evidently made up his mind that his daughter Margaret should marry a man called William Hawkyns. But mindful of the church's rules of free consent, he had consulted with his brother, the prior of Hertford, and reported to his daughter that 'it is his wil and myn also that thou shalt have thi free liberte to take an husbond wher thou wilt and not to take Hawkyns but it com of thyne own stomak.' Margaret, it was said, dutifully assured him that 'I may wel fynd in myn hert to hav[e] hym to my husbond and hym wil I have and noon othir.' A trothplight followed, the banns were published once and preparations for the wedding were put in train. Then it emerged that Margaret had a liking for another man and declared that 'I wil nevir have Hawkyns.' 'Thou hor,' retorted her father, 'while [*sic*] diddist not thow tel me this befor?' and gave her a 'stripe' with a piece of wood used as a 'key clogge'. One of the issues in the subsequent lawsuit was

---

[51] LMA, DL/C/207, fos. 60v–64r; on George Monoux, see *ODNB*.

whether this constituted coercion. Unquestionably, it seems that Margaret
had also been subjected to pressure by others when it appeared that she
was wavering. One of her father's neighbours, apparently a relative, since
he called her 'cosyn Margarete', told her to 'stablissh your mynd, and
I pray send Hawk[yns] sum word of comfort.' According to this account,
Margaret was 'ashamed' for having spoken ill of Hawkyns and hence felt
apprehensive that he would 'love me the worse'. It is not clear whether she
was merely vacillating, as Shannon McSheffrey thinks, or more purposefully trying to put Hawkyns off. Either way, she clearly had limited room
for manoeuvre – despite her father's promise of 'free liberty' – and the
upshot was that the couple did eventually get married.[52]

Coercion was more blatant in a case of 1530, to the extent that witnesses
found unacceptable and reprehensible; indeed, this was not a mere spousals
suit but an attempt to declare a contract invalid on the grounds of force and
fear. Robert Wansworth wanted his daughter to marry a man called Robert
Browne, whom he welcomed to his house as a suitor. But she despised him
as a 'kyng of apes and kyng of sprates', preferring her own choice, William
Sarnell. Her father threatened that 'if thow wyll not leve William Sarnells
company and lene to Robert Browne, I wyll breke a leg or an arme of
thyne; and if thow . . . [will] not be ruled by me, gete the owt of my dores
and thow [will] never have any part of my goodes and I will not know the as
my child and thow shall not have me as thy fader.' There was evidence that
he had threatened her with a trencher and beaten her with a 'metyerd'
(measuring rod) till her arms were black and 'blody' colour and that she
was found on the banks of the Thames bare-legged in her petticoat, saying
she wished to drown herself.[53]

As stated earlier, the possibility of contracting a binding union by means
of an informal spousals ceremony not only generated uncertainty but also
facilitated fraud, and the cases already examined indicate that some individuals did not treat their vows at all seriously. This was true not only of the
principals but also on occasion of others with an axe to grind. In 1530,
a widow, on the point of entering into a contract with a servant of Sir
Richard Grey, admitted that she had made some sort of promise to the
servant of the wealthy Enfield gentleman Robert Wroth but was willing to
commit herself 'so that I may be discharged and redd from thother man . . .
and that fownd no contract of matrimony'. Grey, having heard her account

---

[52] LMA, DL/C/A/001/MS09065B, fos. 11v–15r (quotations fos. 12r, 14r, 14v); the case is discussed at
length in McSheffrey, *Marriage, Sex, and Civic Culture*, pp. 74–7.
[53] LMA, DL/C/208, fos. 120v–122r, 123v–124r, 126v–128r (quotations fos. 120v, 123v). For allegations of
an even more severe beating, see DL/C/208, fo. 165r.

of the earlier bargain, advised her that she might safely go ahead.[54] Some men were charged with the offence of 'selling' wives. This had nothing to do with the marketplace wife sales recorded for the eighteenth and nineteenth centuries but implied that men who had made marriage contracts with particular women had relinquished their rights to other men in return for a cash payment. Sometimes this was an extra-judicial way of settling a dispute when two men claimed a contract with the same woman; on other occasions circumstances had changed, and the man no longer wanted to marry the woman in question. In a Surrey case in 1512, the couple had contracted marriage on condition of obtaining their parents' good will and had promised to wait for each other for seven years till this might be achieved and assuming that each was still content to take the other at the end of that time. The wait was apparently too long for the man, who 'sold' his betrothed for 3s. 1d. Whatever the circumstances, the practice was at odds with the church's principle that a binding contract created an indissoluble union, and even a conditional contract could not be lightly put aside.[55]

However, the incidence of spousals suits – about ten a year in medium-sized jurisdictions such as the archdeaconries of Chichester and Leicester around 1520 – was not so great as to suggest complete chaos. In addition, in every jurisdiction, a few individuals faced disciplinary prosecutions for breaking off marriage contracts and solemnizing marriage with someone else. The fact that such people were reported to the courts suggests that the practice was not simply taken for granted. Indeed, the fact that an individual was supposed to have made a contract that was afterwards disregarded was apparently viewed as disreputable and was sometimes dragged up again years later in legal proceedings or otherwise.[56] Harrington stressed that any pretended marriage made in defiance of a binding contract was 'of none effecte and they lyf in a dampnable adultery'.[57] There are indications that this message was internalized and in times of difficulty could surface in the guise of a bad conscience and bitter remorse. Thus, in a case in the Chichester consistory court in 1520, it was reported that a sick woman, in danger of death, lamented to her supposed spouse, 'Housband, I have shewed you dyvers tymes that ye and I wer not true man and wif: that is the cause we do not thryve nor prosper. I pray God forgeve you and me also, for we have lyved in advoutry as long as we have byn maryed together.'[58]

---

[54] LMA, DL/C/208, fos. 167v–168r, cf. fos. 168v–169r, 170r, 170v, 172r; cf. Elvey (ed.), *Courts of the Archdeaconry of Buckingham*, p. 263 (the evidence in this case may have been suspect, however).
[55] LMA, Ac. 62.7, fo. 78v.   [56] E.g. ROLLR, 1 D 41/11/1, fo. 32r.
[57] Harrington, *Commendacions of matrymony*, sig. C3r–v.   [58] WSRO, Ep.I/10/2, fo. 62v.

Fame, Reputation and Slander Suits

Today, 'fame' is something to which, by definition, few can aspire. In Tudor England, its meaning was quite different. 'Good fame' was an almost tangible social good to which anyone, however poor or humble, could lay claim. It meant to be in good repute or 'credit' among one's neighbours and associates and hence free to live life and pursue diurnal tasks without harassment or the immediate threat of having one's honesty and credit called in question. To be of 'bad', 'ill' or 'evil' fame, however, or even to be 'suspect', was a dangerous and potentially deteriorating social condition. Even the honest actions of such a person were liable to be misinterpreted. He or she might find it hard to get employment or to secure a loan or other credit. The person also was in danger of court action. A dog with a bad name is half hanged. A late fifteenth- or early sixteenth-century man or woman with a similar handicap might indeed be in danger of a similar fate or at least of being brought before the justices, the manor court or the officers of the bishop or archdeacon. Ill-repute fully proven could amount to 'infamy', a legally defined state with tangible consequences that effectively barred the individual concerned from recourse to the courts or from enjoying other social benefits.[59]

Sometimes it was possible, with the aid of the parish priest, to dissipate suspicions locally. Thus, in 1520, the curate of Marsh Gibbon (Buckinghamshire) admitted that 'last Sunday week he divided the consecrated host between John Ladyman and Elizabeth Clark ... at their request ... that by this means they should be reputed innocent of the crime of incontinence that was risen against them ... Elizabeth having first been contracted in marriage with William Newenton but the latter refused to have her ... until she had purged herself in this manner.' He was reprimanded – the judge instructed that the correct procedure was to hold a special mass at which the suspected persons would receive the sacrament to demonstrate that they were innocent – but it was accepted that the priest had acted 'in pure innocence not out of malice but with a good mind'.[60]

But often it was necessary to appeal to higher authority. Thus it was that one of the most important social and legal services offered by the

[59] Janet Coleman, 'Scholastic Treatments of Maintaining One's *Fama* (Reputation/Good Name) and the Correction of Private "Passions" for the Public Good and Public Legitimacy', *Cultural and Social History*, 2 (2005), 23–48.

[60] Margaret Bowker (ed.), *An Episcopal Court Book for the Diocese of Lincoln, 1514–20* (Lincoln Record Society 61, Lincoln, 1967), p. 136.

ecclesiastical courts in fifteenth-century England was redress against slander. At this point they effectively had no competitors. In the high middle ages, borough courts had exercised slander jurisdiction, but for reasons that are at present unclear, it had withered away by 1400. The king's courts, however, had not yet developed a law of defamation.[61] In the church courts, various remedies were available. People who claimed that they had been slandered and feared the consequences – whether general loss of reputation, credit and standing or the danger of actually being prosecuted for crimes of which they had been accused – could appear voluntarily before the courts and offer to vindicate their reputation by means of 'compurgation'. That is, they undertook to produce a specified number of neighbours, themselves of good repute and usually of equal status to the accused, who were prepared to take a formal oath that they believed the defamed person to be innocent of any crime and of good name and fame. Often theft or some other secular crime was the matter at issue, in which case it was most commonly a male who sought to recover his reputation. But many of these voluntary compurgations centred on accusations of sexual transgression and could involve women as well as men. Indeed, such cases are often hard to distinguish from more routine prosecutions for adultery and fornication, of the kind that will be discussed in Chapter 3.[62]

By no means all defamation cases in the church courts were voluntary. People who habitually defamed their neighbours, or subjected them to verbal abuse, were liable to prosecution.[63] Such offenders were often women, sometimes labelled 'scolds', but 'common defamers' also included men. Again, someone who had defamed a particular individual might on occasion be reported to the courts for disciplinary action.[64] As will be seen, this was a particularly common form of proceeding in the London commissary court, to the extent that such cases formed a high proportion of disciplinary prosecutions in some years; they will be discussed in that context in Chapter 6. But outside London, suits between parties were the

---

[61] R. H. Helmholz (ed.), *Select Cases on Defamation to 1600* (Selden Society 101, London, 1985), pp. xlviii–lxxv. On canonical defamation, see also Ian Forrest, 'Defamation, Heresy and Late Medieval Social Life', in Linda Clark, Maureen Jurkowski and Colin Richmond (eds.), *Image, Text and Church, 1300–1600: Essays for Margaret Aston* (Toronto, 2009), pp. 142–61.

[62] For typical cases, see Elvey (ed.), *Courts of the Archdeaconry of Buckingham*, pp. 96, 115, 122, 151.

[63] For a particularly striking example in 1521, when up to forty 'honest women' crowded into court to make their complaint, see Elvey (ed.), *Courts of the Archdeaconry of Buckingham*, p. 313, trans. in P. J. P. Goldberg (ed.), *Women in England, c.1275–1525: Documentary Sources* (Manchester, 1995), p. 229.

[64] Prosecutions of this sort are the main focus of L. R. Poos, 'Sex, Lies, and the Church Courts of Pre-Reformation England', *Journal of Interdisciplinary History*, 25 (1994–5), 585–607.

most common means of seeking redress against slander. The church courts could not offer cash damages, but they could excommunicate a convicted defamer or (the usual procedure) order him or her to make a formal and usually public apology. Exceptionally, the record of a Leicestershire case of 1535 detailed the precise form of words:

> Wher as I have spokyn herbefore slaunderous worddes against your goode nayme ande fame, more off males [malice] then off trouth ande off a hasty mynd, I dyde speke them unadvyssly, wherfor I besych you off your gudnes to forgyffe me ande I intend never so doo more for I know no yll by youe.[65]

Mostly cases did not proceed so far. Frequently the litigants settled their differences between themselves, often almost as soon as legal proceedings began or even before; sometimes cases were referred to arbitrators or otherwise settled out of court with an apology or compensation in cash. In an Essex case in 1494 involving an unmarried woman accused of fornication, the original slander was uttered in church, in the presence of the parish priest, the woman's father and another man. The victim and her accuser each nominated two representatives (all males), who shortly afterwards met with other men on neutral ground (probably an alehouse) in an attempt to settle the matter by mediation. The defamer confessed that he had spoken in spite but refused to comply with the mediators' order that he should publicly disavow the slander in the parish church. It was only then that the matter was taken to court.[66]

From around 1500 the royal courts began to insist that the church courts should not consider any matters that touched on the temporal jurisdiction, so slanders of theft and suchlike were gradually squeezed out. Because these secular matters had mostly concerned men, the change – which affected different jurisdictions at different times – had an effect on the gender ratio among litigants, especially plaintiffs. As late as 1520 at Chichester, where the courts were still hearing slanders of theft and other secular crimes, sixty-six of eighty-eight identifiable defamation suits were brought by men, mostly against other men, and a further two were commenced by married couples. The presence of ten clerical plaintiffs biases the figures slightly, but even so, it is clear that the prosecution of defamation suits was far more characteristically a male than a female activity. It was as the common-law restrictions on the church courts' jurisdiction began to bite that the balance shifted. When imputations of theft and other secular crimes were removed, sexual slanders predominated in the church courts. Overall, the numbers of

---

[65] ROLLR, 1 D 41/11/2, fo. 190v.   [66] LMA, DL/C/A/002/MS09065, fo. 183(184)r-v.

cases went down, but the proportion of women plaintiffs rose, though not necessarily to form a clear majority. Thus, in the archdeaconry of Leicester, between December 1524 and February 1527, fifty-seven defamation suits are recorded. In only a minority of these is the nature of the slander made evident, but overwhelmingly these cases concerned sexual matters. There are a few miscellaneous non-sexual slanders of ecclesiastical cognizance – revealing the secrets of the confessional, burying a dead child in a field, Lollard heresy – but imputations of theft and the like are notable by their absence. Of the fifty-seven suits, thirty were brought by men and one other by a married couple. Women thus made a better showing among plaintiffs in this court, accounting for the other twenty-six suits. If the male total is deflated to remove the bias caused by clerical plaintiffs, men and women emerge as more or less equally prone to bring defamation suits.[67]

Slander and Sexual Regulation

Studies of later periods, for which more abundant sources survive, have shown that sexual slander suits cannot always be taken at face value and that it is potentially misleading to read off from them attitudes towards sexual transgression. Suits were often enmeshed with other disputes, over land, cash transactions, neighbourhood clashes and the like, and the basic cause of rancour and enmity was often remote from sexual matters. Individuals from a wide range of social positions might be involved, but characteristically litigants were householders and their wives of middling substance in town and country. Sometimes they were prominent in their local societies, although not truly eminent in status. It may be that, as in later periods, sexual slanders were sometimes part of a process whereby such individuals jockeyed for local position and prestige in conflicts that might have been simmering for many years. More generally, it is clear that many slanders were uttered by way of insult or in hot blood during the course of other quarrels. In such circumstances, the victims of slander were as apt to resent the affront to their position as to fear any real loss of reputation: they resorted to litigation to heal their wounded pride or simply get their own back rather than to clear their names.[68]

---

[67] WSRO, Ep.I/10/2, *passim*; ROLLR, 1 D 41/11/1, *passim*.

[68] Martin Ingram, 'Law, Litigants and the Construction of "Honour": Slander Suits in Early Modern England', in Peter Coss (ed.), *The Moral World of the Law* (Cambridge, 2000), pp. 143–6, and the references there cited; Elvey (ed.), *Courts of the Archdeaconry of Buckingham*, pp. xviii–xix, 267, 268, 270.

This is particularly helpful in understanding why abusive epithets were brought to court as slander suits. In point of fact, much scurrilous and spiteful invective was not actionable. The essence of the English canon law of slander was redress against accusations of *crime* whereby an individual might be defamed among 'good and grave' men. Actions could be brought for abusive 'words of reproach' with no obvious criminal content, but this jurisdiction was used sparingly in this period. Clergymen, with their position to defend and enjoying privileged status in the courts, were most prominent among litigants suing for abuse. Many of the matters they complained of, though directed against individuals, in fact had a generic element in implying that all who bore the clerical tonsure were disreputable. In 1520, the subdean of Chichester sued a man for calling him 'pollshorn prest', while the prior of Sele reacted similarly to the imputation that he was a 'poldeshoron whorson and poldeshoryn fryar'.[69] As will be seen in Chapter 8, it is even more understandable that priests should want to vindicate their credit when abused in terms that suggested sexual immorality.

Lay people sometimes brought suits for epithets such as 'knave' and 'harlot' – the latter word applied to both men and women in this period – especially when they were linked with charges of extortion or dishonest dealing in couplets, such as 'false extortioner' and 'polling knave'. 'Harlot', which when applied to females was roughly equivalent to the term 'whore', in certain contexts may have implied sexual transgression on the part of males also.[70] 'Knave' also may have had a possible sexual dimension, as it certainly did later.[71] 'Whoremaster', a biting word that meant a habitual sexual transgressor, was occasionally the grounds for action. However, the most powerful sexually charged word applied to men, and the one most often used – on its own or coupled with practically anything else – was 'cuckold'. Like the modern (and much milder) epithet 'bastard', this word was regularly employed as a generalized term of abuse, often with little real content. Its power to wound, however, lay in the fact that it could carry a specific and very damaging meaning, namely, that the wife of the man in question was, or had been, sexually unfaithful. The plain word could be embroidered with adjectives. 'Stark' or 'strong' implied that the condition was inveterate and beyond remedy. 'Poor cuckold' expressed more openly what was in all cases implied, that the situation arose from the man's own

---

[69] WSRO, Ep.I/10/2, fos. 18r, 106r.
[70] Cf. Poos, 'Sex, Lies, and the Church Courts', 591–2, which arbitrarily excludes this possibility.
[71] Ingram, 'Law, Litigants and the Construction of "Honour"', pp. 156–7.

inadequacy – sexual, economic or otherwise. 'Wittol' signified that the man was not only a cuckold but also knew about it and yet did nothing. Obviously, the jibe of cuckoldry was more damaging if it was coupled with a specific account of the wife's supposed misdoings, but it is plain that even on its own the word was humiliating and deeply wounding. That there were not more prosecutions for this slander was because cuckoldry was not in itself a crime (and so only marginally within the courts' competence) and no doubt also because many men preferred not to advertise the fact that they had so been taunted.

There was no equivalent word applied to women. The counterpart was the word 'whore', which referred to women's own sexual transgressions. The word did not, as it does in some usages today, imply a prostitute. It could denote any sexually transgressive woman – a single act of adultery, for example, made a whore – though in fact there were often implications of promiscuity. Even more than 'cuckold', however, the word was often used as a vulgar term of abuse, with little or no real content. It was in fact the standard means of expressing hostility and contempt towards any woman in practically any situation. In some cases before the courts, the word had been used in this general sense, and reputation was hardly at issue: the plaintiff was, in effect, suing for the affront or had seized upon the word 'whore' as a handy means of bringing the defendant into court.

This was by no means invariably so, however. Some slanging matches were indeed based in deep resentment of sexual misdoing. In 1520, Anne Petit of West Angmering (Sussex) sued Elizabeth Yong for calling her 'strong hore'. But Yong immediately began a counter-suit, and a witness reported how he had heard Petit, standing at Yong's door, charge her with adultery: 'thou kepist my housband her[e] lyke a strong hore as thou art and so will I prove the.'[72] However, there are indications that the use of the word 'whore' on its own, without any corroborating claim of specific sexual misdoing, could cause a woman's reputation to be brought in question or have other serious consequences. Not least such slander might give an excuse to a jealous or discontented husband – who might himself be fearful of the taint of cuckoldry and anxious to assert himself – to ill-treat his wife. In 1494, a Middlesex woman who parted two female assailants was for her pains abused by one of them as a 'strong hoore'; as a result, her husband turned on her with the words, 'Walk, art thou a strong hoor? It shalbe provid whedir it be so or no or evir thou come mor in my bed.' In a Whitechapel case in 1524, a woman slandered Katherine Ratclyf as 'a

<hr>

[72] WSRO, Ep.I/10/2, fos. 94r, 110v.

stronge erraunt hoore and a weddyd mannys hore'. As a result of the
rumours raised in the parish, it was said, her husband would have turned
her out if her friends had not dissuaded him, while Katherine herself was so
intimidated by so much disgrace that she scarcely dared to go out of the
house.[73]

Gowing's argument that the reputations of men and women were
'incommensurable' is at best an overstatement, if applied to this period.[74]
It is certainly true, as many of the cases so far cited imply, that sexual
reputation was more central to the female persona, while society in general – though not necessarily the courts, as will be seen – was apt to regard
the sexual transgressions of women more seriously than those of men.
More specifically, it is plain that men sometimes boasted of their sexual
exploits and even claimed publicly to have had relations with particular
women in a way that females did not. In the Essex case of 1494, cited earlier,
the defamer was a disappointed suitor, and 'because she woold not have
me, therfor I seid I lay by her that she shuld be loth to any othir man.'[75]
More usually, however, these admissions were made in a peer-group
situation, often in alehouses and sometimes when the men concerned
were the worse for drink, or they were confidences that were betrayed by
male companions, sometimes out of jealousy or a desire to do mischief.
In any case, male boasters ran the risk of being brought to book. Cases in
the archdeaconry of Leicester in the early 1520s indicate that when a man
admitted or was proved to have incriminated himself in this way, he was
immediately subjected to discipline or forced to undergo compurgation.
This happened to Richard Leeys, who claimed to have had sex with
Elizabeth Deyne of Hoby, and to Arthur Yerland of Stathern, who allegedly boasted that he could have Isabel Braybrooke at his good pleasure.[76]

There is ample evidence from this and other jurisdictions that men
could be highly sensitive to slurs of sexual misconduct. Robert Jonson of
Chiltington (Sussex) sued when slandered for committing fornication
with a certain Joan at Wode, while Ralph Hyton of Kirkby Mallory
(Leicestershire) took action because a man said that he had begotten
a certain woman with child.[77] These cases jostle with those brought by

[73] LMA, DL/C/A/002/MS09065, fos. 184(185)r, 184(185)v; LMA, DL/C/207, fo. 306r.
[74] Laura Gowing, *Domestic Dangers: Women, Words, and Sex in Early Modern London* (Oxford, 1996),
    pp. 109–10 and chaps. 3–4, *passim*; cf. Ingram, 'Law, Litigants and the Construction of "Honour"',
    pp. 151–7.
[75] LMA, DL/C/A/002/MS09065, fo. 183(184)r.   [76] ROLLR, 1 D 41/11/1, fos. 3r, 10v.
[77] WSRO, Ep.I/10/2, fo. 92r, cf. fo. 125r; ROLLR, 1 D 41/11/1, fo. 25r, cf. fo. 38r. See also Elvey (ed.),
    Courts of the Archdeaconry of Buckingham, pp. 258, 261–2.

women, usually married, to clear their sexual reputations. Joan Boycot of Chichester, for example, sued a woman for declaring that she had 'had a childe or [i.e. ere] she was maryed when she dwellid with the goodman of the Swan', while Emmota Hargrave of Oadby (Leicestershire) took similar action to clear herself of the implications of a statement that 'hyr husband wasse a cukewould'.[78]

Gowing also implies, as have other commentators, that women used their tongues more often and more adeptly than men in pursuing their quarrels and grievances and in particular excelled at spinning scandalous tales that had the ring of truth. These ideas are debatable. Men certainly used words to taunt and humiliate opponents or to claim their rights, but they probably resorted to physical violence more than women did, and they were more readily brought to court for their blows than for their words. However, it is clear that both men and women played a role in evaluating reputations and upholding standards of personal morality and in doing so aired potentially defamatory facts and opinions. But, as will be seen more fully in later chapters, men had more opportunities to do this in official roles and in institutional contexts – as local churchwardens or members of juries, for example. In contrast, women's views were more likely to be voiced informally, either as gossip or in face-to-face confrontations on the streets. A case from St Christopher le Stocks in London in 1529 provides a good example of the latter. A local woman 'exclaimed' against the parish priest – unjustly, it was said – alleging that he had kept her for years and was the father of the child she bore in her arms. But the 'honest good and substancyall wyffes of the ... parish' to whom she appealed judged that 'ther owt no credens to be gevyn to suche a shameles woman which was not ... abashyd oppynly to declare and pronounce hirself vycious and yll of hir levyng.'[79]

Yet males were as prominent as females among those accused of being defamers, and some demonstrated salty rhetoric, ready wit and a keen eye for scurrilous detail. In Leicestershire in 1525, Thomas Dylkys of Kirkby Mallory challenged another man: 'William Calver, yff thow kepe noughty pakkes, harlettes and qwennes and flyrtes with them thow shall not flyrt with me.' But in the last resort perhaps women did take the prize for the most effective tale-bearing and invective. In the same year, Cecily Ball of Coleorton reported that John Taytnell, evidently a baker, 'dyd cast Johanna Hunnyluffe apone hys muldyng bord and the bord went gyge a goge.' (A moulding board was a table for kneading large masses of dough,

---

[78] WSRO, Ep.I/10/2, fo. 26r; ROLLR, 1 D 41/11/1, fo. 31r.   [79] TNA, SP 1/40, fos. 176r, 177r.

and the last phrase was probably pronounced 'jig a jog'.) In 1531, Alice
Adcoke of Leicester, upset at Katherine Care's suggestion that she was 'off
yll disposicion' with her suitor, indeed his 'harlot ande hore', responded
thus:

> [Y]ff thy moder and thy selffe have made a fals ly off me I shall tell a trew
> tayle off the . . . Thow sent me dyveres and many a tymme for Sir Christofer
> the curet off Saint Leonardes to cum and speke with the ande so I dyde.
> I dyd see hym ly in naked bed with the ande that I wyll make good apone
> a bouke [i.e. swear to]. I wasse thy bawde, wherfor I ame sore [i.e. sorry] that
> so I wasse. This that I have seid I wyll make good ande prove.[80]

These defamation suits are revealing in many ways. The slanders were
often uttered maliciously and in pursuit of other quarrels; mixed motives
also tainted the reasons why cases were brought to court. Nonetheless, they
hint at what must have been a constant swirl of gossip and rumour about
sexual behaviour that was transgressive in the sense of being at odds with
the standards of Christian morality that Harrington took for granted. They
also suggest the processes whereby suspicions of ill fame gradually accumulated and were eventually brought into sharp focus by being publicly
uttered in ways that deliberately 'outed' individuals as adulterers, cuckolds,
whores and so on. The altercations and accusations that occurred in
street and marketplace, inns and alehouses, workshops and private dwell-
ings are redolent of endemic tensions in small-scale communities and the
importance in a face-to-face society of unblemished reputation. This is an
essential part of the context of active efforts to police sexual conduct.[81]

It is of equal importance to note the linkages among the various
elements discussed in this chapter. The paths towards matrimony were
tortuous and the processes of matchmaking highly flexible. Albeit within
a framework of parental influence and community supervision, young
people – often in service and perhaps remote from their families, if indeed
they had not outlived father, mother or both – had considerable scope to
work out their own destinies. But once achieved, marriage was a decisive
event that both conferred status and entailed responsibilities. Married
householders, as the backbone of society, played an important role in
policing personal behaviour and social relations, in the sexual as in other
spheres of life. Men were more likely than women to do this through
institutional channels, but both had a part to play. All the indications are
that sexual slander suits were brought less by maids or bachelors seeking to

---

[80] ROLLR, 1 D 41/11/1, fos. 7r, 22r; 1 D 41/11/2, fo. 121v.
[81] A similar argument is made by Poos, 'Sex, Lies, and the Church Courts'.

safeguard their marriage chances than by married women anxious to preserve their reputation for honesty and respectability or by husbands determined to avoid the ignominy of being called a cuckold. They were, in short, a further reflection of the centrality of marriage, household and family in social life and in the construction of both male and female identity.

Shame

Not only was marriage an institution of central political, economic, social and cultural significance, but it was also the only framework within which sexual relations could be licitly pursued. As was noted earlier, virtually no one was prepared to voice the contrary opinion, even if they thought it. There were some soft or ambiguous terms that might be used to cloak sexual transgression, such as 'leman' (though this was gradually going out of use) or 'mistress' (slowly coming in), but all the evidence is that much harsher words sprang more readily to minds and lips – 'whore', 'whoremaster', 'harlot', 'cuckold'. Anyone who pursued a sexual relationship outside marriage was vulnerable to such abuse. The corollary was that sexual reputation, in the sense of being 'clear' (as contemporaries said) of any suspicion of fornication, adultery or other sins of the flesh, or of aiding and abetting them, was widely understood to be a positive good that was closely related to social status and personal identity.

This was true even though numerous individuals acted otherwise. In a right-minded Christian of either gender, it was thought, apprehension of sexual transgression should arouse a sense of guilt and a troubled conscience. In the public arena, the counterpart of these emotions was shame – so vividly evoked by the women of St Christopher le Stocks in 1529 – a biting sense of status or character damaged or destroyed.[82] Late fifteenth- and early sixteenth-century England, as indeed the whole of Western Europe, had inherited from Aristotle the idea that 'shame' was an intensely unpleasant emotion, expressed in reddened cheeks and downcast eyes, that was not in itself a virtue but which could act both as a bridle to restrain misconduct and a spur to better behaviour. Hence *erubescentia* ('blushing') was a common synonym. Aristotle saw it as

---

[82] Shame differs from guilt partly in that it depends on the fact or apprehension of public exposure. It can also be experienced as a result of circumstances – as diverse as poverty, loss of bowel control or the misdeeds of family members – that are in no way the 'fault' of the individual or at least are involuntary.

becoming in youth, who naturally had much to learn, but disgraceful in adults. Christian ethics nuanced this view while not effacing it. Medieval theologians developed the idea of 'good' and 'bad' shame. The latter was the bitter emotion suffered by condemned criminals or those who were unrepentant. It was by definition dishonouring and destructive. But if the painful and humiliating lessons of shame – if necessary, reinforced by penance or corporal punishment – were embraced with faith and repentance, they could lead a person's soul to God and be a means towards reconciliation of the criminal or sinner with his or her neighbours.[83]

Famously, Norbert Elias linked the 'civilizing process' with advancing thresholds of shame and embarrassment in relations between the sexes, as also in other areas of bodily comportment. His account is too schematic to serve as a template for this study, while his chronology – focusing on the sixteenth century as the crucial period of change – is manifestly at odds with much of the evidence presented here.[84] Yet the subject of shame is of undoubted importance. Both as a concept and as an experience, it flits constantly in and out of subsequent chapters. Though only occasionally brought to the foreground either in legal discourses or in the statements of witnesses and accused people, it was implicit in many of the procedures of the courts and in particular in the practice of penance and punishment. It is important not least because it draws attention to some of the ambiguities inherent in the system of social discipline discussed in this book. It was the task of the courts – primarily those of the church but, as will be seen, many secular tribunals too – to punish sexual sin. Yet even to bring someone into question was to defame them and so subject them to public obloquy and shame in ways that might prove irreversible. Canon lawyers debated how this dilemma should be handled in Christian society. St Matthew's gospel taught that the first step towards the reform of a sinner should be brotherly exhortation in private, followed by admonition before witnesses. Only if this proved ineffective should the matter be 'told to the church'. But in what circumstances exactly should charitable admonition give way to legal action? There was room here for considerable differences of interpretation.[85]

---

[83] This is one of the main themes developed by the contributors to Bénédicte Sère and Jörg Wettlaufer (eds.), *Shame between Punishment and Penance. La honte entre peine et pénitence* (Florence, 2013). See also Katharina Behrens, *Scham: zur sozialen Bedeutung eines Gefühls im spätmittelalterlichen England* (Göttingen, 2014).

[84] Norbert Elias, *The Civilizing Process: The History of Manners and State Formation and Civilization*, trans. Edmund Jephcott (Oxford, 1994 edn.), p. 492 and *passim*.

[85] Edwin D. Craun, 'The Imperatives of *Denunciatio*: Disclosing Others' Sins to Disciplinary Authorities', in Mary C. Flannery and Katie L. Walter (eds.), *The Culture of Inquisition in Medieval England* (Cambridge, 2013), pp. 30–44.

On this partly depended whether the courts at particular times and in particular places were more or less active in combating sin and whether they themselves sought out information or relied on others to report accusations. Once individuals were before the courts, there were further choices to be made. Should investigations be kept as secret as possible, or should they be made public to ensure that the truth came out? When offenders were actually convicted, should they be subjected to rigorous, shaming penalties, both to mortify them and to deter others, or should the courts exercise mercy or leniency in the hope that this would better bring sinners back to God or heal social relations in local communities? These issues – which still have resonance today – will repeatedly crop up in subsequent chapters as they examine the mechanisms of sexual regulation as they worked in practice in England before, during and after the Reformation.

CHAPTER 3

'Bawdy Courts' in Rural Society before 1530

The church courts were known colloquially as the 'bawdy' or 'bum courts'. This undignified appellation was partly metaphorical, implying that the men who ran the courts were themselves disreputable. No doubt there *was* some underhand dealing and simple slackness, but the same could be said of any law court of the time. However, careful examination by modern historians has largely exonerated the church courts of egregious corruption or inefficiency.[1] More basically, the nickname reflected the fact that in rural areas – the main focus of this chapter – these courts were far and away the most important official agents of sexual discipline. Manor courts were involved to some extent but in most places only marginally. Church court records and procedures are therefore key to understanding how sexual regulation operated, and to gauging its scope and intensity, in much of England in the fifty years or so before the Reformation.

This chapter serves several purposes. Since references to the disciplinary activities of the church courts will recur throughout this book, some of the basics of how they operated are explained at this point and their distinctive features emphasized. Historians' understanding of the workings of similar institutions in other parts of Europe is at present limited, but what is known suggests that the pre-Reformation English church courts operated an unusually intense regime of regulating the sexual lives of lay people.[2] This chapter also highlights the ways in which the late fifteenth- and early

---

[1] Brian L. Woodcock, *Medieval Ecclesiastical Courts in the Diocese of Canterbury* (London, 1952), esp. pp. 48–9, 106, 111–12; Margaret Bowker, 'Some Archdeacons' Court Books and the Commons' Supplication against the Ordinaries of 1532', in D. A. Bullough and R. L. Storey (eds.), *The Study of Medieval Records: Essays in Honour of Kathleen Major* (Oxford, 1971), pp. 282–316; Margaret Bowker, 'The Commons Supplication against the Ordinaries in the Light of some Archidiaconal Acta', *Transactions of the Royal Historical Society*, 5th Series, 21 (1971), 61–77 (abridged version of preceding article); Ralph Houlbrooke, *Church Courts and the People during the English Reformation, 1520–1570* (Oxford, 1979), esp. pp. 52–3, 271–2.

[2] Henry Ansgar Kelly, 'Inquisition, Public Fame and Confession: General Rules and English Practice', in Mary C. Flannery and Katie L. Walter (eds.), *The Culture of Inquisition in Medieval England* (Cambridge, 2013), pp. 8, 20.

sixteenth-century courts differed from their post-Reformation counter-parts. To facilitate comparison with the later period, the scope, intensity and effectiveness of the courts' activities in the sphere of sexual regulation will be closely examined. The courts' relationship with local communities will also be scrutinized. By 1500, the courts had already been operating for many generations. While their efforts to raise moral standards were not always appreciated, were by no means universally successful and undoubtedly offended individuals, they could also be formidable agents of moral discipline, commanding considerable support in the parishes.

Church Court Records: Through a Glass Darkly

The courts were conducted in the name of the bishops, each with authority over one of the twenty-one dioceses into which England was divided,[3] and of archdeacons, who exercised jurisdiction over specific geographical areas – characteristically the size of a small county – within each see.[4] Formerly rural deans may have played a role in sexual discipline, but by the late fifteenth century there is little trace of such activity. Occasionally bishops, more frequently the archdeacons, presided over their courts themselves. But by the period in question, they mostly delegated these judicial responsibilities to legally qualified personnel who filled the diocesan offices of chancellor, vicar-general or official principal (by the late fifteenth century these were beginning to be combined in one person) or, at the archdeaconry level, bishop's commissary and archdeacon's 'official'. Records were maintained, and processes issued, by administratively trained registrars and their deputies and scribal assistants; suitors in the courts were represented by ecclesiastical lawyers called 'proctors' and citations and such like were delivered by the 'apparitors' or 'summoners'. These messengers of the courts were literate but otherwise lowly individuals. But the other personnel were men of substance with an array of professional qualifications. The top jobs were held by men of some eminence, often doctors of canon law, civil law or both. But even the less exalted judges, such as archdeacons' officials, often held the degree of MA or LLB. So also did some proctors, though they could also be trained by apprenticeship, and indeed for everyone concerned, long practice and experience in the courts

---

[3] Counting Bath and Wells as one and including the four Welsh dioceses, but excluding Sodor and Man, which covered the Isle of Man but was otherwise in Scotland, albeit it was part of the northern province of the English church. In 1541 Henry VIII created several new dioceses.

[4] This ignores complications, notably the existence of 'peculiar' jurisdictions exempt from the authority of the bishop.

were the only means of acquiring real competence. Apparitors were not clerics, and by the early sixteenth century it was coming to be accepted that registrars need not be. Judges and proctors, however, were still required to be ordained members of the clergy, and it may be presumed that the ethos of the courts was distinctly clerical as well as legal and professional.[5]

As the qualifications of their personnel indicate, by 1500 the English church courts were formalized, well-established institutions administering the canon law of the church according to orderly, recognized procedures – albeit with scope for local variation and some idiosyncrasies. But only a small fraction of their records survives today, and those that do are not easy to interpret. In order to understand them, it is necessary to establish some basic administrative facts. The contentious business of the courts fell into two main divisions, 'instance' causes (or suits between parties) and 'office' or disciplinary jurisdiction. Instance suits included most matrimonial and defamation causes, of the kinds discussed in Chapter 2, but also comprised such matters as testaments, tithes and other ecclesiastical dues. As noted in Chapter 1, in the late fifteenth century they also included actions for debt in the guise of 'breach of faith' or perjury suits, though from around 1500 the royal courts challenged the church's right to adjudicate such cases, and their numbers dwindled. Some of these causes were handled summarily and recorded very briefly. But, in general, instance actions were likely to be fully documented in formal citations, elaborate 'libels' or statements of the case, witnesses' depositions, and – in the small minority of cases that were pushed to a finish – sentences expressed according to set forms in stylized language. The reasons are obvious. The matters at issue were often weighty, and more fundamentally, the litigants were there to foot the bill. The difficulties of reconstructing this kind of litigation lie not in the paucity of information originally recorded but in the fact that the proceedings of any one suit are characteristically scattered among many pages of court registers and numerous individual documents. More basically, many of these materials have simply perished with time.

The way disciplinary jurisdiction was exercised and the kinds of record it generated were very different. In the remote past, criminal prosecutions had been initiated either by the Roman law procedure of accusation – which required a specific accuser willing to risk incurring the penalty of the

---

[5] For detailed information on the qualifications of pre-Reformation church court personnel, see Woodcock, *Medieval Ecclesiastical Courts*, pp. 37–49, 113–23; Margaret Bowker, *The Secular Clergy in the Diocese of Lincoln, 1495–1520* (Cambridge, 1968), pp. 13–37; Houlbrooke, *Church Courts*, pp. 24–9.

crime if he or she failed to prove the case – or denunciation to the ecclesiastical authorities. The cumbersome nature of these procedures had led to the development of 'inquisition', which enabled judges to bring cases on the basis of 'common fame' and to investigate the facts by putting the accused on oath. This was not the same as acting on the basis of mere rumour. The latter, explained the fifteenth-century canonist William Lyndwood, was 'a particular assertion, of uncertain authorship and deriving solely from suspicion'. Or it was when 'any part of the neighbourhood says something, but not the greater part' or when 'a few say something, but not publicly'. Fame, however, was the 'shout of disapproval of the whole neighbourhood'.[6]

In England, inquisitorial procedure was nonetheless used very flexibly, though (as will be seen) a procedure known as 'compurgation' offered a ready means by which the innocent could clear their names. In practice, the actual term 'inquisition' was used only in a small minority of cases where particular attention was paid to the formalities of procedure – for example, where it was judged necessary to prove the existence of a 'fame' by the oaths of witnesses. Characteristically, disciplinary or criminal prosecutions in English dioceses were said to derive from the office of the judge and were described as 'office' or 'correction' cases. By this means quite large numbers of suspects could be brought to court.[7]

Defendants in such cases were naturally disinclined to pay substantial fees. Moreover, many were poor and could not pay. Justice had perforce to be swift and reasonably cheap. Hence, procedure was summary, and recording was extremely terse. Even if a case extended over several sessions, the memoranda of what was done were often consolidated into an inch or so of writing space. Disciplinary or 'correction' cases seem to have been regarded as ephemeral, not necessarily worth recording with much care or formality. So minutes of cases or the records of whole courts might be fitted in as occasion served – as rough notes on the back of other documents, for example, or in blank spaces found in the registers without reference to chronological order. Greater order and formality were probably more usual by the early sixteenth century but were by no means universal, and records still tended to be extremely brief.

Reconstructing what went on from such materials – and in particular assessing the numbers and intensity of prosecutions, to make comparisons with later periods – is fraught with difficulties. These are compounded by

[6] William Lyndwood, *Provinciale (seu constitutiones angliae)* (Oxford, 1679), pp. 113–14n.
[7] Kelly, 'Inquisition, Public Fame and Confession', pp. 8–20.

the administrative complexities of the period. In many areas there were overlapping jurisdictions. Courts might be held by a bishop's commissary and by the archdeacon's official, and the bishop's consistory or audience court might be hearing cases too. Unless records of all these courts survive and their mutual relationship is understood, it is impossible to be sure how many cases were heard in total. Again, things become a little easier after about 1500. In the interests of effective discipline and, sometimes, because of financial pressures resulting from the migration of some kinds of business to other courts, from the closing years of Henry VII onwards the offices of bishop's commissary and archdeacon's official were often amalgamated.

'Top Down' or 'Bottom Up'? The Role of Visitations

From one point of view, the church courts were authoritarian institutions with a mission to impose Christian standards on the mass of the population. Indeed, they were one major means – the hearing of confessions by parish priests was another – whereby the church was still striving to achieve the aims of the pastoral reform movement initiated by the Fourth Lateran Council of 1215. However, it is plain that – even in disciplinary cases, as opposed to party and party suits – ordinary people played an important role in bringing cases to court. They were thus active collaborators or at least complicit in what the courts did. More basically, as with other tribunals in this period, the church courts were to an extent embedded in local society and dependent on co-operation at the parish level in almost everything they did. The system they embodied was thus neither 'top down' nor 'bottom up' but a combination of the two.

Bearing on these issues is the relationship between action at or immediately following 'visitations' and jurisdiction exercised at other times. Visitations were tours of inspection carried out by bishops and archdeacons or by their deputies and officials. Ian Forrest has argued for the 'transformation of visitation' in the thirteenth century, suggesting that it was then that the practice became much more systematic and extended to the regulation of the religious and sexual lives of lay people as well as the clergy. Part of the argument is that this development occurred in tandem with the development of secular courts, both seigneurial and royal – all these courts increasingly relied on the participation of village elites, in the sense of substantial peasants and local office holders as jurors or fact-finders. Forrest has gone so far as to draw parallels with the far-reaching involvement of the 'middling sorts' with the ecclesiastical and secular courts of late Tudor and early Stuart England.[8]

These are cogent arguments, but the similarity of late medieval and early modern ecclesiastical visitations should not be exaggerated. As will be seen in Chapter 10, from the later sixteenth century onwards, visitations were unquestionably the pivot of episcopal and archidiaconal administration, used to elicit a wide range of information – including accusations of sexual misdoing – from the elected representatives of each parish, called 'church-wardens' and 'sidemen'. Disciplinary cases could arise by other means, but in the Elizabethan and Jacobean church those based on churchwardens' presentments overwhelmingly predominated.

Before the Reformation, things were different. There were some exceptions: for example, in the diocese of Winchester – where unusually the bishop exercised the right to visit annually – it would seem that visitations were carefully conducted and already in the 1520s were prob-ably the major source of disciplinary business.[9] But, in most dioceses, visitations, whether episcopal or archidiaconal, were neither so regular nor so searching.[10] To cite a well-known example, Archbishop Warham conducted a visitation of Canterbury diocese in 1511, but there is no indication that he had held one previously since coming to the see in 1503, while Brian Woodcock found that late medieval archidiaconal visitations in the same diocese were 'little more than formal annual tours, the chief object of which was the collection of procurations' (payments due from the incumbents of parishes).[11] This concurs with the comments of Christopher St German, writing critically of the church and its jurisdiction in the early 1530s, who claimed that the general view was that visitations were mainly used as a fiscal device and 'comenly they refourme nothynge'.[12]

---

[8] Ian Forrest, 'The Transformation of Visitation in Thirteenth-Century England', *Past and Present*, 221 (November 2013), 3–38.

[9] Houlbrooke, *Church Courts*, pp. 29, 44.

[10] R. N. Swanson, *Church and Society in Late Medieval England* (pbk edn., Oxford, 1993), pp. 163–5; A. Hamilton Thompson (ed.), *Visitations in the Diocese of Lincoln, 1517–1531*, 3 vols. (Lincoln Record Society 33, 35, 37, Hereford, 1940–7), Vol. I, pp. xx, xxii–xxiv, xli, ciii–civ.

[11] K. L. Wood-Legh (ed.), *Kentish Visitations of Archbishop William Warham and his Deputies, 1511–1512* (Kent Records 24, Maidstone, 1984), p. x; Woodcock, *Medieval Ecclesiastical Courts*, p. 68; cf. Ralph Houlbrooke, 'Bishop Nykke's Last Visitation, 1532', in M. J. Franklin and Christopher Harper-Bill (eds.), *Medieval Ecclesiastical Studies in Honour of Dorothy M. Owen* (Woodbridge, 1995), pp. 113–29.

[12] Christopher St German, *A treatise concernynge the division betwene the spiritualtie and temporaltie* (London, [1532]), fo. 36r.

The visitors did seek information from the parishes. Lists of questions occasionally survive.[13] But there were no lengthy 'books of articles', as there were later, and it is plain from the returns that visitations of different archdeaconries by a single bishop on the same tour of inspection could follow markedly different agendas. Historians' understanding of what went on is complicated by the fact that the record of particular visitations was sometimes shaped by jurisdictional disputes among archbishops, bishops, archdeacons, religious houses and churches claiming 'peculiar' or 'exempt' status; indeed, such conflicts may have determined whether individual records were preserved in the registry or simply discarded when their immediate usefulness was past.[14] That said, the main concerns were generally understood to be the fabric and ornaments of churches and the conduct of the clergy serving the cure. Whether rectors or vicars resided was a big issue. Clerical celibacy was another major focus of attention, but, as will be seen in Chapter 8, even in this area the returns are by no means a reliable guide to the incidence of offences. They are even less so with regard to lay people's transgressions.

The parishioners responsible for making the returns varied from jurisdiction to jurisdiction. Sometimes, as later, the prime responsibility lay with the churchwardens, who appeared on their own or with other 'parishioners'. But sometimes presentments were made by 'inquisitors' or 'questmen', who might, but did not necessarily, include the wardens. Cross-referencing to other local sources and incidental evidence both indicate that the people who made the presentments were generally drawn from the middling and upper middling ranks of village society, overlapping with the men who served as manorial jurors and the like.[15] But the real opinions of such people cannot simply be read off from the reports they made. Close scrutiny of the returns indicates that unless there was clear proof, they tended to be cautious in framing accusations. Almost always, only a minority of parishes actually reported matters amiss, and even then they were sparing of information. The parishioners were equally reluctant to state plainly that 'all is

---

[13] E.g. Worcestershire Archive and Archaeology Service, 009:1 BA 2636/11, Visitation Book of Hartlebury (marked 43700), fo. 46r (1468).

[14] Ian Forrest, 'The Survival of Medieval Visitation Records', *Archives*, 37 (April 2012), 1–10.

[15] L. R. Poos, 'Ecclesiastical Courts, Marriage, and Sexuality in Late Medieval Europe', in Troels Dahlerup and Per Ingesman (eds.), *New Approaches to the History of Late Medieval and Early Modern Europe: Selected Proceedings of Two International Conferences at the Danish Royal Academy of Sciences and Letters in Copenhagen in 1997 and 1999* (Copenhagen, 2009), p. 193. See also Beat A. Kümin, *The Shaping of a Community: The Rise and Reformation of the English Parish, c.1400–1560* (Aldershot, 1996), pp. 31–40.

well' (*omnia bene*). From visitations that were recorded in the greatest detail, it is evident that the great majority of inquisitors or churchwardens maintained a studied silence; they said or deposed 'nothing'. The reasons for this pattern of behaviour are not far to seek. Usually wardens and questmen were in office only for short periods. They had to watch their backs – a neighbour delated to the courts might next year serve them in like kind – and could not afford to appear too officious. Church officials, for their part, knew better than to press them too hard in public. It was better to act discreetly so that if there were suspicions in the minds of the parochial representatives or rumours circulating locally, they could be sifted carefully and only cases with real substance brought into the open.

It is true that the church authorities did occasionally prosecute churchwardens for failing in their duty.[16] In 1520, John Lander of Lurgashall (Sussex) was brought to court for perjury in not presenting as required in the archdeacon's last visitation: on his re-appearance a few days later, he came up with the names of three couples suspected of illicit sexual relations.[17] But such cases were so rare and visitation reports of lay sexual transgressions so sparse and intermittent that it is clear that the authorities simply chose not to rely on these public statements by churchwardens as a source of information.[18] But, as will be evident throughout this chapter, this did not necessarily mean that local people were unwilling to co-operate with the courts, far less that they were indifferent to sexual transgression or other scandals. The courts seem to have had little difficulty in bringing to light numerous additional cases, based variously on information from local clergy, disgruntled neighbours, 'common voice and fame' and the detective activities of summoners. Importantly, this meant that accusations voiced by women – whether publicly or in the exchange of gossip – undoubtedly played a part.[19]

The courts may have had a vested interest in obscuring exactly how cases came to their attention. According to William Tyndale's hostile account in 1528, judges customarily refused to tell defendants how the charges against them had originated:

---

[16] Cf. R. H. Helmholz, *Roman Canon Law in Reformation England* (Cambridge, 1990), pp. 106–7.
[17] WSRO, Ep.I/10/2, fos. 90r, 93r.   [18] Cf. Woodcock, *Medieval Ecclesiastical Courts*, p. 69.
[19] L. R. Poos, 'Sex, Lies, and the Church Courts of Pre-Reformation England', *Journal of Interdisciplinary History*, 25 (1994–5), esp. 585–6, 604–7; Poos, 'Ecclesiastical Courts, Marriage, and Sexuality', pp. 193–5.

Yf they desyre to knowe their accusers, naye saye they, the mater is knowen well ynough and to moare then ye are ware of. Come, laye youre hande on the boke, yf ye forswere your selfe, we shall bringe proves, we will handle you, we will make an ensample of you.[20]

Between the leaves of court books there survive occasionally roughly written scraps of paper, sometimes in several hands, that suggest what went on behind the scenes. Starting with notes of suspicions, often in vague terms, the list was gradually amplified and details filled in. Thus, an entry in a Leicestershire example from around 1490 – the list as a whole was not confined to sexual offences – was first written as 'Item Robert Cache usyng lecher[y]'; later 'husbandman' was appended to his name, and 'with Elene Ketyll' added to complete the charge. Further down was noted, 'Item the vicar of Stapulford drawyng to a woman wheras hyll suspecyns is had'; the woman's name, Margery, was added later. Then the notes switched to Latin, and a memorandum recorded that Robert Taylor's wife was suspected of adultery with Thomas Lukas deceased. Perhaps he had implicated her on his deathbed.[21]

Some visitation returns survive simply as lists of clergy and church-wardens or other representative parishioners (*parochiani*), together with their presentments – chiefly concerning clergy and church repairs with a sprinkling of lay morality cases and other offences such as talking in church, neglecting divine service, quarrelling, cursing and sorcery – and brief notes of action taken. Usually such returns are very ill written and flimsy. Others, normally better penned and more substantial in make-up, have associated with them entries that record additional cases. Often these are clearly distinguished from visitation presentments by means of a distinctive formula, such as, 'A notatur cum B super crimine adulterii' (A reported with B on the crime of adultery) or 'contra A objicitur quod . . .' (it is objected against A that . . .). Especially with regard to sexual transgressions, the extra cases add substantially to the total number. Thus, the volume recording two visitations in the archdeaconry of Leicester in 1510 includes forty-five sexual transgression cases deriving from present-ments and a further thirty-seven additional charges.[22]

---

[20] William Tyndale, *The Obedience of a Christian Man, 1528*, facsimile edn. (Menston, Yorkshire, 1970), fo. 77v.

[21] LA, DIOC/Viv 2, fo. 36r; a similar note is printed in Woodcock, *Medieval Ecclesiastical Courts*, p. 133.

[22] LA, DIOC/Viv 5, fos. 38(*bis*)r–95v. Some 135 individuals were named, including three married couples. The totals include a few cases of bigamy or irregular marriage.

The Intensity of Prosecutions: The Archdeaconries of Chichester and Leicester

Often the records of disciplinary prosecutions make it difficult to be sure what derives directly from visitation presentments and what from other sources. This is true of two otherwise well-ordered books relating, respectively, to the diocese of Chichester from January 1520 to January 1521 and to the archdeaconry of Leicester between November 1522 and July 1523. The latter, which consists almost entirely of disciplinary cases, generally introduces them with the formula 'officio detectus' (or 'detecta', 'detecti') with a note of the alleged offence. In later times in this jurisdiction, as elsewhere, such terms usually referred to churchwardens' presentments. But this was plainly not so in 1522–3, though the book does include a few cases that apparently relate to visitations. The Chichester volume was a general court book, including much instance and probate material as well as disciplinary prosecutions. Although nominally relating to the whole diocese, it was in fact devoted primarily to business from the western archdeaconry of Chichester. However, for this area it effectively amalgamated the jurisdiction of the bishop and the archdeacon, since by this time the powers of the latter had been limited by agreement to on-the-spot correctional activity during visitations. The record covers both the consistory court, which sat regularly at Chichester, and the circuit courts of the bishop's commissary, which sat in local churches in the rural deaneries. The disciplinary cases were generally introduced by the formula 'notatur quod/super . . .' (reported that/for . . .). As with the Leicestershire record, there are some cases that must have emerged, directly or indirectly, from visitatorial activity, but the bulk apparently did not derive from churchwardens' presentments. In fact, separate registers were compiled of the latter, though unfortunately none survive to collate with the 1520–1 record.

In the archdeaconry of Chichester, as in Leicester, if the corresponding visitation returns were available, the tally of disciplinary prosecutions would be that much greater. Incomplete as they are, the surviving records indicate an impressively high level of correctional activity, particularly in the sphere of sexual regulation. At Chichester in these twelve months the consistory and the commissary courts together handled about 195 to 245 disciplinary cases of all kinds. (The different totals depend on exactly how a 'case' is defined, in particular, whether multiple defendants are counted individually, and whether cancelled cases are included, bearing in mind that entries were often struck through, not because a mistake had been made but because process was complete or it had been decided to take no further action.) In over fifty cases in the total, mostly involving sole defendants, the nature of the offence was not specified, though it is probable that sexual transgression was actually at issue in many of them. Sexual matters were definitely at issue in about a hundred cases (the total number of *persons* involved being much greater), while there were in addition a number of disciplinary prosecutions relating to marriage.

Admittedly at this time the administration of Chichester diocese was in the process of a vigorous overhaul, instigated by Bishop Robert Sherburne, assisted by his chancellor William Fleshmonger, his commissary John Worthial and the registrar John Stilman.[23] But a similarly vigorous disciplinary regime is found elsewhere. The Leicester record for 1522–3 yields more clear-cut figures than Chichester. Setting aside a handful of instance actions (tithe, perjury, violence against a cleric and defamation), the total number of cases recorded was about 140. Two of these related to common defamers, while a further thirty-four concerned a variety of non-sexual matters including sorcery, failure to attend church, talking in church and a few clerical faults. Just over 100 cases, involving some 174 persons, related to sexual transgressions. These figures are of similar order to those reported from elsewhere around the same time or somewhat earlier. In the consistory court of Canterbury in 1474, for example, 158 charges are recorded, of which 110 related to sexual transgressions.[24] These numbers must be understood in relation to the demographic stagnation that persisted well after 1500. The total population of Sussex in the 1520s – of which the archdeaconry of Chichester comprised less than half – has been estimated at 60,000, while the population of Leicestershire around the same time was probably fewer than 40,000.[25] The conclusion must be that the intensity of prosecution was as great as, if not greater than, in late Elizabethan and Jacobean times – generally viewed by historians as the peak of the 'reformation of manners'.[26]

The geographical spread of cases was also quite extensive. It has been suggested, particularly with regard to archdeaconry courts, that in practice

---

[23] Stephen Lander, 'Church Courts and the Reformation in the Diocese of Chichester, 1500–58', in Rosemary O'Day and Felicity Heal (eds.), *Continuity and Change: Personnel and Administration of the Church of England, 1500–1642* (Leicester, 1976), pp. 215–37, 280–4.

[24] Woodcock, *Medieval Ecclesiastical Courts*, p. 79.

[25] Julian Cornwall, 'English Population in the Early Sixteenth Century', *Economic History Review*, 23 (1970), 38; R. B. Pugh (ed.), *The Victoria History of the County of Leicester*, Vol. III (London, 1955), pp. 137–8.

[26] Martin Ingram, 'Reformation of Manners in Early Modern England', in Paul Griffiths, Adam Fox and Steve Hindle (eds.), *The Experience of Authority in Early Modern England* (Basingstoke, 1996), pp. 47–88. See Chapter 10 for comparative figures.

their powers were confined mainly to areas close to the main centres of ecclesiastical administration and that their grip on outlying areas was much more lax.[27] The evidence needs to be evaluated carefully because some courts – as has been seen in the case of the Chichester consistory – deliberately restricted their activities to certain geographical areas, more remote regions being dealt with by other tribunals.[28] In the record for 1520–1, it is observable that not only was there little business from the archdeaconry of Lewes but also that there were relatively few prosecutions from the more easterly parts of Chichester archdeaconry. However, elsewhere in the jurisdiction, cases were quite evenly distributed, and there is no reason to doubt that the reach of the court extended to its northern, western and southern borders. In the archdeaconry of Leicestershire, the borough of Leicester itself and certain other urban centres generated a disproportionate number of cases, but otherwise business arose from all over the jurisdiction, including some parishes on its very periphery.

Sexual and Marital Transgressions before the Courts

What sexual transgressions came before the courts and in what form, how did this compare with the profile of the post-Reformation courts, and what can be inferred about underlying patterns of behaviour and social attitudes? The following discussion is based mainly on the record of prosecutions in west Sussex (archdeaconry of Chichester) and Leicestershire in 1520 and 1522–3, respectively (Table 3.1), though other examples are occasionally introduced. Clerical immorality is the subject of Chapter 8; here the focus is on lay people. Sins 'against nature', namely, sodomy and bestiality, were in theory the gravest of all sexual offences. But, as was noted in Chapter 1, cases came to court so rarely that they can effectively be discounted. The next gravest offence in the church's book was incest.[29] In practice, however, this likewise did not always attract the condemnation that might have been expected, as indeed continued to be the case after the Reformation.[30] The fact is that the church had taken

---

[27] David Crawford, 'The Rule of Law? The Laity, English Archdeacons' Courts and the Reformation to 1558', *Parergon*, New Series, 4 (1986), 164–6.

[28] Cf. Woodcock, *Medieval Ecclesiastical Courts*, pp. 32–5.

[29] Lyndwood, *Provinciale*, pp. 62, 314; Priscilla Heath Barnum (ed.), *Dives and Pauper*, 2 vols. in 3 parts (Early English Text Society 275, 280, 323, London, 1976–2004), Vol. I, Part 2, p. 58; Venetia Nelson (ed.), *A Myrour to Lewde Men and Wymmen: A Prose Version of the* Speculum Vitae (Heidelberg, 1981), p. 166.

[30] Martin Ingram, *Church Courts, Sex and Marriage in England, 1570–1640* (Cambridge, 1987), pp. 245–9.

Table 3.1 *Disciplinary Prosecutions in West Sussex (1520)*
and Leicestershire (1522–3): Cases Concerning Illicit Sex

Archdeaconry of Chichester, Jan–Dec 1520[a]	
Clerical incontinence	11
Bestiality	1
Incest	2
Adultery (stated or inferred)	12
Incontinence, etc.	37
Illicit pregnancy/child out of wedlock	17
Common whore, etc.	8
Bawdry	11
Total	99
Archdeaconry of Leicester, Nov 1522–July 1523	
Clerical incontinence	14
Adultery	24
Incontinence	49
Illicit pregnancy/child out of wedlock	2
Common whore, etc.	3
Promiscuous (male)	1
Expelling wife	1
Bawdry	8
Total	102

[a] Excluding cases in which the nature of the charge is unspecified.

some of the sting out of the concept by making the range of relationships of kinship and affinity, within which marriage and hence sexual relations without marriage were forbidden, so extremely wide. They extended to the fourth degree of kinship – that is, even to third cousins – and there were further restrictions based on 'spiritual' relationships between godparents and godchildren. It was impossible to enforce the prohibitions consistently, and inevitably there was an insistent demand for dispensations to allow marriages when the relationship between the parties was relatively distant.[31] Some people – whether innocently or otherwise – entered into marriages within the forbidden degrees, only to have them declared null

---

[31] Sir Frederick Pollock and Frederic William Maitland, *The History of English Law before the Time of Edward I*, 2nd edn., 2 vols. (Cambridge, 1898–9), Vol. II, pp. 543–4. See also Jack Goody, *The Development of the Family and Marriage in Europe* (Cambridge, 1983), esp. pp. 134–46 (though his explanation of the facts is controversial).

and void when the matter came to the attention of the authorities. Some unscrupulous individuals only started investigating how closely they were related by kinship or affinity to their spouse when they sought some means of annulling a marriage that had become irksome or inconvenient.[32]

On account of all these complexities, matters of 'incest' sprawled uneasily across the boundary between 'instance' and 'office' business in the church courts, and it is often unclear how far the people caught up in these situations were morally culpable. In typical cases in the archdeaconry of Chichester in 1520, William Godfrey of Laughton received a stern injunction that within a fortnight after the post-childbirth 'purification' of his 'pretended wife' Emmelina Petibone, he should withdraw from her company unless he could exhibit a papal dispensation; meanwhile, he was on no account to 'commit' with her. Robert Ax of Lewes, however, and his 'pretended wife' failed to appear to answer charges *ex officio*, whereupon they were suspended from church attendance, and the judge 'took the cause into his own hands'.[33]

Still, such cases were by no means common, and just as rare, if not more so, were prosecutions involving incest between close family members. In these circumstances, condemnation was more clear-cut. There were two cases in the archdeaconry of Chichester in 1520. William Hardham of South Stoke had got with child a young woman who was described as his 'daughter' but was probably his stepdaughter. William Gobull of Rumboldswyke was accused of 'adultery with his wife's daughter' and with his uncle's daughter too and was moreover suspected of using sorcery, but he denied all the charges.[34] The occasional cases that cropped up in other jurisdictions suggest that when incest was known or suspected, the relationship most commonly in question was between a man and his stepdaughter, but connections with a niece, an aunt, a sister or the wife's sister are also found.[35] Sometimes judges commented on the 'gravity and notoriety' of such crimes, suggesting that they aroused considerable scandal locally.[36]

---

[32] But cf. R. H. Helmholz, *Marriage Litigation in Medieval England* (Cambridge, 1974), pp. 77–87, emphasizing the paucity of nullity suits on the grounds of consanguinity and affinity.

[33] WSRO, Ep.I/10/2, fos. 64v, 89v, 101v.   [34] WSRO, Ep.I/10/2, fos. 17r, 23v, 24r.

[35] E. M. Elvey (ed.), *The Courts of the Archdeaconry of Buckingham, 1483–1523* (Buckinghamshire Record Society 19, Welwyn Garden City, 1975), pp. 50, 107–8; LA, DIOC/Viv 5, fo. 94v; Christopher Harper-Bill (ed.), *The Register of John Morton, Archbishop of Canterbury, 1486–1500*, 3 vols. (Canterbury and York Society 75, 78, 89, Leeds and Woodbridge, 1987–2000), Vol. III, pp. 148–9, 177.

[36] Margaret Bowker (ed.), *An Episcopal Court Book for the Diocese of Lincoln, 1514–1520* (Lincoln Record Society 61, Lincoln, 1967), p. 94.

In England, concern about bigamy was to peak around 1600.[37] A century earlier it was a much less urgent issue but not, apparently, because it was little regarded or widely tolerated. The term 'bigamy' was rarely employed in court records, since in medieval usage it could simply refer to the second marriages of widows or widowers. Offenders were accused more specifically of having two wives or husbands alive at the same time and, occasionally, even three. Men were prosecuted for this offence more often than women. This pattern was so prevalent elsewhere in Europe that Sara McDougall characterizes bigamy as a 'male crime', plausibly arguing that men were regarded as primarily responsible for upholding the integrity of marriage and hence more culpable.[38] In the English cases it was often not made explicit that the first and any subsequent unions had actually been solemnized, but this seems to have been the usual presumption. Thus, in the archdeaconry of Chichester in 1520, Thomas Tryssell was reported for having one wife in Marlborough (Wiltshire) and another in Horsham. At the same court session, the second wife, Anne Wells alias Tryssell, successfully petitioned for a sentence of annulment. This case was typical in that the other spouse lived a considerable distance away, and it is plain that these bigamous situations were facilitated by both poor communications and the fact that geographical mobility was easy and common.[39]

However, cases were not numerous, and defendants were occasionally able to make a plausible claim either that they believed on good grounds that their former spouse was dead or that the earlier marriage had been duly annulled.[40] There is no indication of a 'crisis of marriage', as McDougall has found in fifteenth-century Champagne.[41] The pattern of cases seems indicative not of a society in which bigamy was rampant but rather of one characterized by widespread popular understanding of marriage law, acceptance of the importance of solemnizing matrimony and sharp-eyed vigilance on the part of clergy, churchwardens and neighbours. The incidence of a related form of prosecution supports

---

[37] See Chapter 12.

[38] Sara McDougall, 'Bigamy – A Male Crime in Medieval Europe?', *Gender and History*, 22 (2010), 430–46; but cf. Sara McDougall, *Bigamy and Christian Identity in Late Medieval Champagne* (Philadelphia, 2012), p. 6.

[39] WSRO, Ep.I/10/2, fos. 31v, 32r; cf. LA, DIOC/Viv 5, fo. 89r.

[40] Harper-Bill (ed.), *Register of John Morton*, Vol. III, p. 170; Thompson (ed.), *Visitations in the Diocese of Lincoln*, Vol. I, p. 38; and cf. Bowker (ed.), *Episcopal Court Book*, p. 140 (note, however, that in this case the defendant was also accused of incest with his daughter, which may throw doubt on his trustworthiness).

[41] McDougall, *Bigamy and Christian Identity*.

this conclusion. Bigamy usually presupposed the earlier desertion of a wife or husband, and this, at least, must have been highly visible to the neighbours of the spouse left behind. If such situations had been at all common, presentments and reports of desertion would presumably have flowed into the courts in some numbers. Philippa Maddern claimed that such cases were far more common than historians have recognized, but her examples were drawn from a range of jurisdictions covering a large area of England over a lengthy period from 1350 to 1500.[42] More focused sampling shows that they were rare. Thus, no cases at all were reported from the archdeaconry of Chichester in 1520 or the archdeaconry of Leicester in 1522–3.[43]

Prosecutions dealing with other illicit relationships between men and women formed the great bulk of the courts' activities in the sphere of sexual regulation. But to recover the precise outlines of what was done is not easy, not least because of the imprecise nature of the labels used by the courts.[44] In theory, there was a more or less clearly defined hierarchy of sins.[45] Adultery, sometimes qualified as 'double' or 'single' adultery, depending on whether or not both partners were married, was regarded as particularly reprehensible, though discussion of this offence was complicated somewhat by the issue of the double standard. Some commentators, while recognizing that the sins of either party were equal in the eyes of God, opined that adultery on the part of a married woman caused the greater harm because it threatened to confuse inheritances and caused strife between men. An alternative approach was to argue that men were more culpable because they were held to be more reasonable than women and hence bore the greater responsibility for restraining their lusts. Others, of whom William Harrington is an example, eschewed these debates and simply emphasized the heinousness of adultery in all circumstances.[46] Also viewed with great gravity was *stuprum*, or the violation of a virgin. Other

---

[42] Philippa Maddern, 'Moving Households: Geographical Mobility and Serial Monogamy in England, 1350–1500', *Parergon*, 24 (2007), 69–92.

[43] For a Buckinghamshire case, see Thompson (ed.), *Visitations in the Diocese of Lincoln*, Vol. I, p. 47; and for Suffolk cases, see Harper-Bill (ed.), *Register of John Morton*, Vol. III, pp. 185, 200, 204.

[44] Ruth Mazo Karras, 'The Latin Vocabulary of Illicit Sex in English Ecclesiastical Court Records', *Journal of Medieval Latin*, 2 (1992), 1–17.

[45] James A. Brundage, *Law, Sex and Christian Society in Medieval Europe* (Chicago and London, 1987), pp. 246–51.

[46] Barnum (ed.), *Dives and Pauper*, Vol. I, Part 2, pp. 67–8, 71–2; William Harrington, *Commendacions of matrymony* [title page mutilated] (?1515), sig. D1r. See also Ruth Mazo Karras, 'Two Models, Two Standards: Moral Teaching and Sexual Mores', in Barbara A. Hanawalt and David Wallace (eds.), *Bodies and Disciplines: Intersections of Literature and History in Fifteenth-Century England* (Minneapolis, 1996), pp. 129–31, and the references there cited.

sexual relationships between unmarried people were called 'fornication', generally reckoned to be the least grave of the sins of the flesh, save for activities that fell short of full intercourse. Thus Lyndwood described fornication as a 'mediocre' sin. However, certain circumstances aggravated it. When a man resorted to a woman regularly, or even kept her in his house on a permanent basis, the relationship could be referred to as 'concubinage'. This term, though largely reserved for the clergy, was sometimes applied to the irregular ménages of lay people.[47]

In actual court usage, these categories were not used consistently, and some had little practical relevance. Explicit prosecutions for *stuprum* are rarely found in the English courts. The reason probably lies in the fact that 'stupre', to use the rather uncommon English equivalent, was akin to rape, which before the later sixteenth century was itself not clearly differentiated from abduction. But rape was a common-law offence and as such not cognizable in the church courts.[48] The terms 'adultery' and 'fornication' were not always used in court records or were employed spasmodically and inconsistently. The phrase 'adultery or fornication' was sometimes used as if the terms were virtually interchangeable. More often, the unspecific term 'incontinence' was preferred to anything more definite, or people were said simply to have 'committed' or 'offended' with others, or they were 'reported together' or 'noted' for a 'fame' or 'crime' between them. Partners in sin were not always named, and the marital status of offenders frequently went unspecified. Sometimes the facts were simply not available: in particular, churchwardens and parishioners often had to report that such and such a young woman was pregnant or had given birth, but 'by whom is unknown'.[49] However, it cannot be assumed that the absence of a mention of an illegitimate child or illicit pregnancy meant that the relationship had not borne fruit.

Despite the uncertainties, some clear patterns can be identified. It might be imagined that fornication cases – sexual transgressions between unmarried people – would heavily predominate. They certainly did so in the late sixteenth century and early seventeenth century, and much the same may have been true in the late fourteenth century.[50] A similar pattern

---

[47] Lyndwood, *Provinciale*, pp. 10, 62, 314.
[48] Henry Ansgar Kelly, 'Statutes of Rapes and Alleged Ravishers of Wives: A Context for the Charges against Thomas Malory, Knight', *Viator*, 28 (1997), 361–419.
[49] Variants on this formula were numerous.
[50] Ingram, *Church Courts, Sex and Marriage*, pp. 259, 265 and chaps. 7 and 8 *passim*; Katherine L. French, *The Good Women of the Parish: Gender and Religion after the Black Death* (Philadelphia, 2008), p. 213.

has been reported for some parts of continental Europe around 1500.[51] In early Tudor England, however, it is clear that always a substantial, sometimes even a large proportion of sexual immorality cases involved adultery in the modern sense – that is, one or both parties were married. The term itself was frequently, if irregularly, used in that sense in court records, and even when it was not, there are often explicit indications that a married man, a married woman, or both were involved. On this basis, minimum estimates of the proportion of adultery cases can be made. In the record of the Chichester courts in 1520 – where the scribe was particularly prone to use unspecific terminology – it was some 16 per cent, whereas in the archdeaconry of Leicester in 1522–3 it was about 30 per cent. Even this higher figure may well be an underestimate. The records of Cardinal Morton's visitation of the diocese of Norwich in 1499 indicate that adultery was at issue in 67 per cent of the incontinence cases in the archdeaconries of Norfolk and Norwich (not a complete record but only cases referred to the consistory court) and 51 per cent in the archdeaconries of Sudbury and Suffolk (a register of all visitation presentments and proceedings). This is the closest thing we have to a true picture because it is clear that Morton's agents used the terms 'adultery' and 'fornication' with an unusual degree of precision and consistency, while in an exceptionally high proportion of cases the marital status of one and often both parties was plainly specified.[52] The same record indicates that adultery cases involving married men were more numerous than those involving married women. Instances of 'double adultery', where both parties were married, and cases involving married women and single men were in a minority.

The Leicestershire archdeaconry material for 1522–3, which frequently specifies when defendants were household servants, reveals that a very common form of adultery was a liaison between a married man and his maidservant. This is consistent with what can be gleaned from the more laconic records of many other jurisdictions. In some other adultery cases, the woman was not a servant, at least as far as we know, but was none-theless installed in the house. Sometimes, in either situation, the man had

---

[51] Thomas D. Albert, *Der gemeine Mann vor dem geistlichen Richter: Kirchliche Rechtsprechung in den Diözesen Basel, Chur und Konstanz vor der Reformation* (Stuttgart, 1998), pp. 195, 214, 344; Ruth Mazo Karras, 'The Regulation of Sexuality in the Late Middle Ages: England and France', *Speculum*, 86 (2011), 1010–39.

[52] Based on analysis of WSRO, Ep.I/10/2; ROLLR, 1 D 41/13/1; Harper-Bill (ed.), *Register of John Morton*, Vol. III, pp. 148–60, 168–239. The figures comprise allegations of illicit sexual relations between lay people, excluding the few cases of incest. Clerical incontinence cases have been omitted from the calculations, as have cases of lay people accused of promoting or condoning the sexual transgressions of others.

actually thrown his wife out. A woman of Syston (Leicestershire) was, however, able to turn the tables before this could happen. The charge made clear that the husband had been 'defamed' by his own wife; he was able to secure favourable treatment by promising to dismiss the maidservant and henceforth to stop seeing her. An Evington (Leicestershire) man in 1509 took outrage further. He was charged with 'living suspiciously with the daughter of one Stephen, a swineherd of that town … he keeps the said woman in his house at night against the wishes of his wife and all the parishioners.' To justify himself, he claimed to know that 'his said wife had been legitimately contracted to another man before she married him', so that his union with her was null.[53]

A quite different situation arose when a man's lawful wife was not on the scene – perhaps left behind in another parish – and he had established an irregular relationship to fill the gap. The 'new woman' might be single, widowed or herself a married person estranged from her spouse. Thus John Thorp of Coston (Leicestershire) was detected in 1522 'for adultery with one Margaret Richardson of the same place, because, as is said, the man has a wife living and the woman a husband'. Such cases could be hard to distinguish from bigamy. Another Leicestershire case in the following year illustrates a further complication. Elizabeth Fox confessed that Master Libeus Dygby, scion of a leading gentry family, had sexual relations with her when his wife was still alive, but she only became pregnant after her death. She denied that Dygby had promised her marriage or that either of them had planned for the wife's eventual decease. Either circumstance would have made the offence more serious, since in church law a man who committed adultery was explicitly debarred from marrying his mistress in the event of his wife's death.[54] Another aggravating factor was repeated or habitual adultery, which might earn the culprit the epithet of 'common adulterer' with other signs of communal disapprobation. John Keyn of Witherley (Leicestershire) in 1523 was accused with three woman and also charged with not observing the sabbath.[55]

Spanning the categories of adultery and fornication, and invariably viewed seriously by the ecclesiastical authorities, were cases in which men 'kept' or 'held' women for lengthy periods. These terms often denoted some form of financial support and referred to situations in which men

[53] ROLLR, 1 D 41/13/1, fo. 27v; LA, DIOC/Viv 5, fo. 31r.
[54] ROLLR, 1 D 41/13/1, fos. 2v, 21r; Harrington, *Commendacions of matrymony*, sig. C2v.
[55] ROLLR, 1 D 41/13/1, fo. 19r. For other cases of multiple adultery, see WSRO, Ep.I/10/2, fos. 10v, 49v.

were either deliberately cohabiting with women without marrying them – relationships that Ruth Mazo Karras refers to as 'unmarriages' – or, more discreetly, maintaining them elsewhere.[56] This kind of relationship may have been quite prevalent in parts of northern England, Wales and the Welsh borders – a fact reflected in the more frequent use of the term 'concubine' in court records in those areas.[57] As will be seen in later chapters, it was also quite common in the metropolis. Elsewhere in southern England the phenomenon was primarily associated with nobles and gentlemen.[58] Lower down the social scale, in rural areas at least, it was much less common, but cases did occasionally surface. Thus, in 1519, the curate of Eastwell (Leicestershire) reported that for a period of twelve years William Brabyson had 'incontinently' kept Agnes Cryspin and had begotten seven children on her. A more aggravated case was that of Richard Hoghton, a weaver of Cranoe (Leicestershire). In 1510 he was accused of having been 'taken in fornication with a vagabond the summer before last, and he yet keeps in his house another man's wife and, as the parishioners believe, has lived and at present still maintains a suspicious and bad life with her'.[59]

Even without the aggravating circumstance of cohabitation, fornication was sometimes roundly condemned. Thus, in 1510 it was reported that Robert Burbage of Ratcliffe on the Wreak (Leicestershire) 'wickedly commits the grave crime of fornication' with his former servant.[60] But the seriousness with which non-adulterous relationships were regarded, both by the courts and by society at large, depended in great measure on whether or not marriage was, or had originally been, a likely outcome. In many fornication cases the possibility of marriage was very much at issue; indeed, in some cases the couple had already entered into a binding union or signalled their intention to do so. Thus, from Loughborough in

---

[56] Ruth Mazo Karras, *Unmarriages: Women, Men, and Sexual Unions in the Middle Ages* (Philadelphia, 2012).

[57] Llinos Beverley Smith, 'A View from an Ecclesiastical Court: Mobility and Marriage in a Border Society at the End of the Middle Ages', in R. R. Davies and Geraint H. Jenkins (eds.), *From Medieval to Modern Wales: Historical Essays in Honour of Kenneth O. Morgan and Ralph A. Griffiths* (Cardiff, 2004), pp. 76–80; Margaret Lynch et al. (eds.), *Life, Love and Death in North-East Lancashire, 1510 to 1538: A Translation of the Act Book of the Ecclesiastical Court of Whalley* (Chetham Society, 3rd Series, 46, Manchester, 2006), pp. 4, 29–30, 53, 84–7, 94, 95. See also Katharine Carlton and Tim Thornton, 'Illegitimacy and Authority in the North of England, c.1450–1640', *Northern History*, 48 (2011), 23–40.

[58] Lawrence Stone, *The Crisis of the Aristocracy, 1558–1641* (Oxford, 1965), pp. 662–4; Barbara J. Harris, *English Aristocratic Women, 1450–1550* (Oxford, 2002), pp. 82–6.

[59] Thompson (ed.), *Visitations in the Diocese of Lincoln*, Vol. I, p. 26; LA, DIOC/Viv 5, fo. 91r.

[60] LA, DIOC/Viv 5, fo. 56r.

1509, it was reported that William Nawntell 'lives suspiciously with Joan Bell ... he lies in her house nightly *solus cum sola* and says that he is to contract marriage with her but has not done so'.[61] As was seen in Chapter 2, already by this period it was generally accepted that a church wedding was required to ratify a contract in words of the present tense and turn it into a socially and legally acceptable marriage, and such cases further emphasize that the courts were not prepared to allow couples in the liminal state – L. R. Poos calls it a 'twilight zone' – between contract and wedding to cohabit.[62] But how consistently were cases reported to the authorities? Newcomers sometimes aroused suspicions about their marital status.[63] Beyond that, it was probably a matter of degree: a prosecution for fornication was likely to occur only if a couple's intention was uncertain, if solemnization was unduly delayed or if the spousals had subsequently been challenged or repudiated. The courts' function then was to examine the issues and, if the contract appeared good, order the couple to ratify it without delay. Sometimes courting couples had begun sexual relations without any clear intention to get married. However, if on appearing in court they were willing to take each other as man and wife, they were usually let off with a caution and ordered to solemnize their union.

While it was expected that couples would not set up house together permanently without proceeding to solemnization, it did not follow that they remained completely chaste before marriage. The early sixteenth-century moralist William Harrington, it will be recalled, sternly insisted that any sexual intercourse between contract and solemnization was a deadly sin.[64] But there is no indication either that this was reflected in popular understanding and practice or that the courts themselves made any significant effort to enforce the principle. On the contrary, it is very striking that in this period the church courts simply did not normally prosecute newly married couples for antenuptial incontinence, whether or not the woman had become pregnant. Such prosecutions, which were to become increasingly common in the later years of Elizabeth's reign and utterly routine in many areas by the early seventeenth century, were not entirely unknown before the Reformation. But they were exceedingly rare and not always quite what they seem at first sight. In the archdeaconry of

---

[61] LA, DIOC/Viv 5, fo. 18r; cf. Thompson (ed.), *Visitations in the Diocese of Lincoln*, Vol. I, p. 38 (Amersham); Elvey (ed.), *Courts of the Archdeaconry of Buckingham*, p. 159.
[62] L. R. Poos, 'The Heavy-Handed Marriage Counsellor: Regulating Marriage in Some Later-Medieval English Local Ecclesiastical-Court Jurisdictions', *American Journal of Legal History*, 39 (1995), 297.
[63] *Ibid.*, 294.   [64] Harrington, *Commendacions of matrymony*, sig. A4v.

Chichester in 1520, it was reported of William Knyllar of Burpham 'that he begot his wife with child before he married her'. But the circumstances were complicated. An earlier entry indicates that he had originally been charged with this offence before there was any talk of marriage between the couple, and the woman had also been accused with another man.[65]

Marriage contract claims featured in many other fornication cases. For one thing, there was a definite overlap between matrimonial suits brought by instance procedure and disciplinary prosecutions. This is often not readily apparent when the two types of business were entered in different books, but it is plain enough in, for example, the general court books maintained in this period in the archdeaconry of Chichester. Thus in 1520 Robert Bowley of Pulborough was put to penance when he publicly confessed that he had committed fornication with Margaret Malyvery of Chichester; at the same time, Margaret was suing him for marriage, unsuccessfully as it turned out.[66] More commonly, a case came up as an ordinary charge of fornication or illicit pregnancy. But, once before the judge, one of the partners – almost always the woman – claimed the man in marriage on the basis of a matrimonial contract or, at the least, alleged some kind of promise of marriage. In 1522, for example, William Humberston of Wymeswold (Leicestershire) confessed incontinence with Alice Wright, his father's servant. She likewise admitted the charge but also claimed him for her husband. This case was wholly typical in that the man flatly denied any promise of marriage, and in the absence of witnesses, that was that.[67] However, there were variations on this sad theme. In the archdeaconry of Leicester in 1510, Robert Coke of Barrow confessed 'communication and treaty of marriage' with Joan Cheytyll, after which he begot her with child. He also admitted that he gave her some silver pattens and a fur girdle, while she gave him a silken lace 'in token of dowry' (*in signum dotale*). Clearly, these were not poor people. He even publicly declared that he was willing to take her to wife if she could demonstrate that she was free to marry, but she was unable to do this, and the case was dismissed. Evidently there was another contract in the background, from which Joan was unable to shake herself free.[68]

In contrast, an Ilston widow, Margaret Cowper, finally secured her object. Richard Dalle confessed making a contract but prevaricated, alleging that it was without his proper consent. Faced with the judge's

---

[65] WSRO, Ep.I/10/2, fos. 19v, 125r; cf. Bowker (ed.), *Episcopal Court Book*, pp. 133, 139.
[66] WSRO, Ep.I/10/2, fos. 90v, 91r, 102r, 118v; for other cases, see *ibid.*, fos.11r, 18r (Oviatt/Saull), 12v, 14v, 61r–v, 66r, 69r (Martyn/Bartlett), 47r (Paynter/Foke).
[67] ROLLR, 1 D 41/13/1, fo. 7v.   [68] LA, DIOC/Viv 5, fo. 54v.

scepticism, he promised to take her to wife. But over six months later he again appeared in court, still unwed, claiming that Margaret had another husband still alive; he proved contumacious when the judge tried to press matters. Eventually, Margaret and he turned up together and admitted that they had resumed sexual relations. The judge ordered them to solemnize their marriage. Still Dalle tried to wriggle out of his obligations, but once the judge had managed to secure his appearance again, he gave him no further chance to escape. In open court Richard Dalle was forced to enter into a binding contract in the presence of a half dozen or more witnesses, three of them being notaries public. He left the court a married man, save, of course, for the church wedding that presumably followed soon after.[69]

Obviously, both adultery and fornication prosecutions could involve the complicating fact of illicit pregnancy or the birth of one or more children out of wedlock. But in this period these additional facts were far less regularly reported than they were to be by the early seventeenth century.[70] The focus of the Leicester archdeaconry act book for 1522–3 was illicit sexual relations, not babies and big bellies: the latter were mentioned only incidentally or when the fact of pregnancy was all the court had to go on since the father's identity was unknown. The registrar of the Chichester courts in 1520, who used the semi-technical terms 'adultery' and 'fornication' comparatively rarely and often eschewed even the broader term 'incontinence' in favour of various other descriptors and circumlocutions, more often noted illicit pregnancies and out-of-wedlock births: references occur in almost a quarter of cases.

Visitation returns and records developed from them yield more references to parturition, both because this was of concern to local communities and because an illicit pregnancy or birth provided the kind of clear evidence that churchwardens and questmen often felt they needed before they would make a presentment. Thus the register of proceedings at and after the two visitations of the archdeaconry of Leicester in 1510 refers to pregnancies or births in about 65 per cent of adultery and fornication cases; it is striking that in this record suspicions of pregnancy and illicit births were also meticulously noted in cases of clerical incontinence. In this jurisdiction, the focus on parturition was probably not just a reflection of parochial concerns. Both the officials who conducted the visitations and the registrars who made up the record were clearly interested in the fate of

[69] *Ibid.*, fo. 62v.
[70] Cf. Poos, 'Ecclesiastical Courts, Marriage, and Sexuality', p. 185; Ingram, *Church Courts, Sex and Marriage*, pp. 259–81.

the offspring of illicit unions. In all the records, the fruit of illicit relationships was not described in derogatory language as 'base-born', 'bastards', 'spurious' or 'illegitimate', as was commonly the case later. The parents were on trial, not the children.

In fact, the ecclesiastical courts had some general responsibility for the well-being of infants. In particular, a thirteenth-century canon directed that

> women be monished that they nourish their children warely and that they lay not the younglings nigh to them in the night lest they oppress them. Also they may not leave them in their houses where is fire, or nigh hand to the water, alone without a keeper, and let this be shewed them [by their parish priests] every Sunday.[71]

Court records reveal a trickle of prosecutions, which very occasionally impinged on sexual transgressions if the neglectful couple were fornicators or adulterers.[72] More generally, the courts had the power to look after the material and spiritual interests of children born of illicit relationships. They could also defend the interests of unmarried mothers when these were deemed to have been unfortunate or the victims of exploitation and deceit rather than willing partners in sin. Most records of disciplinary proceedings for the period contain some references to such activities, but their sporadic nature inevitably casts doubt on the consistency and efficacy of the courts' work in this sphere, as do occasional reports that orders had been neglected.[73]

That the courts could on occasion take a careful line is indicated by the proceedings arising from two visitations in the archdeaconry of Leicester in 1510. The record includes summaries of fifteen orders (including one re-imposition of an order after complaint of neglect) and one report of an order imposed by another authority. These represented the great majority of cases in which an order was likely to be of use. (Little could be done if, for example, a woman had fled with her baby.) While one of the orders related to a case of clerical incontinence, the rest concerned ordinary lay people. The orders were to provide baptism and religious education,

---

[71] J. V. Bullard and H. Chalmer Bell (eds.), *Lyndwood's Provinciale: The Text of the Canons Therein Contained, Reprinted from the Translation Made in 1534* (London, 1929), p. 133.

[72] E.g. LA, DIOC/Viv 5, fo. 39r; cf. DIOC/Cj 4, fo. 49r; WSRO, Ep.I/10/2, fo. 67v.

[73] E.g. ROLLR, 1 D 41/13/1, fo. 18r; Elvey (ed.), *Courts of the Archdeaconry of Buckingham*, pp. 258, 259 n. 4; cf. Houlbrooke, *Church Courts*, pp. 77–8. More generally (covering the period 1350–1500), see Philippa Maddern, '"Oppressed by Utter Poverty": Survival Strategies for Single Mothers and their Children in Late Medieval England', in Anne M. Scott (ed.), *Experiences of Poverty in Late Medieval and Early Modern England and France* (Farnham, 2012), pp. 41–62.

clothes, food and other maintenance or (in most cases) all these elements. Orders were imposed on the men if they were forthcoming. If not, the obligation was placed on the women: clearly, the priority was to see to the needs of the child rather than to ensure male responsibility. However, the order could be modified if the man turned up later, and the arrangements were anyway subject to some negotiation between the couple.

For example, Joan Hayward of Frisby on the Wreak was initially ordered to ensure that the child was baptized and taught the Catholic faith – that is, the Pater Noster, Ave Maria and Creed – and to provide all necessaries for it. But when the father, Richard Gamyll, appeared in court a week later, the maintenance responsibilities, to extend till the child came of age, were transferred to him. Later the couple appeared in court together to register a 'concord' between them: Richard had agreed not only to pay for the maintenance of the child but also to give Joan 20s. or necessaries (*utensilia*) of similar value when she should demand them. In return, she undertook never to molest him further on account of this offence.[74]

While there were a few repeat offenders, most of those accused of adultery and fornication had transgressed with only one named person. In a class of their own were individuals, overwhelmingly females, who were actually prosecuted for promiscuity. As will be seen in subsequent chapters, such cases were more characteristic of larger towns and cities and the metropolis. They were relatively uncommon in predominantly rural areas, but nonetheless some did occur. Various formulations were used. Sibil Birkby of Kegworth (Leicestershire), it was said in 1510, 'lives suspiciously with divers persons'. Elizabeth Howles of East Dean (Sussex) in 1520 was described as a 'common whore'. In the same year, Juliana Davy of Petworth (Sussex) was first reported merely for incontinence, though no partner was named, then a few weeks later denounced as a 'whore'. In Leicestershire in 1522–3, Joan Forran of Aston Flamville was said to be 'of evil disposition', while Alice Wattes of South Croxton was reported as being 'of bad fame'. The latter was subsequently denounced as a 'common whore' and indeed admitted that she had been publicly defamed as 'strong houre' – a further reminder that the term 'whore' was not merely an abusive epithet used in slanging matches but could refer to women's actual behaviour and carry adverse legal consequences.[75] The root meaning of the Latin term *meretrix*, which was invariably used in

---

[74] LA, DIOC/Viv 5, fos. 56v and 38(*bis*)r–95v *passim*.
[75] E.g. *ibid.*, fo. 52r; ROLLR, 1 D 41/13/1, fos. 8r, 8v, 15v; WSRO, Ep.I/10/2, fos. 4v, 56r, 65v.

these records to convey the English term 'whore', was one who sets out her stall for sale. Whether the women prosecuted in these terms actually charged money for their services is usually unclear. They may have done – or received food, drink, clothing and the like in lieu – but this was rarely mentioned. This suggests that the issue of most concern to those who framed the accusations was that the women were sexually available to many men, if not all comers. The sense of hardening local suspicion about such matters is aptly caught in the accusation against Agnes Blayke of Hinckley (Leicestershire) in 1523, detected for incontinence 'and reputed among her neighbours to be common'.[76]

Among the individuals reported to the Chichester consistory court for promiscuity in 1520 was 'Joan, the daughter of the woman keeping the alehouse at Stopham bridge'.[77] The alehouse-keeper herself was at risk because aiding and abetting sexual offenders was itself an offence. Prosecutions for so doing were fewer in number than those for adultery, fornication and the like but by no means an insignificant item of court business. Depending on jurisdiction, they generally accounted for between 5 and 20 per cent of all sex-related offences. Sometimes individual cases are hard to distinguish. A report that a man was keeping a suspect woman in his house might mean merely that he was shielding her or that he was thought to be conducting an illicit relationship with her himself. He might be doing both, of course.[78] However, women accused of aiding and abetting might on other occasions be cited as principals. Thus, in 1523, a widow called Emmota Taberer of Slawston was first reported for 'bawdry' and ordered not to receive suspicious persons in her house; shortly afterwards, she was in court again for incontinence with one Consciens 'and as it is asserted the said Emmota confessed that . . . [he] knew her twice'.[79]

The English word used for condoning, aiding or abetting sexual transgressions was 'bawdry', and someone guilty of these offences, whether male or female, was a 'bawd'. The Latin equivalent of the latter term was *pronuba*, and there were various abstract nouns derived from this such as 'pronubacia'. However, these words seem to have been associated most often with the more or less full-time activities of professional brothel-keepers and their

---

[76] ROLLR, 1 D 41/13/1, fo. 29v. On the term 'meretrix', see Ruth Mazo Karras, *Common Women: Prostitution and Sexuality in Medieval England* (New York and Oxford, 1996), pp. 11–12, 147 n. 35.

[77] WSRO, Ep.I/10/2, fo. 13r.

[78] E.g. ROLLR, 1 D 41/13/1, fo. 20v. For examples of ambiguous reports, see WSRO, Ep.I/10/2, fos. 89r, 103v, 123r.

[79] ROLLR, 1 D 41/13/1, fos. 21v, 24r.

associates, and they were used comparatively rarely in a rural context. 'Leno' as a noun, meaning 'pimp' or 'bawd', was even more rarely used. Instead, the sense was conveyed by some variant of *lenocinium* or *fovet lenocinium*. The latter phrase meant to promote, maintain or uphold (literally to 'foster') bawdry. It could cover a wide range of circumstances, usually centring on the provision of house-room or other space. Thus it could refer to keeping a brothel, in the sense of premises where 'whores' were or could be made available. But equally it could mean making a room available for a couple who wished to pursue an illicit relationship or simply providing cover for them or helping them to avoid detection or capture. It could mean taking in vagabonds or persons who were 'suspect' in a general sense – thieves, night-walkers and so on – with the additional implication that these undesirables were allowed to indulge in out-of-wedlock sex. Sometimes people accused of 'promoting bawdry' were at one time or another guilty of all these activities. As has been seen, illegitimate births were not usually the focus in prosecutions for fornication in this early period, and they were even less so in cases of aiding and abetting. In fact, 'fostering bawdry' only occasionally meant 'harbouring' an illicitly pregnant woman or providing a safe house for her delivery. This form of the offence is much more characteristic of a later period – the decades around 1600.[80]

The records of cases of sexual transgression and related matters rarely include direct information on the wealth or standing of the accused. Unusually, the account of proceedings at and after the visitation of Norwich diocese in 1499 does give the occupations of some of the defendants. They included the bailiff of Stow (Norfolk), presumably a man of means, a parchment-maker and sundry bakers, butchers, carpenters, smiths, tailors and mariners. Plainly this does not mean that these trades were exceptionally prone to sexual licence, simply that the scribe did not bother to record the occupations of agriculturalists, who (of whatever precise social status) probably accounted for the bulk of male defendants.[81] In this record and others there are occasional indications of poverty, but they are rare.[82]

But there is another kind of status to consider, for which more evidence is available. As noted earlier, many of the women accused of adultery with married men were in fact their maidservants. Female servants also featured prominently in other sexual incontinence cases.

---

[80] Cf. R. H. Helmholz, 'Harboring Sexual Offenders: Ecclesiastical Courts and Controlling Misbehavior', *Journal of British Studies*, 37 (1998), 258–61.

[81] Harper-Bill (ed.), *Register of John Morton*, Vol. III, pp. 152, 153, 156, 170, 195, 204, 205, 225, 232, 233, 235.

[82] E.g. *ibid.*, p. 150; Thompson (ed.), *Visitations in the Diocese of Lincoln*, Vol. I, p. 37, cf. Bowker (ed.), *Episcopal Court Book*, p. 134 (Robert Radclyff).

For the most part, probably, their sexual partners were young unmarried men, some of whom were themselves said to be in service, while no doubt others were at that stage of their lives – either wage labourers or working for fathers or elder brothers.[83] These life-cyclical features are themselves revealing of the social status of many of the accused, but they make it hard to trace them in local records to discover further information. The difficulties of that task are compounded by the fact that faced with prosecution or burdened by an illicit pregnancy, many accused individuals temporarily or permanently abandoned their communities or even went right out of the court's jurisdiction. The records are peppered with notes to the effect that this or that individual – both men and women but generally rather more of the latter – had 'left' (*recessit*) or 'fled' (*aufugit*). They amounted to nearly 15 per cent of the accused in the archdeaconries of Suffolk and Sudbury in 1499, and though the record of that visitation was exceptionally well kept, there is no guarantee even here that the list was complete.[84]

It is nonetheless of value to compare the names of alleged offenders with tax lists and other topographically specific records, especially in the early 1520s, when Henry VIII's military and financial exactions, ruthlessly organized by Cardinal Wolsey, led to the creation of highly detailed (though, of course, not unproblematic) tax and muster lists. For the reasons already implied, most of the women and some of the men simply cannot be traced. But plausible linkages can be established in other cases and reveal plainly that the accused individuals came from a wide social spectrum, including poor and middling people, but extending into the ranks of the most substantial elements in local society.[85] On the basis of a similar exercise, Stephen Lander found that 'as many as one in seven of those cited to the [Chichester] consistory court in 1524 to answer office charges were amongst the most substantial men in their communities'.[86] Similarly, E. M. Elvey, collating archdeaconry of Buckingham records

---

[83] E.g. ROLLR, 1 D 41/13/1, fos. 2r, 3r, 5r, 5v, 6v, 7r, 7v, 9r, 9v, 10r, 10v, 12r, 12v, 16r, 19v, 20v, 21r, 22r, 23r, 26v, 27v, 28r, 28v, 29v, 30r (females), 6r, 19v, 29v, 30r (males).

[84] Harper-Bill (ed.), *Register of John Morton*, Vol. III, pp. 168–239 *passim*.

[85] Based on collation of church court records for the archdeaconries of Chichester and Buckinghamshire with Julian Cornwall (ed.), *The Lay Subsidy Rolls for the County of Sussex, 1524–25* (Sussex Record Society 56, Lewes, 1956); A. C. Chibnall and A. Vere Woodman (eds.), *Subsidy Roll for the County of Buckingham, Anno 1524* (Buckinghamshire Record Society 8, 1950); A. C. Chibnall (ed.), *The Certificate of Musters for Buckinghamshire in 1522* (Buckinghamshire Record Society 17, 1973).

[86] Stephen James Lander, 'The Diocese of Chichester, 1508–1558: Episcopal Reform under Robert Sherburne and its Aftermath', unpublished PhD thesis, University of Cambridge, 1974, pp. 82–3.

with a variety of local sources, identified a number of high-status defendants in adultery and fornication prosecutions. Sir Roger Dynham, for example, brother of Lord Dynham, was defamed of adultery with the wife of one of his servants in 1489, while Thomas Rokes, senior of Fawley, accused of adultery with Alice Powlyn in 1494, is identifiable with the individual who served as sheriff of Bedfordshire and Buckinghamshire in 1477 and 1486.[87]

Aims and Outcomes

From this discussion it will be evident that the correctional activities of the church courts served many purposes. Among them was the punishment of the guilty, if they could be so proved, and behind that lay the church's aspiration to bring sinners to real repentance. Local people might well share these aims, especially when the circumstances were blatant and had provoked scandal, but were often prepared to be pragmatic when the issues were less clear-cut. For their part, the courts did not wish to disrupt social relations further than was essential to achieve condign punishment, and like all courts in the period, they tended to be circumspect in handling people of high status – both with a healthy regard for the reprisals that such individuals might unleash if they felt themselves demeaned or slighted and because to humiliate prominent individuals could have a detrimental effect on the ties of deference that were so important in local society. Especially when illicit pregnancy was at issue, there were also matters of compensation and support to consider, which might on occasion override the imperative to inflict punishment.

From another point of view, the courts were just as concerned to offer defamed individuals the means to clear their names. Even if suspicions were strong, the matter could not be usefully pursued if the accused did not confess and there was no means of proof. It was better, in such circumstances, to offer a decisive means of cauterizing rumour and suspicion rather than letting them fester and perhaps infect other social relations. Compurgation was this means – having denied the charges, the accused was required to produce a specified number of neighbours, usually of the same sex and status, prepared to back up the denial by taking an oath that they believed him or her to be innocent. After a successful purgation, the judge formally re-admitted the accused into a state of good fame and

---

[87] Elvey (ed.), *Courts of the Archdeaconry of Buckingham*, pp. xviii, 70–1, 148, 252; cf. Thompson (ed.), *Visitations in the Diocese of Lincoln*, Vol. I, p. 39; Bowker (ed.), *Episcopal Court Book*, p. 129.

ordered that the alleged offence should be spoken of no more – unless, as sometimes happened, fresh matter came to light or the offence was renewed.

The multifarious aims made for flexible proceedings and, occasionally, complicated outcomes, and finding out what happened is not helped by imperfect record keeping. In view of this, it is useful to compare findings from the archdeaconries of Leicester and Chichester with those from other jurisdictions. In the archdeaconry of Buckingham in the late fifteenth century, the end of many cases was signalled by the Latin word *pax* (literally 'peace') implying simply that some kind of resolution acceptable to the registrar had been achieved. The discontinuous records for the period suggest that in this area successful compurgation was a common outcome, especially in adultery and bawdry cases.[88] Few who attempted the test failed to clear themselves; even an Amersham man ordered to produce eight compurgators was able to do so.[89] Yet the procedure was by no means a formality. Well-recorded cases specified the names of the oath helpers, while occasionally their credentials were subjected to close scrutiny.[90] From this it is clear that they were real people, drawn from the neighbours of the accused person, not legal parasites who could be picked up for hire at the doors of the court. Moreover, compurgation was not an automatic escape route. Roughly the same number of cases ended with the award of penance, usually after one or both parties had confessed.

The records of other jurisdictions with a predominantly rural population provide even less evidence that compurgation was an easy option. In the visitation of the archdeaconries of Sudbury and Suffolk in 1499, twice as many people accused of sexual offences confessed and were immediately enjoined penance than attempted compurgation. Of the latter, only a minority is known to have purged successfully, including those who were allowed to do so on their own oath alone. Approaching half failed the test or defaulted by not turning up. In the remaining cases the record is incomplete – perhaps more likely an indication of failure than of a successful purgation, though we cannot be sure. The pattern in the Chichester courts in 1520 is partially obscured by the fact that in some 40 per cent of sex and sex-related cases the record was left incomplete. But only five people are known to have cleared themselves by compurgation, whereas sixteen were assigned penance. It is true that a further thirteen

---

[88] For an example of failure, see Elvey (ed.), *Courts of the Archdeaconry of Buckingham*, p. 154; for successful purgations in non-clerical sexual incontinence cases, see *ibid.*, pp. 21–2, 49, 64 and *passim*.

[89] Elvey (ed.), *Courts of the Archdeaconry of Buckingham*, p. 188.

[90] *Ibid.*, pp. 22, 64, 70–1, 84, 99–100, 107–8, 148, 246, 250, 261–2.

were dismissed without either penance or a compurgation order. But some of these had already been suspended from church for a period and were probably judged to have been humiliated enough; others were given an 'admonition', presumably a severe telling off from the judge; yet others received a stern injunction – for example, a Chichester man suspected for adultery was peremptorily told 'to remove the woman this night'.[91] A clearer indication of the limits of compurgation as an escape route for culprits comes from the archdeaconry of Leicester in 1522–3, where fewer cases were left incomplete. Again a certain number of defendants (especially those accused of promoting immorality) were dismissed with a caution or an injunction. But thirty-seven people were ordered to do penance, five of them after failed attempts at compurgation, whereas only fifteen were actually able to clear themselves by this means.

Those found guilty of sexual transgressions, either by their own confession or after failing to 'purge', were usually ordered to undergo some form of public penance. Just as much as the forms of public repentance ordered by the post-Reformation Scottish kirk sessions, this was very much a 'performance' with strong dramatic elements.[92] The basic method was for the culprit to walk before the cross in the parish procession on a Sunday or major feast carrying a candle of a specified value (usually a halfpenny or a penny, but sometimes as much as 8d.). The procession ended, the penitent had to stand or kneel in church during the first part of high mass, sometimes reciting prayers or psalms, and then at the offertory to deliver the candle – sometimes this was expressed as 'offer wax' – to the officiating priest or place it before the principal image in the church. But there were many variants. More often than not the penance was ordered to be repeated on two or three occasions, sometimes on the understanding that the last 'day of penance' might be remitted if the others were duly and penitently performed. Often penitents were told to go barefoot, barelegged or both; women were occasionally ordered to leave their hair unbound, a potent symbol of degradation. Worse still was to do penance dressed only in a shirt (men) or smock (women), sometimes with the addition of a penitential white sheet draped about the body. In purely physical terms, these conditions must have made for a miserable experience, especially in wet or windy weather in inclement seasons. But in a society in which dress was such an important marker of wealth and

---

[91] WSRO, Ep.I/10/2, fo. 129v.
[92] Margo Todd, *The Culture of Protestantism in Early Modern Scotland* (New Haven and London, 2002), chap. 3.

status, to be thus stripped almost bare must have been a deep humiliation. Significantly, culprits were rarely expected to suffer such shame more than once; if the penance was repeated, it was normally in ordinary clothes on the second or third occasion.

There were other variations. Milder penances – for a fornicating couple who agreed to get married, for instance – might take place entirely in church, whereas it was sometimes ordered that a person performing part of a penance in the church building should stand or kneel on a platform to ensure complete visibility.[93] If an illicit pregnancy or childbirth was at issue, the penitent (whether male or female) might be ordered to perform some ritual centring on the font. As another refinement, in the early sixteenth century it became common to order the penitent to carry a rosary in one hand as well as the usual candle in the other. At a time when the church was constantly on its guard against heresy – even though committed heretics were apparently few in number – this symbol of orthodox devotion signalled that though the culprit had sinned, perhaps grievously, he or she was a faithful believer, in no way doctrinally at odds with the Catholic community, and willing to submit to the church's authority.

The severity and elaboration of penances broadly corresponded to the gravity of the offence. Blatant incest, for example, was likely to attract a stiff penalty, while adultery tended to be more harshly treated than fornication. Sometimes particular circumstances account for the more spectacular penalties. For example, a man who had begotten a child on a woman of hitherto unblemished reputation and refused to marry her despite her avowal that they were lawfully contracted might be made an example. But it is impossible on the basis of surviving information to explain all the variations. Presumably judges took into account the circumstances of the case, their impression of the culprit, his or her reputation and attitude, the degree of scandal that the offence had aroused and so on. But probably there was an arbitrary element too. Some judges were stricter than others, and different culprits got slightly different treatments even from the same judge.

In one important respect, penances tended to become less severe as time went on. The few surviving court records from the fourteenth century indicate that at that time sexual offenders and those who infringed the laws of marriage, whether male or female, were often ordered to be whipped.[94]

---

[93] E.g. ROLLR, 1 D 41/13/1, fo. 14v.

[94] Andrew John Finch, 'Sexual Morality and Canon Law: The Evidence of the Rochester Consistory Court', *Journal of Medieval History*, 20 (1994), 261–75; Lindsay Bryan, 'Marriage and Morals in the

It is not clear how severe these whippings were, in other words, whether they were intended to be a serious form of corporal punishment rather than a ritual humiliation. But, whatever the degree of physical pain, they were surely deeply humiliating. Submission to one's parish priest was also accentuated, since it was normally he who wielded the whip. This degree of harshness may have reflected a determination on the part of the fourteenth-century authorities to make Christian sexual morality a reality for ordinary people. In ordering whippings, in other words, they were not merely punishing individuals but sending a strong message.

To an extent these practices, and the motives underlying them, continued into the fifteenth century. A formulary book for the diocese of Lincoln stated that the culprit should 'at each corner of the churchyard, humbly kneeling, receive from the curate of the same church a whipping (*fustigaciones*) with a rod according to the custom'.[95] Late fifteenth-century records of the archdeaconries of Buckingham and Leicester show that such 'discipline' or 'correction' (as it was euphemistically called), while not ordered invariably, was by no means unusual.[96] But after 1500, the situation was in flux. Whereas around 1510 whipping was still being prescribed in Leicestershire, at least in some cases, the record for 1522–3 does not specify the actual details of penalties but records them as one or more days of penance 'in common form'. It seems unlikely that this included 'discipline'. Certainly penitential whippings were only rarely, if ever, applied in Buckinghamshire by this period. There is likewise little trace of them at Chichester in the early sixteenth century, nor in the diocese of Norwich. Winchester diocese appears to have been unusual in persisting with the practice of penitential flogging on more than an occasional basis right up till the Reformation.[97]

Was the gradual abandonment of whipping forced by lay people's reluctance to undergo it? By the early sixteenth century, flogging with a whip was beginning to establish itself as the standard punishment for vagrants, and while this penalty took a different form from penitential discipline and was no doubt much more drastic, it may have made corporal discipline for lay people seem less appropriate and hence less acceptable in

---

Fourteenth Century: The Evidence of Bishop Hamo's Register', *English Historical Review*, 121 (2006), 467–86.

[95] Quoted (in the original Latin) in Bowker (ed.), *Episcopal Court Book*, p. xv.

[96] E.g. Elvey (ed.), *Courts of the Archdeaconry of Buckingham*, pp. 96, 149, 164.

[97] Houlbrooke, *Church Courts*, p. 46.

the ecclesiastical context.[98] Yet there is no clear evidence of lay opposition, and the reasons for the decline of this form of penance are in any case more complex. Some canon lawyers themselves seem to have had reservations about the licitness of penitential whipping, at least in the case of people of higher status.[99] More broadly, there was clearly a long-term trend towards more lenient penances. Centuries before, imprisonment and lengthy periods of fasting had been considered appropriate for major sexual sins such as adultery. The penances of the high and late middle ages, though rigorous to the extent that the rod was often employed, were nonetheless more moderate than earlier.[100] The changes of the early sixteenth century may be seen as a continuation of this development, not a concession extorted from a reluctant church but an effort to encourage penitence by making ecclesiastical discipline less drastic. By this stage, the clergy may in any case have felt more confident that despite numerous lapses on the part of individuals, the basic principles of Christian sexual morality were accepted by lay people. However, the shift was slow and halting, and the exact pattern depended on personalities as much as on general trends and policies. Thus Bishop Atwater of Lincoln, in his court of audience, rarely ordered penitents to receive corporal punishment, whereas William Mason, his commissary in the archdeaconry of Leicester and president of Atwater's consistory court, was plainly less reluctant to do so.[101]

With or without the 'discipline', public penance was clearly an experience that most wished to avoid if they could. The well placed and the wealthy could hope for favourable treatment. From a modern perspective, such discrimination appears monstrous, but it could be accommodated by contemporary expectations of law and social practice. It could in any case be argued that it was not to the common good to expose a prominent individual to public shame and obloquy or that to exact a substantial payment 'for pious uses' was of more benefit to the Christian community than to force a wealthy man to walk in his shirt. It was in these terms that the practice was to be defended by the ecclesiastical authorities against the 'Commons'

---

[98] Martin Ingram, 'Shame and Pain: Themes and Variations in Tudor Punishments', in Simon Devereaux and Paul Griffiths (eds.), *Penal Practice and Culture, 1500–1900: Punishing the English* (Basingstoke, 2004), esp. pp. 52–5.
[99] Lyndwood, *Provinciale*, pp. 53–4, 96, though the statements are not clear-cut and the terminology relating to higher status is ambiguous. I am grateful to Ralph Houlbrooke for comments on these texts.
[100] Thomas N. Tentler, *Sin and Confession on the Eve of the Reformation* (Princeton, NJ, 1977), pp. 1–18.
[101] Bowker, *Secular Clergy*, pp. 21–2.

Supplication against the Ordinaries' in 1532.[102] But undoubtedly there were some very dubious cases. As was noted earlier, in 1520 William Hardham of South Stoke (Sussex), evidently a man of considerable substance, was convicted of begetting a child on his daughter or stepdaughter. Submitting to correction, he was ordered to pay 20s. 'in pious uses', namely, 13s. 4d. to the cathedral and 6s. 8d. in the form of bread to be distributed to the poor in Chichester marketplace on the Saturday following. This was a swingeing financial penalty, but the offence was grave and scandalous, and it is difficult to imagine that anyone, except perhaps Hardham himself, regarded this as a truly satisfactory outcome.[103]

Anyway, the practice continued, albeit on a very limited scale. Occasionally judges imposed a straightforward pecuniary penance without, apparently, any ado at all. Thus, at Chichester in 1520, Peter Bullaker – who was the third highest taxpayer in Storrington in 1524 – was ordered, as his penance for getting a woman with child, to provide twelve shillings' worth of bread for the curate to distribute to the poor.[104] More usually defendants had to beg for the favour, and sometimes a miniature psychic drama was played out in court. The culprit was first terrorized with an order for a severe penance before the judge 'of his grace' or 'for the greater benefit' agreed to commutation. As usual, there were many variants. Penances might be only partially commuted, for example. Thus, in 1510, William Tailor of Ashby de la Zouch had not only to donate 20d. towards the repair of the chapel on the west bridge at Leicester but also to offer a wax candle into the hands of his parish priest 'when the greater part of the people are present'; still, this was preferable to the original sentence of having to perform public penance on three successive Sundays. Again, commutation might constitute the compensation and child support that were, as noted earlier, sometimes awarded to unmarried mothers.[105] Women occasionally benefited from commutation orders themselves. Thus, in 1510, Joan Rowse, the daughter of a widow of Stathern (Leicestershire), was ordered as penance for bearing a child out of wedlock to go on pilgrimage to Lincoln Cathedral, make an oblation of 4d. before the high altar there and fast on every vigil of the Virgin Mary for the next year.[106] Predictably, however, it was mainly males who commanded

---

[102] Henry Gee and William John Hardy (eds.), *Documents Illustrative of English Church History* (London, 1896), p. 163.
[103] WSRO, Ep.I/10/2, fo. 23v. The record says that he had impregnated his daughter, but her surname was different, and she was probably his stepdaughter.
[104] WSRO, Ep.I/10/2, fo. 13r; Cornwall (ed.), *Lay Subsidy Rolls*, p. 46.
[105] LA, DIOC/Viv 5, fo. 81v; ROLLR, 1 D 41/13/1, fo. 29v.   [106] LA, DIOC/Viv 5, fo. 69v.

the resources and influence to secure commutations. Yet, even for men of substance, this was a concession that could never be taken for granted, and judges sometimes used the threat of penance with great skill to secure an outcome that they considered just. In a Buckinghamshire case in 1520, a gentleman's son protested that he would rather kill himself than do penance. But he only secured dismissal by agreeing to marry his partner in fornication.[107]

Whether considering commutation or not, judges were more inclined to be merciful if culprits readily submitted to correction and showed themselves penitent. Stubbornness or defiance was met with corresponding harshness. This is well illustrated by the remarkable case of William Banckes, a widower of Loughborough (Leicestershire) in 1525–6 – a local cause célèbre that bears on a number of the other themes discussed in this chapter. Unusually, the original visitation presentment is recorded in English, together with details of who made the detection:

> The churchwayrdens of Loughborow, Richard Grenesmythe, William Cotes and John Sayrson; the names off honest men electe to be with them, Thomas Wood for the churche gayt, Edward Dennam for the byggynge, Richard Androw for the markett stede, Henry Barton for the baxster gayt, Richard Manard for the hygh gayt, and John Androwe for the hall gayt and wood. Be hitt knowen to your mastershipe that all we by one assent and consent have present and doo present unto your mastership apon a verey trouth the myslyvinge and the evyll disposicion of one William Banckes dwellynge emonges us that the seid William Bankes hathe kepped oon Elizabeth Everingham otherwisse called Elizabeth Pater Noster sens Whitsontyde in our parishe by the whiche Elizabeth he hath hadd ij children; and the said Elizabeth is his wyffes broder['s] doughter and alsoo she was her godmoder, and also he kepped her in his wyffis dais and yett doith contynue to yll example of other.[108]

Banckes was duly cited to court, and at first, all seemed to go smoothly. He appeared, confessed the offence and swore to fulfil the commissary's injunctions. The order to abstain from Elizabeth Everingham's company, unless in church or other 'honest places' and in the presence of 'honest persons', was standard, though no doubt not to Banckes' liking. But the penance that the judge chose to impose was a severe one, including 'discipline' at the hands of the curate at the four corners of the churchyard. At this point, Banckes played his trump card, claiming that he had already

---

[107] Elvey (ed.), *Courts of the Archdeaconry of Buckingham*, pp. xviii, 252.
[108] LA, Bishop's Register 26, fo. 130v (the full proceedings are recorded on fos. 124v, 129v, 130r–133v).

been punished for the offence by the previous commissary in the archdeaconry of Leicester, Richard Parker. The latter, however, was close at
hand and rapidly disclaimed this suggestion. He had indeed punished
William Banckes, but only for the first child begotten on Elizabeth
Everingham. The second child amounted to a fresh charge, indeed
a graver one since Banckes was guilty of recidivism.

Banckes evidently went away unhappy with this interpretation, and it
was soon reported that he had performed no part of the penance newly
assigned to him. Cited to appear again, he defaulted and was suspended
from entry into the church. Eventually he turned up again with a fresh
expedient. He had been into the neighbouring jurisdiction and obtained
'letters of correction' – in effect, a disguised form of commutation – from
the court of the archdeacon of Nottingham. Such a tactic was wholly
characteristic of litigants in this period; whether in the ecclesiastical or
the secular courts, individuals were inclined to exploit the complexities of
the system as far as they could to achieve the best possible outcome. In this
instance, though, Banckes' manoeuvre failed, since the official to whom he
had recourse had no jurisdiction in Loughborough. Banckes begged for
absolution nonetheless but refused to take the usual oath to obey the
mandates of the judge, storming out of the court with the words, 'I will
nott sweer nor doo no pennaunce for you, nor ye shall not be my juge for
I doo intend to goo to a superior judge.'[109]

The commissary promptly excommunicated him and, after the statutory forty days, took the unusual step of seeking the aid of the temporal
power. A *significavit* was directed to the king to obtain a writ *de excommunicato capiendo*, and Banckes was in due course arrested and imprisoned in
Leicester gaol. Several weeks later he appeared in a chastened frame of
mind and submitted to a remarkable series of exemplary penances.
Barefoot, bare-legged and bare-headed, with a rosary in one hand and
a one-pound wax candle in the other, he was paraded three times round
Loughborough market, the summoner leading the way with a white rod in
his hand and shouting at the top of his voice, 'This man William Banckes is
injoyned by his ordinary John bischopp of Lincoln to doo this pennance
for his myslyvinge and his great disobedience unto Christes churche.'[110]
Then he went back to prison till the following Sunday, when he performed
an elaborate series of penitential acts in the church and churchyard of his
home parish. These included being beaten on the hands and head by the
curate wielding a black rod while Banckes said the *Confiteor* and the priest

[109] *Ibid.*, fo. 132v.   [110] *Ibid.*, fo. 133r.

intoned the *Misereatur*. After the procession, he went straight back to prison, only to re-emerge to face a similar ordeal the following Sunday. On each occasion the curate made the same announcement, publicly in the middle of the nave, as the summoner had done in the marketplace, before Banckes (still excommunicate) was hustled out of the church in an act of ritual exclusion.

After the end of mass on the second of these Sunday performances, the bishop's commissary sat judicially in the church and summoned Banckes before him. Just in case anyone had still not grasped what was going on, he recited, in English and in plain language, the sequence of proceedings taken against Banckes. At the end of all this, Banckes dropped to his knees and in a plaintive voice said, 'I requyre [i.e. beg] you, Master Comyssary, for the reverence off Christes passion and in the way of charyte, I may be absolvyd and restored ageyne to the lyberties of Christes churche', whereupon the judge released him from the sentence of excommunication. 'And so', the record continues, 'all the parishioners there present went out, to the estimated number of a thousand Christian people, crying out publicly, "Our lord God save the byschope of Lincoln and all his, for this man is well reformed to grace to goode insample of all husse."'[111]

Sexual Transgressions, Local Opinion and Manor Courts

Since this account was inscribed in the bishop of Lincoln's formal register, it may be unwise to take its message of universal satisfaction at the conclusion of these proceedings too literally. Yet the case is both unusual and interesting in offering some direct evidence of popular support for the church's punishment of sexual offenders. But this was an extreme case, and as the preceding discussion indicated, it is unlikely that in rural society on the eve of the Reformation there was a single, uncomplicated view of sexual transgressions and how they should be dealt with. To summarize the findings of this chapter, it is probable that virtually everyone, men and women alike and of all social ranks, paid lip service to the notion that adultery was reprehensible. But this did not stop many people doing it. Married men were particularly prominent among those who succumbed to temptation, and their maidservants – close at hand and (whatever their own desires) in a weak position to say no – were particularly vulnerable to their attentions. But men could range much further afield in search of illicit sex, while some married women were also willing to transgress. Attitudes

[111] *Ibid.*, fo. 133v.

towards sexual relations between unmarried people were much less clear-cut and vastly complicated by courtship customs and the marriage quest in a society where matrimony was the only realistic career option for most women. It is probable that males and females alike took calculated risks, some more foolish than others. Inevitably women were in a more vulnerable position than men, who benefited both from the biological fact that they could not get pregnant and from a multitude of social circumstances and cultural assumptions that favoured them. No doubt everyone thought it a sorry matter if an unmarried woman of hitherto sound reputation found herself pregnant. But did it necessarily follow that the man should marry her? For the men who made these decisions, whether solid farmers and tradesmen or court officials, the matter hardly required thought. In numerous cases modest compensation was the best that could be expected. But many unmarried mothers did not get even this. The number noted in the records as 'fled' or 'gone' suggests that many decamped as quickly as possible. How they (and their babies) fared can for the most part only be conjectured.

Most of the cases of sexual transgression coming from predominantly rural areas seem to have been in the nature of occasional lapses rather than inveterate misbehaviour. But some men, especially those of higher status, kept mistresses on a long-term basis, either cohabiting with them in their own houses or maintaining them elsewhere. Presumably they thought that the ordinary rules did not apply to them. Moreover, there were some women who gained the reputation of being common whores and a few men who were noted as habitual adulterers or whoremongers. People in settled society were also troubled by the sexual activities of the vagabond men and women who occasionally passed through. All these people could hardly have behaved as they did had it not been for householders who were prepared to receive people of dubious reputation without asking too many questions, perhaps offering premises for couples to meet illicitly, harbouring pregnant women on occasion and providing, if necessary, facilities for their lying-in. There were men for whom a young daughter or step-daughter was a market opportunity, men who turned a blind eye to their wives' infidelities either because they had no choice or because there were profits or benefits to be had.

Although the courts that primarily dealt with sexual transgressions were ecclesiastical and run by the clergy, they were clearly dependent on the vigilance of churchwardens and other local lay people to make them work. Visitations were generally less important as a source of information than they were to be after the Reformation and were hampered by the habitual

reticence of local churchwardens and questmen. But they were supplemented by a variety of more informal mechanisms that enabled the officers
of the courts to tap into local suspicions and resentments. When sexual
transgressions were blatant or prolonged, neighbours of both sexes and all
social ranks could become increasingly exasperated and more than ready
to assist the courts. As several cases have illustrated, constables – the local
agents of secular policing – were sometimes also brought in to lend a hand.
On occasion, justices or other local gentlemen likewise intervened.

Against this background it is not surprising to find that some local
secular courts entertained cases of sexual transgression, especially egregious
instances of habitual misbehaviour and the blatant upholding or condoning of immorality. Marjorie McIntosh, in particular, has emphasized that
some manor courts exercising leet jurisdiction took upon themselves to
deal with such matters as 'nuisances' and breaches of good order, just as
they punished scolds, quarrellers and brawlers, receivers of vagabonds,
harbourers of thieves and the like. The language of such manor court
presentments is skewed to reflect the secular concerns of the courts in
which they were made, but in other respects they have similarities with
church court prosecutions. In 1460, for example, jurors in the manor of
Loughborough (Leicestershire) – William Banckes's parish – presented
a man for receiving an adulterous couple in his house, along with other
presentments for scolding, wrongfully offering hospitality at night and at
other illegal times and playing dice and cards.[112]

Such cases are suggestive, but it is doubtful if they should be seen as
a 'clear invasion' of ecclesiastical jurisdiction.[113] They look more like
a supplement to the church courts rather than a hostile challenge and
from another point of view simply reflect a degree of jurisdictional fuzzi-
ness in this period. A relatively late Sussex case shows further that action by
manorial jurors could be instigated or supported by figures much higher up
the social scale. It was reported that in 1537 the countess of Arundel called
before her two men of West Dean, informing them that one of their fellow-
parishioners 'kepith shrewde rule with his servant . . . wherfor I will that
now at your next lawe day that ye present hir that she be avoided out of the
parishe, for it is my lordes mynde' – presumably she was referring to
William Fitzalan, the eleventh earl – 'that ther shalbe no such rule kept'.
In this case it is striking both that it was the woman, not the man, who was

---

[112] Marjorie Keniston McIntosh, *Controlling Misbehavior in England, 1370–1600* (Cambridge, 1998),
p. 141.
[113] Paul Seaver, 'Introduction', in 'Symposium: Controlling (Mis)Behavior', *Journal of British Studies*,
37 (1998), 237.

to bear the brunt of this action and that the householder himself resisted the intervention: the individuals who made the presentment at the countess's behest were sued for defamation in the bishop's consistory court.[114]

In any event, such prosecutions probably did not occur in the great majority of rural communities at this time. Loughborough, a populous market centre and stopping place on the main road from London through Nottingham to York, is typical of the sort of places that were, according to McIntosh's analysis, most likely to throw them up.[115] Yet, even here, as search of the surviving late fifteenth- and early sixteenth-century court rolls indicates, they were rare.[116] To take another example, in Battle (Sussex) a woman was fined for receiving whores (*meretrices*) in 1474; Agnes Petyt was regularly presented between 1474 and 1482, accused of being a bawd (*pronuba*) and keeping a suspect house; while in 1477 a widow was presented for being a public or common whore. But there had been no comparable prosecutions between 1470 and 1474, nor were there any in the admittedly broken series of court rolls for the next fifty years. Between 1524 and 1530, three men were presented for keeping suspect houses or taverns – it is not clear that they were bawdy houses – but that is all.[117] As a phenomenon, such prosecutions are interesting both as an indication of the underworld activities that existed in some communities and the neighbourhood response marked by the use both of church courts and varieties of secular courts to deal with them. But in rural areas, it would seem, sexual regulation was mostly the prerogative of the church courts. It was otherwise in the context of larger urban centres, and it is to the towns and cities of Yorkist and early Tudor England that we must now turn.

---

[114] WSRO, Ep.I/10/5, fos. 113r, 114r–v.

[115] McIntosh, *Controlling Misbehavior*, chaps. 6 and 7 *passim*.

[116] Based on search of Huntington Library, Hastings Collections VI: Manorial Papers, Box 21, nos. 6 (2) (1455–6), 8 (1459–60), Box 22, nos. 4 (1486), 5 (1488–9), 7 (1492–3), Box 23, nos. 1 (1494–5), 2 (1496–7), 3 (1501–2), 4 (1503–4), 5 (1504–5), 6 (1505–6), 7 (1507–8).

[117] Mavis E. Mate, *Daughters, Wives and Widows after the Black Death: Women in Sussex, 1350–1535* (Woodbridge, 1998), p. 47; cf. Huntington Library, Battle Abbey VI, Manorial Papers, BA 648–55 (1470–1), 739–46 (1482–3), 756–71 (1500–1, 1509–10), 809–14 (1519–20), 832–41 (1524–6), 856–7 (1530–1).

CHAPTER 4

Urban Aspirations
Pre-Reformation Provincial Towns

Sexual transgressions were reported from rural parishes, whether in the form of visitation presentments or by other means, only in small numbers. In a particular year there might be one or two, perhaps as many as four cases from a single village. Many parishes would yield no cases at all. Moreover, such prosecutions as occurred were mostly run-of-the-mill cases of adultery, fornication and illicit pregnancy, occasionally varied by accusations of bawdry and the like. Small market towns were much the same, but major provincial urban centres show a different pattern. It was not merely that their larger populations generated cases in larger numbers and more regularly. In addition, the profile of urban prosecutions reveals more persistent problems of sexual transgression that contemporaries clearly regarded as disorderly, often associated with inns and alehouses and verging on or including prostitution. In what were, by contemporary standards, sizeable towns and cities – though none was truly very large in this period – such features were magnified.

In these urban situations, ecclesiastical courts were by no means the sole institutions prosecuting sexual transgressions. At least in principle, religious guilds imposed strict standards of behaviour on their members, including sexual probity.[1] At a more public level, a number of secular courts were involved too, co-existing or interacting in complex ways with church tribunals. While historians have been aware of this fact for some time, there have been few attempts to gauge the intensity of such activity or to chart its exact contours; and where such attempts have been made, the tendency has been to downplay the efforts of civic authorities. Helen Carrel, for example, states that in practice towns were 'not particularly anxious to prosecute morality cases', however keen they were to *legislate* on

---

[1] Ben R. McRee, 'Religious Gilds and Regulation of Behavior in Late Medieval Towns', in Joel Rosenthal and Colin Richmond (eds.), *People, Politics and Community in the Later Middle Ages* (Gloucester, 1987), pp. 108–22.

such issues.[2] In contrast, the evidence presented here shows just how far-reaching and important urban jurisdiction over sexual transgressions actually was in the late fifteenth and early sixteenth centuries.

Complementing the work of Carrel, Philippa Maddern and others, this chapter further emphasizes that these efforts should not be seen merely in terms of a pragmatic response to perceived disorder – important though this was, both for urban magistrates and for the local officers and jurors on whom they were dependent to identify offenders. They were underpinned by a powerful ethos in which Christian morality blended with a sense of right order and ideas of 'the common weal' or 'the worship of the town'. Indeed there are strong signs that in the late fifteenth and early sixteenth centuries this moral vision was being articulated more clearly and thereby brought into sharper focus within the framework of ideas of good rule that encompassed the realm as a whole and united the crown and civic authorities in a common endeavour.[3] This ethos was later appreciated by the Elizabethan Protestant antiquarian and local official John Vowell, alias Hooker. 'Yn theise dayes', he recorded in his history of Exeter, 'the citie was so well governed as it was not better yn any age before. For the mayere and magistrates applyed theyre offices, exequuted justice, punyshed vice and dyd governe in truthe and diligens.' Writing at a time when the city was redoubling its efforts against sexual transgressors, he noted with particular approval that his early Tudor namesake, John Hooker, was during his mayoralty 'very severe and sharpe agaynste all notoryose offenders, specially adulterers and whoremongers whom he spared not to punyshe accordinge to theire desertes'.[4]

For the most part the actual records of proceedings against sexual transgressors in Yorkist and early Tudor provincial towns and cities survive only in fragments, if at all. When there are substantial survivals, they tend to be partial in coverage: church court records may survive in the absence of those of borough and city courts, or vice versa.

---

[2] Helen Carrel, 'Disputing Legal Privilege: Civic Relations with the Church in Late Medieval England', *Journal of Medieval History*, 35 (2009), 291–2.

[3] On the general context, see Philippa Maddern, 'Order and Disorder', in Carole Rawcliffe and Richard Wilson (eds.), *Medieval Norwich* (London, 2004), pp. 189–212, 382–6; Helen Carrel, 'The Ideology of Punishment in Late Medieval English Towns', *Social History*, 34 (2009), 301; Carrel, 'Disputing Legal Privilege'. For later development of the ideas of 'common weal' and 'commonwealth', see Paul Slack, *From Reformation to Improvement: Public Welfare in Early Modern England* (Oxford, 1999), chap. 1; Phil Withington, *The Politics of Commonwealth: Citizens and Freemen in Early Modern England* (Cambridge, 2005).

[4] Walter J. Harte, *Gleanings from the Common Place Book of John Hooker, Relating to the City of Exeter (1485–1590)* (Exeter, n.d.), pp. 19, 32. Proceedings against sexual offenders in Elizabethan Exeter are discussed in Chapter 10.

Nonetheless, something of the distinctive profile of sexual offenders and offences, the action taken against them and variations in different towns and cities may be recovered by analysing synoptically the records that happen to survive from a number of locations. The following discussion is based mainly on Colchester, Leicester, Nottingham and Salisbury, with some material also from Exeter and sidelights and comparisons from Coventry and elsewhere.[5]

Leicester and Salisbury

Let us consider Leicester and Salisbury first. The former was a long-established shire borough dominated in the thirteenth and fourteenth centuries by the castle of the earls of Leicester, and it remained an important town throughout the late middle ages. The site of an abbey and several friaries and centre of a relatively independent archdeaconry (though not an episcopal see), it boasted half a dozen parish churches and several hospitals; the elaborate two-storey buildings of Wigston's Hospital were started in 1513. It had a lively civic consciousness that exploded into conflict in 1489. In that year, in accordance with a recent act of parliament, the mayor and Twenty-Four, together with forty-eight of the 'wiser' inhabitants nominated by them, elected Roger Tryng as mayor 'in the name of the whole community'. The commonalty, however, allegedly of 'little substance and discretion', followed past custom and at an assembly of burgesses elected another man as mayor. In the event, the will of the richer inhabitants prevailed, reflecting the pattern of increased oligarchic control that characterized many urban communities in the later fifteenth century. Economically, however, the borough was by this time well advanced along a pathway of slow decline. Though a wide range of occupations, including bell founding, was represented within the town, Leicester's main economic activities centred on locally marketed textiles, tanning and shoemaking and trade in wool. Inevitably, therefore, its fortunes declined in line with those of the surrounding agricultural region. In 1377, Leicester ranked seventeenth among English towns with 2,302 taxpayers, suggesting a total population of 4,000 or more. In 1524–5, its ranking in terms of

---

[5] For additional material, consistent with the arguments presented here, see Ann J. Kettle, 'City and Close: Lichfield in the Century before the Reformation', in Caroline M. Barron and Christopher Harper-Bill (eds.), *The Church in Pre-Reformation Society: Essays in Honour of F. R. H. Du Boulay* (Woodbridge, 1985), pp. 158–69; Ann J. Kettle, 'Ruined Maids: Prostitutes and Servant Girls in Later Medieval England', in Robert R. Edwards and Vickie Ziegler (eds.), *Matrons and Marginal Women in Medieval Society* (Woodbridge, 1995), pp. 19–31.

tax-paying population had fallen to thirty-third, its actual population having by this time declined by probably well over 30 per cent.[6]

Salisbury offers something of a contrast. New Sarum had developed rapidly after the bishop of Salisbury had around 1220 determined to transplant his see from the exposed and arid site of Old Sarum to the confluence of the rivers Avon and Nadder. The location had encouraged the growth of textile and leather industries and trades associated with them, so that by the late fourteenth century the city was among the wealthiest and most populous in the realm. In the poll tax returns of 1377, its tally of 3,373 taxpayers (including the suburb of Fisherton) placed it seventh in rank among English urban centres. This figure represented a population upwards or downwards of 6,000, among whom weavers, tuckers, dyers and tailors were prominent, as also to a lesser degree were tanners, glovers and parchment-makers. The subsidy returns of 1524–5 indicate the extent to which Salisbury maintained its standing and prosperity into the sixteenth century. At that point it ranked eighth in terms of tax-paying population and seventh in terms of taxable wealth. Salisbury never had impressive fortifications (earthen banks rather than walls sufficed), but in other respects its physical aspect and social amenities were commensurate with its status. Apart from the cathedral, set apart in a large walled close, the late medieval city also boasted two large friaries, a college and two hospitals. To serve less spiritual needs, there was a clutch of inns, including the George, as well as innumerable alehouses. The combination of a numerous and supposedly celibate clergy, a large population including not only local inhabitants but also visiting merchants and traders and the easy availability of drink undoubtedly contributed to the city's policing problems.[7]

Despite its size and importance, Salisbury remained a seigneurial borough under the control of the bishop. His officers kept a view of frankpledge and other courts and acted as justices. However, the mayor and four aldermen, assisted by constables and serjeants, also had an eye to the maintenance of order. The civic community, including members of the two councils, the Twenty-Four and the Forty-Eight, met regularly in an assembly or 'convocation' to deal with pollution, slander and contempt of

[6] D. M. Palliser (ed.), *The Cambridge Urban History of Britain*, Vol. I: *600–1540* (Cambridge, 2000), pp. 307–9, 383, 442–3, 447, 461, 616, 624, 627, 629, 632, 758, 762; Alan Dyer, *Decline and Growth in English Towns, 1400–1640* (Basingstoke, 1991), pp. 21, 42.

[7] Palliser (ed.), *Cambridge Urban History*, Vol. I, pp. 123, 141, 177–8, 373, 442–3, 458, 543, 596, 599–600, 606, 758, 761, 765; David R. Carr, 'From Pollution to Prostitution: Supervising the Citizens of Fifteenth-Century Salisbury', *Southern History*, 19 (1997), 24–41.

city officers and other threats to order and harmony. These included the activities of 'common women'. Early in the fifteenth century the convocation seemed willing to countenance their living within the town, so long as they were confined to a certain location – first Friary Lane and later Culver Street. But in 1452 they were ordered out of the city and, on pain of imprisonment, forbidden to enter it for any length of time unless they wore striped hoods. (As it happened, fine striped cloths or 'rays' were a Salisbury speciality, but the use of ray hoods to denote prostitutes was characteristic of many urban communities.) Leicester, for its part, legislated against various moral offences, apparently for the first time, in 1467; in particular, it ordered 'that no bordell be holden withinne this town, bawdery ne bawde dwelling, but that the firdeborowe [frankpledge] next dwelling utter them to the courte'.[8]

Unfortunately, there survive no detailed records to show how the activities of common women and other sexual transgressions were dealt with by the secular courts of either of these towns in the fifteenth century. It is to church court records that we must turn for further insight. The three parishes of the city of Salisbury were within the jurisdiction of the subdean of the cathedral, who exercised quasi-archidiaconal authority subject to the oversight of the bishop. An act book survives for a short period in Edward IV's reign: analysis of the record for 1477, which appears to be complete, shows that much of the work of the court consisted of debt suits, but there were also considerable numbers of defamation causes and many disciplinary prosecutions (Table 4.1). The latter consisted primarily of cases variously described as adultery, fornication and incontinence and the like. But some of these involved accusations of promiscuity, while there was in addition a significant number of cases of aiding and abetting sexual offences (*lenocinium*), characteristic of a town of this size.[9]

The proceedings of visitations of the six parishes of the town of Leicester in 1509 and 1510 indicate a broadly similar pattern. There are fewer cases, as is to be expected in a much smaller town, but the records are more discursive than those from Salisbury and include telling detail. Moreover, whereas at Salisbury the source of accusations was generally unspecified, at Leicester it is clear that the charges were mostly brought by churchwardens and other

---

[8] Carr, 'From Pollution to Prostitution', 36 and *passim*; Mary Bateson et al. (eds.), *Records of the Borough of Leicester: Being a Series of Extracts from the Archives of the Corporation of Leicester*, 7 vols. (London, Cambridge and Leicester, 1899–1974), Vol. II, p. 291.

[9] WSA, D4/3/1, fos. 3r–24r, 59r–64v. See also Roy Martin Haines, 'The Jurisdiction of the Subdean of Salisbury', in his *Ecclesia Anglicana: Studies in the English Church of the Later Middle Ages* (Toronto and London, 1989), pp. 53–66, 264–71.

Table 4.1 *Proceedings in the Court of the Subdean*
of Salisbury, 1477

Instance suits:	
Breach of faith/perjury [debt]	42
Defamation	20
Matrimonial	4
Tithes/dues	3
Testamentary	3
Total	72
Office cases:	
Bigamy	2
'Adultery'	16
'Fornication'	11
'Incontinence', etc.	2
Aiding/abetting sexual offences	9
Questionable marriage	1
Common defamer	1
Non-sexual offences	6
Unspecified	4
Total	52
Grand total	124 (excluding 11 probates)

parishioners, who came to make their presentments in groups of four to twelve. It may therefore be safely inferred that they reflect the concerns of ordinary local people.[10] Some of the offences are indistinguishable from those commonly found in rural areas, albeit with the occasional hint of the urban context. Thus, one man was 'defamed by his adversaries in the ward' (*per suos berttatis emulos*) that he had fathered a child on his maidservant. Another case was suggestive of a couple on the run, seeking the relative anonymity of the town. Christopher Maltby was said to 'occupy and keep in fornication Emmota Blackeburn of the same place; they sleep together at night in the house of Henry Staton'. In court, they admitted that, after contracting marriage, they had lived together in fornication in the house of one of them in Doncaster, and afterwards at Oakham they had cohabited for

---

[10] LA, DIOC/Viv 5, fos. 71r–72r, printed in W. G. D. Fletcher (ed.), 'Documents Relating to Leicestershire, Preserved in the Episcopal Registers at Lincoln', *Associated Architectural and Archaeological Societies Reports and Papers*, 22 (1893–4), 109–12.

a whole year. They were ordered not to keep house together and indeed to abstain from each other's company until marriage had been solemnized between them, and before they did that, they had each to exhibit a certificate of the decease of their former spouses. Were they indeed dead? The judge was suspicious, but the woman at least was able to specify the churchyard in which her late husband was buried.[11]

Many other cases were even more strongly redolent of disorder. In the Michaelmas vistation of 1510 it was said that Katherine Green 'promotes bawdry' between a townsman and a vagabond. Helen Tromell was accused of 'living suspiciously' with a named man 'and others'. Agnes Burton, 'lying at the sign of the Rowndell', lived suspiciously with Robert Thomson, 'lying at the sign of the Star'. One Elizabeth, surname unknown at the time of presentment (later identified as Hockerton), lying at the 'iij steppys' was suspected with the same man as Helen Tromell. Matilda Eliet 'lies by night' with Christopher, the servant of William Metcalf, 'jailer'. Margaret, surname unknown, servant of Alice Gilbert, 'lives suspiciously with divers men' and was taken in the act with one of them. Four women were accused of living suspiciously with a certain Longkayshire, Christian name unknown, 'lying in Leicester Abbey'. To complete the seedy picture, Agnes Walkar was reported for defaming a priest, 'saying that she caught the same priest between Agnes Bradley's legs'.[12]

Further light on this murky scene is shed by other reports from earlier visitations. In particular, it is plain that the town's inns and alehouses were a prime site of disorderly sexual activities. In 1490 it was reported that Alice Biscoppe 'on the south wall of the town' kept a common alehouse open in time of matins and high mass and was suspected of promoting bawdry. In four inns – the George, the Ram, the Unicorn and the Lion – it was said that a number of 'very bad women' were kept, tapsters (*propinatrices*) 'in form and figure like whores'. Women working in these and similar establishments were frequently cited to court under the name of 'Tapster'. It was not their real name, of course, if indeed they had one: it was a sobriquet that aptly conveyed their function in life, serving ale and servicing men. Less often males were similarly typecast. In a somewhat earlier return, 'John Ostiler' at 'the sign of the Bear' was reported for 'adultery with divers women'.[13] It was a similar picture in late-fifteenth-century Salisbury. Disciplinary proceedings in 1477 involved seven women who were said

---

[11] LA, DIOC/Viv 5, fos. 5v, 71v.   [12] LA, DIOC/Viv 5, fo. 71r–v.
[13] LA, DIOC/Viv 3, fo. 39r; DIOC/Vj 3, fos. 8r, 8v. See also Ruth Mazo Karras, *Common Women: Prostitution and Sexuality in Medieval England* (Oxford and New York, 1996), p. 72.

to be tapsters or were given the surname 'Tapster': they included Edith, tapster at the Three Cups; Emma, tapster at the Mitre; and Margaret, tapster at the George.[14] The following year, Marion Tapster at the sign of the Saracen's Head was in trouble, as was William, surname unknown, lately 'hostilarius' of the Angel, with Alice, servant and tapster (*clipsidera*) at the same inn. In 1478 there was also mention of 'French Joan' and 'Irish Kate': these more colourful sobriquets are perhaps an indication of unequivocal professional status.[15]

How adequate were the powers of the church courts to police this kind of world? Certainly the ecclesiastical authorities pursued these and other urban sexual offenders with some vigour. The record of proceedings following the Leicester visitation of 1510 is very incomplete, but in at least two-thirds of cases an appearance was entered, and several individuals are known to have been put to penance. The much fuller record from Salisbury shows that in 1477 nearly seventy individuals were cited in connection with sexual offences. Strikingly, the court secured the appearance of the great majority of them, in some cases after they had been suspended for their initial contumacy. Of the small minority who failed to turn up, several were marked 'recessit', indicating that they had left the city. Of those who appeared, thirteen are known to have cleared themselves by compurgation, whereas ten failed the test or defaulted. The success rate was boosted by defendants – all women – facing accusations of 'bawdry' or aiding and abetting sexual offences. They were more likely than other individuals to deny the charges against them and better able to produce the necessary compurgators. However, it does not seem that this was the result of sharp practice. One compurgator did act for two women accused of bawdry on separate occasions, and another was herself to be brought to court for the same offence a few months later. But the great majority of the compurgators were, as far as can be seen, the respectable neighbours that they were supposed to be.

Those who confessed charges, in whole or in part, or were convicted after failing to clear themselves by compurgation were dealt with in a variety of ways. A good number of people accused of fornication or incontinence – and even a couple initially reported for adultery – claimed that they were contracted to marry and sought favour on these grounds. In some cases untoward circumstances were discovered, such as doubt whether a former spouse was dead. But mostly what was really at issue was failure to solemnize a marriage within a reasonable time. Like its rural counterparts, the court

---

[14] WSA, D4/3/1, fos. 10r, 12v, 59r, 60v, 63r, 63v, 64v.   [15] *Ibid.*, fos. 69r, 73r, 77r, 84v.

clearly regarded it as important to insist on solemnization, and couples in these circumstances were generally ordered to arrange a wedding without delay and meanwhile to abstain from sexual relations or even from consorting together on pain of penance if they defaulted.

Some of the cases where marriage was not in prospect – whether because the relationship was adulterous or for other reasons – were likewise dealt with by injunction rather than penance. The offenders swore to renounce the illicit relationship, sometimes in addition paying what was probably a substantial sum to 'compound with the office'. Why the judge chose this course of action is not always clear, but sometimes the entreaties of influential friends or *generosi* were mentioned or 'hope of amendment' was noted. It would seem that the rigours of public penance – though whipping was never ordered – were reserved for the most serious and obdurate cases. Penance was actually performed even more rarely than it was imposed. Rather than undergoing the humiliating ritual, several culprits allowed themselves to be excommunicated or simply left the city.

It is true that the occasional well-placed individual was able to pervert the system. John de la Haye (or Delahayse) – who, it would appear, had recently been sued for marriage by two different women – was brought to court again for fornication with Edith, the tapster at the Three Cups, with a certain Joan Meslin and with other, unnamed women. Ordered to purge with six hands, he defaulted. The fact that he was in prison – presumably for some other offence – held proceedings up for a while, and when a sentence of suspension eventually brought him to court, he refused to do penance. After a further suspension, he made show of submission and was ordered to do penance, barefoot and dressed only in his shirt, in his parish church on the following Wednesday and on Passion Sunday in the cathedral. But again he reneged. Finally, 'by special grace and at the instance of many worthy people', he was allowed to compound. There can have been little real hope of amendment, and soon he was again in trouble with three more women, including 'Frenche Jone'.[16]

But this particularly blatant case of misplaced leniency was not characteristic of the court, which spent a great deal of time harrying offenders and did not hesitate to cite people anew if suspicious behaviour was renewed. There are signs, moreover, that their activities were backed up by local gossip and ridicule. In January 1478, John Wymborne was cited for adultery with Alice Norton. Despite several appearances, the couple could not clear themselves by compurgation, but they strongly denied any real

[16] *Ibid.*, fos. 62r, 77r, 94r.

wrongdoing; and at this stage, the court did not press the matter beyond ordering them to avoid each other's company at suspicious times and places. However, in October they were cited again for renewing the offence. Wymborne admitted that 'he was in the house of the said Agnes around ten of the clock in the night, contrary to the injunction previously imposed', but he continued to deny the fact of adultery and on this occasion managed to produce five compurgators. Yet, his troubles were not over. He was already embroiled in one defamation suit to clear his name, and in November he had to sue another fellow-parishioner for repeating a rumour that he had been 'found between the legs of a certain woman'.[17]

Nottingham

In the absence of detailed records of their court proceedings, it can only be conjectured how far and in what ways the secular authorities in these two towns dealt with sexual offenders. But the borough of Nottingham, less than twenty-five miles north of Leicester as the crow flies, is unusual in preserving a substantial, though discontinuous and sometimes fragmentary, series of sessions files, which may serve as a proxy for the absent Leicester records. To be sure, Nottingham was smaller than Leicester; in 1377 there were 1,447 taxpayers, indicating a total population of between 2,500 and 3,000. But its status as a shire town and archdeaconry (rather than episcopal) centre, together with an economic profile similarly based in the agriculture of the region, makes it roughly comparable. Like Leicester, it was probably in a state of gradual economic and demographic decay in the fifteenth century, though the likelihood that the community was under-assessed in 1524–5 makes the scale of this decline hard to estimate.[18]

The Nottingham borough sessions, held four times a year, included presentments made by juries representing the eastern and western parts of the town, respectively, and by the town constables. The jurors tended to be of higher social status than the constables, drawn from the wealthier rather than the poorer trades and having a greater chance of proceeding to higher civic office; overall these presentments thus gave voice to middling and upper-middling male householders – social groups comparable to the

---

[17] *Ibid.*, fos. 67r, 67v, 82r, 83r, 83v, 89r.
[18] Palliser (ed.), *Cambridge Urban History*, Vol. I, pp. 609–10, 627, 632, 758, 762; Dyer, *Decline and Growth*, pp. 21, 42, 65, 67, 70, 74. On the economic, social and political background more generally, see David Marcombe, 'The Late Medieval Town, 1149–1560', in John Beckett (ed.), *A Centenary History of Nottingham* (Manchester, 1997), pp. 84–103.

churchwardens and questmen who provided information to the church courts.[19] The offences named encompassed assaults, thefts, occasional homicides, trading offences and a wide variety of 'nuisances' and other disorders. Strikingly, among these were numerous charges concerned with 'bawdry' and other sexual offences. These presentments jostled with others that were evidently their natural concomitants: keeping 'misrule' or ill-governed houses; harbouring vagabonds, thieves, or other dangerous persons; playing or promoting unlawful games such as cards and dice, presumably for money; receiving servants and allowing them to waste their masters' goods and money on food, drink and idle activities; scolding and quarrelling, especially on the part of women; nightwalking and nocturnal disturbances; and 'bribery' or petty theft. In practice, particular individuals were often accused of several of these offences in the same or successive courts. The details of repeated presentments evoke a world of ill-regulated alehouses and lodgings, in crowded tenements and back alleys, where the more disorderly inhabitants – including servants and apprentices – whored, gambled, stole, embezzled, quarrelled, occasionally ran riot and sometimes ended up dead.

As this context indicates, secular court jurisdiction over sexual matters had a rather different focus from the work of the ecclesiastical courts, though there were areas of overlap. Whereas the church was primarily interested in lapses from Christian morality, in sinful behaviour that was often conducted as far as possible secretly and out of the gaze of prying neighbours, town courts were more centrally concerned with the raw demands of maintaining public order. The Nottingham evidence, some of it in English rather than the more opaque legal Latin, indicates a number of variations on this general theme. In 1463, the burgesses, much like their counterparts in Leicester in 1467, had made ordinances 'agaynst light women', 'agaynst kepinge of bawdy howses', and 'for alehowses receyvinge suspicious persons or kepinge theyr howses open after 9 of the clock'.[20] The earliest surviving presentments relating to these matters charge inhabitants with keeping 'bordel' and enormity in their houses, sometimes linked with receiving servants or one or more of the other offences just listed. Sometimes the charge might be elaborated into, say, 'lenocinium, bordellum et malam gubernacionem', or the

[19] Judith Mills, 'Continuity and Change: The Town, People and Administration of Nottingham between c. 1400 and c. 1600', unpublished PhD thesis, University of Nottingham, 2010, pp. 218–23.
[20] W. H. Stevenson *et al.* (eds.), *Records of the Borough of Nottingham*, 9 vols. (London and Nottingham, 1882–1956), Vol. II, p. 425.

associated disorders were spelt out: 'making outcries such that the neighbours and other liege subjects of our lord the king cannot sleep in their
beds', for example.[21] English renderings included such phrases as 'ffor
bordur oldyng' and 'for herberyng boudes and idell pepell'.[22] At times,
there may have been some elision of the ideas of 'bawdry' and 'boarding'
or 'bordering' in the sense of providing food or lodging. Thus, in 1524,
the jurors listed 'they that we put wp for scholders [i.e. scolds] and
borderars of men[s] servantes', while in the following year one William
Nyckolson was presented 'for borderyng of serten persons be nyght and
suffer[ing] theryn bawdry to be kepte'.[23] However, as the frequent
association with the Latin word *lenocinium* makes clear, the prime meaning of the term 'bawdry' and its variants was the usual one of aiding and
abetting sexual offences, primarily by providing premises where such
encounters could take place.

Yet there was also a creeping tendency for the term 'bawdry' to include
the actual commission of sexual offences. By this means, offences that
might more obviously be subject to ecclesiastical jurisdiction were brought
within the purview of the borough court. Some presentments named not
only householders but also the people engaged in sexual relations under
their roof. Thus, in 1500, a widow was charged with 'border holdyng don
on Annes her maydon holdon be Tohmas [sic] Wadyngham'.[24] A sizeable
proportion of the individuals presented for promoting bawdry – upwards
or downwards of 50 per cent in any given year – were female, and it is clear
that some of these provided not only the premises but also the actual sexual
services.[25] In other cases, charges of 'bawdry' or 'keeping bawdry' seem to
have referred primarily to the actual commission of sexual transgressions
rather than to aiding and abetting them. Thus, in 1515, William Perkynsun
was accused of bawdry with his 'leymon', or mistress, while in 1529, Roger
Atkynson and Emot Wode were presented 'for kepyng of bawdrye
togedder'.[26] These cases jostled with a minority of other presentments in
which couples were explicitly charged with fornication or adultery or
women were presented as harlots, common whores and the like. In an
unusual formulation, in 1516, Richard Pellet and his wife were presented
'for pleysur of other for to use hir selfe a comon woman'.[27] In a combined
presentment in 1514, Thomas Kappok and Cicely Welforthe were reported

---

[21] NA, CA 3b/5; CA 7b/6; CA 9d/1.   [22] NA, CA 9a/2, CA 9d/2.   [23] NA, CA 26a/2, CA 26b/5.
[24] NA, CA 10a/6 (for the Latin version, see CA 10a/5).   [25] NA, CA 13c/10.
[26] NA, CA 20b/1, CA 30a/2.
[27] NA, 21c/1 (in the original the word 'of' is repeated, apparently in error); cf. 23c/5 ('comon herlat').

for 'fornekacyon en the scherche yerd', while Thomas Granger, smith, was accused of 'bawdre en hys hows with [the] sam persons'.[28]

The loss of many records makes it hazardous to generalize about the numerical incidence of cases. But what survives suggests that presentment was sporadic and largely at the discretion of constables and presentment juries. In some years, only a few cases of a sexual nature were brought forward. However, there were occasional 'drives' – which may or may not have been instigated by higher authority – when large numbers of offenders were named. Thus, in October 1484, there were sixty-six charges of keeping 'bordel' involving fifty-one separate persons, of whom twenty-two were female and twenty-nine male.[29] The women included nine widows; almost all the rest were designated 'housewife', the husband's name being also specified in a few cases. The men were mostly labourers and artisans, plying a miscellany of trades including mason, tiler, shoemaker, tailor, glover, barker (tanner), litster (dyer), shearman and horner.[30]

The year 1505–6 also saw a bumper crop of presentments, perhaps stimulated by the renewal of the borough charter in June 1505 or reflecting a moral panic triggered by the high mortality which – to judge from probate evidence – afflicted the town between 1503 and 1506.[31] On this occasion, the range was wider, including not only sexual offences but also prosecutions for scolding (mostly women), playing bowls (a wholly male offence) and various other disorderly activities. Prosecutions that were explicitly related to sexual transgressions implicated twenty individuals (eight males and twelve females, of whom seven were identified as widows and one as a housewife) for variations on the theme of bawdry, mostly aiding and abetting, but including one case in which a man and a woman were said to be common fornicators as well as practising bawdry. Three other men were charged with 'occupying' named women, evidently in fornication or adultery, while another woman was identified as a 'common whore' and hedge-breaker.[32]

Apart from naming large numbers of persons, jurors and constables could underscore their concerns by pointing an accusing finger at individuals in prominent social positions. In 1505–6, Richard Copeland's wife,

---

[28] NA, CA 15b/4.

[29] Possibly this was in response to Richard III's 1483 proclamation 'for reformation of manners', on which, see Chapter 7.

[30] NA, CA 4/1, 3, 9.

[31] Stevenson *et al.* (eds.), *Records of the Borough of Nottingham*, Vol. III, pp. 96–8; Marcombe, 'Late Medieval Town', p. 84.

[32] NA, CA 13a/2; CA 13b/8, 9; CA 13c/6, 8, 10.

Alice, was named along with many others for 'border haldyng'; but in her case the accusation went on to name Sheriff Johnson 'for okkepyng the sam womon' and – in a situation neatly reflecting the hierarchical principle – the sheriff's servant, William Danson, for 'okepyng' Alice Copeland's servant.[33] Some presentments may have arisen from the endemic tensions that existed between the small group of aldermen, who (in accordance with the charter granted by Henry VI in 1449) effectively dominated government in the town, and the burgesses and commonalty; but this is hard to demonstrate.[34] As will be seen in Chapter 8, more often the targets of this kind of pointed accusation were priests or parish clerks.

Colchester

A suggestive comparison is provided by the records of the tri-annual 'lawhundreds' and sessions of the borough of Colchester – a much larger and more prominent urban centre. On the site of a Roman town and major pre-Roman settlement, surrounded by imposing walls that were proudly depicted in the new civic seal of *c.* 1400, and with a well-established right to return members to parliament, Colchester was in some respects the natural capital of Essex. But in fact it was never the shire town and merely the centre of an archdeaconry within the diocese of London. On the basis of cloth manufacturing and a local and international trade in textiles, it had grown and prospered in the later fourteenth century and early decades of the fifteenth to attain a population of perhaps 8,000. But there were many setbacks thereafter, and the period 1425–1525 witnessed a reduction in immigration from surrounding areas, a fall in population of perhaps a third and a contraction in industrial output, trade and consumption. Investment in land became a more marked feature of the economy, and there was some influx of gentry into the community, not least to occupy legal positions. Nonetheless, textiles remained the greatest single source of wealth, albeit the control of cloth-making became increasingly concentrated in fewer hands.[35] This contraction was paralleled by oligarchic tendencies in the town's system of governance. In the course of the fifteenth century, aldermen were increasingly demarcated from other members of the council; eventually, a new constitution, introduced in

[33] NA, CA 13c/10.   [34] Marcombe, 'Late Medieval Town', pp. 89, 92–3.

[35] Palliser (ed.), *Cambridge Urban History*, Vol. I, p. 18–19, 339, 442–3, 568, 758, 761, 765; Dyer, *Decline and Growth*, pp. 31–2, 70, 73; R. H. Britnell, *Growth and Decline in Colchester, 1300–1525* (Cambridge, 1986), pp. 159, 183–6, 201–2, 209–12, 216, 230–5, 263.

1523–4 during a period of recession in cloth exports and a sharp increase in royal taxation, ensured that high office was monopolized by the wealthier burgesses and reinforced their security of tenure. Since this meant that wealth inexorably carried with it the responsibilities of public service, it was not necessarily to their economic benefit; but it did enhance their sense of honour and 'worship' and, probably, their commitment to maintaining order.[36]

Records of proceedings against sexual offenders in Colchester reveal some themes familiar from the Nottingham evidence, but the precise pattern of prosecutions was significantly different. A late-fourteenth-century list, in Latin, of offenders to be presented at the lawhundreds included 'those who receive common whores within the borough against the ordinance', whereas a list in English from the middle of the following century included 'all comen women beying withyn this towne' and 'ravissours of women, maydenys, or menys servaunts'. Complementary to these ordinances relating to such explicitly sexual matters were articles inquiring of 'al maner vacabunds, dise pleiers, and riotours that wake be nyght and sclepe be daye, and of all such as haunte customably the tavernys, ale housys, and riotts, and of al such as gon up and downe and do nought, and [no] man can sey from whens they com' and of 'al comen chiders and brawlers to the noyauns of ther neyghbours'.[37]

These provisions furnished the basis for a range of prosecutions in which promoting or maintaining bawdry – aiding and abetting – was relatively less prominent than at Nottingham, while there was correspondingly greater emphasis on actual sexual transgressions, including matters of fornication and adultery. All these offences, as the presentments and indictments were at pains to spell out, were brought within the orbit of secular justice on the principle that they were the source of quarrels, debates and nocturnal disturbances, sometimes to the danger of the inhabitants – the king's liege people, as the common phrase went – or to the officers of law and order. In some years, as at Nottingham, the sexual transgressions of the clergy seem to have been particularly targeted,[38] but most of the offenders were laypeople. The pattern was established well before the Tudor period. To take the year 1476–7 as an example, a total of ten men and six women were named for various combinations of adultery, whoredom and bawdry. Some of them were in question more than once,

---

[36] Britnell, *Growth and Decline*, chap. 15.
[37] William Gurney Benham (ed.), *The Oath Book or Red Parchment Book of Colchester* (Colchester, 1907), pp. 2–4, 223.
[38] See Chapter 8.

while a few unnamed women were also involved. To cite but a few cases, William Johnson, brazier, was presented as a common bawd (*pronubus*) between John Parker, mercer, and Thomas Cheveyn's wife, Joan; Thomas Kirkby, John Parker's servant, was charged with the same offence – no doubt he was a go-between – and with being a common nightwalker; while Johnson's wife was named as a common scold among her neighbours. In a less usual formulation, John Grene, loader, and John Whiteryk, junior, were charged with habitually committing adultery (*solent communiter adulterari*) with Agnes Thursteyn, who was herself named as a common whore. A fuller was said to be the 'common maintainer of the said Agnes in her misdeeds', while her own mother acted as her bawd. Another striking case featured the mercer John Parker, when he found himself in trouble again for another adulterous relationship. In a creative use of the law, a trespass indictment was made to serve the turn of the prosecutors, who probably included the husband. It was said that in Easter week Parker had assaulted the wife of Robert Hamlyn and 'with her committed adultery, whereby quarrels and debates have been made at night between the people of the lord the king and against the peace'.[39]

There is a gap in the records for 1485–1509. When the rolls resume in the reign of Henry VIII, the basic pattern persists, and numbers of cases remain at about the same level; but some changes are nonetheless evident. The charge of keeping or maintaining 'ill rule' (*malum regimen*) was now very common. This phrase was associated with diverse disorderly and antisocial activities, including unregulated ale selling; 'riot' in the sense of dissolute behaviour; unlawful games such as 'tables', cards, dice and tennis (all linked with gambling); receiving servants; lodging beggars; nightwalking; theft; hedge-breaking and even 'ferettyng in the nyght'.[40] However, as some presentments made explicit, ill rule was often synonymous with 'bawdry' and could imply either activities that cloaked or supported sexual immorality or actual sexual transgression, including adultery and fornication.[41] In 1514, for example, a weaver named Thomas Crane was indicted at the October session of the peace on the grounds that daily he kept ill rule with Thomas Sutton's wife, openly fornicating with her.[42] However, less ambiguous terms were still frequently used, either instead of or in addition to the language of 'ill rule', and on occasion, the moral implications were spelt out. Thus, in 1530, a married woman was

---

[39] Essex RO, Colchester BR, D/B5 Cr 76, mm. 2r, 2v, 11r, 21r.
[40] *Ibid.*, D/B5 Cr 93, m. 16r; D/B5 Cr 99, mm. 5r, 5v, 9v (ferreting); D/B5 Cr 112, mm. 2v, 5r; D/B5 Cr 116, m. 14r, 14v.
[41] *Ibid.*, D/B5 Cr 86, mm. 12v, 22r; D/B5 Cr 93, mm. 2v, 20r.   [42] *Ibid.*, D/B5 Cr 86, m. 5r.

presented for ill rule, 'bawdry' and keeping a whore (*meretrix*) and her child in her house, while in the same year, in blunt English, a man was reported 'for kepyng of too wenchys with chyld in hys howse'. Occasionally, the jurors employed religious language: in 1515 it was said that a miller 'keeps a whore against the law of God'.[43]

In the 1520s, English phrases were increasingly used in the record. They included some vivid and striking turns of phrase, strongly redolent of moral indignation. The roll for 1526–7 includes presentments for 'maynteynyng of Syr John Fuksmaster and other knaves' and maintaining a woman identified as 'rede petycote', while one man was accused of 'maynteynyng his wyfe in yll rule with prysts and other knavys and he gothe up and down and dothe nought'. In 1534, a woman of Holy Trinity parish was presented 'for yll rule and hulsteryng [i.e. sheltering] of naghty drabbs'.[44] The roll for 1529 includes an inquest to determine whether a woman deliberately took deadly medicines to destroy the child in her womb – a further indication that sexual transgression and its consequences were of real concern to local officers.[45]

Punishments

It is thus clear that by the late fifteenth and early sixteenth centuries, the prosecution of sexual offenders was a well-established practice in the secular courts of many provincial towns. But how serious were the penalties? The point is clearly of importance in evaluating the intensity of moral regulation in pre-Reformation urban centres. Is it the case that the authorities, while paying lip-service to the principle of punishing sexual misdeeds, in practice imposed penalties so light that they could be ignored? Certainly the indications are that a pecuniary mulct was regarded as appropriate in most cases, though it should not be assumed that these fines were a disguised form of licensing, implying an underlying toleration. If they had indeed been treated as a fiscal device, they would surely have been much more regularly and consistently levied at set rates, and the sense of moral outrage that clearly underlay some of the charges would have been absent. In Colchester, offenders were fined varying amounts, commonly 3d., 6d., 12d., 20d. or 3s. 4d. in the late fifteenth century. Even at that time larger mulcts of 6s. 8d. or 10s. were

[43] *Ibid.*, D/B5 Cr 86, m. 22r; D/B5 Cr 99, m. 9r.
[44] *Ibid.*, D/B5 Cr 97, mm. 2v, 19r; D/B5 Cr 103, m. 20v.   [45] *Ibid.*, D/B5 Cr 99, m. 5v.

sometimes made, and the level of fines seems to have been generally higher by the late 1520s. The variations are hard to interpret, but it would seem that the highest sums were levied on habitual offenders who had been fined lesser amounts on previous occasions.[46] It was much the same in Nottingham. Some offenders were explicitly said to have been 'pardoned'. But most of the individuals prosecuted in 1505–6 were fined sums ranging from 2d. to 3s. 4d., whereas someone from outside the town who was maintaining a bawdy house within it was mulcted of a hefty 6s. 8d.[47]

Moreover, it is possible that some culprits, whether in Colchester or in Nottingham, were expelled from the town or subjected to imprisonment or corporal punishment. Certainly there were precedents in some other provincial towns and cities. Thus, in Coventry in 1439, it was ordered that 'William Powet, capper, and his paromour be caried and lad thorowe the town in a carre in exaumpull off punnyshment off syne, and that alle other that be proved in they same syne, ffrom thys tyme fforward shall have the same peyne.' Likewise in Gloucester around 1504, it was ordered that sexual offenders should suffer a spell of imprisonment in a specially made 'hutch' (partitioned to divide off the men from the women), while 'alle abomynable qwenys lyvyng viciously to the opyn fame and knowleg of the comynaltye' should be 'takyn and putt in oone of the commyn halyers cartes within the saide towne, so that they may be conveyed frome ward to ward rounde aboute the same towne … disgysed with frontelettes of papyr and ray hodes'.[48] The paper placards presumably carried a note of the offence, whereas the 'ray hood' was a striped head covering similar to those prescribed for the 'common women' of Salisbury and, as will be seen, was the characteristic badge of convicted prostitutes in London.

Similarly, referring to proceedings in Exeter around 1486, John Hooker wrote both of offenders who were 'corporall[y] punyshed' and those who 'payed for theire redemption with moneyes', while the Chamber Act Book for 2 June 1525 records a decision that Joan Luter

> schalbe carried abowte the cite yn a carte with a ray howde apone heir hede accordyng to the cusementes by dyvers ynquestes ageynst heir

[46] E.g. *ibid.*, D/B5 Cr 76, mm. 2r, 2v, 11r, 21r; D/B5 Cr 78, m. 10r; D/B5 Cr 79, m. 16v.
[47] NA, CA 13a/2; CA 13b/8, 9; CA 13c/6, 8, 10, *passim*.
[48] Mary Dormer Harris (ed.), *The Coventry Leet Book: or Mayor's Register, Containing the Records of the City Court Leet or View of Frankpledge, A.D. 1420–1555*, 4 parts (Early English Text Society, Original Series 134, 135, 138, 146, London, 1907–13), Vol. I, p. 192; *Historical Manuscripts Commission, Twelfth Report*, Appendix, Part IX (London, 1891), pp. 435–6.

presentyd and accordyng to the ponysmentes of suche luyde persons yn the cite of olde tyme used and custumyd and after to banesse the cite yncontynent.[49]

From later records it is clear that 'cusements' were accusations made by juries of presentment at the 'sessions of the peace' and 'lawdays' held several times a year. Evidently there was already an established custom that notorious offenders, after repeated presentments against them, could be driven in obloquy around the city before being expelled. Luter's case was transcribed into Hooker's 'abstracte of all the orders and ordynances' of the city and became one of a number of precedents used to justify the carting and banishment of notorious 'whores' and other sexual offenders in Exeter in the reign of Elizabeth and beyond. Here post-Reformation developments were clearly, indeed self-consciously, related to earlier precedents.[50]

It may be that recourse to public shame punishments of this kind was particularly associated with large towns. Gloucester, it is true, probably had scarcely more than 3,000 inhabitants around 1500. Coventry was among the most prominent towns of late medieval England, with a population that had probably approached 10,000 in 1377, albeit in decline during the course of the fifteenth century. Meanwhile, Exeter – unlike most of the towns that have been discussed so far in this chapter – experienced marked growth from the fifteenth into the sixteenth century. As the see of the bishop of Exeter, a county town, a regional centre of trade and manufacture, and a stopping-point for travellers to and from Cornwall and south, west and north Devon, it enjoyed many advantages. The number of its poll tax payers in 1377 indicates a population of perhaps 3,200, but a case can be made for 5,000 or more in the fifteenth century. By the 1520s, this important international port and emergent provincial capital may have had 6,800 inhabitants.[51] In a more crowded urban environment such as this, the carting of common women and other sexual offenders served not merely to punish individuals by exposing them to open shame but also

---

[49] Harte, *Gleanings*, p. 18; John M. Wasson (ed.), *Records of Early English Drama: Devon* (Toronto, Buffalo and London, 1986), p. 126.

[50] John Vowell, alias Hooker, *The Description of the Citie of Excester*, ed. Walter J. Harte, J. W. Schopp and H. Tapley-Soper, 3 parts (Devon and Cornwall Record Society, Exeter, 1919–47), Part III, pp. 863, 876. See also Chapter 10.

[51] Dyer, *Decline and Growth*, pp. 34, 72–3. On the city and its population in the fifteenth century, see Nicholas Orme, 'Access and Exclusion: Exeter Cathedral, 1300–1540', in Peregrine Horden (ed.), *Freedom and Movement in the Middle Ages: Proceedings of the 2003 Harlaxton Symposium* (Donington, 2007), p. 269.

played a role in public communication, making it possible to send a powerful message to the wider populace.

Sexual Regulation and Urban Ideology

The fragmentary nature of the surviving records, and their complete absence in many cases before about 1450, makes it impossible to speak with certainty of changes in the intensity of prosecutions. But, as noted earlier, what is apparent in the records of a number of towns in the late fifteenth century, extending into the early sixteenth, is a more elaborated and explicit statement of measures against sexual transgression, especially (but not confined to) the activities of 'common women', or prostitutes. What did this betoken? As the foregoing reviews of the fortunes of Colchester, Exeter, Leicester, Nottingham and Salisbury have illustrated, many towns in this period suffered long-term decline punctuated by periodic recession; the success of those that defied this trend was the result of particularly favourable circumstances and in any case merely relative. It is plausible to suppose that hard times tempted poor women to offer sexual services in return for money or other reward and that the late-fifteenth-century ordinances of places like Coventry and Leicester represented the reaction of the civic authorities to what was perceived to be a growing threat to the order of urban society.

Jeremy Goldberg, who originally developed this argument on the basis of York records, has presented it in terms of a change in the sexual division of labour and depicted increasing hostility to common women as part of a process whereby women were systematically squeezed out of legitimate employment opportunities as the fifteenth century progressed. Moreover, he speaks of women being driven onto the streets, insisting that casual contacts centred on street walking, rather than organized activities in brothels, were the characteristic form of prostitution in England in this period.[52] But, of course, it was not only women who saw trade in sex as an economic opportunity. From the court records of Leicester, Colchester, Nottingham and elsewhere, it is apparent that while some women were working on their own account, others were managed – not necessarily

---

[52] P. J. P. Goldberg, 'Women in Fifteenth-Century Town Life', in John A. F. Thomson (ed.), *Towns and Townspeople in the Fifteenth Century* (Gloucester, 1988), pp. 107–28; P. J. P. Goldberg, *Women, Work, and Life Cycle in a Medieval Economy: Women in York and Yorkshire, c.1300–1520* (Oxford, 1992), pp. 149–57; P. J. P. Goldberg, 'Pigs and Prostitutes: Streetwalking in Comparative Perspective', in Katherine J. Lewis, Noël James Menuge and Kim M. Phillips (eds.), *Young Medieval Women* (Stroud, 1999), pp. 172–93.

coercively – by men who provided contacts and protection and were the tenants or proprietors of more or less 'safe' houses in which sexual activities could take place. In some cases the business was in effect a husband and wife team. The corollary was that the sex trade in many late-fifteenth-century towns was not merely (or not so much) a street problem as one partially concealed in ill-regulated households, and it was these above all that town ordinances were designed to control.

One of the most characteristic figures offering sexual services in late-fifteenth-century towns was the female tapster, the ubiquitous maid of all work serving pots of ale and cups of wine in inns and alehouses. In the short term, the availability of this kind of work may be regarded as at odds with Goldberg's vision of narrowing employment opportunities for women.[53] Longer-term developments, however, sit nicely with his model. As Judith Bennett has shown, the prominent role that women occupied in the fourteenth- and fifteenth-century ale trade diminished after 1500. The growing popularity of hopped beer enforced a change in the production process that demanded much greater capital organization and so disadvantaged women. At the same time, the production and sale of drink were increasingly brought under the control of male house-holders in the name of public order. This process was to intensify with the introduction from 1552 of statutory licensing measures and their increasingly strict enforcement in the later sixteenth century and beyond.[54] But in many towns and cities the process was already under way by the turn of the century. As early as 1463 in Nottingham, taverners were ordered not to admit suspect persons and to close by 9 p.m., while the ordinances issued in Coventry in 1492 virtually equated the term 'tapster' with the idea of the prostitute. In Exeter in 1522, according to John Hooker, the mayor 'fyndinge the many incommodyties which dyd arise and growe by the common alehouses and typlyng howses by reason of drunckenness, whoredome and other evells, which yn theym were maynteaned, he wold not suffer any one to kepe any such howses but that he shold be first bound for kepinge of good rule.'[55] Eventually this *indirect* means of regulating illicit sexual activity – by strictly licensing the proprietors of drinking establishments and imposing on them the responsibility for preventing sexual transgression on their premises – was to be of enormous importance.

---

[53] But cf. Goldberg, 'Women in Fifteenth-Century Town Life', p. 117.

[54] Judith M. Bennett, *Ale, Beer and Brewsters in England: Women's Work in a Changing World, 1300–1600* (Oxford and New York, 1996).

[55] Goldberg, 'Women in Fifteenth-Century Town Life', p. 118; Harte, *Gleanings*, p. 30.

Interpretations that see increased efforts at sexual regulation merely in terms of a straightforward response to perceived problems of disorderly behaviour are not, however, adequate in themselves. The framework of religious and moral ideas needs to be considered, as also the legal and constitutional context. As was emphasized in Chapter 2, the fact that public discipline extended to include sexual behaviour and the internal conduct of households represented a distinct vision of 'order' and 'disorder', deriving ultimately from Aristotle but more firmly rooted in an Augustinian vision of the relationship between human and divine affairs. As Maddern has emphasized, this vision had particular resonance in late medieval towns, whose rulers charged themselves with the meticulous supervision of almost all aspects of civic life and assumed a close connection between individual behaviour and the 'good rule' of the entire city or borough. Since they themselves formed a 'corporation' and conceived the whole community in terms of a 'body', to control the physical bodies of individuals was for urban governors an important undertaking both actually and symbolically.[56]

Closer examination reveals a variety of inflections of this fundamental religious and moral schema. Strikingly, at Gloucester around 1504, the lawday court invoked the kind of providential rhetoric that is more usually associated with the Protestant regimes of the late sixteenth and seventeenth centuries, enacting ordinances against the 'to excidyng nowmbre' of bawds and strumpets, 'which, yf hit be not shortly remedyed and punysshed, hit is to be feryd leste allemyghty God wole caste his greate vengeaunce upon the said towne in shorte tyme'. More typical was the muted providentialism expressed in Leicester in 1484. To justify the division of the borough into twelve wards, each under the authority of an alderman, the ordinance evoked 'the grete displesour of almyghty God, and utter distruccion of this said toun, without due remedy therin be had'.[57]

Also striking for their religious content are the ordinances enacted by the court leet of Coventry in 1492. Indeed, Goldberg has gone so far as to interpret them as a coherent and radical programme promoted by a specific group of citizens with Lollard leanings.[58] The town's jurisdiction over sexual

[56] Maddern, 'Order and Disorder', pp. 197, 205–10.
[57] Bateson et al. (eds.), *Records of the Borough of Leicester*, Vol. II, p. 306; *Historical Manuscripts Commission, Twelfth Report*, Appendix, Part IX, p. 435; cf. Slack, *From Reformation to Improvement*, p. 35.
[58] P. J. P. Goldberg, 'Coventry's "Lollard" Programme of 1492 and the Making of Utopia', in Rosemary Horrox and Sarah Rees Jones (eds.), *Pragmatic Utopias: Ideals and Communities, 1200–1630* (Cambridge, 2001), pp. 97–116.

offences was in fact very well established; at intervals throughout the fifteenth century, the mayor's registers record a series of ordinances to punish 'men of worship' or civic officers who were guilty of 'avowtery' or fornication or were otherwise 'vicious of his body' and to deter innholders and other house-holders from keeping 'bawdry' or, more specifically, maintaining any 'woman of evell name, fame or condicion to whom eny resorte is of synfull disposicion, hauntyng the synne of lechery'.[59] Nonetheless, it may be that in 1492 there was a group with a distinctive moral outlook that they were concerned to impress on their fellow townsmen. A case can be made for regarding this set of ordinances as exceptionally coherent, while one of its most striking measures, forbidding all unmarried women under fifty from taking houses or chambers on their own account and directing them instead into service with a master, is unusually far reaching in its scope – so much so indeed that within a few years it had to be mitigated.

In other respects, however, the ordinances reveal much the same aspirations and outlook as are found in other towns of the period, and certainly their content is from a doctrinal point of view entirely orthodox. Suggestive comparisons may be made with both Colchester and Nottingham, both of which were, as has been seen, highly active against sexual offenders. Colchester had a persistent Lollard presence, but there is no discernible connection with its regime against moral offenders, at least as far as laypeople are concerned.[60] Nottingham, however, had no Lollard tradition; quite the contrary. It was noted for the production of alabaster religious images marketed in England and abroad; its three parish churches were the focus of a powerful lay piety laced with pride and emulation, while its commitment to up-to-date forms of charitable endow-ment was reflected in the grammar school founded in 1512 by the widow of an alderman.[61] It may after all be a mistake to emphasize the Lollard presence in Coventry. Undoubtedly there existed a group of committed Lollards, mostly male artisans but including more women than usual. A few of the latter were of elite status. But the higher-status men caught up in the investigations that Bishop Geoffrey Blyth eventually conducted in 1511–12 may be plausibly seen as expressing a distinctive form of lay piety centred on the reading of parts of the Bible in English rather than actual heresy.[62]

---

[59] Harris (ed.), *Coventry Leet Book*, Vol. I, p. 118, Vol. II, pp. 278, 545.
[60] Measures against the clergy are considered in Chapter 8.
[61] Marcombe, 'Late Medieval Town', pp. 93–7.
[62] Cf. John Fines, 'Heresy Trials in the Diocese of Coventry and Lichfield, 1511–12', *Journal of Ecclesiastical History*, 14 (1963), 160–74; Imogen Luxton, 'The Lichfield Court Book:

These religious inflections must also be seen in the context of the relationship between the ecclesiastical and secular authorities within cities and boroughs. The church had a long-established authority for exercising jurisdiction over sexual offenders and policing morals more generally. Civic leaders, however, had to bid for moral authority and justify their intervention in this sphere. As Carrel has emphasized, at best, this could lead to a competition over who should 'govern most virtuously'. It is true that emulation could at times generate tension, if not conflict. One symptom – further discussed in Chapter 8 – was the periodic singling out of immoral clergy for special attention by the civic authorities. In some towns also there were clashes over jurisdiction. According to the later testimony of John Hooker, his namesake's actions as mayor in Exeter in the late fifteenth century 'caused and bredd some differens betwene hym and the clergie', who claimed that the punishment of 'adulterers and whoremongers' was 'incydent onely unto theire chardge and office'. The background was a long history of friction between the civic and ecclesiastical authorities within the city.[63] Yet, even so, there was much common ground. By 1517 the leading citizens of Exeter were accustomed to attending mass and sermon in the cathedral on Sundays and major feasts, while in 1521 the mayor regularly heard mass said by his chaplain in the chapel of St Katherine's beside the north quire aisle. In this light, the punishment of sexual offenders by civic authorities looks like the expression of committed Catholic lay piety, not wholly dissimilar from the moral activism that many towns were to display within the changed framework of Elizabethan Protestantism.[64]

Within the framework of contemporary understandings of Christian religion and morality, more secular impulses towards enacting measures against 'common women' and other sexual offenders were also important. These included the desire to define and perhaps extend the jurisdiction of the town; emulation with other urban communities and the quest for honour or 'worship'; and dialogue with the crown, employing the language of their mutual duties and the desirability of cooperation in maintaining good rule and order to the benefit of the citizens and the realm as a whole.

A Postscript', *Bulletin of the Institute of Historical Research*, 44 (1971), 120–5; Shannon McSheffrey, *Gender and Heresy: Women and Men in Lollard Communities, 1420–1530* (Philadelphia, 1995), chap. 2, esp. pp. 3–45.

[63] Carrel, 'Disputing Legal Privilege', pp. 288, 290, 296; Harte, *Gleanings*, p. 19; Hannes Kleineke, 'Civic Ritual, Space and Conflict in Fifteenth-Century Exeter', in Frances Andrews (ed.), *Ritual and Space in the Middle Ages: Proceedings of the 2009 Harlaxton Symposium* (Donington, 2011), pp. 165–78.

[64] Orme, 'Access and Exclusion', pp. 276, 280. Cf. Chapter 10.

Since the exercise of urban jurisdiction depended on royal charter or at least the tacit approval of the king's courts, and since urban communities could gain or lose favour with the crown, these three themes were seamlessly connected. They are found inextricably entwined not only with each other but also with religious issues in the rhetoric of civic ordinances.

The first known Leicester ordinances concerning sexual immorality were enacted four years after the town acquired its charter in 1463; similarly, the prominent place that matters of bawdry occupied in the proceedings of the borough court of Nottingham can plausibly be related to the ample charter granted to the town by Henry VI in 1449, which formed the basis for the moral ordinances of 1463.[65] Both Leicester in 1484 and Gloucester around 1504 presented themselves as being the subject of 'rumour' and 'sklaunder', 'abomynable spokyn of' for disorderly behaviour within their walls; Gloucester lamented that it was 'to abomynable spokyn of in alle England and Walys'. Ameliorative action thus was essential to restore their honour. Gloucester, moreover, knew where to look for models of best practice: its new 'hutch' for the punishment of sexual offenders was to be as 'usid in the worshipfull citie of London and in the towne of Bristow'.[66] (Bristol itself had earlier determined that 'forasmoche as at all tymes this worshipfull toune ... hath take a grete president of the noble citee of Londone in exerciseing theire laudable customes, it is therfore requisite and necessarie unto the hedde officers of the saide towne of Bristow to know and understonde the auncient usages of the saide citee of Londone.')[67]

There was a tendency not merely towards emulation of more famous towns but also to look to the highest authority in the land. The self-conscious recognition of a symbiosis between town and crown in the repression of disorder and vice is well illustrated by Henry VII's response to the legislation made in Gloucester around 1504:

> Trusty and welbelovyd, we grete you well and be enformed the [i.e. that] ye of your circumspect myndes have accordyng to our lawez made certayne good ordynaunces and lawedabyll constitucions to be observed and kept amonges you for the publike and commen weale of our townne ther ... with the which your politique demeanyng we be right wele content and pleasid:

---

[65] Cf. Marcombe, 'Late Medieval Town', p. 93.

[66] Bateson et al. (eds.), *Records of the Borough of Leicester*, Vol. II, p. 306; *Historical Manuscripts Commission, Twelfth Report*, Appendix, Part IX, p. 435.

[67] Lucy Toulmin Smith (ed.), *The Maire of Bristowe Is Kalendar, by Robert Ricart, Town Clerk of Bristol 18 Edward IV* (Camden Society, New Series 5, London, 1872), p. 93.

and therfore straytely charge you to putt the said liefull ordynaunces in plenary execucion withoute undue favour or parcialite.

In 1485, in similar terms, the king had reminded the mayor and corporation of Coventry that 'ye have auctorite to provide, make and establisshe ordenaunces and rules amonges yow for the universall wele and pollitique guiding of our said citie.'[68] This is not to say that in particular cases the concerns of town and crown were wholly congruent, nor that sexual transgressions as such were high on the list of royal priorities. In the case of Gloucester around 1504, the language of the king's letter suggests that his main concern was unlawful retaining and associated disorders; it should probably be seen in the context of a series of initiatives taken in the early years of the sixteenth century to secure royal government in Wales, the Marches and adjacent areas.[69] More generally, the crown did sponsor 'reformation of manners' but its interest spanned a wide range of matters – unlawful games, excess in apparel, idleness and vagabondage featured most prominently in proclamations and parliamentary legislation. As will be seen in later chapters, the alliance between crown and town in promoting sexual regulation was stronger in territories where the monarch had a more regular presence, in London and Westminster. Nonetheless, the link with crown policy was important in provincial towns and cities to reinforce the self-image of their governors as guardians of politic order and good rule.

This chapter has revealed in more detail than has hitherto been attempted the lively efforts of both the ecclesiastical and secular authorities in provincial towns to police sexual transgression, the contours of which took a distinctive form in the urban context. Contrary to what some historians have supposed, at least by the late fifteenth and early sixteenth centuries, city and borough magistrates were active in actually prosecuting offenders, not merely legislating against them. The sanctions the church courts employed were their usual mixture of neighbourhood pressure, judicial admonition and the threat of public penance. Secular penalties were most commonly financial, though the sums levied were by no means always negligible. Moreover, by the early sixteenth century, if not before, some towns were insisting on their right to inflict more severe public punishments on egregious offenders – precedents that were to be seized on by early Elizabethan proponents of moral reformation.

---

[68] *Historical Manuscripts Commission, Twelfth Report*, Appendix, Part IX, p. 437; Harris (ed.), *Coventry Leet Book*, Vol. II, p. 523.
[69] S. B. Chrimes, *Henry VII* (London, 1972), pp. 245–57.

As always, in exercising this jurisdiction, the authorities depended on the co-operation at the neighbourhood level of constables and jurors, churchwardens and questmen and indeed of ordinary people annoyed, threatened and outraged by the scandal and disorder often associated with sexual transgression. In practice, their conscientiousness and zeal varied, and prosecutions were sporadic. Nonetheless, as Carrel and Maddern have stressed, it is important not to lose sight of the ideological dimension of these activities. In the world of these pre-Reformation civic authorities, the policing of bawds and strumpets within their cities and boroughs was not merely a mundane issue, a matter of controlling misbehaviour, but more positively and imaginatively a means 'to thencreasyng of vertue and the commyn welth' of civic communities that vied for royal favour and aspired to be reputed among the best in the realm.[70]

---

[70] *Historical Manuscripts Commission, Twelfth Report*, Appendix, Part IX, p. 435.

CHAPTER 5

Stews-Side?
Westminster, Southwark and the London Suburbs

Even in the largest provincial towns, the bulk of the population at least paid lip service to Christian standards of sexual morality and neighbourhood values hostile to blatant transgression. There were moral grey areas, for example, dilemmas surrounding the making of marriage and what to do if a couple split up, and, of course, there were numerous lapses on the part of individuals. But, on the whole, the paths of right and wrong, the acceptable and the unacceptable, were clearly marked out. The tapsters and their associates who made their living in what was at best an uneasy relationship with prevailing moral standards were thus relegated to the margins of society. As will be seen, in the city of London, things were less clear-cut, but at least in principle the authorities there were strongly hostile to illicit sex. In Westminster, Southwark and the suburbs, however, sexual services were available on a professional or semi-professional basis, catering not only to local demands but also to the needs of customers from the adjacent city of London and elsewhere.

The terms 'common women' and 'single women' – Southwark had a graveyard especially for them – signalled that there were some females who clearly did not match the stereotypes of maid, wife or widow. Plainly also there were many men, whether of high status or otherwise, clerical or lay, denizens or visitors, who did not intend their sexual activities to be confined within the channels approved by the church and respectable society. A further class of women and men saw a means of making a living by bringing these two groups together. The result was an unusually complex situation in which the usual standards of behaviour could not always be taken for granted, and the difficulties of regulating sexual conduct were, accordingly, particularly acute. The problems were epitomized in the notorious Southwark stews – premises that were actually licensed for prostitution – but the whores of Westminster, Holborn and St Giles's were almost equally famous.[1]

---

[1] Edward F. Rimbault (ed.), *Cock Lorell's Bote: A Satirical Poem* (Percy Society, London, 1843), printed by Wynkyn de Worde around 1510, alludes to their well-known haunts.

The thrust of this chapter is that, nonetheless, opinion hostile to blatant sexual transgression had a powerful voice in these suburban areas, and the official agents of law enforcement were by no means supine. Particularly in Westminster and Southwark, a network of courts – among which secular tribunals were at least as prominent as those of the church – mounted sporadic but cumulatively impressive totals of prosecutions against sexual vice. They could not eliminate it, nor in truth did they attempt to do so. But the wheels of justice constantly harassed those, both men and women, who sought to profit from sexual sins. Neither lay nor ecclesiastical authorities willingly accepted the anomalous licence of the stews, which came under considerable pressure long before the Reformation. The temporary closure they suffered in 1506 foreshadowed their final abolition forty years afterwards.[2]

Westminster

A document relating to law enforcement in 1519 spoke of London's 'suburbes and other villages adjoinant'.[3] This reflected the fact that even settlements at a distance from London, especially those on the main thoroughfares into the city, had some of the characteristics of suburbs and might experience particular problems of policing sexual and other forms of misbehaviour. But the suburbs proper north of the Thames clustered close to the walls on the east, north and west of the city itself. Some were ordinary parishes, jurisdictionally indistinguishable from country villages. Some were located in parishes that spanned the city walls. Many were complicated by the proximity of religious houses and jurisdictional liberties. Of special significance was the liberty of Westminster, south-west of London further up the Thames. Before the Reformation, it comprised the town or vill, more or less coterminous with St Margaret's parish, and the less developed parishes of St Clement Danes, St Mary le Strand and St Martin in the Fields.[4]

Westminster had developed round the twin poles of the Benedictine abbey and the royal palace, and as time wore on, the crown became an increasingly powerful presence. But in 1512 much of the old palace (apart from Westminster Hall) was destroyed by fire, and for some years

---

[2] Cf. Ruth Mazo Karras, *Common Women: Prostitution and Sexuality in Medieval England* (New York and Oxford, 1996), pp. 22–3.

[3] TNA, SP 1/18, fo. 227r.

[4] Gervase Rosser, *Medieval Westminster, 1200–1540* (Oxford, 1989); J. F. Merritt, *The Social World of Early Modern Westminster: Abbey, Court and Community, 1525–1640* (Manchester, 2005), pp. 5–8.

thereafter the most prominent secular household was Cardinal Wolsey's residence at York Place. In 1530, after Wolsey's fall, Henry VIII began to build a massive palace complex, with substantial parkland adjoining, on the same site, and eventually Whitehall emerged as the pre-eminent location of the royal household. In 1539, the dissolution of the monastic community changed the situation even more drastically, though the great abbey was reconstituted as the cathedral of the new – and destined to be short-lived – see of Westminster.[5]

In size, the settlement was equal to many major provincial towns. Following the Black Death its population faltered, slumping below 2,000 in the early fifteenth century, but it was on the increase again from about 1475 and reached upwards of 3,000 in the early decades of the sixteenth.[6] Together with the abbey, the law courts, government departments and the royal household were major sources of employment, both directly in the form of household positions and other offices and indirectly via the numerous services that the individuals who staffed these institutions required from day to day. The effect was magnified by the swarms of visitors who came periodically to Westminster to attend court and parliament and to sue or be sued at law. The result was an economy in which victualling, drink-selling and other retailing, servicing and finishing trades (such as tailoring and barbering), as also the provision of such amusements and recreations as tennis, archery and bowls, dominated over primary production. Moreover, it was an economy based very largely on what Gervase Rosser has described as 'the entrapment of the consumer'.[7]

Inevitably these conditions generated an insistent demand for sexual alongside other services, especially as a large proportion of the potential clientele – comprising clergy, officials and visitors on some sort of business – was male. At the same time, they created numerous marketing opportunities for those willing to sell their own or others' bodies or at least connive at such traffic by renting rooms or premises with no questions asked.[8] Even individuals of substance and considerable local standing stood to gain so much that they might be drawn into this kind of trade to an extent that was much less usual in the provinces. However, the royal presence in the area also cut in an entirely different direction. The crown was the embodiment of order, and the dignity of the monarch, his courts and officers argued against the toleration of disorderly and unseemly

[5] Merritt, *Social World of Early Modern Westminster*, pp. 25–7.
[6] Rosser, *Medieval Westminster*, pp. 168–77.   [7] *Ibid.*, pp. 161, 215–17 and chap. 5 *passim*.
[8] *Ibid.*, pp. 143–4, 216, 218, 244.

activity of any kind in the vicinity of the royal household. As will be seen, this apparently did not prevent one of Henry VII's courtiers from keeping a brothel within the precincts of the palace of Westminster. Yet, during Wolsey's ascendancy, the *alter rex* was an immediate presence in the neighbourhood, strongly opposed to public manifestations of vice and disorder.

King's Bench Indictments for Sexual Vice

The royal court itself was policed by a tribunal known as the court of the Marshalsea, whose jurisdiction extended to a radius of twelve miles, but little is known of its operations in this period. An institution with more general jurisdiction was the King's Bench, the importance of which in the regulation of the late fifteenth- and early sixteenth-century sex trade has hitherto not been sufficiently recognized.[9] Much of its activity comprised the hearing of 'pleas' or suits between parties – its jurisdiction was parallel but not identical to that of the court of Common Pleas – and, on the 'crown' side, the exercise of a supervisory function in criminal matters. However, King's Bench also had direct jurisdiction in the county of Middlesex, and a marked feature of its activities there in the late fifteenth century and early sixteenth century was the prosecution of petty offences and local nuisances.[10] The jurors who vetted these charges were apparently drawn from Middlesex freeholders; comparison with information from local sources indicates that only a small minority came from Westminster, where King's Bench normally sat.[11] But it would seem from incidental contemporary references and by analogy with later practice that the prosecutions were ultimately based on information from local constables. Together these petty office holders and jurors spanned the middling social ranks, and ordinary householders were hence able to give voice to a wide range of concerns about matters as diverse as roaming pigs and blocked watercourses. Tellingly, however, many of them related to sexual commerce.[12]

[9] But for a later period, see Faramerz Dabhoiwala, 'Prostitution and Police in London, c.1660–1760', unpublished DPhil thesis, University of Oxford, 1995, pp. 100–2, chaps. 4 and 5 *passim*. A few early Tudor cases are cited in Rosser, *Medieval Westminster*, pp. 143–4.

[10] The indictments are found in the King's Bench term files or 'Ancient Indictments'; process was entered on the 'rex' portion of the court's plea rolls (TNA, KB 9, KB 27).

[11] Based on comparison of samples of grand jury lists (entered on the reverse of some indictments) with information on local office holders compiled by Rosser, *Medieval Westminster*, Appendix VIII.

[12] *Ibid.*

Such presentments (or 'indictments', as they technically became when they were found to be 'true bills' by the grand jury and sent for trial), though formalized in Latin with only an occasional admixture of the vernacular, were not altogether stereotyped and covered a range of different offences with a sexual dimension. Some individuals were accused of receiving suspicious men and women, including thieves and robbers. In these cases, any sexual aspects of the offence were implicit. A more explicit charge was that of receiving suspect men – thieves and robbers were stated or implied – and allowing them to have carnal copulation with their 'whores' (*meretrices*). Sometimes they were said to allow lechery (*luxuria*) and vice. A variant was a charge of encouraging or inciting immoral behaviour. Very commonly householders were charged with keeping brothels (*lupanarie*), keeping common 'bawdry' (*pronubacia*) or maintaining houses of bawdry (the English 'bawdryhouses' occasionally appears, as does the term 'blynde inne').[13] It is plain from the context that all these pursuits implied some form of sexual traffic or at least the toleration of illicit sexual activity. Some accusations had an anticlerical tinge or at least reflected a concern to spotlight clerical as well as lay immorality in that it was specifically stated that the customers included priests, whether seculars or regulars. Sometimes individual men and women, or husband and wife teams, were accused of being 'bawds' (*pronube*). At least till the end of the fifteenth century, women (who might or might not be married to a bawd or accused of being a bawd themselves) were liable to prosecution as a common whore (*meretrix*).

Many presentments, often comprising long lists of offenders, went into some detail. Their language offers some insights into the concerns and objections that sexual traffic aroused. An indictment in Hilary Term 1486, having rehearsed how it was by law prohibited that any man or woman in the realm should keep any 'commune hospicium vel petyt hostre seu pronubariam' at any town's end, went on to accuse six women of receiving into their houses thieves, robbers, vagabonds, whores and suchlike and allowing them to lie together and commit fornication.[14] Often it was stated that the congress of whores and other suspicious persons had occasioned clamours, outcries, quarrels, suits and discords to the disturbance of neighbours and to the extent that honest people could scarcely pass through the vicinity by day or by night – or hardly dared do so – without danger to their lives.[15] The phraseology was stereotyped, but there is no

[13] TNA, KB 9/435, m. 76; KB 9/437, m. 70.   [14] TNA, KB 9/369, m. 44.
[15] TNA, KB 9/387, mm. 22, 23.

reason to doubt that the disorder was real and a persistent social nuisance. Sexual transgressions were often coupled with other forms of misbehaviour, notably scolding, drinking, gambling and unlawful games such as tables, cards and dice. Sometimes it was stated that the bawds had 'basely' received money to allow sexual transgressions to take place.[16] Occasionally, a religious dimension was introduced. Thus it was sometimes emphasized that fornicators had not been legitimately coupled together by the law of the church or that receiving men and women to have illicit sexual relations was not only in breach of the king's peace but also 'to the great displeasure of God'.[17]

Some indictments ended with the statement that the activities of which complaint was made were 'to the great disturbance of the lord king's people and in bad example to other offenders to transgress in like sort unless due remedy be not speedily provided'.[18] This was true of what was in other respects also among the most detailed charges in these records, the indictment of Maud Galthrop 'huswiff' of Rotherhithe in Surrey in 1483. The indictment stated (in Latin) that she

> and other unknown rioters and disturbers of the peace of the lord king evilly associated with many other suspicious male pimps and women lightly disposed, not like Christian people regarding the law of God but like partners in crime setting aside and scorning the fear of God and his commands and according to the lust of their bodies living carnally and damnably and most abominably and intending thus to live viciously day in and day out, ... in divers secret places in Westminster ... did keep, frequent and carnally occupy within their houses common brothels basely erecting *le stewesside* and for filthy lucre permitting all kinds of riotous and suspect persons, whether regular clergy, seculars, or laymen, to lie there carnally with divers whores and did so often from day to day whereby divers quarrels and discords were raised there to the great nuisance of all the neighbours living there and against the peace of the king himself.[19]

Plainly this was a notorious case, and an effort was being made to make an example of Maud Galthrop. But it is notable in showing that most of the ideas and vocabulary that featured in later presentments were already current before the beginning of the Tudor period.

---

[16] TNA, KB 9/397, m. 34; KB 9/424, m. 43.
[17] TNA, KB 9/369, m. 44; KB 9/477, m. 18. On the use of religious language by lay jurors, see Shannon McSheffrey, 'Jurors, Respectable Masculinity, and Christian Morality', *Journal of British Studies*, 37 (1998), 270, 274–6; Marjorie McIntosh, 'Response', *ibid.*, 297.
[18] TNA, KB 9/433, m. 17.   [19] TNA, KB 9/363, m. 9.

Table 5.1 *King's Bench: Middlesex Indictments for Keeping Bawdy Houses, 1501–5*

		M	F (w)	HW	Total persons
1501	Hilary	—	—	—	—
	Easter	1	5 (3)	2	10
	Trinity	2	3 (1)	3	11
	Michaelmas	2	8 (2)	7	24
	Total	5	16 (6)	12	45
1502	Hilary	10	18 (6)	13	54
	Easter	6	18 (8)	15	54
	Trinity	2	7 (1)	3	15
	Michaelmas	1	5 (1)	6	18
	Total	19	48 (16)	37	141
1503	Hilary	9	12 (4)	2	25
	Easter	—	—	—	—
	Trinity	5	9 (4)	6	26
	Michaelmas	2	3 (1)	1	7
	Total	16	24 (9)	9	58
1504	Hilary	1	0	1	3
	Easter	3	5 (3)	1	10
	Trinity	1	4 (2)	1	7
	Michaelmas	4	15 (7)	1	21
	Total	9	24 (12)	4	41
1505	Hilary	6	2 (1)	0	8
	Easter	5	16 (5)	2	25
	Trinity	12	7 (3)	0	19
	Michaelmas	5	3 (1)	3	14
	Total	28	28 (10)	5	66

Key: M = male defendants; F = female (w = widows); HW = married couple

The impact of these prosecutions may be illustrated by a closer look at cases recorded in the five years 1501–5 (Table 5.1). This period witnessed over 350 charges (counting husband and wife as separate defendants, as did the court, and including some repeat prosecutions). The peak year was 1502, when over 140 people were prosecuted, most of them in the Hilary and Easter terms, in what was evidently some kind of purge. The totals in the other years, more characteristic of the pattern of prosecutions in the late fifteenth and early sixteenth centuries, were upwards and downwards of fifty. Almost all the accusations in this particular half decade were variants on keeping a brothel, though the precise form of words varied from case to case. There were few indictments simply for being a whore. The significance of this may be that the court concentrated its efforts on householders, who might be brought to heel by arrest or distraint of goods, whereas the court's procedures were ill adapted to deal with unattached females of no fixed abode. But, in any case, it was probably already emerging as a principle that illicit sexual activity was less properly a common-law offence than keeping a bawdy house. About a fifth of the charges related to places in Middlesex other than Westminster. A good proportion of these came from St John Street and neighbouring Turnmill Street in Clerkenwell – as might be expected from the reputation of these localities – while there were significant numbers also from St Giles in the Fields and Holborn in the northern part of the area between London and Westminster. Finsbury to the north and Stratford le Bow, lying east of Mile End, yielded small clusters of prosecutions, while the rest originated in a variety of suburban parishes and some places a little further away, such as Kensington and Uxbridge. But the great bulk of charges (over 280 of them) related to the parishes that comprised the liberty of Westminster. There were a few from St Martin in the Fields (where little building had taken place by this date), a score from the small parish of St Mary le Strand and over ninety from St Clement Danes. The rest (some 60 per cent of the total) either came from St Margaret's parish or were simply said to be of Westminster.

Matthew Baker, esquire, was charged with keeping whores and bawds in a house actually within the palace of Westminster itself. He was, in fact, one of Henry VII's courtiers, an esquire of the body and close to the king. He was a frequent jouster and known to have hunted with Henry. He seems to have had a reputation for violent and high-handed behaviour. Yet he received visiting ambassadors at his home, taking them and their messages to and from the king, and himself served several times as ambassador in France, receiving a gold collar from Louis XII in 1507. In 1502 he was granted the keepership of the palace of Westminster, and presumably his association with bawds and whores within the precincts was a business venture associated with this position. Interestingly, in his will he bequeathed the sum of twenty pounds and two feather beds to 'Johane dwellyng at Kyllyngworth and to the childe she goth withall', no doubt a reference to his own provision for recreational sex.[20]

This King's Bench case is unusual not only for its location but also for the high social status of the offender, though there may have been a few other reasonably well-heeled individuals among the defendants, including one called 'gentleman' and a number described as 'beerbrewer'. Otherwise, a wide range of occupations was specified, many (though not necessarily all) implying low status. The stated callings of male defendants in Westminster included baker, barber, bookbinder, butcher, carpenter, cobbler, cook, cooper, cutler, fletcher, fuller, gardener, haberdasher, innholder, labourer, minstrel, pardoner, pinner, saddler, shearman, shoemaker, skinner, spurrier, tailor, tanner, taverner, victualler and yeoman; one man was described as a vagabond, while the occupation of another was simply stated to be 'bawd'. The locations outside Westminster threw up a few more trades, including cordwainer, glazier, paintmaker, parish clerk, sawyer, smith and 'gongfermer' (latrine scourer), but the social profile of defendants does not seem to have been much different. Both in Westminster and in other places in Middlesex, female defendants were not usually given a specific occupational label. If they were not designated 'singlewoman' or 'widow' or simply said to be someone's wife, they were ascribed the ambiguous status of 'spinster' or 'housewife'. However, a few of the Westminster women had sobriquets that suggest that they traded on their well-known status. Eleanor Gybbes was known as 'Paynted Nell', while Joan Barbour, wife of Thomas (who was indeed a barber), went by the name of 'Jane of Paradyse' or 'Joan Aparadyce'. But this may not have been an indication of the quality or the nature of the service offered, any more than were such appellations as 'the wife of Purgatory' and 'Margaret of Hell' – Paradise, Purgatory and Hell were the names of three tenements adjacent to Westminster Hall.[21]

The indictments themselves only occasionally indicate the outcome of cases, but cross-checking with the crown section of the plea rolls and with the controlment rolls (brief notes of process used to monitor the progress of cases) reveals what usually happened. A few charges were quashed because of insufficiency (e.g. if a name was not given in full). Some defendants were fined sums of twenty shillings, ten shillings, or 6s. 8d. – quite hefty penalties at the beginning of the sixteenth century. Most

---

[20] Steven Gunn, 'The Courtiers of Henry VII', *English Historical Review*, 108 (1993), 37, 39–41, 43, 45–6. 'Kyllyngworth' is Kenilworth, where Baker had established a country residence.

[21] Rosser, *Medieval Westminster*, p. 144.

defendants did not respond to court summonses, and many ended up by being outlawed or (the equivalent for women) 'waived'. The effects of such an outcome are unclear. In theory at least, outlawry entailed various legal disabilities, but some defendants probably incurred this penalty because they had absconded or simply moved on. Probably the main effect of prosecutions was not so much to subject offenders to exemplary punishment as to harass them and undermine their local reputation. Certainly the King's Bench proceedings must be understood in the context of the concurrent activities of the local courts and their officers.

The Westminster View of Frankpledge

Jurisdiction in Westminster was mostly exercised by the abbey, and the main policing and law enforcement agency in matters short of felony was the view of frankpledge or manor court. Prosecutions took the form of presentments or 'verdicts' formulated on the basis of local knowledge by twelve jurors called 'chief pledges' or 'headboroughs', a body which by the beginning of the sixteenth century at the latest had become self-electing. Rosser's work indicates that these jurors were characteristically substantial (rather than rich) local residents, ranging from minor royal officials and lawyers resident in the liberty to innkeepers and tradesmen such as chandlers, bakers, carpenters, masons and tailors.[22] A petition from Abbot John, dating most probably from 1511, reveals the defects of this system of government. While this document refers primarily to issues concerning the sale of victuals, its strictures seem to be applicable also to the various prosecutions for disorderly behaviour characteristic of this local court.[23]

The basic framework for the imposition of penalties was a medieval statute of uncertain date that bakers or brewers who broke the assize (i.e. infringed the regulations concerning weights and measures) should be 'amerced', or fined, for the first, second or third offence but thereafter, on the grounds that the offence was 'grievous and often', 'he shall suffer punishment of the body, that is to wit, a baker to the pillory, and a brewer to the tumbrel.'[24] Since in Westminster the local court met only once a year, on the Monday after St Barnabas (11 June), bringing offenders to book was a protracted business and could only be achieved if they were prosecuted in four successive courts. The effects on the prosecution of brothel-keepers and the like can be seen from the court rolls, which survive,

---

[22] *Ibid.*, chap. 7.   [23] Printed *ibid.*, pp. 362–5.   [24] *Statutes of the Realm*, Vol. I, p. 201.

albeit in a broken sequence, from 1364 to 1514.[25] In 1512, under the heading
'bawdes et meretrices [whores]', two married couples, five men and
a married woman were presented as bawds (several being singled out as
operating in Charing Street and 'near the bars'). Six women, one of them
specified as being married, were presented as whores; five of them were said
to operate in King Street, the main thoroughfare of Westminster. All these
offenders save one were amerced in the sum of 20d. The next year, under
the same heading, only two married couples were presented as bawds,
suffering the same penalty, while in 1514 'nothing' was entered under
'meretrices et bawdes'. Undoubtedly the system could be cranked up to
take rigorous action. Thus, in 1508, a total of thirty-one people (half of
them women) were ejected from Westminster for being 'ill governed of
their bodies'. But it was apparently difficult to achieve this level of severity,
and in normal circumstances the presentments in the local court were
merely subsidiary to the more numerous indictments of offenders in King's
Bench.[26]

Privy Searches and the Westminster Gatehouse Court

Abbot John's petition was cast in the form of a parliamentary bill. But
while a statute relating to the assize of wines and victuals was passed in 1511,
it did not address the defects in Westminster's system of local regulation.
More important was a wide-ranging proclamation of the same year
designed in general to improve peace-keeping and more specifically to
enforce measures against unlawful games, idleness, vagabondage and unregulated ale selling. On the basis of an act of Richard II, it authorized
searches for 'vagabonds, idle people and suspect persons living suspiciously', who on arrest were to be set in the stocks on bread and water
for twenty-four hours and then made 'to avoid the town'. This may have
been done on occasion before 1511, but there is tangible evidence that after
the proclamation, 'privy searches' were carried out vigorously.[27] Most
notably, in 1519, proceedings against sexual offenders were part and parcel
of a massive drive, instigated by Cardinal Wolsey, against vagabonds
and other suspect persons in London, Westminster, the suburbs and
surrounding towns and villages. A powerful body of commissioners was
appointed, including such leading figures as the duke of Norfolk and Lord

---

[25] WAM 50699–50782; TNA, SC 2/191/66 (stray dated 1510).
[26] WAM 50773, 50775–7; Rosser, *Medieval Westminster*, p. 244.
[27] Paul L. Hughes and James F. Larkin (eds.), *Tudor Royal Proclamations*, 3 vols. (New Haven and
London, 1964–9), Vol. I, pp. 85–93 (quotation p. 89), cf. pp. 17 (1487), 32–4 (1493).

Darcy. A search was ordered for the night of Sunday 17 July and another for Wednesday 22 October

> all at one houre ... and in the mean while to be kept very secritt, and the parties therin suspiciously taken, as well men as women, to be committed to warde, ther to remayn till Friday on the morning next comyng, and then to be brought in personally before the lordes [of the council] with a certificat of their names.

The surviving returns form a bulky dossier. Exactly how the offenders were dealt with is not known, but in any case the sheer scale of the operation is impressive.[28]

Even more so is the evidence of local action taken in Westminster, where – as noted earlier – Wolsey's household was at that time a dominant presence. A court held at the Gatehouse on 20 August 1519, dealing with presentments made by the abbot of Westminster's bailiff, the headboroughs and constables, was evidently supplementary to the annual view of frankpledge.[29] A few of the individuals named had been, or were soon to be, indicted in King's Bench, but otherwise the proceedings were independent of that court too. Apart from a few miscellaneous matters, such as keeping 'evil rule' and defying the constables, the cases heard at the Gatehouse overwhelmingly concerned scolding, bawdry and lechery. There were seventeen presentments for scolding, eighteen for bawdry, eleven for lechery, six for scolding and bawdry and three for lechery and scolding.[30] In addition, a woman was presented 'for lechery [of] hir owne body and [being] bawde to hir owne doughter', while a married couple living in the Strand were in trouble 'for lechery and for logyng of suspecyous personys and resortyng of vacaboundes and pyke purcys'.[31] Another notable feature is that the great majority of cases were directed against women. Very few men were prosecuted as individuals. In about half the cases, the defendants were a married couple, but in almost all these instances it is plain from the wording of the subsequent proceedings that the wife was the main target; the husbands were brought in question

---

[28] TNA, SP 1/18, fos. 227r–257v (quotation fo. 228r), abstracted in J. S. Brewer, J. Gairdner, R. H. Brodie et al. (eds.), *Letters and Papers, Foreign and Domestic, of the Reign of Henry VIII*, 21 vols. and Addenda (London, 1862–1932), Vol. III, Part 1, pp. 126–9.

[29] WAC, 0045/001 (photostat copy; archival stamps indicate that the original manuscript formed part of the 'Westminster Chapter Muniments', but its whereabouts are at present unknown; references are to the modern pagination). I am grateful to Faramerz Dabhoiwala for originally bringing this item to my attention in the form of a mid-twentieth-century typescript abstract.

[30] In a few other cases the nature of the charge is unclear on account of either the obscurity of the original wording or damage to the document.

[31] WAC, 0045/001, pp. 15, 26.

because they were held to have some responsibility for their wives' beha-viour. When wives were named without their husbands, it is sometimes clear that the latter were absent. Thus proceedings against Joan Brygeman, presented 'for bawdry and scoldyng', were respited because she was looking after a bedridden woman, so she was given 'lycensse till Michaelis next or ellys that hir husbond com and kepe housse with hir'.[32] About a third of the women named alone were described as widows. There were probably also a few single women, though (as will be seen) these were for the most part dealt with in a different way.

The Gatehouse court, it would seem, summoned people to appear personally and give an account of themselves. Sometimes this went badly wrong, as when the headboroughs sent the bailiff and constables for Elizabeth Bolton, wife of one of the 'yemen of the kinges kechyn', 'desyr-yng hir to come to the courte', to which she replied 'that she wold not com ther for non of all the chorllys'. Clearly, she was a tough nut, since it was also reported that she did 'vex and trobyll hir neigburs wrongfully in the lawe, as by accions of the peace, of good aberyng, with many other; and also in dispisynge of the hedborus and other the kynges officers in callyng them cankerd chorllys with many other dispiteffull wordes'. But this degree of recalcitrance was unusual.[33]

Certainly the court had at its disposal some powerful sanctions. Scolds were ordered to 'amend' on pain of being sent to the cucking stool. Some culprits were imprisoned for short periods or 'committed to ward' until they found sureties for their good behaviour. Indeed, the production of two such sureties, invariably men (and men of some substance at that, able and willing to give bond in the sum of ten pounds as a guarantee of future 'good demenor' or to 'keep good rewyll'), was the most effective means of placating the court. The court's ultimate sanction was simply to order the culprit to 'avoid' the town, in some cases after a prior period of imprison-ment. Again, a few individuals were defiant or used their connections to secure concessions. Thus Elizabeth Hardyng, wife of one of Cardinal Wolsey's scullery men, ordered out of Westminster for bawdry, scolding and unstated other misdemeanours, 'beryth hir so sore on my lo[r]d cardenays sarvants that she wol not avoyde for no man'. Likewise, the widow Elizabeth Wylson, committed to ward for refusing to leave the town after her conviction for bawdry, 'layd for hirself that she hade sherttes and other stoff of servantes of my lorde cardenalles'. She was allowed some respite but still had to 'departe the towne within vj days aftyr my lordes

[32] *Ibid.*, p. 19.   [33] *Ibid.*, p. 7.

grace his comyng home, upon payne of inprisonment'.[34] Even those accorded favourable treatment were evidently given not only a stiff talking to but also firm guidelines for future behaviour. Elizabeth Davy was brought to court for 'bawdry and evell ruyll keypyng of hir owne body and for onlawfull gaming, as disyng and cardyng, with other evyll reulyd personys thedyr resortyng'. Perhaps because she was married to one of the king's servants, she was warned to amend rather than simply ordered out. But the husband, it would seem, was admonished that 'ther shall no harlottes be in no chambre within his howsse, nor in no close house, with no company of men, but in open places within the same howsse, and that byneth [beneath], as it may honestely be ussed'.[35]

The intensity of this burst of legal proceedings is notable. Counting the married couples as two persons, some eighty-nine individuals were brought to court on this single occasion. If the miscellaneous cases and the presentments simply for scolding are discounted, this still leaves sixty people accused of offences directly relating to sexual transgressions. But these numbers do not represent all that was done. Even before the court met, charges against a further forty-four people had been resolved by their departure from Westminster. Thus three women and one married couple had 'avoided' for scolding, six women and two married couples had departed for bawdry and a further three women and a married couple had gone for various combinations of scolding, bawdry and lechery, while three more women had 'avoided' for unstated reasons. Seven 'single-women', three widows, two wives named on their own and two married couples had 'avoided' for lechery. Further, the labourer Thomas Nicholas 'hath avoyded a syngle woman which was logid withyn his house', while three other men and a widow were said to have similarly ejected from their houses single women, evidently suspected of lechery.[36]

This volume of cases dealt with by this court was clearly exceptional, as is shown by comparison with the record of another court held at the Gatehouse in June 1523 (when parliament was in session at the London Blackfriars). Unlike the session of 1519, this court dealt with numerous defective pavements, nuisances and assaults, while an important part of its activities was the regulation of innholders, 'tipplers', vintners, beer- and ale-brewers, bakers, cooks and poulterers. But the residue of its business concerned scolds and quarrellers and sexual or sex-related offences similar

---

[34] *Ibid.*, pp. 10, 11.
[35] *Ibid.*, p. 6. The presence of the husband in court is inferred from the wording.
[36] *Ibid.*, pp. 35, 38.

to those dealt with in 1519; however, they were far fewer in number, comprising only nineteen individuals (eleven women, six men and one married couple).[37] Nonetheless, the burst of activity reflected in the proceedings in 1519 remains impressive as an indication of what could be done.

It is plain that sexual regulation was a regular feature of life in Westminster on the eve of the Reformation. Illicit activities, especially brothel keeping, were the subject of constant surveillance. Despite the limitations of the view of frankpledge, it was on occasion possible to ratchet up this activity and deal with offenders with some severity. Evidence from around 1520 indicates that late medieval statutes, refreshed by the authority of a recent royal proclamation, were used as the basis for a system of policing that could be thorough and far reaching. It is unfortunate that, owing to the loss of the records of the church courts operating in Westminster, little is known about the treatment of the common run of cases of adultery and sexual relations between unmarried people. A lucky survival means that we do have some information on this subject for the London suburbs south of the river.

Southwark

The borough of Southwark lay across the Thames opposite London Bridge, but its various manors sprawled all along the south bank between Lambeth and Bermondsey. By the standards of the time, its population was large and, in the early sixteenth century, growing fast. Though the number of inhabitants slumped to little more than 2,000 in the wake of the Black Death, by 1550 there were more than 8,000 – a rate of growth boosted by immigration from most parts of England save for the most remote areas, but particularly from London, Middlesex, the south east and East Anglia.[38]

Though clothing, shoemaking and other trades were plied in the borough, especially where rentals were cheaper, the economic heart of Southwark was sustained above all by innkeeping (including such famous establishments as the Tabard and the Green Dragon), together with brewing and other forms of victualling. To judge by the returns of the lay subsidies of 1524–7, Southwark ranked twelfth in taxable wealth in England as a whole – behind such major provincial centres as Salisbury,

---

[37] WAM 50778. Two of the women (Christian Browne and Alice Edwardes) had also been indicted in King's Bench in Easter Term of the same year: TNA, KB 9/490, m. 18.

[38] For this and succeeding paragraphs, see Martha Carlin, *Medieval Southwark* (London, 1996).

Canterbury and Reading but ahead of the populous clothing town of Colchester. In the words of Martha Carlin, early sixteenth-century Southwark was thus 'a place of densely packed houses and teeming alleys ... Houses were subdivided, gardens disappeared and hundreds of new tenements were built by speculators'.[39] It was also a locality offering a variety of forms of recreation – bowls, tennis and card-playing were among the pleasures available – and an area where sexual services were both in high demand and much on offer.

In this respect it was significant that jurisdiction in this large and populous area was fragmented. The Guildable manor, held by the crown, encompassed the borough of Southwark immediately to the south of London Bridge. West of this lay the Clink manor, held by the bishop of Winchester, and Paris Garden manor, held by the military order of Hospitallers before 1536. South of these lay the manor of the prior and convent of Southwark, known as the King's (or Queen's) manor after it passed into crown hands at the dissolution of the monasteries. East and south-eastwards lay the manor of the archbishop of Canterbury. This also was acquired by the crown in 1538 and was known henceforth as the Great Liberty manor. The fourteenth and fifteenth centuries had seen repeated attempts by the city of London to extend its jurisdiction into Southwark, and in principle the corporation had achieved this for the Guildable manor by the charters of 1406 and 1444. However, the change had been partially rescinded in 1462, and in practice the jurisdiction remained contested. Ecclesiastical government was slightly more straightforward. The heart of the borough was in the small parish of St Mary Magdalen, and the area to the west was covered by St Margaret's. The southern parts of Southwark were in St George's parish, the eastern parts in St Olave's. South-east of St Mary Magdalen's was the precinct of St Thomas's Hospital, which became a parochial church in 1496. There was yet another church in Southwark, that of the Augustinian priory of St Mary Overy, used for sessions of the ecclesiastical court by the bishops of Winchester, in whose jurisdiction lay Southwark and the rest of the archdeaconry of Surrey.[40]

The Southwark Stews

Notoriously, the bishops were also the patrons of the Southwark stews, licensed brothels situated on Bankside in the jurisdiction of the Clink manor. They were well established by this period, with a history going back

---

[39] *Ibid.*, p. 58. [40] *Ibid.*, pp. 31–6, 72, 85–6, 106–25.

centuries; given a choice, the Yorkist and early Tudor bishops of Winchester would hardly have wished to be associated with such an institution. Indeed, the bishops did not actually own the stews, which were in private possession; they were merely saddled with their jurisdictional oversight. Physically, the stews consisted of a series of houses or inns. There were about eighteen in 1506, called after signs like the Castle, the Bull, the Hart, the Bear's Head, the Unicorn and the Elephant.[41] There survives a detailed manorial customary setting regulations for their conduct; revised in the fifteenth century, its basis is clearly much older.[42] One of the main aims of the ordinances was to restrict the power of the stewholders over the 'single women' and in other ways safeguard their wellbeing. As the preamble states, they 'ought to have theire free goyng and comyng atte theire owne libertees', and this was reinforced by a provision that stewholders who prevented free movement were subject to fine. Every quarter the bailiffs and constables were to search each house to ensure that no woman was kept there against her will. Moreover, stewholders were not to keep women at board, nor were they to lend them more than 6s. 8d. – presumably lest they entangle them in debt. There were severe restrictions on the number of servants that could be maintained in the houses, again to ensure that economic dependence did not force women into the sex trade. Each woman was to pay fourteen pence a week for her chamber and no more.

The provision that no woman who had the 'horrible disease' or 'any sikeness of brennynge' should be kept in the houses seems to have reflected concern more with the well-being of clients than with the welfare of the women themselves (though there was, of course, the danger of cross-infection between inmates), and in other respects the single women of the stews were subject to many restrictions. They could not have their own lovers on pain of prison, fine and cucking stool, nor could they be kept secretly in the stews without the stewholder's permission. They could not wear aprons, the dress of respectable women. Reasonably enough, they were forbidden to drag in customers from the streets, and there were strict rules against fighting and scolding. They were to have only restricted access

---

[41] The exact number, their names and their locations are a matter of controversy: see Henry Ansgar Kelly, 'Bishop, Prioress, and Bawd in the Stews of Southwark', *Speculum*, 75 (2000), 342–88 (though note that his account cannot be taken as definitive, not least because he appears to be unaware of the surviving Southwark church court act book for 1511–15, discussed later).

[42] J. B. Post, 'A Fifteenth-Century Customary of the Southwark Stews', *Journal of the Society of Archivists*, 5 (1974–7), 418–28; Carlin, *Medieval Southwark*, chap. 9; Karras, *Common Women*, pp. 37–43.

to the stews on holy days and when parliament or a royal council was in session at Westminster. Nuns, wives and pregnant women were forbidden entry into the stews altogether. Some measures that affected both stew-holders and the women – a prohibition on spinning, for example – were probably to avoid confusion between respectable and immoral activities. The regulations were of a practical nature, but while they *accepted*, they did not actually *condone* sexual transgression. At many points the language of the customary made clear that what went on was sinful and inherently undesirable.

Only one court roll survives for the bishop of Winchester's manor during the period of the stews' existence. Covering fifteen sessions including two views of frankpledge held from October 1505 to September 1506, it names a total of twenty-two stewholders, including fourteen men and eight women. On each occasion between five and ten of them were presented for various combinations of staying open on holy days, buying and selling women, beating women and keeping them at weekly board in contra-vention of manorial custom. Fines ranged from 12d. to 6s. 8d. in the views and from 4d. to 12d. at the other courts. This gives the impression of the use of amercements less for the purposes of serious regulation than as a fiscal device to the benefit of the bishop of Winchester. Yet the situation was by no means completely stable. Even within this twelve-month period there was considerable turnover: several of the stewholders moved from one set of premises to another, while some disappeared and were replaced by others. More drastically, *The Great Chronicle of London* recorded that in 1506 'the stewis or comon bordell beyond the watyr . . . was ffor a seson inhibyt and closid upp. But it was not long or they were sett opyn agayn, albeit the ffame went that where beffore were occupyed xviij howsys, ffrom hens forth shuld be occupyed but xij.' That is, they were not only tem-porarily closed but also reduced in scale. 'Ffor what happ or concyderacion the sertaynte I knowe nott,' claimed the chronicler.[43]

Behind the closure lay a long tradition of complaint which has left some traces in central court and other records. Around 1473, Ellen Boteler complained that she had been in effect kidnapped. A man named Thomas Bowde came into the house in London where she was and 'asked of her yf she wold have a gode servise [whereupon] the wif of the seid hous aunswerd and seid it wer grete almes that she had a gode master and mastres to abyde with them and do suche service as she coude wheruppon

---

[43] Hampshire RO, 11M59/C1/21/1; A. H. Thomas and I. D. Thornley (eds.), *The Great Chronicle of London* (London, 1938), p. 331.

the seid Thomas desired to have . . . [her] with hym to see his hous uppon lykyng.' In fact, he conveyed her by boat 'to his hous at the stewes syde and there wold have compelled her to do suche service as other his servauntez done there which to do . . . [she] utterly denyed and yet doith and had lever dye then to be of that disposicion'. To compel her, he was suing her on a false action of trespass in the bishop of Winchester's court and had kept her in prison for three weeks. The complaint of false dealing in 'the court of the Clink' was echoed in other petitions, which pointed out that little justice could be expected when cases were tried by juries made up of 'occupyers and kepers of such unclenly and defamy placez' or 'baudes and watermen'. Since the latter commonly conveyed customers to and from the city of London, they were thought to be heavily implicated in the nefarious activities of the stews.[44] In 1491, John Waldron, who had been successively keeper of the Rose, the Flower de Luce and the Bull, testified in the consistory court – only to have his character assassinated. Not only was he a pimp or 'appul squier' and notorious for his habitual association with whores. According to the witnesses against him, he was also a thief, a vagabond and a 'knight of the post' or professional perjurer in Westminster Hall. The archdeacon of Surrey's official had put him to penance for living with a woman whose lawful husband was still alive, and he subsequently cohabited with yet another woman. Waldron's fellow witness, William Alston, was likewise denigrated.[45]

Sexual Regulation in the Southwark Manor Courts

Surviving records of regulatory activity in Southwark not directly related to the stews indicates a similar dislike of brothels, disorderly houses, and sexual transgression generally to that found in Westminster. Since Southwark was outside the immediate jurisdiction of King's Bench, the records of that court contain only occasional references to such activities. But the records of the various manor courts, though fragmentary, are suggestive. The earliest surviving court rolls of Paris Garden from the late fifteenth century include presentments against whores, bawds and suchlike offenders. For example, in 1463, Joan, daughter of John Clement, was reported to be 'a common whore [*meretrix*] to the common nuisance', and it was stated that John Shipman and John Watirman – the surnames may well have been generic – 'keep and

---

[44] TNA, C1/48/191; C1/64/897; C1/363/76. These cases are discussed by Carlin, *Medieval Southwark*, pp. 218–19, 222–3.
[45] LMA, DL/C/A/002/MS09065, fos. 88(89)v–92(93)r; the case is discussed in Shannon McSheffrey, *Marriage, Sex, and Civic Culture in Late Medieval London* (Philadelphia, 2006), p. 178.

maintain her in fornication'. The woman was fined 6d. and the men paid 12d. each. Such sums might be dismissed as inconsiderable, were it not for the fact that they were part of an escalating scale of penalties. Alice Spoforde was presented for a similar offence in 1479 and likewise fined 6d. – but on this occasion it was ordered that she was to be removed. Other cases indicate that removal, or at least the threat of removal, to secure compliance was regularly employed on this manor in Yorkist and early Tudor times.[46] Bawdry and brothel-keeping were the main targets,[47] but occasionally the jurors turned their attention to sexual transgressions of a slightly different nature. Thus, in 1510, Thomas Wayte and Hamlet Sawyer and his wife were presented for permitting a man and a woman to sleep together for a night in their respective houses; piously, the jurors declared that 'according to their conscience they suppose that the said man and woman were not married together'.[48]

The archbishop of Canterbury's manor in the eastern part of Southwark was policed in similar or even more intense fashion, to judge by the surviving court rolls for 1504–11. The view of frankpledge met annually, presentments being made by the 'chief pledges' and the 'great inquest' (*magna inquisicio*); among other means of detection were searches of suspect houses by constables accompanied by a posse of neighbours. In 1504, amid numerous prosecutions for trading offences, reparations and sundry nuisances, two married couples, three men and one woman, were presented for keeping ill rule, receiving men's servants, evilly disposed women living lecherously and suspect persons generally and 'blyndhostry'. There were similar clutches of offenders in subsequent years, but the fact that neither the lists of persons nor the offences were simply duplicated indicates that this was not a licensing system masquerading as regulation. The jurors wanted amendment, and to achieve this, they employed the usual escalating system of fines, eventually leading to an order for amendment on pain of expulsion or a summary order to quit.[49] For example, in May 1511, Maud Dochewoman, said to be 'ill disposed of her body and also keeps whores in her house and entertains suspect persons resorting to them', was ordered to leave the lordship by Michaelmas on pain of 20s.[50] Admittedly, the system had its limits. One man, variously named in the records as Henry Harper and Henry Clator, Cleter, or Sleter, 'harper' by

---

[46] Lambeth Archives, Class VI/1, mm. 3r, 12r; cf. VI/2, mm. 4r, 6v, 17v.
[47] In the sphere of sexual regulation, that is; other offences, such as scolding, quarrelling and brawling, were also of concern and occasioned removal orders: Lambeth Archives, Class VI/2–3, *passim*.
[48] Lambeth Archives, Class VI/2, m. 13r.
[49] Lambeth Palace Library, Estate Document 969, mm. 1r, 4v and *passim*.   [50] *Ibid.*, m. 5v.

occupation, was repeatedly fined and threatened with removal, apparently to little effect. He had installed archery butts and a bowling alley and was no doubt reluctant to lose his investment.[51]

No court records survive for the Guildable manor before 1539. But the proceedings of the court held in October 1540, by which time the manor was under city jurisdiction, indicate a self-confident system, stiffened by the presence of the lord mayor and sheriffs of London. The removal of householders guilty of a variety of forms of 'ill rule' played a regular part in the regime, while the wording of the charges indicates how far the local officers could rely on their fellows in other jurisdictions to help them in their task. Thus, Marion, the wife of John Smythe in 'Peper allye', was presented as 'an yl lyver of her bodye and a great resorter [i.e. receiver] of mens servauntes and a keper of bawdry and hath byn dryven from one place to another'. She was ordered 'to away before Candlemas' (2 February), as was Thomas Bysto's wife for similar offences. In a case that gives a rare insight into the activities of royal justices in this area — sessions of the peace records are lost — 'Patrycke a glovar' was presented 'for that he kepyth another mans wyfe the whych he hath byn commaundyd by the Justys Curson to avoyde and as yet he lyves with her after hys olde custome'. He was likewise ordered out. Others, for this time at least, got off with a hefty fine, even if there was evidence of considerable local hostility. For example, the jury presented 'Master Browgrave gentylman for to be an yl lyver of hys body wyth one Dymockes wyff the whych ys not hys owne wyff and he doth contynew dayly and nyghtly together as man and wyff in towne and countrye contrarye to the lawe of God and the inhabitantes do sore complayn: we payn [him] xiijs. iiijd.'[52]

The Southwark Church Courts

Discussion so far in this chapter has centred on the work of the secular courts. But it is important to realize that week by week, month by month, year in and year out their activities were complemented by those of the ecclesiastical courts. Little work has been done on their impact in the suburbs of London in the early Tudor period for the simple reason that few records survive. As far as is known, there is virtually nothing for Westminster and only fragmentary indications for other suburban areas north of the river. Fortunately, there does survive for Southwark a church court act book covering the period March 1511 to March 1515. Some of the

[51] *Ibid.*, mm. 2v, 3r, 4r, 4v, 5v.   [52] LMA, CLA/043/01/016, fos. 10r, 10v, 11v.

cases recorded are suits between parties – principally matrimonial and defamation – but the great majority are disciplinary prosecutions, largely to do with sexual and sex-related offences. Surprisingly, the volume has hitherto attracted little attention.[53]

The court sat several times a month, usually in the church of St Mary Overy, and was variously presided over by the vicar-general of Winchester diocese, the bishop's commissary or occasionally Bishop Fox himself. The great bulk of cases related to Southwark. But some came from adjacent or nearby parishes, notably Bermondsey, Camberwell, Streatham and Tooting; several from Kingston and Richmond, further up river, while only a few related to other parts of Winchester diocese.[54] Some were specifically said to be visitation detections, but most of the charges had been 'notified' to the court, presumably by local clergy, the neighbours of the accused or the court summoners who were constantly out and about delivering citations and other mandates. Yet again, the contents of this volume show that in contrast to the post-Reformation church courts, charges arising from visitation returns were of subsidiary significance. But it was by no means solely a 'top down' institution imposing values from above, since in a variety of ways local men and women informed the court and participated in its activities.

As is common for this period, the record was often left incomplete, especially when proceedings were protracted, so it is not always possible to trace cases through to a finish. Nonetheless, it is plain that the officials took their duties seriously; on one occasion the archdeacon of Winchester was brought in question for failing to conduct his visitation.[55] They pursued the common run of offenders with vigour, apparently on the basis of a very shrewd knowledge of the neighbourhood and its inhabitants. Defendants who failed to attend court were first suspended from the church and then, if they persisted in their contumacy and there seemed some chance of catching up with them, sentenced to excommunication. Even in the bustling suburb of Southwark, these sanctions were sufficient to bring the great majority of suspects to court to answer charges.

[53] In 1954, this volume of 178 folios was a stray survival among the records of the archdeaconry of Leicester, ref. 1 D 41/50, misleadingly catalogued as an 'Act book of a court of Instance causes'. Later it was transferred to the Greater London Record Office, now London Metropolitan Archives, where it is catalogued as Ac. 62.7 and available on microfilm X003/007. It is noticed in Ralph Houlbrooke, *Church Courts and the People during the English Reformation, 1520–1570* (Oxford, 1979), p. 32.

[54] About 15 per cent of cases were not precisely located; in many of these the nature of the offence was not specified either.

[55] LMA, Ac. 62.7, fo. 17r.

Admittedly, they were not always amenable to discipline thereafter, and some probably absconded. In part, this was because the treatment of defendants was rigorous by the standards of the ecclesiastical courts. Compurgation was by no means a formality. In a few cases the judge allowed the accused to clear themselves on their own oath or called for only one or two compurgators. But the usual tariff was four, five or six 'hands', and the court had no hesitation in demanding seven, eight, or even more if circumstances warranted. The Southwark court also took a strict view of penance. The least that culprits could expect was to lead the parish processions two or three times on successive Sundays, submitting themselves to the priest in the course of mass. Often it was specified that they should go barefoot, bare-legged and bare-headed; sometimes men had to do penance in their shirt, women in their smock. Occasionally, greater severity was ordered, including the 'discipline' or penitential whipping and performance of penance in the marketplace. Thus in 1511 an example was made of Margery Bunche of St Margaret's for bawdry and maintaining suspicious persons in her house. She had to parade round the marketplace on three market days, barefoot and bare-legged, carrying a wax candle in one hand and in the other a rod, with which the curate at length subjected her to 'discipline'. She was also ordered to wear a 'ray hode', the ignominious garb of bawds and prostitutes.[56]

Numerically, the scale of the court's activity is impressive. In 1512, for example, apart from ten suits between parties (eight of which concerned marriage), some 157 prosecutions were recorded (Table 5.2). Since a sizeable proportion of them involved couples, the number of *individuals* brought in question was in fact nearer 200. This indicates an intensity of prosecution far greater than in rural areas such as Leicestershire or west Sussex. In eighteen of these cases, the charge was unspecified, while a further fifteen concerned a range of miscellaneous matters of the kind commonly handled by church courts. There was one case of expressing erroneous opinions and another of swearing 'by the lord' (instead, presumably, of the more usual 'by the mass'), so raising suspicions of heretical leanings. Twenty-one defendants (thirteen of them women) were accused of being scolds or common defamers, a specific victim being named in most cases. The actual words of defamation were rarely spelled out. But in two typical cases a woman of St George's parish accused another of taking a kerchief from her house, while two women had reported that they had seen Martina Kyng of St Margaret's in bed with a young man at the Steelyard (headquarters of the merchants of the Hanseatic League).[57]

[56] *Ibid.*, fo. 6r.   [57] *Ibid.*, fo. 66r.

Table 5.2 *Southwark Church Court Act Book:*
Disciplinary Prosecutions, 1512

Clerical incontinence	4
Adultery	21
Fornication, etc.	4
Illicit pregnancy	2
(Common) whore	7
(Common) whore and bawd	6
Bawdry	36[a]
Contempt of Eucharist, etc. (Bankside denizens)	15[b]
Bigamy	1
Clandestine marriage	2
Issues relating to marriage contracts	2
Marital ill-treatment	1
(Common) scold/defamer	21
Miscellaneous	17
Unspecified	18
Total	157

[a] Includes four married couples.
[b] Includes seven married couples.

The bulk of the cases before the court concerned the sexual transgressions of lay people. (Cases concerning the clergy are considered in Chapter 8.) It is striking that many of them were not dissimilar to those found in the provinces; even in sinful Southwark, the church courts plodded on with the task of upholding Christian morality. To be sure, the judges seem as usual to have had only limited interest in the behaviour of courting couples. Yet, if a man and a woman were known to be cohabiting or otherwise having regular sexual relations, the court did its best to ensure that they were properly married in church. A marriage contract, far less a mere promise of marriage, was evidently not enough to make their relationship licit.[58] But probably the majority of prosecutions were directed against married men, some of whom were accused of having sex with their maidservants. Thomas Manery, accused of adultery with Alice Whitehed, was separately examined about the treatment of his wife;

[58] E.g. *ibid.*, fo. 32r.

he claimed to have received her back into his house and was now ordered to provide her with sufficient victuals.[59]

Predictably, in view of Southwark's association with the sex trade, cases of aiding and abetting sexual offences were relatively numerous: there were thirty-six of them in 1512. These involved thirteen men, nineteen women and four married couples, variously described as bawds or common bawds (*pronube*) or accused of *lenocinium*. A further five women[60] were described as bawds and whores, while seven more were prosecuted simply for being a whore or common whore (*meretrix*). Some of the accused were said to be bawds to named couples, who were themselves prosecuted for adultery. But in most cases the implication was that they were aiding and abetting illicit sex on an extensive scale, presumably for business. Yet none of them confessed the offence. As householders, no doubt with connections and at least some status, they had a reasonable chance of securing compurgators, even when the court set the hurdle very high by demanding a large number; men had a better chance than women. Thus fifteen of the defendants charged solely with bawdry – eight males, five females and two married couples – are known to have cleared themselves by this means.

However, about the same number seem to have failed to secure oath-helpers, though often the outcome is not recorded. One man appeared with eight compurgators, only to see them refuse to take the necessary oath: he was ordered to do penance, barefoot and bare-legged, in the general procession in Southwark on three successive Fridays. One woman, having successfully purged, nonetheless undertook to leave the borough; another was dismissed on condition of good behaviour, otherwise to do public penance.[61] The women charged with being both bawds and whores appear to have been in a more vulnerable position; most of the small number so accused in 1512 probably ended up suspended from church or excommunicated. Of the seven women accused of being whores or common whores, two cleared themselves by compurgation, while in the case of a third, a group of neighbours promised to ensure that she behaved herself in the future.[62] The overall impression is that though there were limits to what it could do, the court was exerting as much pressure as it could on these suspected bawds and whores.

[59] *Ibid.*, fo. 63v.
[60] Six if we include a case from Bermondsey that was crossed out in the record: *ibid.*, fo. 54v.
[61] *Ibid.*, fos. 75r, 76v, 77v.   [62] *Ibid.*, fo. 81r.

The association of Southwark with the sex trade is manifest in various other ways in this volume of proceedings. A man of St George's parish was reported for spending the night with whores in the stews, 'having a wife of his own'.[63] It was reported of one St Margaret's man in 1511 that 'he standith with his swerde and bukler at bawdes dores betyng men and women into the bawdes houses compellyng them to pay mony unto the baudes whether they will or not, forsing honest people therto agaynst there willes, and also he kepys bawdes and al that ben accursed [i.e. excommunicated] in his house.' Rather more venial were the activities of another man of the same parish, said to supply sheets to common bawds.[64]

Most remarkable were the court's dealings with the actual denizens of the Southwark stews. On 22 June 1512, following the feast of Corpus Christi, seven married couples, seven other women and a man were summoned from 'le bank syd'. Most of them confessed to having received the sacrament at the Crutched Friars, Blackfriars, Whitefriars, the hospital of St Mary Rouncivall and similar places in and around London and were thereupon threatened with excommunication 'for contempt of Corpus Christi'. From the fuller record of similar proceedings two years later, it is clear that these people were the bawds or stew house keepers; their profession made them ineligible to receive the rites of the church. In 1514, a full list of their establishments was given, together with a note of the whores – forty-eight in all – working in each. Comparison between the two lists of brothel keepers shows that half those named in 1514 were newcomers. Indeed, the point of the exercise was to exert pressure on them to move; here is one reason for the turnover of brothel keepers noted earlier. In 1514 the keepers of the Unicorn and of the Bull agreed to go, as did another woman and a married couple who were apparently associated with unnamed establishments. In 1512, it would seem, the court was rather less successful, despite the aid of local clergy. George and Margaret Fen confessed that they had received the Eucharist at the Whitefriars; subsequently, their local priest, Master John Eton, undertook on pain of £20, to be paid to the bishop of Winchester, that they would remove from the stews by the beginning of the following February. But Thomas Prowt of the Hart's Horn was openly defiant, saying that 'Master chaunceler is more habyll to make men morderers and thevys then trew or good men.'[65] To the modern eye, threatening to withhold the sacrament to try to change people's behaviour smacks of spiritual brutality. The officers of the church

[63] *Ibid.*, fo. 79r.   [64] *Ibid.*, fos. 25v, 26r.
[65] *Ibid.*, fos. 69r, 74r–v, 144r–145r (quotation fo. 74v).

courts no doubt saw it differently. They were using the spiritual weapons available as a means of combating sin.[66]

Far more than provincial towns and cities, pre-Reformation Westminster, Southwark and some of the adjacent suburbs were inextricably linked with the trade in sex. It could not be stamped out; indeed, it was institutionalized in the Southwark stews and was endemic in and around the palace of Westminster. Its practitioners – 'common' or 'single' women, pimps and bawds – lived lives that were manifestly at odds with conventional Christian morality. One might even describe them as a subculture, though it is striking that some of the bawds still considered themselves part of Christian society to the extent that they sought to receive the sacrament, albeit surreptitiously. The purpose of this chapter has been to demonstrate that the existence of this subculture was not condoned or even tolerated by the ecclesiastical and secular authorities, or by respectable neighbours, any more than other sexual and sex-related transgressions, such as adultery and bigamy. King's Bench, local manor courts, and the church all mounted regular prosecutions to exert pressure on sex traders and other offenders to desist from their activities; when possible, persistent and notorious offenders were expelled. Especially in the light of the new evidence presented here, to describe such policing activities as 'half hearted', mere 'harassment' motivated as much by 'fiscal intent' as real disapproval seems too dismissive.[67] They had at least intermittent support from some powerful figures in court and government, particularly Cardinal Wolsey in the 1510s and 1520s. More generally, they were clearly supported by many local householders in the guise of constables, jurors, churchwardens and other informants, including women. The role of such people is often forgotten by historians prone to view pre-Reformation attitudes towards prostitution and other forms of illicit sex as lax or hypocritical. For if some individuals and couples saw business opportunities in sins of the flesh and were prepared to exploit them, many of the ordinary people who had to live their lives in Westminster and Southwark were plainly affronted by such activities and strove both to restrict them and to subject offenders to what they felt was condign punishment.

[66] Cf. the use by Protestant parish ministers of rejection from the sacrament as a means of promoting 'reformation of manners': Christopher Haigh, 'Communion and Community: Exclusion from Communion in Post-Reformation England', *Journal of Ecclesiastical History*, 51 (2000), 730–1.
[67] Karras, *Common Women*, p. 23.

CHAPTER 6

London Church Courts before the Reformation

Around 1500, the population of London within the walls or under the immediate jurisdiction of the city government may have numbered fewer than 50,000 in normal times, and periodically it suffered savage cuts from plague and other epidemic diseases. Yet, by contemporary English standards, this was an enormous urban settlement. Its teeming streets, lanes and alleys offered far greater opportunities than smaller centres for illicit sexual activity, whether as a commercial or semi-commercial enterprise or simply on the part of individuals pursuing personal liaisons. Visiting gentlemen and officials, together with groups of foreign merchants, augmented the demand of ordinary local inhabitants for sexual services, as did some of the city's numerous clergy. However, the city had traditionally been hostile to the 'whores' and 'bawds' who were thought to infest the city, and in contrast to Southwark and to many continental cities, the existence of licensed brothels was never tolerated.[1] The civic ethos articulated by the rulers of the city of London, and to an extent shared by many citizens lower down the social scale, also condemned other forms of sexual transgression such as adultery.[2] This was the powerful message implicit in the policing activities routinely in operation at the local level and at least sporadically reinforced by exemplary action by the mayor and aldermen on their own initiative or, on occasion, when prodded by the crown or its ministers – the subject of Chapter 7.

Complementing this secular policing, moreover, was the correctional activity of the church courts. As elsewhere in England, they pursued adulterers, fornicators and a variety of other sexual offenders, together

---

[1] Cf. Leah Lydia Otis, *Prostitution in Medieval Society: The History of an Urban Institution in Languedoc* (Chicago, 1985); Jacques Rossiaud, *Medieval Prostitution*, trans. Lydia G. Cochrane (Oxford, 1988).

[2] Shannon McSheffrey, *Marriage, Sex, and Civic Culture in Late Medieval London* (Philadelphia, 2006), esp. chaps. 6 and 7.

with those who aided and abetted them. In London these activities were at times on a very impressive scale indeed, at least in terms of sheer numbers. It is true that this 'system' of moral regulation – if the sum total of ecclesiastical and secular action may be thought of in those terms – had definite limits, and few individuals were subject to the degree of severity that some sexual offenders suffered in the later sixteenth century. There has therefore been a tendency for historians to write off the pre-Reformation regime of sexual regulation in the capital as lax or otherwise imperfect. Even Ian Archer, though rightly hesitant to pronounce on the issue in advance of detailed research, concluded that in contrast to the later sixteenth-century campaigns, 'vigorous action was exceptional and rarely sustained.'[3]

But this is to judge by anachronistic standards. Contemporaries could not know that their successors, in a very different cultural, religious and economic climate, would ratchet up the intensity of policing and the scale of penalties. Early Tudor Londoners had their own distinctive methods of dealing with sexual transgression that are themselves worth close attention. At the same time, study of this period reveals signs of stress and directions of change that make it easier to understand later innovations. If the surviving records are representative, the disciplinary activity of the ordinary church courts in London became quite desultory in the period 1500–29 – a picture offset only by some firm action by the bishop of London's vicar-general against immoral priests and other egregious offenders and in the lower-level courts by some belated efforts at increased rigour on the very eve of the Reformation Parliament. This modifies the influential view, established a generation ago by Margaret Bowker, that it was the *vigour* of the church courts that frightened lay people and provoked a reaction. While they may well have been fearful of heresy trials, it is unlikely that proceedings against sexual offenders aroused much terror.[4] However, *civic* action against sexual offenders, though firmly based on fourteenth-century precedents and well established in practice long before 1500, was certainly not slackening and may have been stepped up in the early decades of the sixteenth century, especially the 1520s.

---

[3] Ian Archer, *The Pursuit of Stability: Social Relations in Elizabethan London* (Cambridge, 1991), pp. 249–50.

[4] Margaret Bowker, 'The Commons Supplication against the Ordinaries in the Light of some Archidiaconal Acta', *Transactions of the Royal Historical Society*, 5th Series, 21 (1971), 61–77; Margaret Bowker, 'Some Archdeacons' Court Books and the Commons' Supplication against the Ordinaries of 1532', in D. A. Bullough and R. L. Storey (eds.), *The Study of Medieval Records: Essays in Honour of Kathleen Major* (Oxford, 1971), pp. 282–316.

London Church Courts and Their Records

The church courts are the most obvious starting point for understanding public efforts towards sexual regulation in pre-Reformation London. This is simply because their work is represented by a quite exceptional accumulation of late fifteenth- and early sixteenth-century records, most of which have already been extensively analysed in what is in many ways an excellent study by Richard Wunderli.[5] He was under the mistaken impression that two act books for the period 1518–29, used by Archdeacon Hale in the nineteenth century, had since been lost, and to that extent his work is incomplete.[6] It must be said that knowledge of the additional materials would not have significantly affected his argument – indeed, he would no doubt have seen them as reinforcing it – but on other grounds some of his interpretations are open to question. In any case, Wunderli by no means exhausted the possibilities of these rich materials, nor have other historians who have since worked on the records.[7] More detailed analysis of the proceedings for sample years provides further insights into the church courts' role in sexual regulation.

The chief ecclesiastical court survivals are registers of disciplinary prosecutions or 'corrections' under the authority of the bishop of London's commissary or legal deputy, covering (with gaps) the period 1470–1529. This court met in Paul's Chain, close to the heart of the city. Complementing the records of this court are the much more fragmentary records of the bishop of London's consistory court, which heard party-and-party suits at sessions usually held in St Paul's cathedral. An act book for 1500–5 and several late fifteenth- and early sixteenth-century volumes in which the 'personal answers' of some of the parties to the causes and the 'depositions' of witnesses are registered suffice to give an indication of the nature of business.[8] For the period 1521–39, there survives also a volume known as 'Foxford', the first in a series of vicar-general's books that illuminate a higher level of ecclesiastical discipline. Apart from licences, dispensations, commissions, admissions to offices and so forth,

---

[5] Richard M. Wunderli, *London Church Courts and Society on the Eve of the Reformation* (Cambridge, MA, 1981).

[6] The volumes survive as LMA, DL/C/B/041/MS09065J/1–2.

[7] McSheffrey, *Marriage, Sex, and Civic Culture*; Stephanie Tarbin, 'Gender, Order and Sexuality in London, 1400–1530', unpublished PhD thesis, University of Western Australia, 1999. For a comparison between material found in the London commissary court, 1483–1503, and the records of the archdeacon of Paris in the same period, see Ruth Mazo Karras, 'The Regulation of Sexuality in the Late Middle Ages: England and France', *Speculum*, 86 (2011), 1010–39.

[8] LMA, D/L/C/1, D/L/C/205–208, DL/C/A/002/MS09065, DL/C/A/001/MS09065B.

this includes sessions of judicial business, normally presided over by the bishop of London's chief deputy, his 'vicar-general in spiritualities', though sometimes cases were heard by other individuals and on occasion by the bishop himself.[9] While the jurisdiction of the vicar-general and the consistory court extended over the whole of the diocese of London, including the county of Essex, the jurisdiction of the commissary was limited to the city of London and the adjacent deaneries of Middlesex and Barking. The commissary court records are therefore particularly relevant to understanding the pattern of sexual regulation in the metropolis.

Impressive though these survivals are for the pre-Reformation period, it is salutary to reflect on what is lacking and how this may affect our interpretation of what remains. We know that the bishop's officers were conducting visitations in this period, as they did later, seeking systematic information from the churchwardens and other representatives of the parishes. This was essential to deal with, among other things, the upkeep and furnishing of churches. Such matters are almost wholly absent from the surviving commissary court books and must have been recorded elsewhere, along with an unknown number of prosecutions relating to other detections arising from visitations. The commissary court records do contain some incidental references to visitatorial activity,[10] and it is quite possible that at certain periods, some, perhaps many, of the cases registered there *did* originate at visitations. But it is impossible to be sure.

Also lost are the records of the visitations, disciplinary prosecutions and other judicial activities of the archdeacon of London. Within the city, his officers had concurrent jurisdiction with the bishop's commissary, in effect sharing the available business. Incidental references in the commissary records show that the archdeacon's court was active throughout this period in handling cases of sexual transgression, as in other matters. In the absence of its registers, the exact scale and range of its activities cannot be determined, but it is known that in later periods its correction business was very brisk, and there is no reason to suppose that this was not true earlier. It may be that the volume of archidiaconal business fluctuated in line with that of the commissary court, but this cannot be assumed. It is therefore hazardous to draw conclusions from totals of cases in the commissary court without

[9] LMA, DL/C/330, partially edited by Colin A. McLaren, 'An Edition of Foxford, a Vicar-General Book of the Diocese of London, 1521–1539, ff. 161–268', unpublished MPhil thesis, University of London, 1973. See also Colin A. McLaren, 'An Early 16th Century Act Book of the Diocese of London', *Journal of the Society of Archivists*, 3 (1965–9), 336–41.

[10] E.g. LMA, DL/C/B/043/MS09064/6, fo. 131v.

knowledge of what the archdeacon's court was doing; reductions in business in one jurisdiction may have been compensated, in whole or in part, by increases in the other.

Prosecution Trends and the Genesis of Accusations

Especially in view of the restricted area to which they refer, the most striking feature of the surviving commissary court records for the late fifteenth century is the huge number of cases they contain. Taking due account of population, the intensity of prosecution was much greater than in rural areas such as Leicestershire and west Sussex and greater too than in contemporary Paris.[11] Equally striking is a fall in the number of cases after 1500. In 1490, a peak year, over 1,500 defendants were named; in 1472, there had been over 1,300. The inter-annual figures are marked by violent fluctuations, and some of the intermediate years saw much lower totals. In 1486, for example, there were about 500 cases. By the 1510s, numbers were consistently down to about 300 a year and fell even further in the next decade. In view both of the high late fifteenth-century totals and of the apparent fall in numbers later, the perennial puzzle posed by pre-Reformation church court records – how cases, other than those which are known to have arisen from visitations, came to the attention of the authorities – is particularly critical.

Unfortunately, the evidence is not clear-cut. Archdeacon Hale was 'inclined to believe' that the apparitors or summoners – the officers responsible for issuing summonses or citations on defendants – were the main means by which offenders were detected. There is some correlation between the numbers of summoners and the volume of cases. In 1524, only four summoners were named, whereas in the mid-1490s, there was a substantial team of fifteen or more. In 1512, there were still about a dozen, though the bulk of the work was done by four or five of them. But Wunderli sees the numbers of summoners as reflecting rather than determining the volume of business and disputes their role as initiators of prosecutions, pointing out that direct indications of detective activities on their part are rare in the records.[12] There were some, however: for example, in 1495, Giles Barbour claimed that no-one accused him of the crime of

---

[11] The comparison with Paris rests on the numbers provided by Karras, 'The Regulation of Sexuality', 1018–19 and *passim*; however, she makes the point that in terms of rates of punishment the disparity was much less. On rural England, see Chapter 3.

[12] William H. Hale, *A Series of Precedents and Proceedings in Criminal Causes . . . 1475 to 1640; Extracted from the Act-Books of Ecclesiastical Courts in the Diocese of London* (London, 1847), p. lvii; Wunderli,

adultery with his maidservant but the apparitor, James Patenson.[13] Moreover, the scarcity of direct references to accusations by summoners does not preclude the possibility that behind the scenes they acted in a variety of ways to invite or encourage prosecutions, and almost certainly they played a part in the process by which actual prosecutions were filtered out from a deeper reservoir of suspicions, accusations, rumour and gossip – whether malicious or otherwise.

But Wunderli is undoubtedly correct to assume that their activities were buoyed up by information generated at the local level. Some of the informants were parish priests, though their duties as confessors and their desire to maintain harmony within their flock probably prevented them from taking a very active role. But the great majority of informants appear to have been the neighbours and close family members of the people they accused. All this is consistent with what has been observed in Southwark, where the church courts explicitly drew on a variety of sources of information in addition to visitation presentments.[14] Particularly interesting in the case of the London commissary court is that individuals of quite high status were occasionally netted. In 1471, Master Robert Bassett, alderman of Aldgate ward, was brought in question for adultery with his maidservant, while in the early 1490s, Grace, an illegitimate daughter of the late King Edward IV, was twice named in fornication cases.[15] In 1491, Lewis of Caerleon, Henry VII's court physician, was prosecuted for committing adultery with his servant Margaret and begetting two children on her; on each occasion he sent her into the country to give birth. The unusually elaborate charge, strongly redolent of local indignation, concludes with the statement that he 'cares neither for God, nor for the lord king whom he serves, nor for the law, nor for the ministers of the law. He has a young wife who is certain of these things, as are all his neighbours.'[16]

This was by no means the only case to specify the grounds for suspicion. Some of these appear flimsy in the extreme, though it must be understood that the details noted by the scribes were mere memoranda, intended as aids to identification and perhaps as a starting point for questioning; they were not a full statement of evidence. For example, in 1470, it was recorded

London Church Courts, pp. 37–8; Richard M. Wunderli, 'Pre-Reformation London Summoners and the Murder of Richard Hunne', Journal of Ecclesiastical History, 33 (1982), 211–14; cf. Tarbin, 'Gender, Order and Sexuality', pp. 159–65; McSheffrey, Marriage, Sex, and Civic Culture, pp. 155–6. The estimates of the numbers of summoners working in 1495, 1512 and 1524 are based on my own examination of the records.

[13] LMA, DL/C/B/043/MS09064/6, fo. 100v.   [14] See Chapter 5.
[15] McSheffrey, Marriage, Sex, and Civic Culture, p. 146; Wunderli, London Church Courts, p. 89.
[16] Quoted in McSheffrey, Marriage, Sex, and Civic Culture, p. 171.

that William Wyen of St Andrew Hubbard committed 'adultery with Margaret Harper alias Isabel Harper, wife of a tailor dwelling in *le aley* by the church called *Fanchirche*, the token whereof is that he gave the said woman *rollys de pynnys*', while Agnes Johnson of St Margaret Pattens likewise committed adultery with Roger Clerk, 'the token whereof is that she drank with him in the house of *le butler* on Tower Hill in Whitsun week'. A few prosecutions were based on self-accusation or ill-advised boasting: thus, in 1471, it was said that Cecily Boweer was 'a whore and called her husband *cocolde*, saying that she gave birth to a child by a priest with the knowledge of her husband'.[17] Many others were solidly grounded in the fact of illicit pregnancy[18] or in blatant circumstances, some of which involved dramatic revelations that must have occasioned a considerable local stir. For example, in 1498 the wife of John Haslopp of St Mary Matfelon (Whitechapel), seizing a ladder, climbed up and looked through the window of his chamber, discovering him in bed with his mistress.[19] Numerous other offenders, as will be seen in Chapter 7, were brought to the attention of the courts because they were already in trouble with the secular authorities.

How far did these neighbourhood accusations reflect a consensus of values between local people and the courts? Why individuals took exception to other people's sexual transgressions is rarely stated, and the grounds for action may have been different from (or more complicated than) moral disapproval based on strongly felt Christian ethics. Many accusations were probably self-interested. Others may have represented efforts by neighbours to deal with disharmony between spouses, either to intervene on behalf of husband or wife or, more impartially, to minimize the local tensions generated by marital conflict or deception.[20] Some accusations were no doubt simply malicious. That said, there appears to have been at least a rough-and-ready congruence between what the courts claimed to be doing and the attitudes and prejudices of many local inhabitants. Occasionally, large groups of people crowded into court to bear witness against some notorious offender, and in such cases it is hard not to detect in London, as in some of the provincial cases considered in earlier chapters, a strong sense of moral outrage. If foreigners – such as 'Lombards',

---

[17] LMA, DL/C/B/043/MS09064/1, fos. 16v, 109v.
[18] E.g. LMA, DL/C/B/043/MS09064/1, fo. 142v. [19] LMA, DL/C/B/043/MS09064/8, fo. 96r.
[20] L. R. Poos, 'The Heavy-Handed Marriage Counsellor: Regulating Marriage in Some Later-Medieval English Local Ecclesiastical-Court Jurisdictions', *American Journal of Legal History*, 39 (1995), 291–309, deals mainly with rural areas, but his insights are equally applicable to the urban context.

'Easterlings' or 'Spaniards' – were implicated, as was true in a regular minority of cases, these feelings might be sharpened by the undercurrent of xenophobia that was to erupt so spectacularly in the 'Evil May Day' riots of 1517.[21]

The topographical distribution of cases reveals some marked features. A few parishes – St Giles without Cripplegate, St Gregory by St Paul's, St Helen Bishopsgate – are notable for their absence, despite being quite large. This is simply because they were subject to the dean and chapter of the cathedral and exempt from the jurisdiction of the bishop of London's commissary. Thus records from these parishes do not survive. Another independent jurisdiction that has left no records was St Katharine's Hospital east of the Tower – a significant hole in the commissary's net because it was notorious as a nest of bawds and whores.[22] Otherwise, prosecutions flowed in from all parts of the city and its liberties, but certain parishes generated a disproportionate number. This was true of a few locations well within the walled area, such as the riverine parish of All Hallows the Great. But mostly the 'disorderly' parishes were in the northern and eastern environs of the city – St Botolph Aldgate, St Botolph Bishopsgate, St Mary Matfelon (Whitechapel), St Stephen Coleman Street – and, even more, in the western suburbs – St Botolph Aldersgate, St Bride and, above all, St Sepulchre. These were large, mainly poor parishes on the fringes of city government.[23] In Elizabethan and Jacobean times, Bridewell offenders were to be drawn mainly from the same areas. Later sixteenth- and early seventeenth-century developments were indeed to intensify the pattern, but it was already well established at the end of the fifteenth century.[24]

Though most of the cases before the London church courts concerned illicit sex in one way or another, this was not true of all. There were also sporadic or occasional prosecutions concerning witchcraft, sorcery and blasphemy, lax religious observances, trading on Sundays and holy days, debt in the guise of 'breach of faith', non-payment of tithes and other dues to church and clergy and a few miscellaneous matters. In some periods the registers also included matters concerning probate, the administration of intestate estates, the withholding of

[21] E.g. LMA, DL/C/B/043/MS09064/6, fos. 109r, 113r, 147v, 169r, 185r; on 'Evil May Day', see Susan Brigden, *London and the Reformation* (Oxford, 1989), pp. 129–33.
[22] Sidelights on St Katharine's are offered in Chapter 7.
[23] Based on analysis of cases from 1495; see also Wunderli, *London Church Courts*, p. 28.
[24] See Chapter 11.

legacies and other testamentary issues. For the rest, the tally of commissary court business was made up by prosecutions for scolding or
various forms of verbal harassment and the closely related offence of
defamation. Before 1513, by which time the determination of common
lawyers to limit the church courts' slander jurisdiction affected their
business, these cases included a minority of non-sexual slanders such as
imputations of murder and theft. But throughout the period, sexual
defamation predominated. Some cases were indeed scarcely distinguishable from prosecutions for adultery or fornication – an accusation of
sexual misdoing was at issue, and the form of prosecution depended on
whether the onus of justification lay with the person slandered with
sexual transgression (who might then have to undergo compurgation to
clear his or her name) or with the accuser. For this reason, the following
analysis treats slander cases alongside those for sexual transgression.
But, although many cases, whether of actual sexual transgression or of
slander, implicated members of the clergy, the issues that this particular
fact raises are not addressed at this point. This chapter is mainly about
lay people; clerical immorality is the focus of Chapter 8.

Sexual Mores and the Pattern of Prosecutions in 1495

The pattern of prosecutions is best understood by considering in detail
the proceedings for sample years. Among other advantages, this method
serves to emphasize how much the pattern of business changed over time,
and cautions against interpreting the material as a straightforward linear
sequence. The proceedings for 1495 may be taken as a starting point
(Table 6.1). This was not one of the peak years, but the tally of just over
a thousand cases by Wunderli's reckoning does indicate a very brisk rate
of business. Moreover, this sizeable figure implies a much larger number
of individuals who to a greater or lesser extent were brought in question.
Many prosecutions were against married couples, while a smaller number
involved multiple defendants. Furthermore, Wunderli's tallies of prosecutions for adultery, fornication and the like are based on the numbers of
individuals named first in the act book entries and hence, it may be
inferred, the prime target of the court's attentions. Many of their sexual
partners were named, even when there was no indication that they were
separately prosecuted. The very large number of cases, closely examined,
makes it possible to get a real insight into the moral climate of late
fifteenth-century London – indeed, in its main outlines, the picture is
probably true also for the early decades of the sixteenth century, less well

Table 6.1 *London Commissary Court Prosecutions, 1495*

	M	F	HW	Total
Defamation	95	113	26	234
Adultery	220	80	—	300
Fornication	66	24	—	90
Other incontinence	2	1	—	3
Common whore	—	55	—	55
Bawdry	22	50	42	114
Erroneous opinions on sex	1	—	—	1
Marriage issues	3	4	—	7
Other offences	—	—	—	191
Unknown	—	—	—	19
Total				1,014

Key: M = male; F = female; HW = married couple.

covered though these are by the surviving records. If even half of what was alleged in court had substance, this was a city teeming with illicit sex. Yet it was by no means a lawless society, and many people were eager to bring sexual transgressors into question, whether by formal or informal means.

Including a small number of cases where the matter at issue is unknown, the miscellany of prosecutions that did not deal with sex, marriage or defamation made up about a fifth of the total in this year. While it would be beside the point to analyse them in detail, some of these cases are worth a comment because they shed interesting light on the relationship between the court and the wider society at this moment in time. If there were few prosecutions for not attending church or failing to observe holy days, this was evidently because persistent behaviour of this sort was rare. Participation in church services was part of social identity, and negligence or dissent was the sign of a bad lot and socially stigmatized. Thus John Richardson was brought in question not only for being suspect in faith and disobedient to the church but also for beating his own mother. But London was large enough and sufficiently complex both socially and culturally to produce the occasional individual who challenged the church's claims despite the risk of heresy charges. Robert Bonde of St Gabriel Fenchurch, a fruiterer, withheld tithes and other church dues, claiming that he was bound to pay them by 'nother goddes law nor manys law'. He refused to be sworn, saying defiantly, 'and ye make me force bere a fagat avant Pollis grosse [i.e. Paul's Cross] I will not swere uppon a boke ... I will not swer for all the men on lyff' and brushed off the sentence of excommunication with 'tut for this curse ye shall blesse me agayn'. On another occasion he had asserted that 'the preste hathe no more power to curse me then I hym and I sett not a turde for hys curse.' 'These wordes towche heresy, then ye shal be a loller,' warned the judge drily.[25]

Bonde's defiance was exceptionally self-conscious. It was less unusual for the court officials to face abuse, if only on the spur of the moment from exasperated defendants, or for spiritual sanctions to be set at naught by recalcitrant individuals. When he did not get the answer he wanted, one man (in fact, a priest) told the commissary 'than me thinkkith ye be nane juge for me'. Simon Phyppys of St Andrew Hubbard said, 'I wyl not set for no curse' and 'I wil not swer for no man alyve.' One Taylour of St Andrew Baynard Castle said openly in the Dragon inn, 'I wyl not aper for no man' and before the commissary said, 'I set not by the curse on[e] strawe,' whereas the wife of Thomas Sympson of St Stephen Coleman Street abused the summoner and other court officers, saying, 'A thou false knave and false ye be al.'[26]

Such cases are a reminder that respect for the courts was by no means universal. Yet disgruntled expressions of this sort – which usually provoked a vigorous reaction from the judges – were in fact just a minor element swamped in the sheer mass of ordinary prosecutions. Approaching a quarter of the cases in 1495 were complaints of defamation. Business on this scale – far exceeding that found in provincial jurisdictions around the same time – indicates a society that was very concerned indeed with matters of reputation, in a context in which people of ill-fame faced an ever-present threat of court action. But legal dangers were only one dimension of what was suffered by victims of defamation. It also brought into question their local standing and social identity and, more basically, attacked their sense of personal integrity. In St Swithin's parish in 1494, a woman was slandered with having had a child by a priest. 'Thow liest upon me!' she responded bitterly, and when the defamer – in this case a man – later sought her pardon, she declared, 'Thow art never abyll to make me amendys.'[27]

---

[25] LMA, DL/C/B/043/MS09064/6, fos. 102v, 104r.   [26] *Ibid.*, fos. 113v, 123r, 124r, 160r.
[27] LMA, DL/C/A/002/MS09065, fo. 227(228)r–v.

The numbers are all the more striking in that the cases that came to court cannot possibly have reflected the full range of invective exchanged on the streets of late fifteenth-century London. As was seen in Chapter 2, the canon law of defamation was mainly concerned with the imputation of crimes or at least words that could be interpreted as imputing a crime.[28] Mere abuse or disparaging invective – such as calling someone a base fellow, fool, boy or ass – was unlikely to find legal remedy, even though it could be extremely wounding and provoking, especially in exchanges between individuals touchy about their status. However, at this point, the court was still hearing cases concerning a wide range of issues, not just offences subject to ecclesiastical jurisdiction, so sexual slanders jostled with those to do with secular crimes. The victims in these cases were mostly men.[29] This still left a large number of cases that had to do with sex.

Procedurally, the court facilitated actions by deliberately blurring the normal distinction between 'office' (disciplinary) and 'instance' (party-and-party) causes. Cases were prosecuted on the grounds that the accused were 'common' defamers or 'disturbers' of their neighbours (terms used interchangeably for men and women) or 'common' scolds (mostly women) – in other words, the imputation was that they were habitual or inveterate offenders or had defamed and harassed many of their neighbours. About a quarter of cases were simply of this type, and presumably arose from neighbourhood complaints reported to the court via the usual channels. In the great majority of cases, however, the charge of being a common scold or defamer was supplemented by the information that in particular – or 'in especial' as it was sometimes written in English – the accused had slandered one or more specific individuals. These individuals clearly had an interest in the case, and it is plain, from the fact that they often appeared in person, that they had been instrumental in bringing cases to court – perhaps by themselves reporting them directly to the summoners or other court officers, perhaps indirectly via complaints to clergy, church-wardens or other leading parishioners. If cases of this sort could not be settled easily, what usually happened was that the defendants underwent compurgation to clear themselves of the 'general' charge – that their offence was 'common' – while the specific slander was remitted to the bishop's consistory court to be tried by 'instance' procedures, which included the formal examination of witnesses.

---

[28] See Chapter 2.
[29] LMA, DL/C/B/043/MS09064/6, fos. 92r, 99r, 107r (falsehood/perjury), 108v, 111v, 135r (theft), 168v, 176r (murder).

In light of the findings of previous chapters, it will come as no surprise that in London as elsewhere women were the main targets of sexual slanders. Some were specific – accusations of adultery, bigamy, having children by other men or having borne children before marriage. But more common were generic terms of sexual abuse. Variants on the term 'whore' were predictably prominent, with 'harlot' running a close second. The bare words hardly convey the force of such accusations, since as usual they were often made more powerful and hurtful by reiteration, by associating them with other moral failings that were not necessarily strictly defamatory or by being embroidered with telling detail. Characteristic examples were 'strong hore and proud herlat', 'strong horre and herlote and a landloper' (i.e. renegade or vagabond) and 'strong hore and herlot . . . I coude have taken her betwene a mannys legges'.[30]

Another significant cluster of aspersions against women, though numerically far fewer than accusations of whoredom, were slanders of being a bawd, whether with reference to particular clients ('strong bawde and yn aspecial Master Paston his bawde') or as mere abuse ('olde baude, balde baude and hore baude')[31]; sometimes 'bawd' was coupled with other accusations of whoredom or theft.[32] Married couples were also a frequent target of slanders of bawdry, and some men were similarly defamed. Taking all the cases together, defaming people of being bawds was much more common in London than in the courts of rural England, reflecting primarily the ubiquitous presence of the sex trade in the capital but also the unusual prevalence of a wide variety of sexual transgressions in the metropolitan setting and the many circumstances in which individuals might be thought to have aided and abetted them.

More characteristic of male victims was to be slandered as 'whoreson' or 'cuckold', words that in principle reflected on the sexual misbehaviour of their mothers or wives, though in practice they were often bandied about as mere terms of abuse. However, the majority of male victims complained of slanders of clear-cut sexual or marital transgressions, such as adultery or bigamy, and the more generalized terms of abuse were sometimes given substance with further detail. Thus Richard Thirlthorp of St Bartholomew the Less called Robert Tomson 'strong cocold', going on to allege that he had sold his wife to a certain Thomas Butler for ten marks and moreover had another wife living.[33] Occasionally, men were accused of being

---

[30] *Ibid.*, fos. 150r, 156r, 181v. As will be seen in Chapter 8, variants on 'priest's whore' were likewise frequent.
[31] *Ibid.*, fos. 94r, 129r   [32] E.g. *ibid.*, fos. 143v, 188r.   [33] *Ibid.*, fo. 124v.

inveterate sexual offenders – 'strong horemonger and vouterer' – with or without the addition of other abusive epithets.[34] Such outbursts indicate that male sexual transgressions were by no means always taken for granted or condoned. Husbands and wives, or whole groups of neighbours, were sometimes comprehensively slandered with portmanteau terms of abuse. 'Whores and bawds'; 'whores and maintainers of bawds'; 'whores, thieves and bawds'; 'whores, harlots, thieves'; 'whores, knaves and thieves' and 'whores and strong priests' whores': these were characteristic combinations, reflecting the kinds of neighbours that people did not want.

At this distance in time, many of these slanders appear intemperate, if not trivial. As in the provinces, cases often arose out of interpersonal tensions and neighbourhood disputes that really had little or nothing to do with sex. In some cases, the term 'whore' was being used not with reference to specific sexual transgression but rather in the much more general sense of 'worthless and deceitful woman', or this and other sexual slanders were seized upon in tit-for-tat altercations simply because they were the handiest means of denigrating and humiliating someone to whom one bore ill-will. Elizabeth Hore of St Mildred Poultry upbraided Margery Renald, 'A, thow dame, thy moder stole me a poding, thow prowde drabbe and skotysh hore, bring home the poding thy moder stole', while John Warde of St Nicholas Shambles warned Alice Merys, 'Knowyst not thow that menne know the wel inough, that thow wert the dethe of thy husbande and causid hym to be slayne lyk a hore as thow arte.' Margaret Garter of Whitechapel, accused of slandering Amy Wilson, admitted that 'she callid me hore and I callid her agayn likewyse.'[35]

Yet, in this metropolitan setting, even apparently trivial slanders could have serious consequences. At first sight, Geoffrey Coo's gibe to his servant Edmund, 'Goo knave and skowre a hole that was not skowrid not of all this forthnyght', was no more than a coarse joke. Yet the woman who complained, Margaret Wilson of St Michael Queenhithe, undoubtedly had cause for concern: she had been cited to court for adultery with Edmund and for being a common whore. Likewise it was said that Andrew Gressopp of St George Pudding Lane, who slandered the wife of the 'drawer' at the Saracen's Head as a whore, 'thus ... accuses her to the archdeacon's official'.[36] Cecily Guysnes of St Sepulchre's, who declared that 'this xx[ti] winter I had never no good woman dwelling with me' was herself treated as a bawd as well as a defamer, presumably on the assumption that she was

---

[34] *Ibid.*, fo. 184r.   [35] LMA, DL/C/B/043/MS09064/6, fos. 89v, 103r, 164r.
[36] *Ibid.*, fos. 89r, 97r.

responsible for the bad character of this succession of servants and might well have profited from their transgressions.[37] In London, slander on the open street, however trivial at first sight, was undoubtedly part of the system of moral policing, one of the means whereby suspicions were crystallized and bad reputations were confirmed and publicized in ways that were likely to bring offenders to the notice of the church courts, the civic authorities or both.

But of greater significance are the even larger numbers of cases in which people were brought directly in question for sexual and sex-related offences. In line with the pattern of slanders, prosecutions for 'bawdry' or aiding and abetting sexual offenders were far more prominent than in rural areas or even in provincial towns. Commonly, defendants were charged with being a common bawd (*communis pronuba*) or with bawdry (*pronubacia*); less often it was said that individuals 'fostered' or promoted bawdry or immorality (*fovet lenocinium*). One of these variants was the prime charge in well over a hundred cases – of which 44 per cent were directed against women, 18 per cent against men and the rest against married couples. Bawdry was also a subsidiary charge in many other cases of defamation or sexual transgression. A few of the accused were in trouble for what in a later period was called 'harbouring': that is, providing shelter for illicitly pregnant women during the time of their delivery and while they recovered afterwards. However necessary it might be, such behaviour was clearly discountenanced. Thus Mary Rychcrosse, a cypress dyer of St Martin Vintry, was said to have had 'from year to year and at present has a woman pregnant in her house to the evil and pernicious example of others'.[38] But mostly what was at issue was not harbouring pregnant women but actually assisting couples to have illicit sex, either by procuring, acting as a go-between or providing accommodation of some sort. These premises did not include the Southwark stews, since they were outside the jurisdiction of the commissary of London. However, there were frequent references to alehouses, taverns and inns – the signs mentioned included the Angel, the George in Lombard Street, the Key of St Andrew, the Swan near Newgate and the Woolsack in St Sepulchre's.[39] But most of the premises involved were private houses, and if they were brothels, it was only in an informal sense or on a temporary basis. This is consistent with the official stance that bawdy houses were not to be tolerated in the city itself. Apart from landlords or landladies of inns and similar

---

[37] *Ibid.*, fo. 138v.　　[38] LMA, DL/C/B/043/MS09064/6, fo. 130v.
[39] *Ibid.*, fos. 111v, 128r, 172r, 174v, 179v.

establishments, the status and occupations of accused bawds were a miscellany – males among them included a buckle maker, butcher, cypress dyer, founder, pinner, purser, shoemaker, tailor and a vestment maker. Only one of the women was specifically said to have been a widow, but there may have been others hidden among the females accused on their own. 'Mother (*moder*) Plum' and 'Mother Tomson' were evidently middle-aged or older women.[40]

As the variety of premises and occupations suggests, there was no clear dividing line between commercial and non-commercial activities. Some of the accused were complicit in occasional or even casual liaisons. Others were lodging women whom men visited regularly, treating them as concubines or long-term mistresses. In either case, such assistance usually had to be paid for. Furthermore, many 'bawds' were active in arranging sexual services as a regular business proposition. Several men were said to be bawds to their own wives. In other cases, men, women or married couples were accused of being bawds to their daughters. More commonly, householders were charged with being bawds to female servants or other women residing with them. The exact circumstances are often hard to fathom; in particular, it is hard to know how much agency the women had – whether willing participants or victims of exploitation.

A case against a certain Brian Studbery and his wife contained the most graphic account of a clandestine brothel. In their house in St Mary Colechurch, they were said to keep a private corner for committing sexual transgressions, ingeniously using the customers' 'tabs' scrawled on a board or on a wall as a means of disguising payment for illicit sex. The word on the street was that 'yff ye will have a fayr gentilwoman go to Bryan['s] taverne and ther stryk out one of the skoris and pay ij^s and spede your erand and go your weys.' Less well served were the customers of Thomas Heavison of St Sepulchre's, prosecuted in 1494. He was charged with committing adultery with his servant and also acting as her bawd, but there was more to it than that. He led her to guests and visitors to the house and knowingly allowed her to have sex with them; he then made his wife go to the rooms to take the couple in bed together, forcing the men concerned to pay money to avoid being reported for immorality. That such a scam was possible underlines the extent to which this was a society under surveillance. While sex outside marriage was possible, even commonplace, liaisons had to be conducted with circumspection, and there was the ever-present danger of discovery.[41]

---

[40] *Ibid.*, fos. 98v, 147r.   [41] *Ibid.*, fos. 5v, 126r.

Women charged with bawdry were often accused also of being whores or common whores, or where a husband and wife were prosecuted together, the man was said to be a bawd and his wife a whore – much as the two epithets were often coupled in cases of slanderous words. In addition, there were fifty-five women against whom the prime charge was that of being a common whore (*communis meretrix*). These may well have represented the hard core of women involved in the sex trade. Yet the charges against them were by no means wholly stereotyped. Sometimes they were accused of being whores to whole groups or classes of people, such as 'Lombards and priests' or 'married men, single men, ordained men and other priests' or 'apprentices of the city'; this reinforced the imputation of promiscuity.[42] But in well over 40 per cent of cases, one or more male partners were specifically named; in this sense, these were quite firm charges of sexual transgression, comparable to accusations of adultery or fornication with particular men. As will be seen in Chapter 8, a sizeable proportion of the women charged with being common whores were accused of transgressing with priests. However, the clients of a certain Joan Burdet look to have been a selection of high-status professionals, not all of whom were clergy. She was accused with 'divers priests', including the Master of St Bartholomew's Hospital – at this time Thomas Crewker – while the names of 'Master Bennett' and one Skynner, 'attorn[ey] in le yeld hall', were added to the charge.[43]

Designated 'common whores' were not the only habitual offenders, however. Collating the names of the women identified as the partners of men prosecuted for adultery and fornication reveals many who were in trouble on only one occasion but also some who were repeatedly in question and were probably professionals or semi-professionals. The most notable were Katherine Saunders alias 'Flying Kate', named four times or more in 1495; Agnes or Nan Coverdale, named six times at least; Katherine Wright, named on seven occasions; Joan Popy alias 'Little Joan', named at least six times; and Joan Tankard, named with six men and mentioned in other cases in ways that suggest that she made premises available for illicit rendezvous.

'Fornication' and 'adultery' were the main categories of sexual transgression found in these records. Even more than in rural areas, the latter was very prominent. In 1495 there were ninety prosecutions for fornication but

---

[42] *Ibid.*, fos. 89v, 110r, 118v.
[43] *Ibid.*, fo. 182v; Norman Moore, *The History of St Bartholomew's Hospital*, 2 vols. (London, 1918), Vol. II, pp. 114–17.

more than three times as many (around 300) that used some variant on the language of adultery.[44] In both adultery and fornication cases, many of the sexual partners of the individuals cited to court were not, as far as can be seen, separately prosecuted. The names or identities of some of them were simply unknown, but most were actually named, whereas the remainder were either partially named – 'Alice his maidservant' and the like – or at least given some kind of circumstantial description, such as 'the landlord of *le grene Dragon*' (a famous Southwark inn).[45] The record includes nearly 400 references of this kind. While some were repeat offenders, over 350 separate individuals were thus mentioned in addition to the principal defendants. In a little over one case in ten, an illicit pregnancy or illegitimate birth was mentioned; the proportion was slightly higher among women named as the prime defendant in fornication cases. Evidently this was seen as a significant issue but does not seem to have been the overriding concern of those who detected offenders.[46]

While it is clear that – as is commonly the case in pre-Reformation church court records – the terms 'fornication' and 'adultery' were used quite loosely and sometimes interchangeably, there were broad differences between the two categories. Those accused of fornication plainly included many young people who were not yet married but were eligible to be so. Their sexual activities were evidently regarded as understandable, perhaps natural, even though they were supposed to be reprehensible. It was probably considerations like these that made the lesser charge of fornication seem appropriate and also explain why there were far fewer prosecutions for this offence than for adultery; a blind eye was turned in many cases. Some of those who were accused were simply unlucky. Agnes Marle 'was taken by her mistress' having sex with Thomas At Hilton, while the maidservant of Mistress Campion, reported for a similar offence with Thomas Leving, confessed but said she only 'committed' once.[47] Other couples were prosecuted because although they had entered into a contract of marriage, they seemed to be deferring the actual solemnization in church for far too long. However, some men clearly never planned to marry but instead were keeping women in long-term relationships or as concubines.

[44] About a dozen such cases may be set aside for the moment because, though the Latin for adultery was used in formulating the charge, they were basically about bigamy. These cases are discussed later as a point of comparison with bigamy cases in 1512.

[45] LMA, DL/C/B/043/MS09064/6, fo. 155v.

[46] This is consistent with the fact that (as noted earlier) harbouring pregnant women accounted for only a minority of 'bawdry' cases.

[47] LMA, DL/C/B/043/MS09064/6, fos. 118r, 188v.

Predictably enough, maidservants sometimes slipped into this role.[48] There were also habitually promiscuous fornicators like William Sharpe of St Mary Magdalen Old Fish Street, notorious for relations 'with many women married and single' and in particular with Elizabeth Saunder alias Besse Freyr; his activities with her had been well noted, for the charge specified the day of the offence and the fact that he had received her in his chamber for two hours, the doors and windows of the house being closed.[49] Males were the prime defendants in the great majority of 'fornication' cases. Setting aside for the moment the 13 per cent or more who were priests, the social status of the accused varied quite widely, including some from quite high-status occupations.

The bulk of the principal defendants in the 'adultery' cases were likewise male. An even higher proportion – about 15 per cent – were priests, a circumstance that will be addressed in Chapter 8. Otherwise, their social status varied widely. If anything, there were rather more individuals of high rank among the accused adulterers than among the fornicators, including Master John Warde, alderman of Bishopsgate ward, former mayor and shortly to be elected member of parliament for London for the third time.[50] Much less eminent but locally prominent was the beadle of the ward of Farringdon Without, resident in St Bride's parish.[51] A wide range of trades were represented among other alleged adulterers.[52] Some defendants were clearly poor, but most were probably of middling wealth. The status of the accused women was less often noted. 'Magistra scolamaster' of St Nicholas Cole Abbey, who was indeed the schoolmaster's wife, was in trouble on one occasion.[53] Otherwise, the few women distinguished with courtesy titles were in question with members of the clergy.[54] All these facts about the status and identity of the accused suggest that court officials tended to use the term 'adultery' not only in the case of married people, especially householders, but more generally to denote people in some position of authority. In other words, these were offenders who ought to have known better. Noticeable also is that a significant proportion of the alleged adulterers were described in terms that suggested that they were repeat or even habitual offenders – another circumstance

---

[48] E.g. LMA, DL/C/B/043/MS09064/6, fo. 145r. [49] LMA, DL/C/B/043/MS09064/6, fo. 153r.
[50] LMA, DL/C/B/043/MS09064/6, fo. 102v; Alfred B. Beaven, *The Aldermen of the City of London*, 2 vols. (London, 1908–13), Vol. I, pp. 35, 273.
[51] LMA, DL/C/B/043/MS09064/6, fo. 182r.
[52] They included baker, capper, cobbler, cutler, draper, dyer, fishmonger, fuller, girdler, linen weaver, miller, pointmaker, pouchmaker, purser, shearman, shoemaker, skinner, tailor, wiredrawer and goldwiredrawer.
[53] LMA, DL/C/B/043/MS09064/6, fos. 186v, 187r. [54] *Ibid.*, fos. 93r, 122v; see also Chapter 8.

that probably made the charge of 'adultery' seem appropriate. It is clear from some cases that the Latin word *adulter* stood proxy for the English 'whoremaster' or 'whoremonger'.[55]

A few of these alleged adulterers were what we would today refer to as bigamists, a point to which we shall return. Many were behaving in ways similar to the more inveterate fornicators. Some, whether laymen or clergy, were serial users of prostitutes. Others were 'keeping' – the term implied longer-term relationships, usually involving financial support – one or more women, some of whom were described as their concubines or more familiarly as their whores. In the provinces, instances of such behaviour were few and far between. In London, they were, if not commonplace, at least a much more recognizable feature of the social landscape. While some of these women were maintained in inns or alehouses or elsewhere, a striking number of men seem to have carried on long-standing relationships with servants or other females in their own households. Particularly blatant was the case of Vincent van Baven of St Alban Wood Street; he was said to be a common adulterer, especially with a certain Margaret 'whom he keeps beside him just like his own wife, though she is not, having a husband beyond seas'.[56] For lawful wives, the consequences of the husband's adultery could be dire. At Stratford le Bow it was said that George Sayer's liaison with another woman caused his wife's death, whereupon he married the mistress. Prat the 'podingman' of St Margaret Bridge Street, accused of adultery with his servant, was said to have got rid of his wife by poisoning her. The behaviour of Smyth the brewer was little better: he not only committed adultery with his servant but brutally beat his wife and threw her out of the house.[57]

Not all wives allowed themselves to be passive victims. The wife of the Brentford almshouse keeper, for example, on discovering that he was keeping another woman, attacked her and broke her arm. Richard Ady, cited to court for adultery with his maidservant, incriminated himself by the rueful admission that 'I had sorow inoughe of my wyff therfor.'[58] While male adultery can hardly have been an uncommon occurrence, it nonetheless had the potential to arouse much bitterness and resentment. Equally, though there were habitual offenders and men who conducted long-term relationships, such behaviour usually led to a build-up of local disapproval which would sooner or later result in legal action. Against this background, it seems likely that most acts of adultery committed by

[55] *Ibid.*, fos. 34r, 187v.   [56] *Ibid.*, fo. 158r.   [57] *Ibid.*, fos. 141r, 174r, 179r.
[58] *Ibid.*, fos. 90r, 143r.

London men were opportunistic and that the commonest form of liaison was with an ordinary maidservant as occasion offered. The archetypal adulterer was probably someone like Thomas Tryfelde of St Mary Fenchurch. According to his maidservant Elizabeth, he had had sex with her twice on the pallet in her chamber, each time on a Sunday when his wife was at church.[59]

Changing Patterns of Prosecution in the Early Sixteenth Century

The main contours of illicit sexual activity in late fifteenth-century London, so vividly revealed in the voluminous records of those years, probably remained much the same in the early decades of the new century. Some of what went on was similar to the patterns of behaviour common elsewhere in England, including surreptitious sexual activity between courting couples and the usual run of opportunistic extramarital encounters, especially between masters and maidservants. More distinctive of the metropolitan environment were a lively, albeit clandestine sex trade and the relative frequency of more or less long-term irregular relationships, facilitated by the urban topography, the sheer availability of potential partners of various social ranks and perhaps the example of foreigners living in the city.[60] The will that Diego Sanchez, a Spaniard resident in London, made in 1537 reveals that he had maintained a long-standing liaison with his 'sclave' Joan; his wife was instructed to keep this woman as her servant for two years before freeing her and also to bring up and eventually endow the two female children that she had borne. One of Sanchez' two sons was also stated to be a bastard.[61]

To take a few native English examples of lengthy relationships from 1529 – the last complete year for which commissary court records survive before the Reformation – Roger Wright of West Ham was said to have lived with Margery Stafford for twelve years continuously, while William Locke of an unnamed parish had lived in fornication for a year with Margaret Dixon 'as his wife'; quite why the first case had taken so long to come to court is unclear, though since the man had been suspended from the services of the church, the matter had apparently not passed

---

[59] *Ibid.*, fo. 107r.
[60] For some points of comparison, see Ruth Mazo Karras, *Unmarriages: Women, Men, and Sexual Unions in the Middle Ages* (Philadelphia, 2012).
[61] Ida Darlington (ed.), *London Consistory Court Wills, 1492–1547* (London Record Society, 1967), p. 62.

completely unnoticed.[62] Margery Nevell of St Peter Cornhill was accused of 'incontinence' with William Goddescoke, Hugh Egerton and Sir Henry Spyt (probably a priest). She confessed adultery with Egerton for a period of four years, receiving from him occasional payments – sometimes 12d., sometimes 20d., sometimes 2s.[63]

However, early sixteenth-century London was clearly still very much a society subject to the surveillance of neighbours, who might not be able to prevent sexual transgressions but could usually bring them to light. Gossip was rife among both men and women. As one accused adulteress protested, she could not 'restrain the tongues of men who will speak evil of her'.[64] In 1512 it was a matter for comment that Hugh Acton of St Antholin's had kept Agnes Lynne for three years, while Robert Smyth, a barber of St Sepulchre's, had long maintained an adulterous relationship with a woman in the Middlesex parish of Hornsey, 'whereby great infamy has arisen among the people'.[65] Sexual misdoing, especially if sustained, could arouse enormous resentment that frequently boiled over into abuse on the open streets. With a fine display of invective, in 1512, John Bekkett and his wife challenged Alice Taverner: '[T]hou art a brodell herlotte and was kepped at rak and mawnger in Pater Noster Rew, fals fylth we know itt well ynough.'[66] In contrast, some defendants claimed to be offering their victims wholesome advice rather than spitefully defaming them. Thus Joan Bakster claimed that she spoke 'with a mind to turn him to good' when she accused John Percyvall of adultery with Thomas Worthyngton's wife, having heard the accusation from another woman.[67] More commonly, defamers claimed justification or offered to 'prove' their accusations. They presented themselves as accusers rather than slanderers.[68]

But if the social context had not much changed between the late fifteenth and the early sixteenth centuries, the same is not true of the pattern of prosecutions found in the commissary court. If the record for 1495 is compared with that for 1512 – a date chosen to provide a point of comparison with the surviving Southwark materials – the changes that had occurred in less than two decades appear quite drastic.[69] It is not simply that there were far fewer cases in 1512, between 325 and 350 instead of over a thousand in 1495. Nor is it merely the fact that, as Wunderli has noticed,

[62] LMA, DL/C/B/041/MS09065J/2, fos. 153r, 153v.   [63] *Ibid.*, fos. 163v, 166r, 170v.
[64] LMA, DL/C/B/041/MS09065J/1, fo. 38r (1519).
[65] LMA, DL/C/B/043/MS09064/11, fos. 46v, 49v.   [66] *Ibid.*, fo. 67v.   [67] *Ibid.*, fo. 46v.
[68] E.g. LMA, DL/C/B/043/MS09064/11, fos. 39r, 42r, 67v, 71r.
[69] LMA, DL/C/B/043/MS09064/11, fos. 32r–88v comprise the record for 1512.

the record of proceedings was more formal and detailed, marked in particular by the greater use of witnesses, especially in slander cases. More basically, the composition of the business was quite different. Far and away the most common kind of case in 1512 concerned defamation: there were over 150 prosecutions of this nature. Moreover, though defendants were generally described initially as *common* defamers, it is evident that the real substance of the very great majority of cases was a specific slander, brought to the attention of the court by one or more individual complainants. In other words, these were party-and-party suits masquerading as disciplinary prosecutions; in some cases, this was underscored by the fact that after the initial entry, prosecutions were continued in the manner of instance suits in the form 'Smyth *contra* Jolybrand', 'Sheperd *contra* Kynkhorn' and so forth.

In contrast, genuine 'criminal' cases – in the sense of disciplinary prosecutions – were quite few in number, hardly more than in the Southwark church court in the same year, even though the latter served a much smaller and less populous area. Thus there were only forty-one cases described in terms of adultery, thirty-nine cases of fornication and a further seventeen cases of sexual transgression referring ambiguously to either fornication or adultery or expressed in different terms – often with reference to the outcome of the illicit relationship, notably an illicit pregnancy or illegitimate child.[70] In addition, there were five prosecutions of women said to be common whores; eleven cases of bawdry; nineteen cases of repudiating, impeding or deferring the solemnization of marriage contracts; one case of clandestine marriage; and seven cases of bigamy. The tally of cases in 1512 was made up by thirty-five miscellaneous cases (thirty-nine if prosecutions with more than one defendant are counted as multiples) – mostly concerning tithes and other 'spiritual' dues, together with a few testamentary cases and prosecutions for clerical faults, neglect of religious duties and contempt of court.

Wunderli hypothesizes that the reduced numbers of cases resulted from a collapse of public confidence in ecclesiastical justice, but, as Susan Brigden has observed, this suggestion raises puzzles of its own, since the collapse would have had to be catastrophic in scale and extremely sudden.[71] Wunderli's complementary argument, that Londoners had recourse instead to the secular courts, is equally open to question. Undoubtedly

---

[70] However, in some cases described as 'fornication' or 'adultery', the fact of illegitimacy or illicit pregnancy was also noted.

[71] Wunderli, *London Church Courts*, pp. 4, 23, 61–2, 102, 137–8; cf. Brigden, *London and the Reformation*, pp. 146, 199.

the existence of a parallel system of civic justice over sexual offenders – to be explored in Chapter 7 – did offer an alternative means of action. But while the court of aldermen may have increased its activity in the sphere of sexual regulation in the 1510s, and certainly did so in the 1520s, the scale of its operations remained numerically quite small and cannot possibly have compensated for the drastic fall in commissary court prosecutions. At the same time, there is no reason to think that the city's lower-level wardmote courts were notably more active in the early sixteenth century than they had been in the late fifteenth. It might be asked why, in any case, should people not use both sets of courts as they undoubtedly did to some extent. Yet, as will be seen in Chapter 7, there is some evidence that by the early sixteenth century people were indeed choosing to report cases *either* to the wardmote inquest *or* to the church courts. As a consequence, levels of business in the latter would have suffered.

Probably it is a mistake to seek one single reason for the decline in numbers of commissary court prosecutions; more plausible is to imagine a combination of changing circumstances. One possibility is that the surviving record represents no more than a subset of the disciplinary cases that were actually prosecuted, so that the apparent fall in numbers is, at least in part, an optical illusion. As noted earlier, the records of the archdeaconry court have been lost, while it could well be that the bishop's officers were by this time – as was the case in the later sixteenth century – keeping a separate series of records of visitation proceedings which do not survive. The absence of such visitation records could go far to explain the fall in numbers. Indications of the means by which cases were brought to the attention of the court in 1512 may offer some support for this hypothesis. The overwhelming majority of cases were introduced with the formula *notatur officio* or *notatur officio fama publica referente* – delated to the office or brought to the attention of the office on the report of common fame. Visitation presentments by churchwardens and the sworn men of the parishes were implicitly excluded. Particular informers seem to have been involved, though they were rarely identified. A prosecution against Joan Brown for adultery, her husband living in Ware, was said to be 'by Kyrkham', who was one of the summoners of the court.[72]

Alternative explanations, assuming that the fall in numbers was a real one, are perforce equally speculative. Epidemic disease was certainly responsible for very high mortality in London in the years around 1500,

---

[72] LMA, DL/C/B/043/MS09064/11, fo. 36r.

and this may have been a cause of reduced numbers of prosecutions in the early years of the new century.[73] But other factors must be brought into play to explain why the change was perpetuated. The miscellaneous cases recorded in 1512 reflect one important jurisdictional shift that had occurred since the late fifteenth century – debt suits in the guise of prosecutions for 'breach of faith' had been virtually eliminated. This had been achieved by aggressive action by judges in the royal courts, threatening to use the fearsome weapon of 'praemunire' proceedings if the spiritual courts continued to handle temporal matters. (They had not yet acted to ban slanders of secular crime from the church courts, so a sizeable proportion of the defamation cases – approaching 15 per cent – still concerned imputations of theft, perjury, false dealing and even murder, but they were soon to do so.)[74] It is possible that the fear engendered by these tactics deterred lay people from having recourse to the church courts on other matters, even the sexual transgressions that had traditionally been the staple of their business, or that ecclesiastical court officials became extremely circumspect about handling them. But if so, this was an effect confined to London: there is no sign of a similar impact on disciplinary proceedings in the diocese of Chichester or the archdeaconry of Leicester, discussed in Chapter 3. Jurisdictional wrangles within the church may also have been a factor. Already the episcopate of Richard Hill (1489–96) had been marked by conflicts with Archbishop Morton, and cases concerning the usurpation or contempt of the commissary's jurisdiction were unusually prominent in the closing years of the century. But whether this was a cause or a consequence of declining activity is a moot point.[75]

To approach the issue from another angle, the number of cases recorded in 1495 and other years of similarly high, or even higher, totals is quite astonishing, seemingly without parallel before or after the Reformation. Quite possibly this surge in prosecutions in Yorkist and early Tudor times represented a self-conscious 'push' on the part of the ecclesiastical authorities, a determined effort to bring the sexual behaviour of Londoners in line with Christian standards. Not enough is known of the commissaries of this period, William Wylde and Richard Blodwell, to infer how far they themselves may have promoted such a policy. But it is certainly consistent with the episcopal priorities not only of Richard Hill, a pastorally minded bishop who conducted visitations with care, but

---

[73] Wunderli, *London Church Courts*, pp. 21–3.
[74] R. H. Helmholz, *Roman Canon Law in Reformation England* (Cambridge, 1990), pp. 30–4.
[75] *ODNB*, Richard Hill; Hale, *Precedents*, pp. 46–7, 52, 63–4; cf. Wunderli, *London Church Courts*, p. 16.

also of his long-serving predecessor Thomas Kempe (1448–89), an able and devoted diocesan.[76] At the same time, the impetus may not have been wholly ecclesiastical. Comparable efforts to impose 'order', albeit not on the same massive scale, are visible in some secular courts.[77]

Yet, from an administrative standpoint, to maintain such a high level of activity indefinitely was probably impossible; as has been seen, even in the late fifteenth century, very high numbers of prosecutions were not sustained every year. It may also be that such intensity of legal action came to seem undesirable from a pastoral or neighbourly point of view, especially since – as will be demonstrated later – relatively few prosecutions led to convictions. This state of affairs could hardly fail to generate resentment, or at least a sense of futility. Already in the later fifteenth century people were highly sensitive to slurs on their reputation; they may have become more so as time went on, discouraging charges of sexual transgression unless they were well founded. At the same time, clergy and lay people alike may have come to feel that many matters of suspect sexual behaviour were better dealt with in the privacy of the confessional than in the open forum of the church courts, especially if, as may indeed have been the case, the practice of regular confession was better observed in the early sixteenth century than it had been a generation or two earlier. As was seen in Chapter 2, it had always been an issue in canon law in what circumstances it was right to go beyond the private reproof or admonition of suspected transgressors to bring them to court, thus exposing them to public obloquy. In the London commissary court in the late fifteenth century, the hurdle had apparently been set extremely low; people might be brought in question on the slightest suspicion and expected to defend their reputation publicly. In the new century, in contrast, the bar was raised much higher, and the court became primarily a defender of people's reputations against unjust or maliciously motivated charges.

As usual, the contribution of individuals to changing policies is hard to pinpoint. In office as commissary during the watershed years around 1500 was John Perot. As little is known of him as of his predecessors and indeed also of his successors in the 1500s and the 1510s. The bishop of London from 1496 to 1501 was Thomas Savage, later archbishop of York, a DCL from Padua and a trusted servant of Henry VII – in fact, the president of

---

[76] *ODNB*, Thomas Kemp, Richard Hill. On the commissaries, see Hale, *Precedents*, pp. 1, 30; G. D. Squibb, *Doctors' Commons: A History of the College of Advocates and Doctors of Law* (Oxford, 1977), pp. 3, 7, 10, 22, 46, 116, 121.

[77] Marjorie Keniston McIntosh, *Controlling Misbehavior in England, 1370–1600* (Cambridge, 1998), pp. 68–81.

the king's council in the later 1490s. His successors in the next twenty years were William Warham, translated to Canterbury in 1503, William Barons (1504–5) and Richard Fitzjames (1506–22). All these men were notable for firm action against heretics, and indeed the revival of prosecutions against Lollards, beginning in the 1490s and intensifying in subsequent decades, may be another relevant factor in explaining changes in the numbers and make-up of cases in the London commissary court. On this perspective, they may in part reflect a reorientation of the church's priorities from the detection of routine sexual offenders to the hunting out of heretics.[78] It is not inconceivable, indeed, that a much more scrupulous approach to disciplinary prosecutions in general – evinced by more self-consciously legalistic procedures and a decline in the number of cases – was a deliberate attempt to offset public fears of anti-heretical activities. While there is no reason to assume any significant level of popular support for Lollardy in the metropolis, the city may have been unsettled by the burnings in 1494 of the widow of a former mayor and her eighty-year-old mother and by the abjurations and book burnings at Paul's Cross in 1496.[79]

The Pattern of Prosecutions in 1512

Since it is by no means certain that we are comparing like with like, detailed, point-by-point comparison of the proceedings for 1512 with those of 1495 would be futile. But certain differences are worth highlighting because they seem to reflect the evolving preoccupations of the ecclesiastical authorities. In the later year the institution of marriage was much more prominent in the record. In 1495, bigamy cases did not have a particularly high profile. There were in fact twelve of them, but this represented a tiny proportion of the total number of prosecutions, and as noted earlier, the offence was usually described in terms of adultery. This usage in fact followed gospel terminology, the underlying logic being that a bigamous relationship was not a real marriage but an illicit sexual union.[80] A case from St Bride's is noteworthy simply because the female defendant was prepared to express defiance. Accused of being contracted to

---

[78] On the drive against heresy, see John A. F. Thomson, *The Later Lollards, 1414–1520* (London, 1965), chap. 6; Brigden, *London and the Reformation*, chap. 2; Craig D'Alton, 'Heresy Hunting and Clerical Reform: William Warham, John Colet, and the Lollards of Kent, 1511–1512', in Ian Hunter, John Christian Laursen and Cary J. Nederman (eds.), *Heresy in Transition: Transforming Ideas of Heresy in Medieval and Early Modern Europe* (Aldershot, 2005), pp. 103–14; Craig D'Alton, 'The Suppression of Lutheran Heretics in England, 1526–1529', *Journal of Ecclesiastical History*, 54 (2003), 228–53.

[79] Thomson, *Later Lollards*, pp. 155–8.   [80] Mark X.11–12; Matthew V.32; Luke XVI.18.

another man while her first husband was still alive, she retorted that if 'I can not be wede after my owne will I wil be wede at a lawley [i.e. lawless] chirch and aske no man non leve': the case was immediately remitted to a higher court.[81]

The eight bigamy cases recorded in 1512 were relatively much more prominent in the record for that year and suggest that this issue was now more explicitly on the court's agenda. But far from giving the impression that even in the crowded streets of London bigamy was either common or taken for granted, they reflect the vigilance of the authorities and careful local scrutiny. In some cases it was apparently the process of securing solemnization that had led to inquiries that had raised suspicions of bigamy. John Gray of St Mary Magdalen Milk Street, for example, was brought in question in 1512 for the dual offence of publishing the banns of marriage between him and Emery Bartilloter, already having a wife called Katherine living in Ely, and for cohabiting with Emery without solemnizing the union. His explanation was that his first wife was dead and that he had solemnized marriage with his current wife at Hertford, but the court sent him away to secure proof.[82]

The general context, it is clear, was one in which it was assumed that for a marriage to be properly recognized, there had to be a church wedding. Prosecutions relating to disputed marriage contracts give the same impression. The standard charge was refusing to proceed to solemnization,[83] and in several instances the banns of marriage had already been read.[84] Of course, such cases could be taken straight to the consistory as party-and-party suits. But in 1512 about twenty cases came before the commissary – significantly more than in 1495 and representing a far larger proportion of the total number of prosecutions. But while the underlying circumstances were various, it is noticeable that many of these cases had a strong disciplinary element; either the person reneging on the contract was threatening to marry someone else and/or the couple was accused of having had sexual relations – indeed in several cases a baby was already on the way. Some men had seduced a woman by promising marriage, only to abandon her later – some added insult to injury by boasting of their conquest. In cases both of bigamy and of neglect of solemnization, such phrases as 'to the notorious derision', 'mockery' or 'delusion' of the sacrament of marriage occur repeatedly.

<hr />

[81] LMA, DL/C/B/043/MS09064/6, fo. 173v.   [82] LMA, DL/C/B/043/MS09064/11, fo. 66v.
[83] There were also a few cases of 'jactitation', or boasting (i.e. fraudulent claiming) of marriage or impeding the marriage by one means or another.
[84] E.g. LMA, DL/C/B/043/MS09064/11, fos. 74r, 87r.

The impression overall is of a much more self-conscious promotion around this time of the dignity of marriage.[85]

Another big difference between the pattern of cases found in 1512 compared with the late fifteenth century was the very small number of women prosecuted as 'common whores', though the sex trade no doubt continued to flourish. But, as noted earlier, even in 1495 the courts had paid little attention to the most notorious professionals; they were really interested only in individuals willing to repent, or at least make some act of contrition, which did not include women of this kind. It is possible that this attitude was becoming even more pronounced in the early sixteenth century. Alternatively, it may have been felt that common women should properly be left to the secular tribunals, the activities of which will be discussed in Chapter 7. Perhaps on the same principle, cases of aiding and abetting sexual offences were also strikingly rare – in 1512 the commissary handled barely a third of the number of such cases dealt with by the Southwark church court in the same year – and relatively few of those that did occur were clearly associated with the professional sex trade. To be sure, many among the three men, six women and two married couples prosecuted for this offence were said to be 'common' offenders. John Patryk of St Sepulchre's and Margaret Bapethorp of St Andrew Holborn – the latter said to be a 'most vile bawd' – were accused of promoting bawdry between any couple that wanted it, while John Mystylbroke and his wife of St Mildred Bread Street habitually kept suspect women in their house.[86]

The Pattern of Prosecutions in 1519 and 1529

In October 1529, a woman up before the commissary for maintaining bawdry in her house broke out, 'You have callyd me a bawde and I shal meyt with you lyke a powle shorne pryst and a vengeance then take the and yf I am a baude I am your bawde and thy name be Master Doctor Clyff.' This was William Clyffe, Bishop Cuthbert Tunstal's commissary-general since 1522. Referring to the summoner, she added, 'I shall cawse hys crowne to be knockyd . . . lyke a false thefe and false poulyng knave.' There had been other – less elaborate or less fully recorded but essentially similar – outbursts earlier in the year, and it is tempting to link such

---

[85] E.g. *ibid.*, fo. 74r; LMA, DL/C/B/041/MS09065J/1, fos. 112v, 127r; Hale, *Precedents*, pp. 95–6.
[86] LMA, DL/C/B/043/MS09064/11, fos. 61r, 73r, 83v.

expressions of discontent with the impending attack on the privileges of the church, shortly to be unleashed in the Reformation Parliament.[87] Yet, in truth, such attacks were nothing new; similarly striking examples can be found earlier in the 1520s and indeed in any decade for which records survive; some choice examples from 1495 have already been cited.

Nonetheless, there are some hints of strain, the result not so much of attacks from without as of internal tensions. In 1522 and 1523 there was a quite exceptional sequence of cases centring on contested jurisdiction, triggered by the vacancy between the death of Bishop Richard Fitzjames in January 1522 and the consecration of Tunstal in October. Many featured individuals accused of citing persons without proper authority, sometimes with the purpose of compounding with them for money – in other words, of using church discipline as the basis of a protection racket. The main area of contest, it would seem, was between the jurisdiction of the bishop's commissary and that of the archdeacon of London. But the audience court of Cardinal Wolsey, an institution that generated frequent complaints yet whose activities are poorly documented, undoubtedly had the capacity to complicate further an already complex jurisdictional situation. While probate and party-and-party suits were probably affected most, there are some indications that disciplinary business was also being transferred to the cardinal's court.[88]

In this fraught context, it is exceptionally difficult to evaluate the significance of levels of business in the commissary court in the decade before the Reformation Parliament. Sampling of particular years reveals even fewer cases than in 1512, which itself (it will be recalled) yielded a much lower total than in 1495 and even fewer than the peak years of the late fifteenth century. But there were marked inter-annual fluctuations, while the make-up of the case load also varied from year to year. The record for 1519, covering city parishes only, included almost 150 cases, though more than seventy other people were named as partners in sexual transgressions without themselves necessarily being subject to separate prosecutions. Much of the reduction in numbers was simply the result of far fewer cases of defamation – only twenty-three in 1519 compared with over 150 in 1512. A decline in the number of slander cases is to be expected because by this time the secular courts had taken action to prevent the spiritual judges

[87] LMA, DL/C/B/041/MS09065J/2, fo. 201v, cf. fos. 169v, 176v, 185v, 199r. On Clyffe and Tunstal, see *ODNB*.
[88] LMA, DL/C/B/041/MS09065J/1, fos. 126r, 127v, 128r, 131v, 132r, 142v; Hale, *Precedents*, pp. 97–8; Sir Henry Ellis (ed.), *Original Letters Illustrative of English History, 3rd Series*, 4 vols. (London, 1846), Vol. II, pp. 41–2.

from hearing slanders of theft and the like.[89] But the scale of the decline is startling, and it is noticeable that cases were recorded in little detail – often the defendant was simply accused of being a scold or common defamer, and when a particular victim was specified, the actual words of slander were rarely given.

However, the record for 1529 shows some recovery in numbers of defamation cases. Over eighty of them were registered this year, nearly two-thirds of the defendants being women.[90] While many were simple accusations of scolding – overwhelmingly directed against women – or of being a common defamer of the neighbours, a specific victim was named in about half the cases, and in a few instances the actual words or substance of the slander were given. Possibly this represented a crackdown on loose talk likely to lead to poorly founded accusations to the church courts. Two other circumstances boosted the overall total of prosecutions in this year to over 200 (a further thirty-six individuals being named as sexual partners but not separately prosecuted). Firstly, the record included cases from the out-of-town deaneries of Middlesex and Barking. Secondly, there were markedly more prosecutions for bawdry than there had been in 1519. It might almost be said that this year witnessed a drive against them; as will be seen, comparison with the records of the secular courts suggests that this may have been part of a concerted effort.

In contrast, the numbers of sexual transgressions recorded in 1529 were down on the figures for a decade earlier, as also – for no apparent reason – were the figures for certain other offences, such as bigamy. Nomenclature had changed markedly. This year only a minority of cases were described in terms of 'adultery' and only one in terms of 'fornication'; mostly the scribe used the general term 'incontinence' or referred to cases in terms of their outcome, such as illicit pregnancy, with the result that it is even more difficult than usual to infer the underlying circumstances. What is clear is that the proportion of female defendants in sex cases this year was exceptionally high (nearly 60 per cent). A factor that contributed but did not in itself determine this pattern was that no clergy were brought in question, while priests and monks were also much less in evidence than previously among the alleged partners of the women prosecuted for sexual offences.

---

[89] R. H. Helmholz (ed.), *Select Cases on Defamation to 1600* (Selden Society 101, London, 1985), pp. xlii–xlv; Wunderli, *London Church Courts*, pp. 67–8.
[90] Defamation or scolding was the first named charge against eighty-two individuals, while one person against whom the main charge was bawdry was also accused of being a scold. The total falls a little if married couples are counted as one, though in fact at this time the court was apparently treating them separately.

This does not mean, however, that the church courts were ignoring cases of clerical immorality or that the issue was of no public concern. As will be seen in Chapter 8, some cases were being dealt with elsewhere and with considerable rigour.

In this year, too, there were no explicit prosecutions for being a 'common whore', nor other indications of professional prostitution. Unless cases were entered in other series of records now lost, it must be presumed that women who qualified for such epithets were now thought to be entirely the business of the secular courts. But the case of Margery Nevell, mentioned earlier, alerts us to patterns of behaviour that were at least very closely allied. Indeed, a feature of the prosecutions for 1529 is the relatively high proportion of cases of alleged promiscuity, sometimes linked explicitly to individuals accused of promoting bawdry or otherwise suggestive of murky circumstances. Thus William Randoll was charged not only with incontinence with three named women but also with receiving bribes not to report them to the authorities, knowing them to be reputed among their neighbours as 'impudicis' (shameless or unchaste).[91] But most of the prosecutions alleging multiple sexual contacts were directed at women. Alice Ivyns, 'at the steyre' in St Clement Danes, was one of several individuals, some of them married, accused of adultery or incontinence 'with many'.[92] Juliana Cockes of St Andrew Hubbard was likewise accused, four men being named in particular; Joan Wellys was said to be her bawd. Similarly charged was Elizabeth, servant of Alice Olyver of St Sepulchre's, herself accused of keeping bawdry in her house. Sometimes the bawds themselves were also accused of promiscuity. Such a one was Anne Johnson, likewise of St Sepulchre's; Sibil, Johnson's maidservant, was also reported to be pregnant.[93]

Outcomes

Plainly, the numbers and pattern of commissary court cases varied considerably both in the long term and from year to year; even within the 1520s there were marked fluctuations. Much more consistent, at least until the very eve of the Reformation Parliament, was the manner in which the accused, including convicted defendants, were treated by the courts. The patterns have been analysed extensively by Wunderli with reference

---

[91] LMA, DL/C/B/041/MS09065J/2, fo. 198r.
[92] LMA, DL/C/B/041/MS09065J/2, fo. 166v; cf. *ibid.*, fos. 161r (Agnes Fen), 188r (Joan Abbott), 204r (Joan, wife of Leonard Cooper).
[93] LMA, DL/C/B/041/MS09065J/2, fos. 192v, 193r, 193v, 196v.

to the total body of commissary court activities.[94] Here the focus is on cases directly concerned with regulating sexual behaviour. The task is complicated by the fact that especially before 1500 when the numbers of cases before the courts were often very large, the record of many prosecutions was left incomplete. In particular, many entries consist merely of the suspect's name and parish and a brief account of the charge; sometimes there is a note that the person was cited, but often nothing further. It is likely, but not certain, that the defendant was actually cited, failed to come to court and was therefore suspended for contumacy. At any rate, it can be reasonably assumed that these persons never appeared, if not because they were contumacious, then because the courts failed to pursue them. In a smaller number of cases, it was made explicit that the accused had not responded to the citation and had therefore been suspended from church both as a penalty for their contumacy and as a means of exerting pressure on them to appear to answer the charges.

To give some specific figures, in 1495, about 550 people were charged as principals in various sexual offences, including bawdry. Slightly fewer than 300 (about 54 per cent) are recorded as having made an appearance; just over thirty of these (10 per cent of those who attended) had been suspended from church before they became amenable to discipline. Men, it would seem, were somewhat more likely to appear than female defendants. Of the accused who never appeared, forty-three were explicitly sentenced to suspension, whereas in over 200 cases the record was simply left blank. In 1512, when there were far fewer cases, the appearance rate was higher. Of 140 accused, 106 (over 75 per cent) entered an appearance, twenty-two of whom (nearly 21 per cent) after first being suspended from church. Of the thirty-four individuals who did not turn up, twelve are known to have been suspended, while in the case of the remaining twenty-two, the record was left blank. The even smaller numbers in 1529 yield results broadly comparable to those in 1512. There were seventy-eight accused, of whom fifty-nine (just over 75 per cent) made an appearance, as many as twenty of them (nearly 34 per cent) having first been suspended from church. In the case of the great majority of those who never appeared, the record was simply left incomplete. Evidently the court officers rarely noted suspensions, unless defendants subsequently turned up in court – in which case, they had to secure absolution before the case could proceed further.

Seemingly, the courts accepted that many defendants would never submit to discipline. At one level this is hardly surprising, since all the

---

[94] Wunderli, *London Church Courts*, pp. 142–7 and *passim*.

legal institutions of the period, secular and ecclesiastical, faced difficulties in securing the appearance of defendants. In any case, some culprits no doubt made themselves scarce before process was issued against them; the officers of the court had to be realistic about what could be achieved. But contumacy was a real problem nonetheless. Very occasionally the courts were provoked into more draconian action when they faced real defiance. In 1512, Dominic Lumley, a Lombard of St Christopher le Stocks, confessed to keeping a woman in his house as his wife and begetting a child on her, though he had a wife in his own country. It was said that 'by all means he escapes unpunished and has boasted ... that ... he will keep the said woman in spite of his Ordinary and the authority of his court'. The judge met his defiance with excommunication and threatened him further with a writ *de excommunicato capiendo*, which could have landed him in gaol.[95]

The judges occasionally showed a similar kind of zeal when they were faced with circumstances that they regarded as unusually serious or particularly reprehensible. Clearly exploitative was James Taylor's seduction in 1512 of a mentally deficient woman (*mulierem fatuissimam*), Agnes Pipard, who became pregnant as a result. This offence came to the attention of the court through a deliberate act of public denunciation by a neighbour, John Bywater, and the judge required four sureties for Taylor's submission 'for committing fornication with the said Agnes Pipard who is innocent and lacking discretion as by the confession of the said woman many times examined is to be presumed'. In the same year, the court likewise took very seriously the fact that a certain Agnes Swalowe was pregnant by Edward Clyfford, one of the mayor's officers. The couple claimed that they were contracted and intended to marry, but the commissary insisted that 'to avoid or at least allay the grave scandal' that had arisen, Clyfford should remove the woman from his house and refrain from being alone with her before the wedding. He was also ordered to perform penance, albeit in a reduced form in his usual clothes, later commuted into a money payment of 10s.[96]

But mostly cases were dealt with in routine fashion. The bulk of defendants who actually entered an appearance denied the charges against them. A few were simply dismissed or allowed to clear themselves 'by their own oath', but most – in the usual manner of the church courts – were ordered to undergo compurgation with the help of a varying number of their neighbours. Most defendants were ordered to purge themselves with three, four or five 'hands', but larger numbers of compurgators were

[95] LMA, DL/C/B/043/MS09064/11, fos. 74r, 77v.   [96] *Ibid.*, fos. 59r, 73v.

required in serious or highly notorious cases. The relatively easy availability of oath-helpers in the metropolitan environment and the fact that the compurgators had to travel no great distance to perform their task made compurgation in pre-Reformation London less of a hurdle than it was in the predominantly rural areas surveyed in Chapter 3, and only occasionally is there any indication that this state of affairs was questioned by parishioners. In 1495, Alice Berell of St Clement Danes was reported not merely for being a common scold, a quarreller among her neighbours and a 'grave and common defamer' but also for purging herself on oath 'to the grave danger of her soul'.[97]

In any event, in 1495, in approaching two-thirds of the sex-related prosecutions (including bawdry but excluding defamation), the defendants purged successfully, were otherwise dismissed, or their cases remitted to other courts. For them, prosecution in the commissary court had involved merely trouble, expense and possibly some shame or loss of face – in a case in 1512, a man declined the opportunity to purge himself, fearing 'greater scandal and future disparagement'.[98] But some groups of defendants did find it easier to clear themselves by compurgation than others. In 1495, those charged with bawdry – mostly householders – had a success rate of over 75 per cent. Women accused of adultery, fornication or being a common whore (the last often coupled with charges of bawdry) achieved success rates that were only slightly lower. But of males charged with adultery and fornication, fewer than 50 per cent were able to clear themselves. This suggests that many of the accused men faced strong local disapproval.

Of the remaining defendants, a small proportion were convicted for failing to produce compurgators as required or because some interested party challenged the procedure and the oath-helpers refused to swear. Most of the convictions resulted from the confession of the parties, sometimes accompanied by pleas for lenient treatment. As usual, the stock penalty imposed by the courts was penance, whose bite lay at worst in public shame and humiliation. In physical terms, culprits were not very harshly treated, since the bishop of London's commissaries – unlike their counterparts in some other parts of the country, including the bishop of Winchester's official in Southwark – rarely, if ever, imposed the 'discipline' of penitential whipping. London penances took a basically standard form that did not change much between the late fifteenth century and the very eve of the Reformation Parliament. This involved leading the parish procession on

97 LMA, DL/C/B/043/MS09064/6, fo. 169r.   98 LMA, DL/C/B/043/MS09064/11, fo. 57v.

Sunday, usually barefoot, bare-legged and bare-headed, carrying a candle which in the course of the following mass was offered to the priest or before the principal image of the church. But judges used their discretion in deciding how many times penance should be performed, while there were numerous variations in detail. Sometimes, but not invariably, a lesser form of penance was ordered if a fornicating couple undertook to marry.[99]

In practice, however, the severity of the penance was less of an issue than it might seem, since in late fifteenth- and early sixteenth-century London it was very common to allow culprits to commute it into cash. The form in which such transactions – variously referred to as fines for remission of penance, compositions and the like – was entered in the record is often opaque. But it does seem that in the years around 1500 perhaps half the men enjoined penance, but fewer of the women were able to evade public exposure in this way. However, there were striking changes afoot in the decade or so before the Reformation. The record for 1519 shows that although commutations were still being allowed, the culprits did not get off with a simple money payment. Instead, they were ordered to perform some personal devotion, including giving alms to the poor, fasting, saying prayers or psalms, privately offering candles to images or going on pilgrimages (sometimes barefoot) to neighbouring shrines, such as Our Lady of Willesden. This changed the emphasis of penance from public humiliation to private contrition. By 1529, further changes had occurred. In that year no commutations were authorized, perhaps in response to the kinds of public criticism that were soon to be voiced in the Commons' Supplication against the Ordinaries. The penances that were ordered included the traditional elements of public humiliation, such as leading the procession with bare head, legs and feet. But more often than formerly they culminated in an elaborate series of prayers, penitents typically being required to say the Lord's Prayer, the Apostles' Creed and the Hail Mary several times repeated. In this way, even in the context of a public ritual of repentance, the element of personal contrition was emphasized and reinforced.[100]

To conclude, the sexual regulation exercised by the bishop of London's commissary court was not at any point in the late fifteenth and sixteenth centuries notable for its harshness. To be sure, it is plain from defamation proceedings, in which church court disciplinary prosecutions were often

[99] E.g. LMA, DL/C/B/043/MS09064/11, fo. 59r.
[100] E.g. LMA, DL/C/B/041/MS09065J/2, fos. 153r, 178r, 181r, 184r, 193r, 201v, 206r, 207r.

referred to among the ill-effects of accusations, that even a court appearance leading to a dismissal was not to be taken lightly. But essentially this was a system whose efficacy depended not on severe punishments but rather on the constant risk of detection and the resultant publicity, the trouble and expense of attending court and the danger of public exposure and the ritual humiliation of penance. In the late fifteenth century, the sheer numbers of prosecutions – an astonishing level of activity by any standards, especially in peak years – mean that such considerations could not easily be ignored.

For reasons already discussed, it is impossible to be sure whether the precipitate fall in the numbers of cases that the records of the commissary court apparently reveal for the period after 1500 was a true reflection of reality or – at least in part – an illusion created by haphazard record survival. But in a polemical response to Tyndale in 1529, Sir Thomas More claimed that 'not onely the ryche but the pore also kepe open quenis and lyve in open advoutry wythout payment or penaunce or eny thyng almoste onys sayd unto them.'[101] This seems inconsistent with the very high levels of prosecution characteristic of a generation and more previously and, if true for the period in which More wrote, suggests that the intensity of discipline had decreased markedly between the 1470s and the 1520s. It may be, therefore, that the extraordinarily 'high pressure' regime that evidently prevailed in the late fifteenth century had by the eve of the Reformation given way to a 'low pressure' version of the same system. Just why this should have happened is hard to pinpoint, and it is likely that we should envisage a combination of factors. Wunderli's notion of a sudden and drastic collapse in public confidence is problematic in several ways, though there may have been some reduction in active lay support, perhaps reinforced by the pressure that the royal courts were beginning to exert on the spiritual jurisdiction and the fact that a parallel system of *civic* policing of sexual offenders was also available. Administrative overload, a shift of resources towards combating heresy, increasing sensitivity towards public opinion in the context of the anti-heresy drive, more scrupulously legalistic approaches and changing views on the balance to be struck between the internal forum of private penance and the public or external forum of ecclesiastical justice may also have contributed. But, in any case, on the eve of the Reformation, the London church courts were still prosecuting

[101] Thomas More, *The Complete Works ...*, Vol. VI: *A Dialogue Concerning Heresies*, ed. Thomas M. C. Lawler, Germain Marc'hadour and Richard C. Marius (New Haven and London, 1981), p. 350.

substantial numbers of people, the framework of neighbourhood surveillance clearly still existed and the ecclesiastical authorities were by no means supine – so much is evident from the striking innovations in penance visible in the 1520s.

Moreover, the survival of 'Foxford', the record of sessions before the vicar-general from 1521 to 1539, shows that sterner measures of justice were occasionally meted out by the higher authorities of the diocese. By this period, it would seem, this was the main court for dealing with the persistent problem of immoral clergy. Such cases will be discussed in Chapter 8, but lay people also were occasionally targeted for egregious offences, such as obstinate persistence in adultery. In 1531, a particularly severe penance was imposed on a notorious bigamist. After suffering a spell of several weeks in the Lollards' Tower (the bishop of London's prison adjoining St Paul's), he was ordered to parade 'in penitential manner' through Warwick Lane and around the markets of Cheapside and Leadenhall. He carried a wax candle, while fixed to his back were three distaffs and a paper bearing the inscription: 'This man hath iii wyves all iii beyng alyve.' His ordeal over, he was to be returned to prison.[102] This case is interesting in more ways than one. While the intention was clearly to humiliate the particular offender, the nature of the penance suggests that the authorities wanted it to serve a wider educative purpose. They aimed, as we would say nowadays, to send a clear message that bigamy was unacceptable. But marketplace penances of this kind also had close affinities with the spectacular shaming punishments characteristically meted out by the city of London courts. It is to the system of civic justice towards sexual offenders that we now turn.

---

[102] LMA, DL/C/330, fo. 213r. The case is noticed by McLaren, 'Early 16th Century Act Book', 340.

CHAPTER 7

Civic Moralism in Yorkist and Early Tudor London

An adulterer called to account before the bishop of London's commissary in 1495 insisted defiantly that he would keep his mistress 'despite all the spiritual judges and aldermen'.[1] From his point of view, the ecclesiastical and spiritual authorities were working in tandem to repress sexual transgression – an impression that was in large measure a true one.[2] However, there were points of tension between the two jurisdictions and, more basically, many differences in the procedures and institutions they employed and the principles that underlay their activities. The secular counterpart to the church courts' discipline over sexual behaviour in London, underpinned by a distinctive vision of civic morality, has attracted increasing attention from historians in recent years. But none of the existing accounts provides a complete and accurate picture.[3] To an extent the difficulties arise from loss of records and

---

[1] LMA, DL/C/B/043/MS09064/6, fo. 189r.

[2] The livery companies may also have played a part, as they certainly did later, but evidence for the period before 1530 is very limited; for cases of alleged sexual transgression mentioned in company records, see Matthew Davies (ed.), *The Merchant Taylors' Company of London: Court Minutes, 1486–1493* (Stamford, 2000), pp. 236–7; Lætitia Lyell and Frank D. Watney (eds.), *Acts of Court of the Mercers' Company, 1453–1527* (Cambridge, 1936), p. 418.

[3] The most substantial studies confine themselves to the period before 1500: Shannon McSheffrey, 'Men and Masculinity in Late Medieval London Civic Culture: Governance, Patriarchy and Reputation', in Jacqueline Murray (ed.), *Conflicted Identities and Multiple Masculinities: Men in the Medieval West* (New York and London, 1999), pp. 243–78; Shannon McSheffrey, *Marriage, Sex, and Civic Culture in Late Medieval London* (Philadelphia, 2006), chaps. 6 and 7; Shannon McSheffrey, 'Whoring Priests and Godly Citizens: Law, Morality, and Clerical Sexual Misconduct in Late Medieval London', in Norman L. Jones and Daniel Woolf (eds.), *Local Identities in Late Medieval and Early Modern England* (Basingstoke, 2007), pp. 50–70; Frank Rexroth, *Deviance and Power in Late Medieval London*, trans. Pamela E. Selwyn (Cambridge, 2007), first published as *Das Milieu der Nacht: Obrigkeit und Randgruppen in Spätmittelalterlichen London* (Göttingen, 1999). Brief treatments extending into the early sixteenth century include Richard M. Wunderli, *London Church Courts and Society on the Eve of the Reformation* (Cambridge, MA, 1981), pp. 90–1, 94–6; Martin Ingram, 'Regulating Sex in Pre-Reformation London', in G. W. Bernard and S. J. Gunn (eds.), *Authority and Consent in Tudor England: Essays Presented to C. S. L. Davies* (Aldershot, 2002), pp. 79–95; Stephanie Tarbin, 'Moral Regulation and Civic Identity in London, 1400–1530', in Linda Rasmussen, Valerie Spear and Dianne Tillotson (eds.), *Our Medieval Heritage: Essays in*

the patchy nature of what survives. But by carefully collating all the information that does exist, including incidental references in church court records, it is possible to offer a more faithful and comprehensive reconstruction of what was an extraordinarily elaborate multi-tiered system.[4]

Moreover, it was a system underpinned by a powerful ethos of civic morality. It was deeply gendered in several senses. One of its most obvious features was hostility towards 'common women' and the bawds – many of whom were also female – who aided and abetted them. But also important was an assumption that the male inhabitants of the city, including not merely the minority of citizens with full political and economic rights but the whole body of householders and other denizens, should themselves exercise sexual self-control and be vigilant in restraining the sexual behaviour of their servants and other dependants. This vision was strongly reinforced by an explicit appeal to Christian standards and – as Shannon McSheffrey has emphasized – the use of religious language to an extent unusual in the context of secular jurisdiction. Indeed, the standard formula used in proclamations was that bawds, strumpets and whoremongers, 'not fearing God nor the shame of the world', merited exemplary treatment, while their offences were described in such forthright terms as 'ayenst the lawe of God'.[5] Originating in the remote medieval past and developed amid the city's factional conflicts of the reign of Richard II, this ethos and the accompanying mechanisms of social discipline persisted through the decades of Lancastrian rule. In the late fifteenth and early sixteenth centuries they were powerfully reinvigorated – by this time interacting creatively with the crown's own developing rhetoric of 'reformation of manners'. In this way, sexual regulation was far more integral to the government of the city of London than to provincial towns.

Honour of John Tillotson for his 60th Birthday (Cardiff, 2002), pp. 126–36; Stephanie Tarbin, 'Civic Manliness in London, c.1380–1550', in Susan Broomhall and Jacqueline Van Gent (eds.), *Governing Masculinities in the Early Modern Period: Regulating Selves and Others* (Farnham, 2011), pp. 23–45. See also Stephanie Tarbin, 'Gender, Order and Sexuality in London, 1400–1530', unpublished PhD thesis, University of Western Australia, 1999.

[4] The subject of this chapter is set in somewhat wider context in Martin Ingram, '"Popular" and "Official" Justice: Punishing Sexual Offenders in Tudor London', in Fernanda Pirie and Judith Scheele (eds.), *Legalism: Community and Justice* (Oxford, 2014), pp. 201–26.

[5] LMA, Journal 10, fo. 10v. On the use of religious language in secular jurisdictions, see Shannon McSheffrey, 'Jurors, Respectable Masculinity, and Christian Morality', *Journal of British Studies*, 37 (1998), 270, 273–7.

Wardmote Inquests and Sexual Regulation

Institutionally, the system was grounded in the wardmote jury or inquest – sometimes referred to, in the vernacular corruptions current around 1500, as the 'warmolqueste'. The city was divided into twenty-five wards, most of them covering several parishes, presided over by an alderman (Map 2). Aldermen were important figures in the government of the city and dominant at the local level. However, local people did play a part in their selection in that by the fifteenth century it had become the custom for the ward to nominate four candidates, leaving it to the mayor and aldermen to select one.[6] The aldermen were assisted by deputies on an ad hoc basis before 1500 but more regularly later. They were further supported by a number of common councilmen drawn from among the most substantial inhabitants. By 1536, it was said that their 'election belonged to the aldermen', whose choice was merely to be confirmed by the ward.[7] Yet grass-roots initiative was still a reality in that much of the everyday government of the ward was carried out by elected local officials. The senior officer was the beadle, who had general oversight over policing, whereas the routine work of maintaining law and order was the responsibility of constables. There were also officers called 'scavengers', charged with the disposal of waste, who were, in turn, assisted by humble 'rakers'. Together the task of the wardmote inquest and local officers was to keep the ward 'clean' both physically and morally.[8]

The wardmote inquest met and exercised its powers by virtue of the mayor's precept. Formerly, it had been the custom to hold meetings several times a year, and in the late fifteenth century and early sixteenth century it still remained the practice to convene wardmotes whenever the mayor and aldermen thought necessary. Ad hoc meetings could also be held locally at the initiative of an alderman in response to requests from ward residents, since the mayor's precept was taken to confer authority to convene the wardmote at any point throughout the year. But the regular meeting of the wardmote inquest was on 21 December, St Thomas the Apostle's Day, when all householders and other adult male inhabitants of the ward, including wage-workers and servants, assembled as the wardmote

---

[6] Caroline M. Barron, *London in the Later Middle Ages: Government and People, 1200–1500* (Oxford, 2004), pp. 136–41.

[7] Caroline M. Barron, 'Lay Solidarities: The Wards of Medieval London', in Pauline Stafford, Janet L. Nelson and Jane Martindale (eds.), *Law, Laity and Solidarities: Essays in Honour of Susan Reynolds* (Manchester, 2001), pp. 224–5.

[8] *Ibid.*, pp. 225–9.

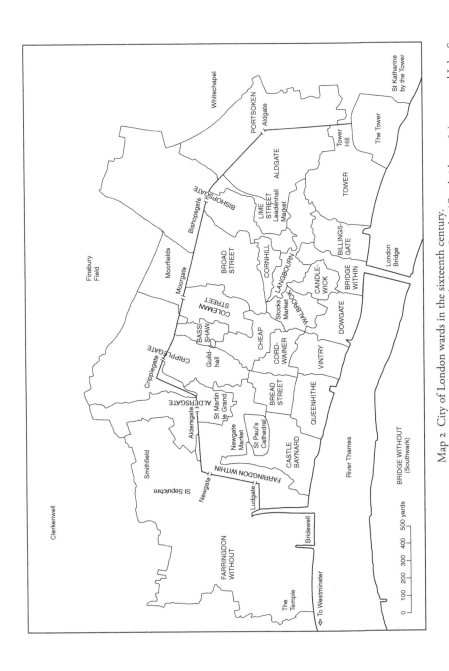

Map 2 City of London wards in the sixteenth century.

(Based on Steve Rappaport, *Worlds within Worlds: Structures of Life in Sixteenth-Century London* (Cambridge, 1989). p. 33; and John Stow, *The Survey of London*, ed. C. L. Kingsford, 2 vols. (Oxford, 1908).)

'for the correction of defaults, the removal of nuisances, and the promotion of the well-being of the ward'.[9]

A jury, numbering twelve or more men according to the custom of the ward, was elected to serve as the wardmote inquest. When the jurors had been sworn in and received their charge, the wardmote adjourned to give them time to find out facts and consider what matters needed to be reformed. They reconvened after Christmas, at which time their 'verdict' of 'presentments' and 'indictments' – the latter term sometimes indicated greater gravity, or at least urgency, but the two words were often used interchangeably – were engrossed on parchment indentures, one part of which was supposed to be referred to the court of aldermen in Guildhall, while the counterpart stayed in the ward. The record of verdicts covered two broad areas. One dealt with defective places, such as dangerous chimneys and decayed pavements, and associated 'nuisances' such as casting offal in the roadway, noisome latrines and blocked ditches. The other dealt with 'defective' people, including sexual offenders. Unfortunately, very few returns survive, whether in original, copy, or abstract. Wardmotes might take place in a local church or church house (as in Farringdon Without), but most of the wards did not have a permanent meeting place. Most commonly, it would seem, the wardmote was convened in the house of the alderman, and the subsequent meetings of the wardmote inquest took place either there or in some convenient inn or tavern; there was certainly no secure place for the storage of records. As a result, many of the wardmote returns kept locally may have had a relatively short life, though early in Elizabeth's reign Aldersgate ward had a chestful of indentures dating back to the last years of Henry VI.[10]

How long the returns sent to the Guildhall were retained is not known, but whatever accumulation existed in 1666 was destroyed in the Great Fire. Some late fourteenth- and early fifteenth-century returns survive among the mayor's records, and as will be seen, some copies and abstracts exist in the Journals of the court of common council and Repertories of the court of aldermen. Otherwise, all that remain for the pre-Reformation period are three stray indentures from Aldersgate ward in the early sixteenth century, one without date and the others dated 1510 and 1528, respectively, and a sequence of fourteen original returns for the suburban, only partly built-up ward of Portsoken, east of Aldgate, for certain years between 1465 and

---

[9] Henry Thomas Riley (ed.), *Munimenta Gildhallae Londoniensis*, 3 vols. (London, 1859–62), Vol. I, p. 36.
[10] Barron, *London in the Later Middle Ages*, p. 123.

1482, plus another, badly damaged indenture for 1508. Portsoken, it should be noted, differed from other wards in that the alderman was not elected. The position was held ex officio by the prior of Holy Trinity, commonly called Christ Church.[11]

Despite (or because of) the paucity of evidence, it has often been assumed that the activities of the wardmote inquests were ineffective. It is certainly true that the surviving returns for 1421–2 and 1422–3, covering the whole of the city, contain a mere sprinkling of charges against sexual offenders, including bawds, strumpets and immoral priests.[12] In the later Portsoken returns, moral offences are much more numerous, suggesting that the system had been considerably cranked up in the interim. Nonetheless, according to Wunderli, only 'prostitutes or pimps' were indicted, and many of the same offenders occurred 'year after year . . . apparently to little avail'. The indentures themselves include no record of punishment and little evidence of other action, so Wunderli's presumption was that nothing was done.[13]

These judgements underestimate the significance of the later fifteenth-century wardmotes in several respects. For one thing, the range of charges proves on examination to be wider and more varied than Wunderli implies. They included numerous imputations of scolding and of other disorderly activities that might or might not have been associated with illicit sex, together with many specifically sexual offences. In particular, there were numerous 'bawds' both male and female; to choose from many examples, in 1476, John Wolflete was charged with 'keeping of his council in bawdry' in respect to his wife. Women supposed to be of light morals and behaviour were variously described as 'common strumpet', 'common puterer', 'common harlot' and 'common harlot of her body'. Some men were accused of 'maintaining' or 'supporting' such women; others were accused of being 'common strumpetmongers', while in 1479 John Johnson, pavior, was presented for being 'an harlot of his body and a common baratour'. Occasionally, people were described as partners in sexual

---

[11] Barron, 'Lay Solidarities', p. 220. It was among the records of Christ Church (transferred to the Court of Augmentations at the Dissolution) that the Portsoken wardmote inquest indentures survived: they have been mostly transcribed by Christine L. Winter, 'The Portsoken Presentments: An Analysis of a London Ward in the 15th Century', *Transactions of the London and Middlesex Archaeological Society*, 56 (2005), 97–161. Quotations in this chapter follow that transcription.

[12] A. H. Thomas (ed.), *Calendar of Plea and Memoranda Rolls Preserved among the Archives of the Corporation of the City of London at the Guildhall, A.D. 1413–1437* (Cambridge, 1943), pp. xxiv–xxx, 115–41, 150–9.

[13] Wunderli, *London Church Courts*, pp. 34–5.

transgression. Thus, in 1471, John Browne and his 'lemman', or paramour, were presented, 'him for a comon strumpetmonger and her for a common strumpet'.[14]

Wardmote Proceedings and the Church Courts

Cross-referencing to the commissary court records offers some perspective on the numbers of such charges and what some of the more ambiguous presentments actually meant. Some historians have surmised that men such as Richard Bryce, described in 1482 as a 'harlot of his body', may have been male prostitutes.[15] But the commissary court records show that there Bryce was explicitly prosecuted for adultery, once with Maud Vyce and twice with Maud Brampton (perhaps in fact the same woman), while his wife was accused of being his bawd – presumably this meant that she was prepared to collude with, if not actually consent to, the relationship.[16] So it seems that Bryce's offence was blatant and repeated heterosexual transgression, the kind of behaviour that both in the church courts and in slanging matches on the streets led to charges of being a 'whoremaster' or 'whoremonger'. In turn, this suggests that wardmote presentments to the effect that a man was a 'common strumpetmonger' imply that he was himself sexually promiscuous, or at least an habitual adulterer or fornicator, rather than a pimp or procurer, as some historians have supposed. But there are ambiguities, and it may be that in some cases the man was both. Such a one, perhaps, was Charles Gentilman, indicted by the Portsoken wardmote inquest in 1467 'for holding and supporting of . . . French Philip', who was herself indicted for 'a common strumpet'; in a subsequent year he was indicted in similar terms, with the additional charge of being a 'common strumpetmonger'.[17]

An obvious difference between the presentments of the wardmote, a secular tribunal, and prosecutions in the spiritual courts is that in the former moral issues overlapped with public order concerns, whereas the

---

[14] Winter, 'Portsoken Presentments', pp. 120, 133, 136, 141.

[15] Gervase Rosser, 'London and Westminster: The Suburb in the Urban Economy in the Later Middle Ages', in John A. F. Thomson (ed.), *Towns and Townspeople in the Fifteenth Century* (Gloucester, 1988), pp. 55, 60, n. 57; Winter, 'Portsoken Presentments', 104–5, 141. This interpretation is rejected by Rexroth, *Deviance and Power*, pp. 201–2. On male prostitutes in sixteenth- and seventeenth-century Spain, see Rafael Carrasco, 'Lazarillo on a Street Corner. What the Picaresque Novel Did Not Say about Fallen Boys', in Alain Saint-Saëns (ed.), *Sex and Love in Golden Age Spain* (New Orleans, 1999), pp. 57–69.

[16] LMA, DL/C/B/043/MS09064/3, fos. 41v, 57v, 136(137)r.

[17] Winter, 'Portsoken Presentments', 116, 118.

church courts were rather more narrowly concerned with sin and personal morality. Frank Rexroth argues further that wardmote presentments tended to ascribe to the individual a persistent *identity* as a bawd, harlot, strumpetmonger, or whatever it might be, with little or no reference to particulars; church court prosecutions, however, were inclined to be much more specific, grounded in accusations of wrongdoing with, or towards, particular individuals. This distinction should not be pressed too far, as specific circumstances were sometimes part of the wardmote charges, while (as was seen in Chapter 6) the church courts did sometimes stigmatize individuals as common whores, habitual adulterers and the like; indeed, charges of being a common scold or common defamer of the neighbours were actually very common. However, Rexroth's point can be accepted as a statement of a broad tendency.[18]

It is related to another difference. To judge by the surviving evidence, at least in the late fifteenth century, moral offences were prosecuted in considerably greater numbers in the church courts than in the wardmotes. In Portsoken ward in the two years 1481 and 1482, some thirty-six individuals were charged with moral and public order offences: they comprised fourteen males and twenty-two females, including eight married couples. Among them were four female scolds, a male barrator and another man described as a scold and barrator, while begging under false pretences, night-walking, keeping petty hostry or receiving suspicious or misruled people were the charges brought against a few other men. Specifically sexual or sex-related offences, occasionally in tandem with matters of public order, were laid to the charge of seventeen women and seven men.[19]

Arising from the parish of St Botolph Aldgate in the commissary court in the same two years were fifteen prosecutions for defamation, overwhelmingly featuring female defendants and mostly consisting of general charges of being a common defamer rather than specifying particular slanders against named victims. There were also twenty-three prosecutions for bawdry, involving as defendants five married couples and a further fourteen women and four men. In addition, there were two cases of bigamy, three prosecutions for being a common whore and three charges of fornication, while the total of sexual offences was boosted by twenty-seven adultery cases, twelve against women and fifteen against men.[20] Most of the fornication and adultery cases specified sexual partners who were

[18] Rexroth, *Deviance and Power*, pp. 206–7.
[19] LMA, COL/AD/05/001, mm. 13–14, printed in Winter, 'Portsoken Presentments', 138–42.
[20] LMA, DL/C/B/043/MS09064/3, fos. 34r–178(179)r *passim*.

not, as far as can be seen, separately prosecuted, while some of the individuals whom the bawds were said to have aided were likewise not themselves the subject of legal process. As a result, the total number of individuals who were in some degree implicated in these prosecutions was considerably greater than the raw totals of cases would at first sight suggest. It should be recalled, moreover, that in all probability the archdeacon of London handled further cases of which we know nothing because the relevant records do not survive, and yet more offenders may have been disciplined during episcopal visitations.[21]

This loss of records may explain why it is that by no means all the scolds and sexual offenders named in the wardmote presentments feature in the commissary court records, though some certainly do. But it may also be that some transgressors were, for one reason or another, pursued only in the wardmote. Thanks to the stray survival of a well-preserved indenture from Aldersgate ward, the relationship between the two courts can again be observed in 1510, and it is striking that in this case there was no overlap. The wardmote presentments included a number of offences that could not be dealt with by the spiritual courts, together with others that would be unlikely (unless there was an unstated sexual component) to lead to church court prosecutions – matters such as night-walking, annoying the neighbours, receiving suspicious people or, in the case of a baker's wife, being so drunk that her behaviour constituted a serious fire risk.[22]

However, five women were named for being a common harlot, 'miswoman' or 'vicious' of their bodies; five men, two women and a married couple were presented for various offences that in the church courts would come under the heading of bawdry; one man was accused of having two wives; while a further three married men were accused of keeping women not their wives – essentially charges of adultery, though that word was not used. None of the individuals concerned can be traced in the commissary court records. In the same year the commissary dealt with twenty or more cases, some involving more than one defendant, from St Botolph Aldersgate and the other parishes that constituted the ward. About half of them were charges of defaming a specific victim who was presumably responsible for bringing the complaint to court, but otherwise there was the usual mix of adultery, fornication, bawdry, disputed marriage and scolding. Subject to the qualification that we do not know what was

[21] See Chapter 6.
[22] LMA, CLC/W/FA/005/MS01499, partly printed in William McMurray (ed.), *The Records of Two City Parishes: A Collection of Documents Illustrative of the History of Ss. Anne and Agnes, Aldersgate, and St. John Zachary, London, from the Twelfth Century* (London, 1925), pp. 29–30.

happening in the other London ecclesiastical courts, it would seem from this evidence that by the early sixteenth century the work of identifying sexual offenders was in effect shared between the commissary and the wardmote. A difference was that the latter was more likely to deal with 'common women' and their bawds and hangers-on, whose activities tended to shade into the broader area of behaviour that threatened public order. As shown in Chapter 6, such offenders were by this time marginal to the commissary court's activities.[23]

Contexts, Aims and Outcomes of Wardmote Proceedings

Any suggestion that wardmote proceedings were merely formulaic is wide of the mark. On the contrary, their form and content appear to reflect the real interests of the jurors who made the presentments and those who supplied them with information. Penny Tucker's investigation of the composition of the inquest juries of Portsoken ward indicates that they were householders of moderate substance. Few of them would rise to higher official positions, though they may have had aspirations to do so.[24] It may be surmised that they wished both to keep in good standing with the civic authorities and establish and maintain their local 'credit'. Denouncing those who stepped out of line – individuals who were often in a more marginal social and economic position than themselves, especially those whose activities had given rise to scandal or were considered a public nuisance – was a powerful means of achieving these aims.

Certainly by the early sixteenth century the language of surviving returns is richly redolent of moral indignation. The Portsoken return for 1508, for example, spoke of 'keeping bawdry in the most abominable ways', while in Aldersgate ward in 1510 John Salforde was presented 'for kepyng of a myswoman shamfully bysyde hys wyffe and for her sake comyth not in company with hys owne wyff'.[25] The same Portsoken return shows also that the wardmote inquest did not necessarily make its return on the basis of the existing knowledge of its members but could take an active role in investigating suspicions and complaints. Indeed, suspects could be 'sent for to the inquest ... to be examined' – not always to good effect, since one culprit 'despised the inquest', while another 'disobeyeth' and had apparently fled.[26] Incidental references in other sources prove that such

---

[23] LMA, CLC/W/FA/005/MS01499 compared with DL/C/B/043/MS09064/10, fos. 49v–87v.
[24] Penny Tucker, *Law Courts and Lawyers in the City of London, 1300–1550* (Cambridge, 2007), p. 232.
[25] Winter, 'Portsoken Presentments', 143; LMA, CLC/W/FA/005/MS01499.
[26] Winter, 'Portsoken Presentments', 143, 144.

interviews were commonplace and, probably, a long-established practice, and that they were part of a process of screening in which various suspicions might be voiced before the jury settled on the list of culprits to be included in their returns. Thus it was reported that John Saunderson of St Peter Cornhill had been called to appear before the 'warmold queste' at Christmas 1511 because his wife had complained that he had ill-treated her and thrown her out of the house – perhaps with the implication that the husband was also an adulterer.[27]

An analogous screening process applied to the election of ward officers and of the members of the wardmote inquest itself, a further indication that their proceedings were in no way an empty ritual. When Roger Wryght was nominated to be of 'le warmolquest' in Farringdon Within in 1523, it was reported that Roger Newesse spoke up: 'Nay, he ys nott worthy to have yt ... there ys a padde [toad] yn the strawe.' The obstacle apparently lay with the ill-behaviour of Wryght's wife, who was thereupon summoned before the inquest.[28] Other incidental references reveal further sidelights on this searching system of local policing. In 1523, Alice Goodryk claimed that the alderman of Walbrook ward had sent for her to inquire whether two local women 'kepe any better rule than they were wont to doo', to which she replied, 'Yeven as they were wont to do soo they doo styll.' Two years earlier a woman who had just let part of her house to a certain Agnes Cockrell grew doubtful of her character and accordingly went to make inquiries in the parish where she had formerly dwelt. 'I ame come to yow to know the maner and condytions of hyr ... she wyll dwell within my howse and I have taken of hyr a peny in ernest.' What she heard in reply confirmed her fears: 'Tak hydd of hyr ... that she do not pute yow clene oughte of your howse for ye shall fynde hyr a crafty dame' or, according to another account, 'she ... ys a brothell of her taylle and she wyll leve no thyng onstolne.' Apart from the implication of theft, the main charge against her was that she had been conducting an illicit relationship which, it was purported, made her an unfit and untrustworthy prospect for a tenant: 'and ye have lett her your howse ye be deceyved for Dyngley her servaunt kepyth her.'[29]

---

[27] LMA, DL/C/206, fo. 170r.

[28] LMA, DL/C/207, fos. 270v–272r. A 'pad in the straw' meant a hidden danger. For a somewhat similar case, see DL/C/A/002/MS09065, fos. 182r–183v, discussed with slightly different interpretations in Ingram, 'Regulating Sex in Pre-Reformation London', p. 89, and McSheffrey, *Marriage, Sex, and Civic Culture*, p. 175.

[29] LMA, DL/C/207, fos. 99v–101r, 102r, 189v.

The further details of this case bring to light other important features of ward government – which indeed extended beyond the city and into suburban areas – that need to be understood if the work of the wardmotes is to be seen in proper context. These were a very active system of neighbourhood watch, involving regular searches, combined with the practice of expelling troublemakers. Agnes Cockrell's former neighbours reported that 'hyr howse was serchyd on a nyghte' and that she and her servant lover 'wer taken togethyr'. It was in fact well established in city custom, several times tested in the royal courts, that constables could enter premises where wrongdoing was suspected and make arrests; usually they were accompanied by posses of other inhabitants who constituted the 'watch' that patrolled the streets at night.[30]

The best evidence of these activities is found not in the exiguous survivals of the city courts themselves – though these do yield some examples[31] – but in the records of the church courts. In particular, throughout this period the registers of the commissary court are peppered with numerous references to such activities, which obviously provided solid evidence on which cases could be reported to the ecclesiastical authorities. In St Sepulchre parish in 1471, for example, Joan Deyse was said to have committed adultery in her kitchen, 'the token whereof is that certain men took her in bed in the said kitchen with the same man, and this was done at the time when *le wache* was made before Easter.' In the previous year, Robert Martin and his wife of Whitechapel were accused of being 'bawds to a certain man and a certain women, who were taken in his house by *le constable* on 6 June in the night-time'.[32] Strikingly, these policing activities were not confined to known brothels or sex-trade professionals; ordinary adulterous relationships were likewise subject to surveillance. They may even have extended to assignations between courting couples, though here the evidence is more ambiguous. In a case in 1473, a man was interviewed by the Broad Street wardmote inquest, 'having been previously detected to the Twelve concerning fornication'; his claim that he planned to marry the woman was a means to secure his release.[33] In another case, reported in

---

[30] TNA, KB 27/854, rot. 18, KB 27/885, rot. 50v, KB 27/857, rot. 72, KB 27/860, rots. 40v, 51v (1475); *Year Book* 1 Hen. VII, 6–7 (1485).

[31] E.g. Philip E. Jones (ed.), *Calendar of Plea and Memoranda Rolls Preserved among the Archives of the Corporation of the City of London at the Guildhall, A.D. 1458–1482* (Cambridge, 1961), pp. 60, 63, discussed in McSheffrey, *Marriage, Sex, and Civic Culture*, p. 181.

[32] LMA, DL/C/B/043/MS09064/1, fos. 15v, 86v. For an example from a consistory court case in 1474, see McSheffrey, *Marriage, Sex, and Civic Culture*, pp. 191–2.

[33] Shannon McSheffrey (ed.), *Love and Marriage in Late Medieval London* (Kalamazoo, MI, 1995), pp. 84–5; for a somewhat similar case, see LMA, DL/C/A/002/MS09065, fos. 196(197)v–197(198)v.

1489, though the events had taken place years earlier, the intervention of the constable was instigated by a father who wished to put a stop to the relationship.[34]

In terms of punishment, the ethos of the wardmotes was harsher than the church courts. As seen in Chapter 6, most of those who bothered to appear before the commissary could expect to secure a dismissal. Even the minority who were ordered to do penance were often able to commute it for a money payment. The results of being in trouble with the civic authorities, however, were variable – discretion amounting to arbitrariness was integral to the system. But the way the various sanctions operated tended to render offending individuals infamous, and the cumulative impact of escalating penalties could be extremely harsh. Thus, whereas the church courts worked to reintegrate offenders into their communities, the civic tribunals tended to do the opposite.

The usual fate of individuals and couples 'taken' by local officers in compromising circumstances was to be led through the public streets to the nearest Counter prison to be confined overnight or more simply to be set in the stocks. Again, there are numerous incidental references to this procedure in church court records.[35] Culprits were dealt with on the morrow by the local alderman. Some were committed for trial at the Guildhall, but probably most were released on finding sureties to be of good behaviour. Apart from the physical discomfort of incarceration, it is plain that the shame of such an experience could be keenly felt. One man, taken with a woman by the constable of Aldgate ward at ten o'clock one night in 1492, described it in terms of 'great opprobrium'. Inevitably, the circumstances were gleefully noted by neighbours. In 1531 it was reported that a year or two before a married woman called Margaret Thompson had committed adultery, or at least had been taken in suspicious circumstances, in a house in St Anne and St Agnes parish in Aldersgate ward. Knowledge of this 'crime' was broadcast throughout the neighbourhood, and as a result, the premises were searched in the middle of the night, and the couple was led to the Counter in Bread Street. One witness added the tell-tale detail that next day the doors of the woman's house stayed shut until midday.[36]

The alderman had the power not only to order temporary imprisonment but also actually to expel troublemakers – including sexual offenders –

---

[34] *Ibid.*, fos. 47(48)v–48(49)v, 52(53)v–54(55)r. The case is reported more fully in Ingram, 'Regulating Sex in Pre-Reformation London', p. 90; and McSheffrey, *Marriage, Sex, and Civic Culture*, pp. 150–1.

[35] E.g. LMA, DL/C/B/043/MS09064/6, fos. 101v, 103r, 125r, 125v, 168v (all 1495); DL/C/B/041/ MS09065J/2, fos. 165r, 167v (1529).

[36] LMA, DL/C/A/002/MS09065, fo. 196(197)v; DL/C/208, fos. 180r–182r.

from the ward. This is what happened to Agnes Cockrell, according to the former neighbours who informed her suspicious new landlady of her 'conversation': she and her manservant were 'brought bothe to the Counter and therfor she was putt oughte of thys warde.'[37] Being caught in the act and imprisoned, especially if it was not the first offence, plainly offered an excellent opportunity for exemplary action. But even if people had not suffered the public disgrace of being led to the Counter, they might nonetheless find themselves ordered to leave the ward. In some cases, it would seem, the mere complaint of one or more neighbours was enough to send them packing. In 1529 it was reported that about two years before, William Bourse of the parish of St Mary Staining (Aldersgate ward) had fathered a child on his maidservant, Joan Stere; the woman gave birth in the hospital of St Mary without Bishopsgate, and the child was nursed at Havering-atte-Bower in Essex. Afterwards the man continued to 'keep' Joan, lodging her with a widow in Carter Lane. This was too much for one witness in the case, who complained to 'le warmoll quest' of their 'ill rule and adultery', whereupon the woman was expelled from the ward of Baynard Castle. William Bourse presumably stayed put, but his reputation was clearly damaged, and the circumstances were brought to light when his credibility as a witness was impugned in the consistory court.[38] The fact that a poor reputation could lead to expulsion is a further explanation of why public accusations in the street were such a marked feature of social relations in London, why they were taken so seriously and hence why matters of slander were (as was seen in Chapter 6) so prominent in the business of the ecclesiastical courts.

Though individuals could apparently be summarily ejected on complaint from a neighbour, probably the most usual grounds for expulsion was the fact of being presented or 'indicted' before the wardmote inquest. This tribunal was a means of weighing local reputations in the balance, with dire consequences for those found wanting. Indeed, Rexroth characterizes the proceedings of the wardmotes as 'ceremonies of status degradation'.[39] The presentments of the jury attached to the individuals they named – the 'common' bawds, harlots, strumpets, strumpetmongers and so forth – the *persistent identity* of inveterate, habitual malefactors. These were 'verdicts', presented as self-evident statements of truth, permanently recorded in duplicate indentures of durable parchment. From such imposed identities, there was no escape.

[37] LMA, DL/C/207, fo. 101r.   [38] LMA, DL/C/208, fos. 36r–37v.
[39] Rexroth, *Deviance and Power*, p. 221.

However, the effect of the presentment was more than merely to inscribe the offenders in a register of public infamy. It put them in jeopardy of draconian further action. The system was discretionary rather than following a simple rule such as the present-day 'three strikes and you're out'. An individual could be presented once, twice or several times without necessarily being ordered out of the ward. But the underlying principle was that expulsion was the prescribed penalty and was liable to be invoked sooner or later. As a witness stated in 1529, 'Each and every person [offending] ... within the city of London is to be presented to the alderman of the ward within which they inhabit by the verdict of twelve sworn men; which persons thus presented the alderman ... shall correct and punish by expulsion from the ward in which they dwell or otherwise as shall seem expedient to the same alderman.'[40] The application of this principle has left traces in the surviving wardmote presentments. The Portsoken return for 1473, for example, 'presented and indicted' Emmota Rygdowne 'for a common harlot and indicted out of another ward the last year'.[41] This phrase 'indicted out of the ward' – sometimes 'indicted out two wards', 'three wards' and so on – is repeatedly found in the commissary court records as evidence that an offence had been committed. Clearly, action at the ward level was one source of information for prosecutions in the church courts.[42]

How these sanctions worked in practice in the case of a single individual is vividly conveyed in a consistory court suit of 1491. John Harries of Fenchurch in Langbourn ward recounted how in the summer, three years before, a certain Margaret Morgan alias Smythe had dwelt with John Han and his wife as an ale server. A colourful character who sang bawdy songs 'inciting to lechery and uncleanness and against good morals', she became very much defamed as a whore and, as such, was 'noted and detected' to 'Master' (Sir Hugh) Bryce, alderman of the ward.[43] On Bryce's orders, Harries (the local beadle) warned her to quit the ward on pain of imprisonment. She moved to the liberty of the royal hospital of St Katharine by the Tower – a noted haunt of prostitutes – where she married but (according to the story) continued to maintain bawdry

[40] LMA, DL/C/208, fo. 2r. This particular statement referred to the offence of 'petty hostry', but the same applied to other moral and public order offences; cf. Riley (ed.), *Munimenta Gildhallae Londoniensis*, Vol. I, pp. 37–9, 312–3, 332, 591–2; Vol. III, pp. 126, 132, 234 (partial translations).

[41] Winter, 'Portsoken Presentments', 126, adopting this editor's dating.

[42] E.g. LMA, DL/C/B/043/MS09064/1, fos. 6v, 8r, 9r and *passim*; DL/C/B/043/MS09064/6, fo. 178r; DL/C/B/043/MS09064/8, fos. 56r, 112v; DL/C/B/041/MS09065J/1, fos. 27v, 131r; see also Wunderli, *London Church Courts*, p. 35.

[43] Alfred B. Beaven, *The Aldermen of the City of London*, 2 vols. (London, 1908–13), Vol. I, p. 168.

and commit adultery for nearly three years. Eventually, the master of St Katharine's received a mandate from the queen, as patron of the hospital, to rid the liberty of bawds and harlots, whereupon Margaret was expelled along with others to the number of forty. She moved back to Fenchurch and set up ale selling in a house to which there was much suspicious resort; expelled again, she took up residence with a notorious bawd, Margery Hor, and was soon in more trouble, and returning back to Langbourn ward she was there barely a fortnight before being ordered out for the third time. She moved to Billingsgate ward only to suffer the same fate. In short, she was repeatedly chivvied from ward to ward, as evidence of her misconduct gradually accumulated. Plainly this treatment did not reform her, but she was constantly denied a settled existence, and her infamous status was gradually reaffirmed.[44]

It will be evident from the examples quoted that this system was by no means even handed in its treatment of the two sexes. The categories of offence specified in the articles of the wardmote meant that more women than men were likely to be presented for sexual and sex-related offences, while 'kept women' and 'common strumpets' were likely to be in a dependent position and hence easier to chase out of the ward than householders. Cases where offenders strongly resisted attempts to expel them from the ward mostly involved men, especially those who enjoyed a powerful or privileged position. But such individuals were not entirely immune. In 1504 it was reported in the court of aldermen that the physician William Paron had 'often and dyvers tymes … been inditid of myslivyng of his bodye and sundrey tymes … chargid and monysshed to avoyde the warde as well by the maire and aldermen as by the aldermen of the warde whereyn he duellyth and that to doo he promisid in a full courte of aldermen'. He had failed to go, however, and so was now imprisoned till further notice. There is little doubt that this was Henry VII's Italian astrologer. In 1502 he had predicted that the queen, Elizabeth of York, would live till she was eighty – only to see her die the following year, aged thirty-seven. Presumably this faux pas had rendered him vulnerable.[45]

[44] LMA, DL/C/A/002/MS09065, fo. 88(89)r–v; cf. Ruth Mazo Karras, *Common Women: Prostitution and Sexuality in Medieval England* (New York and Oxford, 1996), pp. 69–70. On St Katharine's, see Catherine Jamison, *The History of the Royal Hospital of St. Katharine by the Tower of London* (London, 1952), esp. pp. 19–22, 46–7.

[45] LMA, Repertory 1, fo. 168r; C. A. J. Armstrong, 'An Italian Astrologer at the Court of Henry VII', in his *England, France and Burgundy in the Fifteenth Century* (London, 1983), pp. 157–78 (I owe this identification to Steven Gunn).

Exemplary Action by the Court of Aldermen

This response to Paron's intransigence was tailor-made to suit the particular case, but it was part of a broader pattern. The mayor and aldermen intermittently stepped in to make an example of persistent or egregious offenders. Individuals who had already been indicted by the wardmotes, or who were simply notorious, were summoned to the Guildhall. In some cases, it would seem, the verdicts of the wardmotes were simply confirmed; in others, the accused were formally arraigned and tried by a jury drawn from wards across London. They were thus subject to the censure not merely of their local community but of the entire city. Unfortunately, there is no complete and continuous record of these activities, but material in the city of London Journals (records of the court of common council), Repertories (records of the court of aldermen), Letter Books (a sequence of volumes registering important documents and precedents) and related records (notably the custumals known as the *Liber Albus* of *c.*1420 and *Liber Dunthorn* of 1474) enable the main outlines to be traced and provide much detail on individual episodes.[46]

The basis of such exemplary action against sexual offenders lay in ordinances dating from the reign of Richard II, albeit building on earlier practice. This was a turbulent period marked by severe faction fighting, and according to Rexroth, the measures may be seen as part of an attempt by John of Northampton, mayor from 1381 to 1383, to seize the moral high ground and secure public support.[47] A religious dimension was integral, the preamble asserting that the lack of ordinances hitherto had meant that offenders had remained uncorrected 'to the great displeasing of God and to the dishonour of the city'. But the situation was more complicated than simple support for the church or a virtuous contest between the secular and spiritual powers in combating sin. According to the chronicler Thomas Walsingham, the enactment of new ordinances was a rebuke to the ecclesiastical authorities, whom the citizens accused of abrogating their responsibility for the punishment of sin by allowing sexual offenders to commute penances into money payments.[48]

The newly framed ordinances laid down a graduated series of penalties that were to follow the process of indictment, imprisonment and

---

[46] See also Stuart Minson, 'Public Punishment and Urban Space in Early Tudor London', *London Topographical Record*, 30 (2010), 1–16.

[47] Rexroth, *Deviance and Power*, chap. 4.

[48] Riley (ed.), *Munimenta Gildhallae Londoniensis*, Vol. I, p. 457; Vol. III, p. 179 (translation); Thomas Walsingham, *Historia Anglicana*, ed. Henry T. Riley, 2 vols. (Rolls Series 28/1, London, 1863–4), Vol. II, p. 65.

conviction. Immoral clergy were clearly an important target but by no means the only one.[49] Thus, any man convicted of being a bawd or common whoremonger was to have his beard and head shaved, save for a two-inch fringe round the crown, and led off 'with minstrels' for a spell in the pillory. A female bawd was to be punished in much the same manner, except that she went not to the pillory but to the 'thew', an exhibition platform reserved for women. A 'common woman' was to be taken from prison to Aldgate, wearing a 'ray', or striped hood, and carrying a white wand in her hand; led thence with minstrels to the thew, where her offence was to be proclaimed; and then taken through Cheap and Newgate to dwell thereafter in Cock Lane. (In the fifteenth century the Cock Lane provision was deleted.) For a second offence, bawds, whoremongers and common women were to suffer imprisonment in addition to the other penalties, while for a third the punishment was to culminate in expulsion from the city.[50]

Plainly the aim of these measures was not merely to punish individuals by exposing them to shame and public obloquy – though they certainly did that – but also to send a clear message that certain activities were not only reprehensible in themselves but also inconsistent with being a good citizen and offensive to God. The elaborate symbolism, which was not merely striking in itself but differentiated between offences, was a species of moral rhetoric with a powerful educative purpose. Moreover, the parading of culprits through crowded markets and thoroughfares, their public exposure at the pillory and ultimate ejection through the gates of the city were designed to ensure that the message was communicated to as wide an audience as possible. Thus public space was deliberately managed to put sexual transgression, and the city's response to it, literally on the map.[51]

In practice, it is unlikely that the penalties were ever applied consistently and regularly, and with time, their precise details came to be modified. But the spirit of what was intended did persist. Indeed, in 1439, the 'olde ordenaunce' was renewed, albeit in somewhat simplified form, and throughout the fifteenth century variants on what were by now traditional shame punishments were periodically invoked as the 'custom

---

[49] Treatment of immoral clergy is discussed in Chapter 8.
[50] Riley (ed.), *Munimenta Gildhallae Londoniensis*, Vol. I, pp. 457–60; Vol. III, pp. 179–82 (translation).
[51] For an imaginative interpretation of the symbolism embodied in these measures, see Rexroth, *Deviance and Power*, pp. 172–87. On the spatial dimension, see Minson, 'Public Punishment and Urban Space', 3–4. See also Katharina Behrens, *Scham: zur sozialen Bedeutung eines Gefühls im spätmittelalterlichen England* (Göttingen, 2014).

of the city'. Some of the most spectacular instances were noted by city chroniclers; their accounts tended to single out drives against 'common women', though some reflected the fact that male bawds and whoremongers were likewise subject to public punishment.[52] Thus, the so-called Great Chronicle of London recorded that in 1474 (in fact an error for 1473) the mayor, fishmonger William Hampton, 'dyd dyligent and sharp correccion upon Venus['s] servauntys, and cawsid theym to be garnysshid and attyrid wyth raye hodys, and to be shewid abowth the cyte wyth theyr mynstralsy beffore theym by many and sundry market dayes, and sparid noon ffor mede nor ffor ffavour'.[53]

The corresponding records of prosecutions may well be incomplete. But they show that on this occasion over sixty people, most of them indicted by the wardmote inquest of Portsoken but including some offenders from the wards of Aldersgate, Cripplegate, Farringdon Without, Tower and Vintry, were victims of this civic clean-up. Two-thirds were women, most of them indicted as common strumpets and the like and a few as bawds; added to the list later was Trude Garard, who had been 'taken vagarant and walkyng by the stretes of this citee in a mans aray and clothyng . . . [and] by hir own confession . . . lawfully atteynt of that . . . she is a comon strumpet'.[54] But a good proportion of those accused of bawdry were men; four male 'putours', though not included in the ward returns, were tried at the subsequent proceedings in the Guildhall; while a further six men were accused of a variety of sexual offences. They included William Eccham, 'yeoman of the crown', who had been 'taken in Middlesex and endited by thenquest . . . of the warde of Portsokyn' for 'holdyng' a Whitechapel woman, 'in somoche . . . [that her] husbond dare not comme home to his hous'.[55]

More than a third of the accused, it would seem, could not be apprehended; some of them may already have cleared out, bag and baggage. Predictably, of those who were brought to trial, the males were more likely to be acquitted. But some men were convicted and sentenced to spells on the pillory, followed in some cases by expulsion from the city.[56] Along with female scolds, 'common strumpets' fared worst. Not only were they convicted in larger numbers, but also they were punished with greater

---

[52] E.g. James Gairdner (ed.), *The Historical Collections of a Citizen of London in the Fifteenth Century* (Camden Society, New Series 17, London, 1876), pp. 182, 185; Charles Lethbridge Kingsford (ed.), *Chronicles of London* (Oxford, 1905), p. 146 (cf. p. 200: two men pilloried for bawdry and 'putry', and p. 205: man pilloried for bawdry).

[53] A. H. Thomas and I. D. Thornley (eds.), *The Great Chronicle of London* (London, 1938), p. 222.

[54] LMA, Journal 8, fo. 50r.   [55] LMA, Journal 8, fos. 46v–48v (quotation fo. 47r).

[56] LMA, Journal 8, fos. 48r, 49r.

symbolic elaboration and publicly paraded much further round the streets of London. Taken first to the eastern extremity, they were then conveyed to the centre for exposure at the pillory and all the way back again before finally being expelled. Thus they were ordered to 'be ledde with mynstralsy and ray hodes on their hedes and white roddes in their handes from prison to Al[d]gate and from Al[d]gate to the pillory in Cornhill and their the causes to be proclamed and from thens to be conveied thorough Chepe to Newgate and ther to be voided oute of this citee and the fraunchise of the said citee for ever'.[57]

Those expelled from the city faced further punishment if they returned: they were to stand on the pillory for an hour on three market days and then be imprisoned for a year and a day. As late as 1490, when one of the female bawds driven out in 1473 was found to be in London, she was pilloried and sent to prison, and repeated royal writs of *corpus cum causa* and *habeas corpus* failed to get her out.[58] The effectiveness of the purge of 1473, at least in the short term, is suggested also by analysis of the surviving presentments for Portsoken ward. Many of those prosecuted in April that year had already been indicted by the wardmote inquest at its regular meeting the previous December. But the same names do not appear the following year. They had clearly gone from the ward, including not only individuals who had been paraded and expelled but also some of those presumably 'at large' who were not actually brought to trial in the Guildhall.[59]

The city's hostility towards sexual offenders was reiterated the following year, in 1474. In response to a royal writ on behalf of John Denys, a barber surgeon imprisoned after being indicted for bawdry in Tower ward, the mayor and sheriffs likened the conjunction of bawds and whores to that of 'crows and eagles, [which] by their natural instinct flock to places where carrion lies'. In the following decade, in 1483, the city further evoked the imagery of corruption and decay in a proclamation 'for to eschewe the stynkyng and horrible synne of lechery the whiche daily groweth and is used more than it hath been in daies past ... to the grete displesur of Almyghty God and distourbaunce and brekyng of the kyng our soveraign lordes peas and of the politique guydyng of the citee'.[60]

---

[57] LMA, Journal 8, fo. 49r.

[58] LMA, Journal 9, fos. 232(264)r–v, 262(294)r, 263(295)r–v, 265(297)r, 266(298)r, 267(299)v.

[59] The exception is Elizabeth Barcroft or Barecroft. In April 1473, she confessed herself to be a common harlot but was ordered to 'be delivered' and 'not indicted' because she was of Middlesex, not of the city of London: LMA, Journal 8, fo. 47r; cf. Winter, 'Portsoken Presentments', 126.

[60] LMA, Journal 8, fos. 85v–86r, 88r; Journal 9, fo. 17r; Reginald R. Sharpe (ed.), *Calendar of Letter-Books ... of the City of London at the Guildhall. Letter-Book L. Temp. Edward IV–Henry VII* (London, 1912), p. 206.

Yet, despite such rhetoric, apparently no purge on the scale of the prosecutions of 1473–4 was attempted in the last quarter of the fifteenth century. Instead, from year to year there were clusters of prosecutions, or simply isolated judgements, against smaller groups of offenders or individuals singled out for exemplary punishment. Often they were marked by the use of religious language. Sometimes the circumstances were particularly blatant, such as the procuring of very young girls, or the offender was clearly an old hand. In 1494, for example, a man was convicted 'as welle by xij menne after the lawes and custumes of this citee of London for a bawde as by his own confession . . . for conveying of one Alys Wilson of thage of xiij yeres to his house to one Aleyn Redeman by whom the same Alys was ravisshed and devoured'. For this he was paraded and pilloried on three market days and then expelled from the city. At the same time, another man was sentenced to one hour in the pillory and expulsion for being 'a comon putrier of his body'. Both cases were accurately reported by a city chronicler.[61]

Action appears to have intensified in the early decades of the sixteenth century. Indeed, there was a sequence of 'drives' on a more ambitious scale, achieved by means of special large-scale searches ordered by the civic authorities. There were well-established precedents for such action. Thus, in December 1463, aldermen were ordered to make 'due serche' of 'al maner suspecte persones logged and harborwed within your said warde and of al other of whome the cause of their beyng there is unknowen and that ye in al godly hast have afore us the names of al theyme soe that we maie have knowlege of their rule and demeanyng and to make provysion for the guydyng of theyme in kepyng of the peas'. But later precepts were more detailed and commonly specified that the search should take place at a certain time of night. Secrecy was to be preserved beforehand to achieve surprise, hence the term 'privy search' that was common by the time of Henry VIII.[62]

Right from the start his reign witnessed some major initiatives against sexual offenders. In 1510, at least twenty-six individuals were punished, mostly women but including four male bawds and a 'putrer of his body'.[63] The following decade witnessed even more vigorous action. In early February 1520 the aldermen were ordered to commit to prison all 'common bawds' and 'harlots' indicted at the last wardmote so that they could be

---

[61] LMA, Journal 10, fo. 31v; cf. Kingsford (ed.), *Chronicles of London*, p. 200.

[62] LMA, Journal 7, fo. 52v; cf. Journal 11, fo. 109v, Repertory 2, 200r, Repertory 3, fos. 98v, 193v.

[63] LMA, Journal 11, fos. 110r, 111v–112v, 114v–115r; see also *ibid.*, fos. 258r, 264v–265r (1516), 389v, 391r (1519).

arraigned in the Guildhall 'accordyng to the auncyent lawes and custumes of the same citie'; five weeks later there was a follow-up measure. Not all of the resulting batch of accused were found guilty, but it is plain that proceedings were rigorous.[64] A case from the following year gives some insight into the means by which cases were proved. Margaret Byrcheley, indicted in Aldersgate ward as a common woman of her body, 'was demaunded where she lay on Saterday at nyght the vth day of February [five days before her court appearance] and she saide she lay the same nyght at a chaundelers hous'. This statement, it was noted, was 'proved ageyns her'.[65]

In 1523, the mayor and aldermen issued a proclamation against lechery, bawds and strumpets in much the same terms as that of 1483. There survives no record of prosecutions following this proclamation, though a few had preceded it.[66] But exemplary punishments were certainly staged again in June 1529 and recorded in detail. Five women were convicted for being 'persones not dredyng godd ne the shame of thys worlde but contynually usyng thabhomynable custume of the fowle and detestable synne of lechery and bawdry to the gret dysplesure of Almyghty Godd and to the gret noysaunce of their neighbours'. Accordingly, the mayor and aldermen gave judgement that the culprits, wearing ray hoods and carrying white rods, should be paraded through the city with minstrelsy and the rough music of pans and basins. Their offences were to be twice proclaimed, both at the Standard in Cheap and at the pillory in Cornhill, before they were expelled from the city at Aldgate and so banished. In the same month, various other offenders were subjected to similarly severe punishment.[67]

City, Crown and Sexual Regulation

Wunderli describes these activities in 1520, 1523 and 1529 as 'outbursts of reforming zeal' and takes them to indicate that Londoners were losing faith in the church courts and turning instead to the secular authorities for the

---

[64] LMA, Repertory 5, fos. 20v, 29r; the second order is duplicated in Repertory 4, fo. 45r–v. For the proceedings, see LMA, Journal 12, fo. 40r–v.

[65] LMA, Repertory 5, fo. 97(100)r. This foreshadows the interrogation methods used in Elizabethan Bridewell.

[66] LMA, Journal 12, fo. 239r–v; see also Repertory 6, fos. 16v, 23r. For exemplary punishments in 1522, 1523 and 1524, see Journal 12, fos. 169r, 237r, 238r, 277r–v.

[67] LMA, Journal 13, fo. 143v–144v; see also Repertory 8, fo. 43v; Ingram, 'Regulating Sex in Pre-Reformation London', p. 91.

punishment of sin.[68] This is both to overstate the novelty of such drives, since it is plain that they were firmly based in precedents stretching back into the fifteenth century and earlier, and also to exaggerate their impact: while these early sixteenth-century purges were extensive enough to be eye-catching, they were on nothing like the scale of events in 1473. Moreover, as has been seen, the idea of a self-conscious rejection of ecclesiastical authority in the sphere of sexual regulation is hard to substantiate, even though there may have been some *implicit* tension, not least on the issue of clerical immorality, while the probability is that the intensity of church court action did slacken in the early sixteenth century.[69] But throughout the Yorkist and early Tudor periods, the general context was clearly one in which the right of the city authorities to intervene in matters of sexual sin was regarded as axiomatic – irrespective of the work of the church courts, which had a somewhat different role to play.

It is nonetheless necessary to explain why exemplary action against sexual offenders was periodically cranked up, to the accompaniment of strident rhetoric, and why, more generally, the tempo of civic action appears to have increased in the 1510s and 1520s. At a basic level, the city had to maintain at least minimal enforcement of its ordinances to keep alive its claims to jurisdiction. Thus, in 1529 (as on other occasions), the mayor and aldermen insisted that their judgements were 'accordyng to the olde and auncyent lawes and customes of this citie . . . used and tyme oute of mynde contynued'.[70] To an extent, more pronounced peaks of activity by the court of aldermen were attributable to the proclivities of individual mayors, keen to attract the attention – as William Hampton had in 1473 – of city chroniclers and the wider public in London by presenting themselves as enemies of sin.[71] But of more sustained importance was a kind of counterpoint between purely civic concerns and those of the crown and wider political community. This skein of issues involved a number of interrelated elements: the measures that successive kings took to safeguard their position and, more generally, the growing pretensions, if not the power, of the crown; and efforts on the part of the city authorities not only to address what appeared to be growing problems of order within the city but also to respond to crown needs, placate the monarch on occasion and present an image of good civic governance to the world at large.

---

[68] Wunderli, *London Church Courts*, pp. 95–6.   [69] See Chapters 6 and 8.
[70] LMA, Journal 13, fo. 143v.
[71] Cf. Kingsford (ed.), *Chronicles of London*, pp. 187–8, for the efforts of mayors to make a name for themselves and the resulting inconsistency of policy. This is not to say, however, that all mayors set an example of personal probity: see Tarbin, 'Civic Manliness', pp. 41–2.

A perfect fit between civic and royal concerns about sexual morality is not to be expected. Edward IV's court was noted for its licentiousness, while it hardly requires emphasis that Henry VIII personally was no paragon of sexual virtue.[72] Indeed, Shannon McSheffrey has suggested that in the fifteenth century there was tension between 'civic' and 'court' morality and that on occasion the city deliberately asserted its own vision of morality against aristocratic licence. As will be seen in Chapter 9, a similar argument may be made for the years around 1550.[73] In so far as the crown, in association with the interests represented in parliament, embraced 'reformation of manners' in the fifteenth century and early sixteenth century, the measures it sponsored were certainly conceived in favour of substantial if not wealthy employers and against working men, labourers and servants. Apart from the restrictions on dress embodied in sumptuary legislation, the main targets of attack were gambling, illicit games and other activities supposed to lead to idleness and the squandering of masters' money and goods. It was within the same framework of ideas that sexual laxity was condemned, especially if the guilty parties were servants or apprentices.[74] However, the higher the social echelon, the more likely it was to be taken for granted that a man might reasonably command the services of women other than his wife. This mindset is captured in an accusation – whether true or not is beside the point – against a woman called Joan Feltes, reported in 1524: '[T]how dydyst poynt with the duke of Buckyngham for to comme to hys chamber at my lorde Hastynges place, and when thow dydyst cumme there he bad the avante drabbe [i.e. begone, whore] for he hadde mayny ferer than thow wer.'[75]

Nonetheless, there were occasions when the rhetoric of sexual reformation did appeal directly to monarchs. Most remarkably, when Richard duke of Gloucester usurped the throne, he chose to exploit the rhetoric of sexual transgression to besmirch the memory of his deceased brother and condemn supporters of his line, and it may well be that this represented a bid for support by appealing to the sense of civic morality that was by now firmly entrenched in London civic culture. In October 1483, following the collapse of Buckingham's revolt, Richard issued a proclamation 'for the

[72] However 'virtuous' he may have appeared in other respects: David Starkey, *Henry: Virtuous Prince* (London, 2008).
[73] McSheffrey, *Marriage, Sex, and Civic Culture*, p. 173; but cf. Tarbin, 'Civic Manliness', pp. 41–2.
[74] Martin Ingram, 'Reformation of Manners in Early Modern England', in Paul Griffiths, Adam Fox and Steve Hindle (eds.), *The Experience of Authority in Early Modern England* (Basingstoke, 1996), pp. 70, 72–3.
[75] LMA, DL/C/207, fo. 330v.

reformation of manners'. Condemning (among other misdoers) 'orible adultres and bawdes, provokyng the high indignation and displeasure of God', the king accused his opponents of 'letting of vertue and the dampnable maintenaunce of vices and syn', while he for his part claimed to show his love for 'the commen wele of this his reame' in 'puttyng downe and rebuking of vices'. In particular, the proclamation asserted that Thomas Grey, marquess of Dorset, 'not feryng God, nor the perille of his soule, hath many and sundry maydes, wydowes and wifes dampnably and without shame devoured, defloured, and defouled, holding the unshampfull and myschevous woman called Shores wife in adultry'. It was around this time that Elizabeth Shore, erstwhile mistress of Edward IV and now accused of living in sin with one or more of his noblemen, was (as a London chronicler expressed it, with evident satisfaction) 'as a comon harlott put to opyn penaunce, ffor the lyfe that she ledd with the said lord Hastyngys and othir grete astatys'. The following year a parliamentary act, denouncing the reign of Edward IV as a time when 'every good maiden and woman . . . [stood] in drede to be ravysshed and defouled', impugned the late king's marriage with Elizabeth Woodville as clandestine and invalid and hence asserted that 'the said King Edward duryng his lif and the seid Elizabeth lyved togedre sinfully and dampnably in aduultre . . . provokyng the ire and indignacion of oure lord God.'[76]

A more persistent point of linkage between civic and royal concerns was the association between sexual licentiousness and vagrants, referred to by contemporaries as 'vagabonds' or 'mighty beggars', and more particularly their influx into London and presence on the city streets. In July 1473 Edward IV issued a proclamation that evoked political dangers as well as the economic ills of vagrancy. Vagabonds were said to be 'persones beyng stronge and myghty of body to do service in husbondry and other labours', who on various pretexts 'fall into . . . beggyng . . . and so lyvyng ydely will not doo service but wander abought from town to town as vagaboundes'. At the same time, they were responsible for 'sowyng sedicious langages wherby the comon people many tymes be put in gret fere and jeobardy of their lyves and losses of their goodes', while the king for his part strove for 'the pacifying of this reame and restfull governaunce of the same'. While in this text no explicit link was made between vagrancy and sexual

---

[76] Thomas Rymer (ed.), *Foedera, conventiones, literae, et cujuscunque acta publica*, 10 vols., 3rd edn. (The Hague, 1739–45), Vol. V, Part 3, p. 138; Thomas and Thornley (eds.), *Great Chronicle of London*, p. 233; Rosemary Horrox (ed.), *The Parliament Rolls of Medieval England XV: Richard III, 1484–1485; Henry VII, 1485–1487* (Woodbridge, 2005), p. 15.

immorality, it can hardly be coincidence that the city of London registered this proclamation shortly before embarking on its great purge of bawds and strumpets, which thus can be seen as closely related to a broader royal initiative against disorderly elements.[77] It has even been suggested that the purge of 1473 was designed to flush out remnants of the rebellion led two years before by the Bastard of Fauconberg, whose followers were said to be lurking in brothels in and about London after the insurgents' attack on the city was driven off by the citizens.[78]

Major events of interest to the crown repeatedly revived this link between sexual licence and vagrancy and related forms of disorder and clearly underpinned some of the civic drives and exemplary action that have already been noted. The proclamation against lechery of April 1483 was issued on the accession of the boy king Edward V, when his arrival in the city was shortly expected. Its rhetoric evoked the evil of 'strumpettes, mysguyded and idil women daily vagraunt and walkyng aboute by the stretes and lanes of this citee of London and suburbes of the same and also repairyng to taverns and othere private places'. The very similar proclamation of April 1523 was issued on the day parliament assembled at Blackfriars. Reflecting how 'yt hathe pleasyd the kynges hyghnes to appoynt hys most high courte of parlement to be holden here within thys hys citie of London to the grett comforte of all the citezens and other inhabitauntes', the mayor and aldermen charged victuallers not to sell at excessive prices, required that innholders should 'honestly and curtesly entreate' visitors and took measures not only against bawds and strumpets but also against vagabonds, beggars and idle persons.[79]

These linkages spanned the late fifteenth century and early sixteenth century and were not confined to a single dynasty. Yet discontinuities are equally important. Following the purge of 1473, it does not appear that Edward IV consistently promoted the potential symbiosis between Yorkist rule and civic morality, while Richard III's recourse to the rhetoric of 'reformation of manners' sprang from the particular dynastic position in which he had placed himself. His nemesis, Henry VII, fashioned his image of Christian kingship in rather different ways, and during his reign, there is little indication of close congruence between royal and civic action against sexual transgressors, though the city continued such action on its own

---

[77] LMA, Journal 8, fos. 52v–53r.

[78] E. J. Burford, *London: The Synfulle Citie* (London, 1990), p. 108; cf. C. F. Richmond, 'Fauconberg's Kentish Rising of May 1471', *English Historical Review*, 85 (1970), 673–92.

[79] Sharpe (ed.), *Calendar of . . . Letter-Book L*, p. 206; LMA, Journal 12, fo. 239r–v.

account.[80] It is in the early part of Henry VIII's reign that there developed a more regular association, in ways that repeatedly resonated in the judicial activities of the mayor and aldermen of the city of London. In 1513, preparations for the invasion of France included a measure against 'bordel keeping in the host', which forbade both any man to 'hold' a woman in his lodgings overseas and any 'common woman' to approach the host on pain of being 'burned upon the right cheek at the first time' and subsequently imprisoned if she appeared again.[81] At home, Cardinal Wolsey – whose influence in Westminster was noted in Chapter 5 – probably played a key role in forging links between royal policy and London civic moralism. At various points in the 1510s there is evidence of direct contact between the mayor and aldermen on the one hand and, on the other, 'my lord cardynall' and other members of the king's council.

Such contacts were by no means always to the city's advantage, especially in view of recurrent tensions between crown and city. In 1517, following the riots of Evil May Day, the royal government was distinctly admonitory, and the city authorities were correspondingly placatory. On this view, high-profile public punishments were intended to demonstrate to the royal council, including Wolsey, that the city authorities were completely loyal, thoroughly reliable and acting with due diligence.[82] More usually, the sense is of a more straightforwardly co-operative (albeit unequal) relationship reflecting the shared interest of royal government and city authorities alike in maintaining public order, threatened as it seemed to be by vagabondage, epidemic disease, troop movements and other emergencies.[83] In this context, measures to combat sexual sin played an important part. The purge of bawds and harlots that occurred in 1510 was in fact part of a wider campaign in which the king's council clearly played a major role against vagabonds, beggars and suspicious persons generally, the unregulated sale of ale and beer, unlawful games and other disorders. It came in the wake of a series of exemplary prosecutions of perjurers and false questmen (crooked jurors), which was, in turn, clearly related to the disgrace of Henry VII's rapacious servants, Empson and Dudley, at the

---

[80] Anthony Goodman, 'Henry VII and Christian Renewal', in Keith Robbins (ed.), *Religion and Humanism* (Studies in Church History 17, Oxford, 1981), pp. 115–25.

[81] Paul L. Hughes and James F. Larkin (eds.), *Tudor Royal Proclamations*, 3 vols. (New Haven and London, 1964–9), Vol. I, p. 113. There had been no such provision in Henry VII's admittedly much briefer *Statutes and ordenaunces of warre* (1492).

[82] LMA, Repertory 3, fos. 86(89)r–v, (189)193v, 192(196)r; Minson, 'Public Punishment and Urban Space', 8–9; more generally, see Susan Brigden, *London and the Reformation* (Oxford, 1989), pp. 131–2, 150–5, 163–5.

[83] LMA, Repertory 4, fo. 54r–v; Repertory 5, fos. 49r–v, 50v.

commencement of the new king's reign. Just as those convicted of perjury were paraded as far as Fleet Street, presumably to ensure maximum publicity among the legal fraternity, so likewise the whores and bawds punished in 1510 were taken as far as Temple Bar before being ejected from the city.[84] In the following year the crown issued a proclamation enforcing the statute of Winchester and tightening up on law and order generally. Similarly, in 1519–20, civic proceedings against sexual offenders were part and parcel of a massive drive instigated by Wolsey against vagabonds and other suspect persons in London, Westminster and their environs.[85] Crown and city continued to work together. This symbiosis continued into the next decade and was the background of the drives against sexual offenders already noticed. By 1529, however, the context was beginning to change, as 'reformation' of an order different from any seen previously began to unfold.

[84] LMA, Journal 11, fos. 74v–78r, 93r–v, 104v, 109v, 110r, 111v–12v, 114v–15v; Repertory 2, fos. 68v, 70r, 91v, 95r; Letter Book M, fo. 159r–v. The careful choice of route is highlighted in Minson, 'Public Punishment and Urban Space', 9–12.

[85] The proclamation of 1511 and the drive of 1519 are discussed in Chapter 5.

CHAPTER 8

Sex and the Celibate Clergy

By their very nature, sexual transgressions are recurrent, and efforts to combat them are at best only temporarily successful. But certain kinds of illicit sexual behaviour found in the late fifteenth and early sixteenth centuries appear, in retrospect, to be particularly entrenched and, for different reasons, especially likely to provoke scandal. If one was the sex trade – symbolized by the continued existence of the Southwark stews, though unlicensed prostitution in a multitude of premises and locations in towns and cities was probably more insidious – the other unquestionably was clerical incontinence. Indeed, they were linked – the records confirm what contemporaries knew only too well, that members of the supposedly celibate clergy were prominent among those who availed themselves of the services of common women. But, of course, clerical immorality was by no means confined to brothels and the sex trade and took a multitude of forms. How common was it, how much resentment did it arouse among lay people and how and with what success did the authorities – whether ecclesiastical or lay – attempt to deal with it?

Anticlericalism in Question

The topic has become an historiographical vexed issue.[1] Generations of historians steeped in the Protestant tradition believed that sexual transgressions were rife among the fifteenth- and early sixteenth-century clergy and that this contributed to a groundswell of anticlericalism that was assumed to be one of the underlying causes of the Reformation in England as elsewhere in Europe. But from the 1960s new studies, based on detailed research into diocesan archives, have cut the issue down to size in terms of real numbers,[2] while more recently researchers have turned their attention

---

[1] For broader context, see Helen L. Parish, *Clerical Celibacy in the West: c.1100–1700* (Farnham, 2010).
[2] Margaret Bowker, *The Secular Clergy in the Diocese of Lincoln, 1495–1520* (Cambridge, 1968), pp. 117–21; Peter Heath, *The English Parish Clergy on the Eve of the Reformation* (London and Toronto, 1969), chap. 7; Ralph Houlbrooke, *Church Courts and the People during the English Reformation, 1520–1570*

to the implications of the rule of celibacy for the gender identity of clergy subject to it.[3] Janelle Werner has recently challenged the minimizing tendency, arguing that in the diocese of Hereford, levels of clerical immorality in the generations before the Reformation stand comparison with those in many parts of continental Europe. A potential weakness of her argument is that this see extended into Welsh-speaking areas where, it has long been recognized, clerical concubinage was relatively common. Even so, it is striking that in 1531 the vicar of Leominster 'openly flouted canon law on clerical celibacy'. Having been summoned for getting children on two different women, he was so defiant as to state in court that 'carnal pleasure' was 'natural and is not that thing that God takes vengeance for. For a little confession will easily remove it'.[4]

Meanwhile, the work of Christopher Haigh has changed the initial paradigm by not merely questioning the extent of clerical immorality but also casting doubt on the whole idea of anticlericalism as a significant force in any sense in early sixteenth-century English society, far less an efficient cause of the Reformation.[5] Yet this argument is not without problems. Earlier historians' belief that feelings against the clergy were running high in the years around 1530 was based not merely on the assumption that, to make the Reformation explicable, anticlericalism 'must have' existed but also on the observations of contemporaries. Individuals as diverse as Eustace Chapuys, the imperial ambassador, and Edward Hall, the London chronicler, seem to have thought so,[6] whereas in the early 1530s Christopher St German produced a series of works based on the idea that there was 'division betwene the spiritualtie and the temporaltie'. St German was a common lawyer who no

---

(Oxford, 1979), pp. 177–80; Tim Cooper, *The Last Generation of English Catholic Clergy: Parish Priests in the Diocese of Coventry and Lichfield in the Early Sixteenth Century* (Woodbridge, 1999), pp. 170–8.

[3] R. N. Swanson, 'Angels Incarnate: Clergy and Masculinity from Gregorian Reform to Reformation', in D. M. Hadley (ed.), *Masculinity in Medieval Europe* (London, 1999), pp. 160–77; P. H. Cullum, 'Clergy, Masculinity and Transgression in Late Medieval England', *ibid.*, pp. 178–96; P. H. Cullum, 'Life-Cycle and Life-Course in a Clerical and Celibate Milieu: Northern England in the Later Middle Ages', in Gerhard Jaritz and Gerson Moreno-Riaño (eds.), *Time and Eternity: The Medieval Discourse* (Turnhout, 2003), pp. 271–81; Jennifer D. Thibodeaux (ed.), *Negotiating Clerical Identities: Priests, Monks and Masculinity in the Middle Ages* (Basingstoke, 2010). For criticism of some of these works, see Ruth Mazo Karras, *From Boys to Men: Formations of Masculinity in Late Medieval Europe* (Philadelphia, 2003), pp. 161–2.

[4] Janelle Werner, 'Promiscuous Priests and Vicarage Children: Clerical Sexuality and Masculinity in Late Medieval England', in Thibodeaux (ed.), *Negotiating Clerical Identities*, pp. 173 and 159–81 *passim*. On Welsh customs, see Glanmor Williams, *The Welsh Church from Conquest to Reformation*, 2nd edn. (Cardiff, 1976), pp. 340–5.

[5] Christopher Haigh, 'Anticlericalism and the English Reformation', *History*, 68 (1983), 391–407; Christopher Haigh, *English Reformations: Religion, Politics and Society under the Tudors* (Oxford, 1993), pp. 15, 41–51. See also Christopher Harper-Bill, 'Dean Colet's Convocation Sermon and the Pre-Reformation Church in England', *History*, 73 (1988), 191–210.

[6] Susan Brigden, *London and the Reformation* (Oxford, 1989), pp. 172, 198; cf. Haigh, 'Anticlericalism', 391–2.

doubt had an axe to grind; others likewise had their own motives for stirring up bad feelings against the clergy.[7] But it is striking that although Sir Thomas More – likewise a common lawyer yet a staunch defender of the church authorities – took issue with many of St German's arguments, he did not altogether deny his basic premise and clearly feared that such hostility might increase. It seems incontrovertible that there was at least a *perception* that anticlericalism was rife.[8] As to reality, even Haigh admits that London offers at least a partial exception to his arguments. Susan Brigden's detailed study of the metropolis lays considerable emphasis on lay resentment on a wide range of issues, including tithe, mortuaries, pluralism and clerical ignorance and pride as well as immorality, and suggests, moreover, that recrimination and suspicion were exacerbated by fears that heresy proceedings might be used against those who challenged tithes or otherwise criticized the clergy.[9]

Some historians have noted that whatever the situation before the Reformation Parliament, challenges to – even violent attacks on – the clergy manifestly increased in the 1530s and 1540s. Ethan Shagan, who has made this argument most forcibly, does not particularly stress clerical incontinence among the matters at issue. But Robert Whiting, making essentially the same point with reference to the western counties of Devon and Cornwall, views this as a major source of lay resentment.[10] Plainly this upsurge of dissatisfaction occurred in drastically altered political circumstances, as it came to be believed that 'the king and his government had turned against the clergy', while new legislation, such as the harsh penalties against clerical marriage laid down in the Act of Six Articles (1539, modified 1540), increased the range of weapons that disgruntled lay people had at their disposal.[11] But it is hard to believe that the dissatisfactions so forcibly expressed at

---

[7] See e.g. Richard Rex, 'Jasper Fyloll and the Enormities of the Clergy: Two Tracts Written during the Reformation Parliament', *Sixteenth Century Journal*, 31 (2000), 1043–62.

[8] Christopher St German, *A Treatise concernynge the division betwene the spiritualtie and temporaltie* (London [1532]); Christopher St German, *Salem and Byzance* (London, 1533); J. B. Trapp (ed.), *The Complete Works of St. Thomas More*, Vol. IX: *The Apology* (New Haven and London, 1979), esp. pp. 54–5; John Guy, Ralph Keen, Clarence H. Miller and Ruth McGugan (eds.), *The Complete Works of St. Thomas More*, Vol. X: *The Debellation of Salem and Bizance* (New Haven and London, 1987).

[9] Haigh, 'Anticlericalism', 402; Brigden, *London and the Reformation*, pp. 48–68, 151, 204–5. See also P. R. Cavill, 'Anticlericalism and the Early Tudor Parliament', *Parliamentary History*, 34 (2015), 14–29.

[10] Ethan H. Shagan, *Popular Politics and the English Reformation* (Cambridge, 2003), chap. 4; Robert Whiting, *The Blind Devotion of the People: Popular Religion and the English Reformation* (Cambridge, 1989), pp. 126–44. See also Peter Marshall, *The Catholic Priesthood and the English Reformation* (Oxford, 1994), chap. 8.

[11] Shagan, *Popular Politics*, p. 133; 31 Henry VIII c. 14; 32 Henry VIII c. 10.

this time did not draw on long-standing currents of resentment. As Peter Marshall has demonstrated, these formed a set of powerful cultural assumptions and stereotypes that could be readily invoked.[12]

Some examples of aggression towards clerics, whether before or after 1529, certainly seem to reveal a peculiarly venomous strain of contempt and hatred. In a case from Brentford (Middlesex), a priest taken in suspicious circumstances with a woman – he claimed that he had been set up for the purposes of extortion – begged his captor for mercy but met a brutal response: 'Nay horeson thow shalt not eskape us thus for I shalle strippe the starke nakid and bryng the to the constable.' A similar threat of being stripped to the skin and utterly shamed had been made in the London parish of Aldermanbury in 1523. 'Thow knave preste,' thundered Thomas Bukke, taking Thomas Cauland by the bosom and pulling him towards him, 'I shall serche the . . . frome the crowne of thy hedd to the sole of the fote . . . I shall handle the soo that all other knave prestes shal be ware by the.'[13]

As noted in Chapter 1, 'anticlericalism' is a wide-ranging term that invites distinctions between, on the one hand, the failings of individual priests and, on the other, the role of the clergy in government and society and how as an order they used their power. It follows that the unchastity of some priests is only one of a number of issues in the anticlericalism debate. Nonetheless, it is recognized to be of special importance. Even historians who largely accept Haigh's arguments have continued to muse on the potentially corrosive effects of clerical incontinence – on the resentment and shock that individual cases could undoubtedly evoke; on the clergy's *reputation* for lubricity, irrespective of reality; on the scope for lay criticism, satire, even disillusionment inherent in the fact that the church was setting idealistic standards that some clergy simply could not attain.[14] The issue is also highly relevant to the aims of this study, that is, to gauge the intensity and efficacy of the sexual policing of the lay population as well as the clergy. As previous chapters have shown, secular tribunals took an important part in this work, especially in urban contexts. But the church courts were the main agents. If the officials who ran these courts

---

[12] Peter Marshall, 'Anticlericalism Revested? Expressions of Discontent in Early Tudor England', in Clive Burgess and Eamon Duffy (eds.), *The Parish in Late Medieval England: Proceedings of the 2002 Harlaxton Symposium* (Donington, 2006), pp. 365–80.

[13] TNA, REQ 2/11/115, m. 6 (the case is discussed further in Marshall, *Catholic Priesthood*, pp. 147, 155–6); LMA, DL/C/207, fo. 194v (the underlying cause of tension in this case is unclear).

[14] Marshall, *Catholic Priesthood*, chap. 5; G. W. Bernard, *The Late Medieval English Church: Vitality and Vulnerability before the Break with Rome* (New Haven and London, 2012), pp. 69–71.

were in any way tainted by aspersions on the sexual morality of the parish clergy and of monks and friars, their efforts were at risk of being undermined. This chapter addresses the question by examining, in greater detail than has hitherto been attempted, how the fact or suspicion of illicit sexual activity on the part of the clergy was dealt with under various jurisdictions in rural areas, provincial towns and the metropolis. It concludes, more emphatically than most recent assessments, that there existed a real, persistent and by no means negligible problem that provoked a great deal of lay resentment.

Popular and Official Attitudes towards Clerical Unchastity

While secular clerics did not take an explicit vow of chastity, the law and custom of the Western church had for centuries required them to be celibate, and it is plain that to all intents and purposes they were assumed to be as much vowed to celibacy as monks and nuns. Living in the world as they did, cheek by jowl with ordinary lay people, they were in effect a showcase for the church's ascetic ideals and veneration of the celibate life as spiritually superior, and their prime duty of celebrating the mass and administering other sacraments made it all the more important that they should live up to the ideal. 'Men of holy chirche,' asserted the author of *Dives and Pauper*, 'mon betere withstondyn flechly temptacion than weddyd men, for thei owyn to pasyn the peple in connyng and in vertue.' He recommended harsh punishments for priests who 'presumyn to touchyn Godys body or to mynystryn at Godys auter whan they han comounyd with othir mennys wyfis or with her [i.e. their] concubynys'.[15] Ordinary 'incontinence' on the part of the clergy was bad enough, but priests who had sexual relations with women they had baptized or (a more likely event) whose confessions they had received were said to be guilty of the graver sin of 'spiritual incest'.[16]

How far did the ordinary inhabitants of villages and small towns share the conviction that clerical chastity was an important matter? Of pre-Reformation parish priests, David Loades has written: 'Canon law forbade them to marry, but only a minority of them were celibate. Their communities normally accepted that a man needed a woman, and as long as he treated her decently and provided for his children, they were not disposed

---

[15] Priscilla Heath Barnum (ed.), *Dives and Pauper*, 2 vols. in 3 parts (Early English Text Society 275, 280, 323, London, 1976–2004), Vol. I, Part 2, pp. 107, 110.
[16] F. M. Powicke and C. R. Cheney (eds.), *Councils and Synods with Other Documents Relating to the English Church*, Vol. II: *A.D. 1205–1313* (Oxford, 1964), pp. 486, 1015, 1083.

to be critical.'[17] At best, this argument can only apply to otherwise unattached concubines or mistresses – Loades seems not to consider the issue of clergy forming liaisons with married women – but an abundance of evidence suggests that it is simply wrong. It has been shown that testators, in making provision for masses and prayers to be said to speed their souls through purgatory, demonstrated an explicit preference for 'honest' priests, and among the bundle of attributes that constituted 'honesty', sexual continence was very prominent. In contrast, a 'lewd' priest was one given to sins of the flesh and other laxity and was thereby (as numerous petitions and complaints make plain) an object of 'shame'.[18] Such a priest might forfeit all credit and be pushed to the very margins of society. Thus, around 1530, it was reported of the vicar of Haverhill (Suffolk) that 'for his incontinence of his vicious living he was driven from Fulbourn in the county of Cambridge into Sampford in Essex, and from there to Lyttyng Wrottyng . . . in Suffolk, as all the country will testify'.[19] It is no wonder that, as noted in Chapter 2, priests sometimes sought the aid of the courts to defend themselves against accusations. In 1520, for example, Alexander Henryson brought an action for defamation in the Chichester consistory court on the grounds that he had been called 'the sardyng priest of Lymynster', coupling this with a suit for laying violent hands on the clergy. The sense of the word 'sarding' is hard to capture in modern English; 'screwing' and 'shagging' are perhaps the nearest equivalents, but in any case the biting force of the epithet is palpable. It was used again the following year to insult no less a person than the bishop of London's commissary, when a woman charged with promoting bawdry snapped back contemptuously, '[L]oo a knave somner hathe cited me to Pollis Cheyn to the comen sarder.'[20]

Haigh's attempt both to minimize the numerical incidence of sexual transgressions among the clergy, and to deny their importance, on the basis of large-scale but relatively superficial analyses of visitation returns begs many questions.[21] The argument rests on the assumption that visitations were the prime opportunity for parishioners to express disquiet about their priests' sexual morality and that the returns are therefore a good guide to the extent of clerical incontinence itself or of lay concern about it. It is true

[17] David Loades, 'Anticlericalism in the Church of England before 1558: An "Eating Canker"?', in Nigel Aston and Matthew Cragoe (eds.), *Anticlericalism in Britain, c.1500–1914* (Stroud, 2000), p. 5, cf. p. 15, n. 20.
[18] Marshall, *Catholic Priesthood*, pp. 51–9, 152, 161–2.   [19] Quoted *ibid.*, p. 154.
[20] WSRO, Ep.I/10/2, fos. 77v, 87r, 101r; LMA, DL/C/B/041/MS09065J/1, fo. 127v.
[21] Haigh, 'Anticlericalism', 392; Haigh, *English Reformations*, pp. 41–2.

that clerical celibacy was an important focus of investigation to the extent that on occasion a bishop might demand reports on all females living or working in the houses of the clergy, not merely those deemed 'suspect'.[22] But, as seen in Chapter 3, visitation presentments as such are an inadequate guide to the occurrence of sexual transgressions of any sort, far less those of the clergy. Fearful of reprisals and certainly wary of raising scandal unless there was clear proof, the churchwardens and questmen responsible for making these reports always tended to be very circumspect in the accusations they made, and this was especially so when the object of suspicion was a priest. For example, if a young woman had been delivered of child in a vicarage or rectory – an event that was bound to raise suspicion about the morality of the clergyman himself – the circumstance was often carefully expressed in terms of plain fact, and it was left to the authorities to investigate further. Thus, at Sproxton (Leicestershire) in 1510, it was simply stated that the vicar 'has a young woman in his house who is pregnant as the public voice and fame labour'.[23]

Haigh's argument is in any case insensitive to the salience and persistence of clerical incontinence as a matter of concern among both lay people and the church hierarchy. In any one year, in any one jurisdiction, probably fewer than 5 per cent of priests were brought in question for sexual immorality. Assuming that the resultant scandals would remain in parochial memory – especially when (as was often the case) the circumstances were such as seriously to affront local sensibilities or disrupt social relations – it may be inferred that the cumulative effect of such figures was much greater than appears at first sight.

Even when errant clergy submitted humbly to penance, the public response might be far different from the charitable forgiveness envisaged in penitential theory. If Sir Thomas More is to be believed, lay people commonly seized on cases of clerical incontinence, whatever the circumstances, with great glee. It was, he said, with

> moche pyte that we take suche a wretched pleasure in the herynge of theyr synne, and in the syght of theyr shame. Good is it for theym to loke on theyre fautes, but for us were it better to loke lesse to theyrs and more unto our owne. But surely many of us have suche delyte to here of theyr harme that it semeth we be glad when one of them dothe any suche thynge, as we may have occasyon to se them punysshed or hadde in derysyon.

---

[22] E.g. A. Hamilton Thompson (ed.), *Visitations in the Diocese of Lincoln, 1517–1531*, 3 vols. (Lincoln Record Society 33, 35, 37, Hereford, 1940–7), Vol. I, pp. xxiv, 55–98 *passim*.
[23] LA, DIOC/Viv 5, fo. 69r.

He told the story of a young priest who for his unchastity carried a lighted candle in procession, to the great laughter of the onlookers, and 'one mery marchaunt sayd unto the prestes that folowed hym, *sic luceat lux vestra coram hominibus.* Thus let youre lyght shyne afore the people.'[24]

Occasionally, the ecclesiastical authorities worsened the situation by neglecting cases of misconduct, treating them with scandalous leniency or even turning a blind eye. Stephen Lander argues that this was the case in Chichester archdeaconry in the early years of the sixteenth century, when as many as 15 per cent of parishes were troubled by clerical immorality. In a notable clutch of cases early in 1508, the rector, vicar and curate, respectively, of the contiguous parishes of Gates, Sidlesham and Selsey were convicted of incontinence with one or other of two sisters, whose mother was also cited as their bawd.[25] Interestingly, the experienced administrator Richard Fox, bishop of Winchester between 1501 and 1528, was reluctant to subject clergy to 'open penance to theyre noys or infamy', far less punish them with deprivation, even for 'manyfest fornycation or advowtrey' – though this did not mean that he let such offences pass unnoticed.[26] In general, the late fifteenth- and early sixteenth-century church courts did put considerable effort into combating the problem – impossible though it was to eradicate completely – actively assisted on occasion by local people.

Indeed, sometimes they went to extreme lengths. Bishop Longland's visitors in parts of the archdeaconry of Buckingham in May 1519 seem to have inquired minutely about women of any kind in the houses of the clergy. This initiative turned up sundry mothers, sisters and other relatives, no doubt piously ministering to male domestic needs (though an aunt was evidently thought to be suspicious). It also drew attention to female servants who, though not relatives and possibly young, were seen to pose no threat because their clerical employers were themselves aged. But in a number of patently suspicious cases, the clergy were forthwith ordered to get rid of the offending females, and in one case, some very tangled circumstances came to light. At Thornton, the rector was said to keep a certain Joan Thakham in his house. The first entry, itself not altogether

---

[24] Thomas M. C. Lawler, Germain Marc'hadour and Richard C. Marius (eds.), *The Complete Works of St. Thomas More*, Vol. VI: *A Dialogue Concerning Heresies* (New Haven and London, 1981), pp. 296–7.

[25] Stephen Lander, 'Church Courts and the Reformation in the Diocese of Chichester, 1500–58', in Rosemary O'Day and Felicity Heal (eds.), *Continuity and Change: Personnel and Administration of the Church in England, 1500–1642* (Leicester, 1976), p. 218; WSRO, Ep.I/10/1, fos. 36r, 37r, 39r.

[26] P. S. Allen and H. M. Allen (eds.), *Letters of Richard Fox, 1486–1527* (Oxford, 1929), p. 151; Houlbrooke, *Church Courts*, pp. 175, 178, 210.

convincing, indicated that 'the parishioners, however, suspect no ill of her, save that she is not a little proud and gives them proud words'. But a further report suggested that she was 'a common whore who lives within the rectory and keeps there a common tavern; she is also a common scold; the rector lives incontinently with her.' Plainly there was an incipient scandal here, and the woman had to go.[27]

Such thoroughgoing drives were unusual, but the authorities were on the whole very vigilant, so sooner or later egregious cases were bound to come to light. Some of the circumstances thus exposed were extreme. In Chetwode (Buckinghamshire) in 1489, a chaplain was accused of incest with his spiritual daughter, servant of a local householder; of relations with a certain Alice Graunt and of consorting very suspiciously with the wife of a man living in the neighbouring village of Tingewick. At Waddesdon in 1485, the vicar was accused of an adulterous relationship with only one woman, but he was also detected for sorcery, using the psalter and keys to find lost goods. In certain circumstances, even an ill-founded accusation of incontinence could have its uses for the authorities eager to uphold standards. At Lidgate (Suffolk) in 1499, Isabel Laurence was presented for consorting suspiciously with the parish chaplain, Edmund Wynchester. She claimed that the accusation sprang from pure malice and was allowed to clear herself by her own oath. But the judge took the opportunity to examine Wynchester on his knowledge of the sacraments and, finding him seriously wanting, ordered him to give up the cure. In the same visitation, an even more disquieting set of circumstances was revealed at Pettaugh. The rector, John Springe, was accused of keeping a woman in his house. But he was also said to be an excommunicate and was charged with revealing the secrets of the confessional. Like Wynchester, he was found to have inadequate knowledge to serve the cure and was suspended from administration of the sacraments until he was better informed.[28]

Cases where the clergy were ordered out of their parishes raise the interesting question of how this was managed without exacerbating scandal. The courts were certainly aware of the problems and did what they could to mitigate them. In 1519, the rector of Sheepy (Leicestershire) was ordered to undergo penance and then, to avoid scandal, to exchange his benefice for another in a different diocese. He was given a paper to read

---

[27] Thompson (ed.), *Visitations in the Diocese of Lincoln*, Vol. I, pp. 46–7 and 35–54 *passim*.

[28] E. M. Elvey (ed.), *The Courts of the Archdeaconry of Buckingham, 1483–1523* (Buckinghamshire Record Society 19, Welwyn Garden City, 1975), pp. 23, 24, 77–8; Christopher Harper-Bill (ed.), *The Register of John Morton, Archbishop of Canterbury, 1486–1500*, 3 vols. (Canterbury and York Society 75, 78, 89, Leeds and Woodbridge, 1987–2000), Vol. III, pp. 201–2, 229.

from the pulpit, to the effect 'that his parishioners shuld forgive hym and he to forgive them, they to pray for hym and he for them, signyfyng that he must thence *propter peccata sua ad mandatum ordinarii recedere.*' It is unlikely that the switch into Latin deceived anybody, but it may at least have prevented the occasion from being marred by too many sniggers and gibes.[29]

Case Studies: The Archdeaconries of Leicester and Chichester, 1520–3

Illuminating though such examples are, a rounded picture of the church courts' efforts to combat clerical immorality can come only from examining all their proceedings in a given area for particular periods. A fair sample is provided by the Leicester archdeaconry correction book for the period November 1522 to July 1523, especially as the names of the clergy concerned can be compared with those listed in the rolls of the 1526 clerical subsidy. There were 450 or more parish clergy associated with the county at this time, of whom perhaps 360 were actually resident in the parishes. The incidence of cases is in line with the usual finding that fewer than 5 per cent of clerics in a given period were subjected to immorality charges.[30] In these eight and a half months, the court dealt with fourteen cases, one involving the rector of a parish outside the jurisdiction in Nottinghamshire.[31]

Of the Leicestershire clergy, five were beneficed vicars, while the rest appear to have been curates or parochial chaplains. This is similar to the pattern in Winchester diocese in 1527–8, where Houlbrooke found that the majority of clergy accused of incontinence were unbeneficed.[32] The marital and social status of several of the women is unknown, but at least six married women were implicated, while three of the females (one of whom had become pregnant) were the household servants of the clergy concerned. The vicar of Long Clawson was one of those brought in question with a married woman, but he successfully cleared his name with two compurgators in the form of fellow clergy and was still serving

[29] Margaret Bowker (ed.), *An Episcopal Court Book for the Diocese of Lincoln, 1514–1520* (Lincoln Record Society 61, Lincoln, 1967), p. 113.

[30] On numbers of Leicestershire clergy, see J. F. Fuggles, 'The Parish Clergy in the Archdeaconry of Leicester, 1520–1540', *Transactions of the Leicestershire Archaeological and Historical Society*, 46 (1970–1), 25–6, 32–7.

[31] ROLLR, 1 D 41/13/1, fo. 10r and *passim*; cf. Fuggles, 'Parish Clergy', 37–8.

[32] Houlbrooke, *Church Courts*, p. 174n.

the cure in 1526. Likewise ordered to clear themselves by compurgation were the vicar of Croxton Keyrial, accused of relations both with his maidservant and a local married woman; the curate of Misterton, charged with a married woman; and the stipendiary of Tur Langton, similarly accused. (In the last case, three lay and three clerical compurgators were required.) In each of these cases the outcome is uncertain, but all three were still resident in their parishes in 1526.[33]

So was the vicar of Hungerton. He was accused of incontinence with a married woman and ordered to undergo the stiff test of producing three clerics and three lay people to support him with their oaths. He could not do so but requested a special commission to 'inquire of his infamy'. If this cleared him in a technical sense, it can hardly have done his local reputation much good. John Hutchyngton, vicar of Shepshed, was accused with a certain Emmot, wife of Thomas Davy, who was at a later stage brought in question with another man. The circumstances were evidently murky, and Hutchyngton admitted that there was ill-fame against him. He was given the daunting task of clearing himself with the oaths of six fellow clerics and six lay people. Simply to produce so many people all at once cannot have been easy, but he managed it and was still in his benefice in 1526. So also was the vicar of Thornton, who, having succumbed to the sexual attractions of his maidservant, compounded with the commissary.[34]

Unbeneficed clergy were in a less secure position. When brought in question, some no doubt thought it prudent to move on – there was always a high turnover of curates anyway – while others were singled out for exemplary treatment by the court. The case of Dominus William Hopkyn of Breedon on the Hill was remitted to the commissary. What he did in the matter is not known, but Hopkyn was not in the parish by 1526. Neither was John Gorge, chaplain of Stoney Stanton. He and the woman both confessed; she did penance, and he was 'convented before the commissary of the cardinal [Wolsey]' and was soon gone from the parish. The chaplain of Cold Overton confessed only the fame against him and was ordered to undergo compurgation: whether he succeeded or not, he was apparently away by 1526. Master John Bosard of Kibworth – the only graduate in this group – did manage to purge himself in similar circumstances, but by 1526 he was a curate in Northamptonshire.[35]

---

[33] ROLLR, 1 D 41/13/1, fos. 4v, 12v, 19v, 29r; H. E. Salter (ed.), *A Subsidy Collected in the Diocese of Lincoln in 1526* (Oxford Historical Society 63, Oxford and London, 1909), pp. 96, 98, 103, 117.

[34] ROLLR, 1 D 41/13/1, fos. 10r, 23r; Salter (ed.), *Subsidy*, pp. 104, 109, 110.

[35] ROLLR, 1 D 41/13/1, fos. 7r, 25r, 25v, 26r; Salter (ed.), *Subsidy*, pp. 98, 101, 113, 116, 135.

The curate of Ibstock, who also farmed the rectory, was suspended after he got his maidservant with child and failed to turn up in court to answer the charge. Later he was absolved and promised to leave the jurisdiction. Dominus Robert Bartrame of Muston, probably a stipendiary curate, confessed carnal relations and was enjoined a series of severe penances. However, these were *in terrorem* only. Later the judge changed them to two pilgrimages to the image of the Virgin in Lincoln Cathedral and to the Chapel of the Virgin on the south bridge of Leicester. In each case Bartrame was to recite the psalter of the Blessed Virgin and to make an offering to the saint; on the bridge, he was also to give the token sum of one penny to the poor. The sting in the tail of this penance was that Bartrame was ordered to leave the district for at least a year 'on account of the scandal that might arise'. Probably he never returned to Muston and was certainly not there in 1526.[36]

Between January 1520 and January 1521, the consistory and commissary courts of Chichester commenced eleven prosecutions of this type, but only nine clergy were involved, as two were prosecuted more than once. Both beneficed and unbeneficed clergy were implicated, as well as Dominus John Welles, prior of the house of Sele, while several of the women were married.[37] Most of these cases are recorded only briefly, and the outcomes are often unclear, but there is some telling information about Dominus Thomas Combes, vicar of Arundel. In January 1520 he was scheduled to clear himself of an imputation of 'committing' with a certain Elizabeth Hutchyns. Failing to produce compurgators, he was ordered to receive penance. But the matter was clearly complicated. At the same session, Combes brought an instance suit against the mayor and townspeople of Arundel, while they for their part produced articles against him. All these cases dropped from the record, but in April, Combes was back in court, facing an ex officio prosecution promoted by Edward Hurst, the town constable. Hurst recounted how on the Friday night before Palm Sunday he and two sergeants

> toke the saide Thomas and oon Elisabeth Hutchyns in a chamber within Thomas Cranes howse and then he wold have gon forth into the strete at a dore wher stode oon of the sargeantes and then he went from that dor and cum forth at an other dor and stroke at the said . . . [sergeant] with a knyff and hurt his hand and so from ther he went home.

---

[36] ROLLR, 1 D 41/13/1, fos. 9v, 22r, 24v, 25r; Salter (ed.), *Subsidy*, pp. 96, 104.
[37] WSRO, Ep.I/10/2, fos. 8v, 19r, 22r, 31v, 42r, 67v, 81v, 83r, 90r, 113v, 114r, 125r.

Hurst and his officers entered the house and, having found Elizabeth Hutchyns hiding behind a chimney piece, took her before the mayor before setting off for the vicarage to secure Combes. He nearly gave them the slip, but seeing him 'ronne downe a lane with a knyf in his hand', they were soon in pursuit and arrested him. In the presence of the mayor, Combes claimed he had lost his purse. They all went back to the scene of the crime, and the purse was duly found 'hid betwyn the bed and the strawe, and his gowne be the beddes side and his typpett in the hall and his boke apon the bed'. It was all very suspicious, but Combes claimed that he had gone to the house about Easter malt offerings; when Elizabeth Hutchyns came in, he had merely talked with her in the entry by the chamber door. Asked by the judge whether 'Sir Thomas' had offended with the woman, the constable and his companions replied that they rather thought yes than no, but they could not be sure.[38]

Immoral Clergy and the Secular Courts

This case is typical of many in which strong suspicion and local indignation led to stake-outs and ambushes in an attempt to nail the guilty parties. Intervention by the secular authorities was likewise not uncommon, especially in urban contexts. In London, as will be seen, special procedures had been developed to deal with immoral clergy. Away from the metropolis, whether in town or country, another means of invoking the secular law was actually to indict incontinent priests for rape. Some such cases may indeed have involved forcible intercourse without the woman's consent. But it is plain that in many instances the relationship was consensual: the rape charge was used as a legal fiction to bring the matter before the secular courts. Admittedly, the outcome for the priests involved was less dire than might at first sight be supposed. Most cases led to acquittals; indeed, many charges were probably thrown out by the grand jury before they reached the stage of formal indictment. Priests who were convicted could plead 'benefit of clergy', which freed them from the danger of hanging. It must therefore be understood that the purpose of these prosecutions was not actually to get the guilty priests hanged but to expose them publicly and put them to considerable expense and trouble, which might well include a period of pre-trial imprisonment in noisome and dangerous conditions.

The practice was well established by the early fifteenth century, and in some parts of the country, cases occurred in significant numbers. There

---

[38] *Ibid.*, fos. 8v, 42r.

were fourteen in Derbyshire, fifty in Leicestershire and eighty in Warwickshire between 1400 and 1429. Similarly, in Norwich diocese nearly one hundred parochial clergy were arraigned on charges of rape at gaol deliveries between 1423 and 1441, and additional cases were probably prosecuted in sessions of the peace.[39] The near-total loss of early and mid-Tudor assize and sessions records makes it impossible to provide exact figures for the eve of the Reformation, but it is plain both from scattered references in the court of King's Bench and from contemporary comments that the practice continued. Sir Thomas More claimed that 'men know well in many a shyre how often that many folk endyght prestes of rape at the sessyons. And as there ys sometyme a rape committed in dede, so ys there ever a rape surmysed were the women never so wyllynge, and oftentyme where there was nothynge done at all … Ye se not very many sessyons passe but in one shyre or other thys pageant ys playd.'[40]

On this evidence, the church authorities – however active they were by their own lights – struggled to persuade lay people that they were doing enough to deal with immoral priests. There is no indication, at least in the rural areas and small towns that were characteristic of most parts of early Tudor England, that this led to complete disillusionment with the ecclesiastical court establishment or wholesale alienation from the clergy. Far less was there any call for clerical marriage to be permitted, as Protestants were soon to demand. On the contrary, all the indications are that people were at one with the authorities in desiring stricter enforcement of the rules. But this was something that, despite their best efforts, the church courts operating in the generation or so before the Reformation simply could not deliver.

Provincial Towns and Cities

Were things any different in the larger provincial towns and cities? The clustering of religious houses and chantries in urban centres and

---

[39] Edward Powell, 'Jury Trial at Gaol Delivery in the Late Middle Ages: The Midland Circuit, 1400–1429', in J. S. Cockburn and Thomas A. Green (eds.), *Twelve Good Men and True: The Criminal Trial Jury in England, 1200–1800* (Princeton, NJ, 1988), pp. 101–3; R. L. Storey, 'Malicious Indictments of Clergy in the Fifteenth Century', in M. J. Franklin and Christopher Harper-Bill (eds.), *Medieval Ecclesiastical Studies in Honour of Dorothy M. Owen* (Woodbridge, 1995), pp. 221–40.

[40] Frank Manley, Germain Marc'hadour, Richard C. Marius and Clarence H. Miller (eds.), *The Complete Works of St. Thomas More*, Vol. VII: *Letter to Bugenhagen; Supplication of Souls; Letter against Frith* (New Haven and London, 1990), p. 131; cf. TNA, KB 9/347, m. 5 (1478); KB 9/363, m. 2 (1483); KB 9/435, mm. 68, 69, 73, 74, 75 (1504); KB 9/486, m. 7 (1521).

cathedral establishments in episcopal sees inevitably meant a larger and often highly visible clergy presence. At the same time, as seen in Chapter 4, in these environments the sex trade flourished, partly indeed to cater for the clergy. As in rural areas, lay people's response to the inevitable cases of clerical immorality was, for the most part, not hostility to the whole estate of the clergy but simply the demand that they should live up to their ideals. Yet the existence of borough and city courts, claiming jurisdiction over the sexual transgressions of both lay people and clergy, did make it possible to voice accusations that at times had a definite anticlerical flavour.

Nottingham, it has been noted, was staunchly orthodox in its religious complexion. At the same time, it did have a number of moribund hospitals and religious houses,[41] towards which some, though by no means all, of the accusations of clerical immorality were directed. To cite some examples, in 1522, the warden of the Greyfriars and Agnes Waydel were charged with bawdry, Emmot Wode was reported 'for kepyng of bawdre' with 'Sir Roger', the parish priest of St Mary's, while the following year the parish priest of St Peter's was presented with Emma Shaa for 'kepyn mysrule'.[42] Earlier, in 1500, a shoemaker was charged with keeping '*bordellum et lenocinium*' (bawdry and pandering) between a certain woman and the rector of 'Litill Leyk'; the presentment went on to state that, in addition, 'they indyte the same parson and his concubyn for theyr horedome kepyng', while on the same occasion a labourer was presented for keeping bawdry between the parish clerk of St Peter's and his 'concubine'. In the same year, yet another cleric was charged with raping a man's wife. This was probably an instance of the use of rape charges to punish what was in reality straightforward clerical incontinence, since another priest, the warden of the Friars Minor in Nottingham, was named as the couple's go-between and bawd. Equally creative from a legal point of view was the prosecution of John Manby, parish clerk, by means of an indictment for criminal trespass. The charge stated that on a certain day he had, by force of arms with clubs and knives – this was common form and did not necessarily imply real violence – assaulted Elizabeth Haylles. He was not said to have harmed her physically, however, the nub of the charge being that he 'commonly kept and occupied her as his concubine'.[43]

---

[41] David Marcombe, 'The Late Medieval Town, 1149–1560', in John Beckett (ed.), *A Centenary History of Nottingham* (Manchester, 1997), pp. 93–7.

[42] NA, CA 23a/5, 6v, 8; CA 24/2 (the parish priest of St Peter's was also called 'Sir Roger' and may have been identical with the man presented in 1522).

[43] NA, CA 9d/4, 5, 6, CA 10a/5.

The case of Colchester is exceptionally interesting. The bulk of the inhabitants were no doubt orthodox, and conventional piety was not merely strong but, as was commonly the case in these provincial towns and cities, closely enmeshed with the structures of borough government. But this was also an established Lollard centre and in 1526–8 an important focus of Bishop Tunstal's intense investigations into heresy – by now complicated by the infiltration of Lutheran ideas and the circulation of Tyndale's New Testament.[44] In the late fifteenth century there are indications of a sharp eye for clerical misdeeds, though no explicit link with heretical ideas. At the lawhundred court held at Michaelmas 1481, for example, the rector of St Nicholas' church was presented as an habitual adulterer with a certain Alice Waterfalle. At Hilary 1482 he was charged with adultery with both her and another woman, while Alice Waterfalle was prosecuted, along with other women, as a common whore. A church court summoner was reported for being a bawd. At another court in the spring of 1482, another cleric was prosecuted for adultery with a certain Joan, lately the servant of William Danke.[45]

There is a gap in the records in the reign of Henry VII, while sampling of those that survive for the early part of Henry VIII's reign suggests some falling off in presentments of this type. But at the lawhundred in May 1527 the jurors of the south ward – the port area where several alleged Lollards lived – presented a clutch of charges involving clerical immorality, including 'Sir Roger, soul priest at the Hythe' and Dominus John Thixstyll, sacrist of St Botolph's, both for 'ill rule' with married women. Among similar presentments in the following years was the prosecution at the Michaelmas lawhundred in 1529 of Richard Caumond, vicar of St Peter's, for ill rule and 'le mayntenauns' of the same in his parish. For this he was fined the substantial sum of ten shillings, only to be prosecuted again in January 1531 for breaking into the house of Richard Feks and having 'his pleasure and lust' with the latter's wife.[46] In view of the timing, it is hard not to see these presentments as a response first to Tunstal's anti-heresy drive in the late 1520s and then to the parliamentary activities against the clergy from 1529. They suggest that whatever the lay people who mounted these prosecutions may have

[44] Laquita M. Higgs, *Godliness and Governance in Tudor Colchester* (Ann Arbor, MI, 1998), chap. 4, esp. pp. 101–14.
[45] Essex RO, Colchester BR, D/B5 Cr 79, mm. 2r, 16v, 30r.
[46] Higgs, *Godliness and Governance*, pp. 114–15, cf. (on Caumond) pp. 78, 82, 84; Essex RO, Colchester BR, D/B5 Cr 99, m. 5v.

thought of the measures against heretics, they were determined that clerical faults should not pass unnoticed.[47]

Clerical Immorality in the Metropolis

What of the situation in and around the metropolis? Owing to loss of records, disappointingly little can be said about Westminster. As to Southwark, it is perhaps surprising to find that clerical immorality does not emerge as an exceptionally prominent issue. It must be borne in mind, however, that the one surviving ecclesiastical court act book for this period covers only a few years (1511–15) and does not represent the complete activities of the Winchester diocesan courts; some clerical incontinence cases may well have been reserved to the bishop. In the sample year of 1512, four cases were registered, but three related not to Southwark itself but to neighbouring locations, namely, the parishes of Tooting and Camberwell and the monastery of Chertsey, while the provenance of the remaining case – when a priest turned up in court of his own volition and tried to clear himself by offering a parish priest from Canterbury diocese and an out-of-work chaplain as his compurgators – was not stated.[48] But there were occasional Southwark cases in other years recorded in the act book, and some of them reflect considerable lubricious interest and a current of resentment, especially in men but among women also, towards immoral clergy. Thus, in 1514, two women deposed that through an aperture offering a view into the house of Anne Colyns, they witnessed her kissing a priest and otherwise behaving suspiciously. As they told the story, he 'raised . . . [her] lower garments', and they saw him 'standing between her legs and moving his body'. In a defamation suit from St George's Southwark in 1515, Robert Hoknet was said to have taxed a woman with being 'a prestes hore and that he wold showe a tale to Master chaunceler that shuld shame them both'. 'Wherwithal,' he asked rhetorically, 'shuld hir husband and she bye there house but with prestes goodes?' In another case, appeasement was the order of the day. When a chaplain of St Olave's was accused with a sawyer's wife, her husband appeared in court to declare that to the best of his belief the priest was of good name and fame. But prudently the judge ordered the chaplain to seek lodgings elsewhere.[49]

In the city of London itself, the issue of immoral clergy was altogether more fraught. As has been seen, although there were secular reasons of

[47] Higgs, *Godliness and Governance*, pp. 115–16.   [48] LMA, Ac. 62.7, fos. 60r, 64v, 76v, 83v, 92v.
[49] LMA, Ac. 62.7, fos. 131v, 153r [*recte* 163r], 173v.

governance and good order to justify the exercise of civic authority over sexual offenders of all kinds, the mayor and aldermen were never shy of invoking religious and ecclesiastical language in their judgements against malefactors. Moreover, immoral clergy were themselves prominent among the targets of civic justice. Indeed, the ordinances of 1382 included specific measures against them, particularly those taken with a woman in the night time in flagrante delicto. Offenders were to be led to the Tun prison on Cornhill, accompanied by minstrels for maximum publicity; a third offence entailed banishment from the city. Shortly afterwards, the procedure was modified to accommodate the claims of the spiritual jurisdiction. On the morrow of the offence the priest and the woman with whom he had been arrested were to be taken before the mayor and aldermen. If no one came forward to prosecute the charges further, the priest was to be handed over to the bishop's officers, where he was usually able to clear himself by compurgation. However, proclamation was to be made of the offence and the misdeed inscribed on a 'tabula' in the Guildhall so that citizens and other inhabitants might be warned not employ him in any spiritual office. If they did so, they were to pay a fine to the city.[50]

For much of the fifteenth century, the Journals of the court of common council regularly recorded cases of adulterous priests being imprisoned in the Tun. A parliamentary act of 1485, empowering bishops to imprison immoral clergy, may possibly help to explain why such cases disappear from the record around 1480.[51] Yet it is clear from incidental references in church court records that at the local – ward and parish – level the civic authorities continued to make arrests of immoral priests, though by this date they seem to have been incarcerated in the city Counters rather than in the Tun. To take but two examples, in 1494, Dominus William, 'gret tenour' of St Sepulchre's parish, was said to have been 'taken and led to *le Counter* with a certain whore', while in the same year Dominus Richard, priest of the morning mass at St Peter Paul's Wharf, was accused of adultery with Joan Browne, who was taken in his chamber and likewise led to the Counter.[52]

---

[50] Henry Thomas Riley (ed.), *Munimenta Gildhallae Londoniensis*, 3 vols. (London, 1859–62), Vol. I, p. 459; Vol. III, p. 181 (translation); Reginald R. Sharpe (ed.), *Calendar of Letter-Books of the City of London at the Guildhall: Letter-Book H. Circa A.D. 1375–1399* (London, 1907), pp. 189, 389–90. For the period before about 1500, see also Shannon McSheffrey, 'Whoring Priests and Godly Citizens: Law, Morality, and Clerical Sexual Misconduct in Late Medieval London', in Norman L. Jones and Daniel Woolf (eds.), *Local Identities in Late Medieval and Early Modern England* (Basingstoke, 2007), pp. 50–70.
[51] 1 Henry VII c. 4.   [52] LMA, DL/C/B/043/MS09064/6, fos. 9r, 53v.

Surviving records of the Canterbury convocation of 1487, during the archiepiscopate of John (later Cardinal) Morton, indicate both concern about the behaviour of London clergy and the extent to which it had become a public relations issue. It was reported that the preachers at Paul's Cross 'greatly cried out against the church and against ecclesiastics in their absence, and this before lay people, who are always hostile to the clergy'. Admittedly the comment on lay attitudes was a commonplace, echoing the wording of Pope Boniface VIII's bull *Clericis laicos* of 1296. But the preachers – described as 'learned men, both secular and religious' – subsequently appeared before the assembled bishops, and after long discussion, Morton warned them not to inveigh against priests in future, but 'if they knew of any spiritual person who lived ill and irregularly [*enormiter*] or did anything dishonestly, they should detect such a person to their ordinary.' If the ordinary did not correct the malefactor, the matter should be referred to the archbishop, and if he – Morton himself – failed to act, 'then he wished that they should preach against the archbishop and against no other'. A number of London priests also appeared and were duly admonished to reform their ill-behaviour to avoid the 'infamy that had grown on them in the said city'. On this occasion, the ill-behaviour in question was apparently the frequenting of inns, taverns and alehouses, where priests were said to loiter all day. To remedy this, Morton urged that twelve or thirteen of them should eat communally – presumably in imitation of Jesus and the apostles at the Last Supper – and he also ordered them to cut their long hair and not to wear open gowns.[53]

The record says nothing about incontinence as such, but elsewhere – as in a sermon preached by John Alcock, bishop of Ely, apparently to the citizens of London around 1497 – the issues of clerical dress and clerical chastity are juxtaposed.[54] That the latter was a continuing concern is plain from the records of the commissary court around the same time. It is striking that in the sample year 1495 more than thirty of the men charged with adultery – at least 15 per cent – can with reasonable confidence be identified as priests. A further nine clerics, an only slightly smaller proportion, were among the sixty-six men charged with fornication. The exact status of the offending clergy was in most cases unspecified. No doubt

---

[53] Gerald Bray (ed.), *Records of Convocation VI: Canterbury, 1444–1509* (Woodbridge, 2005), pp. 318, 319–20; for a slightly different version of the proceedings, see Harper-Bill (ed.), *Register of John Morton*, Vol. I, pp. 25–6. For the bull *Clericis laicos*, see Ernest F. Henderson, *Select Historical Documents of the Middle Ages* (London, 1896), pp. 432–4.

[54] John Alcock, *Sermo Iohannis Alcok episcopi Eliensis* (Westminster, ?1497), sig. D2r–v. I am grateful to Paul Cavill for this reference.

many were stipendiary curates and chaplains, but several held rectories. Dominus John Love was described as a common adulterer who used priest's garments but was professed to the order of friars. Only one other of the accused priests was said to have been a 'common' offender, with a woman described as his long-standing concubine.[55] But several others were accused of contacts with two or more women, some of whom were either said to be whores or – like Tall Alice and Little Joan – can be identified as such from other references.[56] One unnamed curate was said to have taken a whore to the house of Joan Tankard, a notorious brothel keeper, and offered her money to lie with her. Despite the name, 'Bawdy's wife in the postern gate near the Tower' was not necessarily a professional, and certainly some of the other alleged partners were ordinary women, such as the wife of a waxchandler.[57]

In several cases, however, there were suggestions that women were being kept on a long-term basis. Corroborative detail was supplied by Joan Broune alias Giverson, who confessed that Dominus Thomas Butson had maintained her for two years as his concubine, sometimes in his chamber and sometimes at Westminster, where he paid her living expenses and gave her a gown.[58] A case from 1494 may actually preserve the crude proposition of a priest bent on securing a constant supply of sexual services. Alice Dudley claimed that John Roo, rector of All Hallows London Wall, tempted her with the words 'and ye will let me have my plesuyr of yow, ye nor thy husband shall lak no mony nor good think [i.e. thing] that ye will have ... I have japid Wellis wyff diversse tyms and now that her bely is so gret I cannot cum to her thing.' The court took the matter very seriously and ordered a special session of inquiry in All Hallows church, when eight of the 'more discreet' of the parishioners were to be summoned to inquire of the fame.[59]

Yet more members of the clergy were named as the partners of women cited as the main defendant in adultery cases. Of the few females who bore courtesy titles, Mistress Burton was said to have had two children by the seneschal of St John's, while the Lady de Lewce, resident in St Bartholomew's Hospital, was accused of improper relations with her chaplain.[60] Eighteen other women were accused of adultery with parish priests, curates, parochial chaplains, and members of religious orders. Margaret Sadler was accused of adultery with a friar and a monk of Westminster, while a fletcher's wife was caught between two priests

---

[55] LMA, DL/C/B/043/MS09064/6, fos. 126r, 184v.   [56] E.g. *ibid.*, fos. 97r, 107r, 113r, 125v.
[57] *Ibid.*, fos. 161r, 170r.   [58] *Ibid.*, fo. 146v.   [59] *Ibid.*, fo. 82r.   [60] *Ibid.*, fos. 93r, 122v.

wearing the girdle of the Virgin Mary at Westminster. According to a later account, 'women with chield were wont to girdle with' this relic as an aid to successful childbirth, but there must be a suspicion that this particular woman was using it, with the assistance of the priests, as means of getting pregnant in the first place.[61] A strikingly large proportion (over 30 per cent) of the fifty-five women charged with being common whores in 1495 were accused of serving priests – either named individuals or the clergy as a group. They were somewhat less in evidence in bawdry (aiding and abetting) cases but by no means entirely absent. Joan Gedney of St Sepulchre's, for example, was accused of being a bawd to a chaplain called Sir Roger and many other men, while Marion Butler performed the same service for her daughter and Dominus Richard Westmore.[62]

Inevitably, clerical immorality also featured in prosecutions for defamation. Admittedly many such cases were formulaic slanders of women for being a 'priest's whore' and the like, but some included concrete detail, and a few were highly specific. Margaret Sunday and Anne Swiffte challenged Joan Howe of St Botolph Bishopsgate with being a 'prestes hore, thow was takyn with ij prestes in Edmundton and therfor thow was drevyn owte of the town and ther opynly sette in the stokes'. A priest of All Hallows the Great, William Gylmyn, was slandered twice with having a suspect relationship with his sister: a married couple reported that he had been in her chamber in the middle of the night, while another woman flatly accused him of incest.[63] Taking together all the commissary court proceedings in 1495 – prosecutions not only for slander but also for adultery, fornication and bawdry – over seventy priests were either named or otherwise individually identified as being involved in sexual offences of some sort, several of them more than once.[64] Yet not much rigour is evident in the way they were treated by the court. In about half the cases, the accused failed to turn up or the record of proceedings is incomplete. Most of the others managed to clear themselves by compurgation or were otherwise dismissed. In the few cases in which penance was enjoined, the culprit was allowed to commute it into a money payment.

---

[61] *Ibid.*, fos. 136v, 184v; Eamon Duffy, *The Stripping of the Altars: Traditional Religion in England, c.1400–c.1580* (New Haven and London, 1992), p. 384.

[62] LMA, DL/C/B/043/MS09064/6, fos. 90v, 137v. [63] *Ibid.*, fos. 163r, 172v.

[64] A definitive checklist is impossible to establish because priests were sometimes identified by parish (e.g. the curate of St Benet Fink), sometimes by name and parish and sometimes by name alone, the surname being in any case often omitted. The title 'Dominus' usually denoted a priest but not always. Individuals with the courtesy title 'Master' – which could denote a graduate but was also used to refer to high-status laymen – have not been included unless it is clear that they were priests or religious. References to 'priests', 'friars', etc. as a group are not included in this total.

What was the situation nearly two decades later in 1512? There was a similar mix of specific and unspecific slanders implicating priests. By this time, however, the total number of commissary court prosecutions for sexual transgressions was much diminished, and indeed, even the proportion of those that implicated members of the clergy was somewhat reduced. Priests accounted for fewer than 5 per cent of male defendants, though over 10 per cent of the female defendants were accused of adultery or fornication with clerics. Overall, about twenty clergy, mostly chaplains but including some incumbents, were either themselves the prime defendant, identified as co-respondents or accused of incontinence in more or less specific terms in defamation suits. But the pattern of outcomes was much the same as in the late fifteenth century, and penances were very rare.[65] A case a few years later, in 1519, is notable in having implicated a professor of theology. Tellingly, only his initials, not his full name, were entered in the record.[66]

The figures for 1512 are, of course, merely a minimum indication of clerical involvement in immorality charges in the early sixteenth century. As noted in Chapter 6, the commissary court was only one among a complex of ecclesiastical tribunals and by this period not necessarily the most important for the correction of clerical incontinence. By the 1520s, only a trickle of cases of this nature were appearing before this court – there were none at all in 1529 – but the survival of 'Foxford', the act book of the bishop of London's vicar-general from 1521 to 1539, provides another source of information, as also do consistory court depositions. From the mid-1510s, moreover, the city of London Journals and Repertories – records of the court of common council and court of aldermen – reveal a renewed interest in clerical immorality, a subject on which they had been effectively silent since the late 1470s. Together these sources shed important light on the tensions associated with clerical incontinence in the decade or so before the Reformation Parliament.

The civic records of the late 1510s reveal some highly scandalous cases that led to firm action by the city of London authorities. In 1515, the court of aldermen heard the case of Margaret Hopper, who confessed that since her marriage she had had two children in adultery, the one by a goldsmith and the other by a priest – the latter had 'used her in the detestable synne of advoutrie thees vij yeres'. The woman was forthwith expelled from the city, and the priest was likewise induced to leave. The following year, a woman

---

[65] Based on analysis of LMA, DL/C/B/043/MS09064/11, fos. 32r–88v.
[66] LMA, DL/C/B/041/MS09065J/1, fos. 35v, 37r. For other cases, see *ibid.*, fos. 36v, 38r, 42v.

was indicted by the wardmote inquest of Farringdon Without for acting as a bawd for a priest and a thirteen-year-old girl, while a certain Elizabeth Chekyn was taken in bed lying between two priests and also found 'vagraunt and walkyng by the stretes of this citie in a preestes array and clothyng' – supposedly 'in rebuke and reproche of the ordre of presthod'. The two were sentenced to be paraded through the city to the usual clang of basins and pans, to have their offence proclaimed at the pillory and finally to be expelled. In addition to wearing ray hoods and carrying white rods, as was traditional for female sexual offenders, the bawd had the letter 'B' attached to her shoulder, while Elizabeth Chekyn bore 'on her brest a letter of H. of yelowe wollen clothe in sygne and tokyn of a harlett and on her left shulder a picture of a woman in a preest goun'.[67]

That publicity of this kind was unwelcome to the church may be inferred from a remarkable case in 1521 in which ward and parish officers, together with senior civic officials, were induced to collude with the ecclesiastical establishment to cover up a notorious case of clerical incontinence – with very unsatisfactory results. By this time, William Wych had been a chantry priest in the wealthy parish of St Christopher le Stocks for seven years. There seem to have been problems from the beginning, and successive churchwardens warned him to desist from consorting with a married woman of the parish, Alice Peerson. The fact that she was a willing partner made the circumstances even more sensitive. There was powerful circumstantial evidence, to which neighbours eventually bore testimony in court, that he had had sex with her in the house of a local carpenter, John Chapman, with the active connivance of the latter's wife. As a result, he was commonly defamed of immorality by the greater part of the parish and indeed by most of the inhabitants of the ward. In 1519, the churchwardens, having consulted with 'the graver and more creditworthy' parishioners in accordance with the instructions laid down by the founder of the chantry, warned him that 'yow do nott accordyng to the dedes will' and gave him notice to quit.

Wych refused to go, however, and so was 'detected' to the wardmote inquest. It seems, in fact, that the jury had warned him before, but to no effect. Now they made inquiries of Wych's behaviour in the parish of St Dunstan in the East, where he had formerly lived, and were told that 'Sir William Wych was takyn suspectuously with a wenche in our paryssh.' According to a more colloquial version, 'ther was suche a preste with us

---

[67] LMA, Repertory 3, fos. 36v, 106v; Journal 11, fos. 264v–265r. For other cases involving clergy, see Repertory 5, fos. 52r–v, 98(101)r, Repertory 7, fo. 260(278)v, Journal 12, fo. 238r.

with a whyte hedde and he was fownde in a guttur with Herons whyte petycote' (a contemptuous term for a maidservant). There the outcome had been decisive: '[W]e dyde avoyd hym owte.' Wych was accordingly 'presented' by the wardmote inquest in 1519 and 'indicted' in 1520 – use of the latter term apparently indicating that he was ordered to leave. At this point the ecclesiastical authorities were brought in, and the suspect was required to undergo compurgation. Beforehand, a meeting was held in St Paul's before the bishop of London's vicar-general, the other participants being Wych, the two churchwardens, the rector of the parish, the alderman of the ward and the Recorder of London. To 'avoid greater infamy and scandal', it was agreed that Wych should be allowed to make his purgation secretly without challenge from the churchwardens or other parishioners on condition that he relinquish his office of chantry priest within a certain time. At best, this was dubious practice, but the outcome was disastrous. Wych reneged on the agreement, and at a formal meeting in the nave of St Christopher le Stocks, he outfaced the entire group of officials lined up against him, saying, 'I will not owte for yow all.' To add insult to injury, he proceeded to sue the churchwardens for defamation.[68]

Around the same time there were other cases that reflected awkward tensions between the civic courts and the church. In 1523, the curate of St Botolph Aldersgate was said to have declared that all involved with presenting him to the wardmote inquest were 'acurste' and that those who had named the woman with whom he was suspected 'shall not take their rightes' – that is, receive Easter communion – 'excepte they aske hir forgevenes'.[69] However, the curate of St Christopher le Stocks in 1529 was perhaps more sinned against than sinning; the case of William Wych in the same parish not many years before may have inflamed local sensitivities. He was accused of fathering a child on a local woman but firmly denied the charge and claimed it was malicious. Strikingly, the woman was able to 'exclaim' against him – to neighbours on the streets, to the mayor and aldermen sitting in court, to the diocesan chancellor in the consistory court and directly to Bishop Tunstal himself in his visitation of the city. She received a sympathetic hearing to the extent that Tunstal undertook to examine the priest on oath and promised that if he was found guilty, he 'shuld be ponyshyd in example of all other' and expelled from the diocese. In the event, proceedings in the church court seem to have stalled, provoking the complaint that 'all prystes wyll hold toghether and uphold

[68] LMA, DL/C/207, fos. 32v–33r, 48v, 50v–54r.
[69] LMA, DL/C/330, fos. 44v, 46r; Brigden, *London and the Reformation*, p. 150.

[each] other in myscheff.' But the curate was indicted by the wardmote inquest and – whether or not this was by sinister dealings (as he claimed) – the charge was clearly to the detriment of his 'good name and fame'. Worse still, an action for trespass in the sheriffs' court, on the grounds that he had failed to abide by his agreement to pay for 'dyverse labours, servyses and plesurs' provided by the woman, led to a devastating judgement against him for punitive damages.[70]

Clerical Immorality in London on the Eve of the Reformation

The record of the court of the bishop of London's vicar-general suggests that on the eve of the Reformation Parliament, diocesan authorities at the highest level were attempting to take a firm stand against clerical incontinence but that they faced an intractable problem. Setting aside cases arising from rural Essex, the act book for 1529 records about a dozen prosecutions featuring alleged clerical immorality in and about London. Two of them were cases of defamation rather than clerical incontinence as such, but the details are suggestive of the ignominy associated with this offence. Dominus William Stodard, a priest celebrating at St Michael Queenhithe, was convicted for striking his own mother, drawing blood and slandering her with being a 'priest's whore'. 'A prist hath kept the all thy lief,' he was said to have added. 'I shall write and set up billes in every open place in London that every man shall know the for a prist['s] hore.' In another case, it was claimed that Dominus John Man had given a washerwoman several sums, amounting to the large total of £1 4s. 2d., to induce her to accuse another priest of committing adultery with her and advising her not to confess her sins to her priest. The aim was to secure the victim's dismissal from his position as chantry priest in the church of St John Zachary – a post that Man hoped to obtain in his stead.[71]

The remainder were straightforward cases of actual or suspected clerical incontinence, mostly involving stipendiary priests but including several incumbents. The circumstances were various. One priest was suspect because of his medical ministrations to women; he was ordered out of the city and forbidden to practise medicine within a seven-mile radius. A chaplain of St Benet Fink was ordered not to consort with a certain woman of St Martin in the Fields parish; another priest had to abstain from

---

[70] TNA, SP1/40, fos. 175r–186r (quotations fos. 178r, 179r, 183r); C1/600/46; LMA, DL/C/208, fos. 1r, 3r–v, 6r–v, 10r–v; Brigden, *London and the Reformation*, pp. 64–5.
[71] LMA, DL/C/330, fos. 172r, 173r, 188v.

the company of the servant of the cook at Lincoln's Inn. The celebrant in the monastery of Barking was put to penance in the local parish church for begetting a child on a certain Joan Stone, who herself brought a bill of complaint against him.[72] Dominus Robert West alias Gray, curate of St Andrew Undershaft, confessed that for years he had lived in adultery with a married woman and had four children by her. The matter savoured of protestant heresy, for West was also accused of eating beef on a Friday with two other priests, one of whom was charged with criticizing the bishop for his reaction to the preaching of two leading proto-protestants: 'My lord of London will suffre no man to preche at Powles Crosse but flaterers and dissemblers, for they that say treuth er ponyshed as Bylney and Arthure was.'[73]

Another case featured the curate of St Alban Wood Street, who was taken with a woman in the rectory. Yet another involved clerics operating in tandem to achieve their desires – a scenario that was by no means uncommon, as previous examples in this chapter have shown. In this instance, two women spent the night in the chamber of a priest in St Gregory Paul's Churchyard; he slept with one of them, and a fellow priest slept with the other. Both these cases were reported to the bishop by officials of the city of London. In the latter, indeed, the immoral clergy were surprised by a dawn raid led by the alderman's deputy and the constable of the ward, followed by a large crowd. One of the priests managed to escape, but the other, together with the woman, was paraded through the streets and imprisoned in the Bread Street Counter before being handed over to the ecclesiastical authorities. This is important in demonstrating that the traditional procedure used in the city of London to expose immoral clergy was still in vigorous use.[74] On this occasion, the civic authorities and the citizenry clearly expected exemplary action, and the church obliged. In this and several other cases noted in 'Foxford', the guilty priests were committed to the bishop of London's prison in the Lollards' Tower.[75]

On the basis of mainly fifteenth-century evidence, Shannon McSheffrey concludes that the reactions of ordinary lay people to clerical immorality in London were muted, inferring that 'in general, clergy-lay relationships

---

[72] *Ibid.*, fos. 171r, 180r, 181r, 187r.

[73] *Ibid.*, fos. 174r, 175v, quoted in Colin A. McLaren, 'An Early 16th Century Act Book of the Diocese of London', *Journal of the Society of Archivists*, 3 (1965–9), 339.

[74] LMA, DL/C/330, fos. 176r, 179v, 188v; for other cases of arrest by the constable and imprisonment in the Counter, see *ibid.*, fos. 174v–175r.

[75] LMA, DL/C/330, fos. 172r, 173r, 175r, 176r, 179v, 188v.

worked fairly well.'[76] The responses of lay officials were indeed cautious and legalistic, in contrast to the retributive violence of the French *fabliaux*, which is McSheffrey's arbitrary point of comparison. But they were cautious and legalistic in most things, so this can hardly be taken to imply that all was well. In any case, by the 1510s and the 1520s, circumstances had changed significantly. Much contemporary evidence indicates that the heresy hunts that the church inaugurated, in London and elsewhere, alarmed not merely the main targets but a much wider circle of lay people and led to fears that any criticism of the church was liable to be construed as heresy. In London these fears were undoubtedly heightened by Bishop Fitzjames's intemperate statement at the time of the Hunne affair in 1515 that the citizens were 'maliciouslie set *in favorem hereticae pravitatis*' – an accusation that provoked an immediate protest from the city authorities.[77]

It is surely no coincidence that entries relating to immoral priests, having been absent from the civic records for decades, reappear in the Repertories and Journals about this time. The pity is that we do not have the returns from the wardmote inquests, which would show the extent to which concerns were heightened at the grass roots. Clerical incontinence, always a cause of simmering resentment, was likely to generate even more disgust when the church was claiming a monopoly of the moral high ground. The exposure of immoral clergy was, moreover, an excellent way for lay people to hit back at what they might regard as the unfair exercise of ecclesiastical power or at least to ensure that when the church flexed its muscles, it was not doing so at the expense of lay people while winking at clerical misbehaviour. The church authorities, however much they might suspect the motives of accusers, could hardly condone the sexual misdoings of priests and were inevitably thrown onto the back foot by well-founded cases. For principled critics, including Protestant polemicists, the issue was a godsend, a means of tapping into popular fears and prejudices and an opportunity to link diverse concerns about the church into a powerful sense of resentment. Skilfully yoking the issues of tithe and immorality, the writer of *A supplication of the poore commons* to King Henry VIII mockingly suggested in 1546 that 'yf your hyghnes wolde suffer them ... [priests'] conscience wolde serve them to lye wyth our wives every tenthe nyghte, other els to have everye tenthe wyfe in the paryshe at theyre pleasure.'[78]

---

[76] McSheffrey, 'Whoring Priests and Godly Citizens', pp. 62–3.

[77] E. Jeffries Davis, 'The Authorities for the Case of Richard Hunne (1514–15)', *English Historical Review*, 30 (1915), 477; LMA, Repertory 3, fo. 17(20)v.

[78] Simon Fish, *A Supplicacyon for the Beggers* ... [etc.], ed. F. J. Furnivall and J. Meadows Cowper (Early English Text Society, Extra Series 13, London, 1871), pp. 87–8.

By this date, the tide of political events had been running strongly against the clergy for some time, but at a much earlier stage the issue already packed a powerful punch. A petition prepared for the parliament of 1529, advocating both a partial disendowment of the church and the temporary transfer (on a trial basis) of the ecclesiastical jurisdiction to the crown, is striking for the attention it gives to clerical immorality and, more specifically, for claiming that Henry VII's act of 1485, empowering bishops to imprison offenders, had failed completely. The authors of this document clearly expected their accusations to strike a chord.[79] Likewise, as modern commentators have recognized, the charges of Simon Fish in his *Supplication for the Beggars* of 1529, however exaggerated they appear in retrospect, must have had resonance for contemporary audiences.[80]

Moreover, these audiences were presumably quite large, since free copies of the *Supplication* were distributed in London on the very day that the Reformation Parliament assembled.[81] The claims that the clergy did 'nothing but applie theym silves by all the sleyghtes they may, to have to do with every mannes wife, every mannes doughter, and every mannes mayde, that cukkoldrie and baudrie shulde reigne over all' or that they had 'made an hundreth thousand ydell hores' in the realm were no doubt outragious. That they did not seem so at the time was partly because Fish backed them up with a much more specific suggestion – generally unnoticed by historians – about the prosecution of priests in the city wards and the reaction of Cuthbert Tunstal: '[W]hate a worke there is in London, howe the bisshoppe rageth for endyting of certayn curates of extorcion and incontinency the last yere in the warmoll quest.' The implication is that the wardmote inquests had recently been used by lay people to register dissatisfaction with the conduct of some of the clergy, to the bishop's great displeasure. More claimed that Fish had made this up. While the statement cannot be fully substantiated from the surviving London records, it is certainly not inconsistent with the cases they contain. Whether true or not, for ordinary Londoners it was surely utterly plausible.[82]

[79] R. W. Hoyle, 'The Origins of the Dissolution of the Monasteries', *Historical Journal*, 38 (1995), 301–5.
[80] Marshall, *Catholic Priesthood*, p. 146; Bernard, *Late Medieval Church*, p. 70.
[81] James Davis, 'The Christian Brethren and the Dissemination of Heretical Books', in R. N. Swanson (ed.), *The Church and the Book* (Studies in Church History 38, Woodbridge, 2004), p. 197.
[82] Fish, *Supplicacyon for the Beggers*, ed. Furnivall and Cowper, pp. 6–7, 9; Manley et al. (eds.), *Complete Works of St. Thomas More*, Vol. VII, pp. 116, 327.

CHAPTER 9

Reform and Reformation, 1530–58

Previous chapters have shown that in early Tudor England sexual regulation was already a commonplace of social life. Its intensity fluctuated but overall was at least moderately strict by any standards, and its impact could at times be severe. But certainly among leading churchmen and in some government circles, and potentially also at the grass roots, there was an appetite for further moral activism. It does not follow, however, that what came later was either simply a continuation or a straightforward intensification of the earlier state of affairs. The Reformation period, from the late 1520s to the early 1560s, witnessed drastic and far-reaching yet quite sudden shifts in religious ideas and sensibilities, which combined in complex ways with profound social and economic changes and no less significant developments in government and administration. The speed and nature of these changes were, moreover, affected by a major shift in the cultural context as the expanding output of the printing press accelerated the exchange of ideas and widened the range of available discourses. Simple notions of 'continuity' and 'change' are hardly adequate to capture what occurred.

Nonetheless, the matrix of the past continued to shape the pattern of sexual regulation in middle to late sixteenth-century England. Despite all the dislocations of the Reformation period, some of the most far-reaching proposals for change failed to take effect. These were serious initiatives, based in careful thought. Had they been implemented, they would have profoundly altered the relationship between the secular and ecclesiastical powers and hence the contours of what we would nowadays think of as the secular state. Despite their failure, therefore, they warrant more careful attention than they have received in past accounts. In terms of what did happen and the impact on the ground, some attention is given to the work of the church courts in the 1530s and 1540s. But the focus in this chapter is chiefly on London and its environs. The metropolis became, in effect, a laboratory for the implementation of a far more radical and severe programme of moral reformation, and in the late 1540s and early 1550s, it witnessed a quite extraordinarily intense campaign against illicit sex. Elsewhere – as far as can be seen from the scanty surviving sources – the immediate impact of religious change on sexual manners was less coherent and, for the most part, more muted. In provincial towns and cities and their rural hinterlands, the most striking period of reformation in the sphere of sexual regulation was the early part of Elizabeth's reign.[1] Their story will be resumed in Chapter 10.

Sex and the Reformation

The Reformation, and the humanist debates that preceded and partly overlapped with it, raised society's consciousness of sexual sin to the extent that by the mid-sixteenth century, discourses of immorality had become even more central to religious and political life than they had been before. Those who wished to build a better commonwealth could not be blind to such social problems as the impact of disease and the evils of the sex trade. It had long been recognized that poverty and destitution were both among the causes and possible consequences of prostitution and debauchery. But as the appropriate means of combating poverty came under increasing scrutiny, so the connection was re-emphasized and hence the moral and religious duty (as pious contemporaries saw it) of preventing poor women from sliding into sin.[2] More strikingly, and on a different plane of discourse, sex emerged as a leading metaphor in Reformation polemics. The prophet Ezekiel presented compelling images of Jerusalem transformed into a harlot, while the Revelation of St John included the even more lurid vision of the Whore of Babylon.[3] They formed part of a complex web of highly gendered and sexually charged imagery, deriving from both the Old and New Testaments, that was closely associated with

---

[1] Martha Carlin, *Medieval Southwark* (London and Rio Grande, 1996), p. 228, quotes Derek Keene, *Survey of Medieval Winchester*, 2 parts (Oxford, 1985), Vol. I, p. 390, to the effect that 'cartloads of infamous women were drummed out' of Winchester in 1551–2 and 1563–4. This is based on Adrienne B. Rosen, 'Economic and Social Aspects of the History of Winchester, 1520–1670', unpublished DPhil thesis, University of Oxford, 1975, p. 138. The original sources indicate that in 1563–4 a man was paid 4d. to play the drum ahead of carts in which an unspecified number of 'infames mulieres' were carried, but in 1551–2, apparently only one woman was so punished: see Hampshire RO, W/E1/ 78, 93.

[2] Juan Luis Vives, *De subventione pauperum* [1526], ed. and trans. C. Mattheeussen and C. Fantazzi (Leiden, 2002), pp. 92–3, 100–1, 110–11, 122–3, 138–9, 140–1; William Marshall, *The forme and maner of subvention or helpyng for pore people devysed and practysed in the cytie of Hypres in Flaunders* (London, 1535), sigs. A2r, C8v, E1v; G. R. Elton, 'An Early Tudor Poor Law', *Economic History Review*, 6 (1953–4), 62.

[3] Ezekiel XVI; Revelation XVII.

concepts of the true and false Church, godly and ungodly people, Christ and Antichrist.[4]

Among the issues at stake were a redefinition of Christian vocation and a challenge to monastic values. The more far-reaching Protestant version of these doctrines, built on denial of the efficacy of good works to achieve salvation and related to a fundamental debate on religious vows, was part of the justification for the complete abolition of monasticism and monastic institutions. No matter that when Henry VIII carried out this revolution in England between 1536 and 1540, it was not primarily on these grounds; they were part of the context that made such actions both thinkable and feasible. At the same time, the ideal of Christian marriage was elevated, even though its sacramental nature was denied. Already before the Reformation, works such as William Harrington's *Commendacions of matrymony* (*c*.1515) and Richard Whitford's *Werke for housholders* (1530) represented a powerful current of ideas stressing the importance of the household and marriage among lay people. With strong Protestant inflections, this theme was to be massively reinforced in numerous sermons and conduct books in the middle to late sixteenth century, the archetype being *The christen state of matrimonye* (1541) – Miles Coverdale's translation of a work by Heinrich Bullinger.[5] With some of its most controversial chapters omitted – including a fierce attack on the denial of marriage to the clergy – this was printed in England several times before being banned in 1546, while fuller versions went through many variant editions in the reign of Edward VI.[6]

It is less often noticed that complementing this commendation of marriage was a fierce denunciation of whoredom, adultery and other sexual transgressions, presented as having in recent times 'sore increased . . . and prevayled'. Indeed, in 1543, when the expurgated version of Bullinger's

---

[4] Helen L. Parish, *Clerical Marriage and the English Reformation: Precedent, Policy, and Practice* (Aldershot, 2000), pp. 11–13 and *passim*.

[5] The literature is extensive; more recent contributions include Kathleen M. Davies, 'The Sacred Condition of Equality – How Original Were Puritan Doctrines of Marriage?', *Social History* 5 (1977), 563–80, republished as 'Continuity and Change in Literary Advice on Marriage', in R. B. Outhwaite (ed.), *Marriage and Society: Studies in the Social History of Marriage* (London, 1981), pp. 58–80; Margo Todd, *Christian Humanism and the Puritan Social Order* (Cambridge, 1987), chap. 4; Patrick Collinson, *The Birthpangs of Protestant England: Religious and Cultural Change in the Sixteenth and Seventeenth Centuries* (Basingstoke, 1988), chap. 3; Anthony Fletcher, 'The Protestant Idea of Marriage in Early Modern England', in Anthony Fletcher and Peter Roberts (eds.), *Religion, Culture and Society in Early Modern Britain: Essays in Honour of Patrick Collinson* (Cambridge, 1994), pp. 161–81; Alison Wall, *Power and Protest in England, 1525–1640* (London, 2000), chap. 5; Christine Peters, *Patterns of Piety: Women, Gender and Religion in Late Medieval and Reformation England* (Cambridge, 2003), chap. 13.

[6] Carrie Euler, 'Heinrich Bullinger, Marriage and the English Reformation: *The Christen State of Matrimonye* in England, 1540–53', *Sixteenth Century Journal*, 34 (2003), 367–93.

Christen state of matrimonye was issued in the name of Theodore Basille (the pen name of Thomas Becon), the latter prefaced it with a lengthy disquisition on this theme. Vividly he evoked a society corrupt with 'abhominable whoredome, stynking adultery, wicked fornicacion, and al kynd of uncleannes' and destabilized by shaky marriages, a world of 'preposterous manners' in which 'true wyves ... are neglected and set at nought, but whores and harlottes are embrased, kyssed, kulled and much set by.' Outspokenly, he laid much of the blame on the nobility, whose eagerness to marry their children off at a young age for the sake of riches not only made for ill-fated unions when those couples came to adulthood but also set a disastrously bad example to the 'baser sorte of people'. For a number of reasons, Becon was to get into trouble for this publication. But it was to have an enduring impact. In the more favourable days of 1547, some of the choicest phrases and passages of Coverdale and Becon were reworked into the uncompromising text of the official 'homelie of whoredome and unclennesse', one of a series of off-the-peg sermons ordered to be read in every parish.[7]

A related issue was clerical celibacy. In the early years of the Reformation, the response to complaints against immorality among the clergy was merely to restate the traditional prohibitions and increase in severity the available penalties. The Act of Six Articles (1539) made it a felony for a priest to treat a woman as his wife. To keep a concubine made him liable to forfeiture of all his goods and benefices, while a second offence brought the death penalty. The following year another act mitigated these punishments while remaining very severe.[8] These measures reflected Henry VIII's hostility to the Protestant call for clerical marriage, which was not permitted by statute till 1549 and, after Mary's resolute attempts to restore the status quo, only grudgingly conceded by Elizabeth in the injunctions of 1559 and the articles of religion of 1563.[9] Yet, once

---

[7] Heinrich Bullinger, *The christen state of matrimonye*, trans. Miles Coverdale (Antwerp, 1541), sig. A2r; Thomas Basille [actually Heinrich Bullinger, trans. Miles Coverdale, with a Preface by Thomas Becon], *The golden boke of christen matrimonye* (London, 1543), Preface (quotations sigs. A4v, A5r, A7v, B2r); Ronald B. Bond (ed.), *Certain Sermons or Homilies (1547) and A Homily against Disobedience and Wilful Rebellion (1570): A Critical Edition* (Toronto, 1987), pp. 174–86 and pp. 186–8, nn. 174, 178, 180, 183.

[8] 31 Henry VIII c. 14, cl. v, xx; 32 Henry VIII c. 10 (the wives and concubines of convicted clergy were likewise subject to severe penalties). For prosecutions under 32 Henry VIII c. 10, see Paul Cavill, 'Heresy, Law and the State: Forfeiture in Late Medieval and Early Modern England', *English Historical Review*, 129 (2014), 290.

[9] 2 and 3 Edward VI c. 21, re-enacted by 5 and 6 Edward VI c. 12. On the situation in the early part of Elizabeth's reign, see Eric Josef Carlson, *Marriage and the English Reformation* (Oxford, 1994), pp. 58–64; Parish, *Clerical Marriage*, pp. 227–34.

effected, the shift proved decisive. As will be seen in later chapters, by the late sixteenth century widespread clerical immorality, formerly a major obstacle to effective sexual regulation, was scarcely an issue.

Illicit sex among lay people was in any case a natural target for religious and moral reformers, whether Catholic or Protestant. Incest, adultery, 'harlotry' – a deeply powerful word albeit of uncertain meaning – were among the sexual transgressions plainly forbidden in the Bible, and there was, of course, a long tradition of their condemnation by the church. Moreover, human nature being what it is, transgressions were bound to occur in practice and, to observers steeped in a deep consciousness of sin – or, in less overtly religious terms, of 'disorder' and 'vice' – were wont to be interpreted as a rising tide of immorality. Moralists could expect support from 'honest householders' who did not like what they saw around them. However, more tolerant and permissive strains in popular thinking and, at a practical level, the sheer problems of detecting and proving sexual transgressions made effective policing difficult and were a constant temptation to authorities on the ground to give up the struggle or compromise with offenders. Certainly in London, Westminster and Southwark, the ubiquitous sex trade presented an obvious target for moral reformers, as also did the related practice of 'keeping a whore'.

For those attempting to seize the moral high ground, it was an ideal tactic to champion stricter measures against sexual immorality and to accuse opponents of being soft on sin. This point is made by Ian Archer with reference to the ideology of the English Protestant reformers, who made sexual transgression central to their attacks on the Papacy and the Catholic clergy and could, moreover, revel in the fact that the Southwark stews had been under ecclesiastical jurisdiction in the person of the bishop of Winchester. In that sense they had no small success in appropriating the rhetoric of sexual reformation to the Protestant cause.[10] But it has to be recognized that a not dissimilar policy, albeit with different emphases, was pursued by those of the opposite persuasion in the reign of Mary and by later Catholic apologists. They claimed that the pretended 'reformation' of religion, triggered by Henry VIII's lust for the 'whore' Anne Boleyn and underpinned by a theology of justification that was presented as a morally corrosive invitation to licentiousness, had let loose a torrent of vice. The boasted 'libertye of the gospell', averred John Christopherson, was in reality 'loose libertye', 'carnall libertie', 'the libertie of the fleshe'.

---

[10] Ian W. Archer, *The Pursuit of Stability: Social Relations in Elizabethan London* (Cambridge, 1991), pp. 251–3.

Moreover, the demand for clerical marriage had not only seduced many priests themselves to commit 'abhominable inceste and advoutrye' but had actually led them to become 'preachers of this newe doctrine, and made the people beleve, that licentious livinge … was the libertye of the gospell'.[11] Thus it was not simply Protestant or Catholic theology but the circumstances of confessional conflict itself that led to a ratcheting-up of moral regulation and kept the issue constantly in view.

Shifts in doctrine, theology and pastoral practice nonetheless gave added urgency to the call for action. Although Henry VIII's church was never doctrinally 'Protestant', some traditional beliefs were severely undermined. In particular, the doctrine of purgatory and the necessity of auricular confession were brought in question. Though the latter was upheld by the Act of Six Articles (1539), when it ceased to be compulsory in 1548, its practice seems to have utterly collapsed, suggesting either that compliance had always been reluctant or that its legitimacy had not withstood the Henrician changes.[12] In any case, this represented a major alteration of the framework in which the church courts operated. Previously their work had been complementary to the efforts of priests in the confessional. Now they were at the front line in combating sin. The importance of the *public* regulation of sexual behaviour was thus reinforced.[13]

Changes affecting the doctrine of Providence were also important. The belief that God intervenes actively in the world to bless, warn and chastise his people was a long-established feature of Christian doctrine, and as has been seen, providential ideas intermittently featured in the rhetoric against sexual transgression before the Reformation. However, Protestant stress on the sovereignty of God and the sinfulness of humankind gave it supercharged power. In providential perspective, it was not only blatant sinners themselves who were likely to provoke the wrath of God. Ministers of religion had a duty fearlessly to denounce vice, while officers of the law, from the humble constable to the person of the prince, were charged with punishing it. Failure to act was a grievous affront to the Almighty that might bring down judgements on a city or the whole nation.[14] Everyone knew what had happened to Sodom and Gomorrah and would have

---

[11] John Christopherson, *An exhortation to all menne to take hede and beware of rebellion* (London, 1554), sigs. S3r–v, S5v–S6r, T8v.

[12] Peter Marshall, *The Catholic Priesthood and the English Reformation* (Oxford, 1994), pp. 28–33.

[13] On the broader context, see Anne T. Thayer, *Penitence, Preaching and the Coming of the Reformation* (Aldershot, 2002); Eric Bramhall, 'Penitence and the English Reformation', unpublished PhD thesis, University of Liverpool, 2013.

[14] Alexandra Walsham, *Providence in Early Modern England* (Oxford, 1999).

befallen Nineveh if God had not stayed his hand. It was with such examples in mind that Latimer lamented how 'God is dishonoured by whoredom ... God hath suffered long of his great lenity, mercy and benignity; but he will punish sharply at the length, if we do not repent.'[15] The gradual diffusion of these ideas via sermons and in print helped to change the moral climate.

A related development was a growing emphasis on the literal word of the Bible and a tendency towards Old Testament legalism in thinking about sexual sin. In a sense, this was not new. Harrington, writing around 1515, was by no means the only author to note that 'in the olde law the payn was to be stoned to deth' for adultery, and some passages in More's writing can be read to suggest that he actually approved the introduction of the death penalty for this offence.[16] However, Luther's emphasis was on the power of the gospel to liberate Christians from the heavy sentence that their sins would otherwise have brought upon them. As a consequence, he was in no doubt that the judicial law of Moses inscribed in the Old Testament books of Exodus, Leviticus and Deuteronomy was no longer binding, except in so far as it was identical with natural law. Yet this caveat allowed him to advocate biblical penalties when he thought fit. His successor, Melanchthon, was more inclined to see the gospel as the fulfilment of the law, and this legalistic tendency was taken further by the Swiss reformer Zwingli, who advocated that adultery (among other crimes) should be subject to the death penalty, as it had been in Moses' day. Calvin took the same stance on this particular issue (though in fact his position on the status of the judicial law was characteristically subtle and complex), and this was to weigh heavily with English Calvinists in the reign of Elizabeth and beyond.[17]

Of more immediate influence in the mid-Tudor years were the opinions of the Strasbourg reformer Martin Bucer – invited to England by Archbishop Cranmer and resident there from 1547 until his death in 1551 – and Zwingli's successor at Zurich, Heinrich Bullinger. Bucer's outline for further reformation in England, written in 1550, argued that while the details of Moses' judicial laws were not binding, their substance

---

[15] *Sermons by Hugh Latimer*, ed. George Elwes Corrie (Parker Society, Cambridge, 1844), p. 196.

[16] William Harrington, *The commendacions of matrymony* ([title page mutilated, ?1515]), sig. D1r; Keith Thomas, 'The Puritans and Adultery: The Act of 1650 Reconsidered', in Donald Pennington and Keith Thomas (eds.), *Puritans and Revolutionaries: Essays in Seventeenth-Century History Presented to Christopher Hill* (Oxford, 1978), p. 269.

[17] P. D. L. Avis, 'Moses and the Magistrate: A Study in the Rise of Protestant Legalism', *Journal of Ecclesiastical History*, 26 (1975), 149–72; Richard J. Ross, 'Distinguishing Eternal from Transient Law: Natural Law and the Judicial Laws of Moses', *Past and Present*, 217 (November 2012), 79–115.

in 'matters necessary for the whole commonwealth' unquestionably was, and on these grounds he advocated the death penalty for adultery and a variety of other offences. Yet, while Bucer's *De Regno Christi* was presented to the king, it was never published. In contrast, Coverdale's translation of Bullinger's *Christen state of matrimonye*, likewise urging severity, was (as noted earlier) very widely distributed.[18] Against this background, it is not surprising to find the 'godly imp', Edward VI penning as one of his Latin exercises an oration advocating the death penalty for adultery. The same idea was the capstone of Latimer's repeated invectives against 'whoredom' and 'lechery' in his court sermons.[19] Among leading Protestants, there was near consensus; the dissent voiced by the young John Foxe provoked a sharp rebuke from George Joye.[20]

The Crisis of the Spiritual Jurisdiction

Principle was one thing, practice another. But the far-reaching dislocations of the Reformation period did indeed offer a unique opportunity for major change in the sphere of sexual regulation. Early initiatives were bleakly Erastian, reflecting the suspicion of the church and churchmen that underlay many of the moves of the early Reformation in England. Already in the Commons' Supplication against the Ordinaries of 1532 there were straws in the wind. Apart from its significance as a milestone in the evolution of the Henrician Reformation, historians have most commonly examined the document in relation to its specific criticisms – abuses of excommunication, supposedly excessive fees, delay and expense in the probate of wills, innovations in tithe and rapacity in extracting mortuary dues, profiting from presentations to benefices and so forth. They have on the whole absolved the church of many of these charges, while recognizing that fear and distrust of the ecclesiastical authorities, especially of their spasmodically ferocious campaigns against heresy, were a source of considerable underlying tension.[21]

---

[18] Avis, 'Moses and the Magistrate', pp. 160–1; Catharine Davies, *A Religion of the Word: The Defence of the Reformation in the Reign of Edward VI* (Manchester, 2002), pp. 103, 133 n.144, 153–4, 173 n. 127.

[19] John Gough Nichols (ed.), *Literary Remains of King Edward VI*, 2 vols. (Roxburghe Club, London, 1857), Vol. I, pp. 128–30; *Sermons by Hugh Latimer*, ed. Corrie, pp. 244, 258.

[20] Charles C. Butterworth and Allan G. Chester, *George Joye, 1495?–1553: A Chapter in the History of the English Bible and the English Reformation* (Philadelphia, 1962), pp. 252–4.

[21] The classic discussion is Margaret Bowker, 'Some Archdeacons' Court Books and the Commons' Supplication against the Ordinaries of 1532', in D. A. Bullough and R. L. Storey (eds.), *The Study of Medieval Records: Essays in Honour of Kathleen Major* (Oxford, 1971), pp. 282–316; Margaret Bowker,

But the Supplication's vision of reform was in fact wider and more far-reaching. While the Commons claimed that it was 'not intended . . . to take away from the said Ordinaries their authority to correct and punish sin', they did ask that the latter should not be allowed 'to call any person *ex officio* at their own imaginations without lawful accusation, proved fame by honest witnesses, or presentment in the visi[ta]tion or other lawful presentment according to your laws'.[22] As earlier chapters have shown, the pre-Reformation church courts relied very heavily on unofficial information rather than regular visitation presentments, so this was a shrewd blow at their activities. It is clear too that the proposal was seriously considered, since there survives a draft parliamentary bill to similar effect.[23] Yet the bishops who responded to the Commons' Supplication, while acutely sensitive in general to any assault on 'the laws of the church for repression of sin and reformation of mislivers', hardly seem to have appreciated the potential effects of this particular line of attack, blandly observing that 'a better provision cannot be devised than is already devised by the clergy, in our opinion.'[24]

As the overturning events of the 1530s unfolded, a succession of commentators drew attention to the opportunity for radical and far-reaching jurisdictional reforms that would have transformed the relationship between the ecclesiastical and secular courts. Their arguments reveal both a powerful vein of anticlerical sentiment and how closely sexual regulation was for some contemporaries related to other social and economic concerns. One visionary, identifiable as the minor 'commonwealth' writer and London grocer Clement Armstrong, extolled the virtues of the royal supremacy and exhorted Henry VIII 'thorow your hedd right of faith' to lead his people out of sin. Providing subjects with the means to work and livelihood was the way to ensure that there were 'no idull peple,

---

'The Commons Supplication against the Ordinaries in the Light of some Archidiaconal Acta', *Transactions of the Royal Historical Society*, 5th Series, 21 (1971), 61–77 (abridged version of preceding article). For debates on the origins and political purpose of the Supplication, see G. R. Elton, 'The Commons' Supplication of 1532: Parliamentary Manoeuvres in the Reign of Henry VIII', *English Historical Review*, 66 (1951), 507–34; J. P. Cooper, 'The Supplication against the Ordinaries Reconsidered', *English Historical Review*, 72 (1957), 616–41; M. J. Kelly, 'The Submission of the Clergy', *Transactions of the Royal Historical Society*, 5th series, 15 (1965), 97–119; J. A. Guy, *The Public Career of Sir Thomas More* (Brighton, 1980), chap. 8; G. W. Bernard, *The King's Reformation: Henry VIII and the Remaking of the English Church* (New Haven and London, 2005), pp. 58–63.

[22] C. H. Williams (ed.), *English Historical Documents, 1485–1558* (London, 1971), pp. 732–6 (quotations p. 734).

[23] TNA, SP 2/M, fos. 229r, 230r.

[24] Henry Gee and William John Hardy (eds.), *Documents Illustrative of English Church History* (London, 1896), pp. 154–76 (quotations pp. 165, 174–5).

vacabondes, theffes, harlottes, nor non other werkers of syne and wik-
kidnes in the body of your reame'.[25] For another writer, reform was
primarily the means to cow the clergy once and for all, 'a grete occasyon
of mekenes to verye manye of the clergye'. Underlying such apparently
cynical advice was the claim, again reflecting distrust of clerical power and
pride, that hitherto discipline had been exercised 'only by auctorytye of the
clergye and therfore many of theym have punysshyd the offenders rather
for dysobeyinge theyre decrees then for the offence to god or love of
verteue'. The author also argued that such powers deflected them from
the more fruitful remedies of teaching, preaching and good example, an
optimistic view of what might be achieved by persuasion rather than
coercion.[26]

The author of 'Certen consideracons why the spirituell jurisdiccon
wold be abrogatt and repelled or at the leest refourmed' likewise thought
that the result would be to promote good preaching and teaching of the
word of God, 'and then we shold shortly have more dyvyns then lawyers
wher now yt ys clene contrary.' Brushing aside the objection that the
ecclesiastical jurisdiction was truly spiritual – that is, distinctive in working for the good of the soul – the author argued that the sinner still had
to 'be reconsiled to God by contricon, confession and penaunce and also
by makynge satisfaccon to his neybor whom he hathe offended'. His logic
was that the exemplary and retributive elements of punishment for sin
would be better left to the royal prerogative; and he was confident that,
of the various areas of ecclesiastical jurisdiction, 'matrimony, ffornica-
con, diffamacon, idolatre and suche other myght be reduced to the
kynges court and ther determyned very well appone lawez therfore to
be ordeyned by parlament.'[27]

Even to highly placed contemporaries, such ideas were by no means
fanciful. A letter to Thomas Cromwell of August 1535 definitely recommended the transfer to the temporal courts 'of all suche cryme and causes as
the ecclesiasticall juges have had jurisdiccion hertofore and by thatt meanes
wee shall have butt oon lawe withyn thys reyalme'. Similar advice, probably
from Dr William Petre, coolly appraised which sections of the ecclesiastical
jurisdiction should be transferred, which left to the bishops, and which

---

[25] BL, Lansdowne MS 97, fos. 152r, 153r; see also Ethan H. Shagan, 'Clement Armstrong and the Godly
Commonwealth: Radical Religion in Early Tudor England', in Peter Marshall and Alec Ryrie (eds.),
The Beginnings of English Protestantism (Cambridge, 2002), pp. 60–83; S. T. Bindoff, 'Clement
Armstrong and his Treatises of the Commonweal', *Economic History Review*, 1st series, 14 (1944),
64–73.
[26] TNA, SP 1/99, fos. 196r–97v.   [27] BL, Cotton MS Cleopatra F.II, fo. 250r–v.

abrogated altogether. In 1538, the ambassador, Sir Philip Hoby, looked 'in short time to see provision for the comunaltie concerninge spirituall causes. And to remit them to such as will not deceive God and the kinge.'[28]

Some English contemporaries may have been aware of analogous changes in continental Europe. Those with any degree of legal expertise certainly knew that areas of overlap already existed between the temporal and spiritual jurisdictions, that the boundaries between the two were to some extent shifting and that parliament had already begun to intervene in jurisdiction over sexual crimes. The author of 'Certen consideracons' saw the importance of the act of 1534 that made 'the detestable and abhomynable vice of buggery commyttid with mankynde or beaste' a capital felony without benefit of clergy. From one angle, this measure can be plausibly seen in relation to the impending visitation of the lesser monasteries and, more generally, as part of Henry VIII's campaign of intimidating the clergy. But potentially the act affected lay people too, and jurisdictionally its significance lay in removing an offence hitherto subject to the spiritual jurisdiction – albeit, in practice, cases were extremely infrequent – entirely into the temporal courts. As the commentator observed, since the act was passed, 'the clergye may theryn take no examinacon for the cryme ffor if they shold ther proffes and sentence therappon myght blynde the trouthe upon the triall of ffelonye . . . and that the kynges lawez will not suffer.'[29]

Surveying areas of overlap between the temporal and spiritual courts, the author of 'Certen consideracons' noted correctly that an action of trespass was already available against a man who entered another's house and got his servant with child, on the grounds that he was thereby deprived of her service. Of incest, adultery, fornication and concubinage generally, he observed that 'the examinacon of all thiez by custume perteyne to the clergy, but if a vicyousse housse be kept wheryne suche offensis be comynly used it is to be ynquered of as for a commen anusaunce and to be punyshed by the kynges lawez.' As seen in Chapter 7, not only was this in fact already common practice in London, on the basis of city custom, but the issue had been tested in the royal courts and reported in the Year Books.[30] Clearly, there was scope to push at the boundaries to achieve piecemeal expansion of this area of jurisdiction, and in both local and central courts, there were

---

[28] TNA, SP 1/95, fo. 104r; SP 1/99, fo. 199r–v; Susan Brigden (ed.), 'The Letters of Richard Scudamore to Sir Philip Hoby, September 1549–March 1555', in *Camden Miscellany XXX* (Camden Society, 4th series 39, London, 1990), p. 77.

[29] 25 Henry VIII c. 6; BL, Cotton MS Cleopatra F.II, fo. 251v. On the background, see Bernard, *King's Reformation*, pp. 247–76.

[30] BL, Cotton MS Cleopatra F.II, fo. 251v.

plenty of precedents for those who wished to find them. In the King's Bench in 1504, a glover of St Clement Danes was indicted for keeping another man's wife in lechery and regularly having sexual relations with her. In 1520, a husbandman called Thomas Smyth and Joan, the wife of William Gybbe of Kingsbury (Middlesex), were indicted for living together lecherously in the manner of common adulterers and fined for this offence.[31]

Death for Adultery?

Yet, in the event, no major jurisdictional shift occurred. Not only were the proposals in practical terms too far reaching to be put easily into effect; more importantly, it was in the highest degree unlikely that Henry VIII, having annexed the spiritual jurisdiction to the crown, would countenance its dismemberment. How feasible was the more limited aim of making adultery a secular crime, even in the apparently more favourable circumstances of Edward VI's reign? Death for adultery, effective as a startling rhetorical trope in sermon or pamphlet, was in practice a complex and controversial matter.[32] The examples of Calvin's Geneva and other places on the continent were not much help. They could appeal to the Carolina, the imperial law code of 1532, where the penalty was already laid down.[33] In England, there was no such precedent but, on the contrary, troubling obstacles touching the nature and extent of royal power. In its extreme form, the argument that the Mosaic code should be re-introduced implied that the monarch had no choice in the matter, a clear infringement of the royal prerogative. Moreover, applying the same principles to theft would have involved a reduction in the existing penalty. The Mosaic code prescribed double restitution of the value stolen, whereas according to the common law, larceny to the value of twelve pence or more was a felony punishable by death.[34]

The interests and likely prejudices of lay people also had to be considered. It was all very well for Latimer to invoke the support of the Privy Council and other auditors when he preached against whoredom before

---

[31] TNA, KB 9/435, m. 91; KB 9/482, m. 18; cf. KB 27/1039, unnumbered membrane listing fines and amercements after m. 70; KB 29/152, m. 25r. Cases in local courts are discussed in Chapter 4. For another relevant form of action, see Caroline Dunn, *Stolen Women in Medieval England: Rape, Abduction, and Adultery, 1100–1500* (Cambridge, 2013), chap. 5.

[32] On the broader context, see Thomas, 'Puritans and Adultery', pp. 257–82.

[33] Robert M. Kingdon, *Adultery and Divorce in Calvin's Geneva* (Cambridge, MA, and London, 1995).

[34] Avis, 'Moses and the Magistrate', pp. 166–72.

Edward VI. But the argument for severe penalties against adultery and other forms of lechery was not merely that there were biblical precedents to that effect but that such action was necessary because whoredom was so prevalent. But everyone knew that sexual transgression was not a sin confined to the poor and humble; quite the contrary. It followed that the rich and powerful would find themselves among the victims of greater rigour. Latimer's assumption that the law would apply equally to husbands and wives must also have startled his court hearers.[35]

There was one group who might indeed be in favour of the utmost rigour, albeit not for the most high-minded motives and probably not on a bilateral basis. These were men who wished to rid themselves of adulterous wives – a matter that bore not only on the personal happiness and sense of honour of individuals but also on rights of inheritance and other dynastic concerns. This issue was in any case a topic of interest in Edward's reign because the Protestant reformers, contrary to the teaching of the Catholic church, asserted that adultery was grounds not merely for a judicial separation 'from bed and board' but for a full divorce that recognized the right of the innocent party to marry again. The issues of death for adultery and divorce with the right to remarry were so closely entwined as scarcely to be separable in contemporary discourse. But this was hardly conducive to a favourable hearing of the case for greater rigour towards adulterers, since the other issue was inevitably controversial.

The most notorious case – well known to historians of divorce – was that of William Parr, marquess of Northampton (brother of Henry VIII's last wife), who defied the law to remarry after divorcing his first wife, Elizabeth Bourchier. Appealing to the opinions of Protestant divines, he insisted before the council in the reign of Edward VI that his second marriage to Elizabeth Cobham 'stoode with the word of God, his first wife being proved an adoulteresse', and despite legal obstacles and considerable opposition, he succeeded in having the second marriage ratified by private act of parliament in 1552. So concerned were the other members of the council that ordinary people likewise dared 'to marry and keep two wives' that in 1548 – on the occasion when they considered the circumstances of Northampton's bigamy – they issued a proclamation to combat the trend.[36] Against this background, the prospect of arming disgruntled

---

[35] *Sermons by Hugh Latimer*, ed. Corrie, p. 244.
[36] John Roche Dasent (ed.), *Acts of the Privy Council* . . ., Vol. II: *1547–1550* (London, 1880), pp. 164–5; Paul L. Hughes and James F. Larkin (eds.), *Tudor Royal Proclamations*, 3 vols. (New Haven and London, 1964–9), Vol. I, pp. 421–3; Lawrence Stone, *Road to Divorce: England, 1530–1987* (Oxford, 1990), pp. 303–4.

husbands – not to mention wives – with a powerful weapon against an adulterous spouse was doubly contentious.

The Failure of Canon Law Reform

Attempts to frame a new code of canon law proved equally ill fated. The process had began in 1532, when the clergy conceded that the existing laws should be vetted by a panel of sixteen clergy and sixteen lay lords and members of the lower house of parliament. An act authorizing the appointment of the commission of thirty-two was passed two years later, while in 1544 another act gave the commissioners, when they should be appointed, the power to frame new laws as well as revising the old. All that came of these measures was a partial compilation of existing law now known as the 'Henrician canons'. Revived in the reign of Edward VI, the initiative was now conceived more ambitiously as an opportunity to create an essentially new body of law appropriate to a Protestant church, and the thirty-two commissioners were duly appointed in 1551. Although half were laymen, mostly of distinctly Protestant leanings, there were no peers, while the inner working group, or drafting committee, was dominated by clergy headed by Archbishop Cranmer. This commission finally succeeded in producing a complete new corpus, the *Reformatio legum ecclesiasticarum*, only to see it founder in March 1553.[37]

Relations between some of the lay members of the Privy Council and the bishops – at odds over the secularization of church property and other matters – were extremely strained by this point in Edward's reign, and this, combined with suspicion of clerical pretensions, may be sufficient to explain the rejection of the *Reformatio*. It is in any case likely that parts of the content gave rise to alarm and offence, not least the proposals regarding the punishment of sexual transgressions. Even unmarried offenders 'of whichever sex' were to give 'public satisfaction' – the form of penance was not defined – and to donate what was, by the standards of the time, a swingeing fine of £10 to the poor box of the local church 'or if their means are insufficient . . . as much of their goods as can be conveniently spared'. Regarding adultery, the *Reformatio* took the traditional line of rehearsing the severity of the punishments laid down by the law of Moses and the civil law for such 'awful wickedness' while drawing back from

<hr>

[37] The texts are printed (with translations) and the background is discussed in Gerald Bray (ed.), *Tudor Church Reform: The Henrician Canons of 1535 and the* Reformatio Legum Ecclesiasticarum (Church of England Record Society 8, Woodbridge, 2000).

actually imposing the death penalty. But it did prescribe that a male adulterer should restore his wife's dowry, endow her with half his goods and be condemned to perpetual banishment or life imprisonment. An adulterous wife was to be deprived of her dowry and all other property rights and otherwise to suffer the same penalties as a man. However, the *Reformatio* allowed the innocent party the right to remarry (as it did also in cases of divorce on the grounds of desertion and life-threatening cruelty). It also expressed the pious hope that 'the innocent party should forgive the guilty one and take him or her back again' but did not make clear how such reconciliation would affect the dire punishments enunciated in previous paragraphs of the code. In short, the proposed measures combined severity with impracticality.[38]

Church Courts in the 1530s and 1540s

Meanwhile, how did the church courts' jurisdiction over sexual transgressions fare on the ground? Inevitably the corrosive atmosphere of uncertainty undermined their activities to some extent, but without dealing a fatal blow. Sadly, virtually no disciplinary records are extant for the capital in the 1530s and 1540s. Elsewhere the patchily surviving records indicate that the courts trundled on with varying fortunes in different areas but no great initiatives. Houlbrooke gives the impression that with regard to sexual offences it was business as usual in the dioceses of Norwich and Winchester.[39] The discontinuous materials for the archdeaconry of Chichester suggest – as far as they go – a reduced level of intensity compared with the 1520s.[40] David Crawford's survey of a wide range of archdeaconry records suggests that as a general rule the numbers of disciplinary prosecutions had plummeted by the 1540s.[41] The trend can be illustrated in more detail in the archdeaconry of Leicester, where a correction court act book survives for the period from 1537 to beyond

---

[38] Bray (ed.), *Tudor Church Reform*, pp. 265–79.

[39] But he emphasizes both the difficulty of inferring the volume of correctional business from the surviving records and how profoundly some other aspects of ecclesiastical court business were affected by the changes of the 1530s: Ralph Houlbrooke, *Church Courts and the People during the English Reformation, 1520–1570* (Oxford, 1979), pp. 75–9, 278–81 and *passim*.

[40] Based on study of WSRO, Ep.I/10/5–8, Ep.I/17/1–2. Some disciplinary cases were heard in the consistory court, others in peripatetic correction courts; their records survive only patchily and are hard to piece together.

[41] David Crawford, 'The Rule of Law? The Laity, English Archdeacons' Courts and the Reformation to 1558', *Parergon*, new series, 4 (1986), 170–3.

the end of Henry VIII's reign.[42] It begins with proceedings following Cromwell's vicegerential visitation, while several prosecutions in 1542 are said to have arisen from detections made at an episcopal visitation. However, there are no cases dealing with church fabric or religious observance, so there must have been – as was usual in this jurisdiction – separate records of visitation presentments that have not survived. There were a few unidentified and miscellaneous charges, such as ill treating a wife, plus occasional cases of promoting sexual immorality – but so few indeed as to raise the possibility that the court's jurisdiction over cases of 'bawdry' had somehow been called into question.

Thus, virtually all the prosecutions were for actual sexual transgressions, referred to blandly as 'incontinence'. In the early years their numbers were significant, but they were on the decline. Thus sixty-eight such cases were entered in 1540 and fifty-one in 1545 – well below the levels of 1522–3. These were prosecutions against individuals, the ratio of men to women being approximately 4:3 in 1540 and exactly 2:1 in 1545. But a much greater number of persons was implicated, since in most cases the defendant's alleged sexual partner was named, though he or she was not made the subject of a separate entry. In many cases it is not clear whether any formal proceedings were taken against these 'co-respondents', some of whom were said to be 'late' of their parish and could perhaps not be easily traced. However, a few were marked as having been suspended from the church, presumably because they were expected to turn up in court but did not do so. Occasionally, both parties appeared, whether they had been cited or not. Some of the primary defendants were suspended and occasionally excommunicated if they persisted in their contumacy. But, in general, the court seems to have expected compliance. Successful purgations were rare – not more than eight occurred in 1540, including six men and two women. Most defendants, whether men or women, admitted the charges against them and were put to penance.

Towards the end of this record, the form of penances begins to be recorded in detail, in contrast to the brief notes that had hitherto sufficed. In the archdeaconry of Chichester, penances were often described quite fully throughout the 1530s and 1540s. Penitents, usually clad only in a shirt or smock and barefoot, bare-legged and bare-headed, were required to lead the parish procession on one or more Sundays. In other words, penances remained traditional in form, but this was precisely the point. Throughout all the changes of Henry VIII's reign, his church remained sacramental in

---

[42] The following is based on scrutiny of ROLLR, 1 D 41/13/2, including close analysis of sample years.

focus, and this was reflected in the form that penances took. Offenders carried a lighted candle, and the culmination of the act of penance came when they presented it to the celebrant during the offertory of the mass.

Despite the difficulties faced by the church courts in the 1530s and 1540s, they were clearly by no means supine, and their occasional efforts to take exemplary action in notorious cases suggest that they still kept a finger on the pulse of parish life. In the archdeaconry of Chichester in 1535, for example, fifteen men from three different townships were brought to court to testify to the infamy of an adulterous couple, while in 1546 six men and three women from Horsham, having been detected in the bishop's visitation, were brought to court in a batch to answer charges of adultery or fornication.[43] A case from Fenny Stratford (Buckinghamshire) in 1545, supervised personally by John Longland towards the end of his long tenure of the see of Lincoln,[44] provides especially rich and detailed insights into the reactions of neighbours in a case that had evidently become notorious. It is therefore worth reporting at length. On the basis of 'public fame', Thomas Cosyn was 'detected' for adultery with a widow, Clement Robynson, and in a sequence of court proceedings, the two churchwardens, along with the constable, nine other local men and two women, testified on oath to their knowledge of the affair. They were clearly out to get Cosyn, who was in the service of Lord Grey of Wilton. The fact that his accusers were so numerous argues against any notion that they were maliciously motivated, but in any case, the behaviour of the couple was such that their neighbours were easily able to assume the moral high ground. Indeed, it was claimed that the affair was no longer just a local matter: 'the commen fame is in the countrey of ther yll lyvinge togedre and waye goers comynge to the towne ... mervailethe that the towne dothe suffre the [couple's] abhom[inable dealings].'[45]

As one witness put the matter succinctly, Thomas Cosyn 'did use yll draftes to Clement Robynson in hir husbandes liffe tyme and nowe sence his deathe he dothe use itt worse'. The suspicions of Clement's husband William had been aroused when Cosyn was lodging at his mill – though the details are such as to suggest that the couple's marriage was in dire straits anyway. Robynson had complained to a neighbour that 'whan he

---

[43] WSRO, Ep.I/10/5, fo. 49v; Ep.I/10/8, fos. 71r–72v; for some other striking cases, see Ep.I/10/5, fos. 52v, 53v–54r, 55v, 79v, 123r–v, 129v.

[44] On his career, see Margaret Bowker, *The Henrician Reformation: The Diocese of Lincoln under John Longland, 1521–1547* (Cambridge, 1981).

[45] LA, DIOC/Cj 3, fos. 93r–94v, 96v–98r (quotation fo. 93r–v). 'Abhominable dealings' is a conjectural reading; here and at other points the MS is imperfect.

shulde goo to his naturall reste, his wyffe wolde make hir selffe madde and
renne awaye frome hym.' On one occasion, having seen his wife carry
a shirt into Cosyn's chamber, he threatened the pair with a woodknife,
whereupon Clement 'flewe in . . . [his] face', allowing her lover to make his
escape. The fact that she was taking responsibility for Cosyn's laundry was
picked up by others as a sign of untoward intimacy. A female neighbour
spotted her 'wadinge thrughe the fforde an houre afore daye in hir peticote,
baare leggede, baare neckede and withoute an apron' but with 'twoo shirtes
of Thomas Cosyns in hir lappe'. The neighbour demanded 'where she
hadde bene a progresse', and on receiving the implausible reply that she
had been seeking stray livestock, she 'toke hir by the peticote, sainge doo
you use to fynde shirtes whan you looke [for] beastes?'[46]

A maidservant reported that she had spied on the couple when they took
the opportunity to have sex at Lord Grey's manor at Eton when they were
there on business. She admitted that another of the witnesses 'did promyse
hir a peticote clothe' if she could 'take them togedre'. Not long afterwards,
William Robynson died, but what is striking is that this in no way
diminished local hostility to the affair. Shortly before the court proceedings, a group of people arranged a stakeout of the mill where Clement
was still living. Cosyn was observed to go there in the evening, and
individuals were strategically placed to confront him as he came out next
morning. When it seemed that he might escape by the back door, four men
'mowinge in the meadowes' entered into the spirit of the hunt and
'halowed att hym', crying 'nowe, nowe, nowe goethe the foxe awaye.'[47]

In the face of such intense local scrutiny and the subsequent legal
proceedings, Clement Robynson seems to have vacillated. When
Thomas Cosyn again turned up at her house after the court had ordered
them to avoid each other's company, she 'askede hym whate he didd ther,
sainge thou knowest I am in trouble for the[e] . . . goo thou hence, thou
wilte undoo me'. At a much earlier stage she had lamented 'that she hadde
loste the love of hir husbande for his sake'. Stoutly Cosyn had replied that
'that shulde nott skill ffor she shulde be welcome to hym att all tymes'.
When confronted outside the mill, Cosyn tried to outface his accusers,
disdaining to deny the circumstances and asking one of them, '[W]hate
haste thou to doo with itt?' Seizing the opportunity of a local muster to try
to reach an accommodation, he 'didd reason' with several of his neighbours, insisting that 'he wolde come to the saide Clementes house', but 'all
they sayde naye to itt.' Cosyn was not entirely without support, however.

---

[46] *Ibid.*, fos. 93v, 94r, 97v.   [47] *Ibid.*, fos. 94r, 94v.

He managed to produce six compurgators, but they were rejected because one came from a different village. Another of them accused the bishop, present in court, with being 'a maynteyner and a bearer', claiming that Cosyn's accusers 'wolde nott be soo bolde as they be butt that his lordeshipe dothe beare them'. But the evidence was overwhelming. Clement, at least, was convicted of consorting after being forbidden to do so and ordered to perform public penance.[48]

If the church courts were down, they were certainly not out – or so it would seem if this case was at all representative. Not the least of its points of interest is in demonstrating how the personal involvement of the bishop could help to galvanize procedures. On this basis, in the reign of Edward VI the redoubtable Bishop John Hooper proved able to turn the church courts into effective agents of Protestant advance and moral regeneration in the diocese of Gloucester. Poor record survival makes it hard to be certain that this was an isolated case; Thomas Thirlby, bishop of Norwich, seems to have run Hooper a close second.[49] But, in any event, since Edward VI reigned so briefly, the main impact of Hooper's and others' new thinking about ecclesiastical discipline was to come later, in the early part of Elizabeth's reign. That story is resumed in Chapter 10.

Innovations in Punishment in Henrician London

Historians have long been aware of attempts to reform the ecclesiastical law or to introduce the death penalty for adultery. They have paid less attention to a broader change in the judicial sphere that was by the middle of the sixteenth century beginning to affect attitudes towards the treatment of sexual offenders and did so first in the metropolis. This was a generally harsher attitude towards punishment and, in particular, an increasing recourse to physical penalties. An important part of the cultural context was the use of corporal punishment in the correction of young people. Whipping – for bad behaviour, laziness or simply failure to learn – was so central to school life that the birch was the stock symbol of the master's

---

[48] *Ibid.*, fos. 94r, 94v, 96v, 98r. Cosyn claimed that he was serving Lord Grey at Calais, and proceedings against him were deferred: *ibid*, fo. 101v.

[49] F. Douglas Price, 'Gloucester Diocese under Bishop Hooper, 1551–3', *Transactions of the Bristol and Gloucestershire Archaeological Society*, 60 (1939 for 1938), 51–151; Houlbrooke, *Church Courts*, pp. 79, 210–11. In Salisbury diocese, Bishop John Capon's visitation of 1550 was relatively ineffective – many parishes reported *omnia bene* or failed to report at all, and the crop of sexual offenders was meagre. Returns from the visitation of 1552 were much fuller. Proceedings following the visitation are unfortunately lacking in both cases: WSA, D1/43/1.

authority. In the sixteenth century, corporal punishment was even introduced into the universities. Apprentices were also subject to corporal
punishment, as were servants of both sexes.[50] In the world of the London
livery companies, such discipline could occasionally take extraordinary
forms. In May 1534, an apprentice called John Rolles was brought before
the court of the Drapers' Company having some six weeks before 'gre-
vously mysused hymself' with a maidservant living in the same house; their
master had caught them in bed together. In the interim, 'not regardyng the
schame of the worlde nor dredyng god' – a form of words recalling
numerous judgements against sexual offenders pronounced by the court
of aldermen – 'but in gevyng verey yll ensample to other yong men
apprentices of the same crafte and unyversally to all thapprentices and
servantes of the cetye', he had been boasting of his exploits both within the
craft and outside. It was this publicity rather than the sexual act itself that
determined the severity of his punishment. The wardens secured the
services of 'ij tall men' armed with 'two penyworth of burchen roddes'
and, to secure their anonymity, disguised in 'frokes of canvas' with hoods
to cover their faces, having only 'a space for the mowthe and for the eyen
lefte open'. On a day appointed in the parlour of the Drapers' Hall, in the
presence of the wardens, these men 'withowten any wordes spekyng . . .
pulled of the doblet and schert of the said John Rolles and ther apon hym
beyng naked they spent all the seid roddes . . . to thentent that all other
apprentices that hard therof schuld take ensample by hym and . . . schuld
be afrayed to fall to lyke onthryftenes.'[51]

The tendency in the sixteenth century was for corporal punishment to
move beyond the pedagogical and domestic spheres to become, in its
harsher forms, a staple of judicial punishment. The desire to restrain the
delinquencies of youth was one reason, but of even greater importance was
increasing concern about vagrancy.[52] While there were similar developments in the provinces, the shift is most clearly visible in the records of the
city of London court of common council and court of aldermen. As early as
1510 it was decreed that beggars should be put to work in cleansing the
town ditches; those who evaded this labour should be 'sett in the stokkes ij

[50] Lawrence Stone, *The Family, Sex and Marriage in England, 1500–1800* (London, 1977), pp. 163–7.
[51] Drapers' Hall, Repertory 7(ii), fo. 223r/p. 441, quoted in Laura Branch, 'Faith and Fraternity: The London Livery Companies and the Reformation, c.1510–c.1600', unpublished PhD thesis, University of Warwick, 2011, pp. 49–50. I am extremely grateful to Laura Branch for this reference.
[52] Martin Ingram, 'Shame and Pain: Themes and Variations in Tudor Punishments', in Simon Devereaux and Paul Griffiths (eds.), *Penal Practice and Culture, 1500–1900: Punishing the English* (Basingstoke, 2004), pp. 36–62.

dayes with brede and water and the third day to be beten naked with whippes from Al[d]gate to Newgate' before being banished. In 1517, the 'mighty beggars and vagabonds' in the prisons and cages of the city were ordered to be brought to Leadenhall, marked on the breast with the letter 'V' in yellow cloth 'in signe and token of a vagabund' and 'dryven thrugh-out all Chepe with basons ryngyng afore theym'. Four years later it was ordered that a group of vagabonds noted as 'pryve brybours and pykers' (petty thieves) should be nailed by the ear upon a 'new engyne' attached to the Standard in Cheap, with papers on their heads announcing their offence, while in 1524 able-bodied vagabonds and other suspect persons were ordered to be whipped at a cart's tail in various locations and to be fitted with 'rownde colers of iron' marked with the arms of the city.[53] In later decades the whipping of vagrants became commonplace, especially after this penalty was prescribed in the national vagrancy statute of 1531.

For reasons that have already been implied, the change inevitably affected sexual offenders. The latter were often seen as idle or 'unthrifty' – as in the Drapers' Hall example noted earlier – while, conversely, vagrants were thought to be promiscuous among themselves and with others. In particular, it was assumed that female vagabonds, however poor, did have one commodity to sell and were likely to do so. The humanist Juan Luis Vives said as much, but Londoners did not need learned discourse to instruct them on this matter. It was a commonplace among city magistrates and local officers.[54]

Another physical punishment increasingly applied in London to vagrant women, and hence to female sexual offenders, was ducking. The court of alderman in 1529 ordered seven women, probably prostitutes or 'common women', 'to be had to the cukkyng stole'. In the late fifteenth and early sixteenth centuries the instrument known as the 'cucking stool' was usually a form of pillory used for females, designed to achieve the public exposure of the culprit, not her immersion. So it is not clear in the case from 1529 whether the women were actually ducked.[55] But as time went on, the cucking stool became a ducking stool, and in 1535 it was explicitly stated that a group of 'myghty vagabondes and myswomen of theyre bodyes' were to be taken to Smithfield and 'sett upon the cukkyng stoole and ...

---

[53] LMA, Journal 11, fo. 104v; Repertory 3, fo. 164(168)r; Repertory 4, fos. 76v–77r, 215r.
[54] Vives, *De subventione pauperum*, ed. and trans. Mattheeussen and Fantazzi, pp. 92–3.
[55] LMA, Repertory 8, fo. 43(44)v; cf. Martin Ingram, '"Scolding Women Cucked or Washed": A Crisis in Gender Relations in Early Modern England?', in Jenny Kermode and Garthine Walker (eds.), *Women, Crime and the Courts in Early Modern England* (London, 1994), pp. 58–9; Marjorie Keniston McIntosh, *Controlling Misbehavior in England, 1370–1600* (Cambridge, 1998), pp. 63–4.

wasshyd over the eares'. Thereafter, references occurred regularly.[56]
Ducking, 'dipping' or 'dopping' (as it was variously called) must always
have been a brutal procedure, a shock to the system and perhaps even life
threatening when the immersion was prolonged or occurred in winter, but
it was on the whole less drastic than whipping. When the authorities
wished to be particularly severe, they sometimes combined the penalties,
as in 1536 when Joan Spycer and Joan Halywell were taken to Smithfield
'with papers upon theyre heddes' bearing the legend 'Comon Harlottes',
there to be 'dukkyd yn the water and after to be whypped and . . .
banysshed owt of thys cytie'. Or whipping was used as a deliberate escalation of the punishment, as in 1552 when eight 'common harlots' were to be
stripped to the waist, tied to carts and whipped about the city before being
expelled, because

> neither doppynge in the Theamys nor yet eny other commen sorte of
> ponyshment heretofore ordeyned and appoynted for suche offendours
> which sundry sortes of ponyshment all they or the most parte of theym
> have alredye here dyverse tymes most worthely suffred and wyll nothynge
> steye or refourme theym.[57]

With ducking and whipping at their disposal, as well as the long-
established penalties of parading culprits with rough music, exhibiting
them on the pillory, and banishing them from the city, the London
authorities had a formidable range of weapons to use against notorious
sexual offenders, as indeed also the cheats, perjurers and other offenders
that they commonly dealt with. The 'traditional' forms were, moreover,
not a static legacy but constantly being revised to suit current conditions,
to stigmatize offenders further or simply to add eye-catching features to
attract the crowds to witness the punishment in notorious cases.
The clipping or shaving of offenders' hair, which had been a notable
feature of the penalties prescribed in the ordinance of 1382 but had gone
out of use in the fifteenth century, was revived in 1510 and thereafter
remained available as part of the repertory for occasional use.[58] Sewing
on the garments of offenders letters or symbols signifying their offence was
another innovation that appeared around this time.[59]
Such cases offered precedents for colourful elaborations that became
increasingly common towards the middle decades of the sixteenth century.

[56] LMA, Repertory 9, fo. 104r; cf. Repertory 9, fo. 256v, Repertory 11, fos. 305(329)v, 364(388)
v–365(389)r, Repertory 12, fo. 78(79)r.
[57] LMA, Repertory 9, fo. 178r; Repertory 12, fo. 435(441)r.
[58] LMA, Journal 11, fos. 112r, 114v–115r.   [59] E.g. LMA, Journal 11, fos. 264v–265r, 327r.

To take an example from 1543, a female 'mayntenour of the fylthye synne of lecherye' – she received a child born out of wedlock only to abandon it under cover of darkness, leaving it crying at a merchant's gate – was made to ride 'upon a bare horsebak wyth her face turned towarde the tayll . . . her bodye being garnysshed wyth the ymages of yong infantes and a paper stonding upon her hedde declaring the cause of her ponyshement'.[60] More mundanely, offenders were increasingly paraded in carts – there were older precedents in provincial towns, but in London the first clear reference dates from 1528 – beginning the process whereby the parades that had featured on the streets of medieval London gradually mutated into what by the reign of Elizabeth had become known as 'carting'.[61]

Mounting Pressure: Sexual Regulation in Henrician London

These public punishments did not exist in isolation. As in previous generations, they served as the most exemplary element in a system of moral regulation that remained wide, deep and indeed all-pervasive. Most of the records of routine proceedings against sexual offenders in London in the early Reformation period – whether in the church or in secular courts – have disappeared, and the more informal processes that underlay them were mostly never put into writing. Quantification is therefore impossible, and the extent of church court discipline is particularly obscure. But the records of the court of common council and the court of aldermen – the latter, in particular, far fuller by the middle decades of the sixteenth century than earlier – amply document the main elements of the civic system of sexual regulation and show that they were still in regular use in the 1530s and 1540s. Indeed, activity intensified. In these decades there are frequent references to wardmote presentments and periodic orders for the holding of special sessions to try offenders. There are likewise numerous references to the policing activities of constables and watchmen in the wards, patrolling the streets by night, seeking out malefactors and, if necessary, entering private houses as well as inns and alehouses to make arrests.

Strikingly, there are also many orders for and incidental references to 'privy searches', sometimes confined to single wards but often extending over the whole city and the adjacent suburbs.[62] These were intensive sweeps to identify and arrest 'suspicious persons', who were taken up and imprisoned in stocks or cages or one or other of the London prisons until

---

[60] LMA, Repertory 10, fo. 335r; the same case is also recorded in Journal 15, fo. 30(31)r–v.
[61] LMA, Repertory 7, fo. 260(278)v.   [62] E.g. LMA, Journal 14, fo. 35v (1537).

they could be dealt with. Some of these culprits were imprisoned for short periods; others were fined. In either case they were unlikely to be discharged until they had given sureties for future good behaviour.[63] Expulsion remained another hazard, commonly from a particular ward but sometimes from the entire city; those who returned after formal expulsion from London were subject to imprisonment for a year and a day. Banishment remained the standard culmination of the open shame punishments visited on egregious offenders.

The records also yield evidence of particular concerns and corresponding adjustments of public policy; they also show periodic 'drives' or peaks of activity, motivated by immediate circumstances or by the zeal of individual mayors. One thing offered by the better class of women whose services were available for hire was an appearance of gentility; presumably this was attractive to clients with social pretensions, such as serving men in the households of nobles, bishops, and royal or civic officials, upwardly mobile apprentices or indeed men of higher social rank or economic standing, whether natives or foreigners. This appearance was above all created by means of clothing, perhaps no more than a touch of class like a velvet cap. But such sartorial pretensions were bitterly resented by 'honest' folk, perhaps more by women than by men. Thus, in 1538, the common council considered 'the suplicacon of the wardemote enquest concernyng the evyll example for the gorgyous apparell of the common women of the stewes to the great temptacon of yonge maydens, wyffes and apprentices'.[64] A major escalation in action against sexual offenders occurred in 1543. The chronicler Charles Wriothesley observed that '[t]his yeare the mayor punyshed many harlotes of the stewes by dobbinge in the Thames on a cookinge stoole at the Thre Cranes in the Vintre.' This is supported by numerous entries in the civic records. In February, the 'ponysshment of harlottes and bawdes of the stewys and other comen and incontynent women' was ordered, followed by a sequence of entries relating to the arraignment of offenders presented in the wardmote inquests. The fact that this was a year of scarcity and also of plague may have given added urgency to moral reformation.[65]

---

[63] LMA, Repertory 11, fos. 34(36)v, 38(40)r; Journal 15, fo. 153r.

[64] LMA, Repertory 10, fos. 13v, 27r.

[65] Charles Wriothesley, *A Chronicle of England during the Reigns of the Tudors, from A.D. 1485 to 1559*, ed. William Douglas Hamilton, 2 vols. (Camden Society, New Series 11, 20, London, 1875–7), Vol. I, pp. 145–6; LMA, Repertory 10, fos. 309v, 318v, 338v, 343r; Repertory 11, fos. 10(12)v, 11(13)r; Journal 15, fo. 31(32)r.

More dramatic was the closure of the Southwark stews in 1546. As was shown in Chapter 5, this by no means came out of the blue. There had been complaints for decades and the stews had been temporarily shut down in 1506. Famously, among the first acts of the new Protestant regimes in Augsburg and elsewhere had been to close down the civic brothels, but indeed in all parts of Europe – both Catholic and Protestant – where such institutions had formerly thriven, they were coming under pressure by the early sixteenth century, if not before.[66] In England, the closure was achieved by royal proclamation, and the motives were secular as well as religious, the stated grounds for action being that

> there hath of late increased and grown such enormities as not only provoke instantly the anger and wrath of Almighty God, but also engender such corruption among the people as tendeth to the intolerable annoyance of the commonwealth, and where not only the youth is provoked, enticed, and allowed to execute the fleshly lusts, but also, by such assemblies of evil-disposed persons haunted and accustomed, is daily devised and conspired how to spoil and rob the true labouring and well-disposed men.[67]

An important part of the background were the massive military activities of the 1540s. There was a long history of trying to ensure that the royal host was not troubled by common women; the crown had an interest in ensuring a supply of able-bodied men, rather than specimens weakened by sexually transmitted disease or (according to the notions of the time) simply made effeminate by excessive contact with women, whilst the demobilization of the bulk of the 48,000 men involved in the 1544 seizure of Boulogne heightened fears of vagabonds and idleness.[68] Thus the king himself may have had a direct interest in the closure of the stews. But the involvement of the London authorities may also be readily detected, since the rhetoric of the proclamation, evoking 'the fear of Almighty God and the shame of the world', was closely akin to that found year after year and decade after decade in numerous city ordinances, proclamations and judgements against sexual offenders.[69] Indeed, the closure of the stews was part of a larger campaign waged by the city, which in 1550 decisively

---

[66] Lyndal Roper, *The Holy Household: Women and Morals in Reformation Augsburg* (Oxford, 1989), chap. 3; cf. Leah Lydia Otis, *Prostitution in Medieval Society: The History of an Urban Institution in Languedoc* (Chicago, 1985); Jacques Rossiaud, *Medieval Prostitution*, trans. Lydia G. Cochrane (Oxford, 1988).

[67] Hughes and Larkin (eds.), *Tudor Royal Proclamations*, Vol. I, p. 365.

[68] *Ibid.*, p. 113; C. S. L. Davies, 'Slavery and Protector Somerset: The Vagrancy Act of 1547', *Economic History Review*, 19 (1966), 538.

[69] See Chapter 7.

established its jurisdictional oversight of the Southwark suburban area by the creation of the ward of Bridge Without.[70]

Meanwhile, the stewholders, Bankside victuallers and 'all such persons as have accustomed most abominably to abuse their bodies contrary to God's law and honesty' were ordered to 'depart from those common places and resort incontinently to their natural countries with their bags and baggages, upon pain of imprisonment and further to be punished at the king's majesty's will and pleasure'.[71] This closure, announced by the sound of trumpets, proved permanent. Predictably it did not eliminate prostitution, which already existed in other locations in and about the city; but it was a powerful statement of intent that could be invoked to redouble efforts against sexual sin. 'One thing I must here desire you to reform, my lords,' inveighed Hugh Latimer in his third court sermon before King Edward VI in 1549:

> You have put down the stews: but I pray you what is the matter amended? . . . I hear say there is now more whoredom in London than ever there was on the Bank . . . For God's sake let it be looked upon; it is your office to see unto it.[72]

Civic Purge in Edwardian London

In fact, the mayor and aldermen of London had already commenced a large-scale civic purge. The scale and ferocity of this campaign were unprecedented in London at least since 1473 and probably far exceeded the impact of that episode. It is reminiscent of the purges that occurred in some continental cities, notably Geneva, around the same time. As a major episode in the English Reformation (however defined), it merits more detailed treatment than it has hitherto received. Previous historians have rightly identified the spring of 1550 as a peak period. On 26 April, Richard Scudamore wrote to Sir Philip Hoby that 'they begyn to ponyssh vyce very ernestlye yn London, the lord be praysed therfore', while Wriothesley recorded that this month the lord mayor ordered the aldermen to convene the wardmote inquests to inquire of offenders. The chronicle makes clear that instead of relying on presentments from the last regular meeting of the wardmotes in December, the mayor and aldermen demanded entirely new returns; moreover, offenders named in the wardmote indictments were

---

[70] Carlin, *Medieval Southwark*, pp. 126–7.
[71] Hughes and Larkin (eds.), *Tudor Royal Proclamations*, Vol. I, pp. 365–6.
[72] *Sermons by Hugh Latimer*, ed. Corrie, pp. 133–4.

formally arraigned in the Guildhall, not dealt with in the wards at the aldermen's discretion.[73] Corroboration is found in the city records. On 15 April 1550, a precept was issued for the aldermen to hold wardmote inquests, while in July uncharacteristically generous provision was made for the hiring of carts and other necessaries.[74]

The account of an anonymous Spanish chronicler implies that investigations at the ward level were especially searching, and this may well be true. Equally plausibly, he says that so many offenders were found that the investigators 'were sorry they had had anything to do with it' and that as a result 'very many women were disgraced who had always before enjoyed good reputations.' In addition, he insists that a determined effort was made also to identify male sexual offenders, who were 'carried along on a cart, and people threw dirty water and other filth out of the windows at them'. He concludes by observing that 'many men would have paid large sums to be saved from the disgrace', a comment reminiscent of the language of the *Great Chronicle of London* in describing the proceedings of 1473.[75]

Well before the succession of Edward VI, overtly Protestant writers had been calling on the authorities to live up to their ideals and put the civic machinery of sexual regulation to even more effective use; the medium of print may have increased the impact of such pleas. 'There is a custome in the cytie,' wrote Henry Brinklow in 1545, 'ones a yeare to have a quest called the warnmall queste, to redresse vices, but alasse, to what purpose cometh it, as it is used. If a pore man kepe a whore besides his wife, and a pore mans wyfe play the harlot, they are punisshed as well worthye. But let an alderman, a jentleman, or a riche man kepe whore or whores, what punishment is there?'[76] In what circumstances was this challenge actually taken up? Rapid population increases in London, Westminster, Southwark and adjacent suburbs since the 1520s; the visible increase in numbers of

---

[73] Brigden (ed.), 'Letters of Richard Scudamore', p. 130; Wriothesley, *Chronicle*, ed. Hamilton,Vol. II, p. 36; cf. Charles Lethbridge Kingsford (ed.), 'Two London Chronicles, from the Collections of John Stow', in *Camden Miscellany XII* (Camden Society, 3rd Series 18, London, 1910), p. 45.

[74] LMA, Journal 16, fo. 50(52)v; Repertory 12, fos. 200(201)r, 247(249)v.

[75] Martin A. Sharp Hume (ed. and trans.), *Chronicle of King Henry VIII of England* (London, 1889), pp. 168–9; cf. Chapter 7.

[76] *Henry Brinklow's* Complaynt of Roderyck Mors . . . *and* The Lamentacyon of a Christen Agaynst the Cytye of London, ed. J. Meadows Cowper (Early English Text Society, Extra Series 22, London, 1874), p. 91. Possibly he was thinking of Sir John Allen, who died in 1544; lord mayor in 1525–6 and (unusually) for a second term in 1535–6, he is believed to have had a long-term relationship with a woman who bore him two sons. See Stephanie Tarbin, 'Civic Manliness in London, c.1380–1550', in Susan Broomhall and Jacqueline Van Gent (eds.), *Governing Masculinities in the Early Modern Period: Regulating Selves and Others* (Farnham, 2011), pp. 41–2; *ODNB*, Sir John Allen.

vagrants; and the dislocations of war in the 1540s – all of which could plausibly have generated increasing concern about sexual transgression – were no doubt background factors but do not explain why matters came so dramatically to a head. The timing suggests Protestant influence. Diarmaid MacCulloch emphasizes co-operation between Archbishop Cranmer and the lord mayor of London for the year 1549–50, Sir Rowland Hill. The end of clerical celibacy and the aristocratic marriage scandals of Parr and others had, he asserts, engendered 'an atmosphere of moral panic', which impelled Cranmer to arrange a Paul's Cross sermon on national morality that served as the trigger for Hill's prosecuting drive.[77]

While Rowland Hill was later to be described as the first Protestant mayor of London, there seem to be no contemporary indications that he was a fervent reformer.[78] But irrespective of his personal religious commitments, the campaign can undoubtedly be seen as Protestant in a broad sense, one of a series of civic initiatives in tune with the programme of reform and reformation in church and commonwealth that characterized the reign of the boy king and his leading advisers, both lay and clerical. Cranmer was by no means the only one concerned about sexual transgression at this juncture. The charges against Bishop Bonner in August 1549, leading to his deprivation later in the year, included the accusation 'that adulterie and fornicacon is mayntyned and kept very openly and comonly in the ... citie of London and other places of your diocese wherby the wrathe of God is provoked agaynst our people'.[79] It was indeed easy to single out the metropolis in this way, though whether Bonner was any more negligent than previous bishops in this respect may be doubted. In October, at the suggestion of Bucer, Calvin wrote a letter of advice to Protector Somerset urging him not only to complete the religious reformation but also to 'hold the brydle shorte' to 'punyshe vice'. Observing that 'disciplyne and correccion of vices bee as the senewes for to mayntayne the body in his force and strength', he conceded that in England, as elsewhere, crimes such as theft and extortion were often sharply punished 'for that in those men be offended'. But 'whoredomes' and 'adulteries', along with drunkenness and blasphemy, were treated as 'but a laughing game', even though they defiled bodies, subverted the holy state of marriage and above all were offensive to God. Calvin concluded that 'thys is the cause that so manye tribulacyons bee thys daye upon the yearthe. For insomuche as

---

[77] Diarmaid MacCulloch, *Thomas Cranmer: A Life* (New Haven and London, 1996), p. 455.
[78] Hume (ed. and trans.), *Chronicle*, pp. 167–9; *ODNB*, Sir Rowland Hill.
[79] TNA, SP 10/8, fo. 63v, cf. fo. 107v.

menne pardoneth suche enormities, it must folowe that God must take vengeaunce.'[80]

By invoking the threat of divine providence at a time of national crisis and presenting the punishment of vice as an integral part of government, Calvin made a strong case for the involvement of the secular magistrates in such matters. By the time he received the letter, Somerset had been forced from office and was in prison, but he arranged for a translation to be put into print, two editions appearing early in April 1550.[81] The contents of this pamphlet may have given added impetus to the civic purge already in operation – perhaps especially because of the sympathy that Somerset enjoyed among the populace. However, agreement between the city fathers and those of Edward's advisers who were still on the Privy Council was by no means perfect when it came to the actual punishment of sexual transgressors. As will be seen, certain episodes suggest that on occasion councillors were tempted to protect individuals. As a result, the mayor and aldermen had sometimes to tread warily, yet they were clearly determined to set their face against the lax morality of some courtiers and their hangers-on. More generally, the episode is notable for the vigour with which the city fathers seized the opportunity to give full effect to their powers of punishing vice and indeed to extend those powers if at all possible.

A basic point to emphasize is that the anti-vice campaign was lengthier than has previously been recognized. The campaign was essentially a redoubling of the sporadic moral reform efforts characteristic of the 1530s and 1540s, but the beginning of a more intense phase of action was signalled by an order on 20 January 1547, while Henry VIII was still languishing, that a 'synglewoman' and the wife of a locksmith taken in a house outside Aldgate and 'proved ... to be naught and incontynent of theyr lyvyng' should be thrice 'doppyd' in the Thames and then banished from the city.[82] The records of the court of aldermen for the following three years indicate that action against sexual vice was rarely off the agenda. As usual, the notices that survive are the tip of an iceberg: many of them refer to cases originating in ward searches and wardmote inquest presentments but brought into the court of aldermen because they were contested or thought to require special attention.[83] Some shed vivid light on the

---

[80] John Calvin, *An Epistle Both of Godly Consolacion and also of Advertisement ... to the Right Noble Prince Edwarde Duke of Somerset* (London, 1550); for a different translation, see TNA, SP 10/5, fos. 23–9. For the occasion and dating of this letter, see M. L. Bush, *The Government Policy of Protector Somerset* (London, 1975), p. 110 n. 71.

[81] Calvin, *Epistle*, title page and colophon.   [82] LMA, Repertory, 11, fo. 305(329)v.

[83] E.g. LMA, Repertory 11, fos. 319(343)r, 370(394)v.

impact on the ground. Thus, in February 1548, a woman of London Bridge was evidently fighting hard for her 'honestye' to the extent of taking legal advice. Order was taken for further investigation of the matter between her and the wardmote inquest 'after the examynacion of the seid inquest and the heryng of the reporte of Symon Lowe and of a grett number more of the neyghbours there made by the mouthe of Master Morgan serjaunte att the lawe'.[84]

An apparent innovation – and another indication of specifically Protestant influence – was that the court was prepared to act on reports from local clergy. In May 1549, the court ordered the alderman of Portsoken to expel from his ward one Katherine Hawkyns, having been informed by 'Master Huntyngdon the precher' that she was 'a commen woman of her bodye'. At the same time, however, they complained to Archbishop Cranmer of his 'lewde and slaunderous wordes, demeanour and reylynge . . . in the pulpytt' against the mayor and aldermen. This was John Huntington, one of the most fervent Protestants of the time.[85] Shortly before the court had communicated with Cranmer on another matter, alerting him of the case of a man accused of having two, if not three, wives living.[86]

As well as dealing ad hoc with matters such as these, the court also took care to ensure that public punishments occurred at regular intervals, albeit with due regard to persons and circumstances. In March 1548, for example, two 'singlewomen' were taken in suspicious circumstances in a house in Queenhithe ward. One proved to be pregnant and was pardoned; the other confessed 'her lewde and incontynent lyvyng' and was accordingly ducked and expelled from the city, while the male householder was imprisoned for four days and then discharged with an order to 'avoyde oute of that house and kepe honest rule'.[87]

Finally, the court ordered some truly spectacular punishments as an example, particularly of those whom the authorities saw as 'auncyent commen harlottes of their bodies whom no commen or indyfferent correc-cion or punyshment wyll stey, refourme or withdrawe from their detestable and devylysshe vice and synfull lyfe'.[88] In July 1548 it was ordered that Elizabeth Whytehed alias 'Flouncing Bess' should be led from prison in

---

[84] LMA, Repertory 11, fo. 396(420)r, cf. fo. 397(421*bis*)v.

[85] LMA, Repertory 12, fo. 79(80)r; cf. Brigden, *London and the Reformation*, pp. 400, 492–3, 495. For another case instigated by a minister, see Repertory 11, fos. 455(477)r, 465(487)v, 467(489)r.

[86] LMA, Repertory 12, fo. 78(79)v.   [87] LMA, Repertory 11, fos. 414(438)r, 420(444)r.

[88] LMA, Repertory 12, 128v–129r. The women punished on this occasion were threatened with the loss of an ear if they returned from banishment.

market time 'with basones and other instrumentes and melodie ryngyng and playing before her' to the Standard in Cheap, where she was to be set on the pillory. There her hair was to be 'cutt and rounded as short as her eares', and she was to stand for an hour bare-headed 'with a paper upon her brest' stating her offence before being recommitted to prison 'untyll my lorde mayers pleasure be knowen for the further ordering of her'.[89]

She was said to be an inveterate offender, but there were extra twists to the tale. According to Charles Wriothesley, she was 'a whore of the stewes, and, after the putting downe of them, was taken and banished out of divers wardes of this cittie'. Her exemplary punishment thus signalled that the city fathers were unwilling to tolerate informal prostitution in the wake of the recent closure of the licensed brothels in Southwark. Wriothesley added that the immediate cause of her punishment was that she had been taken with 'one of the kinges trumpeters' in Finsbury Court. While there is no evidence in the city records that this man was punished, the case must have sent a clear message that even well-connected pseudo-gentlemen, who might feel that they had a natural right to sexual services, would do well to be circumspect. Later in the year, the city arraigned William Archer, one of the valets of the king's guard, for ill-living. The woman involved and another man were tried too. All three were acquitted, but Archer was forced to give bond to remove Jane Manwarynge from his house in St Dunstan in the West and henceforth not to keep any woman of unhonest behaviour or suspect name and fame as servant or concubine.[90]

Predictably, women were the main target, but men could not necessarily escape even the most severe punishment, as another exemplary case demonstrates. On the last day of February 1549, the court of aldermen sentenced a butcher called William Abraham, who had not only 'detestably kept and carnally knowen and used' Joan Woodshawe, wife of a fellow butcher living opposite, 'dyrectly ageinst Godes lawe' but also hired men to kill the husband. He was made to ride a horse bareback, his face towards the tail, with a paper on his head inscribed in large letters, 'For lying with an other mans wyfe and hyring of certein persons to kyll her husbonde'. He faced a long ordeal. In that guise, he was to be led from the Bread Street Counter, where he had been confined, to Newgate and thence through St Nicholas Shambles – the place where he dwelt and in any case the main resort of butchers – and Cornhill to Leadenhall. After a pause, the procession was to continue through Gracechurch Street, New Fish Street and

---

[89] LMA, Repertory 11, fo. 451(479)r.
[90] Wriothesley, *Chronicle*, ed. Hamilton, Vol. II, p. 4; Journal 16, fo. 40(42)v.

Thames Street till it reached Queenhithe and thence through Bread Street to the Standard in Cheap. There Abraham was to stand on the pillory till half past eleven, still with the paper on his head and a similar inscription fixed above him on the pillory 'that everye person may easely see and red the same'. Finally, he was to be taken back to the Counter to await further order.[91]

The offence had originally come to light in August 1548, at which point Woodshawe's wife was committed to prison, while Abraham had to give sureties for his further appearance in court. According to Wriothesley, however, one of the men hired to kill Woodshawe was one of the king's guard, and so 'by favor and sute to the kinges counsell and rewardes geven punishment was differred.' At length, however, the mayor secured permission to punish Abraham 'as he and his brethren [the aldermen] should thincke best'. Such was the sensitivity of the case that the culprit 'was sodenlie taken . . . selling fleshe at his shopp and sent to ward not knowing the cause, and commandment geaven to the keeper that no person should speake with him, so that when he came to doe his pennance no person knewe it till he rode aboute'.[92]

Thus the anti-vice campaign of 1550, though exceptionally intense, by no means came out of the blue. There was not much of a lull in subsequent years either. Plainly there was much activity at the ward level, whence more difficult or disputed cases surfaced for the attention of the aldermen, while at intervals the usual special sessions were appointed for the arraignment and open punishment of offenders.[93] Reference to a writ of certiorari sued out of Chancery by a married couple indicted by the wardmote inquest of Farringdon Without, probably for bawdry, indicates that there was sometimes resistance to discipline.[94] Yet the pressure from the mayor and aldermen continued in various forms, including periodic privy searches.[95] Of his own knowledge, John Stow reported that the keeper of the Bread Street counter allowed 'strumpets' to lodge there for four pence a night, 'whereby they might be safe from searches that were made abroad'.[96] The scam must have subverted the vice campaign to some extent but at the same time testifies to its intensity. In October 1551 it was ordered that every week henceforth the aldermen or their deputies should in person

[91] LMA, Repertory 12, fo. 53(55)r–v.
[92] LMA, Repertory 11, fos. 465(487)v, 466(488)r; Repertory 12, fo. 55(57)r; Wriothesley, *Chronicle*, ed. Hamilton, Vol. II, p. 8.
[93] LMA, Repertory 12, fos. 309(311)v, 311(313)v.   [94] LMA, Repertory 12, fo. 299(301)v.
[95] LMA, Repertory 12, fos. 323(325)r, 487(491)r.
[96] John Stow, *The Survey of London*, ed. C. L. Kingsford, 2 vols. (Oxford, 1908), Vol. I, pp. 350–1.

'dylygently inquyre and serche oute all the enormyties and defautes' in their wards and see that offenders were duly punished. Hence, in January 1552, Anthony Sylver, deputy of the ward of Farringdon Without, brought in nine 'commen harlotes', of whom eight were whipped at the cart's tail and then expelled from the city, while the last was spared because she was with child but sent to Newgate instead.[97]

But the court of aldermen had sufficient assurance of popular support to send disputed cases back to the local level for further investigation, as in July 1552, when a married woman accused by the same Anthony Sylver and others was referred to the wardmote inquest to 'inquyre of her' and hear witnesses.[98] Wriothesley's chronicle provides further evidence of the co-operation of local people in bringing notorious offenders to book and perhaps of the resentment of ordinary city folk towards upper-class debauchery. In August 1551, a haberdasher's wife was accused not only of adultery with a gentleman called Nicholas Ballard but also of procuring for him her own daughter and a maidservant of ten or eleven years old:

> which the said Ballard occupied all three carnallie, proved by six substantiall and honest persons of the said warde, putting in a booke in wryting to my Lord Maior of five sheetes of paper of their said factes that daie and tyme, which said persons were endited the daie before by the wardens enquest, and this daie arraigned [in the Guildhall] of the said cryme, which was most detestable to be hearde for the enormitie therof.

The haberdasher himself, his wife and the gentleman were all sentenced to be carted wearing ray hoods and holding white rods, Ballard being after-wards sent to Newgate and eventually convicted for the rape of the under-age girl.[99]

Throughout 1551 and 1552, the exemplary punishments of carting and ducking occurred often enough to remind everyone of the dangers of indulging in sexual sin. Indeed, punishments tended to become even harsher, greater severity being justified on the grounds either that ordinary penalties had been insufficient to deter offenders or of the particular heinousness of the offences. Such aggravating circumstances as an attempt to poison a spouse to facilitate an adulterous relationship understandably provoked outrage, but the aldermen were also highly intolerant of situa-tions where a servant or apprentice had betrayed his master by sleeping

---

[97] LMA, Repertory 12, fos. 403(409)r, 435(441)r.   [98] LMA, Repertory 12, fo. 506(510)v.
[99] Wriothesley, *Chronicle*, ed. Hamilton, Vol. II, pp. 52, 64–5. For the record of proceedings, see LMA, Journal 16, fo. 115(121)v.

with his wife, especially if the adulterous couple had compounded their offence by wasting or stealing the husband's goods. It was on all these grounds that in July 1552 a fruiterer's wife was whipped about the city on two market days, pilloried on the third and then imprisoned, while the man's apprentice, one of her lovers, was also whipped.[100] That such exemplary punishments were noted by city chroniclers, such as Wriothesley and the merchant taylor Henry Machyn, is suggestive of their impact on the public imagination.[101]

In the last months of Edward's reign, action against sexual vice was again stepped up. The instigator appears to have been the lord mayor, Sir George Barne, presumably acting on traditional grounds as he is not noted for Protestant commitment. Indeed, it may have been to emphasize that this morality campaign was fully in accord with established city values, not merely the product of a religion that many saw as new-fangled, that it was deliberately combined with a round-up of vagabonds and a drive against tradesmen giving short measure, selling faulty goods or guilty of other dishonest practices.[102] As a result, states Wriothesley, 'all malefactours feared him for his good executinge of justice.'[103] All these activities are reflected in the city records. A flurry of cases in the fortnight after Epiphany (6 January) inaugurated the drive against sexual offenders,[104] while further well-publicized prosecutions occurred in following months, including (as was usual) occasional instances where the court showed mercy and merely admonished offenders.[105]

Barne's campaign was marked by a number of other notable features. On several occasions an example was made of low-level (but among the populace high-profile) public officials. In March 1553, one of the 'beadles of the poor', convicted of 'the fylthye cryme and offence of fornycacon', was ordered either to marry the woman whom he had 'vyciated' or to be carted round the city with a ray hood, a white rod and basins and pans ringing before him. In May, on the same day that a batch of three 'commen vicyous idle and loytering quenes and vacabundes' were ordered to be whipped round the city, the executioner Lawrence Vigorye was arrested for

[100] LMA, Repertory 12, fo. 504(508)r. For other exemplary punishments, see *ibid*, fos. 359(361)v, 394(400)v, 449(454)r, 509(513)r.
[101] John Gough Nichols (ed.), *The Diary of Henry Machyn, Citizen and Merchant-Taylor of London, from A.D. 1550 to A.D. 1563* (Camden Society, Old Series 42, London, 1848), p. 22; Wriothesley, *Chronicle*, ed. Hamilton, Vol. II, pp. 50–1, 52, 64–5. On Machyn's 'diary', see Ian Mortimer, 'Tudor Chronicler or Sixteenth-Century Diarist? Henry Machyn and the Nature of his Manuscript', *Sixteenth Century Journal*, 33 (2002), 981–98.
[102] *ODNB*, Sir George Barne.   [103] Wriothesley, *Chronicle*, ed. Hamilton, Vol. II, pp. 80–1.
[104] LMA, Repertory 13, fos. 7r, 8r, 9r.   [105] LMA, Repertory 13, fos. 40v, 59r, 66v.

'naughtie and suspecte rule' and committed to prison.[106] Important also was the imposition of city punishments on individuals who came from outside; it would seem that the city fathers were taking the opportunity to stamp their authority on areas beyond the traditional limits of civic jurisdiction. This is evident in the case of some of the trade offenders – the punishment of colliers from Edgware and Croydon, for example[107] – as well as those guilty of sexual misdoing. Thus, in February, a Canterbury surgeon, convicted of hiring an assassin to do away with a man from Chigwell (Essex) 'to the intent to have had hys wyfe (whom he kepte) and his good[es]', was ordered to ride round the city on two market days with his face to the horse's tail, wearing a paper 'declaryng his . . . offence', and then on the next market day to have one of his ears nailed to the pillory.[108]

Another innovation is seen in a case in May where the punishment of an apprentice was separated from that of his fellow culprits and staged in a company hall, apparently to send a firm warning to young men who might be tempted to similar vice; what makes it different from the Drapers' Company case quoted earlier is that the city rather than the company wardens took the initiative, and far from the matter being handled discreetly, it was clearly designed to achieve maximum publicity. Agnes Browne, widow, Anne Richardson and John Lane, water bearer, 'who coulde not denye . . . but that they were idle loyterers, vacaboundes and commen harlotes of theire bodies', were sentenced to be whipped about the city at the cart's tail, while it was further ordered that William Foweler, an ironmonger's apprentice

> who dide playnely confese hymself to have commytted fornicacion wythe the saide Agnes Browne shall tomorowe be whipped nakede at the Ire[n]mongers hall in the presense of a good number of thappreyntesies of the same companye to thintente that they admonyshede by his correccion may the rather eschue the lyke offence.[109]

Of course, there were limits to what the city magistrates could do. Southwark was still in the process of being incorporated within their jurisdiction. In 1550 a Southwark case involving a woman who had been consorting with someone else's husband was referred to the lord mayor, Sir Rowland Hill; it is evident that the matter had been the cause of considerable local resentment, provoking not only the neighbours but also the local

---

[106] LMA, Repertory 13, fos. 26v, 43r; cf. Nichols (ed.), *Diary of Henry Machyn*, p. 32.
[107] LMA, Repertory 13, fo. 18v; Wriothesley, *Chronicle*, ed. Hamilton, Vol. II, pp. 80–1.
[108] LMA, Repertory 13, fo. 19v.   [109] LMA, Repertory 13, fos. 52v –53r.

justices to warn her to desist. Shortly afterwards it was ordered that, just as wardmote courts were kept in the London wards, a special session of the peace should be held annually in what was now the ward of Bridge Without 'for the abolysshement and suppressyon of vyce, synne and evell rule and the mayntenaunce and increase of honestye, good rule and vertue'.[110] But it is by no means clear that the anti-vice campaign so active north of the river had similar impact in the southern suburb. Westminster was, of course, a completely separate jurisdiction, and the Middlesex suburbs were likewise mostly beyond the city's authority; paucity of records unfortunately makes it impossible to form a clear impression of what went on in these places. What appears to be a stray surviving record of the Westminster Gatehouse court in 1545 suggests brisk action against sexual offenders towards the end of Henry VIII's reign, albeit not on the scale of the drive of 1519 discussed in Chapter 5.[111] In Edward VI's reign, indictments of bawdy house keepers in the King's Bench were quite numerous in Easter and Michaelmas Terms 1549, Michaelmas Term 1550 and Easter and Trinity Term 1553; Margaret Barnes, alias 'Long Meg of Westminster', was among those netted. But the scale and ferocity of the London campaign were not fully replicated.[112]

The Foundation of Bridewell Hospital

There was another important and highly innovative dimension to metropolitan moral reform efforts in Edward's reign: the foundation of Bridewell Hospital. Rightly, this is usually seen as part of the city's programme of combating poverty and vagrancy and the social ills associated with them. But its foundation takes on greater meaning when it is seen against the existing background of the city's policing of sexual sin. By the early 1550s, this was taking up no small proportion of the aldermen's time. It made

[110] LMA, CLA/043/01/016, fo. 8ov; Repertory 12, fo. 291(293)v.

[111] WAM 50782. This document is endorsed, 'Presentmentes of defaultes of the courte of Westminster', but there is no proper heading for the actual record. The catalogue merely ascribes it to the time of Henry VIII, but on fo. 3r the dates on which three bloodsheds occurred are given as 12, 26 and 29 May 37 Henry VIII [1545]. Of the various offenders, some forty-five individuals, including eleven married couples, were accused of a variety of sexual offences that boiled down to being a bawd, a common woman or harlot or a bawd and a harlot.

[112] TNA, KB 9/573, mm. 16, 19, 22, 23, 28, 32, 33; KB 9/574, mm. 18, 30, 31, 44, 55; KB 9/576, m. 62; KB 9/582, m. 39; KB 9/983, mm. 39, 41 (including Long Meg, on whom see Patricia Gartenberg, 'An Elizabethan Wonder Woman: The Life and Fortunes of Long Meg of Westminster', *Journal of Popular Culture*, 17, no. 3 (Winter 1983), 49–58; Bernard Capp, 'Long Meg of Westminster: A Mystery Solved', *Notes and Queries*, 45 (1998), 302–4.

sense to delegate some of this activity to a board of governors that included some aldermen but drew most of its strength from the ranks of men somewhat below them. It has always been a puzzle how Bridewell acquired such draconian powers. But they appear readily comprehensible when seen in the context of the privy searches, night watches in the wards, regular presentments by wardmote inquests, the extensive local powers of aldermen and their deputies to warn, fine, and imprison offenders, and even send them packing from their wards, and finally, the terrifying powers of the court of aldermen to order the exemplary punishments of riding backwards, carting, whipping, pillory, cutting of hair, mutilation of ears and finally ignominious expulsion from the city.

The initiatives of which Bridewell formed part went back into the reign of Henry VIII; the context was not only the increasing scourge of poverty and a recognition that there existed different categories of poor people that required diverse responses but also, at institutional and legal levels, the problems and opportunities thrown up by the dissolution of religious houses and the incorporation of Southwark into the city of London in 1550. Ideas that had originated in civic circles and been given an intellectual gloss by humanists such as Juan Luis Vives, Sir Thomas More and Thomas Starkey were now inflected by Protestant doctrine and revitalized by the activism and zeal of Bishop Nicholas Ridley and other leaders of the Edwardian Reformation. They were able, it would seem, to forge effective political bonds with Sir Richard Dobbes, Sir George Barne and other key members of the city elite, at least some of whom were already committed Protestants or in the process of becoming so.[113] By 1552, the city had established or re-established St Bartholomew's Hospital to care for the sick poor, St Thomas's in Southwark for the aged and impotent and Christ's for poor orphan children. However, the city fathers, like some leading churchmen, were convinced that there existed a large residual pool of poverty, characteristically represented by the 'sturdy vagabond',

---

[113] The story of the foundation of Bridewell Hospital has been told often, with varying emphases: see Thomas Bowen, *Extracts from the Records and Court Books of Bridewell Hospital* (London, 1798), pp. 1–9; Edward Geoffrey O'Donoghue, *Bridewell Hospital: Palace, Prison, Schools from the Earliest Times to the End of the Reign of Elizabeth* (London, 1923), chaps. 14 and 15; Paul Slack, 'Social Policy and the Constraints of Government, 1547–58', in Jennifer Loach and Robert Tittler (eds.), *The Mid-Tudor Polity, c.1540–1560* (Basingstoke, 1980), pp. 108–13; Christopher Thomas Daly, 'The Hospitals of London: Administration, Refoundation, and Benefaction, c.1500–1572', unpublished DPhil thesis, University of Oxford, 1994, pp. 221–6; Lee Beier, 'Foucault *Redux*?: The Roles of Humanism, Protestantism, and an Urban Elite in Creating the London Bridewell, 1500–1560', in Louis A. Knafla (ed.), *Crime, Gender, and Sexuality in Criminal Prosecutions* (Criminal Justice History 17, Westport, CT, and London, 2002), pp. 33–60; Paul Griffiths, *Lost Londons: Change, Crime, and Control in the Capital City, 1550–1660* (Cambridge, 2008), pp. 11–15.

and that 'the cause of all this misery and beggary was idleness: and the mean and remedy to cure the same must be by its contrary, which is labour.'[114]

The result was the decision to set up a 'house of occupations', and through the good offices of Bishop Ridley, in 1552, the city achieved the remarkable feat of securing from the king a grant of extensive premises in the palace of Bridewell. Even more remarkably, in 1553 they also obtained a wide-ranging charter that gave a board of thirty governors, embracing six aldermen (to include two former mayors) and twenty-four citizens, extensive powers and duties. Ostensibly the house was to be a training establishment, maintaining a stock of materials to set the inmates on work, supervised by 'taskmasters and taskmistresses' with 'power to correct and punish such as are under their task, if they loiter and be found negligent'.[115] But it was also to be a house of correction, going far beyond the treatment of the poor as ordinarily understood, since the governors were given power, throughout the whole of London and Middlesex, to 'inquire and examine . . . all manner of suspicious houses' such as 'inns, taverns, gaming-houses, play-houses, [and] dancing-houses'; to take up thence not only all 'idle lazy ruffians, haunters of stews, vagabonds and sturdy beggars or other suspected persons . . . and men and women . . . of ill name and fame' but also the 'tenants, masters, owners or keepers' of such establishments; to bring them to Bridewell and, unless they could 'honestly . . . discharge themselves', to punish them at their discretion, using 'such correction and order . . . as to them shall seem most convenient'.[116] Apart from 'haunters of stews', sexual offenders were not mentioned explicitly. But, as noted earlier, it was simply assumed that vagrant women would sell their bodies. Moreover, it had always been understood that sexual offenders of all sorts were included in the category of 'suspicious persons' named in precepts for privy searches – the most obvious model for the powers given to the Bridewell governors. It was to be expected that harlots, bawds and whoremongers would feature prominently, and so it was to prove.

Sexual Regulation in Marian London

How did the succession of Mary affect the practice of sexual regulation? Plainly, her priorities were to restore the Catholic religion, secure her

---

[114] Bowen, *Extracts*, App., p. 3.   [115] *Ibid.*, App., pp. 3, 5.
[116] *Memoranda, References, and Documents Relating to the Royal Hospitals of the City of London* (London, 1836), App., pp. 75–6.

marriage with Philip of Spain and combat the threat of rebellion, sedition and popular criticism that these policies provoked. Inevitably, the city authorities had to toe the line, and their activities in support of church and crown are prominently reflected in the records of the court of common council and the court of aldermen, which refer to hissing and 'hemming' at priests and anti-Catholic pranks such as 'polling' a cat or shaving the crown of a little boy's head. In August 1554, the court of aldermen received from the dean of St Paul's a letter asking for 'theire ayde and helpe for the reformacion and steynge of rangelers and talkers of holye scripture and of the highe mysteries thereof openlie in taverns and commen vyttelynge howses'.[117]

Attention to these matters no doubt squeezed the time available for action against sexual offenders. Yet, in London in the first half of the reign, there is actually little sign of any slackening of effort against them. The city's executioner, imprisoned in Edward's reign, was released in October 1553, but only on his 'earneste promyse' to give up the 'commen harlot' whom he had formerly kept.[118] As before, sessions were periodically ordered for the arraignment of bawds, as were privy searches for the arrest of suspicious persons; the latter were fully in tune with the Marian government's concern to maintain order and suppress unrest and sedition. As usual, a miscellany of sex-related cases cropped up for the court of aldermen to deal with.[119] There was also the usual sequence of exemplary punishments – riding backwards, carting, pillory, public whipping and so forth.[120] Occasionally, these performances had peculiarly Marian resonances, as in November 1553, when a priest was carted for having lived with a concubine and claiming to be married to her,[121] but many were indistinguishable from those of Edward's reign.

Of course, the ecclesiastical authorities in London retained their own means of disciplining sexual offenders, but apparently they were netting no great numbers. The surviving register of proceedings after Bonner's 1554 visitation is overwhelmingly concerned with religious conformity. There were fewer than thirty cases relating to sex and marriage, involving a total of thirty-six persons (twenty-three men and thirteen women). Several

---

[117] LMA, Repertory 13, fo. 193r. For anti-Catholic pranks and demonstrations, see Brigden, *London and the Reformation*, chap. 13, *passim*.
[118] LMA, Repertory 13, fo. 90v, cf. fo. 43v.
[119] LMA, Repertory 13, fos. 176r (sessions for bawds), 173r, 347(348)v (privy watches), 99v, 101v, 115r, 132v, 280v, 288r, 288v (miscellaneous cases).
[120] LMA, Repertory 13, fos. 69v, 75r, 80r, 109r, 137v, 143v, 179r, 257r, 292v–293r.
[121] LMA, Repertory 13, fos. 96v, 99v; cf. Nichols (ed.), *Diary of Henry Machyn*, p. 48.

concerned priests who had married in Edward's reign and were still cohabiting. The remainder were a miscellany, including half a dozen cases of promoting bawdry, several bigamy charges and a few instances of adultery or other sexual transgression.[122]

This paucity of cases may have been one of the reasons why Mary's ecclesiastical establishment challenged not only the use of Bridewell as a penitentiary but also the entirety of the city's jurisdiction over sexual offenders. But this was a long-established element of the city's privileges whose diminution the mayor and aldermen could in no wise countenance, and the representatives sent to treat with the ecclesiastical commissioners on this issue in November 1556 included such staunch Catholics as Sir Thomas White as well as others less in tune with Mary's religious views.[123] A sequence of events in February 1557 reveals clearly the city's stance. Having apparently received a warning letter from the chancellor of the diocese of London, the court of aldermen sent a delegation to the bishop asking him

> not onely for his owne parte quyetely to permyte and suffer the cytye to use and enjoy theire auncyente liberties and customes as well in punyshynge of incontynente lyvers and other offendors as otherwyse, as they and theire predycessors tyme oute of mynde of man have alwayes done, but also to take order with his saide chauncellour and all other his offycers to do the same.

To drive the point home, that same day they ordered that all the 'comen harlottes, bawdes and scoldes' lately presented by the wardmote inquests of Farringdon Without, Cripplegate and Portsoken should be immediately arrested, arraigned and tried. Shortly afterwards, rehearsing the formulae that the delegation had been entrusted to utter to Bishop Bonner, they ordered that a man convicted at the recent sessions of adultery with a married woman should be 'openly punyshyd ... accordynge to the auncyente lawes and customes of this cytye in that behalf tyme oute of mynde of man always lawfully usyd, the requeste of the bysshop of London lately made to understande the evydence gevyn agaynste hym upon his arraynemente notwithstandyng'.[124]

---

[122] LMA, DL/C/614; see also Meriel Jagger, 'Bonner's Episcopal Visitation of London, 1554', *Bulletin of the Institute of Historical Research*, 45 (1972), 306–11. Unfortunately, this is the only surviving record of disciplinary proceedings in the London church courts between 1530 and 1560, so comparisons with later Henrician times and the reign of Edward VI cannot be made.

[123] LMA, Repertory 13, fos. 454(455)r, 456(457)v, 457(458), 478(479)v; Letter Book S, fo. 107v.

[124] LMA, Repertory 13, fos. 478(479)v, 480(481)v; cf. Repertory 14, fo. 14r (another session for the arraignment of bawds and harlots ordered, 10 March 1558).

As late as July 1558, certain citizens complained that they were 'sued and troblyd in the spirituall courte' for giving evidence against a married woman arraigned as a common harlot and secured the assistance of the court of alderman in their defence, but essentially the threat to the city's jurisdiction over sexual offenders had been beaten off.[125] In the case of Bridewell, an even more fundamental danger was that Edward's grant would be revoked, but in the event, the charter was eventually confirmed by Mary in February 1556. It was no doubt galling to the city authorities when a preacher at Paul's Cross in April 1558 stated that an apprentice had been beaten to death within its walls – they complained to the Lord Chancellor of this 'rasshe and slaunderous declaracion' – but it is doubtful if this really did much harm.[126] The records of Bridewell court sessions for this early period are lost, but this and other incidental references show that by now its activities were well under way.[127] Moreover, the 'ordinances and rules' drawn up in 1557 'for the good government of the House of Bridewell' specifically refer to 'the idle strumpet and vagabond', confirming the presence of sexual offenders among the 'lewd and idle sort' subject to discipline.[128]

These disputes over jurisdiction may explain why fewer sexual cases were, in fact, entered in the city records in the closing years of the reign. But equally a simple change in record keeping may have been the cause, while the fact that some cases were now being dealt with by the Bridewell governors, who presumably kept their own records, must also be borne in mind. Certainly some cases were still entered in the Repertories and Journals on much the same pattern as before.[129] Moreover, Machyn's diary indicates that exemplary punishments were still being regularly carried out, even though they cannot necessarily be traced in the surviving official records. Indeed, some of them seem to have been particularly elaborate, plainly designed to convey an educative message to a wide audience. According to Machyn, 'The xvij day of Desember [1557] dyd ryd in a care a yonge man and the woman the wyff of John a Badoo ... and she was the bowd, and she was wyped at the care-ar[se], and the harlott dyd bett her.' Completing this unusually kinetic tableau – perhaps to indicate the grim old age that awaited those who persisted in whoredom – a 'nold harlott of iij skore and more led the hors, lyke a nold hore'.[130]

---

[125] LMA, Repertory 14, fo. 49r.   [126] LMA, Repertory 14, fos. 24v, 29v.
[127] O'Donoghue, *Bridewell Hospital*, p. 156; LMA, Repertory 13, fos. 531(532)r, 557(558)r–v.
[128] Bowen, *Extracts*, App., p. 9.   [129] LMA, Journal 17, fos. 19r–v, 59r; Repertory 14, fo. 70v.
[130] Nichols (ed.), *Diary of Henry Machyn*, p. 161; for other public punishments of sexual offenders, see
   ibid., pp. 78, 98, 104, 107, 111, 112, 123, 156, 160.

All in all, there were differences between the reigns of Edward VI and Mary in the prosecution of sexual offenders by the London authorities but not a complete contrast, nor was there a complete break with practice in the reigns of Henry VIII and his predecessors. The zeal of Protestant leaders, both clerical and lay, as their cause triumphed with the accession of Edward VI, does seem to have given a particular fillip to the attack on sexual vice. Via printed tracts, sermons, word-of-mouth contacts and the repeated spectacle of public punishments, ideas and information must have been circulating with unprecedented velocity. This combination of circumstances explains the intensity of the great purge in the years around 1550. Yet such an escalation was possible because the legal, administrative and moral framework for such action already existed. It can only be conjectured how things would have developed if Mary had lived longer and given birth to an heir – in other words, how the pattern of sexual regulation would have developed in a Catholic context. In the event, Mary's death in November 1558 enabled the Protestants to resume the initiative in reform and reformation of religion and manners.

CHAPTER 10

Towards the New Jerusalem?
Reformation of Sexual Manners in Provincial Society, 1558–80

Conservative religious forces remained strong in the aftermath of Mary's death, and it was only with difficulty and with some concessions that Elizabeth's government achieved a Protestant settlement in the years 1559–63. No one could be confident that the queen would survive to maintain it, and there was even the possibility that she would alter her mind and renege on the Reformation, especially if she were to marry a Catholic prince. However, as time passed, the growing confidence of committed Protestants, particularly among the clergy, but including some lay people too, led them to expect further changes that would bring England closer to the best reformed churches on the continent. These great expectations included measures for reform of people's personal lives and moral outlook. The vigour and creativity of initiatives towards sexual reformation in the early and middle parts of Elizabeth's reign have hitherto received too little attention from historians. They should be recognized as an important dimension of the unfolding English Reformation.

But tendencies in the opposite direction were also important. Moral reform initiatives threw up some tricky jurisdictional issues. In an increasingly law-minded society, in which the boundaries between the spiritual and temporal jurisdictions were being marked out with greater clarity, these conspired to set limits on what could be achieved by the more zealous proponents of godly reformation. There were other obstacles too: the opposition of those who, for a variety of reasons, were not persuaded of the desirability of strict discipline; some people's irrepressible appetite for illicit sex whatever the hazard; and the fact that even the most powerful of currents of reform tended quickly to run into the sands of routine. In combination, these factors make for a complex story. The first section of this chapter explores some broader issues of jurisdiction, penal options and public policy. Subsequent sections focus, respectively, on the impact of the church courts in predominantly rural areas and on experiments in sexual regulation in provincial towns. The important developments that occurred in London are the subject of Chapter 11.

Sex and the Early Elizabethan Settlement

Early Elizabethan moral reformers undoubtedly saw some inspiring examples to follow, not least the new Protestant regime in Scotland.[1] In any case, there were within England strong pragmatic reasons to campaign for sharper measures against vice. Moral discipline was something that Marian churchmen and magistrates had called for too, so this was an issue on which people of widely differing doctrinal opinion could perhaps make common cause. However, there were more partisan concerns. In light of the intense anti-vice campaign waged in London in the late 1540s and early 1550s, it may seem strange that it was widely canvassed that the religious changes of Edward's reign had led to the collapse of moral discipline. But the reformers may have been victims of their own rhetoric – having exposed the prevalence of vice, they were now themselves blamed for it. The suggestion may also have drawn strength from such high-profile cases as the divorce and remarriage of the marquess of Northampton and perhaps also from the fragile state of the church courts resulting from Henry VIII's barrage of 'reforms'. In any event, it was a slur that the new establishment was anxious to rebut.

Thus the 'Considerations' delivered to one of Elizabeth's parliaments, probably early in the reign, included among other issues to be addressed as a matter of urgency 'the amendment of manners, the want whereof hath been imputed as a thing grown by the liberty of the Gospel'.[2] In the House of Lords in 1559, Abbot Feckenham used as one of his arguments against the alteration of religion that 'obedience is gone, humilitie and mekenes cleane abolished, vertuouse, chast and straight lyvyng abandoned'. On the other side, the earl of Bedford twitted Viscount Montague with the suggestion that when he had been in Rome with the bishop of Ely delivering Mary's submission to the Pope in 1554, the cardinals had offered to provide them with whores.[3] The matter became even more salient, and

---

[1] Michael F. Graham, *The Uses of Reform: 'Godly Discipline' and Popular Behaviour in Scotland and Beyond, 1560–1610* (Leiden, 1996).
[2] Dated 1559 in R. H. Tawney and Eileen Power (eds.), *Tudor Economic Documents*, 3 vols. (London, 1924), Vol. I, p. 325. This is consistent with much of the content, but a reference to the staple at Middelburg may suggest a later date: Ian W. Archer and F. Douglas Price (eds.), *English Historical Documents, 1558–1603* (London and New York, 2011), p. 58.
[3] T. E. Hartley (ed.), *Proceedings in the Parliaments of Elizabeth I*, Vol. I: *1558–1581* (Leicester, 1981), p. 31; Norman L. Jones, *Faith by Statute: Parliament and the Settlement of Religion, 1559* (London, 1982), p. 100.

a great deal more sensitive, as a result of Elizabeth's personal affairs. The intensity of Elizabeth's involvement with Robert Dudley led to speculation, and by 1562, it was widely rumoured that she was, as contemporaries understood the term, a whore. As a result, Elizabeth's own behaviour perforce became more circumspect, and these circumstances perhaps help to explain one of her few personal initiatives in the sphere of sexual regulation – the vigour with which she disciplined prominent members of her court who flouted the conventions of sexual decorum.[4] But another obvious way for the regime to regain its credibility was to commit itself to a programme of moral reform.

It was against this background that Alexander Nowell, dean of St Paul's and pillar of the establishment, renewed calls for 'sharper laws for adultery' in a sermon preached before the queen during the parliament of 1563.[5] That this was not mere rhetoric is suggested by comparison with the reform proposals prepared for consideration in convocation the same year. These were not, as was formerly thought, the work of radicals among the lower clergy, doomed to rejection by the bishops. On the contrary, they originated in the circle of Archbishop Parker and incorporated suggestions for revision, if not more substantial contributions, from the bishop of London, Edmund Grindal.[6] Among other concerns was 'the suppressing of the horrible licence and boldness now used in the variety of adulteries and fornications and incest', to remedy which it was suggested that 'some sharper laws be devised'. Another paper, developed from the first, proposed that 'adulterers and fornicators may be punished by strait imprisonment and open shame if the offender be vile and stubborn.' As an example of what they had in mind, the authors instanced 'carting by the civil magistrate' – the kind of shame punishment already well established in London and some other cities and (as will be seen) now rapidly spreading to other provincial towns.[7]

No legislation having resulted from these proposals, at the beginning of the parliament of 1571 – in the wake of the Northern Rising, the conspiracy to unite in matrimony Mary Queen of Scots and the duke of Norfolk, the

---

[4] Susan Doran, *Monarchy and Matrimony: The Courtships of Elizabeth I* (London and New York, 1996), pp. 41–2, 64–5; Paul E. J. Hammer, 'Sex and the Virgin Queen: Aristocratic Concupiscence and the Court of Elizabeth I', *Sixteenth Century Journal*, 31 (2000), 77–97; Johanna Rickman, *Love, Lust and License in Early Modern England: Illicit Sex and the Nobility* (Aldershot, 2008), chap. 1.

[5] Alexander Nowell, *A Catechism Written in Latin*, ed. George Elwes Corrie (Cambridge, 1853), p. 226.

[6] David J. Crankshaw, 'Preparations for the Canterbury Provincial Convocation of 1562–63: A Question of Attribution', in Susan Wabuda and Caroline Litzenberger (eds.), *Belief and Practice in Reformation England: A Tribute to Patrick Collinson from His Students* (Aldershot, 1998), pp. 60–93.

[7] Gerald Bray (ed.), *The Anglican Canons, 1529–1947* (Church of England Record Society 6, Woodbridge, 1998), pp. 725, 736.

papal bull of excommunication and the Ridolfi Plot, all of which raised the political and religious temperature – the forthright Bishop Edwin Sandys warned that the 'vile sin of adultery, in God's commonwealth punished with death, so overfloweth the banks of all chastity, that if by sharp laws it be not speedily cut off, God from heaven with fire will consume it'.[8] In the session that followed, a serious – though as it proved a futile and final – attempt was made to get parliamentary approval of the *Reformatio legum ecclesiasticarum*, with its draconian penalties against adulterers and other sexual offenders.[9] But it was not until 1576 that a bill 'touching adultery and incontinence' emerged from the House of Commons, only to be superseded by a Lords' bill 'for the punishment of avowtrie and incest', which got no further than a single reading.[10] A more limited measure that parliament did enact that year gave justices of the peace the power to examine the circumstances of the birth of bastard children likely to be chargeable to the parish in which they were born, to make orders for their support and, at their discretion, to punish the parents.[11] Yet, still pursuing the wider objective, the members of the lower house of convocation in 1580 'earnestly ... desired ... some more strait punishment to be assigned by ecclesiastical judges for adultery, whoredom and incest than now by ecclesiastical laws they can do, whether it be by imprisonment joined with open penance, or otherwise'.[12]

Reforming the Church Courts

By this time the obstacles to such aspirations were patent. They raised contentious issues about the relationship between the spiritual and temporal power, and given that the queen was opposed to further ecclesiastical reform, there was small chance that such difficulties would be addressed. The increasingly vociferous complaints of the 'hotter sort of protestants' who ardently desired further reformation served only to strengthen the

---

[8] *The Sermons of Edwin Sandys*, ed. John Ayre (Cambridge, 1841), p. 50; for the occasion, see Hartley (ed.), *Proceedings in the Parliaments ... 1558–1581*, p. 243.

[9] G. R. Elton, *The Parliament of England, 1559–1581* (Cambridge, 1986), pp. 207–8. The circumstances and the reasons for the failure of this attempt are very obscure: see Gerald Bray (ed.), *Tudor Church Reform: The Henrician Canons of 1535 and the* Reformatio Legum Ecclesiasticarum (Church of England Record Society 8, Woodbridge, 2000), pp. lxxvii–xcix.

[10] *Journals of the House of Lords*, Vol. I, p. 740; Elton, *Parliament of England*, pp. 51, 300; Keith Thomas, 'The Puritans and Adultery: The Act of 1650 Reconsidered', in Donald Pennington and Keith Thomas (eds.), *Puritans and Revolutionaries: Essays in Seventeenth-Century History Presented to Christopher Hill* (Oxford, 1978), p. 273.

[11] 18 Elizabeth I c. 3.   [12] Bray (ed.), *Anglican Canons*, p. 766.

obstacles; the queen was inclined to see even minor changes as the thin end of the wedge. There was, however, an alternative route to greater severity – to make greater use of powers inherent in existing practice in the ecclesiastical courts. It had always been at the judge's discretion to prescribe how many times public penance should be performed by an individual culprit; to make multiple penances the norm would automatically increase severity. Also well established was the practice of ordering penance to be performed in the marketplace of a local town (either instead of or as well as in church), thus recruiting secular space and the public humiliation associated with urban shame punishments to penitential purposes. Common in the fourteenth century, by the eve of the Reformation this practice had become rare without ever going out of use. But it had been revived by Bishop Hooper in the diocese of Gloucester in Edward VI's reign and was also used under Mary in some places.[13] As Dave Postles has shown, this practice was now seized on by those who advocated stricter discipline.[14]

Yet another possibility was the use of whipping as an element in ecclesiastical penance. As seen in earlier chapters, this was another practice that had been commonplace in the late middle ages but had become unusual by the early decades of the sixteenth century. It was never explicitly forbidden in the Elizabethan church, though it had possibly been rendered illegal by a 1552 act of parliament (designed to combat religious contention rather than to affect the nature of penance) that declared that anyone who struck another in church or churchyard was ipso facto excommunicate.[15] There was at least one attempt at vigorous revival in the 'peculiar' court of Southwell, which exercised jurisdiction over twenty-five parishes within the archdeaconry of Nottingham. In January 1567, John Eaton and Joan Warryner of Bleasby were ordered to appear in Southwell Minster the following Sunday

> bare headed, and naked frome the myddles upward with sheites about the nether partes of their bodies after the manner of penytentes and shall knele in queare there untill the preist goo to reade the homylye of adultrie: and then thaie shall stand bothe together before him, and here it redde and when the homylye is doone William Garlan[d] be redye with a birche rod, and shall gyve either of the parties three strypes appon theire bare shoulders: and then

[13] F. Douglas Price, 'Gloucester Diocese under Bishop Hooper, 1551–3', *Transactions of the Bristol and Gloucestershire Archaeological Society*, 60 (1939 for 1938), 90–4. For examples in Mary's reign, see WSA, D1/43/2, fo. 4r; D1/39/1/1, fos. 56r, 70v, 87v.

[14] Dave Postles, 'Penance and the Market Place: A Reformation Dialogue with the Medieval Church (c.1250–c.1600)', *Journal of Ecclesiastical History*, 54 (2003), 441–68.

[15] 5 and 6 Edward VI c. 4.

thaie shall goo upp and knele where thaie kneled before untill service be donne.

This penance, surely intended to be painful as well as humiliating, was actually carried out. It is not clear who was responsible. In principle, the entire chapter of the collegiate church sat as judges, but in practice, the most active individual was Robert Cressy, who also served as the official of the archdeacon of Nottingham. But while penances in these two jurisdictions were mostly fairly similar – as might be expected from this duplication of office – no use of corporal punishment is to be found in the Nottingham court minutes. Indeed, the whipping of the Bleasby couple was unique even at Southwell, though on several occasions in 1568 Robert Cressy did order women to be carted – an even more dubious penalty for a church court to employ.[16]

Setting aside the Southwell case, it seems that the use of corporal punishment by the ordinary church courts rapidly withered away in what was undoubtedly the uncongenial legal climate of Elizabethan England.[17] On the basis of the writ *Circumspecte agatis* (1286) and inferences drawn from a sequence of statutes, common lawyers became more and more convinced that the ordinary censures of the church should be limited to admonition, penance and excommunication, with the corollary that they could touch neither life, limb nor property. As Sir Edward Coke was to put it in Cawdrey's case in 1591:

> The ecclesiastical law and the temporal law have several proceedings, and to several ends; the one being temporal, to inflict punishment upon the body, lands, or goods; the other being spiritual, *pro salute animae*, the one to punish the outward man, the other to reform the inward.[18]

---

[16] NA, SC/8/1/1/1, fos. 49r, 53r, 56r and *passim*; cf. Nottingham University Manuscripts and Special Collections, AN/A 1, *passim*. John Lee, the registrar of both courts, was responsible for the detailed record made of the various penances, and it is possible that he played some part in devising them. A few examples of carting prescribed by kirk sessions, albeit at a somewhat later period, are given in Margo Todd, *The Culture of Protestantism in Early Modern Scotland* (New Haven and London, 2002), pp. 142–3.

[17] Marjorie Keniston McIntosh, *Controlling Misbehavior in England, 1370–1600* (Cambridge, 1998), p. 113–14, cites a case from Durham in 1580, but inspection of the source shows that in fact the church court judge wrote to the Durham city authorities requesting them to whip and cart the offending couple, so this was not a straightforward case of ecclesiastical penance: see James Raine (ed.), *The Injunctions and Other Ecclesiastical Proceedings of Richard Barnes, Bishop of Durham, from 1575 to 1587* (Surtees Society 22, Durham, 1850), p. 126. It is nonetheless possible that further isolated cases will come to light.

[18] Sir Edward Coke, *The reports ... faithfully rendered into English* (London, 1658), p. 343; cf. F. M. Powicke and C. R. Cheney (eds.), *Councils and Synods with Other Documents Relating to the English Church*, Vol. II: *A.D. 1205–1313* (Oxford, 1964), pp. 974–5.

The trend towards the severity of penances was undercut from another direction. Allowing sinners to 'commute' their penances, either in whole or in part, into money payments had been discountenanced but never forbidden by the medieval church. Indeed, as earlier chapters have shown, the practice had been employed quite freely in some areas. Zealous Protestants regarded it as an abuse and clamoured to have it forbidden; it is said that Bishop Hooper had never allowed it in any circumstances. Yet, in a society in which personal credit and reputation were already highly valued and, if anything, became more so in the later part of the sixteenth century, the possibility of avoiding the shame of public penance was an attractive one to people of substance and standing. Moreover, the Elizabethan church hierarchy, as had their predecessors, considered that it was not necessarily in the interests of good order to expose prominent individuals to public opprobrium. So they continued to sanction commutation, though efforts were made to insist that the power was used sparingly, that the money was used for 'pious uses' (especially poor relief) and that some element of personal contrition was retained.[19] But if in this respect the church was able to make sinners 'smart by the purse', the ability to imprison was firmly denied, as also was the imposition of fines in the ordinary sense. It was only by virtue of royal authority exercised through commissions for causes ecclesiastical – in other words, the High Commission, based on statute from 1559 – that churchmen could fine and imprison.[20]

The Elizabethan High Commission was primarily intended, and in practice mainly used, to combat Catholic recusancy and to harass other religious dissidents. Yet it could also act against notorious sex offenders and those who impugned the laws of marriage. In the diocese of York, where a good series of High Commission act books survives, the court handled more than 120 cases concerning the moral behaviour of the local gentry in the period 1562–1603. Such figures hardly add up to a major campaign, but neither are they negligible.[21] Unfortunately, the only surviving Elizabethan proceedings of the High Commission in Canterbury province relate to commissions in particular dioceses; none dates before 1574, and most are

---

[19] Bray (ed.), *Anglican Canons*, pp. 214, 222–3, 246–9.

[20] Roland G. Usher, *The Rise and Fall of the High Commission*, 2nd edn. with introduction by Philip Tyler (Oxford, 1968), pp. 22, 24, 45, 145–6. See also Christopher W. Brooks, *Law, Politics and Society in Early Modern England* (Cambridge, 2008), p. 101.

[21] Claire Cross, 'Sin and Society: The Northern High Commission and the Northern Gentry in the Reign of Elizabeth I', in Claire Cross, David Loades and J. J. Scarisbrick (eds.), *Law and Government under the Tudors: Essays Presented to Sir Geoffrey Elton* (Cambridge, 1988), pp. 195–209.

for the later part of the reign.[22] But they do show that the commissioners not only fined and imprisoned but also had recourse to precisely the kinds of aggravated penances, combining elements of spiritual discipline with various forms of corporal punishment and public shame, that convocation had called for in 1563. For example, in 1575, Thomas Grenewaie of Coulsbourne (Gloucestershire) – who had already been in prison awaiting trial – was ordered to be handed over to the sheriffs of Gloucester and

> putt in the pillorie with a paper on his hedd wrytten with these wordes, for horrible incest with his owne sister, in great lettres, and there to remayne from one till two of the clock this daie in the markett place, and then to be taken downe and whypped aboute the citie at a cartes tayle; and on Mondaie next being markett daie to be sett in the pillorie at Cirencester with the like paper on his hedd the space of two howres.[23]

To this extent the moral activists got what they wanted.

Severity of punishment was not the only issue that animated churchmen as they sought to revive the ecclesiastical courts and make them a more effective instrument of godly reformation. Nor was this the only line of policy that was pursued with regard to penance or otherwise. Probably the most permanent and far-reaching change, originating earlier but consolidated under Elizabeth, was increased emphasis on archidiaconal and episcopal visitations. As noted earlier, before the Reformation they were not as regular and systematic as they became later, nor were they necessarily the main means by which matters of sin were brought to the attention of the courts. The need to monitor compliance with liturgical and doctrinal changes in the 1530s, 1540s and 1550s made them more and more central, and in the reign of Elizabeth, visitations became the linchpin of ecclesiastical discipline. An associated development was the use of printed articles of inquiry, setting out in detail the matters on which information was required. Indeed, it has been aptly said that the survival of such articles, often substantial pamphlets of twenty pages or so, represents one of the most 'conspicuous signs' of the vigour of episcopal administration in the period.[24] To be sure, most of the specific articles related to matters of church property and furnishings, liturgy, religious observance and the

---

[22] R. H. Helmholz, *Roman Canon Law in Reformation England* (Cambridge, 1990), pp. 46–7.

[23] F. Douglas Price (ed.), *The Commission for Ecclesiastical Causes within the Dioceses of Bristol and Gloucester, 1574* (Bristol and Gloucestershire Archaeological Society, Records Section 10, Bristol, 1972), p. 98; see also Peter Clark, 'The Ecclesiastical Commission at Canterbury, 1572–1603', *Archaeologia Cantiana*, 89 (1974), 183–97, esp. 190.

[24] Helmholz, *Roman Canon Law*, pp. 105–7; see also R. B. Outhwaite, *The Rise and Fall of the English Ecclesiastical Courts, 1500–1860* (Cambridge, 2006), pp. 57–8.

like; sexual transgressions themselves warranted only brief entries. But this belied the importance attached to them by the courts and by local people alike.

Later sixteenth-century bishops were expected to visit their dioceses regularly, conducting a 'primary' visitation soon after appointment to their see and 'ordinary' visitations thereafter, usually at three-yearly intervals. Regular archidiaconal visitations were harder to enforce, and it is notable that the canons of 1571 merely reaffirmed the medieval obligation to visit once a year, as had the abortive 'articles for ecclesiastical government' of 1563. In practice, however, bi-annual visitations became standard, as envisaged by the *Reformatio legum*. The canons of 1571 also included regulations for the annual election of churchwardens and instructed that at bishops' and archdeacons' visitations they should make regular and faithful presentment of matters that required correction. The same canons envisaged that they should be aided in their task by a number of 'sidemen', or '*selecti viri*', assistants who often appear in the records as 'inquisitors' or 'questmen'.[25] Although these arrangements were already standard practice, in the Elizabethan context the effect was to place the prime responsibility for reporting offenders on lay representatives of the parishes. Indeed, churchwardens became liable to prosecution if they failed to exhibit 'bills of presentment' or if those bills omitted known offences – a notable increase in the pressures to which they were subject compared with pre-Reformation times.[26] It is true that throughout the late sixteenth century and into the seventeenth century, the courts continued to hear some cases on the basis of 'informations' from apparitors or other informants. In some jurisdictions, such as the diocese of Ely, prosecutions of this type remained quite numerous. In most areas, however, they became increasingly rare relative to visitation presentments – the reverse of the situation prevailing before the Reformation.[27]

The effects on the relationship between the courts and the parishes were double edged. Especially in the early stages of imposing the Elizabethan settlement, the church courts were at the cutting edge of Protestant advance, and the result was a great expansion of the range of disciplinary matters that they dealt with and an increase in the numbers of cases before the courts. Thus, in contrast to the situation prior to the Reformation, the registers of

---

[25] Bray (ed.), *Anglican Canons*, pp. 182–3, 190–6, 752–3; Bray (ed.), *Tudor Church Reform*, pp. 352–3.

[26] Helmholz, *Roman Canon Law*, pp. 106–7. Prosecutions of churchwardens for failure to report offenders were not unknown before the Reformation but were very rare.

[27] Martin Ingram, *Church Courts, Sex and Marriage in England, 1570–1640* (Cambridge, 1987), pp. 44, 231, 352.

the Elizabethan courts are stuffed with numerous cases concerning religious belief and observances – especially failure to attend church or to receive the communion. These depended upon the regular reports from the church-wardens, and in this sense, the revitalized visitation system represented the recruitment of local energies and knowledge on the ground to enforce a programme of religious change dictated from above. The initiative was all the more effective because in other spheres too – notably poor relief and anti-vagrancy measures – parliament and the central government were gradually placing increasing emphasis on parish administration.[28] However, reliance on the presentments or 'detections' of churchwardens and sidemen potentially gave parishioners greater power to inflect the pattern of reported offences, especially the sexual transgressions that still formed a staple of court business, to reflect local prejudices and concerns. More broadly, it meant that the disciplinary work of the courts was, more than ever, the outcome of a complex negotiation between ecclesiastical officials and lay people. Both had their own agendas to pursue.

A related issue was how far it was expected that disciplinary matters should be reported to the courts for determination or simply handled at the local level. A basic form of congregational discipline had been implied by rubrics in the Prayer Books of 1549, 1552 and 1559, which had prescribed that if anyone intending to receive the Holy Communion

> be an open and notorious evil liver, so that the congregacion by him is offended, or have done any wrong to hys neighbours by word or dede, the curate havyng knowledge therof, shal cal hym, and advertyse hym, in any wise not to presume to the Lordes table, until he have openly declared him self to have truely repented, and amended his former naughty lyfe, that the congregation may therby be satisfyed.[29]

A more comprehensive blueprint, based on the disciplinary model laid down in St Matthew's gospel,[30] was sketched in the royal injunctions of 1559 and further elaborated in the clutch of policy documents associated with the convocation of 1563. Though admittedly even the most formal of these reform proposals – known as the 'articles for ecclesiastical government' – did not receive official approval, they are important in revealing the lines along which a broad spectrum of churchmen were

---

[28] Marjorie Keniston McIntosh, *Poor Relief in England, 1350–1600* (Cambridge, 2012), chaps. 5 and 8.
[29] Brian Cummings (ed.), *The Book of Common Prayer: The Texts of 1549, 1559, and 1662* (Oxford, 2011), p. 124, cf. p. 19.
[30] Matthew XVIII.15–18.

thinking. In any event, the congregational foundation of discipline was stated authoritatively in the canons of 1571:

> If any offend their brethren, either by manifest adultery or whoredom or incest or drunkenness or much swearing or bawdry or usury or any other uncleanness or wickedness of life, let the churchwardens warn them brotherly and friendly, to amend. Which, except they do, they shall personally show them to the parson, vicar, or curate, that they be warned more sharply and vehemently of them, and if they continue so still, let them be driven from the holy communion till they be reformed.

This did not mean that the church courts had no role, however. On the contrary, the importance of reporting notorious and intractable cases was emphasized. The 1571 canons continued: 'And that all which live unchastely and loosely be punished by the severity of the laws according to their deserts. The same churchwardens shall present those adulterers, whoremongers, incestuous [persons,] drunkards, swearers, bawds and usurers to the bishop's and archdeacon's visitation.'[31] Plainly, the courts were expected to deal with such cases both vigorously and rigorously. But this was not simply a matter of harsher penalties, as discussed earlier; thoughtful churchmen wished to go deeper. Thus the 'articles for ecclesiastical government' put the emphasis less on punishment than on effectual penance in the sense of measures to induce contrition 'to the intent that the fruits of repentance may better appear'.

This approach arose out of the more basic need to replace traditional forms of penance, associated with Catholic understandings of the doctrine of atonement and now rejected, with a version consistent with Protestant doctrine. Early Elizabethan practice built on earlier initiatives in the reign of Edward VI, notably those of Bishop Hooper in Gloucester diocese. Whereas he had retained some traditional features, including the wearing of a sheet and, especially in more serious cases, going barefoot and bareheaded, he had abolished the carrying of candles and the repetition of paternosters, replacing them with demands for plain declarations of the nature of the offence committed and direct appeals to God and the congregation for forgiveness.[32] The 1563 'articles' proposed that there

---

[31] Paul L. Hughes and James F. Larkin (eds.), *Tudor Royal Proclamations*, 3 vols. (New Haven and London, 1964–9), Vol. II, pp. 123, 127, 128; Bray (ed.), *Anglican Canons*, pp. 193, 195, 756–7.

[32] Price, 'Gloucester Diocese under Bishop Hooper,' 87–97. For similar developments elsewhere, see Ralph Houlbrooke, *Church Courts and the People during the English Reformation, 1520–1570* (Oxford, 1979), p. 46; Ralph Houlbrooke, 'Church Courts and People in the Diocese of Norwich, 1519–1570', unpublished DPhil thesis, University of Oxford, 1970, p. 78.

should be appointed in every church a location called 'the place of penitents' where offenders convicted of notorious sins

> shall every Sunday and holy day in the time of common prayer, both
> morning and evening, and at service time, sit, stand or kneel from the
> beginning of divine service until the end, except the time of the holy
> communion, in which time they shall depart out of the church. And thus
> from time to time [in effect from week to week] the said . . . offenders shall
> continue and stand in the said place so long as shall be appointed for any
> such gross fault . . . and until they show true and unfeigned tokens and signs
> of repentance.[33]

While these proposals were fated not to receive official approval, court
proceedings of the 1560s and 1570s reveal that something of their spirit
was being put into effect locally. In some areas, dedicated judges made
great efforts to bring sinners to repentance – a process involving close
liaison with the local minister and the community, conceived of as 'the
congregation'. In London, the bishop's chancellor John Hammond
adopted an extremely thorough 'hands on' approach. A surviving act
book for 1574–5 vividly reveals him rigorously examining not only offenders themselves but also people they produced to clear their names;
devising elaborate penances, including the wearing of 'papers' to pro-
claim the offence; ordering culprits to confer with the local minister
about 'the state [they] now stode in before God and towchinge his
church' and requiring churchwardens to see 'earnest tokens of repentaunce and desyer to be reconsyled to the churche of God' before
offenders were allowed to do penance. Thus Oliver Wallett of St
Michael Bassishaw was reported to the court for suspicion of sexual
immorality with a widow called Agnes Haywarde. He denied the offence
but failed to clear himself. As a result, it was ordered that after first taking
advice from the parish minister about his spiritual condition, he should
the following Sunday 'stande in the churche porche . . . from before the
begynnynge of mornynge prayour unto the begynnynge of the
sermon . . . with a paper over his heade wherin shulde be written his
offences'. Only if he showed signs of penitence should he

> be suffred to come into the churche and sholde stande there in some open
> place all the sermon tyme where he may beste be sene of all the congregacion
> and at such tyme as shulde be assigned hym by . . . [the minister] he shulde
> openlye confesse his aforesaid offences with declaracion of his hartye

---

[33] Bray (ed.), *Anglican Canons*, p. 756.

repentaunce . . . and desyer all the people to forgyve hym and to praye with hym to God to be forgeven at his handes and to staye hym hereafter with his grace, that he fall not ageyne to the lyke synne, nor gyve lyke offens to his churche.[34]

Similar efforts were made in the archdeaconry of Leicester. To take one of the most striking examples, in 1568, William Tette, an inhabitant of the emerging godly stronghold of Ashby de la Zouch, was, on being convicted of fornication, ordered to

> come to the paryshe churche . . . one Sondaye nexte when they rynge to servis and beyng naked savyng one lynen clothe to hyde hys secrettes, coveryd with a heyre clothe and hys heade spryngkeled with asshes, shall stande in the porche tyll suche tyme as the ministre goythe to servys, then he to go into the churche and theyre to stande with a whyte rodde in hys hand by the minstre tyll suche tyme as the homelie off adulterie be redde, and then fawlyng flatt to the grownde shall saye thes wordes folowyng beyng in the dxix [*sic* for 119] salpme, my sowle clevethe to the duste O qwycken thow me accordyng to thy worde; rysyng then shall desyre all the congregacon to praye for hym and that hys penaunce maye be an example to all them for that hys offence.[35]

Such cases indicate that some of those responsible for running the ecclesiastical courts were animated by a powerful vision of moral reform. The close attention to the spiritual state of the penitent; the use of highly dramatic, emotionally charged forms of penance; the careful use of space to symbolize first the separation of the sinner from the congregation and then his or her reconciliation and reintegration; the orchestration of congregational responses; more generally, the understanding that the ritual of penance should be part of a wider process of spiritual and moral education, both for the individual penitent and for the whole congregation – all these features are reminiscent of the practice of 'performing repentance' as it was developing in the Scottish kirk sessions at roughly the same time.[36]

---

[34] LMA, DL/C/615, pp. 25–6, 29. In the event, the penance was mitigated because Wallett agreed to marry the woman. The background was his reluctance to accept responsibility for her pregnancy despite considerable pressure exerted by neighbours: see LMA, DL/C/212, pp. 69–73.

[35] ROLLR, 1 D41/11/3, fo. 148r.

[36] Todd, *Culture of Protestantism*, chap. 3. Comparison with Scotland raises complex questions that cannot be pursued here. Among other complications is the fact that kirk sessions were established first in urban centres; it is doubtful whether they had much of a presence in the Scottish countryside before the 1580s. A useful introduction to the issues is provided by Felicity Heal, *Reformation in Britain and Ireland* (Oxford, 2003), pp. 457–63.

322 Towards the New Jerusalem?

Case Studies: The Archdeaconries of Leicester and Chichester

So how did the courts fare on a practical, day-to-day basis? The records of what the church courts of provincial England were doing to punish sexual transgressions some ten or fifteen years into the reign of Elizabeth and the nature of those offences survive in greater abundance than from earlier periods. Moreover, the sources are by this time becoming more detailed, characteristically making greater use of the vernacular. At this point it should be noted, except in some cities and boroughs, these courts bore almost the entire burden in this area of jurisdiction. As seen in Chapter 3, even before the Reformation, manor courts were not much concerned with sexual regulation, and by this period, such involvement had become rare. However, the act of 1576 giving some authority in bastardy cases to justices of the peace had not yet been passed. Parish constables sometimes took a part in helping churchwardens to bring sexual offenders to book, while justices of the peace may have lent a hand on occasion, but this was the limit of secular involvement in rural areas.

Historians' views of the church courts' effectiveness have been much influenced by F. Douglas Price's studies of Gloucester diocese. In the reign of Edward VI, the uncompromisingly protestant Bishop Hooper had turned the consistory court into a model of discipline. Under his Elizabethan successor, Richard Cheyney, it plummeted into inefficiency, slackness and corruption. Much of the blame, it appears, lay with his notorious chancellor, Thomas Powell, who was forced to resign in 1579. Yet Cheyney himself was not a whole-hearted supporter of the new religious regime, and undoubtedly his negligence and half-heartedness contributed to the problems.[37] If this was an extreme case, Gloucester was not necessarily the only diocese in which lack of effective leadership was an obstacle to godly discipline. It has been assumed that elsewhere conservative survivors from the Marian years, serving as diocesan chancellors or archidiaconal officials, had little incentive to make the system work. The same was supposedly true of registrars, who

[37] Price, 'Gloucester Diocese under Bishop Hooper', esp. pp. 87–97; Price (ed.), *Commission for Ecclesiastical Causes*, pp. 2–5; see also F. Douglas Price, 'The Commission for Ecclesiastical Causes for the Dioceses of Bristol and Gloucester, 1574', *Transactions of the Bristol and Gloucestershire Archaeological Society*, 59 (1937), 61–184; F. Douglas Price, 'The Abuses of Excommunication and the Decline of Ecclesiastical Discipline under Queen Elizabeth', *English Historical Review*, 57 (1942), 106–15.

often held life patents and so enjoyed a particularly well-entrenched position.[38]

That laxness and inefficiency were by no means universal may be illustrated from the records of the archdeaconry of Leicester for the year 1570 and of the archdeaconry of Chichester for 1574. The latter is a particularly telling case. As has been seen already, there were many signs that from early in Elizabeth's reign 'godly' Protestantism was developing strongly in Leicestershire. Sussex, however, has been seen as an area where religious conservatism was strong, and the early Elizabethan bishops of Chichester, William Barlow (1560–70) and Richard Curteys (1570–82), faced an uphill struggle.[39] In both jurisdictions, it should be recognized that matters concerning sex and marriage were by now only a segment of the courts' activities, even setting aside their party-and-party jurisdiction. The hundreds of detections for non-sexual matters reveal a church that was in many respects still fragile after the vicissitudes of the last two generations but working purposefully to eliminate the vestiges of Catholic worship, to quieten religious tensions, to provide sufficient sermons to preach the Protestant message, to nurture an adequate Protestant ministry and, among lay people, to inculcate a basic knowledge of doctrine and enforce a reasonable level of church attendance and at least annual reception of the communion. In the sphere of personal morality, the work of the courts was strongly skewed. There were only a few reports of drunkenness, cursing, witchcraft and quarrelling – prosecutions for scolding being somewhat more numerous in Leicestershire than in west Sussex, for whatever reason. As was the case before the Reformation, sexual transgressions heavily predominated among the moral failings dealt with by the courts.[40]

To see these sexual transgressions in perspective, it is necessary to review the cluster of ideas and practices centring on marriage and reputation. If these are again viewed (as they were in Chapter 2) mainly through the lens of slander cases and disputed marriage contracts, many continuities with the pre-Reformation situation are immediately evident. Yet it is plain that by the 1560s and 1570s, some changes and developments were also

---

[38] Houlbrooke, *Church Courts*, pp. 24–7; Ralph Houlbrooke, 'The Protestant Episcopate, 1547–1603: The Pastoral Contribution', in Felicity Heal and Rosemary O'Day (eds.), *Church and Society in England: Henry VIII to James I* (London and Basingstoke, 1977), pp. 93–4.

[39] Roger B. Manning, *Religion and Society in Elizabethan Sussex: A Study of the Enforcement of the Religious Settlement, 1558–1603* (Leicester, 1969). It should be noted that at Chichester, unlike most dioceses, the jurisdiction of the archdeacons had become subsumed in that of the bishop, albeit the pattern of at least twice-yearly visitations was maintained.

[40] The comparison is complicated by the fact that jurisdiction over most of these matters was shared with the secular courts.

under way. By this time, defamation suits in the church courts overwhelmingly centred on sexual transgressions, imputations of theft or other secular offences no longer being admissible.[41] Both in west Sussex and in Leicestershire, suits occurred regularly in the 1560s and 1570s but not in particularly large numbers; apparently, they were brought with some circumspection. That said, many were tit-for-tat accusations springing from quarrels, occasionally reflecting long-standing and deep-seated tensions but more often arising spontaneously from the irritations of neighbourhood life in villages and small towns. In these, women were prominent, especially as plaintiffs, and more or less elaborate variants on the epithet 'whore' were the most common insults. Since that word commonly served as a simple term of abuse, its sexual content was often more apparent than real. But in many defamation cases sexual reputation was indeed centrally at issue and reflected a society in which people's personal behaviour was subject to intense scrutiny and an accusation of sexual transgression could be both personally wounding and socially damaging, even if the individual escaped formal prosecution. Undoubtedly, female reputation was most at risk; accusations of having had a child before marriage or of being an adulteress were easy to make and hard to refute. But men's sexual reputation was clearly vulnerable too, particularly if they were married householders or persons in a position of responsibility. The apparently generalized charge of being a 'whoremonger' or 'whoremaster' clearly aroused bitter resentment. Slanders of adultery or of fathering a bastard child were even more of a threat; around 1570, a Leicestershire man was said to have told his wife that if a child was 'fathered on hym he would suerly make away hymself'.[42] As earlier, husbands were also prone to be disparaged, indeed exposed as less than a man, by their wives' infidelities. Hence the term 'cuckold' continued to pack a powerful punch.

In the making of marriage, it was still true that a mere declaration between a man and a woman in words of the present tense could create a binding union. Such 'spousals' usually involved also the clasping and unclasping of hands and were often accompanied by the exchange of gifts or 'tokens'. An act of parliament of 1540 provided that henceforth a solemnized and consummated marriage should supersede an unsolemnized and unconsummated contract. But this measure, clearly

---

[41] R. H. Helmholz (ed.), *Select Cases on Defamation to 1600* (Selden Society 101, London, 1985), pp. xliii–xlvii. Slanders of witchcraft or drunkenness occasionally featured, while some courts still entertained generalized words of abuse (such as 'knave') on the principle that they were 'words of reproach' that 'broke the rule of charity'.

[42] ROLLR, 1 D 41/4/65.

designed to meet the current matrimonial needs of Henry VIII, was repealed in 1549, and the traditional position restored.[43] Whereas by the early seventeenth century spousals suits were to become very rare and extremely difficult to prosecute successfully, in the 1560s and 1570s they were still a fairly regular, though by no means very numerous, item of ecclesiastical court business – upwards or downwards of five a year in Leicestershire and west Sussex.

By this period plaintiffs in spousals suits were usually male and were pursuing not merely a woman but also the property that she could be expected to bring to the marriage. When women sued, it was usually because they needed to vindicate their reputation, especially if they were pregnant.[44] The underlying circumstances were very various, reflecting not only the perennial tensions between individual autonomy and family pressures but also the capricious and sometimes duplicitous behaviour of individuals. Whatever the circumstances, judges at this time had no hesitation in ordering a couple to solemnize marriage if the spousals were in due form and adequately witnessed or if the recalcitrant party confessed on examination. As was emphasized in earlier chapters, even before the Reformation, a spousals ceremony – however elaborate and witnessed by members of the family and others – was not generally regarded as completing the marriage process. The key event was the wedding in church, and it was only after this that the couple were free to set up house together and in that sense publicly recognized as husband and wife. This was even more so in the early reign of Elizabeth; the fact that in the interim the church had ceased to recognize marriage as one of the sacraments made no difference. Indeed, in the new doctrinal situation it was felt to be even more vital, in the interests of social order, to insist on the due performance of an ecclesiastical ceremony to set the seal on a marriage. As early as 1538 the injunctions of Thomas Cromwell had required parishes to maintain a register of marriages – there was no question of publicly recording *contracts* – along with baptisms and burials. Compliance had been patchy at first but became general in Elizabeth's reign. Both the first and second Edwardian prayer books had included an order for 'the solemnization of matrimony'; the 1552 version was repeated in 1559.[45]

---

[43] 32 Henry VIII c. 38; 2 and 3 Edward VI c. 23.
[44] I intend to discuss these issues more fully on another occasion. Meanwhile, see also Diana O'Hara, *Courtship and Constraint: Rethinking the Making of Marriage in Tudor England* (Manchester, 2000), p. 109 and *passim*.
[45] Cummings (ed.), *Book of Common Prayer*, pp. 64–71, 157–64; Richard Adair, *Courtship, Illegitimacy and Marriage in Early Modern England* (Manchester, 1996), p. 181.

The importance attached to weddings in due form emerges particularly clearly in west Sussex, where the issue of whether the couple had signalled their intention to marry by having the banns called in church, or otherwise making arrangements for solemnization, was prominent in many of the spousals suits of the 1560s and 1570s. The implication is that a marriage contract, however binding, was conventionally regarded merely as a step towards the ultimate goal of a church wedding – a principle nicely captured in one female defendant's assertion in 1574 that 'ther was never any talke betwene them of any solempnizacion of matrymony for they never went so farr.'[46] The broader context was one in which the 'commendation' of the married state – a theme already well established before the Reformation – was powerfully preached not only in works intended for private reading, such as Bullinger's *Christen state of matrimony* and its successors, but also in the official homily 'Of the state of matrimonie', designed to be read openly in parish churches throughout the land.[47] At the same time, such works roundly condemned adultery and 'whoredom', the reissued homily of 1547 still lamenting that 'thys vice is growen into suche an height that in a maner emong many it is compted no sin at al, but rather a pastyme, a dalliaunce, and but a touche of youthe, not rebuked but winked at, not punyshed but laughed at.'[48]

Within this context, what was the pattern of prosecutions for sexual offences? In both west Sussex and Leicestershire, the exact profile of cases had altered since earlier times, as also had the language in which charges were expressed. Most noticeable is a shift in balance from the pre-Reformation focus on cases conceived in terms of 'adultery' – though these had by no means disappeared – to those centred on cases of sex between unmarried people, especially when they involved illicit pregnancy and bastardy. As will be seen, by the end of the century, this shift was to be even more in evidence. There are two obvious explanations, by no means mutually exclusive. The first is that the more vigorous valorization of matrimony and insistence on the wedding ceremony as signalling entry into the married state had affected attitudes, perhaps making adultery less common – or at least less blatant – and certainly increasing sensitivity to sexual activity *before* marriage.

---

[46] WSRO, Ep.I/11/1, fo. 40v.
[47] *The second tome of homelyes* [STC 13663.7] (London, 1563), fos. 255v–266r. (This is one among a number of issues in that year.) In 1575, a new edition of Coverdale's translation of Bullinger's text was published. See also Chapter 9.
[48] Ronald B. Bond (ed.), Certain Sermons or Homilies *(1547) and* A Homily against Disobedience and Wilful Rebellion *(1570): A Critical Edition* (Toronto, 1987), p. 174.

The second is that by this time, the population was already on a steep upward curve in both Leicestershire and Sussex. Again, the commendation of marriage may have played a part, in combination with a reduction in mortality. Certainly courtship was active, and hence illegitimacy, an inevitable side-product, was an increasingly visible social phenomenon and causing anxiety. 'Why ... shulde we kepe other mens basterdes?' demanded one of the collectors for the poor in Graffham around 1570.[49]

Further differences emerge when the evidence is examined in more detail. In west Sussex (Table 10.1) there were markedly fewer sexual and sex-related cases than there had been in the same archdeaconry half a century earlier in 1520–1, despite the increase in population.[50] This is yet another reminder that sexual regulation was not necessarily more intense (at least in terms of numbers) after the Reformation than it had been before; though the exact significance of the reduced caseload is hard to assess given that patterns of behaviour were changing as well as the profile of prosecutions. The total of sixty-seven cases[51] included isolated instances of bigamy, marital separation and breach of the regulations concerning banns, two cases of aiding and abetting and a clutch of reports of dubious marriage contracts or delayed solemnizations. But in the great majority (fifty-six) the defendants were accused or strongly suspected of sexual transgressions.[52] Only ten of these cases are clearly identifiable in the record as instances of adultery, in the sense that one or both partners was married; usually it was the female's marital status that was made apparent. Moreover, the term 'adultery', or the cognate 'advowtry', was used very sparingly, whether in English by churchwardens or in Latin by the court officials.[53] It was not that adultery was condoned; quite the contrary to judge by such presentments as that of a South Stoke man, said to 'use moche the companye of one

---

[49] WSRO, Ep.I/11/1, fo. 15v; Adair, *Courtship, Illegitimacy and Marriage*.

[50] Unfortunately, there is no satisfactory basis for a population estimate, since the 1563 ecclesiastical return does not survive for this area.

[51] Most 'cases' included both a man and a woman. A few were presented, or at least entered in the act book, more than once; these duplicates have not been separately counted, unless a second liaison was at issue or the circumstances reported were substantially different. One or two cases had already been reported the previous year.

[52] This includes one case of defamation so circumstantial as to bring the slandered individuals into real question. A Broadwater man was said to have 'slandered one John Vevians wyf and saithe that one Henry Bold did co[mmit] with her advowtry': WSRO, Ep.I/23/4, fo. 19v.

[53] E.g. WSRO, Ep.I/17/3, fos. 20v (Alice Brownrigge), 24r (John White Junior). The word 'adultery' was used a little more freely by the churchwardens of Horsham in 1575: *ibid.*, fo. 28r–v.

Table 10.1 *Disciplinary Prosecutions in the Archdeaconry of Chichester, 1574: Sex and Marriage Cases*

Adultery	10
Fornication (including seven cases involving illicit pregnancy)	10
Other illicitly pregnant/child out of wedlock	24
Incontinence, etc.	5
Suspicious living	7
Privy contract/delaying solemnization	5
Asking banns twice on one Sunday (clergyman)	1
Bawdry/aiding and abetting	2
Filthy talker, etc.	1
Bigamy	1
Unlawful separation	1
Total	67

Note: This table collates information from both the relevant detection book (WSRO, Ep.I/17/3) and the corresponding register of presentments (WSRO, Ep.I/23/4).

Armestronges wyf in our towne which we do not well lyke of'.[54] But it would seem that cases were few or that clear evidence was hard to obtain, and while sometimes efforts were made to settle cases locally, church-wardens were reluctant to poke about too much for fear of causing trouble.[55] Two cases were brought to court as the result of boasting on the part of the man, and in one of them it is plain that action was taken not merely to bring him to book but also to clear the names of the women he had slandered.[56]

The word 'fornication' was employed more readily by churchwardens, while the Latin version and its derivatives were much used by court officials. The generic words 'incontinence' and 'carnal copulation' also featured in some cases. But whatever terminology was employed, the nub of many cases was that an unmarried woman or (in several cases) a widow was illicitly pregnant or had actually given birth to a bastard child. In 1574, more than 60 per cent of cases were of this type. Partly this prominence of

[54] *Ibid.*, fo. 8r (this was actually a case from 1573).   [55] E.g. *ibid.*, fo. 25v.
[56] *Ibid.*, fo. 24v, cf. fo. 21r (Edward Osborne).

illegitimacy cases simply reflected the fact that a visible pregnancy was proof positive that a sexual transgression had occurred. But it is clear also that already during this period it was considered of the utmost importance to establish paternity, to ensure that the child was properly maintained and, perhaps more importantly in the eyes of local people, to ensure that the charge did not fall on the parish.

The record gives some insights into local procedures. Supposing that the identity of the father was not self-evident, various means were used to elicit his name. Commonly, an unmarried mother was interrogated 'in the extremity of travail' by the midwife and other women, who exhorted her in the name of God to speak the truth, threatened her with divine punishment if she lied and even withheld their help if she proved reluctant to provide the father's name.[57] It was also common to 'examine' the woman and the suspected father before unofficial tribunals of local notables.[58] Tracking the history of courtships and marriage negotiations was another common-sense way of establishing paternity. But it was recognized that by no means all illicit pregnancies arose from bona fide courtships. As was the case before the Reformation, when maidservants were in trouble, suspicion often fell on the master of the household or perhaps his son or other relative.[59] In view of the intensity of local investigations and the fact that churchwardens presumably had reasonable knowledge of what went on in their mostly small, face-to-face communities, it is striking that in as many as a fifth of the illicit pregnancy cases in 1574, the father was said to be unknown or was simply not named in the presentment. Churchwardens may have preferred to refer the matter to higher authority rather than risk naming a father themselves, or it may simply be that the surveillance of unmarried women was often not very close. Lack of vigilance would explain the otherwise surprising fact that there were so few cases of aiding and abetting – in the form of 'harbouring' or giving shelter to unmarried women until they were delivered or of moving them from place to place to help them escape punishment.

In contrast to these cases of illicit pregnancy were a number of accusations of suspicious circumstances rather than clear-cut sexual transgressions.[60] They had strong affinities with the presentments concerning unsolemnized

[57] E.g. *ibid.*, fo. 20v. For examples from other areas, see Houlbrooke, *Church Courts*, p. 77; Ingram, *Church Courts, Sex and Marriage*, p. 263; Laura Gowing, *Common Bodies: Women, Touch and Power in Seventeenth-Century England* (New Haven and London, 2003), pp. 159–64.
[58] E.g. WSRO, Ep.I/17/3, fo. 18r–v.
[59] *Ibid.*, fos. 13v, 15r. This case first came up in 1573 but was reported again in 1574: *ibid.*, fos. 19r, 23r.
[60] E.g. *ibid.*, fos. 16v, 24v.

marriage contracts, mentioned earlier, as also with spousals litigation.[61] What was usually at issue was that the couple were 'betrothed' or 'contracted' in marriage, or the banns had been asked between them, yet no wedding had ensued. In some instances they were said to 'dwell in one house together' or to have 'kept house as man and wyf', which obviously aroused overwhelming suspicions that sexual relations had begun[62]; in others, they were said to 'kepe company together', which did not necessarily imply cohabitation.[63] There are signs that churchwardens chivvied couples in this position to get them to wed, and in some cases the couple had indeed got properly married by the time the case came to court.[64] Thus, while there is no indication that either local people or court officials were prepared to accept an unsolemnized union as a 'marriage', the objective of resorting to the courts seems rather to have been to induce couples to regularize their unions than to subject them to public punishment for premarital sex.

Leicester archdeaconry was a larger and more populous jurisdiction. The ecclesiastical returns of 1563 listed nearly 9,000 'families'; depending on assumptions about household size, this suggests a total population upwards or downwards of 50,000.[65] Predictably, therefore, the area yielded a higher number and slightly greater range of prosecutions (Table 10.2) than the archdeaconry of Chichester. Moreover, the authorities in this incipiently puritan area were patently more zealous in pursuing certain offences, including prenuptial fornication. A few cases are illuminated by the vernacular statements of principals or witnesses, surviving as 'examinations' interleaved in the act book. But the original presentments have not survived, and we are mostly dependent for our knowledge of the charges on the terse Latin summaries made by the court officials. This difference in record keeping complicates comparisons with the Chichester material; nonetheless, many similarities as well as some differences are discernible.

A feature of the proceedings in 1570 was an inquiry into women living in the houses of the clergy. In itself this is reminiscent of pre-Reformation investigations, but quite different was the fact – as also indeed was the case in the Sussex record – that clear-cut cases of clerical immorality were now

---

[61] One case was dealt with, albeit very summarily, as a spousals suit: WSRO, Ep.I/23/2, fo. 27v.
[62] WSRO, Ep.I/17/3, fo. 24v; Ep.I/23/4, 21r.
[63] E.g. WSRO, Ep.I/17/3, fos. 13v, 19r, 23r; Ep.I/23/4, fo. 1r.
[64] WSRO, Ep.I/17/3, fo. 23r; cf. *ibid.*, fo. 19r, where a couple were said to have been keeping company together 'to our reproves'.
[65] Alan Dyer and D. M. Palliser (eds.), *The Diocesan Population Returns for 1563 and 1603* (British Academy Records of Social and Economic History, New Series 31, Oxford, 2005), pp. xli–l, 214–26.

Table 10.2 *Disciplinary Prosecutions in the Archdeaconry of Leicester, 1570: Sex and Marriage Cases*

Women in houses of the clergy	14
Adultery	14
Fornication	42
Illicitly pregnant/child out of wedlock	16
Incontinence, etc.	5
Suspicious living	11
Bawdry/aiding and abetting	22
Forbidding banns	2
Clandestine marriage	1
Bigamy	2
Unlawful separation	7
Total	136

a rarity. In most of the fourteen reported cases – sometimes coupled with other charges, such as frequenting alehouses and failing to provide sermons or homilies – there was no specific accusation of immorality. The women were generally servants or in a few cases relatives of the clergyman, but in any case their presence was deemed to be suspicious or unseemly, and they were ordered out.[66] Only two cases gave real cause for concern. The curate of Freeby was lodging in the same house as a woman accused of fornication with another man. The curate of Wigston – also charged with possession of 'superstitious' books – was even more reprehensible in lodging a woman, apparently a maidservant, in the same chamber where he slept, perhaps because the only other available sleeping space was occupied by his mother. This situation persisted for four years till the 'privy watch' discovered it, and the woman was removed. In both these cases the minister denied illicit sexual relations.[67]

Another case involving a clergyman was the prosecution of the vicar of Melton Mowbray for having taken another wife, even though the woman from whom he was separated in Mary's reign was still alive. Strains arising

---

[66] ROLLR, 1 D 41/13/6, fos. 22r (*bis*) (mother and two maidservants), 23r (sister-in-law).

[67] *Ibid.*, fos. 25r, 44v, 56r, 59r. For a rather similar case, represented by examinations but not to be found in the formal record, see fos. 22a [paper slip between leaves], 58r.

from the transition to a married clergy were otherwise not in evidence.[68] Among the prosecutions against the laity rather than the clergy, there was one other bigamy case in 1570 – a Leicester man with a wife in London had married again – and a few miscellaneous cases concerning marriage without banns and the forbidding of banns. It would seem that bigamy and issues to do with the actual celebration of marriage were not of major concern either to court officials or locally.[69] However, seven married couples were brought in question for unlawful separation; in five cases it was the men who were the actual subject of prosecution, and two of them countered the charges by accusing their wives of adultery. In one of these cases, the matter was patched up on condition that the wife asked her husband's pardon in open church on Sunday; the other turned into an instance suit. This relatively large total of separation cases contrasts with both pre-Reformation Leicestershire and contemporary west Sussex and suggests a climate of greater vigilance, paralleling the pattern of prosecutions for illicit sex.[70] While much of the zeal probably came from officials, a degree of popular support is suggested by the fact that one of the separation cases arose because a man publicly announced the facts in court.[71]

There were eighty-eight cases of actual or suspected sexual transgression,[72] together with twenty-two prosecutions for aiding and abetting. The latter total, in particular, is far more striking than the corresponding number for Chichester archdeaconry and is accounted for mainly by the vigilance of the court. Householders named in presentments as having pregnant women in their houses – whether their maidservants or others – were routinely cited to explain the circumstances. Many were able to show that what had happened was no fault of theirs. A few were charged with culpable negligence – a father for allowing his son to have sex under his roof and a master for allowing two servants of opposite sex to share a chamber[73] – while occasionally individuals were brought in question for more active efforts to promote or cloak sexual transgression.[74] Cases of 'harbouring' pregnant women – that is, taking them in, sometimes for money, providing lodgings till they gave birth and usually allowing them to

---

[68] *Ibid.*, fo. 42v.   [69] *Ibid.*, fos. 2v, 11r, 41v, 47v.

[70] *Ibid.*, fos. 37v, 53v, cf. 44r (dismissed because the couple – the man was also accused of being a drunkard – were aged and unable to cohabit). For other separation and marital disturbance cases, see *ibid.*, fos. 10r, 41r, 53v.

[71] *Ibid.*, fo. 41v; cf. Chapter 3.

[72] Discounting a few re-entries of essentially the same case and the instances of clerical immorality discussed earlier.

[73] ROLLR, 1 D 41/13/6, fos. 47r, 51v, 52r.   [74] E.g. *ibid.*, fos. 8v, 9r, 35v, 45r

depart without punishment – were apparently rare at this early stage of Elizabeth's reign. For reasons that will be spelt out in Chapter 12, they were to become more prevalent later.

Of the straightforward cases of sexual transgression in 1570, about one in six was described in terms of 'adultery' – usually the Latin word and its derivatives in this record. The menfolk concerned were usually house-holders, in all probability mostly married, some in trouble for relationships with their maidservants.[75] In one case a man had actually left his wife to consort with another woman; in another an adulterer's wife featured because venereal disease was at issue, and there was controversy about who had infected whom.[76] In some instances the words 'fornication' and 'adultery' were used indiscriminately, and in several 'adultery' cases it is clear that at least by the time the matter was dealt with in court the couple were free to marry. In one such case the liaison had apparently continued for fifteen years, and it may be that it was only now that marriage had become possible.[77]

Nearly half the cases were described in terms of 'fornication'. The indications are that many of the accused were young, some of them servants (including some cases where fellow-servants were accused together). Their freedom was constrained in many ways but not so nar-rowly as to preclude the possibility of occasional acts of surreptitious sex. Female servants may have been particularly vulnerable, but daughters kept at home were not immune. There are incidental glimpses of when and where: 'the facte was done in her masters howsse, he beyng at Leicestre at the cowrte abowte Eyster laste paste; and the seconde tyme was done in a closse when she wentt a mylkyng; and the thyrde tyme was in her masters howsse he beyng from home.'[78] Commonly, the number of times the couple had had sex could be counted on the fingers of one hand, though some did admit to more frequent, even regular intercourse.

Cases in which couples were explicitly accused of being contracted or betrothed but not yet married were fewer in Leicestershire than in west Sussex. However, in a large proportion of 'fornication' cases it is clear that marriage was (or had been) in the offing. Seven were actually cases of ante-nuptial fornication, in the sense that the couple were already married by the time they came to court. This is another type of case that was to become much more common later; the fact that an appreciable number of prosecu-tions was in evidence at this stage suggests an unusually rigorous moral

[75] E.g. *ibid.*, fos. 3r, 55r, cf. fos. 19r, 22v, 59v.   [76] *Ibid.*, fos. 10r, 11v, 38r.
[77] *Ibid.*, fo. 25v, cf. 1 D 41/11/3, fo. 159r.   [78] ROLLR, 1 D 41/13/6, fos. 36v, 48(a)r, cf. fo. 57r.

climate in this particular county. In nearly as many cases, one or both of the parties alleged a contract of marriage or expressed the intention of marrying, though the men concerned sometimes rebutted these claims. A further eight couples went through a form of contract in open court before the judge and were thereupon ordered to solemnize marriage as soon as possible. In several other cases, more or less serious marriage negotiations were in the background, to the extent that the court proceedings may be seen as the continuation of courtship by other means. Indeed, there was some overlap with formal marriage contract litigation. In the best documented of these cases, the woman claimed that the man had promised her marriage if he could obtain a farm from his landlady, that she had only consented to sex after that promise and that the man had taken responsibility for the child that resulted by putting it to nurse. His story was that they had had sex before the promise and not since, though he admitted that the child was his, that the promise was conditional on his gaining the farm and that she had acknowledged before six of his neighbours that he never made her an absolute promise. Despite these denials – which were shaped by the technicalities of the law of spousals and were evidently designed to forestall the possibility that the judge would declare them man and wife on the spot – the man reiterated that if he could get the farm, he would marry her. Reportedly his mistress put the matter the other way round: 'excepte he wolde marie her he shulde never have hys ferme'.[79]

A further sixteen cases were defined not by the use of the term 'fornication' but simply by the fact that the women were described as being illicitly pregnant or as having given birth to a child out of wedlock. One was really a case of antenuptial fornication and hence barely distinguishable from those already discussed.[80] On the whole, however, the circumstances of this clutch of cases seem to have been more remote from the normal processes of courtship and marriage. In some cases, the father's name was either unknown or not stated; in others, the men clearly had no intention of marrying the women concerned, though they may have used a hint or promise of marriage as a means of seduction. Women left isolated in this way were in a particularly vulnerable position, and some took flight. The detailed examination of Judith Grene of Hinckley illustrates how they might be pushed from pillar to post; how they fared depended partly on what resources they could call upon and partly on the actions of men and women who wielded some power locally. Grene confessed that her master, Richard Collens of 'Wyken', an unidentified place near Burbage in

[79] Ibid., fos. 14r, 25v, 48r, 48(a)r; 1 D 41/11/3, fos. 160v–161r.   [80] ROLLR, 1 D 41/13/6, fo. 4r.

south-west Leicestershire, had had sex with her six times between Michaelmas (29 September) and Martlemas (11 November), whereupon she left his service and went to Hinckley, where she stayed with an uncle till New Year. She then moved to the neighbouring village of Sketchley, where she stayed with another uncle till Easter. By this time her pregnancy must have been obvious, and the vicar of Hinckley's wife and her mother 'searched' her and induced her to name the father. The women informed Collens, who thereupon sent a man to 'carry' her to Stanton in the Stones (Derbyshire) to a cousin of the bailiff of Hinckley, with whom she remained for a month, before being conducted home again at her request. All this movement generated further suspicions. While it was reported that 'the rumour goythe so in the cowntre' that Collens was the father, it would seem that the bailiff, Thomas Dylkes, was also in question.[81]

The circumstances of most of the remaining cases are obscure, but two stand out for shedding light on the possibilities of illicit sex in ill-governed households. Robert Smythe of Little Dalby plainly viewed his master's behaviour with a 'wench' with suspicion and resentment; whether his motive was moral disapproval or sexual jealousy is an open question. He reported that after all three had fetched a load of hay, 'he wentt with hys carte into the strete and lokyd over hys fore horsse and he sawe hys master kyssyng of the sayde Alice and then he wentt to the parlore dore and theyre he sawe hys master and the sayde Alice one the bedde nexte the barne walle to yll occupied to be spoken off.' The maid herself described how her master 'strogelyd with her', 'used her very unhomelye' and on one occasion came into her bed and had sex by force. He had 'dyvers tymes sens sawte to have yt of her butt he never hadd ytt', she said with what sounds like bitter defiance. The man was married. There was likewise unseemly behaviour, verging on rape, in a Kirby Bellars household, though in this case there is no mention of a wife. Two men apparently took the opportunity of their master's occasional absences to share a bed with a maidservant, but they all denied actual intercourse. The woman did, however, claim that the household head 'came to her bedde and wolde have hadde knowledge of her body butt she withstode hym and forther she sayethe that he asalte[d] her dyvers tymes bothe in the howsse and in the feldes butt he never had hys wyll'. He for his part denied sex but admitted that on New Year's Day he went to her bed and 'gave her a clappe one the buttocke'.[82]

---

[81] *Ibid.*, fo. 59v.   [82] *Ibid.*, fos. 57r–v, 58r.

Despite these occasional glimpses of murky circumstances, the overall impression is that in Leicestershire the strictures of premarital sexual regulation were quite tight and only slightly more relaxed in west Sussex – by no means as licentious as the homily against adultery and whoredom supposed. As will be seen later in this chapter, the moral climate of urban centres had changed considerably by the later sixteenth century, and a similar evolution may have been occurring in these rural areas. Concubinage or anything like it scarcely features, and strikingly, compared with the pre-Reformation situation, there were no women described as common whores or the like. Supported by a good deal of assistance from churchwardens, other local officers and ordinary people, the courts policed actively. Given that they had no powers to make arrests and in the last resort were wholly dependent on spiritual sanctions, they were also quite effective in bringing defendants to court.[83] In the archdeaconry of Leicester some 85 per cent of men accused of sexual offences appeared in court, mostly after initial citation but some after first being suspended from church attendance. The corresponding figure for women was just under 70 per cent, reflecting the fact that many pregnant women simply made themselves scarce. Individuals accused of aiding and abetting, mostly male householders, were even more amenable. The archdeaconry of Chichester court was less efficient, managing to secure the appearance of just fewer than 70 per cent of men accused of sexual offences but only about 50 per cent of women. Even more than in Leicestershire, the lower rate of compliance among females reflected the difficulty of dealing with women who gave birth to illegitimate children. Of twenty-one such women named in the record for 1574, only six were actually brought to court.

In both areas, accused sexual offenders who did appear were treated quite rigorously – on the whole more harshly than before the Reformation. Only a few were dismissed because the evidence was too flimsy or because they managed to clear themselves by compurgation. On those who confessed or were otherwise convicted, the Chichester court tended to impose swingeing penalties, continuing a pattern that had been established under Bishop Barlow in the 1560s. It may be that the authorities resorted to severity precisely because local regulation was not as tight as it might have been, and they wished to make an example. Even the more lenient

---

[83] Appearance rates in the archdeaconry of Leicester in 1570 were aided by an act of general pardon passed in 1571 (13 Elizabeth I c. 28). This gave individuals who had failed to appear the previous year an incentive to seek absolution.

sentences usually involved repeated acts of public penance performed in church, the culprit being dressed in a white sheet and sometimes going barefoot and bare-headed for greater humiliation. Quite often the severity of sentences was increased by additional acts of penance to be performed in the marketplace of towns such as Chichester and Petworth; sometimes it was specified that the culprit should wear a paper advertising the offence.[84]

In the archdeaconry of Leicester, where local regulation was tighter, the judges seem to have displayed more flexibility. Marketplace penances were reserved for egregious cases, especially when culprits had added perjury to their other sins, for example, by trying unsuccessfully to clear themselves by compurgation.[85] Moreover, the kind of tailor-made penance described earlier in the case of William Tette was already giving way to routine. The standard penance was performed publicly in church on a Sunday or major feast day, the culprit wearing a white sheet. In cases of adultery or unmitigated fornication, only occasionally was it commuted into a money payment either in whole or in part. But in the relatively numerous cases where the offenders were already intending to marry or agreed to do so, the judge was often content with a simple confession in church at the time of solemnization, albeit usually supplemented by a contribution – the sums varying from a shilling or two to 6s. 8d. – to poor relief funds or other charitable uses. These milder penalties were not a formality, however, and when necessary, the judge took care to send a clear message. At Dalby Chacombe, where a case of prenuptial fornication had apparently been winked at by the vicar as well as by the churchwardens and 'sworn men', the couple were sternly ordered to make a plain declaration of their offence and 'desyre all the people to praye for them and to take example at them'.[86] This case suggests strongly that the relatively rigorous moral regime in Leicestershire owed much to 'top down' initiatives by the court, though as usual there was much local support for the disciplining of notorious offenders.

Provincial Towns and Cities

Secular courts in towns and cities were another important focus of innovation in the sphere of sexual regulation in the first half of Elizabeth's reign. London will be examined in Chapter 11; here provincial centres are the

[84] E.g. WSRO, Ep.I/17/3, fos. 21r, 21v, 25v, 26r. For practice in the 1560s, see Ep.I/10/13, fos. 10r, 12r, 12v, 14v, 19r, 19v, 22r, 25r, 27r.
[85] ROLLR, 1 D 41/11/3, fos. 158r, 159r.
[86] ROLLR, 1 D 41/13/6, fo. 9v and schedule of penance between fos. 24 and 25.

subject of attention. As seen in Chapter 4, well before the Reformation many of them were self-consciously pursuing regimes of social discipline in which sexual regulation played a prominent part. Unlike the church courts, they were not primarily interested in repentance and the sinner's relationship with God; rather, the imperative was to subject egregious offenders to exemplary punishment and/or to drive them out of town. Their special powers in this sphere, based on city or borough custom, were attractive to proponents of 'reformation of manners', not least those of puritan persuasion who yearned for further reform in the English church. In Exeter, John Vowell alias Hooker looked back with approval on the rigour of some of his pre-Reformation predecessors. But new initiatives could be problematic, raising as they inevitably did some thorny legal issues, including the danger of transgressing jurisdictional boundaries. Apart from the obvious possibility of conflicts with the spiritual courts – a highly sensitive issue in the wake of all the changes that had occurred by 1559 – the royal courts at Westminster were apt to look askance at idiosyncratic borough and city customs unless they were clearly permitted by charter or prescription.

Outcomes were strikingly diverse. Faced by challenges, some towns tacitly abandoned their claims to jurisdiction over sexual offences, except as far as statute allowed. Others, especially larger towns with a long history of punishing whores, bawds and the like, were able not only to maintain and even extend their activities but also to increase the severity of punishments. This was a period when 'carting' – trundling offenders around town or market – was increasingly used by urban magistrates as a shaming punishment for sexual offences. To an extent, it was also possible to have recourse to the harsher physical punishment of whipping. Nonetheless, such towns had to be circumspect, and there are interesting examples of experimentation with legal procedures to achieve the object of greater regulation and sharper punishment while guarding against legal challenge. A few towns and cities – notably Leicester, among those surveyed here – had by the later part of Elizabeth's reign emerged as models of a successful alliance between magistracy and ministry.[87]

As is well known, in the 1560s and 1570s, certain towns that innovated too radically were rapidly brought to heel. The 'Order of Northampton' (1571), promoted by the zealous Protestant preacher Percival Wiburn, had affinities with the 'Ecclesiastical Ordinances' of Calvin's Geneva. Many of the regulations set out in this document were concerned with church

---

[87] On 'magistracy and ministry', see Patrick Collinson, *The Religion of Protestants: The Church in English Society, 1559–1625* (Oxford, 1982), chap. 4.

services, communion, sermons, catechizing, spiritual exercises and the abolition of ceremonies seen as superstitious. But there were also orders for social discipline. In particular, there was said to be

> a wekelye assembly every Thursdaye after the lecture by the maiour and his bretherne assisted with the preacher, mynister and other gentlemen appointed to them by the bisshopp for the correction of discorde made in the towne, as for notorious blasphemy, whoredome, drunkenes, raylinge agaynst religyon, or the preachers thereof, skowldes, rybauldes and suche lyke, which faultes are eche Thursdaye presented unto them in writinge by certein sworne men, appointed for that cervice in eche parisshe, so the bisshoppes aucthoritie and the mayours joyned together beinge assisted with certein other gentillmen in comyssion of peace, yll lyeff is corrected, Goddes gloary sett fourthe and the people brought in good obedience.

This mingling of ecclesiastical and secular jurisdictions could not fail to arouse alarm, and the bishop of Peterborough, Edmund Scambler, having initially supported the initiative, rapidly backtracked when he appreciated the potential significance for ecclesiastical government. As a result, the order was suppressed, and Wiburn was suspended from preaching.[88] At Bury St Edmunds (Suffolk) in 1579, a group of godly justices devised a somewhat similar regime of draconian penalties directed against 'suspected papists' and sinners of various kinds, including sexual offenders. Even more obviously than the 'Order of Northampton', these provisions both exceeded the law of the land and infringed on ecclesiastical jurisdiction and so were immediately challenged by Bishop Edmund Freke of Norwich.[89]

The Bury orders prescribed that bawds, fornicators, adulterers, incestuous persons and anyone found either with child or to have fathered a child 'before open solempnizacion of mariage' were to be tied to the whipping post for the whole of the 'lordes daie' and the night before or after, to have their hair cut off if they were female and then on market day to receive 'thirtie strypes well layed on till the blood come'.[90] The impression is of an extra twist of cruelty that went beyond mere severity. Yet their offensiveness in the eyes of the authorities lay less in their rigour than in innovating without legal

---

[88] TNA, SP 12/78, fo. 243v; W. J. Sheils, 'Erecting the Discipline in Provincial England: The Order of Northampton, 1571', in James Kirk (ed.), *Humanism and Reform: The Church in Europe, England, and Scotland, 1400–1643. Essays in Honour of James K. Cameron* (Studies in Church History, Subsidia 8, Oxford, 1991), pp. 331–45.

[89] Elliot Rose, *Cases of Conscience: Alternatives Open to Recusants and Puritans under Elizabeth I and James I* (London, 1975), pp. 158–68; Collinson, *Religion of Protestants*, pp. 158–63.

[90] BL, Lansdowne MS 27, no. 70, fo. 155r.

sanction and transgressing jurisdictional boundaries. The fact was that many towns, simply on the basis of existing custom, had the potential to punish sexual offenders with a severity that approached that of the Bury justices, so long as they paid due regard to legal niceties. But how far they proved able and willing to do so depended on a combination of local circumstances. The following case studies illustrate this diversity.

One town in which the opportunity was not seized – perhaps surprisingly – was Nottingham. Prosecutions for keeping bawdry, receiving vagabonds and harlots and variants on these offences remained commonplace in this town throughout the 1530s and 1540s, though none of the surviving files for this period yields anything like the number of cases that had occasionally occurred earlier.[91] In 1539 the mayor himself was presented for 'lak of dew execusyon' on 'serten bawdy persones' dwelling in the town, while in 1544 a chantry priest was prosecuted for 'kypeng of bawdri' with a married woman, 'offending god therin and also our kynges lawes'. There were also occasional prosecutions for actual fornication or adultery on the part of lay people, as when it was reported of a man and his maidservant in 1537 that 'we thynk the[y] lyffe in awouttre [avoutry] and not after the lays of god.'[92] Sexual offenders were still being prosecuted in Mary's reign, their behaviour being now described in terms of 'whoredom' as well as the established variants on the vocabulary of 'bawdry'.[93] The Elizabethan sessions records are unfortunately fragmentary until the very end of the reign, but the rolls that survive do contain many presentments of tipplers, drunkards, swearers, blasphemers, nightwalkers, scolds and quarrellers and people who neglected the communion or other church services, as also frequent prosecutions for keeping 'ill rule' or receiving 'unlawful', 'ill', 'bad', or 'evil' company in service time or otherwise.[94] There was even the occasional case of witchcraft.[95] However, cases referring explicitly to sexual transgressions were by this time rare, the most notable example occurring in 1575 when a bell founder was presented for keeping his daughter (by that time pregnant) as a 'common hore or strumpett' in his house, 'which is bothe odius unto god and his people of this towne'.[96] There was apparently no innovation in punishments either. 'Carting' does not seem to have been introduced till 1604, and then only for scolds.[97]

This lack of interest in sexual delicts is in marked contrast to the late fifteenth and early sixteenth centuries. It may be that such matters were in

---

[91] NA, CA 31–46 *passim*; cf. Chapter 4.   [92] NA, CA 37/4, 38/1, 42c/5.   [93] NA, CA 47b/5, 7.
[94] NA, CA 48–58 *passim*.   [95] NA, CA 56/38.
[96] NA, CA 49/4, 8; for other cases, see CA 50a/12; CA 54/132; CA 57/18, 47.   [97] NA, CA 59/8, 51.

this period dealt with by the justices in petty sessions but have left no trace in the surviving records. Alternatively, they may have been tacitly ceded to the jurisdiction of the ecclesiastical courts, which in 1577 went as far as to cite a Nottingham alderman on the basis of a 'common fame' that he had 'committed fornicacion with one unknowne in the fieldes'. This was a surprisingly insubstantial charge for a man in a prominent position to be called to answer – though immediately on his appearance he was allowed to clear himself with the oaths of 'three honest men', and it may be that he welcomed his day in court to clear his name of an unsavoury rumour.[98] In any event, the archdeacon of Nottingham was the formidable John Louth, and his court was among those that in the early part of Elizabeth's reign imposed elaborate penances, often involving exposure in the marketplace, on sexual offenders hailing not only from the town itself but also from surrounding villages. In 1568, for example, it was ordered that Richard Stanley

> shall resorte to the parishe churche of St Maryes . . . upon Saturday next and from thence to go rounde aboute the markett place after the manner of a penitent, bare headded, bare legged, bare footed with a sheet aboute hym betwene xj of the clocke and one and the paritor to go before hym with a white rodd in his hand and so to retorne agayne to the saide parishe churche and allso two Sundayes or holy dayes next to come to the sayde parishe churche and there to kneele after the manner of a penitent untyll the minister or curat go to readd the homyly which shalbe agaynst adultry and then to go and stande before the pulpytt untyll the same bee finished and then to go and kneele in the churche untyll service bee donne.[99]

The small borough of Devizes (Wiltshire) presents a different picture, illustrating how the active policing of sexual offenders by secular authorities could be reined in by jurisdictional challenge. The earliest surviving records of the borough court, from the reign of Mary, show that at this time the mayor and corporation had no compunction about taking strong action against adulterers and other sexual offenders.[100] This continued to be so in the early part of Elizabeth's reign. Admittedly, many cases involved tangled circumstances, often including an element of vagrancy, which might have been the justification for secular involvement. Yet there was also a succession of straightforward sexual offences, which the mayor and burgesses punished with a variety of shaming punishments and with

---

[98] Nottingham University Manuscripts and Special Collections, AN/A 3/1/4, fo. 34r.
[99] Nottingham University Manuscripts and Special Collections, AN/A 1, fo. 33r, cf. fos. 18v, 31v, 47r, 49r.
[100] See Prologue.

banishment. Thus, in December 1559, a couple were 'punyshed in the open stockes for playinge the knave and the whore together', while in May 1560, the mayor and burgesses ordered that a man and a woman whom he had made pregnant should be 'bette aboute the towne with basons and commaundyd to avoyd the towne'. In June the same year, a man and his mother were 'punyshed' – probably whipped – and also gaoled for having 'carnall copulacyon together beinge haynos and ungodlye'. All these and other cases – together suggesting a brisk rate of prosecution in a comparatively small urban community – could well have been dealt with by the spiritual jurisdiction. Indeed, a case in December 1560 suggests the use of procedures similar to those courts. Examined concerning a rumour that he had had a child by his sister-in-law, a man was ordered 'to bringe in his purgacion for to dischardge himselfe'.[101]

Yet, in 1576, this jurisdiction was challenged, though not directly as a result of proceedings against sexual transgressors. The mayor, Richard Gyfford – who in another quarrel was called 'godly cokscome'[102] – received a complaint that the parson of Devizes St John, Patrick Blare, had assaulted and verbally abused a townsman and his wife and another woman in the churchyard. When the mayor sent the constable and sub-bailiff to command him to appear before him, Blare struck them and 'most contemptuously denied the commandement and the auctoryty', asserting that 'he would not observe the quens peace at the mayors commaundement.' For good measure he called the mayor knave and his wife whore, threatening to 'have the proddest knave of them all into the Flete [prison]'. Subsequently he declared that 'yf there ys any justice that ought to correct him ought first the mair to certifie the ordinarie of Sarum [the bishop of Salisbury] or ells to certifie the high commissioners for causses ecclesiasticall.'[103] Clearly this was a man with a relatively sophisticated grasp of jurisdictional issues. Blare was backed up by a local justice, Sir Henry Sharington, who declared that in matters of vice 'the mayor of the Devizes hath no more auctoryty to punish then his horse.'[104] Thereafter there was a diminishing number of cases that dealt with sexual transgressions, except as allowed by the bastardy provisions of the act of 1576 or

[101] WSA, G20/1/11, fos. 4r, 10r, 10v; G20/1/12, fo. 5v.
[102] WSA, G20/1/13 [unfoliated], 6 April 1576.
[103] WSA, G20/1/13 [unfoliated], 7 Jan. 1576, 11 Jan. 1576.
[104] Ibid., 27 Jan. 1578 (reverse of folio). In his own household, it should be noted, Sharington had no qualms about administering arbitrary punishment: see Linda Pollock, With Faith and Physic: The Life of a Tudor Gentlewoman. Lady Grace Mildmay, 1552–1620 (London, 1993), p. 28.

tangentially under vagrancy legislation. In this small town, secular jurisdiction over sexual offenders was being gradually squeezed out.[105]

The much larger town of Colchester is notable both for striking innovations in sexual regulation and for weathering challenges to its jurisdiction. Since the complex story has already been discussed by several historians, it may be dealt with quite briefly here.[106] As shown in Chapter 4, the town had a long-standing tradition of prosecuting sexual offenders. What happened between 1529 and 1558 is more confused. While the rate of prosecution was quite brisk in the later part of Henry VIII's reign, such cases were far less in evidence under Edward VI and Mary; the great purge of Edwardian London was not echoed in Colchester. Yet such cases had not disappeared. At least until 1589, when the nature of the borough court rolls changes, some presentments of sexual transgressions were still entered in the records of the thrice-yearly lawhundreds and sessions, as they had been for generations, while increasingly cases of bastard-bearing, fornication, adultery and the like were dealt with by the bailiffs and justices in petty sessions. There was a new development in May 1566, when the two bailiffs, three justices and three aldermen met together with the archdeacon of Colchester, James Calfhill, and the town preacher, William Cole, to deal with cases of sexual transgression. This may have reflected another attempt to mingle secular and ecclesiastical jurisdictions, similar to those which were to provoke trouble with the authorities in Northampton and Bury St Edmunds; though in the event the archdeacon – a noted proponent of moral reformation – did not feature in future sittings of the Colchester justices.[107]

In practical terms, a far more important development was the introduction of carting or 'riding the tumbrel' as a routine punishment for sexual offenders in place of the fines – admittedly quite steep on occasion – that had previously been the norm. A tallow chandler and a shoemaker's wife, together with a bow maker and a widow, were punished in this way in December 1562, even though the second couple had apparently been

---

[105] WSA, G20/1/13 [unfoliated], 14 Feb. 1576; G20/1/15, fos. 13r, 14v–15r, 19v (there was also a case of attempted child abuse: *ibid.*, fo. 23v); G20/1/16, fos. 63r, 65r, 67r, 78r, 126v, 133v.

[106] Mark S. Byford, 'The Price of Protestantism. Assessing the Impact of Religious Change on Elizabethan Essex: The Cases of Heydon and Colchester, 1558–1594', unpublished DPhil thesis, University of Oxford, 1988, chap. 5; Laquita M. Higgs, *Godliness and Governance in Tudor Colchester* (Ann Arbor, 1998), esp. pp. 258–63; Richard Dean Smith, *The Middling Sort and the Politics of Social Reformation: Colchester, 1570–1640* (New York, 2004), esp. pp. 145–65, 181–98.

[107] Essex RO, Colchester BR, D/B5 R6 (Entry Bk, 1565–71), fos. 214v, 215r; cf. Byford, 'Price of Protestantism', pp. 165–7.

discussing marriage.[108] Even greater severity was evident in May 1566, the occasion when Archdeacon Calfhill was present. A mariner of St Leonard's parish was examined about 'a comon and publique cryme of incontynencye' with his maidservant, who had fallen pregnant, and on conviction was ordered to be 'carted in the tumbrell and drawen throughe the market in grettest assemblye' and in addition to pay the large sum of £10 in three equal portions to the poor of Colchester and of the universities of Cambridge and Oxford. The alternative was on the 'next market daye in open markett to be drawen att a cartes arse and to be sharpely whypped'. Being 'putt to his chose', he opted to ride the tumbrel and pay the fine. A labourer and another woman, found guilty the same day of 'fylthye whoredom', were not given the choice but simply were sentenced to be whipped in the open market.[109]

Thereafter, carting became a firmly established element in the repertory of punishments inflicted by the borough magistrates. Additional severities occasionally provoked resistance. In 1567, the bailiffs and commonalty faced quo warranto proceedings in Queen's Bench for imprisoning men and women in the Moot Hall for adultery and imposing fines on them.[110] In 1575, a major stir was created when John Lone, a wealthy mariner and ship-owner – engaged, it would appear, in a variety of more or less shady activities, including smuggling – was carted together with the wife of his business associate, William Collins. Lone's treatment aroused widespread resentment and led to a libelling campaign against the magistrates, whereupon Benjamin Clere and Robert Motte, the bailiffs of Colchester, brought a Star Chamber case against the supposed authors. Lone not only denied involvement in the libelling campaign – protesting that he could 'neither wright nor reade nor cannot nor never could' – but challenged the lawfulness of his punishment. While he did not question the practice of carting as such, he raised several objections about his own treatment, not least the fact that he had not been taken in the act but merely convicted on the basis of suspicious circumstances. Lone further claimed that he had been imprisoned for fourteen weeks and was eventually taken to the cart so heavily guarded that 'when . . . [he] was sene it was axed whither he were carried to hanginge or not'. He and the woman were 'throwen into a tumbrell' and carted along an extended route, far lengthier than was customary, all round the town and indeed beyond the

---

[108] Essex RO, Colchester BR, D/B5 Sb 2/1, fos. 1v (recognizance), 19v (judgement); cf. Higgs, *Godliness and Governance*, p. 261 (misdated to 1563).

[109] Essex RO, Colchester BR, D/B5 R6, fos. 214v–215r.

[110] TNA, KB 9/617, m. 7; cf. Higgs, *Godliness and Governance*, pp. 260, 261n.

walls into the eastern suburbs, 'as never anye before that tyme had the like punishment for anie such offence duelie proved'.[III]

The political fallout from this case led to the destruction of Benjamin Clere's career, and henceforth the borough magistrates became more circumspect. It is reasonable to infer, as does Richard Dean Smith, that this was the reason why for two decades from 1576 the town resorted to the trial of some sexual offenders by means of special juries convened to bring charges 'against whores, fornicators and adulterers', the usual punishment being to ride the tumbrel.[112] Some of these prosecutions took the form of indictments in which a man was charged with entering the house of another man and 'not having God before his eyes but seduced by the instigation of the devil', enticing his wife to consent to adultery. In the case of single women, the charge of entering another man's house was omitted. Laquita Higgs assumes that the reference to consent is a legal fiction and that these were really rape cases. They are more plausibly seen as an attempt to bring adultery within the scope of common law.[113] But this tactic was itself vulnerable to Queen's Bench writs of *corpus cum causa*, as was found in 1589 when a weaver named Isaac Lucas was indicted for adultery with the wife of Peter Dributter, a Flemish refugee.[114]

By the later part of Elizabeth's reign the punishment of sexual offenders in Colchester had settled into a pattern, aided by good relations between the ecclesiastical authorities and the borough magistrates in this area of considerable puritan influence. The church courts dealt as usual with incest, adultery, fornication, illicit pregnancy and the harbouring of unmarried mothers. The justices in petty sessions dealt with many cases of bastardy and illicit pregnancy and with forms of behaviour likely to lead to a similar outcome. Often the main aim seems to have been to ensure that there was adequate financial provision so that unmarried mothers and their offspring did not require poor relief. But apart from such prudential considerations, the magistrates regarded fornication and adultery as in themselves highly offensive both to God and to the good order and reputation of the town. Some magistrates were no doubt more strongly motivated by religious conviction than others – and in the context of the

---

[III] TNA, STAC 5/C81/23; STAC 5/C70/2, m. 2; see also STAC 5/C69/29; STAC 5/C79/30. The Lone affair is discussed at length in Byford, 'Price of Protestantism', pp. 194–208, and briefly in Higgs, *Godliness and Governance*, pp. 259–60; Smith, *Middling Sort*, pp. 121–2.

[112] Smith, *Middling Sort*, p. 123; by 1595, thirteen such juries had been assembled, but they were only occasionally convened thereafter.

[113] Essex RO, Colchester BR, D/B5 Cr 141, m. 13r; D/B5 Cr 144, m. 13v; D/B5 Cr 145, mm. 23r, 31v; D/B5 Cr 146, m. 22v; cf. Higgs, *Godliness and Governance*, p. 262.

[114] Essex RO, Colchester BR, D/B5 Cr 150, mm. 25r–v, 26r–v, 32v.

Elizabethan regime, such conviction was bound to be Protestant – but more obviously secular considerations were so closely entwined that it is hard to draw the distinction.

Certainly disordered households, where a husband was pimping his wife or incest was involved, could not be tolerated. Likewise, liaisons between householders and their maidservants were not condoned, especially if they led to an illicit pregnancy. Manifest adultery with a married woman was also likely to lead to trouble, even though it was assumed that men should manage their own wives and others were not always eager to intervene. The magistrates were thus inclined to make an example of egregious offenders and subject them to the public ignominy of carting. But well-heeled victims of this policy had the financial resources and legal sophistication to fight back. Smith's analysis of the social status of individuals accused of sexual offences indicates that though at all times most of the women who became illicitly pregnant were of poor or obscure status, up to the 1580s, male offenders came from a fairly wide social spectrum. Thereafter they tended to be confined to the poorer ranks – whether because men of higher standing were leading more moral lives (or at least were more circumspect) or because the authorities were reluctant to confront them.[115] Carting sexual offenders around the town was still a feature of Colchester by the end of the century, but it was by now a more occasional occurrence and became even less common in subsequent decades.

Exeter, as a large provincial capital, is of exceptional interest.[116] Not only did it have, as was seen in Chapter 4, a long tradition of civic action against sexual offenders; in the reign of Elizabeth it evinced a proud yet shrewd awareness of that tradition and a willingness to build on it. Its practice had been to banish egregious sexual offenders, as it did other undesirables. This was developed into the regular practice of carting delinquents out of the city or, as a more severe sanction, whipping them tied to the 'cart's arse'. It was a matter of record that in 1525 Joan Luter had been 'carried abowte the cite yn a carte with a rayhowde apone heir hede' and then banished.[117] Mindful of the need to demonstrate precedents in an age of keen legal consciousness, the city chamberlain, John Vowell alias Hooker, entered this case, along with others from early in Elizabeth's reign and associated

---

[115] Smith, *Middling Sort*, pp. 179–80, 184, 187.
[116] On the city in this period, see Wallace T. MacCaffrey, *Exeter, 1540–1640: The Growth of an English County Town*, 2nd edn. (Cambridge, MA and London, 1975).
[117] John M. Wasson (ed.), *Records of Early English Drama: Devon* (Toronto, Buffalo and London, 1986), p. 126. For the background, see Chapter 4.

regulations, in his 'abstracte of all the orders and ordynances ... enacted and ordayned by the maiors and common councell ... of Excester ... for the good goverment of the sayde citie and commonwelth'.[118]

The records of actual proceedings are lacking for the later part of Elizabeth's reign, but the material for the earlier part, especially the 1560s, is unusually rich. Already in Mary's reign, the jurors at the regular 'lawdays' and 'sessions' held for the three 'quarters' of the city regularly brought 'accusements' against a variety sexual offenders, some of whom were banished. A leading proponent of severity appears to have been Walter Staplehill, mayor in 1556, commended by Hooker for his punishment of 'all lose and disordered persons', albeit he thought him 'over miche blynded yn poperye'.[119] The records of lawdays and sessions held during 1560, early in the reign of Elizabeth, suggest at first sight a falling off in zeal. Though many other nuisances and disorders were brought to light, explicit prosecutions for sexual transgressions were rare.[120]

Yet subsequent years saw a scattering of cases of women with illegitimate children, 'not to be suffred here in the cytye', and other accusations of sexual misdemeanour. In October 1563 there was a case reminiscent of pre-Reformation times, when the 'great inquest' presented 'Sir Humfry Hardynge priest taken suspiciously with Johan Corvener the wyffe of Hugh Corvyner dwellynge yn the paryshe of Seynt Maryes a Fryday at nyght last past the xxij of October 1563 at x of the clocke'.[121] By the early 1570s, the record includes regular constables' presentments in addition to those of the lawhundreds and sessions. As a result, rather more sexual delicts appear, recorded in greater detail and sometimes with an account of the subsequent jury trial.[122]

But the intensity of sexual regulation in the city can only be properly appreciated in the light of the chance survival of proceedings before the mayor and justices early in Elizabeth's reign.[123] The record covers a wide variety of offences, not always clearly distinguished, including petty theft, scolding and various other disorders. But each year in the period 1560–4,

[118] John Vowell alias Hooker, *The Description of the Citie of Excester*, ed. Walter J. Harte, J. W. Schopp and H. Tapley-Soper, 3 parts (Devon and Cornwall Record Society, Exeter, 1919–47), Vol. III, pp. 863, 876.
[119] Walter J. Harte, *Gleanings from the Common Place Book of John Hooker, Relating to the City of Exeter (1485–1590)* (Exeter, n.d.), p. 20. It may be that Staplehill tried to use moral reform as a means of uniting 'honest men' who might otherwise be divided by religion in a city that was still highly unsettled in the wake of the Western Rebellion.
[120] E.g. DHC, Exeter City Archives, Sessions Records, Miscellaneous Vol. 100, pp. 35, 40
[121] *Ibid.*, pp. 59, 98. [122] *Ibid.*, p. 204; cf. pp. 200, 203.
[123] DHC, Exeter City Archives, Chamber Act Book 4, pp. 1–363.

when the minutes appear to be particularly full, there occurred some ten to twenty cases concerned mainly with sexual transgressions. That it was well understood that the mayor and justices exercised unusually extensive powers of summary justice is shown by a letter from the earl of Bedford's secretary in 1560. Sending them two 'errant whores and suspeciose and idle persons lyeng about my lordes house at Clist in the hedges to the greate hurte of his servauntes', he requested 'allthoughe it be out of your countie' that 'ye havinge a towne of justice will do so muche for my lordes sake as to cause them the next markett daye to be whipped and scorged ... because in the countrey ... we have not so good a punyshement'.[124] The majority of individuals brought in question that year were women – single women, wives and widows. This probably reflects the slant of long-established ordinances directed mainly against common women or whores, and the underlying assumption seems to have been both that women had less of a stake in the city than male householders and that they carried more responsibility than men for sexual disorder. Nonetheless, the condemnation of the magistrates was not confined to women and in subsequent years the proportion of men and women punished was somewhat more equal.[125]

A tucker or clothier called Richard Taylour, a married man, apparently literate and of reasonable substance, tried to evade punishment by challenging the jurisdiction. Evidence of his 'incontynent lyffe' with Joan Smithe included 'presumptiones' based on their being seen together in various locations, letters she had sent him, and her 'open confession which she justified before ... [his] face'. At first Taylour submitted and 'confessed him selfe to have lyved inordynatly and wantonly', but 'prayeng of favour ... and promysyng amendement of lyffe' he was released of the 'extreme punyshement' and instead ordered to pay the considerable sum of £5 10s. to the poor. Dissatisfied, he sent the bishop of Exeter a lengthy petition, claiming to have always enjoyed the reputation of a man 'both just in worde and deede of honest conversacion name and fame, no fylthie lyver worthie for the same and other his good qualyties reposed of God in him to be well spoken of, never spotted untill now of late with any notoriose or sklunderose cryme emonge the whole number of this worthie citie'.

The bishop was hardly likely to countenance any suggestion that adultery was a minor fault, and in fact, Taylour himself described it as 'so fylthie a crime'. Rather, he claimed that the woman who had accused him was 'of

---

[124] *Ibid.*, p. 42.   [125] *Ibid.*, pp. 10, 11, 17, 19, 24, 43, 45, 46, 47–8, 56, 60, 69–70.

smale good name and fame moved by some lewde persons and ungodly perswasions', 'seeking the overthrowe of him and his utter shame and undoyng, the contynuall enemytie betwen him and his wiffe to be as a monster whereat to wonder in a Christian congregacion' – a revealing insight into the public and private consequences of male infidelity in provincial town society. The mayor and aldermen, he asserted, likewise acted 'to revenge olde malyce and grudges', treating him with 'crueltie' yet leaving 'moche open and evydent frayltie and fleshly fall unpunysshede emonge the better sort of them and yet wyncked at'. Crucially he asserted that the civic magistrates were 'men mete to here temporall causes and not matters apperteyning to your Lordships correction appoynted by the lawe ecclesiasticall'. 'The case is spirutuall,' he went on, 'the partie accusinge me taken yn your Lordships ffee and the matter determynable before you as mere ecclesiasticall judge', and called on the bishop 'for conscience sake' to call the matter before the church court. What he wanted was the chance to clear himself by compurgation. There is no evidence, however, that this had any effect on the conduct of the case before the Exeter magistrates, though in fact slightly more than half his fine was eventually remitted upon his 'gentill submission'.[126]

Far from seizing on such cases to vindicate the church's claims to jurisdiction over sexual offenders, Bishop William Alley was himself not averse to invoking the aid of the mayor and aldermen in punishing sin. In 1564 he sent them one Joan Estman with a request that she should be twice whipped and carted through the marketplace 'for dyvers approvid offensis of whoredom ... comytted with severall persons'.[127] By this time, indeed, the magistrates were ordering the use of the whip with increasing frequency to add physical pain to the 'open shame' of the cart and the deprivations of banishment. They did so in measured fashion, often specifying the number of strokes, the frequency with which they were to be administered and the locations where the whippings were to take place. Those considered to be the most reprehensible offenders obviously received the harshest treatment. Thus, in 1564, Thomas Logan was discharged from the Salisbury gaol delivery, only to be arrested in Exeter for 'havynge too wyffes folowenge hym'. He was ordered to be 'whipped at the cartes tayle in the open market ... yn the myddle of the fysh markett, yn

---

[126] *Ibid.*, pp. 115, 129–30. A copy of the petition was entered fourteen pages after the record of the first hearing before the mayor and justices, but at what point the original was submitted to the bishop is not clear.
[127] *Ibid.*, p. 255.

the myddle of [the] butter markett, yn the meale markett, yn the whet
market, yn the malte markett, at the west gate, at the beare corner, at
St Peters churche, at the east gate, at the lytle conducte at St Martyns lane
and the guyldhall, at every of the saide places syxe strypes.' The 'elder
woman' was to receive five stripes at each place and the younger three. This
example illustrates not merely the increasing use of whipping but also the
fact that by 1564 a much greater proportion of cases concerned immigrants
and people passing through Exeter than had been the case at the beginning
of the decade. This increase in judicial action may have been a response to
the vagrancy act of 1563, or it may be that more people were on the roads.
Here, as in other towns on major route-ways, the issue of sexual regulation
was becoming increasingly entangled with that of vagrancy.[128]

Even so, the jurisdictional issues remained sensitive. In May 1570,
immediately after the death of the complaisant Bishop Alley, the High
Commissioners in London wrote in sharp terms to the mayor of Exeter:

> Wheras we are crediblie enfourmed that you and others your predeces-
> sours . . . have of late tyme and do daylye presume and take upon you to
> enquire of incontinente livers and such like spirituall causes and further to
> procede to the corporall punishmente of the offendours which rightlie
> apertayneth to the hearinge and determynynge of your ordinarie and other
> ecclesiasticall judges . . . ye[a] and some once called before the ordinarie
> and according to the ecclesiasticall lawes, theire cause determyned you
> eftsones have convented the said person and punsyshed him by your
> aucthoritie for the same faulte. By which your indirecte dealinge you do
> not a litle prejudice and derogat the quenes majesties ecclesiasticall lawes
> and in continuance of time suffred unrefourmed yt may brede greate
> inconvenience. We have thought good to putt you in remembraunce of
> your dutie in that behalf and withall in her majesties name straightlie to
> charge and commaund you that from henceforth you for your parte do not
> attempte or presume by your self or any of your offycers to enquire, ordre,
> punishe or correcte any person offendinge in the premisses untyll you shall
> alledge and prove before us sufficient cause to the contrarie.

To make certain that the message went home, the letter was to be read
publicly before the mayor and aldermen in the town hall and afterwards
registered. It is unfortunate that the records of policing activities for the
next few decades after this date are very imperfect, so the impact of the
letter is hard to gauge. Such as they are, the records show that cases did not

---

[128] *Ibid.*, p. 250. On the broader penal context, see Martin Ingram, 'Shame and Pain: Themes and
Variations in Tudor Punishments', in Simon Devereaux and Paul Griffiths (eds.), *Penal Practice
and Culture, 1500–1900: Punishing the English* (Basingstoke, 2004), pp. 36–62.

cease immediately, but within a few years there does seem to have been a marked reduction in civic involvement in sexual regulation compared with the 1560s.[129]

The borough of Leicester presents a different case. As the centre of the archdeaconry, the church courts were certainly active in the town, but there is no sign of jurisdictional conflict, and in an environment that was becoming increasingly 'godly' – much influenced by Henry Hastings, earl of Huntington[130] – the exemplary punishment of sexual offenders by the secular authorities became a regular occurrence in the late sixteenth century. Working papers of the Leicester borough justices survive only from the later part of Elizabeth's reign and then only in part,[131] but important information on their judicial activities can be gleaned from the chamberlains' accounts, which record expenditure on public punishments. Already in 1552–3 the accounts had recorded payments 'for iiij papers to set uppon the crosse for the punysshement of horedom and brybere', while in 1556–7 there was payment for another 'paper to sett upon a womans heed', probably for whoredom.[132] Payments for the carting of delinquent women 'throughe the marckett place' or 'abowte the towne' likewise occurred in 1568–9 and 1574–5, while yet more cases, some involving whipping as well as carting, occurred in subsequent decades.[133] The relatively full records of the 1590s reveal a very tight regime of sexual regulation, in which the carting and whipping of notorious offenders interlocked with church court prosecutions and the handling of routine bastardy cases by justices of the peace. Even those of high status were not immune. In 1595, Master Robert Roberttes, a member of the council of Twenty Four, appeared before the mayor and other burgesses charged with the 'moste filthie and lewde cryme' of begetting a child on a Leicester widow. Despite his denials, he was discharged from the council 'untill suche tyme as he ... shall cleire hymself ... by due and lawfull meanes'.[134]

---

[129] DHC, Chanter 41, pp. 51–2; cf. Exeter City Archives, Sessions Records, Miscellaneous Vol. 100, pp. 200, 203, 204, 225, 260, 392.

[130] Catherine F. Patterson, *Urban Patronage in Early Modern England: Corporate Boroughs, the Landed Elite, and the Crown, 1580–1640* (Stanford, CA, 1999), pp. 194–201.

[131] ROLLR, BR II/18/1–7 (Hall Papers Bound, 1583–1606); no formal sessions rolls survive for this period.

[132] ROLLR, BR III/2/21, 24; Mary Bateson et al. (eds.), *Records of the Borough of Leicester: Being a Series of Extracts from the Archives of the Corporation of Leicester*, 7 vols. (London, Cambridge and Leicester, 1899–1974), Vol. III, pp. 71, 87 and n., where the editor is in no doubt that these papers were 'worn by strumpets when carted'.

[133] ROLLR, BR III/2/36, 42, 54, 55, 61, 64.

[134] Bateson et al. (eds.), *Records of the Borough of Leicester*, Vol. III, p. 318.

Perspectives

From the foregoing it is plain that in public policy debates in the early decades of Elizabeth's reign, as also in the practice of the church courts and the government of urban magistrates, there was evident a lively interest both in the bridling of sexual sin and the use of sharper penalties as a means of doing so. Church courts in many areas in the 1560s and 1570s suddenly started to use multiple penances, to pay elaborate attention to arrangements for staging the ritual and to insist in many cases on penance in the marketplace as well as in church. At the same time, town after town had recourse to carting or to other forms of corporal punishment for sexual offenders. These policies can be seen as 'Protestant' in several senses. The crucible in which they were generated was renewed Protestant Reformation under Elizabeth; the experiments in public penance, with antecedents in policies begun under Edward VI, were clearly attempts to reshape a traditional institution to suit the new doctrinal and ecclesiological position; and some of the leading figures involved – such as John Vowell alias Hooker in Exeter and James Calfhill in Colchester – plainly identified themselves as godly Protestants. However, some of the urban initiatives in particular had antecedents in Mary's reign or earlier, and more generally, almost all the early Elizabethan initiatives in sexual regulation built on traditions that long predated the Reformation. There was nothing distinctively Protestant in the aspiration to combat sexual sin, and indeed, its appeal was by no means simply religious. It meshed with wider concerns about order and hierarchy, heightened by growing problems of poverty and vagrancy. At its most basic level, it was supported, if not driven, by powerful prejudices that had existed for generations among ordinary men and women who saw themselves as 'honest' and strongly resented those who would not conform to conventional morality – especially if they did so blatantly or in the pursuit of profit.

What impact did these policies have? To committed Protestants seeking to combat sexual vice in provincial England, the New Jerusalem no doubt seemed an elusive vision. Church discipline had been only very partially reformed, and on the ground, the ecclesiastical courts, though by no means ineffective, found themselves dealing with an unending procession of adulterers, fornicators and unmarried mothers. Magistrates in towns and cities also faced intractable circumstances. These urban authorities – at least those more zealous for sexual discipline – must also have felt frustrated that their efforts were often undercut by jurisdictional challenges. Yet it is plain in retrospect – and may well have been evident to contemporaries themselves – that there were in train some major shifts that went beyond the 'correction' of individuals and amounted to a degree of social transformation. One of these has already been emphasized in Chapter 9, but it bears repetition. Though individual cases still cropped up occasionally, clerical incontinence was no longer a major issue – an important precondition for other developments that were by the early seventeenth century to make the English clergy *stupor mundi*.

If the pattern of sexual regulation in Elizabethan towns is compared with that of the late fifteenth century, another broad change comes into focus – the decline of the sex trade, even in the larger centres. In 1560s Exeter, for example, there were plenty of cases of 'bawdry' and 'evil rule', but most of them consisted simply in lodging 'kept' women or providing accommodation for couples from outside the city whose marital status was suspect or worse. Adulterers and other lechers were often constrained to take their pleasure in gardens or ditches, presumably for want of safer and more comfortable accommodation. Only occasionally are there indications of organized prostitution or anything like it, and even these are equivocal. In December 1564, two married women were whipped at the cart's tail and banished for bawdry. They had apparently organized the provision of sexual services, but procuring suitable women was only achieved with an element of deception. One victim described how Margaret Wylssedoune 'dyd entyse her to her house at a brekfast', only to abandon her to the mercies of a 'master of defense'. Another, who 'cryeth vengeaunce' on the woman who had led her into whoredom, had been abused by a Frenchman and others.[135] An altogether more discreet and consensual arrangement was revealed in Leicester in 1588. A maidservant of Mistress Kiffyn explained that during the last assizes a man brought a woman to the house, where 'Master Crumwell' lay with her 'in the greene chamber alone'. Next day the woman said that she had received 10s. or a mark (13s. 4d.) or 'such a triffle'; the visitor gave the maidservant 6d. and 'bad her buy her pynes with yt'.[136]

The situation appears to have been quite different from the decades around 1500, when the inns and alehouses of Leicester and other towns were served by women with the generic surname of 'Tapster' whose sexual behaviour was often dubious at best. The disappearance of the clergy as a major source of custom was one factor in this change. Others were shifts in the organization of the brewing trade and the way it was regulated in towns, the effect of which was gradually to squeeze out females. If from

[135] DHC, Exeter City Archives, Chamber Act Book 4, pp. 269–70.
[136] ROLLR, 1 D41/13/12, fo. 68v.

a twenty-first-century perspective this seems like further patriarchal restrictions on the economic opportunities open to women, it did help to reduce the challenges to public order faced by contemporaries. Further, from the mid-sixteenth century onwards the entire drink trade was increasingly subject to tight regulation, in part through local initiatives but also through national legislation that consolidated a system of licensing enforced by county and borough justices. To an extent, the church courts were also involved, policing instances of 'ill rule' in service time and punishing drunkards – albeit usually not in large numbers in Elizabeth's reign – in a way that had not been attempted before. These changes were gradual, but their cumulative effect is very noticeable in any series of local records in the late sixteenth century. As an important side effect, in provincial towns and cities the sex trade was pushed to the margins to the extent that in the policing records of towns as diverse as Salisbury, Leicester and Exeter, it is scarcely visible by the end of the sixteenth century. This was not the case in London, however, and it is to there that we must now turn.

CHAPTER 11

Brought into Bridewell
Sex Police in Early Elizabethan London

In Elizabethan London, the regulation of sexual behaviour was dominated by Bridewell Hospital. Foreign visitors remarked on it, some of them struck by the paradox that what had been built as a palace had become a penitentiary.[1] It generated numerous literary representations.[2] As an institution it was unique. The name became a generic term for houses of correction, many of which were established either in the late sixteenth or the early seventeenth century in accordance with the provisions of an act of 1576.[3] But the scope of these later foundations did not match the original. London Bridewell was simultaneously a workhouse, a prison and a place where whipping and hard labour as a means of 'correction' were routinely administered. Characteristically, these punishments were ordered on the spot by a court made up of governors of Bridewell Hospital. Remarkably, these exercised the power, without reference to justices of the peace or other authority, to issue warrants, enforce attendance, examine suspects and determine cases at their discretion, in accordance with the provisions of the royal charter of 1553. The court of governors punished people for a wide range of offences, but among them sexual transgressions were very prominent. Undoubtedly, therefore, Bridewell represented the greatest innovation in the sphere of sexual regulation in England throughout the whole period from the late fifteenth to the early seventeenth century. Among the arguments of this chapter is to stress that nonetheless its

---

[1] Caroline Barron, Christopher Coleman and Claire Gobbi (eds.), 'The London Journal of Alessandro Magno, 1562', *London Journal*, 9 (1983), 144; Derek Keene and Ian Archer with Emma Pauncefort and Ann Saunders (eds.), *The Singularities of London, 1578. Les Singularitez de Londres, noble, fameuse Cité, capital du Royaume d'Angleterre: ses antiquitez et premiers fondateurs, by L. Grenade* (London Topographical Society 175, 2014), pp. 65, 107, 109, 138; Gottfried von Bülow (ed.), 'Journey through England and Scotland Made by Lupold von Wendel in the Years 1584 and 1585', *Transactions of the Royal Historical Society*, New Series, 9 (1895), 233 (I owe this reference to Tracey Sowerby).
[2] William C. Carroll, *Fat King, Lean Beggar: Representations of Poverty in the Age of Shakespeare* (Ithaca, NY, and London, 1996), pp. 108–24.
[3] 18 Elizabeth I c. 3.

activities are in many ways best understood against the background of the *traditional* pattern of sexual regulation in the city of London.

The Powers of Bridewell Hospital: Scope and Limitations

As was seen in Chapter 9, Bridewell began its work in earnest in 1555 and, despite disputes over the scope of its jurisdiction, continued it for the remainder of Mary's reign. The first surviving court book commences in April 1559, at which point the institution was clearly fully functioning. For the rest of Elizabeth's reign (and indeed throughout the Stuart century and beyond), it handled large numbers of cases. Exactly how many remains uncertain, not merely because of gaps in the records[4] but also because there are discrepancies between the numbers of entries in the court books and figures given in the annual 'certificates' of persons maintained or otherwise dealt with issued by the board of governors from the end of the sixteenth century onwards.[5] On this basis, Ian Archer has suggested that around 1600 the court book recorded barely more than a third of the individuals actually dealt with.[6] But some of these must have been prisoners sent there by other courts or authorities, such as the 'Spaniardes' mentioned in 1602 and the 'recusantes papistes and puritans' that in 1601 the governors asked to be removed 'for that there is not sufficient rome in this hospitall to sett vagrantes and idle people on worke'. The annual certificates may also have included poor people who were relieved by the house but were not actual offenders; they certainly included children.[7] Any who were in question yet were omitted from the record were in all probability people taken up and discharged between formal sessions of the court. If, as seems likely, these comprised individuals who were judged to require neither further interrogation nor 'correction' in the form of whipping or hard labour – the main business of the recorded court sessions – the court books

<hr>

[4] Court books survive for the periods April 1559 to June 1562, March 1574 to November 1579, February 1598 to July 1610 and from July 1617 onwards. The originals are held by Bethlem Museum of the Mind, Beckenham, via whose website digitized images are available. The series is hereafter cited as BCB followed by the volume number.

[5] For a detailed discussion of this issue and a time series of committals to Bridewell as far as they can be recovered from extant sources, see Faramerz Dabhoiwala, 'Summary Justice in Early Modern London', *English Historical Review*, 121 (2006), 796–822. But in a personal communication, Paul Griffiths has cautioned against assuming that the numbers provided by the 'certificates' are accurate.

[6] Ian W. Archer, *The Pursuit of Stability: Social Relations in Elizabethan London* (Cambridge, 1991), p. 238; even accepting the totals on which this assessment is based, it cannot be assumed that discrepancies on a similar scale existed earlier in the reign.

[7] BCB 4, fos. 208r, 296v; Thomas Bowen, *Extracts from the Records and Court Books of Bridewell Hospital* (London, 1798), pp. 22, 25, 26.

as they stand do capture the bulk of more serious offenders. At any rate, they can provide minimum figures for the summary justice administered by Bridewell and in particular for the disciplining of sexual transgressors. These figures were substantial and increased over time. In 1560, for example, around 540 offenders were dealt with. Just under half of these were described as vagrants or accused of petty theft, fraud and similar crimes. But some 275 individuals were in trouble solely or chiefly for sexual or marital offences. In 1575, the total number of offenders had risen to about 700, and of these, as many as 440 were accused of sexual transgressions. Since cases of this type were often investigated in detail, they must have taken up most of the governors' time.

Despite such evidence of brisk activity, an important theme in existing accounts is to stress the limits of Bridewell's ability to police sexual transgressions and indeed its failures. Archer and others have documented how in the late 1570s the governors mounted a determined campaign against the sex trade. Among their targets were brothel-keepers, such as Gilbert and Margaret East, Elizabeth Raynbowe and – never actually prosecuted – 'Black Luce' Baynham; a network of prostitutes, including Thomasine Breame, Mary Dornelly, 'Little' Katherine Jones, Elizabeth Kirkham and Ann Levens; and their pimps or 'carriers', such as Henry Boyer and William Mekins, who also procured 'men's wives' and other women prepared to provide sexual services on a casual or part-time basis. Collating the information from this 'drive' with other evidence, Archer has been able to identify at least a hundred bawdy houses around this time, most of them in outlying areas such as Clerkenwell, St John Street, Shoreditch, Aldgate and St Katharine's, but including some in the heart of the city. Most of them were small affairs, maintaining two or three 'whores' on the premises or simply letting out rooms for the purposes of sex trade; sometimes women were summoned as necessary to meet the needs of clients. Such establishments did not, however, represent the limits of commercial sex. Men of standing often kept 'private whores' for their exclusive use, maintaining them in victualling houses or other lodgings. At the other extreme, unknown numbers of women – some of them vagrants – worked the streets and alleyways.

What made the Bridewell governors' initiative of the later 1570s distinctive is their targeting not merely the common run of 'whores' and 'harlots' – who had hitherto borne the brunt of prosecutions – but also the proprietors of well-resourced brothels and even their male clients.[8] But the

---

[8] The distinctiveness of the profile of Bridewell cases in 1576–7 is clearly evident in Archer, *Pursuit of Stability*, p. 239 (Table 6.1).

latter included foreign merchants, embassy staff, courtiers' and noblemen's servants, gentlemen of the inns of court and some prominent citizens, and hence, the efforts of the Bridewell authorities brought them into collision with a host of awkward individuals who, if not highly placed themselves, had powerful backers. Robert, Lord Dudley, later earl of Leicester, was one leading courtier prepared to shield some offenders; another was the earl of Worcester, who owned the premises where the notorious bawd Mistress Higgens operated. In the face of so many obstacles, the Bridewell governors' ambitious campaign eventually ground to a halt.[9]

More fundamentally, Paul Griffiths has emphasized the extent to which Bridewell's jurisdiction was contested throughout the reign of Elizabeth and even beyond.[10] Admittedly there is little indication at this stage of serious friction with the ecclesiastical authorities, as had plagued the city authorities under Mary.[11] Indeed, in the early 1560s, Edmund Grindal, as bishop of London, occasionally sent offenders straight to Bridewell.[12] At first sight this complaisance is surprising. By the 1570s, the London church courts were themselves handling considerable numbers of sexual offenders in parallel with Bridewell. But the one surviving record of disciplinary prosecutions from the early part of Elizabeth's reign suggests that initially the new hospital must have robbed them of much business. The archdeacon of London's act book for 1562–3 is concerned mainly with testamentary matters and religious offences, especially failing to attend church, not receiving communion and working on Sundays and holy days. There were also a fair number of prosecutions for scolding, slander, quarrelling, drunkenness and swearing, as also for allowing people to drink during service time. A clutch of people were prosecuted for receiving suspect persons, with no explicit suggestion that the latter were sexual transgressors. Cases that definitely concerned sex and marriage were in a small minority, and among these, marital disharmony, unlawful separation and bigamy or attempted bigamy were prominent. There were fewer than a dozen prosecutions for adultery, while cases of illicit pregnancy, suspected incontinence, harbouring pregnant women or promoting

[9] Archer, *Pursuit of Stability*, pp. 211–15, 231–3; Duncan Salkeld, *Shakespeare among the Courtesans: Prostitution, Literature, and Drama, 1500–1650* (Farnham, 2012), pp. 135–9 and *passim*. For the metropolitan sex trade, see also Paul Griffiths, 'The Structure of Prostitution in Elizabethan London', *Continuity and Change*, 8 (1993), 39–63.

[10] Paul Griffiths, 'Contesting London Bridewell, 1576–1580', *Journal of British Studies*, 42 (2003), 283–315.

[11] See Chapter 9, but cf. Paul Griffiths, *Lost Londons: Change, Crime, and Control in the Capital City, 1550–1660* (Cambridge, 2008), pp. 237–8.

[12] BCB 1, fos. 205v, 220v.

bawdry were even less numerous.[13] Some offenders asked to be dismissed on the grounds that they had been either punished or exonerated in Bridewell – pleas that, with due safeguards, the court was willing to admit.[14]

A treatise probably dating from the 1580s, variously attributed to Francis Bacon or (apparently less likely, since he was himself a governor) William Fleetwood, concluded that the terms of Bridewell's charter were fundamentally at odds with common and statute law, indeed with Magna Carta itself, and hence that 'proceedings in Bridewell upon the accusation of whores taken by the governors ... are not sufficient to call any man to answer by any warrant by them made, without indictment or other matter of record.'[15] The background was a long string of complaints, from the beginning of the reign onwards, from individuals aggrieved by their treatment in the hospital. In 1577, a substantial goldsmith, Anthony Bate, brought a Star Chamber suit against Robert Winch, the treasurer of Bridewell, on the grounds of charges of sexual immorality supported by false and suborned evidence. Bate eventually lost and was forced to make an abject submission, but the case dragged on for years and caused acute embarrassment.[16] In 1588, another Star Chamber case was brought against the city of London sheriffs, Thomas Skinner and John Catcher, for ordering the whipping of two gentlewomen 'of good behaviour' as common harlots, and against Roger Warefield, erstwhile treasurer of Bridewell, for seeing the sentence carried out. The sheriffs were found to have acted contrary to due process and suffered a spell in prison as well as being ordered to pay compensation and make a public apology to the women.[17]

---

[13] LMA, DL/AL/C/009/MS09055, covering the period 6 April 1562 to 8 July 1563. It should be noted that the stranger churches in London – the French numbering nearly 1,800 people and the Dutch nearly 2,000 in 1568 – had their own means of discipline: see Andrew Pettegree, *Foreign Protestant Communities in Sixteenth-Century London* (Oxford, 1986), pp. 182–94.

[14] *Ibid.*, fos. 103r, 119v. In one case the court did petition the 'masters and keepers' of Bridewell to produce one of the inmates, apparently without effect. This was Margaret Bell, entered in the Bridewell register as Margaret Floude alias Bell, in trouble for being in mixed company at the house of Margaret Barnes alias Long Meg at Ratcliff and sleeping with one of the men. Admitted to the hospital on 25 March, she was 'well whipped' on 8 April and committed again to work, eventually being released on 6 June 'uppon hope of amendment'. *Ibid.*, fo. 3r, cf. BCB 1, fo. 204v.

[15] 'A Brief Discourse upon the Commission of Bridewell', in James Spedding, Robert Leslie Ellis and Douglas Denon Heath (eds.), *The Works of Francis Bacon*, Vol. VII: *Literary and Professional Works* (London, 1859), p. 513; for the various surviving manuscripts and discussion of authorship, see Griffiths, *Lost Londons*, pp. 225–7.

[16] Griffiths, 'Contesting London Bridewell', 292–310; Griffiths, *Lost Londons*, pp. 217–19, 223–4; Archer, *Pursuit of Stability*, pp. 232–3.

[17] Christopher W. Brooks, *Law, Politics and Society in Early Modern England* (Cambridge, 2008), pp. 402–3.

Such high-profile cases were obviously few in number, minute in relation to the large numbers dealt with week in and week out in Bridewell, but they bring into sharp focus the issue of how the governors were able to get away with treating multitudes of people in such a draconian fashion. Part of the answer is simply that many of them were of low status and unable to defend themselves, but there is more to it than that. A clue is provided by Lord Treasurer Burghley's judgement in Skinner and Catcher's case: while censuring the sheriffs for their actions in that particular instance, it acknowledged that the punishment of sexual transgressions was enshrined in the customs of London. As previous chapters have shown, these powers were extremely well established and had been vigorously exercised, certainly for many decades, if not continuously for centuries. The court of aldermen formally punished indicted offenders with fines, imprisonment and a variety of public shame punishments. By this time, 'carting' had become the routine form, but the traditional symbolic embellishments remained in use, while the punishment still generally culminated in banishment.[18]

Thus, in June 1563, it was ordered that no less a personage than a doctor of physic should

> accordinge to the aunciente good lawdable and godly lawes and customes of the said cyty be sett in a carte with a ray hode upon his hedde and a white rodde in his hande and so be ledde thurrough all the most open streates and merket places . . . with pannes and basons ringinge before him unto one of the utter gates of the said cytye and there to be expelled and put out . . . nevermore to retorne . . . and that [on the way] he be steyed in sundry of the said merkett places whilest open proclamacion be made of his said offences.

He had been found guilty of 'the most filthie vice and cryme of lecherey and fornicacion by him of longe tyme very abominably usid and committed' not only with two young women – both said to have been virgins before he deflowered them and one of whom was only fifteen years old – but also with seven others that he kept in his two city houses. Obviously, this was a spectacular case, not least because, as the city chronicler Henry Machyn noted, the culprit was dressed in a coat and cap of velvet and a damask gown lined with the same rich material.[19] But more mundane

---

[18] The court sometimes allowed the culprit back on condition of future good behaviour: e.g. LMA, Repertory 15, fo. 485v.

[19] LMA, Repertory 15, fos. 248(251)v–249(252)r; John Gough Nichols (ed.), *The Diary of Henry Machyn, Citizen and Merchant-Taylor of London, from A.D. 1550 to A.D. 1563* (Camden Society, Old Series 42, London, 1848), p. 309.

cases are noted regularly in the records of common council and the court of aldermen in the 1560s and 1570s.

Such cases were tried by jury at special sessions for 'bawds and scolds' – in fact, mostly sexual offenders – held at irregular intervals throughout the year. The most common means by which cases came to court was as a result of indictment by the wardmote inquests. This is an indirect indication, in the absence of the original records which have mostly been destroyed, that these courts were still handling a steady stream of complaints of sexual transgression; indeed, in 1579, as part of a wide-ranging set of measures to deal with poverty, idleness and petty disorder, the city ordered that wardmote courts should be held more frequently.[20] Yet it is evident that, as in earlier times, indictment did not automatically lead to formal arraignment and trial in the Guildhall. Depending on their record and character and the gravity of the alleged offence, culprits might be allowed a more or less lengthy period of grace. Such discretion was usually exercised informally at the local level, but sometimes the express agreement of the court of aldermen was sought. Thus, in November 1559, it was decided that a man of the parish of St Mildred Poultry who had been twice indicted for 'evyll rule' should be permitted to remain there 'for a tryall of hys amendement' until Christmas, and then if he 'be founde by the wardmote inquest styll to contynewe his mysorder ... he shalbe punysshed accordynge to the lawe and clere removyd thense.'[21]

Policing at the ward level did not, of course, depend entirely on the machinery of the wardmote inquest. It remained the case that the aldermen and aldermen's deputies, on the basis of arrests made by constables and the watch and information from ordinary citizens, exercised formidable powers of summary justice. People found committing sexual offences – whether as part of the sex trade or otherwise – could be imprisoned overnight in one of the Counters and made to give bonds for their good behaviour. As in times past, they might even be summarily expelled from the ward. In a case that is well documented because malice was alleged, a goldsmith of St Katherine Cree described how in 1566 he and his wife Avice or Avys were 'called before the aldermans deputy of the ward ... [who] laide unto the seid Avys that she was a naughtie woman of her body, and ... did within a while after ... put this respondent and the seid Avys

[20] *Parliamentary Papers*, 1840, Vol. XIX, Part 1, Thirty-Second Report of the Commissioners for Inquiring concerning Charities, Part VI, p. 395; on sessions for bawds and scolds, see Archer, *Pursuit of Stability*, p. 218.
[21] LMA, Repertory 14, fo. 256r; cf. Repertory 15, fo. 516v.

out of the ward'. It was, he alleged, merely 'upon the false reporte of some of her neighbors'. In 1566, Anthony Sylver, deputy of the ward of Farringdon Without – and known to have been active in the civic purge of the years around 1550 – was himself publicly denounced to the alderman by the local constable. It was alleged that Sylver, having 'kept a hoore' in his house, had 'conveyed her away' in the time of plague (presumably 1563); she had given birth to two children by him, and he had eventually married her to his stepson. The accuser had a grudge against Sylver, but the case nonetheless shows how even people of high standing in the ward could be vulnerable.[22]

Sexual vice was to an extent also within the jurisdiction of the city of London and Middlesex sessions of the peace and gaol delivery, convened at least eight times a year. Virtually no Elizabethan records survive for the city sessions, while those for Middlesex are imperfect. But the latter indicate that there was a steady trickle of prosecutions against bawdy house keepers and occasional indictments of other sexual offenders.[23] In areas where they were active, the powers of courts leet were another resource against trouble-makers. This was true in Southwark, which despite the extension of city authority reflected in the creation of the ward of Bridge Without in 1550 still retained much of its earlier structures of policing. Between 1560 and 1562, for example, the court of the 'liberty of Southwark' expelled several female 'evil livers' and ordered men who harboured pregnant women to 'avoid' them; the penalties for failing to comply were variously stiff fines, imprisonment, the cucking stool and the cart.[24] Meanwhile, in the city, the livery companies occasionally lent a hand, usually to punish errant apprentices.[25] At an even more basic and informal level, householders in both London and the suburbs used physical correction against errant or recalcitrant servants and apprentices as a matter of course. Household

---

[22] LMA, DL/AL/C/011/MS09056, fo. 35v; DL/C/210, fos. 13v–15v.

[23] John Cordy Jeaffreson (ed.), *Middlesex County Records (Old Series)*, 4 vols. (London, 1886–92), Vol. I, pp. 35, 67, 89 and *passim* (selected cases); Vol. II, pp. 247–87 (numerical analysis of 'true bills' on the surviving rolls).

[24] LMA, CLA/043/01/016, fos. 262v, 276r, 281v, 282r, 290v; see also Lambeth Archives, Class VI/4, fo. 11r. Local courts presumably continued to operate in Westminster also, but their records have not survived. Sampling of the Queen's Bench indictment files indicates that a stream of prosecutions for keeping bawdy houses in Westminster and elsewhere in Middlesex continued to be brought, but on nothing like the scale of the early sixteenth century. Policing in Westminster was soon to be strengthened by the creation of the Court of Burgesses by act of parliament in 1585: see J. F. Merritt, *The Social World of Early Modern Westminster: Abbey, Court and Community, 1525–1640* (Manchester, 2005), chap. 7.

[25] Steve Rappaport, *Worlds within Worlds: Structures of Life in Sixteenth-Century London* (Cambridge, 1989), pp. 208, 209.

discipline was indeed supposed to be the bedrock of the well-ordered commonwealth, though in practice it was no doubt highly imperfect.[26]

Paradoxically, the highly innovative activities of the Bridewell court in the 1560s and 1570s are best understood in relation to these highly *traditional* means of combating idleness and vice.[27] To an extent, the work of the governors was in effect a delegation of a part of the power of the court of aldermen, some members of which always had a place on the board. More generally, it is noticeable from the outset of Elizabeth's reign – indeed from the last year of Mary – that the court's 'Repertories' include less judicial business than earlier, especially in relation to sexual offenders. While some cases continued to be heard there, it is evident that there had been a shift of focus. Sometimes, indeed, the aldermen explicitly referred cases to the new institution, or shared the handling of cases with the governors. Thus, in late April 1563, the court of aldermen ordered Katherine, the wife of a certain William Staunton, accused of 'myslyving', to spend a week in the Counter and then to be removed to Bridewell 'to be examined and ordered according to her desartes'. Within a fortnight she was back, along with her husband, having meanwhile been 'lawfully atteynted of bawdrye before Sir Martyn Bowes knight and alderman ... and other the governors of the said howse'. In accordance with their order, the couple were now ordered to be carted round the city and then recommitted to Bridewell to be whipped.[28] The handling of this matter was in full compliance with an order of September 1560, which specified that cases requiring public punishment should be referred back to the court of aldermen to authorize the execution of the sentence.[29] But it is doubtful whether this scrupulous policy was always adhered to. As will be seen, in the early years of Elizabeth's reign Bridewell quite frequently had recourse to the public shame punishments that hitherto had been the preserve of the court of aldermen.

But much of what the Bridewell governors did was not so much a substitute for the work of the court of aldermen as a systematization, extension and reinforcement of policing activities at ward and street level. More particularly, Bridewell was there to patch the rents in the over-stretched fabric of household discipline. Primarily, it offered a means of dealing with vagrants and others who were – or imagined to be – outside

---

[26] But for its limitations, see Archer, *Pursuit of Stability*, pp. 215–18.

[27] Cf. Penny Tucker, *Law Courts and Lawyers in the City of London, 1300–1550* (Cambridge, 2007), p. 315.

[28] LMA, Repertory 15, fos. 232v, 240r.

[29] LMA, Repertory 14, fo. 372v; see also Griffiths, *Lost Londons*, pp. 238–9.

the effective confines of the household. In addition, it offered support to householders who felt themselves threatened by unusually recalcitrant or transgressive servants or apprentices or who simply wished for a more severe and formal punishment to be imposed on such as had committed misdeeds within their gates. Finally, it tried to bring to book householders and householders' wives who were not merely failing to keep order but were *themselves* involved in sexual transgressions or actively promoting them. Even passive support or mere compliance was viewed as a criminal dereliction of duty by the governors of Bridewell, as indeed was the connivance of servants within these 'disordered' households.

The Ethos of the Bridewell Governors and Their Agents

Further insight into these priorities may be obtained through a close look at proceedings in sample years. The focus of succeeding paragraphs is therefore on 1560, the first full calendar year for which records survive, and 1575, immediately before the governors attempted their ill-fated drive against bawdy house keepers and their clients. The record kept during that campaign provides an important point of comparison. On the basis mainly of evidence from their wills, Archer argues that at least six of the most active governors in 1576–7 were 'puritans', the implication being that their zeal was motivated by committed Protestantism.[30] Godly intent is also indicated by the presence of religious language in the Bridewell registers at this time, usually at the point where accused individuals submitted themselves to the court and craved favourable treatment. Thus Richard Watwood, confessing numerous charges of 'bawdrye and whoredome', protested that 'he is verye sorrye and cryeth God mercye hartely for yt and hopeth that God of his mercye will forgeve hym and desyreth this worshipfull courte to be good and mercyfull unto hym and consider his estate for his creditt sake and his wyfe and childe upon hope of his amendment.' Similarly, a 'stranger', Cornelius Nollett, lamenting that the numerous temptations on offer made it 'harde that a man should be honest here', confessed 'that indeede by intysinges of evill persons he hath offended God with dyverse evill women' and offered to pay £10 to the relief of the poor 'to spare his ponishment for this tyme'. One case seems to embody a comment by the scribe or examining governor. The lengthy confession of an apprentice, John Dowgill, concludes: '[H]e sayeth upon his fayth that all the faltes and follyes he hath heretofore done to this daye and according to his promyse

---

[30] Archer, *Pursuit of Stability*, pp. 253–4.

to me faythfully made I hope he will amend his former lewde lyfe which I pray God geve hym grace so to do.'[31]

Prima facie the same religious inflection is to be expected in the record for the sample years. Some of the governors involved in the campaign of 1576–7 were already on the bench in 1575. If it is hard to determine the deeper religious identities of the most active, including the alderman Sir Alexander Avenon and Thomas Gardener, the treasurer, it is at least clear that Bridewell at this time had close connections with the city Recorder, William Fleetwood, whose Protestant commitment is not in doubt. An associate of William Cecil and also linked with the earl of Leicester – he featured as his 'mad recorder' in *Leycester's Commonwealth* – his hostility to Catholics was as evident as his zeal for order. The record for 1560 was apparently written by Richard Grafton, whose Protestant credentials extended back to the 1530s, when he assisted Thomas Cromwell in the printing of the English Bible. His initials are liberally scattered throughout the pages of the Bridewell register, and he sometimes refers to himself directly in the text.[32]

Occasionally, the religious prejudices of the governors did manifest themselves, as in 1560 when a woman was accused, among other things, of 'kepyng of a nomber of stynkyng bones and other toyes for reliques, in the which she put affiaunce and worshipped theim'.[33] But overall religious language is much more sparingly used in the two sample years than in 1576–7; in fact, there was only one case where sexual transgression was explicitly condemned in such terms and that by one of the defendants. Accused in 1575 of being part of a confederacy of servants and apprentices to leave their masters and flee overseas, and also of having sexual relations with the wife of a complaisant waterman, Fulk Mounslowe begged the governors 'to suppresse and put downe the hospitalitie of the saide John and Jane [Harding], which allureth and entyceth many yonge men to their utter ruyne and decay, not onelie in expendinge and consumynge their goodes and good name, but also entisinge them to suche inconveniensies that are and be abhomynable and detestable before the face of God'.[34] Even in this language there is little to distinguish it from the kind of moral rhetoric that had been current for generations among city of London

[31] BCB 3, fos. 96r, 115r.
[32] Archer, *Pursuit of Stability*, p. 43; P. R. Harris, 'William Fleetwood, Recorder of the City, and Catholicism in Elizabethan London', *Recusant History*, 7 (1963–4), 106–22. On Grafton, see *ODNB*.
[33] BCB 1, fo. 101v.
[34] BCB 2, fo. 222v, cf. fos. 183v, 187r, 194v. (All references to BCB 2 are to the modern archival numbering.)

authorities. Certainly in neither year was the language of the Bridewell court books conspicuously *Protestant*.

The same is true of the bulk of the language of these records. The terms 'adultery' and 'fornication' – the stock in trade of clerical moralists – were used very sparingly, while 'incontinence', an ecclesiastical court commonplace, had no place in Bridewell. The harshest words most commonly used to stigmatize female sexual transgressors were 'harlot' and 'common harlot', though 'strumpet' and 'whore' were also part of the lexicon. To be sure, 'harlot' featured prominently in English translations of the Bible, but the word had a long history in the language of the street and also as an equivalent for the Latin *meretrix* in fifteenth- and early sixteenth-century civic records. It is true that earlier the term 'harlot' had sometimes been used not only of women but also of men – with the general meaning of an unprincipled or immoral person, whether in a sexual or a non-sexual sense – whereas in Bridewell by 1560 it referred solely to sexually transgressive women. But this narrowing of signification reflected a broader change in usage and cannot be used to demonstrate either the egregious godliness of Bridewell governors or that the text of the Bible ran always in their heads.

Other terms had even less of a biblical resonance. Habitual male sexual transgressors were roundly condemned as 'whoremasters' or – a term that in these records often, though not invariably, carried a sexual charge – simply as 'knaves'. Again, once someone had been identified as a 'knave', it required no great stretch of the imagination to assume that he was in fact a 'whoremasterly knave', an 'idle knave' or a 'base rogue'. Condemnation slid easily from term to term, and the combinations were endless. Again, this was street language, yet the Bridewell governors resorted to it freely without, apparently, any sense of inappropriateness or need for restraint. Other words of the street and everyday moral condemnation, applied to both men and women, included 'naughty', usually with a sexual meaning, and 'lewd' and 'wanton', the latter perhaps the less condemnatory but both broader than the merely sexual. Heinous deeds were described, in roughly ascending order of turpitude, as 'shameful', 'base', 'filthy', 'wicked' or 'abominable'. Again this was a language that had been well established for generations and would have been instantly recognizable in the court of aldermen, the wardmote inquest or the discourse of ordinary householders in alehouse, street or market.[35]

---

[35] On the language of the Bridewell registers more generally, see Griffiths, *Lost Londons*, chap. 5.

The usual terminology for sexual congress was blunt. Males were commonly said to have had 'the carnal use' or simply 'use' of the body of females, a phrase that may have had a whiff of commerce about it, or men and women were described as having 'abused themselves'. Women, and occasionally men, were said to have 'committed whoredom'. Taken as a whole, the language of the records may be described as highly moralistic but not in any obvious way reflecting specifically Protestant commitment. This is consistent with the fact that the governors of Bridewell, though they initiated some cases themselves, were dependent on a vast range of individuals and agencies to bring to their attention the bulk of offenders. The single most important group of agents was aldermen's deputies trying to keep their wards clean and decent; some of these were themselves governors of Bridewell, but many were not. Other accusers included aggrieved masters and mistresses; on occasion, parents or other relatives; outraged spouses; pregnant women trying to get men to accept responsibility for the plight they were in; diligent watchmen, constables, and other local officers, sometimes backed up by scandalized neighbours; sometimes Middlesex justices, the city sheriffs, or the Recorder; and occasionally the exalted figures of city aldermen or even the lord mayor.[36]

Certainly some of these individuals were committed Protestants: Thomas Mowntayne, for example, a married clergyman deprived, imprisoned, and threatened with loss of life under Mary, but in 1560 parson of St Pancras, sent in his maidservant 'suspected to be a myslyvver', whereupon she was committed to labour till discharged on 'hope of amendment' some two months later.[37] But it is implausible to imagine that all the agents of prosecution were animated by a common Protestant purpose or indeed any other confessional commitment. What did unite them was adherence (or at the least lip service) to the civic morality that for many generations had underpinned action against sexual transgressors. As an institution, Bridewell Hospital was new, and as will be seen, some of its procedures for ascertaining the truth were highly distinctive. The severity with which it treated large numbers of offenders was also novel. But the underlying principles for action were not. That said, there were some developments as

---

[36] These impressions are backed up by close analysis of the record for 1560 and 1575. Sources of referral were only occasionally made explicit in the first volume of minutes (1559–62); information is fuller in the second volume (1574–6) but still very incomplete. For this reason, the material does not lend itself to precise quantitative analysis.

[37] BCB 1, fos. 49r, 67r. For Mowntayne's own account of his 'troubles', see John Gough Nicols (ed.), *Narratives of the Days of the Reformation* (Camden Society, Old Series 77, London, 1859), pp. 177–217.

Table II.I *Charges Brought against Individuals for Sexual and Sex-Related Offences in Bridewell, 1560*

	M	F	Total
Harlot, whore, etc.	—	98	98
Harlot and bawd	—	13	13
Prenuptial sex	6	4	10
Illicit pregnancy/paternity	8	5	13
Other fornication/adultery	39	15	54
Incest	2	2	4
(Attempted) buggery	3	—	3
Other (attempted) child sexual abuse	7	1	8
Victims of such abuse	1	3	4
Abuse of 'innocents'	2	—	2
Sexual harassment	3	—	3
Bawd/aiding/complicit	23	24	47
Marriage fraud/bigamy	7	4	11
Wife beating	1	—	1
Miscellaneous	1	3	4
Total	103	172	275

time went on, as a comparison between proceedings in 1560 and in 1575 will demonstrate.

Bridewell Business in 1560

Table II.I summarizes the charges against the 103 men and 172 women brought into Bridewell for sexual or sex-related offences in 1560.[38] A few miscellaneous cases are of interest in revealing the limits of the governors' concerns. An apprentice was whipped for mockery of 'one of the officers of this citie', having hung cuckold's horns outside his house and on the door of the church on the latter's wedding day. But defamation – whether by signs or otherwise – was not a regular item of court business. Likewise, there was but a single case of wife-beating; even then the man was also accused of abusing his neighbours, a more common charge in Bridewell but not of concern here. Also unique was the case of Ellen Philpot, brought

[38] Since a few were in trouble more than once, the number of separate individuals was slightly smaller.

in 'as a person suspect of evell lyvyng for that she together with her lewde mastresse did beate their master most unhonestly upon the bare body'. The governors were clearly uneasy about this behaviour, but because 'no further matter was proved', she was discharged.[39]

The largest group of sexual offenders in 1560 – nearly 100 out of a total of 275 – were women to whom the words 'harlot', 'whore', 'strumpet' or analogous terms were applied. The great majority were described as 'common', implying an established identity and at least some involvement with the sex trade. A few were on a slippery slope leading towards that status. Ellen Wall, for example, 'accompted a harlot', claimed that a butcher had had the use of her body on promise of marriage, while Lore Style confessed that she had 'commytted whordome' with a man 'who had long bene an entiser of her to that lewdenes, and he gave her in rewarde viij pistallettes'.[40] Others on the edge of the group were women reported by their suspicious husbands on more or less solid grounds; in two out of the four cases, the wife was also accused of stealing from her spouse or planning to make off with his goods.[41]

Of the women described as 'common' harlots, a few were said to be 'kept' by particular men in long-term relationships. Such a one was Alice Deryck alias Anne Nokes of Clerkenwell, sent in by the Recorder and other Middlesex justices of the peace with a request that she should be set to labour and not delivered without their knowledge. It was said that John Bridges, a merchant taylor, had 'lyved in adultery' with her for twelve years, during which time she had borne him eight children of whom he maintained the three who were still alive. Released on recognizance to look after her children, she was again in trouble later in the year, having been found in a suspicious house in St Mary Spital. (This was probably the long-established 'house of evell rule', currently kept by one Castell, curate of St Mary Ludgate, in the precinct of St Mary's; it was mentioned in several other cases.) But there was no proof against her, and a tailor named John Rice put in bond to marry her himself and thereafter 'as moche as [in] him lyeth to maynteyn and kepe her in honesty of life'.[42]

In a few of the other cases, one or more male partners were named, though often in such vague terms as 'one Messenger' or 'one Thyggyns'.[43] Occasionally, enough detail is given to convey a clearer impression of the clientele. To judge by names, a Welsh circle seems to have formed around Margaret Jones, who had been found in the house of Florence Evance, 'an

[39] BCB 1, fos. 55v, 74r, 75r.   [40] *Ibid.*, fos. 105r, 113r.   [41] *Ibid.*, fos. 55r–v, 71r, 71v, 72v, 78r.
[42] *Ibid.*, fos. 93r, 94r, 107(*bis*)r; cf. fo. 66r.   [43] *Ibid.*, fos. 69r, 86v.

olde bawde'. She confessed that she had often been 'abused' there and named seven men: an ostler at the Three Crowns in Southwark; John Evance, 'Master Sackviles man'; Thomas Ap Robertes, 'my Lord of Arondelles man'; Davy Williams, servant of a baker called Best; John Williams, 'Kelsys man the brewer'; Richard, a servant of Lord Strange; and David Ap Edwardes, servant with a goldsmith at the sign of the Star in Foster Lane.[44]

No partners were named with most of the 'common harlots'. Either they were too numerous to mention, or the women had been taken up on suspicion or on the basis of their haunts or their lifestyle. Indeed, several were recidivists, with a history of previous appearances in Bridewell; about 15 per cent were also accused of being 'pickers' (petty thieves), 'runagates' or drunkards, while others were variously pregnant or suffering from the pox. Characteristically, they had been taken up by constables or other local officers in suspicious houses in or around London: Elizabeth Alforde alias 'Fayre Besse' was found in the Castle near Barking Church, while Anne Bailife, a 'gadder about in sondry places', confessed that divers men had abused her in the Saracen's Head at Islington. Some were described in such terms as 'straggelyng naughty packes . . . suspeciously taken in the feldes'.[45] Some of these individuals were vigorous characters, though their feistiness was not appreciated by the governors. Ellen Ronyon attracted adverse attention 'for that as a filthy harlot [she] in shamefull maner turned up her clothes and bragged of the bewtye of her filthynes'.[46] But not a few were clearly in an abject condition. Margaret Bloke, whom the matron of the hospital 'found . . . in a bawdy house', had 'the pockes and a sor legg'. Like her, Alice Mathew, 'taken in the open stretes as a common filth', was discharged because she was 'full of the pockes'.[47]

Altogether brisker was Agnes Browne, a haberdasher's wife, whom the constable had caught 'crepyng thorough a gutter wyndow' into the house of John Mosse, haberdasher, 'in her petycote and bare legged'. This suggests a degree of enthusiasm beyond the call of professional duty. Indeed, she may have been pursuing what today would be regarded as an extramarital affair, though it was insisted that she was a 'notorious harlot' who had been thrice before 'accused and found fautye'. (For his part, the man claimed 'only that he came thether to brekefast'.)[48] In truth, the taking of money for sexual services was rarely made explicit in the record for 1560, though plainly it did occur. Thus Katherine Davyes, maidservant

[44] *Ibid.*, fo. 74v. 'Master Sackvile' was presumably Thomas Sackville, later Baron Buckhurst and earl of Dorset; 'my lord of Arundel' was Henry Fitzalan, the twelfth earl; while Lord Strange is identifiable as Henry Stanley, later fourth earl of Derby.

[45] *Ibid.*, fos. 83r, 86v, 106r.   [46] *Ibid.*, fo. 107v.   [47] *Ibid.*, fos. 88r, 107v.   [48] *Ibid.*, fo. 97r.

in a house in Seacoal Lane, reported that her mistress 'did procure her unto whordom sondry tymes' with one Master Peckam and others 'and allwayes soche money as [she] . . . did get in this lewde maner . . . tooke yt to her use'.[49]

The other accusations of sexual transgression in the record for 1560 covered a very wide range. Although the main outlines emerge clearly enough, any attempt to assign them to precise categories is bound to be artificial, reflecting the fact that the governors themselves did not observe clear boundaries, whether legal or otherwise. A case of incest between brother and sister, described as 'abhomynable', and another where a woman and her brother-in-law were accused of 'most filthely' committing 'most stynkyng whordome' together stand out for the vigour of the condemnatory language used in the record.[50] As was noted in Chapter 1, cases of sex between males very rarely came before the courts. But at this stage of Elizabeth's reign – before the renewal of the 'act for the punishment of the vyce of sodomye' in 1563 – Bridewell did manage to trawl up a few cases of buggery or the attempted buggery of youngsters, including a boy of ten.[51] But these are perhaps better seen not as a separate category but among a diverse group of about twenty cases – mostly viewed very seriously by the governors – that together make sense in terms of the abuse of more or less vulnerable individuals. They included the enticement of young women away from their masters or mistresses, encouraging a sixteen-year-old boy to have sex, sundry rapes or intended rapes, the sexual abuse of young girls ranging from fourteen to eight years old and the abuse of 'innocents' – that is, mentally deficient young women. Most of the perpetrators were men or youths, and their victims, it would seem, were generally regarded as free of blame. But this was not true of all. The twelve-year-old Ellen Lewes was 'most shamefully defyled by ij Italians, namely Gasperyn and Anthony, [both] whiche . . . most filthely agaynst nature defyled . . . [her] in the fundament', as a result of which she needed medical treatment. But while the men were punished, along with the woman who had procured her, so also was the young girl herself.[52]

At the other extreme from these utterly reprehensible cases were couples who intended to get married but had simply not waited for the wedding before having sex. This was encouraged by the fact that, in London as in provincial England, it was still common for couples to enter into binding marriage contracts which made them 'man and wife before God' in

[49] *Ibid.*, fos. 63v–64r.   [50] *Ibid.*, fos. 64r, 85r.   [51] *Ibid.*, fos. 86v, 99r, 106v.
[52] *Ibid.*, fos. 64v, 65r, 65v, 71v.

372 Brought into Bridewell: Sex Police in Early Elizabethan London

advance of the church wedding.[53] In 1560, the governors seem still to have
considered such behaviour to be largely out of their purview. Thus the half
dozen cases (involving ten accused individuals) were slightly out of the
ordinary, involved unlucky circumstances, or the man needed some pressure to get him to wed. However, these cases reflect what has been
a recurrent theme in this book, that only marriage in church was accepted
as the means to form a proper union. A couple of 'notabell cutte purses'
had been taken at midnight copulating in Seacoal Lane, having been sent
to the Counter for a similar act in Billingsgate less than a week earlier.
Nonetheless, they were released 'for that they do profese to mary'.
The curate of All Hallows Staining, a man who should have set an example,
had made a woman pregnant; now they 'plighted their trouthe eche to
other to marry together' before two of the governors. A woman complained that a Welsh tailor had 'upon promes of mariage abused her body
and . . . begotten her with chyld', but he readily undertook to marry her
when called before the governors. More equivocal was the case of Margaret
Burrell, 'suspected to be a lewde woman'. She confessed that a man
variously described as a grocer or a skinner had often 'abused' her, 'promysyng her mariage'. But he was 'suspected to be a whoremonger' and so
was whipped and peremptorily ordered to marry her within a month on
pain of being banished from the ward.[54]

Everybody knew that promises of marriage could easily be made for
purposes of seduction or deceit, and some did not scruple even to go
through fraudulent ceremonies. A butcher was in trouble 'for that upon
a contract of matrimony he defyled and begat with chylde Alice Martyn'.
In the presence of six of the governors he contracted himself again,
promised to marry her as speedily as possible, and even entered bond
to perform the promise, but it appears that rather than doing so he
absconded. A woman was brought in for having 'in most lewde
maner . . . assured her selfe to sondry men to thentent to deceave theim
of soche goodes as theye have in possession', and the matter 'evydently
proved'. A tapster of the Hanging Sword in Fleet Street was accused of the
male version of much the same scam, but in his case it was concluded that
'all thinges did not apere to be true that is reported of him.' Another man
had come close to committing himself to a woman who was unaware that

[53] Many disputes relating to such contracts are recorded in LMA, DL/C/A/002/MS09056
(Archdeaconry of London Deposition Book, 1566–7). See also Laura Gowing, *Domestic Dangers:
Women, Words, and Sex in Early Modern London* (Oxford, 1996), chap. 5; Loreen L. Giese,
Courtships, Marriage Customs, and Shakespeare's Comedies (Basingstoke, 2006).
[54] BCB 1, fos. 88v, 91v, 94r, 108r.

he already had a wife alive.[55] Then there were five cases of actual bigamy, some of them involving the usual uncertainties and tangled circumstances. A freeman of the merchant taylors, employed as a cook, was unsure whether his first wife was alive. For 'thadvoydaunce of synne' he was ordered to produce a certificate of her decease or leave the city forever, and meanwhile not merely to avoid the second wife's company but also to construct a wall to separate them.[56]

Also related to courtship were some of the ten cases centring on children born out of wedlock; together they brought thirteen people to Bridewell. Several of them were maidservants hauled into court by masters or mistresses as soon as it became obvious that they were pregnant, or the male servants, apprentices or journeymen held to be responsible. Sometimes masters were accused of doing the deed. Slightly more unusual was the case of John Hollyngbrygg of St Dunstan in the West, 'fre of the clerkes' – the Company of Parish Clerks – accused of maintaining in his house a 'naughty woman' now with child. In fact, she had been with him for several years and had borne three children but would not acknowledge any of them to be his.[57] Occasionally paternity cases were strongly contested, to be resolved eventually with a formal order backed up by bonds.[58] The city had an interest in ensuring that public authorities were not charged with the maintenance of illegitimate children, but in 1560 this emerges in the records as still only a very minor concern, certainly not one of the main themes of Bridewell proceedings. Such matters were admittedly of more regular concern to the governors of Christ's Hospital, whose duties included the examination of pregnant single women to establish paternity and enforce maintenance. But there too the numbers of cases in the early 1560s were small.[59]

The remaining sex offenders – not dealt with in the preceding paragraphs – comprised fifteen women and thirty-nine men. Some of the women seem not much different from those described as 'harlots'.

[55] *Ibid.*, fos. 77v, 80r, 101r, 110r–v, 112r.

[56] *Ibid.*, fo. 76r; for the other bigamy cases, see *ibid.*, fos. 67r, 74v, 81v, 87v.

[57] *Ibid.*, fos. 67v, 68v; for other pregnancy/paternity cases, see fos. 50r, 51v, 62r, 66v, 82v, 96r, 101v, 103v, 104r.

[58] *Ibid.*, fos. 100r–v.

[59] Christopher Thomas Daly, 'The Hospitals of London: Administration, Refoundation, and Benefaction, c.1500–1572', unpublished DPhil thesis, University of Oxford, 1994, pp. 333–9; Carol Kazmierczak Manzione, 'Sex in Tudor London: Abusing Their Bodies with Each Other', in Jacqueline Murray and Konrad Eisenbichler (eds.), *Desire and Discipline: Sex and Sexuality in the Premodern West* (Toronto, 1996), pp. 87–100; Carol Kazmierczak Manzione, *Christ's Hospital of London, 1552–1598: 'A Passing Deed of Pity'* (Selinsgrove, PA, 1995), pp. 58–61, 145.

Margaret Dickson alias Germyn, for example, was apprehended in the Windmill at the Old Jewry, 'playeng the whore' with a student of the Outer Temple.[60] Then there were the usual short- or long-term liaisons between fellow servants and maidservants having sex with their masters. One of the last was the victim of a goldsmith who, having 'abused' her, 'to cloke and color the same sought by dyvers of his frendes to have her punysshed and founde fawty', principally to avoid paying her the sum of £3 6s. 8d., an award brokered 'by certeyn of his honest neghbours'. To their credit, the governors made him pay up and then let the woman go free.[61] A brewer's wife was brought in 'at the request of her housband ... suspected to use the company' of another man, while four other women – respectively, the wives of a goldsmith, a merchant taylor, a painter stainer and a clothworker – were accused of conducting extra-marital affairs. The last had 'filthely abused herselfe' with a surgeon. Another had taken advantage of her husband's absence, only to see her lover apprehended by the constable at eleven o'clock at night as he emerged from her bed. Allegedly the goldsmith's wife 'in filthy maner used herselfe unto the housbandes of ij severall women'. She had 'befor this bene warned to advoyde' the company of one of them, a cloth-worker, by the wardmote inquest, 'and yet she doth not leave yt'. Now she was also in trouble for consorting with a glasier, but since 'ther aperd no acte to be done', she was discharged.[62] These cases reveal how the mechanisms of neighbourhood watch made it extremely hazardous for women to conduct adulterous affairs. However, the numbers of such cases were small, and the governors dealt with them circumspectly, probably reluctant to intervene between husband and wife unless they had very strong grounds. The wardmote inquest and the system of informal admonition that underpinned it were more important as first lines of defence if the husband himself had (as contemporaries saw it) failed to keep his wife in check.

Of the remaining thirty-nine male sex offenders, two were described as masterless, one was a law student, nine (just under a quarter) were servants or apprentices, while most of the remainder appear to have been house-holders, including a Dutchman.[63] They were by no means all poor – indeed, some were clearly substantial citizens – and a wide range of occupations and company allegiances was represented.[64] There were a merchant taylor and four other tailors, two mercers, two haberdashers,

---

[60] BCB 1, fo. 102r.   [61] Ibid., fo. 81v.   [62] Ibid., fos. 56r, 62v, 65r, 75r, 77r, 96v.
[63] But one was described merely as having a 'chamber' near Billingsgate: BCB 1, fo. 103v.
[64] On the involvement of members of one company, see Ian W. Archer, The History of the Haberdashers' Company (Chichester, 1991), p. 124.

a draper, a silkman, two goldsmiths, two butchers, a fishmonger, a hosteller, a pinner, a fletcher and a labourer. One servant was said to have behaved stubbornly and also to have 'moost filthely abused himselfe' in his master's house in an otherwise unspecified manner.[65] Mostly the charges were more specific, and many involved named women. Indeed, more than half of the men were linked by name with women who also came before the court in 1560, though they had not necessarily been prosecuted together. (Some had been named in court and subsequently arrested.) The most striking thing about this group of men is that the majority of them were accused of sexual relations with women described as harlots or common harlots. Admittedly, some of these cases were a little more complicated than this might suggest. John Thomas of Kilburn, found in the company of a 'lewde harlot', claimed that he wished to marry her and had promised to do so after the death of his wife.[66] But many were what would nowadays be seen as serial users of prostitutes; the most inveterate of them were bitingly described as 'common whore-monger' or 'common lecher'.[67]

In line with previous civic practice – as indeed with the church courts and other tribunals – the governors punished not only sexual transgressors as such but also those who assisted them. Indeed, there was an overlap, since some women were prosecuted as both harlots and bawds, mostly on the same occasion. A further twenty-four women and twenty-three men (including one married couple) were separately prosecuted for 'bawdry' or related offences. Overall, some sixty individuals, more than a fifth of all those in trouble for sex-related offences in 1560, were implicated for aiding and abetting. The governors of Bridewell construed in this sense a broader range of activities than the court of aldermen had been wont to deal with – more compendious indeed even than the most zealous church courts before the Reformation. A haberdasher of St Sepulchre's – admittedly the husband of a notorious bawd and harlot – was even brought in on the grounds that 'he is thought to be both a cockholde and wytholde.' (A 'wittol' was a cuckold who was aware of his condition and did nothing about it.)[68] Servants were treated as culpable even if they were merely complicit in sexual transgression, aware of what was going on without informing the authorities. However, they might be let off if they turned informer once in court.[69] One Stepney ale drawer, 'suspect[ed] to be a cloker of bawdry', claimed stiffly that the sight of harlots and strangers

---

[65] BCB 1, fo. 55v.   [66] *Ibid.*, fo. 49r.   [67] *Ibid.*, fos. 50r, 86r.   [68] *Ibid.*, fo. 97v.
[69] E.g. *ibid.*, fo. 84v.

congregating in the house where he worked had 'greved and offended his conscyence', while his equally scrupulous wife, much to the displeasure of their mistress, had 'dryven from thence a nomber of harlottes'.[70] Also subject to prosecution were go-betweens and people who provided rooms in which illicit sex could take place. Another kind of assistance was attempting the rescue of women taken by the officers of Bridewell; the several men accused of this offence in 1560 included a 'master of fence', who was trying to free his wife.[71]

But the governors were most interested in hardened bawds – neatly defined in one case as 'a buyer and seller of women' – of whom many, though by no means all, were themselves female.[72] Robert Farrer, a Houndsditch carpenter, was 'suspected to kepe shamefull and filthy rule', he and his wife having 'consented to make their owne daughter a harlot, and also caused soche evell ensample to be geven in his sayd house that he gave occasyon unto ij of his children the one a boye and the other a wench of thage of xj and xij yeres to be bothe naughty together'. Anne Tuckesse, wife of a Southwark cobbler who was himself suspected of complicity, had 'filthely consented unto the defylyng of a wenche of xij yeres of age by ij severall straungers'. This was the anal rape case noted earlier.[73] Accusations like this were often 'stoutly denied', and no wonder, since the governors treated them extremely seriously and were prepared to mete out condign punishment. In 1560, seven bawds were ordered to be carted, which usually entailed banishment from London as well as 'open shame' – not to mention physical discomfort and danger – as they were trundled through the streets. Another culprit was imprisoned in the Counter; several others were expelled from London or simply from the ward in which they were living; three were whipped. Whipping within the walls of Bridewell, it would seem, was regarded as a lesser penalty than carting.

How do these penalties compare with the treatment of other offences? All four of the individuals convicted of incest in 1560 were carted; 'to receave the open ponyshment that so filthy a man ought to have', it was explained in one case.[74] Otherwise, this exemplary penalty was used only occasionally. The most notable victim was Thomas Langham, variously called fishmonger and brownbaker, who had been taken with a married woman whom he had apparently 'kept' for more than a year. He confessed his 'filthy doyng' and had in any case 'befor this tyme . . . bene accompted

---

[70] *Ibid.*, fo. 87r.   [71] *Ibid.*, fos. 95r, 96r.   [72] *Ibid.*, fo. 83v.   [73] *Ibid.*, fos. 61r, 62r, 64v, 67v.
[74] *Ibid.*, fos. 64r, 85r.

a comon lecher and . . . bene in this house for the same'. His sentence is a sidelight on criticisms of Bridewell: the governors, considering 'how slaunderous it wil be to suffer soche a notorious person to passe unponysshed, namely for that it is sayd the beggerly harlottes are ponysshed, and the riche eskape', 'with one mind' agreed to have him carted. His punishment evidently attracted considerable attention and was noted by the city diarist or chronicler, Henry Machyn.[75]

Exceptional in the opposite sense was a small group of cases, all involving men of standing, in which the culprits were allowed to avoid physical punishment by agreeing to pay fines (admittedly substantial ones), usually directed towards the building of the riverside wharf. What these cases show is that the governors, while not averse to *prosecuting* individuals of substance, were inclined to mitigate their zeal when it came to actual *punishment*. Their motives were not dissimilar to those of church court judges when they allowed penances to be commuted. In the case of Robert Wolman, for example, a mercer convicted of being 'an adulterer and comyttyng of whoredome' with a common harlot, the governors reflected that this was 'the firste tyme of his deteccion and also that he is a man of callyng in a company of moost worship and hath a good wyfe and great famelye'. Therefore 'upon his moost humble submyssion . . . after exhortacion and admonicion given for the amendement of his lyfe', they decided to discharge him on condition that he paid for a hundred feet of new wharf.[76] As a further safeguard of their credit, the names of some of these men were entered in the court book as initials only, RKG or MMM.[77]

Only slightly less favoured were men allowed to requite their offences with a penalty similar to ecclesiastical penance. A fletcher from St Botolph Aldgate, 'suspected to have kept a naughty woman in his house', confessed having sex with his maidservant 'but . . . in soche penytent and humble maner with bewaylyng of his synne that mercy was taken upon him'; moreover, his neighbours 'made most earnest sute for him'. The governors therefore ordered that he 'upon Sondaye nexte commyng openly in the parishe before the most parte of the parisheners . . . shall confesse his sayd faute and most humbly beseche theim to forgeve him and they forgevyng him his matter to ende for this tyme'. Further conditions were that he should abstain from the woman's company, and if she eventually gave birth he should give her £3 6s. 8d. 'in her pursse' and himself maintain the child.[78]

---

[75] *Ibid.*, fos.50r–51v, 52v; Nichols (ed.), *Diary of Henry Machyn*, p. 223.
[76] BCB I, fo. 91r; for similar cases, see fos. 53v–54r, 97v, 98r.   [77] *Ibid.*, fo. 54v.
[78] *Ibid.*, fos. 70v–71r.; cf. fos. 56v–57r.

378 Brought into Bridewell: Sex Police in Early Elizabethan London

Implicit or explicit in all these concessions was the condition that the culprit should henceforth 'advoyde and flye from whordom and filthynes or any soche lyke lewde lyvyng' or else to suffer 'open peyn and ponyshment'; bonds for good behaviour were commonly taken.[79] In any case, not all men were favoured, especially those who were blatant or defiant. A mercer, who had not only been 'sondry tymes admonysshed of his lewd and naughty life' but also 'advaunted and bragged of his filthynes' was committed to 'close prison with a payr of fetters of iron'. Likewise, another man, 'for his lewde stoutnes and wantones, consumpcion of monye and accompanyeng of harlottes', was punished 'in irons'. A hosteller at the Cross Keys, Gracechurch Street, 'accused to be a common whormonger', was whipped as well as being ordered to pay forty shillings towards the new wharf.[80] More particularly, men guilty of offences that the governors regarded as especially despicable – child abuse, for example, or breaches of trust such as seducing a master's daughter – could expect little mercy. A man convicted of buggery was 'whipped openly in the pillory' by order of the lord mayor.[81]

Fines, carting, the pillory, iron fetters and the like were relatively unusual penalties. So also was whipping, reserved in these early days of Bridewell for the more serious and reprehensible cases of sexual transgression. It was used more regularly for non-sexual offenders, but even so only about one in three men and one in four women accused of vagrancy, petty theft and the like were whipped. It was in fact only in the middle decades of the sixteenth century that whipping was becoming established as a regular part of the repertory of judicial punishment, and it is in this context that its relatively sparing use by the early Elizabethan governors of Bridewell needs to be understood.[82] This background also helps to explain the outrage expressed by some of the early victims of Bridewell whippings, which appear to have been of a judicial level of severity – as opposed, say, to corporal punishment inflicted in schools and households – even if they were administered within the walls of the 'house'. In 1560, Margaret Grenewood, a painter's wife, complained bitterly that she had been 'whipped untyll she might torne her fynger in her fleshe'.[83] The majority of sexual offenders, whether men or women, were simply detained in Bridewell for periods ranging from a few days to several months

---

[79] *Ibid.*, fo. 57r. [80] *Ibid.*, fos. 70r, 86r, 108r. [81] *Ibid.*, fo. 99r.
[82] Martin Ingram, 'Shame and Pain: Themes and Variations in Tudor Punishments', in Simon Devereaux and Paul Griffiths (eds.), *Penal Practice and Culture, 1500–1900: Punishing the English* (Basingstoke, 2004), pp. 52–8.
[83] BCB 1, fo. 95r; see also Griffiths, *Lost Londons*, p. 14.

before being released – sometimes into service or on bond for good behaviour or other condition. Some may have been detained for longer, though this is difficult to establish. Presumably all the inmates were kept at work, but some were specifically said to be 'committed to the labour of the house' or 'committed to the mill' – the latter seems to imply punitive hard labour. A widow of Clampard's Alley, 'taken in comyttyng of whoredom' with a man whom she refused to name, was committed to work specifically 'to tame her', 'for that she was a fatte cranke quene and well able to labour'.[84]

To summarize, the activities of Bridewell were deeply rooted in well-established civic traditions of restraining vice – indeed, much of what the governors did would have been as familiar to the magistrates of, say, Exeter as they were to the aldermen and common councillors of London. The new institution did make it possible to discipline larger numbers of individuals on a systematic basis, while the availability as penal options of a combination of incarceration, forced labour and corporal punishment greatly increased the intensity of discipline – even though whipping was used quite sparingly at first. Many register entries do not specify from which part of London the case originated, but there is enough information to suggest the main patterns. Cases were drawn quite widely from the city and its immediate environs, but most came from peripheral areas and the suburbs, including Southwark. The wards of Aldersgate and above all Farringdon Without, to the north west and west of the city, were most in evidence. To be sure, these areas were close to Bridewell itself. But they were also populous and close to the thoroughfares leading to Westminster. Precisely the same area had generated by far the greatest number of cases in the commissary court in the late fifteenth century. Of the various categories of offender that Bridewell dealt with, those deemed to be 'harlots' and their 'bawds' were most likely to come from the peripheral areas and the suburbs. Men accused of adultery, whoremongering and the like – some of whom were undoubtedly of substantial wealth – were more likely to live in the central business quarter of the city.

Bridewell Business in 1575

Comparing the record for 1575 (Table 11.2) with that of 1560, these solid citizens from the central parishes are less in evidence. Otherwise the topographical distribution of cases – as far as it is revealed by the record –

---

[84] BCB I, fo. 93r.

Table 11.2 *Charges Brought against Individuals Present in Court in Bridewell for Sexual and Sex-Related Offences, 1575*

	M	F	Total
(Accused with) common harlot	6	74	80
(Accused with) harlot	8	14	22
(Accused with) whoremaster	7	3	10
Prenuptial sex	18	16	34
Illicit pregnancy/paternity	34	41	75
Kept/keeping woman	9	6	15
Wicked company/companying with harlots	2	6	8
Use/abuse of another's body (i.e. illicit sex)	42	50	92
Suspicious company/behaviour	7	9	16
Attempting chastity	1	—	1
Indecent exposure	1	1	2
(Attempted) child sexual abuse/victims	2	3	5
Other sexual misbehaviour	1	2	3
Bawd/aiding/complicit	28	24	52
Marriage fraud/bigamy	9	3	12
Slander/false accusation	5	5	10
Miscellaneous	3	—	3
Total	183	257	440

was recognizably the same, except that riverine locations in the wards of Castle Baynard, Queenhithe, Vintry, Dowgate, Bridge Within and Billingsgate were now somewhat more in evidence, as also were the eastern suburbs in Stepney parish and the increasingly notorious locations of Turnmill Street and St John Street in the rapidly expanding northern suburb of Clerkenwell. In many other respects, the features of the new regime of sexual regulation revealed by the record for 1560 were simply present in accentuated form in 1575. It is immediately obvious that the number of sexual offenders being dealt with had increased sharply – from about 275 in the earlier year to about 440 (183 men and 257 women). In addition, there were another sixty or more named individuals (about twice as many men as women) who featured among the culprits in 1575 but, for one reason or another, appear not to have been physically present in court. Establishing exact totals is impossible because of the way cases were handled. Individuals were brought into court, examined, detained or sometimes temporarily released, only to be brought into court again and further examined – sometimes on several occasions. Meanwhile, other individuals whom they had implicated, or against whom related charges had been made, were brought to court in turn, as also were informers, witnesses and occasionally whole groups of neighbours or other interested parties. It is sometimes not easy to say when one case ended and another began. In other words, this was a highly inquisitorial system in which the governors sought actively to winnow out the facts, striving to uncover as much as they could about any given set of circumstances and to apportion guilt and innocence.

The record sheds vivid light on the methods used by the governors to discover the truth.[85] Assiduously, they searched for discrepancies in the stories they heard and carefully weighed the evidence, even when it was merely hearsay. Perhaps they knew the story of Susannah, whose innocence Daniel had demonstrated by examining her accusers, the two elders, one by one and showing that their testimony differed; perhaps they just used their common sense.[86] Rich and Bullocke, accused of bigamy, said his first wife was 'an evell woman of hir bodie' and had not been with him for seven years, but her examination revealed that they had been together recently 'so that by circumstances of examynacion he is proved to be an evell person'.[87] The approach of the court was also highly sceptical of any denial, with a marked tendency to assume guilt on merely circumstantial grounds. Thus Anne Watson was 'greatelie suspected by the governours by reason of hir fondnes in attire'.[88] More striking was the practice of deliberately confronting accusers and accused. Already in 1560 it was common to find individuals who first denied the offence brought to the point of confession when their sexual partners or well-informed witnesses 'avouched to their face' the facts of the case. By this means, even men of wealth and standing found themselves convicted on the word of common harlots, including long-term denizens of Bridewell.[89] By 1575, the method had become systematized and was in routine use. For example, when Alice Swingles appeared 'uppon suspicion to be a harlott of hir bodie', she at first denied that any 'ill persons' resorted to her or that any evil had been committed in her house. However, the alderman's deputy gave evidence against her, while her twenty-two-year-old apprentice and a twenty-year-old maidservant delivered their testimony 'before hir face'. One of her supposed clients then offered telling evidence about goings-on in her house and on her

---

[85] See also Griffiths, *Lost Londons*, pp. 247–51.   [86] 'Apocrypha, History of Susanna', verses 48–62.
[87] BCB 2, fo. 204v.   [88] *Ibid.*, fo. 116v.   [89] E.g. BCB 1, fos. 50r–v, 85r, 86r.

denial was 'called before hir face to face'. Other witnesses were also produced, with the result that Swingles crumbled and submitted herself to the governors.[90]

Differences in the pattern of cases in 1575 compared with 1560 may be understood partly in relation to these thoroughgoing investigative practices, which facilitated the prosecution of both partners in sexual transgression. In 1575, numerically fewer women, and proportionately far fewer, were simply accused of being 'common harlots'. Even adding in those who were spared the epithet 'common' but nonetheless referred to as 'harlot', the number remains smaller than in 1560. The 'harlots' tended to be accused of offences with named men, as indeed were some of those labelled 'common', and they were really part of a wider category, a huge range of suspected sex offenders investigated by the governors in which the focus was sometimes on the men, sometimes on the women, but overall showing no great bias for or against either sex. These involved cases of men 'keeping' women for more or less lengthy periods, sometimes as virtual concubines. 'Keeping company' with harlots was another category; somewhat similar was the case of a woman warned henceforth not to keep 'wicked companie' or 'rune from hir frendes'.[91] Cases of suspicious behaviour were various. One man had to explain why someone was found locked in a chest when the watch came to search his house. Another was 'taken ... verie suspiciouslie in a poore mans howse ... sittinge by the ffier, and one which he saieth sholde be his wiffe ... who he hathe kepte heretofore as a harlotte'.[92] A small number of men, but more than in 1560, were accused of being whoremasters.

There remains a large number of cases where the basic charge was that men and women had 'abused' each other's bodies or men had had the 'use of the body' of particular women. A few examples will illustrate the extraordinary variety of circumstances that the governors uncovered, though not all cases were as convoluted as these. A subordinate of the Knight Marshal – an officer with jurisdiction over offences committed within the royal household and the twelve-mile 'verge' that surrounded it – complained that his wife had committed adultery with his manservant. The latter confessed both to this and to a relationship with another woman but accused the complainant of having sex with her also. All four had become infected with a sexually transmitted disease. The wife also accused her husband of fathering a child on yet another woman, who was brought to court to give her side of the story. In another case, a householder became

[90] BCB 2, fos. 150r–151r, 152v.   [91] Ibid., fo. 177r.   [92] Ibid., fos. 192r, 202v.

acquainted with a woman at supper with 'the earle of Worcesters man' at the Bell in Newgate Market. He took her home, and over a period of about a week he and four other men had sex with her, including a three-in-a-bed scenario on one occasion. The householder's manservant was also implicated. After a long spell in Bridewell, one of the men, a bookbinder, finally fulfilled his promise to marry the woman.[93]

If these cases are redolent of extremely flexible moral standards, others are more equivocal and testify to the difficulties and hazards of conducting an extramarital affair. Mary Daie of Whitechapel recounted how her neighbour James Forman attracted her attention from the street as she sat at work in a window. 'I have had a good mynde to the[e] a good while this twelmoneth and more,' he declared, 'and I colde never speake with thee till nowe.' Circumstances were briefly propitious: her husband was out 'a shootinge', Forman's wife had gone into London and his 'folkes' were in his garden drying clothes. It seems that Mary Daie had a reason for seeking solace outside her marriage, since he promised to get her with child. At any rate she agreed to have sex; the couple subsequently met at an alehouse to discuss a place of meeting, and she appointed the house of Joan Jackson in Houndsditch and persuaded her to allow them to use a room. Two weeks later they met as arranged, and twice more in subsequent months; each time Forman gave Mary Daie sixpence which she passed to Jackson. But the couple were observed by neighbours, who reported the matter; the enraged Forman denounced them as 'an alley of evell neighbours'.[94]

Other differences between 1575 and 1560 are evident. Although in some respects the governors still had scant regard for legal niceties, they were now quite careful to respect the jurisdiction of other courts. Thus they decided not to proceed in a case of incest 'for that the matter toucheth not this howse but the civell [i.e. ecclesiastical] lawe'.[95] Similar scruples may also explain why there were now no cases of buggery, again a statutory felony since 1563,[96] though instances of the sexual abuse of young girls – some of which could no doubt have been indicted as rapes – did occasionally crop up.[97] Cases of marriage fraud and bigamy were also proportionately fewer. While bigamy was not to become a felony till 1604, one of the

---

[93] *Ibid.*, fos. 91r, 91v, 93r, 93v, 95r, 112v, 133v.   [94] *Ibid.*, fos. 96v–97r, 98r, 103r, 106r, 107r–v.
[95] *Ibid.*, fo. 167v.   [96] 5 Elizabeth I c. 17.
[97] By an act of 1576 (18 Elizabeth I c. 7), all cases of sexual intercourse with girls under ten were to be treated as rapes without benefit of clergy: see Martin Ingram, 'Child Sexual Abuse in Early Modern England', in Michael J. Braddick and John Walter (eds.), *Negotiating Power in Early Modern Society: Order, Hierarchy and Subordination in Britain and Ireland* (Cambridge, 2001), p. 66.

five instances of this offence was referred to the bishop of London's chancellor, which again may indicate respect for other jurisdictions.[98]

Cases of antenuptial sex, where one or both the parties claimed to be 'sure' or intent on marriage, were not proportionately more numerous in 1575 than in 1560. But though they were variously treated according to circumstances, on the whole they were now viewed less tolerantly. Increasingly, the governors acted on the principle – by no means new but hitherto often ignored – that wedding must come before bedding. Two cases will illustrate the framework of constraint in which they arose. A maidservant stayed out late, met a man in Billingsgate, hid him under her bed after surreptitiously introducing him into her mistress's house and then spent the night with him. In court, they both said that they were 'sure', and he affirmed that he would marry her when he next came home from sea. For this 'wickednes', both were whipped. A woman of St Giles in the Fields was 'broughte in by the baliffe, constables and other neighbours' for sleeping with a tailor 'contyneweallie for iij weekes together last past savinge two nightes'. Her maidservant testified against the couple, who claimed they were 'sure'. The man was bound over both to solemnize the marriage shortly and 'not at anie tyme in the meane tyme kepe companie with ... [her] unlawfullye', and both were whipped for good measure. Presumably the neighbours thought that in this case the licence allowed to courting couples was sliding towards cohabitation and took a firm stand that was in turn supported by the Bridewell governors.[99]

Cases involving pregnancy and paternity were strikingly more numerous in 1575 than they had been in 1560. Some involved highly dubious circumstances or had moral dimensions beyond the mere fact of illicit pregnancy. Cecily Steadman, recently married to a shoemaker, complained that her child was begotten by Sergeant Aldersaie, 'one of Master sheriffes officers' in the house of William Goodderidge; she claimed that she had been inveigled into the act – many times repeated – by Goodderidge's wife, who urged her to take an abortifacient when she fell pregnant. Goodderidge had informed the shoemaker that the child was Aldersaie's and she was 'an arrante whore', whereupon he 'put hir awaie' until the governors persuaded him to take her again.[100] In another case, a servant denied having sex with a young woman who later proved pregnant. According to her story, he 'required good will of hir, and that she wolde

[98] BCB 2, fo. 154r. Most of the other bigamy cases had arisen in areas remote from London, so it may not have seemed appropriate to refer them to Dr Hammond: *ibid.*, fos. 141v, 142r, 144v, 147r, 160v, 204v.
[99] BCB 2, fos. 100v–101r, 199v–200r.   [100] *Ibid.*, fos. 198v–200r, 201r–v.

consente to him, and he wolde marrie her'. Apparently suspicious of his intentions, she had asked, 'Howe maie wee live, for I am a poore mayde and have nothinge?' The court was particularly scandalized by his response, to the effect that both his aunt and his uncle 'wolde not live longe, and then he was suer of his landes and goodes'. But later the woman named other men as the father. In this case the governors persisted with their interrogations throughout 'the tyme of hir correction', using the whip not merely for punishment but as a means to establish the truth.[101] Yet tangled cases like this were exceptional. Most were the usual run of illegitimacy cases, where men who had got a woman with child were reluctant, or unable, to 'make hir amendes' through marriage.[102] The increased numbers since 1560 reflected the early stages of the Elizabethan baby boom.

Some offenders had been sent from, and likewise a few were referred back to, Christ's Hospital, which by now was itself handling a significant number of paternity cases – over forty in 1575.[103] In Bridewell as in Christ's, many cases were resolved by compelling the presumed father (or his relatives or master) to enter sureties to save the city from charges; in some, the man undertook to marry the woman, either of his own free will or after some persuasion. But whereas the governors of Christ's Hospital rarely ordered any kind of additional punishment, between a fifth and a quarter of the offenders brought to Bridewell – rather more women than men – were whipped. Such treatment foreshadowed the provisions of the act of 1576, which empowered justices of the peace to examine the circumstances of bastard births in cases where the child was likely to become chargeable and to impose punishment at their discretion. It was of this act that Recorder Fleetwood commented, 'th'example wherof will do muche good here in London.'[104]

Indeed, the rigorous punishment of culprits was a marked feature of all categories of Bridewell cases in 1575. Admittedly, the governors themselves eschewed public carting as a punishment – this was left to the court of aldermen and the justices in sessions – though they did occasionally send culprits to the Counter to be tried 'by order of lawe'.[105] They also sometimes threatened to have egregious offenders sent to Newgate as rogues or

---

[101] *Ibid.*, fos. 104v–105r, 151r, 153r–v.   [102] *Ibid.*, fo. 153v.

[103] *Ibid.*, fos. 139r, 154v, 163r, 181v, 193r, 193v (sent from Christ's Hospital), 116v, 123r, 218r (sent to Christ's Hospital); paternity cases dealt with in Christ's Hospital in 1575 are recorded in LMA, CLC/210/B/001/MS12806/002, fos. 118r–140v.

[104] Thomas Wright (ed.), *Queen Elizabeth and her Times: A Series of Original Letters*, 2 vols. (London, 1838), Vol. II, p. 64.

[105] BCB 2, fo. 149v. In 1577 two men were given the choice either to pay a large fine of £24 each (to buy two lighters for the use of the hospital) or 'to ride in a carte according to the lawe': BCB 3, fo. 146v.

(more commonly) whipped about the city 'at a cartes arse'.[106] Another ploy was to warn culprits that if they were brought in again they could expect to receive 'a hundred stripes' – a terrifying level of punishment.[107] However, the governors were not utterly obdurate. Some culprits were spared because they were sick, others because they seemed repentant; many were eventually discharged 'on hope of amendment'. The court also had an eye to the desirability of keeping married couples together. After extensive investigation, John Holgate's wife admitted having an illicit relationship with an apprentice tailor. She desired 'mercie and favour of the governours', who thereupon pardoned her 'for that she is a mans wiffe and they lothe to breake howsholdes'.[108] But such favourable treatment was hardly to be looked for. A large proportion of offenders were ordered to receive 'correction', a euphemism for what was evidently a severe whipping.

In association with informal action by aldermen's deputies, the annual meetings of the wardmote inquests, privy searches, regular policing activities conducted by local constables and centring on the Counter prisons, proceedings before the court of aldermen in the Guildhall and action by the London and Middlesex justices, not to mention proceedings in the church courts, the work of the governors of Bridewell undoubtedly represented by any reasonable standard a tight system of sexual regulation and one which from the point of view of individuals must have seemed at least intermittently terrifying. Plainly much premarital and extramarital sexual activity nonetheless went on. But anyone who engaged in such pursuits did so at considerable risk and at the least had to be extremely circumspect. Particularly for the less well off, especially for women but also for men, getting caught out could have drastic consequences. In such circumstances, those concerned with law enforcement might well feel that the system was by no means ineffective. After a particularly vigorous drive against vagrants, masterless men and other disorderly elements in January 1582, Recorder Fleetwood went about London and 'found not one rooge stirring'.[109] In the early part of Elizabeth's reign, it is not inconceivable that the governors of Bridewell may occasionally have felt the same complacency about harlots and whoremasters.

Yet, it is easy to see why around 1575 both the governors and the city fathers more generally felt that there were dimensions to the problems of sexual regulation that were both growing in seriousness and escaping their

[106] E.g. BCB 2, fos. 127r, 154v, 159v.   [107] E.g. *ibid.*, fos. 87r, 116v, 121r, 132v, 141r.
[108] *Ibid.*, fos. 165r, 166v, 167r, 167v.
[109] Wright (ed.), *Queen Elizabeth and Her Times*, Vol. II, p. 166.

attentions. Again comparing the record for 1575 with that for 1560, it is striking that numbers of cases of aiding and abetting had grown very little and as a proportion of the total had markedly *decreased*. Many of those netted were small game, servants accused of complicity with the sexual transgressions of their masters or mistresses or such individuals as goodwife Joan Jackson of Houndsditch, who allowed James Forman and Mary Daie the use of a chamber and 'in the meane tyme . . . wente for a pott of ale'.[110] There were some intimations of a regular sex trade. Of Rachel Rogers it was said that 'she wolde go to the dore and if she sawe anie men she wolde call them in, and aske them if they wolde go uppe into the chamber, and burne a cople of fagottes and then abuse themselfes together.' Premises in Holborn were said to be the resort of such notorious whores as Jane Trawse, Mistress Breame, Mary Painter and 'mannye harlottes and other yonge gentlemen'; it was even reported that a secret passage, scarcely big enough for one to squeeze through, had been made for conveying away suspect persons when the house was searched.[111] The proprietor, John Hollyngbryg, 'gentleman' was transferred from Bridewell to the Middlesex sessions, where he was indicted both for keeping a brothel and for being himself an adulterer and fornicator; on his confession, he was sentenced to be carted.[112]

There were also indications of the involvement of high-status people in the market. Hollyngbryg, it was said, 'weareth the Lorde Ambrose liverye',[113] while the name of Master or Captain Carowe recurs several times in the record for 1575. Among other things it was alleged that he had sent Elizabeth Humphrey 'a paire of corcked slippers and willed hir to hier . . . Katherine [Price], and that he wolde give the saide Katherine xls. a yere, and the saide Elizabeth hir howse rente free' on condition that she 'sholde kepe hir for his owne use'. (As a result, Katherine Price became infected with a venereal disease and was later reported as being in Bedlam.) Dorothy Cleveley of St Clement Danes was accused of 'wickedlie' betraying her servant, a widow, into the predatory hands of Master Edmund Verney. According to the victim's own account before four members of the wardmote inquest of Farringdon Without, she had been tricked by a promise of being taken to service. Instructed to 'washe hir ffeete [and] to putt on a cleane smocke', she was taken by a 'preist' to a chamber near the Whitefriars, where she received 4s. and the promise of a petticoat in

---

[110] BCB 2, fo. 96v.   [111] *Ibid.*, fos. 142v, 207r.
[112] Jeaffreson (ed.), *Middlesex County Records*, Vol. I, p. 95 cf. above, p. 373.
[113] BCB, fo. 142v. 'Lord Ambrose' presumably refers to Ambrose Dudley, though he had been created earl of Warwick in 1561.

return for spending the night with Verney – who was indeed careful to inspect her feet beforehand.[114]

The governors had heard stories of this sort many times before – as indeed had the court of aldermen in previous generations. One of the first cases recorded in the surviving Bridewell court books in 1559 concerned 'a yong mayde' conveyed by boat to Durham House. A waterman had rescued her, 'havyng compassion of the wenche who lamented and bewayled the matter, sayeng she was betrayed' by a tailor named Thomas Hall. By the woman's own account, she was talent-spotted by a Spaniard, who bargained with Hall and his wife to procure her for forty crowns. When she proved unwilling, Hall – who was subsequently carted for this offence – told her 'thou art a very foole, he is a goodly gentleman and will geve the soche a reward as maye bothe do the and us good.' When 'in thend' she consented, she was taken to the Blackfriars to the house of one who 'there striped her and . . . pu[t] upon her all freshe and gaye gere with a muffeler of velvet' in preparation for the client, who was none other than the count of Feria, Philip II's representative in England.[115] Of a different stamp was Ellen Remnaunt, repeatedly in Bridewell as a 'lewde woman',[116] but she likewise had tales to tell of a network of contacts to procure women for men in high places. In October 1559 she described how on last being released 'she departed the same nyght to the goodwife Taverner inhabityng in the Grene Arbour in the Lytle Bayly, and she conveyed her unto Long Megg at Westmynster, and then she conveyed her by water unto the prince of Swethyn, who had the use of her body all night'. Presumably this was Duke John of Finland, emissary of Gustav Vasa on behalf of his eldest son Eric for the hand of Queen Elizabeth.[117]

London had never been simply a trading and manufacturing community. Its premier status among the towns of England; its close proximity to the royal court, to sittings of parliament and to the law courts at Westminster; the increasing attraction of the metropolis to the nobility and gentry – all these circumstances gave it a special status and ensured that there would always be a demand for sexual services from high-placed

---

[114] *Ibid.*, fos. 179v–180v, 208r, 209v.

[115] BCB 1, fos. 4r–5r; on Feria, see M. J. Rodríguez-Salgado and Simon Adams (eds.), 'The Count of Feria's Dispatch to Philip II of 14 November 1558', *Camden Miscellany XXVIII* (Camden Society, 4th Series 29, London, 1984), pp. 306–9.

[116] But it is interesting to note that in 1562 she proved attractive to the son of the matron of Bridewell, who defied the governors' attempts to stop him consorting with her and eventually promised to marry her: BCB 1, fos. 200r, 210v.

[117] BCB 1, fo. 42r; on the Swedish embassy, see Susan Doran, *Monarchy and Matrimony: The Courtships of Elizabeth I* (London and New York, 1996), pp. 30–1. On Long Meg, see Chapter 9.

people and their hangers-on. Some of these – foreign merchants or members of ambassadors' households – took for granted a sexual regime a great deal more flexible than the one that ordinary Londoners were used to. Even in English society, not all courtiers, aristocrats and gentry, however much they might pay lip service to Christian morality, expected those strictures to apply to themselves. Nor, crucially, did many of their retainers and servants. In other words, the principles of the sumptuary laws prevailed. What was reprehensible in the poor was the prerogative of the rich and powerful, and their retainers and servants felt that in this respect, at least, Jack was as good as his master. To take a more modern perspective, what the governors of Bridewell uncovered in the middle years of Elizabeth's reign was a situation reminiscent of Prohibition. They had sought to eliminate sexual vice by criminalizing it and imposing harsh sanctions on those they caught stepping out of line; the effect had been to spawn an underworld.

It is easy to see why in 1576–7 the governors of Bridewell, with what they no doubt saw as the solid achievements of the past fifteen years under their belts, felt confident enough to launch an assault on this other world of sexual transgression. It is equally plain to see why they failed. But, more fundamentally, within a few years they were facing a set of changes of a completely different order, which were ultimately to prove overwhelming. The population of England, stagnant till the 1520s and subject to many dislocations in the mid-Tudor years, was by now in a period of sustained growth. Even more so was the population of London, or rather the metropolitan area, comprising not only the city but also Westminster, Southwark and the northern and eastern suburbs. By 1603, the population of this vast area was to exceed 200,000, creating a very different social and cultural context for the exercise of sexual regulation. The shift into that new world will be traced in the final chapter of this book.

CHAPTER 12

Regulating Sex in Late Elizabethan Times
Retrospect and Prospect

It has often been assumed that serious efforts to restrain illicit sexual behaviour by means of legal sanctions were a post-Reformation phenomenon. Ruth Karras, for example, has characterized fifteenth-century measures against prostitution as 'halfhearted attempts at eradication, combined with large dollops of regulation including both harassment and fiscal intent', concluding that 'fundamental attitudinal change, including increased social control and the regulation of male as well as female sexual behaviour (especially among the lower classes), did not come until the late sixteenth century.' In contrast, Faramerz Dabhoiwala, as prologue to his study of the *decline* of the legal regulation of sexual behaviour in the eighteenth and nineteenth centuries, paints an entirely different picture. He asserts that by 'the later middle ages, extra-marital sex had come to be continually policed by a dense network of jurisdictions'; indeed 'the main trend over time was towards ever-tighter control and punishment of non-marital sex, by secular and ecclesiastical authorities alike.' The idea that sexual regulation was fundamental to the social order was in fact 'over-determined', in the sense that 'many different patterns of thought underpinned sexual discipline and were invoked in its justification.'[1]

The latter view derives from the most recent research and is undoubtedly closer to the truth, yet itself begs many questions. The purpose of this book has been both to refute the first approach and to offer a more precise and nuanced picture than the second by examining in some detail the pattern of sexual regulation in London and provincial England in the century or so from the late fifteenth to the late sixteenth century: the courts concerned, the agencies involved in working them (including the local interests on which they heavily depended), the pattern of prosecutions, the

---

[1] Ruth Mazo Karras, *Common Women: Prostitution and Sexuality in Medieval England* (New York and Oxford, 1996), pp. 23, 137; Faramerz Dabhoiwala, *The Origins of Sex: A History of the First Sexual Revolution* (London, 2012), pp. 9, 11, 27.

jurisdictional conflicts that sometimes arose, the occasional institutional innovations and – no less important but far less easily explicable or even detectable – the numerous gradual changes and developments in procedures and punishments. An effort has also been made to determine what the people who used these legal procedures thought they were doing, not merely in terms of the grand ideas that underpinned public policies but also the more pragmatic reasoning that led individuals or groups to mount prosecutions and informed the decisions of judges and other officials in their handling of the cases that came before them. All these issues have been related to the underlying patterns of sexual transgression – as far as they can be discerned – and how they changed over time. If less attention has been paid to such issues as sexual identity, this is because they are extremely elusive in the sources on which this study is based.

Retrospect

Inevitably, it is a complex story, but the main conclusions are plain.[2] Already in the fourteenth century, if not earlier, the church, through its network of local courts, was attempting to enforce Christian sexual morality, while London and many provincial town governments were also claiming some jurisdiction over sexual transgressors. Owing to poor record survival, the extent and intensity of these efforts are hard to evaluate. But by the late fifteenth and early sixteenth centuries, the agencies of legal regulation were unquestionably highly active, albeit spasmodically so. In rural areas, manor courts were occasionally involved in sexual regulation. Justices of the peace may also have played some role, though since this was largely informal it has left few traces. The church courts were by far the main agents of discipline. But in the larger towns and cities, such as Leicester, Nottingham, Colchester and Exeter, the efforts of the church courts were often paralleled by those of secular courts, acting on the basis of royal charters or simply local custom.

In the metropolitan area, the pattern of sexual regulation was exceptionally complex. In Southwark, behaviour was policed by a mosaic of manorial jurisdictions as well as by the courts of the bishop of Winchester. Westminster was a special case. The abbey had its own courts, while large numbers of prosecutions against brothel keepers were mounted in the court of King's Bench. Secular jurisdiction over sexual

---

[2] The following paragraphs summarize the main arguments of previous chapters. For the most part, references are given only when a particular historian is named or new information is introduced.

offences was most elaborately organized in the city of London. Its three-tiered system included regular searches at ward level, backed up by a ubiquitous and often prurient neighbourhood watch, leading to the temporary imprisonment of detected offenders and summary expulsion at the discretion of the local alderman; formal presentments, on at least an annual basis, at wardmote courts; and exemplary action by the court of aldermen, taking the form of intermittent prosecutions against egregious individuals and occasional drives directed against whole swathes of offenders. The most notable of these purges before the Reformation was in 1473, though there were bursts of activity, along with some innovations in procedures and the presentation of punishments, in the 1510s and 1520s. The London church courts were also exercising jurisdiction over sexual offenders. At least in the late fifteenth century, they were astonishingly active in terms of numbers of prosecutions – far more so than their counterparts in rural England or the ecclesiastical courts in contemporary Paris.

To think of these activities simply in terms of a response to disorder, or 'controlling misbehaviour', is insufficient and in some respects misleading – important though these ideas are in helping to explain the developing symbiosis between the ecclesiastical and secular courts and local society. Powerful ideologies underpinned the work of all the courts and helped to shape the pattern of their business. Much of the work of the church courts represented an attempt to impose on the laity a version of the discipline and authority that it aspired to exercise over the clergy. The fact that clerical discipline – in particular, the obligation to live a celibate life – was still in some respects unfinished business complicated matters. But the project, while ambitious, was by no means wholly unrealistic and clearly capable of attracting support among lay people. In modern terms, the framework of sexual regulation was resolutely heterosexual. Same-sex activities, which nowadays are assumed to be quite widespread and are by many taken for granted – albeit discountenanced by certain religious organizations and still the target of hostility from some groups – were in theory strongly condemned but in practice largely ignored. If they were repressed, it was by silence rather than by active persecution.

In the period before the Reformation, the church was mainly concerned to get lay people to respect the institution of marriage. This made sense for many ordinary people, for whom marriage and household were institutions of prime economic, social and personal significance, the framework within which gender identities were expressed and offspring were born and brought up. Hence the courts and local people alike had an interest in prosecuting blatant adultery, as also fornication on the part of individuals who had no intention of getting married. However, amorous relations between couples at an advanced state of courtship were often winked at. As was sometimes stated explicitly in their records, the church courts acted 'in favour of marriage'. Secular courts were more directly concerned with matters that impinged on public order, especially prostitution. But there was a powerful overlap with the church courts' work since households were seen as the fundamental units of local government. Beyond this, when borough and city courts intervened in the sphere of sexual regulation, they were often making some kind of statement. To an extent this might imply criticism of the ecclesiastical authorities, if the latter were felt to be failing in their duties. It might also reflect conflicts of jurisdiction. More positively, civic authorities were bidding for the moral legitimacy that came with the successful exercise of good governance and more basically demonstrating their adherence to orthodox Catholic piety. Londoners' claims to Christian morality were particularly explicit in the language of the city courts. The rhetoric of reforming sexual manners was also an important element in the city's relationship with the crown, increasingly so in the early decades of the sixteenth century. To an extent, indeed, the city acted at the bidding of the royal government.

Yet, despite the importance of rhetoric and ideology in inflecting the language and shaping the pattern of sexual regulation, the realities of sexual behaviour on the ground were also important in determining what the courts – whether ecclesiastical or secular – tried to do and what they could and could not achieve. Compared to the situation around 1600, they had to contend with some intractable phenomena. The first was the tendency of men of substance and position, and their serving men, to maintain mistresses (in contemporary parlance, to 'keep whores') either on a live-in basis as concubines or in some convenient lodging house. In London, the same pattern extended further down the social scale. Since both married and unmarried men acted in this way, the practice overlapped with a second phenomenon, the salience of adultery in the pattern of sexual transgression. More casual and opportunistic forms of adultery, including sex with maidservants, seem to have been more widespread than they were at the end of the sixteenth century. A third feature, which again overlapped with the practice of 'keeping a whore', was a very active and quite widespread trade in sex. The Southwark stews, increasingly the subject of complaint by the early decades of the sixteenth century, were only the most visible end of this business. Illicit bawdy houses and a host of 'strumpets' or 'common women', who might or might not be permanently attached to such establishments, plied their trade in Westminster, the London suburbs and to an extent in the city itself. Most were unmarried – the term 'single woman' was often used in the sense of 'prostitute' – but some had husbands; how far the latter were complicit, or indeed actually coercive, is usually unclear. In any event, married women and widows were prominent as bawds. Women who acted on a full-time or occasional basis as prostitutes – sometimes in the guise of tapsters serving ale in inns and tippling houses – were also a marked feature of many provincial towns and cities, as were the male and female bawds who accommodated and no doubt exploited them. Even in the countryside were to be found a scattering of women whom contemporaries identified as 'common whores'.

Since members of the clergy were prominent among the clients of prostitutes, these phenomena overlapped again with a fourth striking feature of illicit sexual practice in the decades around 1500 – clerical immorality. If fewer than 5 per cent of the clergy in any given jurisdiction were annually brought in question for incontinence, this was nonetheless a significant minority, and the cumulative impact of the associated scandals was considerable. This was particularly so in London, where the civic procedures for dealing with sexually immoral clergy, established in the late fourteenth century, were designed to ensure maximum publicity. Such was the power of these procedures and the popular glee and venom unleashed when offenders were brought to book, that even innocent priests – or so they claimed – were vulnerable to entrapment scams, violence and extortion.

In trying to deal with clerical immorality, the ecclesiastical authorities were in a dilemma. Certainly they did not condone it; on the contrary, many bishops, archdeacons and church court officials were strongly committed to the ideal of clerical celibacy and eager to enforce it as much as they could. However – as in the case of child abuse in the modern church – they were wary of compromising the reputation of the institution as a whole. No doubt in some cases, moreover, they were also reluctant to let what might be a single lapse destroy the career of men who were otherwise good priests. More basically, they were aware of the frailty of the flesh. In the late 1520s, the London vicar-general's court dealt with egregious cases with a severity that was no doubt designed to be exemplary, but elsewhere and at other times the record appears much patchier. It is doubtful if any degree of severity was adequate to assuage popular fury and distrust. This is why, when the crown seemed to turn against the power and privileges of the clergy in the 1530s, the issue of clerical immorality proved so inflammatory.

Attitudes towards the sexual transgressions of lay people and the views of those who transgressed are more difficult to decipher. Karras is one among a number of historians who suppose that some people, or particular groups, lived lives that were more or less self-consciously at odds with the prevailing ethic that all sexual activity outside marriage was illicit.[3] This is most plausibly so in the case of the 'single' or 'common' women of Southwark, Westminster and a few other places, since they and the men who supported and managed them were clearly stigmatized as inveterate traders in sex. But we do not really know how they saw themselves, and as was seen in Chapter 5, some of them did their best to stay within the Christian community by receiving the Eucharist – even though the church officially denied it to people of their profession.

It would seem that most other women, single or married, who sold their bodies or otherwise engaged in extramarital sex did so surreptitiously and tried to maintain a façade of respectability in the face of the constant threat of being denounced as a whore by outraged, hostile or merely spiteful neighbours. We know little of the circumstances and motives that led some women to enter into long-term relationships as 'kept' women or concubines, but there is little sign that such arrangements were a preferred option to the legal certainty and social status of marriage. Despite the fact that some of them persisted for years on end, there is likewise little indication that such relationships were regarded tolerantly by neighbours – apart from those who provided lodgings or otherwise benefited directly from the arrangement.

On the whole, men had less to lose than women from engaging in illicit sex and could therefore more openly defy or simply ignore the church's strictures. But they were by no means immune from censure – especially if they occupied positions of authority – and the derogatory label of 'whoremonger' or 'whoremaster' was clearly one that men wished to avoid. It was noblemen, gentlemen and their servants and other men of similarly high status who were most likely to assume that the usual strictures against fornication and adultery did not apply to them. In other words, they behaved as though sex was subject to the sumptuary laws. Nonetheless, some were targeted for prosecution, especially by the London church courts. Interestingly, a number of high-profile cases of sexual transgression

[3] Ruth Mazo Karras, *Unmarriages: Women, Men, and Sexual Unions in the Middle Ages* (Philadelphia, 2012).

involved physicians. No doubt their privileged access to women's bodies was a source of temptation. Moreover, steeped as they were in the Galenic tradition, some of them may have seen sex more in terms of physical need than of morality. Their neighbours, however, may have been especially outraged by what they saw as a betrayal of trust.

Whether the church was too soft on the sexual sins of the laity was no doubt a matter of opinion. There may well have been pious lay people who aspired not only to live a life of rigorous personal morality themselves but also to use all the means they could to compel others to do so and felt that existing procedures and sanctions were inadequate. More generally, it is plausible to suppose that many ordinary people found the sex trade and its associated disorders an annoyance and wished for stricter measures to be taken against it; some may have resented the hypocrisy implicit in the behaviour of men of higher status who 'kept whores'. But, as far as can be seen, these issues attracted little debate or overt criticism before 1529, so it is hard to know whether they contributed in any significant way to a sense of unease that the church was not altogether living up to its ideals. The situation in London is a possible exception. As noted earlier, in the late fifteenth century, church court prosecutions were very numerous indeed, yet there were relatively few convictions, and public penance was rare. It is hard to imagine that those who favoured strict morality were satisfied with this state of affairs. Unless it is an optical illusion caused by loss of records or shifts in the pattern of business between courts, numbers of prosecutions were far fewer in the decades after 1500. Perhaps this change was a sign of disillusionment or dissatisfaction with the church courts, though it may simply have represented an adjustment to more administratively manageable and socially acceptable levels of prosecution or a shift in disciplinary focus away from sexual transgressions towards matters of heresy.

With the benefit of hindsight, it is plain that both in the metropolis and elsewhere, ecclesiastical zeal for reform of lay people's sexual transgressions, if it had not actually diminished, was at least taking less harsh and intrusive forms around 1500 than it had a century earlier. In the fourteenth century, penances imposed for sexual offences had often involved the public whipping of the penitent round the church or at the four corners of the churchyard. These practices persisted in some areas into the late fifteenth century, but by the early sixteenth they were rare. Another form of severity, public penance in the market of a major town, still persisted, but only on a very occasional basis to mortify egregious offenders, especially those who had been defiant of ecclesiastical authority. Even when more lenient penances were ordered, they were very often commuted into a money payment or the performance of private pieties. It may be that the church, consciously or otherwise, was willing to temper rigour for the sake of compliance. But in the late fifteenth and early sixteenth centuries, the secular authorities – with the partial exception of the city of London – also tended to restrict severities against sexual offenders. In some provincial boroughs and cities, it was in principle possible to parade offenders round the town or even expel them from the community. In practice, money fines – less humiliating and divisive – were usually preferred, though sometimes they were imposed on an escalating basis, and it would be a mistake to underestimate their cumulative bite.

But this moment of leniency was a fleeting one. Well before the Reformation, there are signs of the revival and extension of harsher attitudes towards punishment. This trend may be traced in many sources but emerges with particular clarity from the records of the city of London. Civic penalties against offenders of various kinds, including sexual transgressors, were already robust. But from the early years of the sixteenth century there is evident a clear tendency to supplement traditional shame punishments (often linked with short periods of imprisonment, so already there was a physical element) with measures designed to inflict a measure of pain or, at least, bodily discomfort. Partly this was a matter of extending the practice of corporal punishment, already very common in the home, school and workplace, to the judicial sphere. Of course, this involved an increase in severity – public whipping on the bare shoulders rather than the application of birch rods to the buttocks. But other penalties were also in evidence, including ducking in water.

A major stimulus was the growing problem of homelessness and the migration of the poor, which contemporaries perceived as vagrancy. Vagabonds were thought to have no shame, so the only way to deter them was by physical correction. Contemporaries' perception that numbers of vagabonds were on the increase could only reinforce this attitude. The link with sexual offenders was a straightforward one, since vagrants were generally thought to be promiscuous, and in particular, it was assumed that female vagrants would sell their bodies for cash, food or lodging. Even well-heeled prostitutes and those who abetted them were considered to be harbingers of misery. They tempted servants and apprentices to misappropriate their masters' goods and married men to misspend resources that should have been used to maintain their wives and families. This powerful linkage between sexual transgression and poverty, idleness and waste, forged in what was already a rapidly expanding metropolis in the early sixteenth century, was to have profound consequences in the future.

The broader context was the spate of governmental and religious reform begun in the 1530s, driven not only by practical concerns but also by new visions – partly stimulated by continental developments – of what might be possible in a well-ordered, godly commonwealth. The Henrician Reformation had far-reaching effects, intensified by the much more thoroughgoing Protestant Reformation under Edward VI. Following the submission of the clergy, the breach with Rome and the establishment of the Royal Supremacy, the entire jurisdiction of the church courts was brought into question. Indeed, it was seriously proposed that much of their business, including the punishment of sexual offenders, should be transferred to the secular courts. In the event, this wholesale shift of jurisdiction was not attempted. Instead, the disruptions of the 1530s and 1540s, and the atmosphere of uncertainty that they generated, temporarily corroded the morale of the church courts. Less is known about their activities than would be desired – for example, from 1529 there is a large gap in the London commissary court records, while survival of church court records of this period in the provinces is very patchy – but in areas where records are extant, it is clear that the numbers of disciplinary cases had fallen sharply by the 1540s.

In the absence of fundamental reform sponsored by the state, did the secular courts de facto take up the slack – as they might easily have done in the cities and boroughs that exercised jurisdiction over sexual offenders? In the short term there is little sign that they did, or at least not consistently – as is perhaps hardly surprising amid the bewildering changes of the late 1540s and 1550s. But in London, an escalation of civic discipline did occur, resulting in a series of events that deserves to be better known as a striking episode of the English Reformation. The trend began in the 1530s and intensified in the 1540s. A notable milestone was the suppression of the Southwark stews by royal proclamation in 1546. Protestant pamphleteers and preachers, such as Henry Brinklow, Thomas Lever and Hugh Latimer, insistently linked religious Reformation with moral reform. They had a powerful means of leverage. For generations, city rhetoric had denounced sexual vice, while the complex of civic institutions that existed to combat it was a permanent reminder of the city's aspirations in this sphere. The reformers had therefore simply to challenge the mayor, aldermen and citizenry to live up to their own ideals. In the reign of Edward VI, Archbishop Cranmer and Nicholas Ridley, bishop of London, helped to goad the mayor and aldermen into action. At the grass-roots level there was clearly enthusiastic support from at least some sections of ordinary London society. The result was a moral purge, comparable with similar episodes on the continent, remarkable not only for its intensity – especially at its peak in 1550 – but also for its duration from the last weeks of Henry VIII's reign in 1547 to his son's last days in 1553. Even in Mary's reign it had not entirely fizzled out, despite disputes over jurisdiction between the ecclesiastical and city authorities and the determination of the crown to shift the focus to the restoration of Catholic doctrine and worship.

A permanent legacy of this crucible of moral reform was the establishment of Bridewell Hospital in 1553 – a highly distinctive element in the complex of city hospitals, including also St Bartholomew's, St Thomas's, Christ's and Bethlem, that were founded or re-founded to attend to the physical and moral state of London's poor. Bridewell undoubtedly represented the most striking institutional innovation in the sphere of sexual regulation to emerge in the period surveyed here. But, paradoxically, innovation owed much to tradition. Historians have debated whether the ideas that underpinned the working of Bridewell owed most to Protestant zeal, humanist reform programmes or direct observation of on-the-street needs. But the notion that the 'idle poor' extended to sexual offenders of all sorts, the massive (though not exclusive) emphasis on this kind of transgression in the early decades of Bridewell's existence and the extraordinarily draconian powers that its governors wielded – these remarkable features are best seen in the context of the city's long-established policing powers. The regime of sexual regulation administered by wardmote inquests and aldermen's deputies, supported at the local level by beadles, constables and neighbourhood watch, and at the apex of city government by the lord mayor and court of aldermen, continued to operate throughout Elizabeth's long reign. But Bridewell in effect took over some of this work and also strengthened the system by acting as a forum for the examination and punishment of offenders.

Historians have stressed that from the start Bridewell's powers were questioned and continued to be so throughout the reign of Elizabeth. It is likewise well known that when the governors made an unprecedented attempt, in the winter of 1576–7, not merely to clean up the network of bawdy houses in the city and suburbs but also to prosecute their clients, they found themselves opposed by entrenched vested interests, backed in some cases by powerful courtiers. The resulting collision exposed the limits of their powers. Yet, an equally striking impression from the records of the 1560s and 1570s is the enthusiastic support that Bridewell received from many local people. This was not merely a top-down regime of moral discipline but one that tapped into powerful grass-roots concerns and raw emotions. Among both the governors and deputies who headed the institution and drove its activities and the local officers and ordinary people who brought offenders to them, there were undoubtedly some committed Protestants. But this cannot have been true of all, and it is striking that – except fleetingly during the campaign of 1576–7 – there was little in the language of Bridewell's court minutes that was distinctively religious, far less specifically Protestant.

Nor was it the discourse of civic virtue in any exalted sense. It was in fact language more redolent of the streets and ordinary households, the outraged and frequently self-righteous tones of individuals – whether masters, mistresses or servants – who saw themselves as 'honest' folk who not merely disliked the opprobrium, disorder and occasional violence of brothels and disordered households but, more basically, bitterly resented the behaviour of individuals who failed to conform to – or, worse still, actually showed contempt for – a tight moral regime centred on marriage and household. Such voices had been heard in the London streets and wardmotes for generations, but the sympathetic ear that they could expect from the Bridewell governors made them even shriller. It seems inescapable that this stifling moral regime must have generated enormous tensions even among its strongest supporters, and on this view, the sometimes savage hostility to sexual offenders evinced by 'honest householders' – or by servants eager to snitch on errant masters and mistresses – was a displacement of their own frustrations or a temporary reversal of their everyday lack of power. But Shakespeare said it better:

> Thou rascal beadle, hold thy bloody hand.
> Why dost thou lash that whore? Strip thy own back.
> Thou hotly lusts to use her in that kind
> For which thou whip'st her.[4]

Regrettably, only a fragment survives of the records of London's ecclesiastical courts in the early decades of Elizabeth's reign. It is therefore impossible to gauge accurately the relative importance of the spiritual jurisdiction in handling cases of metropolitan sexual transgression. The indications are that in the early 1560s the church courts were hearing only a few straightforward cases of illicit sex and concentrating instead on bigamy and unlawful separation. For a moment the term 'bawdy courts' was perhaps a misnomer. Yet, within a decade, cases of fornication,

---

[4] *King Lear* IV.6.

adultery and the like were again on the increase. But whatever the situation with regard to numbers of cases handled, self-evidently Bridewell's hand was by far the heavier in terms of the punishments meted out. London was, of course, exceptional. Setting aside a few other major urban centres, elsewhere in Elizabethan England sexual regulation still depended over-whelmingly on the church courts. This fact represented a major element of continuity. Yet, at the beginning of the reign, what the courts could and could not do, and what form they were to take, were by no means set in stone.

Some of the issues, especially initiatives associated with the 'hotter sort' of Protestants or self-styled 'godly' (soon to be stigmatized by critics and opponents as 'puritans'), are well known to historians and have usually been seen in terms of failure. Thus parliamentary efforts to introduce the death penalty for adultery, in line with Mosaic law and current practice in Calvin's Geneva, did not succeed. The attempt in the parliament of 1571 to revive the Edwardian *Reformatio legum ecclesiasticarum* – a revised body of canon law appropriate to a Protestant church, including strict penalties for sexual offences – likewise foundered. More general proposals for a radical restructuring of the existing church courts, to make them conform with the model of Protestant 'discipline' that the godly favoured, also came to nothing. It has generally been assumed that in the early decades of the reign, the church courts on the ground were struggling, even if the parlous state of the diocese of Gloucester is now seen as atypical. The creation of the courts of High Commission has sometimes been seen as both sympto-matic of this fragility and inadvertently a cause of further weakness. Even historians who reject this view – such as R. H. Helmholz and indeed the present writer – and emphasize rather the resilience of the church courts have tended to identify the middle years of Elizabeth's reign as the key period of revival, when new brooms began to sweep in ecclesiastical court registries.[5]

This book has drawn attention to creative developments in ecclesiastical discipline in the 1560s and 1570s – important not merely in institutional terms but also in modifying the relationship between the courts and local communities and altering the contours of sexual regulation. The strength-ening of the visitation system was an essential means of enforcing religious change. One of its effects was to transform the shape of disciplinary court

---

[5] R. H. Helmholz, *The Oxford History of the Laws of England*, Vol. I: *The Canon Law and Ecclesiastical Jurisdiction from 597 to the 1640s* (Oxford, 2004), p. 290; Martin Ingram, *Church Courts, Sex and Marriage in England, 1570–1640* (Cambridge, 1987), pp. 13–14.

business, vastly increasing the numbers of prosecutions for such offences as not attending church or failing to receive the communion – not to mention outright 'recusancy', or refusal to participate, which also came to be prosecuted in the secular courts according to the terms of a growing battery of penal statutes. Despite this new tilt in the pattern of business, prosecutions for sexual and marital offences continued to be brought in considerable numbers. But the fact that the bringing of charges was increasingly the responsibility of churchwardens meant that they were even more likely than in pre-Reformation times to be filtered through parochial interests.

Documents associated with the convocations of the 1560s and 1570s, including the canons of 1571, reflect debates about other changes in ecclesiastical discipline. Moves towards a more congregational focus, emphasizing the duty of churchwardens to warn and admonish errant parishioners before taking matters to court, complemented the new stress on visitations. The nature and purpose of public penance also came under scrutiny. Work had already been done in the reign of Edward VI to bring the penalty in line with Protestant doctrine and liturgy, abolishing its association with procession and doing away with the carrying of candles; these changes were now re-effected. Beyond that there were clearly several different strands of thinking that were not altogether consistent with each other. One was to make penance more severe. Ideas of reviving penitential whipping or assimilating penance with the civil penalty of carting found in towns and cities fell foul of the hardening common-law doctrine that the penalties of the spiritual courts should touch neither life, limb nor property. More viable was to increase the element of public humiliation by the greater use of penances performed in the marketplace. But such penances had already been in occasional use before the Reformation and were revived in some places in Mary's reign, so the practice was not distinctively Protestant. It was probably also recognized that severity and publicity in themselves were not necessarily conducive to true and heartfelt contrition and repentance. Indeed, they could be counterproductive, either by nourishing resentment in the sinner's heart or simply by deterring the culprit from submitting to penance at all. Hence another line of thinking was to make sure that penances – whatever their precise form – were sincere and that the culprit was brought to a state of true repentance. Initiatives and experiments reflecting all these lines of thinking can be traced in many dioceses and archdeaconries in the 1560s and 1570s.

Where good records survive for the years around 1570, as in the archdeaconries of Chichester and Leicester, the church courts can be observed fighting resolutely on several fronts. At a basic level they had to oversee the maintenance of church buildings and other ecclesiastical property, to make sure that churches were properly furnished and equipped to perform the liturgy laid down in the new *Book of Common Prayer* and to keep the clergy up to the mark. They also had to work hard to promote the advance of Protestantism by encouraging qualified clergy to preach, making sure that parishioners absorbed the basics of Christian doctrine by learning the catechism and enforcing at least minimum standards of church attendance and participation in the Holy Communion. Remarkably, they still had time to combat sexual transgressions. The effectiveness of the courts and their precise pattern of business varied somewhat from area to area depending on local conditions and the vigour and efficiency of ecclesiastical officials. On the whole, the impact of the courts was neither dramatically more or markedly less than before the Reformation. Rather, the pattern was shifting somewhat. There was still considerable emphasis on adultery and disordered households, but increasing attention was being paid to courtship patterns leading to marriage, premarital sex and illegitimate births.

In part, this was a consequence of the greater reliance on visitations as a source of information and hence on parochial perceptions and concerns. Also important was the changing demographic situation, as marriage rates rose and the Elizabethan baby boom got under way. But the changing pattern also reflected a gradual but eventually marked shift in people's behaviour. 'Common women' were less in evidence, and it seems that concubinage arrangements or maintaining 'kept women' had become less acceptable. Though the processes are hard to trace, it is likely that these changes were encouraged by the religious and moral reappraisals of the Reformation years. Clearly, the hierarchy of the reformed church was keen to associate Protestantism with strict sexual morality, albeit within a frame of reference that, despite the fact that it was no longer counted among the sacraments, in practice venerated the institution of marriage even more than it had been before.

More broadly, Protestant rejection of the Catholic idealization of virginity and abandonment of compulsory clerical celibacy led to a new ethic that, on the one hand, extolled marriage and, on the other, promoted the ideal of Christian chastity as something that was required of all Christians, whether men or women, lay people or clergy. In an expanding market for print, these ideas were promoted not only by the official homilies on 'the state of matrimony' and against adultery and all other 'whoredom and uncleanness' but also in the burgeoning genre of household conduct literature. Within this new framework, by the late sixteenth century the clergy themselves were undoubtedly in a position to set a firmer example. It is true that clerical immorality was not swept away altogether so that (for example) F. G. Emmison's search of church court records for the county of Essex for the whole of Elizabeth's reign turns up a variety of unseemly examples. But undoubtedly Ralph Houlbrooke's comment for the dioceses of Norwich and Winchester has general application: what had been 'the most prominent disciplinary problem on the eve of the Reformation, now became one of the least important'.[6]

More tangible than changes in the moral climate in the countryside was a decline in the sex trade in provincial towns. The Alice Tapsters, Maud Tapsters and their like who had serviced men in inns and ale-houses in the late fifteenth century had largely disappeared by the time of Queen Elizabeth. Part of the reason was a shift in the organization of the manufacture of and trade in ale and beer that gradually gave women a less prominent role. But the change was also parcel of a broader complex of developments that made sixteenth-century urban magis-trates increasingly sensitive to issues of 'order' – a word that resonates through the municipal records of the period – and correspondingly determined to impose and maintain it by firm action. The regulation of the drink trade, the gradual development of workable systems of poor relief, measures against vagrancy and the tightening of regulations governing apprenticeship and other kinds of service were important dimensions of these initiatives. They enjoyed a reasonable measure of success because they could command widespread support and because they were underpinned by statutory developments that gave them a firm legal foundation.

The use of borough and city courts to prosecute people specifically for sexual misbehaviour was a more complex issue. The general tightening of the bonds of order argued also for stricter measures against fornicators and adulterers, especially as these transgressions sometimes had links with poverty, vagrancy, alehouse-haunting and other offences. From a more transparently religious viewpoint, firm measures against sexual offenders were no doubt advocated by many town preachers. The simultaneous appearance (or re-appearance) of carting as a penalty against sexual offen-ders in many provincial towns in the 1560s likewise suggests widespread interest in innovation in modes of punishment. The outcome depended on

[6] F. G. Emmison, *Elizabethan Life: Morals and the Church Courts, Mainly from Essex Archidiaconal Records* (Chelmsford, 1973), pp. 218–25; Ralph Houlbrooke, *Church Courts and the People during the English Reformation, 1520–1570* (Oxford, 1979), p. 183.

circumstances. In Nottingham, the borough court largely withdrew from this area of jurisdiction, tacitly ceding sexual regulation to the ecclesiastical courts. But many boroughs and cities, ranging from small country towns such as Devizes (Wiltshire) to major trading and manufacturing centres such as Colchester (Essex), or to a busy regional capital like Exeter (Devon), witnessed determined drives against sexual offenders, targeting not merely such common women and bawds as were still involved in the sex trade but also individual fornicators and adulterers, including on occasion men and women of substance and standing. The elaborate spectacles that were devised to punish those found guilty, characteristically involving carting and rough music and sometimes culminating in summary expulsion from the town, must have occasioned a considerable local stir. Some offenders – usually the less well heeled, especially if they were immigrants or had in other ways laid themselves open to charges of vagrancy – fared even worse, suffering the penalty of the lash in addition to the other indignities.

But the high-profile nature of these punishments, together with the fact that they relied for their justification on borough or city charters or simply local custom, laid them open to challenge. Individual victims, especially the better off, could appeal to the higher authorities of King's Bench or the High Commissioners, or to local episcopal administration, claiming that civic bodies had exceeded their jurisdiction and arrogated powers of punishing sin that rightly belonged to the ecclesiastical authorities. By the 1570s, the puritan challenge to the ecclesiastical hierarchy had made such matters an extremely sensitive issue at the highest political levels; any exercise of jurisdiction that seemed to combine spiritual and secular powers was suspect as incipient presbytery. The scotching of the order of Northampton and of the arrangements for 'godly discipline' attempted at Bury St Edmunds is well known. But, as the examples explored in this book reveal, the impact was much more widespread. Civic jurisdiction over sexual offenders was increasingly subject to challenge in middle to late Elizabethan England. Where it was well entrenched in local custom, as at Colchester and Exeter, it did survive, but it had to be deployed selectively and circumspectly. It no longer burgeoned and flourished as it had in some urban centres early in the reign. A firm, enduring and unchallenged alliance between magistracy and ministry – the exercise of complementary jurisdiction over the whole range of sexual offenders by church courts and borough or city courts – emerged in relatively few places. Of the examples explored in this book, the borough of Leicester most closely fits that model.

In sum, how should these complex changes – a cluster of trends, adaptations and experiments rather than a single shift or event – be seen in relation to two of the big issues of the sixteenth century – religious change and the development of the English state? The main theme of this book has been that sexual regulation was not a creation of the Reformation but was nonetheless inflected by it. Protestant ideas, prefigured by humanist visions of the well-ordered commonwealth, reinforced the importance of marriage and the household family at the same time as they encouraged stricter enforcement of sexual morality, while Reformation polemics more broadly raised people's consciousness of sexual sin. Precisely because a powerful system of sexual regulation was already an entrenched feature of English society, it was relatively easy for activists to demand that the intensity of prosecutions or the severity of punishments should be ratcheted up. Yet, while the secular authorities gave intermittent support to reformation of manners, the rigorous punishment of sexual offenders never became a defining feature of the English state or a self-conscious tool of state building. The exercise of the Royal Supremacy, the failure of schemes for a common-law takeover of church court business, the judges' insistence on a clear division between the secular and spiritual jurisdictions and the rigorous oversight exercised by the royal courts over local jurisdictions – all these features of English government ensured that zealots could never have a free hand.

At the same time, a growing emphasis on statute as the ultimate basis of legal authority meant that any group that wished to increase the penalties for sexual transgressions could do so only through parliament. But the social and professional composition of the House of Commons – dominated by the gentry and including a strong common-law presence – ensured that innovations in this sphere would be accepted only after the utmost scrutiny. Hence, by the later part of Elizabeth's reign, the earlier movement to enact wide-ranging measures against fornication and adultery was making little headway. In 1576 there was a failed bill in the Lords 'for the punishment of avowtrie and incest', while in 1601 the Commons turned down a bill that would have deprived a guilty husband or wife of the rights they held in the lands of the innocent partner. In 1604 another Lords bill, 'for the better repressing of the detestable crime of adultery', got as far as a second reading but was abandoned because it was found 'rather to concern some particular persons than the public good' – perhaps Lord Rich and his wife, Penelope, *née* Devereux, whose long-standing liaison with Charles Blount, Lord Mountjoy (later earl of Devonshire) was notorious.[7] Even quite narrowly conceived measures against bastard-bearing – widely considered an antisocial offence and hence prima facie an appropriate issue for legislation – could not necessarily attract support. Thus, in 1593, a bill to empower justices to 'stock', 'whipp' and 'imprison' the parents of bastard children foundered. Among other objections, members of parliament feared that 'gentlemen or men of quality' might be 'putt to such a shame'. The only anti-bastardy measure that did become law in Elizabeth's reign was included in the 1576 act 'for setting the poor to work and avoiding idleness'. Justices were empowered to take order for the maintenance of poor bastards and, at their discretion, for the punishment of the parents. Statutory sexual regulation was thus focused on the poor.[8] As will be seen, as time went on, this was to become increasingly true of sexual regulation more generally.

Sexual Regulation in Later Elizabethan England

This concluding chapter has now completed its review of the ground covered in this book. What follows looks forward, making links with the developments from the 1570s onwards. Historians are already familiar with many of the main patterns of prosecutions in this later period. But to facilitate comparison with earlier chapters, the discussion is underpinned by analysis of disciplinary prosecutions relating to sex and marriage in the London consistory court in 1589, the court of the archdeaconry of Chichester in 1594 and the court of the archdeaconry of Leicester in 1602, together with sexual immorality cases recorded in the Bridewell Hospital register for 1600. These data are summarized in Tables 12.1 to 12.4.[9]

By now the ecclesiastical visitation system was firmly established, in London as in provincial England, ensuring that the pattern of prosecutions was largely shaped by systematic presentments from the parishes. These returns reveal many local variations, but the overall picture is clear. By the

---

[7] *Journals of the House of Lords*, Vol. II, pp. 271–3; Sylvia Freedman, *Poor Penelope: Lady Penelope Rich, an Elizabethan Woman* (Bourne End, Bucks., 1983), chap. 13.

[8] 18 Elizabeth I c. 3; another bill against bastardy failed in 1596. For the measure of 1593 and the wider context, see Joan Kent, 'Attitudes of Members of the House of Commons to the Regulation of "Personal Conduct" in Late Elizabethan and Early Stuart England', *Bulletin of the Institute of Historical Research*, 46 (1973), 49–50, 51, 53, 68; Keith Thomas, 'The Puritans and Adultery: The Act of 1650 Reconsidered', in Donald Pennington and Keith Thomas (eds.), *Puritans and Revolutionaries: Essays in Seventeenth-Century History Presented to Christopher Hill* (Oxford, 1978), p. 267.

[9] Policing in Westminster had been strengthened in 1585 by the creation of the Court of Burgesses, but no records survive of its proceedings before 1610.

Table 12.1 *Episcopal Visitation of City of London Parishes, 1589: Sex and Marriage Cases*

	M	F	HW	Defendants	Cases
Clandestine marriage:					
Principals	—	1	3	4	4
Minister conducting ceremony	1	—	—	1	1
Marrying woman to conceal illicit pregnancy	1	—	—	1	1
Bigamy	8	6	1	15	10
Unlawful separation	3	8	5	16	16
Inciting to divorce/bigamy	1	—	—	1	1
Living together unmarried	1	1	—	2	1
Antenuptial incontinence/pregnancy[a]	—	3	8	11	11
Whoredom	—	3	—	3	3
Incontinence, etc.	3	11	—	14	12
Adultery[b]	2	3	—	5	3
Fornication[c]	6	8	—	14	8
Child illicitly begotten	20	50	—	70	54
Aiding and abetting:					
Receiving/harbouring pregnant woman/women[d]	18	9	3	30	30
Receiving/harbouring other incontinent persons	10	3	2	15	15
Allowing offender to depart unpunished	20	1	1	22	22
Keeping bawdy house	2	—	—	2	2
Other accessory/to produce offender	7	1	—	8	8
Enticing women to illicit sex	1	—	—	1	1
Venereal disease	1	—	—	1	1
Multiple offences (unlawful separation, aiding and abetting, 'of very evil life himself', etc.)	1	—	—	1	1
Criticizing churchwardens for presenting antenuptial incontinence	1	—	—	1	1
Total	107	108	23	238	206

[a] Includes one case in which a couple said they were betrothed and were thereupon contracted again in court and ordered to solemnize their union.
[b] Includes two cases known to involve illicitly begotten children.
[c] Includes two cases called fornication but involving married women.
[d] One female defendant also suspected of keeping a bawdy house.

Table 12.2 *Disciplinary Prosecutions in the Archdeaconry of Chichester, 1594: Sex and Marriage Cases*

	M	F	HW	Defendants	Cases
Bigamy	1	—	—	1	1
Unlawful separation	2	2	—	4	3
Antenuptial incontinence/ pregnancy	—	—	9	9	9
Adultery	6	6	—	12	6
Bastardy/illicit pregnancy	21	28	—	49	29
Other incontinence, etc.	8	10	—	18	10
Receiving/harbouring pregnant woman	2	2	—	4	4
Total	40	48	9	97	62

Table 12.3 *Archdeaconry of Leicester, Annunciation and Michaelmas Visitations, 1602: Sex and Marriage Cases*

	M	F	HW	Defendants	Cases
Clandestine marriage:[a]					5
Minister conducting ceremony	1	—	—	1	—
Principals	1	—	4	5	—
Other persons present	9	3	—	12	—
Bigamy[b]	7	5	—	12	8
Unlawful separation	2	0	—	2	2
Antenuptial incontinence/pregnancy[c]	—	—	23	23	23
Adultery[d]	10	7	—	17	12
Fornication[e]	31	33	—	64	36
Bastardy/illicit pregnancy	17	24	—	41	28
Other incontinence, etc.	4	3	—	7	7
Aiding and abetting	4	1	—	5	5
Total	86	76	27	189	126

[a] One case also involved antenuptial fornication.
[b] One case also involved antenuptial fornication.
[c] Includes two cases in which the couple solemnized marriage after commencement of proceedings.
[d] So described or inferred from marital status of either defendant; one case is known to have involved illicit pregnancy.
[e] One cancelled case has been ignored.

Table 12.4 *Bridewell, 1600: Sex and Marriage Cases*

		Accused persons						Total persons
		In court			Not in court			
	Cases	M	F	T	M	F	T	
Pregnancy/ bastardy/ paternity	112	70	96	166	41	15	56	222
Sex/suspicious behaviour	52	27	43	70	22	10	32	102
Living together as man and wife	2	2	2	4	—	—	—	4
Common whore, etc.	5	—	5	5	—	—	—	5
Whorehunter/sex with whores	4	4	—	4	—	—	—	4
Taken in bawdy house	5	2	6	8	—	—	—	8
Venereal disease	5	3	2	5	—	—	—	5
Lewd/loose/ suspicious	11	2	9	11	—	—	—	11
Nightwalker	2	—	2	2	—	—	—	2
Indecent/unseemly behaviour	2	—	3	3	1	—	1	4
Bawd ⎫ prosecuted	—	—	3	3	—	—	—	3
Whores ⎬ together	3	—	3	3	—	—	—	3
Clients ⎭	—	—	—	—	2	—	2	2
Bawd/pander/ complicit	10	2	8	10	—	—	—	10
Receiving/ harbouring pregnant women	3	—	3	3	—	—	—	3
Attempted rape	3	3	—	3	—	—	—	3
Attempted bestiality	1	1	—	1	—	—	—	1
Bigamy	10	8	4	12	4	—	4	16
Sexual slander	1	—	2	2	—	—	—	2
(Complicit in) abandoning child	4	—	4	4	—	—	—	4
Miscellaneous/ unclear	2	—	2	2	—	—	—	2
Total	237	124	197	321	70	25	95	416

closing years of Elizabeth's reign, Catholic recusants in most areas had been reduced to a tiny and embattled minority. At the other end of the religious spectrum, the mid-Elizabethan puritan campaign to abolish the episcopate, dismantle the existing ecclesiastical courts and erect instead a presbyterian system of church discipline had proved far too radical. Puritan extremists, exemplified in the scurrilous writings of Martin Marprelate against members of the church hierarchy, had themselves done much to discredit the movement. More basically, in a country involved from 1585 in a bitter war with Spain and in which many people were both fearful of Catholic plots and anxious about what might ensue if the childless queen died (perhaps assassinated) without a clear successor in view, the hierarchy were able to represent even more moderate presbyterians and their sympathizers as politically subversive and potentially dangerous. High-profile trials of the leaders in the High Commission and Star Chamber in 1590–1 effectively destroyed the movement as a political force. To be sure, there remained many puritan activists at the local level, their existence reflected in sporadic prosecutions for such acts of nonconformity as failing to wear the surplice or use the sign of the cross in baptism. Some of them would not be forced into a choice between conformity and suspension from office or deprivation of their benefices till 1604–5, in the aftermath of the Hampton Court conference.[10]

In other respects, these sources reveal a church that was in the process of becoming more settled, even though it still faced challenges. It was now much better served by adequate numbers of able, or at least competent, ministers, while sermons were much more readily available than they had been early in the reign. In London, large numbers of prosecutions for neglect of church attendance, failure to receive communion and related offences reflect not merely the large and growing population of the city and its suburbs – some 200,000 by 1600 – but also the difficulties of enforcing religious obligations in a crowded metropolitan environment with high levels of immigration. Nonetheless, it seems that even in the metropolis most people attended their parish churches reasonably diligently and duly participated in Holy Communion at Easter and sometimes on other feasts during the year. This was even more true in rural areas such as Leicestershire and west Sussex. Irrespective of its spiritual benefits, good

---

[10] E.g. WSRO, Ep.I/17/8, fos. 152v, 168r, 189r, 190v, 200r (prosecutions against Mr Bede Goodacres of Ashurst); ROLLR, 1 D 41/13/26, fos. 11v, 12r, 18v (prosecutions against Mr Bayley curate of Kimcote). For the wider context and examples of local tensions, see Martin Ingram, 'Puritans and the Church Courts, 1560–1640', in Christopher Durston and Jacqueline Eales (eds.), *The Culture of English Puritanism, 1560–1700* (Basingstoke, 1996), pp. 75–80.

standing in the parish church was an important marker of local status and identity, and this fact was a powerful inducement to participation. It was likewise a spur to respectability in sexual behaviour.

Changes in the pattern of prosecutions in matters to do with sex and marriage, in the church courts as in secular tribunals such as Bridewell, were shaped by a number of convergent factors. In one sense they reflected the reinforcement of patriarchal principles inherent in much Reformation thinking on marriage, household and family. The focus gradually shifted from the disciplining of disorderly householders by those who saw themselves as 'honest' (an intra-generational dynamic) to the *inter-generational* restraint of the young and the imposition of firmer controls over courtship, premarital sex and marriage formation. But there were also powerful economic dimensions to this story. In retrospect, it is clear that the passage of the anti-bastardy measure of 1576 reflected the economic and fiscal concerns of the time – pressures that were to increase further by the end of Elizabeth's reign. Reduced mortality and increased fertility were expanding the population apace. The resulting pressure on resources, combined with a variety of changes in land use, helped to fuel price inflation, while the increasing availability of labour drove down the real value of wages.

Regionally and locally, the effects varied, as they did also at diverse social levels and among different occupational groups. But as a rule the numbers of the poor increased, both in absolute terms and as a proportion of the whole population, while their living conditions became increasingly straitened. In most parts of England, moreover, caring for the most vulnerable sections of society was becoming an increasing financial burden and an intricate administrative challenge. The 1590s, marked by a plague epidemic in 1593, a terrible sequence of bad harvests from 1594 to 1597 and the dislocations of war, were particularly stressful. It was in the wake of these disasters that parliament passed the far-reaching poor laws of 1598 (re-enacted with modifications in 1601) – measures that built on and drew lessons from a string of earlier statutes, as also on a host of local urban initiatives that fed into national legislation.

It was from the closing decades of the sixteenth century that these economic forces became a principal driver of sexual regulation. Although the poor laws of 1598 and 1601 did not mention fornication, bastardy or marriage, the connections were plain. In a Christian society it went without question that illegitimate children had to be maintained, and if father or mother was unable or could not be identified, it fell to the parish to provide sustenance, however grudging. In conditions where the numbers of poor people were on the increase, the dangers of this fiscal burden falling on the community were all the greater. Moral strictures were powerfully reinforced by economic concerns, a link reflected in all the samples of prosecutions in the closing years of Elizabeth's reign. Thus, in Leicestershire in 1602, cases of fornication greatly predominated, and in a high proportion it is clear that an illicit pregnancy or bastard birth was at issue. The pattern was even more marked in the archdeaconry of Chichester in 1594 (see Tables 12.2 and 12.3).

It was much the same story in Bridewell in London in 1600 (see Table 12.4). Categories of offence that might have been expected to occur frequently, such as being taken in a bawdy house or reputed a common whore, were not in fact very numerous. This reflected not merely the failure of the governors' earlier campaign against organized prostitution but also, more fundamentally, a re-ordering of priorities. John Howes, contemplating the strained resources and limited objectives of the London hospitals in comparison with the manifest increase in poverty and vagrancy, made one of the characters in his *Famyliar and frendly discourse dialogue wyse* (1587) ask why the governors were 'so carefull and dilligent in searching oute of mens wyves and other gallant gyrles'. The social evils of poverty, the speaker went on, were 'to to apparant in the eies of the people, that heaven and earthe cryeth vengeance, and suerly god can not but be angrie with us, that will suffer our Christian bretheren to die in the streates for wante of relyefe, and wee spende and consume our wealthe and our wytte in searching out of harlotts'. His interlocutor provided the stock response: '[S]ynne dothe so abounde in these daies, that yf there were not sharpe and sever punyshment vice woulde overflowe vertue'.[11] But, in practice, as time went on, vagrancy and other poverty-related issues did become relatively more prominent in Bridewell's agenda, while action against sexual offenders was increasingly inflected by concerns about illegitimacy.

Thus, of 237 sex and marriage cases dealt with by the Bridewell governors in 1600 – implicating over 400 individuals, of whom more than 300 were brought to court – as many as 112 (over 47 per cent of the total) involved bastardy or illicit pregnancy, while a further fifty-two (nearly 22 per cent) featured suspected or known sexual liaisons involving two people, character- istically unmarried. Meanwhile, it would seem that Christ's Hospital no

[11] R. H. Tawney and Eileen Power (eds.), *Tudor Economic Documents*, 3 vols. (London, 1924), Vol. III, pp. 441–2.

longer dealt with illegitimacy cases; in the wake of the act of 1576, which empowered justices of the peace to investigate illicit pregnancies, the numbers of bastardy examinations recorded in the minute books of Christ's declined sharply, and by 1600, they had disappeared.[12] Offenders brought to Bridewell were treated more rigorously and often punished with whipping or incarceration, but the governors' major concern in most of these cases was still to ensure that the parish in question and the city as a whole were 'saved harmless'; the putative fathers of illegitimate children normally had to give bond, backed by sureties, that they would pay the woman's expenses in childbed and subsequently maintain the child. The prominence of illegitimacy cases was even more marked in the sample London church court record for 1589 (see Table 12.1). A very high proportion of prosecutions focused on putative fathers and, even more, on women who were illicitly pregnant or had given birth to bastards; many of them were maidservants.

In London it was well established that householders were responsible for their apprentices and servants. In the church courts this was reflected in sizeable numbers of prosecutions for allowing illicitly pregnant or bastard-bearing servants and/or the putative fathers to depart without punishment or before the matter had been properly investigated. On examination, it often turned out that they had not been culpably negligent but simply unaware. Nonetheless, they were usually required to do their best endeavours to locate the offenders and produce them in court – a quest that often proved fruitless. A large number of householders, whether men or women, were also prosecuted for receiving unmarried pregnant women and allowing them to give birth in their houses. People did this for a variety of motives, including compassion, profit and practicality – the women had to give birth somewhere. But prosecutions of this type complete the picture of a web of social and legal constraints that marginalized, if they did not prevent, illicit pregnancies and illegitimate births. Yet the mesh was wide enough to allow most of the culprits to escape – the bishop of London's officers had little success in bringing bastard-bearers to court.

Although prosecutions of householders for failing to prevent illicit pregnancies or assisting bastard-bearers were so frequent, the other forms of aiding and abetting that had been so numerous in pre-Reformation London were strikingly rare. In the visitation of 1589, there was only one charge of keeping a bawdy house, while prosecutions simply for 'bawdry' or 'fostering' immorality were now absent. This was part of a broader shift observable also in the provinces. As seen in Chapter 10, cases of aiding and

12 Based on examination of LMA, CLC/210/B/001/MS12806/002–3.

abetting were already scarcely in evidence in west Sussex in the early 1570s, though they were still a prominent feature of prosecutions in the arch-deaconry of Leicester around the same time. By the closing years of Elizabeth's reign, they had become rare in both areas, and those that occurred were mostly cases of receiving pregnant women or allowing them to depart without punishment after giving birth. The law had not changed in that it was clearly still possible to prosecute accessories before the fact. Thus, in West Wittering (Sussex) in 1594, a widow was charged with 'suffering Alice Aylmer and John a mylner most part of a night to be in her bedchamber', while at Humberstone (Leicestershire) in 1602 a woman was put to penance 'for being bawde' to a couple accused of incontinence, without any suggestion that bastardy was at issue.[13] The questions asked in visitation articles may have contributed to the change, but this must have been symptomatic of a broader shift of emphasis from the actual commis-sion of sexual transgressions to the socially unwelcome *consequences* in the form of illegitimate offspring. Helmholz, commenting on cases of harbour-ing pregnant women found in church court records after about 1580, correctly relates them to the Elizabethan poor laws and what he terms 'the contemporary mania about bastard children' and presents the phe-nomenon as 'an expansion of ecclesiastical jurisdiction to cover behavior not previously treated as wrongful'. This ignores the fact that correspond-ingly other forms of aiding and abetting featured less and less in the church courts. Overall, there was a steep *decline* in such cases.[14]

Another shift was the increasing prosecution of couples who had already got married (or in some cases were about to do so) for 'antenuptial incontinence' or bridal pregnancy. As previous chapters have shown, in earlier times such cases were not entirely unknown but were very rare in most jurisdictions. Indeed, occasionally, individuals actually claimed that they were little or no business of the church courts – a telling exception to the principle that people rarely voiced their dissent from the church's teachings on sexual morality. In London in 1495, a man was in trouble for affirming that fornication was but 'a smale syn betwene a singil man and singil woman whan they be maryed after'. In 1563, the vicar of Burbage (Wiltshire), urging the dean of Salisbury's officers to pursue a couple whose

---

[13] WSRO, Ep.I/17/8, fos. 206r, 210r; ROLLR, 1 D 41/13/26, fos. 25v, 26r; cf. WSRO, Ep.I/17/8, fos. 205v, 215v, ROLLR, 1 D 41/13/26, fos. 2r, 18r, 39v (cases concerning illicit pregnancies or bastard births).
[14] R. H. Helmholz, 'Harboring Sexual Offenders: Ecclesiastical Courts and Controlling Misbehavior', *Journal of British Studies*, 37 (1998), 258–68; cf. Ingram, *Church Courts, Sex and Marriage*, p. 291 and chap. 9 *passim*.

child was delivered within six weeks of marriage, claimed that 'theyr be some bothe old and yonge that saye playn you hav[e] no lawe to punishe them yf they marye aftereward althowgh that they playd the naghty packes together beffore.' In the same vein, a Norfolk woman declared in 1564 that 'after a cople have talked of matrimonye yt is lawfull for them to have carnall copulacon.' The near coincidence of the last two cases in point of time perhaps reflects popular discussion of the limits of ecclesiastical jurisdiction in the immediate aftermath of the Elizabethan settlement.[15]

As late as 1589, a London man told the churchwardens of Clerkenwell 'that they did more then they oughte to doe [in] presentinge such as are with childe before marriage'. But an example was made of this individual, who was made to kneel in church during Sunday service after the reading of the gospel and confess publicly that he had done wrong thus to 'counsell the churchwardens in ... executinge of theire offyce and charge beinge thereunto sworne'.[16] From about the 1580s onwards, in church courts all over England, cases of antenuptial incontinence and bridal pregnancy increased in number till by the 1620s and 1630s they were commonplace. However, there were local and regional variations in the intensity of such prosecutions, and churchwardens were never as consistent in making presentments as they were in bastardy cases. The judges also showed a degree of tolerance, to the extent that guilty couples often got away with some lesser punishment – penance performed in ordinary clothes instead of the white sheet, confession at the time of marriage rather than on Sunday or even a semi-private confession before the minister and churchwardens.

The data summarized in Tables 12.1 to 12.3 illustrate the pattern of such prosecutions in southern England in the closing years of Elizabeth's reign. In west Sussex, antenuptial incontinence was already a clearly established offence by 1594. In Leicestershire in 1602, such cases were utterly routine, most being recorded formulaically as 'fornication before solemnization'. A few cases were more complex in that the couple got married after they were charged; in one instance they were still unmarried when they came to court but promised to marry immediately. Two cases are interesting in that

---

[15] LMA, DL/C/B/043/MS09064/6, fo. 141r and p. 140 (the latter is a narrow slip, apparently left when most of an otherwise blank folio was cut out of the volume); Ralph A. Houlbrooke, 'Church Courts and People in the Diocese of Norwich, 1519–1570', unpublished DPhil thesis, University of Oxford, 1970, p. 125; WSA, D5/21/1/1 (unnumbered file), letter dated 19 June 1563. In fact, canon law on the issue was not entirely clear-cut and was still being discussed in the early seventeenth century: R. H. Helmholz (ed.), *Three Civilian Notebooks, 1580–1640* (Selden Society 127, London, 2011 for 2010), pp. 99–100.

[16] LMA, DL/C/616, p. 319.

the bridegrooms were clergymen; the case against Arthur Greenough, rector of Glooston, seems to have arisen from malice or misunderstanding, since the churchwardens denied any 'fame'.[17] An unusually high proportion of cases seems to have originated not in churchwardens' presentments but from the reports of third parties or the court's own detective work. By this period, churchwardens were required to submit annual transcripts of parish registers, and these provided a ready means by which registry officials could determine when a birth had occurred suspiciously soon after a wedding. This kind of calculation was much more difficult in London, with its populous parishes and high levels of population turnover. This helps to explain why the bishop of London's visitation of 1589 uncovered relatively few cases of antenuptial fornication, a pattern that was not confined to that year but persisted into the early seventeenth century. It may be that in any case in the capital bridal pregnancy was less common than in rural areas.[18]

Marriage, Divorce and Bigamy

The rise of prosecutions for antenuptial fornication should be seen in a broader context. Traditionally, the stock response to an out-of-wedlock pregnancy had been – unless there was great disparity in wealth and status between the man and the woman or other circumstances that made the union seem undesirable – to encourage, if not compel, the couple to marry. But if they were very poor, this was by no means a desirable strategy from the standpoint of their fellow parishioners, since it was all too likely that, having commenced childbearing, the couple would go on to become 'overburdened' with offspring and fall on the poor rates that way. On this perspective it was far better to prevent prenuptial pregnancies in the first place. While the ideal of premarital chastity was by no means new, the determination to enforce it strictly was certainly an innovation.

Even more radical was a further line of thinking that called in question the right of the poor to marry. Again, this built on traditional values. As was emphasized at the outset of this book, it had always been expected that individuals – men in particular, since they were assumed to be the main breadwinners – should exercise self-restraint and avoid marriage until they were economically competent to maintain a household. This was one

---

[17] ROLLR, 1 D 41/13/25, fo. 49r; 1 D 41/13/26, fo. 6r.
[18] Roger Finlay, *Population and Metropolis: The Demography of London, 1580–1650* (Cambridge, 1981), pp. 149–50.

of the chief underpinnings of late age at marriage, a pattern that was probably well established long before 1500 but intensified in the course of the late sixteenth century and on into the early seventeenth century. But in Protestant thinking, marriage was one of God's gifts that should in principle be available to all, even if in practice some individuals could not attain it. As an Elizabethan defender of the customs of London put it:

> Mariage is an honorable ordinance of God, fit and necessarie for all persons disposed thereunto, to the avoyding of sinne, and maintenance of a comfortable and sociable Christian life. To restraine or prohibit the same either in maides or widowes, (as S. Paule sayeth) is the doctrine of divels. And to indent or condition with any that he or she shall not marrie, is a condition limited against lawe, and by the same pronounced unlawfull and unreasonable.[19]

It was therefore a daring thought to suggest that whole groups of people should be prevented from getting married. Nonetheless, from the later years of Elizabeth's reign there occur cases in which poor people claimed that parish officers or their neighbours in general, sometimes actively abetted by the clergy, had refused to let them marry. Some of the earliest examples suggest that initially the practice was justified on the grounds that the individuals concerned had *forfeited* their right to marriage through promiscuity or irresponsibility. But eventually attitudes hardened into the doctrine that very poor people could be prevented from marrying if their fellow parishioners objected, simply because they were likely to burden the poor rates. It is unknown how common the practice actually was. In London and other prominent towns and cities, apprenticeship regulations probably already served as effective restraints. But cases scattered across a wide area of rural England have been uncovered for the early seventeenth century, though it seems that it was only after the Restoration that contemporaries commented on them as widespread.[20]

Fiscal imperatives and inter-generational conflict were not the only factors leading to greater sensitivity to issues concerning marriage. They reinforced – and were in turn reinforced by – a set of other considerations, among which legal issues left unresolved from the past loomed large. As is well known, and was explained afresh in Chapter 2, it was in principle possible for couples to form a binding union merely by the exchange of

---

[19] *A breefe discourse, declaring and approving the necessarie and inviolable maintenance of the laudable customes of London* (London, 1584), p. 36.
[20] Ingram, *Church Courts, Sex and Marriage*, p. 131; Keith Wrightson, *English Society, 1580–1680* (London, 1982), p. 78; Steve Hindle, 'The Problem of Pauper Marriage in Seventeenth-Century England', *Transactions of the Royal Historical Society*, 6th Series, 8 (1998), 71–89.

words in the present tense. But for centuries the church had insisted that to be properly lawful, marriages should be publicized in advance by the calling of banns – though this could be dispensed with by a licence from the ecclesiastical authorities – and solemnized in church by the parish priest in the presence of competent witnesses. All the evidence reviewed in this book indicates that by the early sixteenth century, and probably well before, the great majority of people conformed to these regulations, indeed took them for granted. They were not seen as irksome regulations imposed by an alien authority; rather, they made obvious practical sense, as well as focusing attention on a single occasion that the couple, their families and their neighbours could celebrate as the wedding day.

Thus, throughout this period, when people thought of marriage, they normally meant marriage in church. Nonetheless, many individuals – for a variety of motives, sometimes linked with the property negotiations between families that preceded marriage in the better-heeled sections of society – did enter into binding marriage contracts or spousals before the wedding, in the expectation that they would be ratified by the ceremony in church. Sometimes these contracts were dishonoured or disputed, so everywhere in the late sixteenth century there continued to be brought, albeit not in very large numbers, lawsuits for the enforcement of spousals. Moreover, since there were no clear rules about how quickly a marriage contract should be solemnized, some couples who were thought to be delaying too long were prosecuted in the church courts, especially if – as undoubtedly sometimes happened – they were suspected of having begun sexual relations or had even set up house together. There were regional variations, perhaps reflecting local economies but probably in many cases simply based in local custom. Thus practice seems to have been somewhat more relaxed in west Sussex than it was in Leicestershire, though in neither area was it socially acceptable for couples actually to cohabit (in the sense of living under one roof as man and wife) for any length of time without proceeding to marriage.

The trend in the closing years of Elizabeth's reign was towards further clarification of the regulations surrounding marriage and stricter enforcement of them. By the early seventeenth century, this was reflected in most areas in markedly fewer spousals suits being brought before the church courts and in the increasing difficulty of securing a positive sentence in favour of a disputed marriage contract. But there were complications. There was a growing tendency for some couples, while accepting the need – indeed themselves eager – for marriage in church, to evade the safeguards of publicity by procuring marriages without banns or licence, outside their own parishes, or at unseasonable times. These became known as 'clandestine marriages', for which there were many underlying motives. They were the recourse of eloping couples, acting in defiance of their families; of poor people whose neighbours were reluctant to see them wed, or who simply needed to marry cheaply; of couples when the bride was visibly pregnant and wished to avoid embarrassment; and, especially in London, of people who simply thought a discreet ceremony out of the public gaze was the fashionable thing to do. These desires were met by so-called lawless churches, where marriages could be procured with few or no questions asked. In the provinces these were 'peculiar' or exempt jurisdictions, subject to little or no higher authority. In London, the chapel of the Tower of London was the usual venue. (It was only in the later seventeenth century that the chapel of the Fleet Prison became popular for this purpose.)[21]

The church hierarchy was hostile to such clandestine marriages; on the whole, so also were parish incumbents, who thereby lost marriage fees. But the wish to take firm remedial action was mitigated by other considerations. Clandestine marriage ceremonies were not merely a practical problem but touched on issues of principle cherished by puritans. Although by the 1590s proposals for wholesale restructuring of the church had been defeated, this did not prevent presbyterians and their more moderate sympathizers from seeking more limited changes in the status quo. Indeed, it may have incited them to do so, as a means of asserting themselves amid the bitterness of defeat or at least of salvaging something from the wreck of their hopes. Among these aspirations was the demand, dating back to the debates launched by the continental reformers and taken up in England in mid-century, that marriage required the consent of parents to be valid, rather than merely the free consent of the couple, as the church had taught for centuries. Irrespective of doctrinal issues and ecclesiological positions, this could be expected to attract support from substantial families eager to prevent the possibility of *mésalliances*. But setting its face against such pressures, convocation in 1597 strongly reasserted the traditional principle that 'consent in marriage is the matter specially to be regarded, and credit of kindred, honour, wealth, contentment, and pleasure of friends, be rather matters of conveniency than necessity in matrimony.' The matter was tied up with the more technical

---

[21] Martin Ingram, 'Cohabitation in Context in Early Seventeenth-Century London', in Rebecca Probert (ed.), *Cohabitation and Non-Marital Births in England and Wales, 1600–2012* (Basingstoke, 2014), p. 37.

question of marriage licences. Bogus dispensations, or licences issued for cash without proper investigation of the circumstances, were a concern to the hierarchy. But puritan criticism ran much deeper, effectively denying the right of bishops to issue licences at all, a position that the hierarchy could not possibly concede. The canons of 1604 gestured towards compromise. Children under the age of twenty-one were forbidden to marry without the consent of their parents or guardians, while marriage licences were to be issued only under strict conditions and required proof of parental consent irrespective of the age of the parties, but marriages made in contravention of these regulations were not declared invalid.[22]

There were links with another running sore in matrimonial law. The principle urged by some mid-century reformers that in cases of divorce for adultery the innocent party should be allowed to remarry had been rejected by the church, but the idea had by no means gone away. The debate was renewed in very controversial terms in the 1590s, while late sixteenth-century church court records from all parts of England, among other sources, reveal a persistent trickle of cases in which lay people from all social levels professed to believe that the principle held good and had acted accordingly – by illegally remarrying after securing a sentence separation 'from bed and board', or indeed in some cases where no formal divorce at all had been pronounced, yet one or both the parties believed that they had a right to separate from their spouse and remarry.[23] Marriage licences were again implicated, since they were widely believed to facilitate these practices, as indeed other forms of bigamy.

It may also be that the rapid rise in population, the increased velocity of migration, the exponential growth of London and other social changes and dislocations of the late sixteenth century made bigamy more likely to occur. So an issue that had long been a matter of recurrent yet limited concern – reflected, as has been seen in earlier chapters, in sporadic prosecutions in the church courts – suddenly assumed the proportions of a major scandal. The matter was extensively aired in the parliament of 1597 – when members of parliament exchanged what Bernard Capp calls 'horror stories' of bigamous, incestuous and otherwise irregular unions – and further publicized in a high-profile Star Chamber case of 1598. The upshot was firm legislation in both the ecclesiastical and secular

---

[22] John Strype, *The Life and Acts of John Whitgift*, 3 vols. (London, 1822 edn.), Vol. II, p. 381; Vol. III, p. 380; Gerald Bray (ed.), *The Anglican Canons, 1529–1947* (Church of England Record Society 6, Woodbridge, 1998), pp. 400–3.

[23] Bernard Capp, 'Bigamous Marriage in Early Modern England', *Historical Journal*, 52 (2009), 539–41; Ingram, *Church Courts, Sex and Marriage*, p. 179.

spheres. The canons of 1597 and 1604 strongly reaffirmed the ban on remarriage after 'divorce' from bed and board and introduced a system of taking bonds from the parties in such separation cases so that those who attempted to evade the law would suffer a severe financial penalty. The parliament of 1604 was to make bigamy a felony.[24] The data from around the turn of the century summarized in Tables 12.3 and 12.4 reflect this concern. Bigamy cases were high on the agenda of the Bridewell governors in 1600 and were investigated with considerable rigour. Even in the predominantly rural archdeaconry of Leicester, the offence was also prominent, eight cases being brought to light in 1602. In addition, a Breedon man was prosecuted 'for receaveing a butcher and a woman into his house who lyve togeather as man and wife and yett the said butcher hath another wife as yt is reported'; he admitted lodging the couple but claimed 'that he hath hard that . . . he is parted from her by lawe'.[25]

Thus, in the closing years of Elizabeth's reign, illegitimacy, marriage and divorce were matters of public concern for a combination of reasons, including rising population (of which contemporaries were becoming increasingly aware),[26] economic stress, financial pressure on parish rate-payers, the polemical fallout from the crackdown on presbyterianism, renewed debates about divorce and remarriage and a moral panic about bigamy that was linked with all these issues. In retrospect, these factors, despite their diversity, may be seen to have created a distinctive cluster of impulses that added up to more intensive policing around the borders of marriage. However, continuing a trend already visible earlier in Elizabeth's reign, adultery as such was less and less prominent in the pattern of prosecutions. The fact that the presentment of sexual offences was now very much in the hands of local churchwardens and questmen, acting through the visitation system, gave them some scope to downplay this issue. This does not mean that they cynically exploited their powers to ensure that adulterers among themselves or others of similar status should

---

[24] Capp, 'Bigamous Marriage', p. 541; Strype, *Life of Whitgift*, Vol. III, pp. 378–80; Bray (ed.), *Anglican Canons*, pp. 242–3, 406–7; 1 James I c. 11. This act did not apply if the husband or wife had been absent for seven years or if the couple had been lawfully divorced in an ecclesiastical court; whether this was intended to include separation from bed and board was unclear, but this interpretation eventually prevailed.

[25] ROLLR, 1 D41/13/26, fo. 32v; the other cases are recorded in *ibid.*, fos. 10v, 16v, 18r, 33r, 37r, 1 D41/13/25, fos. 16v, 19r, 20r. See also Capp, 'Bigamous Marriage', 543, 544–5.

[26] Paul Slack, '*Plenty of People': Perceptions of Population in Early Modern England* (Reading, 2011), p. 5; Mildred Campbell, "'Of People Either Too Few or Too Many." The Conflict of Opinion on Population and its Relation to Emigration', in William Appleton Aiken and Basil Duke Henning (eds.), *Conflict in Stuart England: Essays in Honour of Wallace Notestein* (London, 1960), esp. pp. 176–83.

get off scot free. Rather it would seem that there was a growing feeling that adultery, when it was suspected, should, if possible, be dealt with by some means that avoided public exposure and the scandal that might wreck the marriage. Yet the offence itself was, if anything, increasingly discountenanced. Local office holders could hardly fail to realize that stricter measures against bridal pregnancy and prenuptial fornication demanded that the older generation of established householders themselves should exercise restraint in their own sexual lives. In any case, as was seen earlier, concubinage and the keeping of 'whores' by married men were already on the decline in the early to middle years of Elizabeth's reign, in parallel with the withering away of the provincial sex trade and stricter standards of personal morality among the clergy that clerical marriage made feasible. The aristocracy might evade these tightening bonds of sexual discipline, but ordinary people could not. Parish patriarchs had to live up to the ideals of their own rhetoric.

Sexual Regulation in the Early Seventeenth Century

The peak of concern about bigamy soon passed. The 1604 act did not wholly destroy ecclesiastical jurisdiction over the offence, but thereafter fewer cases came before the church courts. Henceforth, bigamy was mostly prosecuted by indictment at assizes, in some borough courts and at the Old Bailey, but numbers of cases were not large and executions were few and far between. In most other respects the pattern of prosecutions for sexual transgressions found around 1600 was reinforced under the early Stuart kings, as poverty became entrenched, the administration of the poor laws was increasingly well established and it came to be accepted more and more that marriage was a state to which only those who could command a reasonable economic competence could hope to aspire. Church court prosecutions for adultery, fornication, bastardy, bridal pregnancy and the harbouring of unmarried mothers continued to be important in setting out the limits of acceptable behaviour and harassing offenders, albeit the authorities were not invariably successful in actually punishing culprits or inducing a sense of real contrition. Action by justices of the peace under the act of 1576 was a sharper deterrent against bearing or begetting bastard children, especially when a further act of 1610 ordered that the mothers of illegitimate children liable to burden the poor rates should be sent to the nearest house of correction for one year. Even when these harsh measures were not enforced, their mere existence encouraged the fathers and mothers of bastard children to come to some accommodation to ensure that they did not provoke the wrath of parish officials. Administrative measures, particularly the use of bonds 'to save the parish harmless', were probably even more important than judicial means to restrain bastard-bearing and to manage the consequences, notably the accommodation of women in childbed and the maintenance of illegitimate children. This was particularly so in the metropolis, where such measures were very well developed indeed, but was true also in provincial towns and rural areas.[27]

Early seventeenth-century London is distinctive in that in some other respects sexual regulation became demonstrably less intense. The church courts continued to be active, and the pattern of prosecutions evident in 1589 broadly persisted. But already by 1600 the court of aldermen, formerly so prominent in imposing exemplary public punishments on egregious offenders, was handling very few such cases, and numbers dwindled further as time went on. The wardmotes likewise ceased to be active in the prosecution of sexual transgression. Cases of adultery and fornication were to an extent dealt with by the Middlesex and city of London sessions, but from the 1620s the trend was towards increasing focus on the prosecution of keepers of bawdy houses rather than the individuals themselves engaged in illicit sex. Strikingly, the numbers of sexual offenders of any kind dealt with by Bridewell Hospital plummeted after about 1620 and decreased even further in the 1630s.[28]

These changes foreshadowed what by the eighteenth century had become a major social and cultural shift – the decline of legal regulation of consensual sexual activity between men and women. To be sure, the developments leading in that direction were complex, and there were conflicting currents – one has only to think of the notorious act of 1650, which for a period made adultery involving a married women a felony, or the Societies for Reformation of Manners that flourished from the 1690s to the 1720s.[29] But there are some grounds for seeing the early seventeenth century as a period of transition, during which divergent trends may be found in different areas. Unlike the situation in the metropolis, there is no sign in provincial England of the slackening of sexual regulation. Indeed, in these decades some villages and provincial towns – Terling (Essex) and

[27] Walter J. King, 'Punishment for Bastardy in Early Seventeenth-Century England', *Albion*, 10 (1978), 130–51; Eleanor Fox and Martin Ingram, 'Bridewell, Bawdy Courts and Bastardy in Early Seventeenth-Century London', in Rebecca Probert (ed.), *Cohabitation and Non-Marital Births in England and Wales, 1600–2012* (Basingstoke, 2014), pp. 10–32.

[28] Paul Griffiths, *Lost Londons: Change, Crime, and Control in the Capital City, 1550–1660* (Cambridge, 2008), pp. 201–3. I intend to publish on another occasion a detailed account of the changing pattern of sexual regulation in early seventeenth-century London.

[29] The shift and its antecedents are brilliantly analysed in Dabhoiwala, *Origins of Sex*.

Dorchester (Dorset) are well-documented examples – witnessed lively moral reform campaigns in which sexual transgressors were important targets,[30] while diehard zealots, such as Ignatius Jourdain of Exeter, continued to call in the House of Commons for harsher measures against adultery. But the flippant response that Jourdain evoked is suggestive: in 1628 when he 'made a motion in the Parliament concerning the bill against adultery some one or more in the House cried out, "Commit it, Mr Jourdain, commit it!" Upon which a great laughter was occasioned.'[31]

For several reasons, sexual transgression was slipping a little down the agenda of moral reform. The disappearance or at least containment of many of the crying sins of yesteryear – clerical immorality, keeping 'whores', blatant adultery and (except in the London suburbs, where it flourished) the sex trade – made the matter seem in some ways less urgent. Certainly it no longer had the news value that the mid-sixteenth-century Protestant reformers had managed to give it. Even illegitimate births were less of a concern. Whereas around 1600 rate-payers and moralists alike – they could well be the same persons – feared a rising tide of bastardy, the battery of legal and administrative measures that had been rapidly put in place had proved able to contain the threat, to the extent that illegitimacy rates were on the decline by the 1620s. Thus, in most areas of England by the end of James I's reign, sexual regulation, however intense, had become a matter of routine, a financial as much as a moral issue.

Of course, for committed moral activists, whether clergy or lay people, such a situation was inadequate. But even for them, sexual transgression was now only one among a number of crying sins to be denounced and combated. As seen in Chapter 1, 'reformation of manners' was a broad-ranging idea that had never been confined to sexual matters. Yet, for generations, illicit sex had in practice been the most prominent target, particularly for the most consistently active agents of moral discipline, the ecclesiastical courts. Other concerns, such as unlawful games, excess in apparel and usury, had generated sporadic prosecutions and short-lived campaigns but had never been regularly and vigorously pursued. Indeed,

---

[30] David Underdown, *Fire From Heaven: The Life of an English Town in the Seventeenth Century* (London, 1992); Keith Wrightson and David Levine, *Poverty and Piety in an English Village: Terling, 1525–1700*, 2nd edn. (Oxford, 1995), esp. chaps. 5–7; cf. Martin Ingram, 'Religion, Communities and Moral Discipline in Late Sixteenth- and Early Seventeenth-Century England: Case Studies', in Kaspar von Greyerz (ed.), *Religion and Society in Early Modern Europe, 1500–1800* (London, 1984), pp. 177–93.

[31] Cited in Thomas, 'Puritans and Adultery', p. 274; cf. Conrad Russell, *Parliaments and English Politics, 1621–1629* (Oxford, 1979), p. 29. On Jourdain's activities in Exeter, see Mark Stoyle, *From Deliverance to Destruction: Rebellion and Civil War in an English City* (Exeter, 1996), chap. 2.

by the beginning of the seventeenth century, some of these traditional targets ceased to feature on legal agendas, though still subject to the denunciations of moralists. In 1604 the sumptuary laws lapsed, and while it remained possible to mount prosecutions for usury, the taking of moderate interest became an accepted feature of economic life.[32]

Yet, as some moral fears were dissipated, others rose in prominence. Indeed, a feature of the half-century before the civil wars was a major reappraisal of 'reformation of manners' – expressed in a veritable explosion of preaching and print – that still gave plenty of attention to illicit sex but dealt in unprecedented detail with a huge range of other 'sins', 'vices' and 'enormities'. Among these were gaming and card-playing, cursing and swearing, drunkenness and alehouse-haunting, dancing and other popular festivities – by no means new objects of execration but now addressed with far greater urgency and becoming much more prominent in the work of both the ecclesiastical and secular courts. As in the case of sexual offences, economic concerns, the desire to curb what was perceived to be the licentiousness of youth and more general fears of 'disorder' contributed to these efforts.[33] But another reason for urgency was a supposed connection between these activities and breaches of Sunday observance, now re-emphasized in line with changed understandings of the Christian 'sabbath'. This is a major topic in its own right and cannot be discussed in detail here. Suffice to say that this was something distinctively new and capable of generating enormous energy to power vigorous efforts at repression. Adultery, fornication and the like remained targets of attack. But there are grounds for thinking that sabbatarianism, rather than sex, was the real puritan shibboleth of the early seventeenth century.[34]

---

[32] Martin Ingram, 'Reformation of Manners in Early Modern England', in Paul Griffiths, Adam Fox and Steve Hindle (eds.), *The Experience of Authority in Early Modern England* (Basingstoke, 1996), pp. 69–71.

[33] *Ibid.*, pp. 76–81; Wrightson, *English Society*, chap. 6; Mark Hailwood, *Alehouses and Good Fellowship in Early Modern England* (Woodbridge, 2014). Generational conflicts are emphasized by Robert von Friedeburg, 'Reformation of Manners and the Social Composition of Offenders in an East Anglian Cloth Village: Earls Colne, Essex, 1531–1642', *Journal of British Studies*, 29 (1990), 347–85; Paul Griffiths, *Youth and Authority: Formative Experiences in England, 1560–1640* (Oxford, 1996).

[34] Alistair Dougall, *The Devil's Book: Charles I, the Book of Sports and Puritanism in Tudor and Early Stuart England* (Exeter, 2011); cf. Kenneth L. Parker, *The English Sabbath: A Study of Doctrine and Discipline from the Reformation to the Civil War* (Cambridge, 1988).

Bibliography

The following lists the manuscript and printed sources on which this book is based, together with a selection of secondary works bearing directly on the main themes in Britain and Europe before about 1625. Full references are provided in the footnotes to successive chapters.

Manuscript Sources

Bethlem Museum of the Mind, Beckenham

BCB 1–4 (Bridewell Hospital Court Books, 1559–62, 1574–9, 1598–1604, available online as digitized images)

British Library, Department of Manuscripts

Cotton MS Cleopatra F.II, fos. 250–4 ('Certen consideracons why the spirituell jurisdiccon wold be abrogatt')
Lansdowne MS 27, no. 70 (Bury St Edmunds Orders, 1579)
Lansdowne MS 97, fos. 148–53 (Tract by Clement Armstrong)

Devon Heritage Centre, Exeter

Chanter 41 (Diocese of Exeter Act Book, 1568–97)

Exeter City Archives
Chamber Act Book 4
Sessions Records, Miscellaneous Vol. 100

Essex Record Office, Chelmsford

Colchester Borough Records
D/B 5 Cr 71–152 (Court Rolls, 1460–85, 1509–91)

D/B 5 R 4, 6, 7 (Entry Books, 1539–45, 1565–71)
D/B 5 Sb 1/3 (Justices' Book, 1514–23)
D/B 5 Sb 2/1–6 (Examination and Recognizance Books, 1561–1619)
D/B 5 Sr 1–8 (Files and Rolls of Sessions and Gaol Delivery, 1516, 1562, 1576–7, 1583–5, 1588, 1593)

Hampshire Record Office, Winchester

11M59/C1/21/1 (Court Roll of the Clink Manor, Southwark, 1505–6)

Huntington Library, San Marino, California

Battle Abbey VI: Manorial Papers (Battle)
Hastings Collections VI: Manorial Papers (Loughborough)

Kent History and Library Centre, Maidstone

DRb/Pa 7 (Diocese of Rochester Act Book, 1518–23)

Borough of Lambeth Archives Department

Class VI/1–5 (Manor of Paris Garden, Southwark, Court Rolls, 1460–1577)

Lambeth Palace Library

Estate Document 969 (Court Rolls of the Archbishop of Canterbury's Manor, Southwark, 1504–11)

Record Office for Leicestershire, Leicester and Rutland, Leicester

Leicester Archdeaconry Records
1 D 41/4/1–903 (Court Papers, 1526–1603)
1 D 41/11/1–4 (Act Books of Instance Courts, 1524–60)
1 D 41/12/1–6 (*Libri cleri*, 1517–33)
1 D 41/13/1–27 (Act Books of Correction Courts, 1523–1603)

Leicester Borough Records
BR II/18/1–7 (Hall Papers Bound, 1583–1606)
BR III/2/4–74 (Chamberlains' Accounts, 1517–1606)

Lincolnshire Archives, Lincoln

Lincoln Diocesan Records

DIOC/Cj 3–4 (Court of Audience Act Books, 1525–62, 1527–9)
DIOC/Vj 3 (Leicester and Northampton Archdeaconry Visitation Returns, *c.*1469–79)
DIOC/Viv 2–5 (Leicester Archdeaconry Visitation Returns, 1489–1510)

London Metropolitan Archives, Clerkenwell

Ac. 62.7 (Diocese of Winchester Act Book, 1511–15)
CLA/043/01/016 (Southwark Court Leet Book, 1539–64)
CLC/210/B/001/MS12806/001–3 (Christ's Hospital Minute Books, 1556–1632)
CLC/W/FA/005/MS01499 (Aldersgate Wardmote Presentments, 1510)
COL/AD/01/012, COL/AD/01/018 (Letter Books M, 1497–1515, S, 1554–60)
COL/CA/01/01/001–27 (Repertories of the Court of Aldermen, 1495–1602)
COL/CC/01/01/007–26 (Journals of the Court of Common Council, 1462–1602)
COL/CS/01/010 (*Liber Dunthorn*)
DL/AL/C/009/MS09055 (Archdeaconry Court of London, Office Act Book, 1562–3)
DL/AL/C/011/MS09056 (Archdeaconry Court of London, Deposition Book, 1566–7)
DL/C/A/002/MS09065, DL/C/A/001/MS09065B (Consistory Court of London, Examination Book, 1487–97)
DL/C/B/043/MS09064/1–11 (Commissary Court of London, *acta quoad delinquentium*, 1470–1503, 1508–16)
DL/C/B/043/MS09065 J/1–2 (Commissary Court of London, *acta quoad delinquentium*, 1518–29)
DL/C/205–16, 628–9 (Consistory Court of London, Examination Books, 1467–1603)
DL/C/300–1, 614–16 (Consistory Court of London, Office Act Books, 1554–90)
DL/C/330–1 (Vicar-General's Act Books, 'Foxford', 1521–39, 'Croke', 1546–60)

The National Archives, Kew

C1/48/191; C1/64/897; C1/363/76; C1/600/46 (Chancery Proceedings)
KB 9 (King's Bench, Ancient Indictments)
KB 27 (King's Bench Plea Rolls)
REQ 2/11/115 (Court of Requests Proceedings)
SC 2/191/66 (Westminster Manor Court Roll, 1510)
SP 1/18, fos. 227–257 (Searches for Suspected Persons, 1519)
SP1/40, fos. 175–186 (Petition of John Roo, Curate of St Christopher le Stocks, London, 1529)

SP 1/95, fo. 104 (Report on Ecclesiastical Jurisdiction, 1535)
SP 2/M, fos. 229–232 (Draft Bill for Reform of Church Courts, 1532)
SP 10/8, fos. 63v, 107v (Charges against Bishop Bonner, 1549)
SP 12/78, fos. 243–245 (Northampton Church Orders, 1571)
STAC 5/C69/29, C70/2, C81/23 (Star Chamber Proceedings Relating to Colchester)

Nottinghamshire Archives, Nottingham

CA 1–58 (Nottingham Borough Sessions Rolls, 1453–1603)
SC/8/1/1/1–4, SC/8/1/2/1–5, SC/8/1/3 (Southwell Chapter Act Books, 1564–95)

Nottingham University Manuscripts and Special Collections

AN/A 1 (Archdeaconry of Nottingham, Register of Office Causes, 1565–74)
AN/A 3/1/4 (Archdeaconry of Nottingham, Correction Act Book, 1577–8)

Westminster Abbey Muniments

WAM 50760–50777 (Westminster Manor Court Rolls, 1486–1545)
WAM 50778, 50782 (Westminster Gatehouse Court Books, 1523, 1545)

Westminster Archives Centre

0045/001 (Westminster Gatehouse Court Book, 1519 [photostat copy])

West Sussex Record Office, Chichester

Chichester Diocesan Records (available in microform as *The Church Court Records of Chichester*, 38 reels (Brighton, 1986), reels 1–5, 14–15, 20–2, 33)
Ep.I/15 (Register of Bishop Robert Sherburne)
Ep.I/10/1–21 (Consistory Court of Chichester, Instance Books, 1506–1603)
Ep.I/11/1–9 (Consistory Court of Chichester, Deposition Books, 1557–1603)
Ep.I/17/1–10 (Consistory Court of Chichester, Detection Books, 1538–1603)
Ep.I/23/1–7 (Registers of Presentments, 1571–86)
Ep.II/9/1 (Archdeaconry of Lewes, Detection Book, 1550–7)

Wiltshire and Swindon Archives, Chippenham

D1/43/1–2 (Bishop of Salisbury: *Detecta* Books, 1550, 1553, 1556)
D4/3/1 (Subdean of Salisbury: Act Book, 1477–8)
D5/21/1/1 (Dean of Salisbury: Citations, 1561–4)

Worcestershire Archive and Archaeology Service, Worcester

009:1 BA 2636/11, item 43700 (Visitation Book of Hartlebury)

Printed Sources

Alcock, John, *Sermo Iohannis Alcok episcopi Eliensis* (Westminster, ?1497).

Allen, P. S. and H. M. Allen (eds.), *Letters of Richard Fox, 1486–1527* (Oxford, 1929).

Archer, Ian W. and F. Douglas Price (eds.), *English Historical Documents, 1558–1603* (London and New York, 2011).

Barnum, Priscilla Heath (ed.), *Dives and Pauper*, 2 vols. in 3 parts (Early English Text Society 275, 280, 323, London, 1976–2004).

Barron, Caroline, Christopher Coleman and Claire Gobbi (eds.), 'The London Journal of Alessandro Magno, 1562', *London Journal*, 9 (1983), 136–52.

Basille, Theodore [actually Heinrich Bullinger, trans. Miles Coverdale, with a Preface by Thomas Becon], *The golden boke of christen matrimonye* (London, 1543).

Bateson, Mary et al. (eds.), *Records of the Borough of Leicester: Being a Series of Extracts from the Archives of the Corporation of Leicester*, 7 vols. (London, Cambridge and Leicester, 1899–1974).

Benham, William Gurney (ed.), *The Oath Book or Red Parchment Book of Colchester* (Colchester, 1907).

Bond, Ronald B. (ed.), Certain Sermons or Homilies *(1547) and* A Homily against Disobedience and Wilful Rebellion *(1570): A Critical Edition* (Toronto, 1987).

Bowen, Thomas, *Extracts from the Records and Court Books of Bridewell Hospital* (London, 1798).

Bowker, Margaret (ed.), *An Episcopal Court Book for the Diocese of Lincoln, 1514–1520* (Lincoln Record Society 61, Lincoln, 1967).

Bray, Gerald (ed.), *The Anglican Canons, 1529–1947* (Church of England Record Society 6, Woodbridge, 1998).

Bray, Gerald (ed.), *Tudor Church Reform: The Henrician Canons of 1535 and the Reformatio Legum Ecclesiasticarum* (Church of England Record Society 8, Woodbridge, 2000).

Bray, Gerald (ed.), *Records of Convocation VI: Canterbury, 1444–1509* (Woodbridge, 2005).

A breefe discourse, declaring and approving the necessarie and inviolable maintenance of the laudable customes of London (London, 1584).

'A Brief Discourse upon the Commission of Bridewell', in James Spedding, Robert Leslie Ellis and Douglas Denon Heath (eds.), *The Works of Francis Bacon*, Vol. VII: *Literary and Professional Works* (London, 1859), pp. 509–16.

Brigden, Susan (ed.), 'The Letters of Richard Scudamore to Sir Philip Hoby, September 1549–March 1555', in *Camden Miscellany XXX* (Camden Society, 4th Series 39, London, 1990), pp. 67–148.

Bibliography

Brinklow, Henry, *Henry Brinklow's* Complaynt of Roderyck Mors … *and* The Lamentacyon of a Christen Agaynst the Cytye of London, ed. J. Meadows Cowper (Early English Text Society, Extra Series 22, London, 1874).

Bullinger, Heinrich, *The christen state of matrimonye*, trans. Miles Coverdale (Antwerp, 1541).

Butler, Cheryl (ed.), *The Book of Fines: The Annual Accounts of the Mayors of Southampton*, Vol. I: *1488–1540* (Southampton Records Series 41, Southampton, n.d.).

Calvin, John, *An epistle both of godly consolacion and also of advertisement … to the right noble Prince Edwarde Duke of Somerset* (London, 1550).

Chibnall, A. C. (ed.), *The Certificate of Musters for Buckinghamshire in 1522* (Buckinghamshire Record Society 17, 1973).

Chibnall, A. C. and A. Vere Woodman (eds.), *Subsidy Roll for the County of Buckingham, Anno 1524* (Buckinghamshire Record Society 8, 1950).

Christopherson, John, *An exhortation to all menne to take hede and beware of rebellion* (London, 1554).

Coke, Sir Edward, *The reports … faithfully rendered into English* (London, 1658).

Cornwall, Julian (ed.), *The Lay Subsidy Rolls for the County of Sussex, 1524–25* (Sussex Record Society 56, Lewes, 1956).

Cummings, Brian (ed.), *The Book of Common Prayer: The Texts of 1549, 1559, and 1662* (Oxford, 2011).

Darlington, Ida (ed.), *London Consistory Court Wills, 1492–1547* (London Record Society, London, 1967).

Dasent, John Roche (ed.), *Acts of the Privy Council …*, Vol. II: *1547–1550* (London, 1880).

Davies, Matthew (ed.), *The Merchant Taylors' Company of London: Court Minutes, 1486–1493* (Stamford, 2000).

Dyer, Alan and D. M. Palliser (eds.), *The Diocesan Population Returns for 1563 and 1603* (British Academy Records of Social and Economic History, New Series 31, Oxford, 2005).

Ellis, Sir Henry (ed.), *Original Letters Illustrative of English History: 3rd Series*, 4 vols. (London, 1846).

Elvey, E. M. (ed.), *The Courts of the Archdeaconry of Buckingham, 1483–1523* (Buckinghamshire Record Society 19, Welwyn Garden City, 1975).

Fish, Simon, *A Supplicacyon for the Beggers*, ed. F. J. Furnivall and J. Meadows Cowper (Early English Text Society, Extra Series 13, London, 1871).

Fletcher, W. G. D. (ed.), 'Documents Relating to Leicestershire, Preserved in the Episcopal Registers at Lincoln', *Associated Architectural and Archaeological Reports and Proceedings*, 21 (1891–2), 277–329, 22 (1893–4), 109–50, 227–365.

Gairdner, James (ed.), *The Historical Collections of a Citizen of London in the Fifteenth Century* (Camden Society, New Series 17, London, 1876).

Gee, Henry and William John Hardy (eds.), *Documents Illustrative of English Church History* (London, 1896).

Hale, William H., *A Series of Precedents and Proceedings in Criminal Causes . . . 1475 to 1640; Extracted from the Act-Books of Ecclesiastical Courts in the Diocese of London* (London, 1847).

Harper-Bill, Christopher (ed.), *The Register of John Morton, Archbishop of Canterbury, 1486–1500*, 3 vols. (Canterbury and York Society 75, 78, 89, Leeds and Woodbridge, 1987–2000).

Harrington, William, *The commendacions of matrymony* ([title page mutilated,? 1515]).

Harris, Mary Dormer (ed.), *The Coventry Leet Book: or Mayor's Register, Containing the Records of the City Court Leet or View of Frankpledge, A.D. 1420–1555*, 4 parts (Early English Text Society, Original Series 134, 135, 138, 146, London, 1907–13).

Hartley, T. E. (ed.), *Proceedings in the Parliaments of Elizabeth I*, Vol. I: *1558–1581* (Leicester, 1981).

Helmholz, R. H. (ed.), *Select Cases on Defamation to 1600* (Selden Society 101, London, 1985).

Helmholz, R. H. (ed.), *Three Civilian Notebooks, 1580–1640* (Selden Society 127, London, 2011 for 2010).

Henderson, Ernest F., *Select Historical Documents of the Middle Ages* (London, 1896).

Historical Manuscripts Commission, Twelfth Report, Appendix, Part IX (London, 1891).

Horrox, Rosemary (ed.), *The Parliament Rolls of Medieval England XV: Richard III, 1484–1485; Henry VII, 1485–1487* (Woodbridge, 2005).

Hughes, Paul L. and James F. Larkin (eds.), *Tudor Royal Proclamations*, 3 vols. (New Haven and London, 1964–9).

Hume, Martin A. Sharp (ed. and trans.), *Chronicle of King Henry VIII of England* (London, 1889).

Jeaffreson, John Cordy (ed.), *Middlesex County Records (Old Series)*, 4 vols. (London, 1886–92).

Keene, Derek and Ian Archer with Emma Pauncefort and Ann Saunders (eds.), *The Singularities of London, 1578. Les Singularitez de Londres, noble, fameuse Cité, capital du Royaume d'Angleterre: ses antiquitez et premiers fondateurs by L. Grenade* (London Topographical Society 175, 2014).

Kingsford, Charles Lethbridge (ed.), *Chronicles of London* (Oxford, 1905).

Kingsford, Charles Lethbridge (ed.), 'Two London Chronicles, from the Collections of John Stow', in *Camden Miscellany XII* (Camden Society, 3rd Series 18, London, 1910), pp. 1–57.

Latimer, Hugh, *The Sermons of Hugh Latimer*, ed. George Elwes Corrie (Parker Society, Cambridge, 1844).

Legrand, Jacques, *Here begynneth a lytell boke called good maners* (London, 1487 edn.).

Lempriere, William, *John Howes' MS., 1582, Being 'a Brief Note of the Order and Manner of the Proceedings in the First Erection of' the Three Royal Hospitals of Christ, Bridewell and St. Thomas the Apostle* (London, 1904).

Lyell, Lætitia and Frank D. Watney (eds.), *Acts of Court of the Mercers' Company, 1453–1527* (Cambridge, 1936).

Lynch, Margaret et al. (eds.), *Life, Love and Death in North-East Lancashire, 1510 to 1538: A Translation of the Act Book of the Ecclesiastical Court of Whalley* (Chetham Society, 3rd Series 46, Manchester, 2006).

Lyndwood, William, *Provinciale (seu constitutiones anglie)* (Oxford, 1679).

Lyndwood's Provinciale: The Text of the Canons Therein Contained, Reprinted from the Translation Made in 1534, ed. J. V. Bullard and H. Chalmer Bell (London, 1929).

McMurray, William (ed.), *The Records of Two City Parishes: A Collection of Documents Illustrative of the History of Ss. Anne and Agnes, Aldersgate, and St. John Zachary, London, from the Twelfth Century* (London, 1925).

McSheffrey, Shannon (ed.), *Love and Marriage in Late Medieval London* (Kalamazoo, MI, 1995).

Manuale secundum usum insignis ac preclare ecclesie Sarum (London, 1523).

Marshall, William, *The forme and maner of subvention or helpyng for pore people devysed and practysed in the cytie of Hypres in Flaunders* (London, 1535).

Memoranda, References, and Documents relating to the Royal Hospitals of the City of London (London, 1836).

More, Thomas, *The Complete Works . . .*, Vol. VI: *A Dialogue Concerning Heresies*, ed. Thomas M. C. Lawler, Germain Marc'hadour and Richard C. Marius (New Haven and London, 1981).

More, Thomas, *The Complete Works . . .*, Vol. VII: *Letter to Bugenhagen; Supplication of Souls; Letter against Frith*, ed. Frank Manley, Germain Marc'hadour, Richard C. Marius and Clarence H. Miller (New Haven and London, 1990).

More, Thomas, *The Complete Works . . .*, Vol. IX: *The Apology*, ed. J. B. Trapp (New Haven and London, 1979).

More, Thomas, *The Complete Works . . .*, Vol. X: *The Debellation of Salem and Bizance*, ed. John Guy, Ralph Keen, Clarence H. Miller and Ruth McGugan (New Haven and London, 1987).

A Myrour to Lewde Men and Wymmen: A Prose Version of the Speculum Vitae, ed. Venetia Nelson (Heidelberg, 1981).

Nicolas, Sir Harris (ed.), *Proceedings and Ordinances of the Privy Council of England*, Vol. VII: *32 Henry VIII. MDXL. to 33 Henry VIII. MDXLII* (London, 1837).

Nichols, John Gough (ed.), *The Diary of Henry Machyn, Citizen and Merchant-Taylor of London, from A.D. 1550 to A.D. 1563* (Camden Society, Old Series 42, London, 1848).

Nichols, John Gough (ed.), *Narratives of the Days of the Reformation* (Camden Society, Old Series 77, London, 1859).

Nichols, John Gough (ed.), *Literary Remains of King Edward VI*, 2 vols. (Roxburghe Club, London, 1857).

Nowell, Alexander, *A Catechism Written in Latin*, ed. George Elwes Corrie (Cambridge, 1853).

Parker, Sandra Lee and L. R. Poos, 'A Consistory Court from the Diocese of Rochester, 1363–4', *English Historical Review*, 106 (1991), 652–65.

Parliamentary Papers, 1840, XIX, Part 1, Thirty-Second Report of the Commissioners for Inquiring concerning Charities, Part VI.

Poos, L. R. (ed.), *Lower Ecclesiastical Jurisdiction in Late-Medieval England: The Courts of the Dean and Chapter of Lincoln, 1336–1349, and the Deanery of Wisbech, 1458–1484* (British Academy Records of Social and Economic History, New Series 32, Oxford, 2001).

Post, J. B., 'A Fifteenth-Century Customary of the Southwark Stews', *Journal of the Society of Archivists*, 5 (1974–7), 418–28.

Powicke, F. M. and C. R. Cheney (eds.), *Councils and Synods with Other Documents Relating to the English Church. II: A.D. 1205–1313* (Oxford, 1964).

Price, F. Douglas (ed.), *The Commission for Ecclesiastical Causes within the Dioceses of Bristol and Gloucester, 1574* (Bristol and Gloucestershire Archaeological Society, Records Section 10, Bristol, 1972).

Raine, James (ed.), *The Injunctions and Other Ecclesiastical Proceedings of Richard Barnes, Bishop of Durham, from 1575 to 1587* (Surtees Society 22, Durham, 1850).

Read, Conyers (ed.), *William Lambarde and Local Government: His 'Ephemeris' and Twenty-Nine Charges to Juries and Commissions* (Ithaca, NY, 1962).

Riley, Henry Thomas (ed.), *Munimenta Gildhallae Londoniensis*, 3 vols. (London, 1859–62).

Rimbault, Edward F. (ed.), *Cock Lorell's Bote: A Satirical Poem* (Percy Society, London, 1843).

Rodríguez-Salgado, M. J. and Simon Adams (eds.), 'The Count of Feria's Dispatch to Philip II of 14 November 1558', *Camden Miscellany XXVIII* (Camden Society, 4th Series 29, London, 1984), pp. 302–44.

Rymer, Thomas (ed.), *Foedera*, 10 vols., 3rd edn. (The Hague, 1739–45).

St German, Christopher, *A treatise concernynge the division betwene the spiritualtie and temporaltie* (London, [1532]).

St German, Christopher, *Salem and Byzance* (London, 1533).

Salter, H. E. (ed.), *A Subsidy Collected in the Diocese of Lincoln in 1526* (Oxford Historical Society 63, Oxford and London, 1909).

Salter, H. E. (ed.), *Registrum Annalium Collegii Mertonensis, 1483–1521* (Oxford Historical Society 76, Oxford, 1923).

Sandys, Edwin, *The Sermons of Edwin Sandys*, ed. John Ayre (Cambridge, 1841).

Sharpe, Reginald R. (ed.), *Calendar of Letter-Books ... of the City of London at the Guildhall. Letter-Book L. Temp. Edward IV–Henry VII* (London, 1912).

Smith, Lucy Toulmin (ed.), *The Maire of Bristowe Is Kalendar, by Robert Ricart, Town Clerk of Bristol 18 Edward IV* (Camden Society, New Series 5, London, 1872).

Stow, John, *The Survey of London*, ed. C. L. Kingsford, 2 vols. (Oxford, 1908).

Tanner, Norman (ed.), *Kent Heresy Proceedings, 1511–12* (Kent Records 26, Maidstone, 1997).

Tawney, R. H. and Eileen Power (eds.), *Tudor Economic Documents*, 3 vols. (London, 1924).

Thomas, A. H. and Philip E. Jones (eds.), *Calendar of Plea and Memoranda Rolls Preserved among the Archives of the Corporation of the City of London at the Guildhall*, 6 vols. (Cambridge, 1926–61).

Thomas, A. H. and I. D. Thornley (eds.), *The Great Chronicle of London* (London, 1938).

Thompson, A. Hamilton (ed.), *Visitations in the Diocese of Lincoln, 1517–1531*, 3 vols. (Lincoln Record Society 33, 35, 37, Hereford, 1940–7).

Vives, Juan Luis, *De subventione pauperum* [1526], ed. and trans. C. Mattheeussen and C. Fantazzi (Leiden, 2002).

Von Bülow, Gottfried (ed.), 'Journey through England and Scotland Made by Lupold von Wendel in the Years 1584 and 1585', *Transactions of the Royal Historical Society*, New Series, 9 (1895), 223–70.

Vowell alias Hooker, John, *The Description of the Citie of Excester*, ed. Walter J. Harte, J. W. Schopp and H. Tapley-Soper, 3 parts (Devon and Cornwall Record Society, Exeter, 1919–47).

Whitford, Richard, *A werke for housholders* (London, 1530).

Williams, C. H. (ed.), *English Historical Documents, 1485–1558* (London, 1971).

Winter, Christine L., 'The Portsoken Presentments: An Analysis of a London Ward in the 15th Century', *Transactions of the London and Middlesex Archaeological Society*, 56 (2005), 97–161.

Wood-Legh, K. L. (ed.), *Kentish Visitations of Archbishop William Warham and His Deputies, 1511–1512* (Kent Records 24, Maidstone, 1984).

Wright, Thomas (ed.), *Queen Elizabeth and Her Times: A Series of Original Letters*, 2 vols. (London, 1838).

Wriothesley, Charles, *A Chronicle of England during the Reigns of the Tudors, from A.D. 1485 to 1559*, ed. William Douglas Hamilton, 2 vols. (Camden Society, New Series 11, 20, London, 1875–7).

Select Secondary Works

Adair, Richard, *Courtship, Illegitimacy and Marriage in Early Modern England* (Manchester, 1996).

Albert, Thomas D., *Der gemeine Mann vor dem geistlichen Richter: Kirchliche Rechtsprechung in den Diözesen Basel, Chur und Konstanz vor der Reformation* (Stuttgart, 1998).

Archer, Ian W., *The Pursuit of Stability: Social Relations in Elizabethan London* (Cambridge, 1991).

Avis, P. D. L., 'Moses and the Magistrate: A Study in the Rise of Protestant Legalism', *Journal of Ecclesiastical History*, 26 (1975), 149–72.

Barron, Caroline M., 'Lay Solidarities: The Wards of Medieval London', in Pauline Stafford, Janet L. Nelson and Jane Martindale (eds.), *Law, Laity and Solidarities: Essays in Honour of Susan Reynolds* (Manchester, 2001), pp. 218–33.

Barron, Caroline M., *London in the Later Middle Ages: Government and People, 1200–1500* (Oxford, 2004).

Beaulande-Barraud, Véronique and Martine Charageat (eds.), *Les Officialités dans l'Europe médiévale et moderne. Des tribunaux pour une société chrétienne* (Turnhout, 2014).

Beier, Lee, 'Foucault *Redux*?: The Roles of Humanism, Protestantism, and an Urban Elite in Creating the London Bridewell, 1500–1560', in Louis A. Knafla (ed.), *Crime, Gender, and Sexuality in Criminal Prosecutions* (Criminal Justice History 17, Westport, CT, and London, 2002), pp. 33–60.

Bernard, G. W., *The King's Reformation: Henry VIII and the Remaking of the English Church* (New Haven and London, 2005).

Bernard, G. W., *The Late Medieval English Church: Vitality and Vulnerability before the Break with Rome* (New Haven and London, 2012).

Betteridge, Tom (ed.), *Sodomy in Early Modern Europe* (Manchester, 2002).

Boone, Marc, 'State Power and Illicit Sexuality: The Persecution of Sodomy in Late Medieval Bruges', *Journal of Medieval History*, 22 (1996), 135–53.

Bowker, Margaret, *The Secular Clergy in the Diocese of Lincoln, 1495–1520* (Cambridge, 1968).

Bowker, Margaret, 'Some Archdeacons' Court Books and the Commons' Supplication against the Ordinaries of 1532', in D. A. Bullough and R. L. Storey (eds.), *The Study of Medieval Records: Essays in Honour of Kathleen Major* (Oxford, 1971), pp. 282–316.

Bowker, Margaret, *The Henrician Reformation: The Diocese of Lincoln under John Longland, 1521–1547* (Cambridge, 1981).

Boyd, David Lorenzo and Ruth Mazo Karras, 'The Interrogation of a Male Transvestite Prostitute in Fourteenth-Century London', *GLQ*, 1 (1995), 479–85.

Bray, Alan, *Homosexuality in Renaissance England*, 2nd edn. (New York, 1995).

Brigden, Susan, *London and the Reformation* (Oxford, 1989).

Brooks, Christopher W., *Law, Politics and Society in Early Modern England* (Cambridge, 2008).

Brown, Andrew D., *Popular Piety in Late Medieval England: The Diocese of Salisbury, 1250–1550* (Oxford, 1995).

Brundage, James A., *Law, Sex and Christian Society in Medieval Europe* (Chicago and London, 1987).

Brundage, James A., *Medieval Canon Law* (London and New York, 1995).

Bryan, Lindsay, 'Marriage and Morals in the Fourteenth Century: The Evidence of Bishop Hamo's Register', *English Historical Review*, 121 (2006), 467–86.

Burghartz, Susanna, 'Ordering Discourse and Society: Moral Politics, Marriage, and Fornication during the Reformation and the Confessionalization Process in Germany and Switzerland', in Herman Roodenburg and Pieter Spierenburg (eds.), *Social Control in Europe*, Vol. I: *1500–1800* (Columbus, OH, 2004), pp. 78–98.

Butler, Sara M., *Divorce in Medieval England: From One to Two Persons in Law* (New York and London, 2013).

Capp, Bernard, 'The Double Standard Revisited: Plebeian Women and Male Sexual Reputation in Early Modern England', *Past and Present*, 162 (February 1999), 70–100.

Capp, Bernard, *When Gossips Meet: Women, Family, and Neighbourhood in Early Modern England* (Oxford, 2003).

Capp, Bernard, 'Bigamous Marriage in Early Modern England', *Historical Journal*, 52 (2009), 537–56.

Carlin, Martha, *Medieval Southwark* (London and Rio Grande, 1996).

Carlson, Eric Josef, *Marriage and the English Reformation* (Oxford, 1994).

Carlton, Katharine and Tim Thornton, 'Illegitimacy and Authority in the North of England, c. 1450–1640', *Northern History*, 48 (2011), 23–40.

Carr, David R., 'From Pollution to Prostitution: Supervising the Citizens of Fifteenth-Century Salisbury', *Southern History*, 19 (1997), 24–41.

Carrasco, Rafael, 'Lazarillo on a Street Corner: What the Picaresque Novel Did Not Say about Fallen Boys', in Alain Saint-Saëns (ed.), *Sex and Love in Golden Age Spain* (New Orleans, 1999), pp. 57–69.

Carrel, Helen, 'Disputing Legal Privilege: Civic Relations with the Church in Late Medieval England', *Journal of Medieval History*, 35 (2009), 279–96.

Carrel, Helen, 'The Ideology of Punishment in Late Medieval Towns', *Social History*, 34 (2009), 301–20.

Carroll, William C., *Fat King, Lean Beggar: Representations of Poverty in the Age of Shakespeare* (Ithaca and London, 1996).

Cavill, Paul, 'Heresy, Law and the State: Forfeiture in Late Medieval and Early Modern England', *English Historical Review*, 129 (2014), 270–95.

Clark, Peter, 'The Ecclesiastical Commission at Canterbury, 1572–1603', *Archaeologia Cantiana*, 89 (1974), 183–97.

Coleman, Janet, 'Scholastic Treatments of Maintaining One's *Fama* (Reputation/Good Name) and the Correction of Private "Passions" for the Public Good and Public Legitimacy', *Cultural and Social History*, 2 (2005), 23–48.

Collinson, Patrick, *The Religion of Protestants: The Church in English Society, 1559–1625* (Oxford, 1982).

Cooper, Tim, *The Last Generation of English Catholic Clergy: Parish Priests in the Diocese of Coventry and Lichfield in the Early Sixteenth Century* (Woodbridge, 1999).

Crankshaw, David J., 'Preparations for the Canterbury Provincial Convocation of 1562–63: A Question of Attribution', in Susan Wabuda and Caroline Litzenberger (eds.), *Belief and Practice in Reformation England: A Tribute to Patrick Collinson from His Students* (Aldershot, 1998), pp. 60–93.

Craun, Edwin D., 'The Imperatives of *Denunciatio*: Disclosing Others' Sins to Disciplinary Authorities', in Mary C. Flannery and Katie L. Walter (eds.), *The Culture of Inquisition in Medieval England* (Cambridge, 2013), pp. 30–44.

Crawford, David, 'The Rule of Law? The Laity, English Archdeacons' Courts and the Reformation to 1558', *Parergon*, New Series, 4 (1986), 155–73.

Crawford, Katherine, *European Sexualities, 1400–1800* (Cambridge, 2007).

Cross, Claire, 'Sin and Society: The Northern High Commission and the Northern Gentry in the Reign of Elizabeth I', in Claire Cross, David Loades and J. J. Scarisbrick (eds.), *Law and Government under the Tudors: Essays Presented to Sir Geoffrey Elton* (Cambridge, 1988), pp. 195–209.

Cullum, P. H., 'Clergy, Masculinity and Transgression in Late Medieval England', in D. M. Hadley (ed.), *Masculinity in Medieval Europe* (London, 1999), pp. 178–96.

Dabhoiwala, Faramerz, 'Summary Justice in Early Modern London', *English Historical Review*, 121 (2006), 796–822.

Dabhoiwala, Faramerz, *The Origins of Sex: A History of the First Sexual Revolution* (London, 2012).

Davidson, Nick, 'Theology, Nature and the Law: Sexual Sin and Sexual Crime in Italy from the Fourteenth to the Seventeenth Century', in Trevor Dean and K. J. P. Lowe (eds.), *Crime, Society and the Law in Renaissance Italy* (Cambridge, 1994), pp. 74–98.

Davies, Kathleen M., 'The Sacred Condition of Equality: How Original Were Puritan Doctrines of Marriage?', *Social History*, 5 (1977), 563–80.

DiGangi, Mario, 'How Queer Was the Renaissance?', in Katherine O'Donnell and Michael O'Rourke (eds.), *Love, Sex, Intimacy, and Friendship between Men, 1550–1800* (Basingstoke, 2003), pp. 128–47.

Donahue, Charles, Jr, 'Female Plaintiffs in Marriage Cases in the Court of York in the Later Middle Ages: What Can We Learn from the Numbers?', in Sue Sheridan Walker (ed.), *Wife and Widow in Medieval England* (Ann Arbor, MI, 1993), pp. 183–213.

Donahue, Charles, Jr, *Law, Marriage, and Society in the Later Middle Ages: Arguments about Marriage in Five Courts* (Cambridge, 2007).

Emmison, F. G., *Elizabethan Life: Morals and the Church Courts, Mainly from Essex Archidiaconal Records* (Chelmsford, 1973).

Euler, Carrie, 'Heinrich Bullinger, Marriage and the English Reformation: *The Christen State of Matrimonye* in England, 1540–53', *Sixteenth Century Journal*, 34 (2003), 367–93.

Farr, James R., *Authority and Sexuality in Early Modern Burgundy (1550–1730)* (Oxford and New York, 1995).

Finch, Andrew John, 'Parental Authority and the Problem of Clandestine Marriage in the Later Middle Ages', *Law and History Review*, 8 (1990), 189–204.

Finch, Andrew John, '*Repulsa uxore sua*: Marital Difficulties and Separation in the Later Middle Ages', *Continuity and Change*, 8 (1993), 11–38.

Finch, Andrew John, 'Sexual Morality and Canon Law: The Evidence of the Rochester Consistory Court', *Journal of Medieval History*, 20 (1994), 261–75.

Flemming, Rebecca, '*Quae corpore quaestum facit*: The Sexual Economy of Female Prostitution in the Roman Empire', *Journal of Roman Studies*, 89 (1999), 38–61.

Forrest, Ian, 'Defamation, Heresy and Late Medieval Social Life', in Linda Clark, Maureen Jurkowski and Colin Richmond (eds.), *Image, Text and Church, 1380–1600: Essays for Margaret Aston* (Toronto, 2009), pp. 142–61.

Forrest, Ian, 'The Survival of Medieval Visitation Records', *Archives*, 37 (2012), 1–10.

Forrest, Ian, 'The Transformation of Visitation in Thirteenth-Century England', *Past and Present*, 221 (November 2013), 3–38.

Fox, Eleanor and Martin Ingram, 'Bridewell, Bawdy Courts and Bastardy in Early Seventeenth-Century London', in Rebecca Probert (ed.), *Cohabitation and Non-Marital Births in England and Wales, 1600–2012* (Basingstoke, 2014), pp. 10–32, 215–17.

Foyster, Elizabeth A., *Manhood in Early Modern England: Honour, Sex and Marriage* (London and New York, 1999).

French, Katherine L., *The Good Women of the Parish: Gender and Religion after the Black Death* (Philadelphia, 2008).

Fuggles, J. F., 'The Parish Clergy in the Archdeaconry of Leicester, 1520–1540', *Transactions of the Leicestershire Archaeological and Historical Society*, 46 (1970–1), 25–44.

Giese, Loreen L., *Courtships, Marriage Customs, and Shakespeare's Comedies* (Basingstoke, 2006).

Goldberg, P. J. P., 'Women in Fifteenth-Century Town Life', in John A. F. Thomson (ed.), *Towns and Townspeople in the Fifteenth Century* (Gloucester, 1988), pp. 107–28.

Goldberg, P. J. P., *Women, Work, and Life Cycle in a Medieval Economy: Women in York and Yorkshire, c.1300–1520* (Oxford, 1992).

Goldberg, P. J. P., 'Pigs and Prostitutes: Streetwalking in Comparative Perspective', in Katharine J. Lewis, Noël James Menuge and Kim M. Phillips (eds.), *Young Medieval Women* (Stroud, 1999), pp. 172–93.

Goldberg, P. J. P., 'Coventry's "Lollard" Programme of 1492 and the Making of Utopia', in Rosemary Horrox and Sarah Rees Jones (eds.), *Pragmatic Utopias: Ideals and Communities, 1200–1630* (Cambridge, 2001), pp. 97–116.

Goldberg, P. J. P., 'Gender and Matrimonial Litigation in the Church Courts in the Later Middle Ages: The Evidence of the Court of York', *Gender and History*, 19 (2007), 43–59.

Goody, Jack, *The Development of the Family and Marriage in Europe* (Cambridge, 1983).

Gowing, Laura, *Domestic Dangers: Women, Words, and Sex in Early Modern London* (Oxford, 1996).

Graham, Michael F., *The Uses of Reform: 'Godly Discipline' and Popular Behaviour in Scotland and Beyond, 1560–1610* (Leiden, 1996).

Griffiths, Paul, 'The Structure of Prostitution in Elizabethan London', *Continuity and Change*, 8 (1993), 39–63.

Griffiths, Paul, *Youth and Authority: Formative Experiences in England, 1560–1640* (Oxford, 1996).

Griffiths, Paul, 'Contesting London Bridewell, 1576–1580', *Journal of British Studies*, 42 (2003), 283–315.

Griffiths, Paul, 'Building Bridewell: London's Self-Images, 1550–1640', in Norman L. Jones and Daniel Woolf (eds.), *Local Identities in Late Medieval and Early Modern England* (Basingstoke, 2007), pp. 228–48.

Griffiths, Paul, *Lost Londons: Change, Crime, and Control in the Capital City, 1550–1660* (Cambridge, 2008).

Guth, DeLloyd J., 'Enforcing Late-Medieval Law: Patterns in Litigation during Henry VII's Reign', in J. H. Baker (ed.), *Legal Records and the Historian: Papers Presented to the Cambridge Legal History Conference, 7–10 July 1975, and in Lincoln's Inn Old Hall on 3 July 1974* (London, 1978), pp. 80–96.

Haigh, Christopher, 'Anticlericalism and the English Reformation', *History*, 68 (1983), 391–407.

Haigh, Christopher, *English Reformations: Religion, Politics, and Society under the Tudors* (Oxford, 1993).

Haliczer, Stephen (ed.), *Inquisition and Society in Early Modern Europe* (London, 1987).

Haliczer, Stephen, *Inquisition and Society in the Kingdom of Valencia, 1478–1834* (Berkeley, CA, 1990).

Hammer, Paul E. J., 'Sex and the Virgin Queen: Aristocratic Concupiscence and the Court of Elizabeth I', *Sixteenth Century Journal*, 31 (2000), 77–97.

Harper-Bill, Christopher, 'Dean Colet's Convocation Sermon and the Pre-Reformation Church in England', *History*, 73 (1988), 191–210.

Harrington, Joel F., *Reordering Marriage and Society in Reformation Germany* (Cambridge, 1995).

Heath, Peter, *The English Parish Clergy on the Eve of the Reformation* (London and Toronto, 1969).

Helmholz, R. H., *Marriage Litigation in Medieval England* (Cambridge, 1974).

Helmholz, R. H., *Roman Canon Law in Reformation England* (Cambridge, 1990).

Helmholz, R. H., 'Harboring Sexual Offenders: Ecclesiastical Courts and Controlling Misbehavior', *Journal of British Studies*, 37 (1998), 258–68.

Helmholz, R. H., 'Judges and Trials in the English Ecclesiastical Courts', in Maureen Mulholland and Brian Pullan with Anne Pullan (eds.), *Judicial Tribunals in England and Europe, 1200–1700: The Trial in History*, Vol. I (Manchester and New York, 2003), pp. 102–16.

Helmholz, R. H., *The Oxford History of the Laws of England*, Vol. I: *The Canon Law and Ecclesiastical Jurisdiction from 597 to the 1640s* (Oxford, 2004).

Higgs, Laquita M., *Godliness and Governance in Tudor Colchester* (Ann Arbor, MI, 1998).

Hindle, Steve, *The State and Social Change in Early Modern England, c. 1550–1640* (Basingstoke, 2000).

Houlbrooke, Ralph, 'The Protestant Episcopate, 1547–1603: The Pastoral Contribution', in Felicity Heal and Rosemary O'Day (eds.), *Church and Society in England: Henry VIII to James I* (London and Basingstoke, 1977), pp. 78–98, 182–3, 193–4.

Houlbrooke, Ralph, *Church Courts and the People during the English Reformation, 1520–1570* (Oxford, 1979).

Houlbrooke, Ralph, 'Bishop Nykke's Last Visitation, 1532', in M. J. Franklin and Christopher Harper-Bill (eds.), *Medieval Ecclesiastical Studies in Honour of Dorothy M. Owen* (Woodbridge, 1995), pp. 113–29.

Hoyle, R. W., 'The Origins of the Dissolution of the Monasteries', *Historical Journal*, 38 (1995), 275–305.

Hunt, Alan, *Governance of the Consuming Passions: A History of Sumptuary Law* (Basingstoke, 1996).

Ingram, Martin, *Church Courts, Sex and Marriage in England, 1570–1640* (Cambridge, 1987).

Ingram, Martin, '"Scolding Women Cucked or Washed": A Crisis in Gender Relations in Early Modern England?', in Jenny Kermode and Garthine Walker (eds.), *Women, Crime and the Courts in Early Modern England* (London, 1994), pp. 48–80.

Ingram, Martin, 'Puritans and the Church Courts, 1560–1640', in Christopher Durston and Jacqueline Eales (eds.), *The Culture of English Puritanism, 1560–1700* (Basingstoke, 1996), pp. 58–91, 288–95.

Ingram, Martin, 'Reformation of Manners in Early Modern England', in Paul Griffiths, Adam Fox and Steve Hindle (eds.), *The Experience of Authority in Early Modern England* (Basingstoke, 1996), pp. 47–88.

Ingram, Martin, 'History of Sin or History of Crime? The Regulation of Personal Morality in England, 1450–1750', in Heinz Schilling (ed.), *Institutionen, Instrumente und Akteure sozialer Kontrolle und Disziplinierung im frühneuzeitlichen Europa* (Frankfurt am Main, 1999), pp. 87–103.

Ingram, Martin, 'Law, Litigants and the Construction of "Honour": Slander Suits in Early Modern England', in Peter Coss (ed.), *The Moral World of the Law* (Cambridge, 2000), pp. 134–60.

Ingram, Martin, 'Regulating Sex in Pre-Reformation London', in G. W. Bernard and S. J. Gunn (eds.), *Authority and Consent in Tudor England: Essays Presented to C. S. L. Davies* (Aldershot, 2002), pp. 79–95.

Ingram, Martin, 'Shame and Pain: Themes and Variations in Tudor Punishments', in Simon Devereaux and Paul Griffiths (eds.), *Penal Practice and Culture, 1500–1900: Punishing the English* (Basingstoke, 2004), pp. 36–62.

Ingram, Martin, 'Church Courts in Tudor England (1485–1603): Continuities, Changes, Transformations', in Véronique Beaulande-Barraud and Martine Charageat (eds.), *Les Officialités dans l'Europe médiévale et moderne. Des tribunaux pour une société chrétienne* (Turnhout, 2014), pp. 91–105.

Ingram, Martin, '"Popular" and "Official" Justice: Punishing Sexual Offenders in Tudor London', in Fernanda Pirie and Judith Scheele (eds.), *Legalism: Community and Justice* (Oxford, 2014), pp. 201–26.

Ingram, Martin, 'Cohabitation in Context in Early Seventeenth-Century London', in Rebecca Probert (ed.), *Cohabitation and Non-Marital Births in England and Wales, 1600–2012* (Basingstoke, 2014), pp. 33–50, 217–19.

Jagger, Meriel, 'Bonner's Episcopal Visitation of London, 1554', *Bulletin of the Institute of Historical Research*, 45 (1972), 306–11.

Jones, Karen, *Gender and Petty Crime in Late Medieval England: The Local Courts in Kent, 1460–1560* (Woodbridge, 2006).

Kamen, Henry, *Inquisition and Society in Spain in the Sixteenth and Seventeenth Centuries* (London, 1985).

Kamen, Henry, *The Phoenix and the Flame: Catalonia and the Counter Reformation* (New Haven and London, 1993).

Karras, Ruth Mazo, 'The Latin Vocabulary of Illicit Sex in English Ecclesiastical Court Records', *Journal of Medieval Latin*, 2 (1992), 1–17.

Karras, Ruth Mazo, *Common Women: Prostitution and Sexuality in Medieval England* (New York and Oxford, 1996).

Karras, Ruth Mazo, 'Two Models, Two Standards: Moral Teaching and Sexual Mores', in Barbara A. Hanawalt and David Wallace (eds.), *Bodies and Disciplines: Intersections of Literature and History in Fifteenth-Century England* (Minneapolis, 1996), pp. 123–38.

Karras, Ruth Mazo, *Sexuality in Medieval Europe: Doing unto Others* (New York and London, 2005).

Karras, Ruth Mazo, 'The Regulation of Sexuality in the Late Middle Ages: England and France', *Speculum*, 86 (2011), 1010–39.

Karras, Ruth Mazo, *Unmarriages: Women, Men, and Sexual Unions in the Middle Ages* (Philadelphia, 2012).

Kelly, Henry Ansgar, 'Bishop, Prioress, and Bawd in the Stews of Southwark', *Speculum*, 75 (2000), 342–88.

Kelly, Henry Ansgar, 'Inquisition, Public Fame and Confession: General Rules and English Practice', in Mary C. Flannery and Katie L. Walter (eds.), *The Culture of Inquisition in Medieval England* (Cambridge, 2013), pp. 8–29.

Kent, Joan, 'Attitudes of Members of the House of Commons to the Regulation of "Personal Conduct" in Late Elizabethan and Early Stuart England', *Bulletin of the Institute of Historical Research*, 46 (1973), 41–71.

Kettle, Ann J., 'City and Close: Lichfield in the Century before the Reformation', in Caroline M. Barron and Christopher Harper-Bill (eds.), *The Church in Pre-Reformation Society: Essays in Honour of F. R. H. Du Boulay* (Woodbridge, 1985), pp. 158–69.

Kettle, Ann J., 'Ruined Maids: Prostitutes and Servant Girls in Later Medieval England', in Robert R. Edwards and Vickie Ziegler (eds.), *Matrons and Marginal Women in Medieval Society* (Woodbridge, 1995), pp. 19–31.

King, Helen, *The One-Sex Body on Trial: The Classical and Early Modern Evidence* (Farnham, 2013).

King, Walter J., 'Punishment for Bastardy in Early Seventeenth-Century England', *Albion*, 10 (1978), 130–51.

Kingdon, Robert M., *Adultery and Divorce in Calvin's Geneva* (Cambridge, MA, and London, 1995).

Kümin, Beat A., *The Shaping of a Community: The Rise and Reformation of the English Parish, c.1400–1560* (Aldershot, 1996).

Lander, Stephen, 'Church Courts and the Reformation in the Diocese of Chichester, 1500–58', in Rosemary O'Day and Felicity Heal (eds.), *Continuity and Change: Personnel and Administration of the Church of England, 1500–1642* (Leicester, 1976), pp. 215–37, 280–4.

Laqueur, Thomas, *Making Sex: Body and Gender from the Greeks to Freud* (Cambridge, MA, and London, 1990).

Laslett, Peter, *The World We Have Lost: Further Explored* (London, 1983).

Laslett, Peter, Karla Oosterveen and Richard M. Smith (eds.), *Bastardy and Its Comparative History* (London, 1980).

Lidman, Satu, *Zum Spektakel und Abscheu. Schand- und Ehrenstrafen als Mittel öffentlicher Disziplinierung in München um 1600* (Frankfurt am Main, 2008).

Linkinen, Tom, *Same-Sex Sexuality in Later Medieval English Culture* (Amsterdam, 2015).

McDougall, Sara, 'The Prosecution of Sex in Late Medieval Troyes', in Albrecht Classen (ed.), *Sexuality in the Middle Ages and the Early Modern Times: New Approaches to a Fundamental Cultural-Historical and Literary-Anthropological Theme* (Berlin, 2008), pp. 691–713.

McDougall, Sara, 'Bigamy: A Male Crime in Medieval Europe?', *Gender and History*, 22 (2010), 430–46.

McDougall, Sara, *Bigamy and Christian Identity in Late Medieval Champagne* (Philadelphia, 2012).

McIntosh, Marjorie Keniston, *Controlling Misbehavior in England, 1370–1600* (Cambridge, 1998).

McIntosh, Terence, 'Confessionalization and the Campaign against Prenuptial Coitus in Sixteenth-Century Germany', in John M. Headley, Hans J. Hillerbrand and Anthony J. Papalas (eds.), *Confessionalization in Europe, 1555–1700: Essays in Honour and Memory of Bodo Nischan* (Aldershot, 2004), pp. 155–74.

McLaren, Colin A., 'An Early 16th Century Act Book of the Diocese of London', *Journal of the Society of Archivists*, 3 (1965–9), 336–41.

McRee, Ben R., 'Religious Gilds and Regulation of Behavior in Late Medieval Towns', in Joel Rosenthal and Colin Richmond (eds.), *People, Politics and Community in the Later Middle Ages* (Gloucester, 1987), pp. 108–22.

McSheffrey, Shannon, '"I will never have none ayenst my faders will": Consent and the Making of Marriage in the Late Medieval Diocese of London', in Constance M. Rousseau and Joel T. Rosenthal (eds.), *Women, Marriage, and Family in Medieval Christendom: Essays in Memory of Michael M. Sheehan* (Kalamazoo, MI, 1998), pp. 153–74.

McSheffrey, Shannon, 'Jurors, Respectable Masculinity, and Christian Morality', *Journal of British Studies*, 37 (1998), 269–78.

McSheffrey, Shannon, 'Men and Masculinity in Late Medieval London Civic Culture: Governance, Patriarchy and Reputation', in Jacqueline Murray (ed.), *Conflicted Identities and Multiple Masculinities: Men in the Medieval West* (New York and London, 1999), pp. 243–78.

McSheffrey, Shannon, *Marriage, Sex, and Civic Culture in Late Medieval London* (Philadelphia, 2006).

McSheffrey, Shannon, 'Whoring Priests and Godly Citizens: Law, Morality, and Clerical Sexual Misconduct in Late Medieval London', in Norman L. Jones and Daniel Woolf (eds.), *Local Identities in Late Medieval and Early Modern England* (Basingstoke, 2007), pp. 50–70.

Maddern, Philippa C., 'Order and Disorder', in Carole Rawcliffe and Richard Wilson (eds.), *Medieval Norwich* (London, 2004), pp. 189–212, 382–6.

Maddern, Philippa C., 'Moving Households: Geographical Mobility and Serial Monogamy in England, 1350–1500', *Parergon*, 24 (2007), 69–92.

Maddern, Philippa C., '"Oppressed by Utter Poverty": Survival Strategies for Single Mothers and their Children in Late Medieval England', in Anne M. Scott (ed.), *Experiences of Poverty in Late Medieval and Early Modern England and France* (Farnham, 2012), pp. 41–62.

Manning, Roger B., *Religion and Society in Elizabethan Sussex: A Study of the Enforcement of the Religious Settlement, 1558–1603* (Leicester, 1969).

Manzione, Carol Kazmierczak, *Christ's Hospital of London, 1552–1598: 'A Passing Deed of Pity'* (Selinsgrove, PA, 1995).

Manzione, Carol Kazmierczak, 'Sex in Tudor London: Abusing Their Bodies with Each Other', in Jacqueline Murray and Konrad Eisenbichler (eds.), *Desire and Discipline: Sex and Sexuality in the Premodern West* (Toronto, 1996), pp. 87–100.

Marshall, Peter, *The Catholic Priesthood and the English Reformation* (Oxford, 1994).

Marshall, Peter, 'Anticlericalism Revested? Expressions of Discontent in Early Tudor England', in Clive Burgess and Eamon Duffy (eds.), *The Parish in Late Medieval England: Proceedings of the 2002 Harlaxton Symposium* (Donington, 2006), pp. 365–80.

Mentzer, Raymond A. (ed.), *Sin and the Calvinists: Morals Control and the Consistory in the Reformed Tradition* (Kirksville, MO, 1994).

Merritt, J. F., *The Social World of Early Modern Westminster: Abbey, Court and Community, 1525–1640* (Manchester, 2005).

Minson, Stuart, 'Public Punishment and Urban Space in Early Tudor London', *London Topographical Record*, 30 (2010), 1–16.

Monter, E. William, *Enforcing Morality in Early Modern Europe* (London, 1987).

Murdock, Graeme, *Beyond Calvin: The Intellectual, Political and Cultural World of Europe's Reformed Churches, c.1540–1620* (Basingstoke, 2004).

Naphy, William G., 'Reasonable Doubt: Defences Advanced in Early Modern Sodomy Trials in Geneva', in Maureen Mulholland and Brian Pullan with Anne Pullan (eds.), *Judicial Tribunals in England and Europe, 1200–1700: The Trial in History*, Vol. I (Manchester, 2003), pp. 129–46.

Norberg, Kathryn, 'Prostitutes', in Natalie Zemon Davis and Arlette Farge (eds.), *A History of Women in the West*, Vol. III: *Renaissance and Enlightenment Paradoxes* (Cambridge, MA, and London, 1993), pp. 458–74, 540.

O'Donoghue, Edward Geoffrey, *Bridewell Hospital: Palace, Prison, Schools from the Earliest Times to the End of the Reign of Elizabeth* (London, 1923).

O'Hara, Diana, *Courtship and Constraint: Rethinking the Making of Marriage in Tudor England* (Manchester, 2000).

Otis, Leah Lydia, *Prostitution in Medieval Society: The History of an Urban Institution in Languedoc* (Chicago, 1985).

Outhwaite, R. B., *The Rise and Fall of the English Ecclesiastical Courts, 1500–1860* (Cambridge, 2006).

Parish, Helen L., *Clerical Marriage and the English Reformation: Precedent, Policy, and Practice* (Aldershot, 2000).

Parish, Helen L., *Clerical Celibacy in the West: c.1100–1700* (Farnham, 2010).

Payer, Pierre J., *The Bridling of Desire: Views of Sex in the Later Middle Ages* (Toronto and London, 1993).

Pedersen, Frederik, *Marriage Disputes in Medieval England* (London, 2000).

Peters, Christine, *Patterns of Piety: Women, Gender and Religion in Late Medieval and Reformation England* (Cambridge, 2003).

Pollmann, Judith, 'Off the Record: Problems in the Quantification of Calvinist Church Discipline', *Sixteenth Century Journal*, 33 (2002), 423–38.

Poos, L. R., 'Sex, Lies, and the Church Courts of Pre-Reformation England', *Journal of Interdisciplinary History*, 25 (1994–5), 585–607.

Poos, L. R., 'The Heavy-Handed Marriage Counsellor: Regulating Marriage in Some Later-Medieval English Local Ecclesiastical-Court Jurisdictions', *American Journal of Legal History*, 39 (1995), 291–309.

Poos, L. R., 'Ecclesiastical Courts, Marriage, and Sexuality in Late Medieval Europe', in Troels Dahlerup and Per Ingesman (eds.), *New Approaches to the History of Late Medieval and Early Modern Europe: Selected Proceedings of Two International Conferences at the Danish Royal Academy of Sciences and Letters in Copenhagen in 1997 and 1999* (Copenhagen, 2009), pp. 181–207.

Postles, Dave, 'Penance and the Market Place: A Reformation Dialogue with the Medieval Church (c.1250–c.1600)', *Journal of Ecclesiastical History*, 54 (2003), 441–68.

Price, F. Douglas, 'The Commission for Ecclesiastical Causes for the Dioceses of Bristol and Gloucester, 1574', *Transactions of the Bristol and Gloucestershire Archaeological Society*, 59 (1937), 61–184.

Price, F. Douglas, 'Gloucester Diocese under Bishop Hooper, 1551–3', *Transactions of the Bristol and Gloucestershire Archaeological Society*, 60 (1939 for 1938), 51–151.

Price, F. Douglas, 'The Abuses of Excommunication and the Decline of Ecclesiastical Discipline under Queen Elizabeth', *English Historical Review*, 57 (1942), 106–15.

Puff, Helmut, *Sodomy in Reformation Germany and Switzerland, 1400–1600* (Chicago, 2003).

Rappaport, Steve, *Worlds within Worlds: Structures of Life in Sixteenth-Century London* (Cambridge, 1989).

Rexroth, Frank, *Deviance and Power in Late Medieval London*, trans. Pamela E. Selwyn (Cambridge, 2007).

Rickman, Johanna, *Love, Lust and License in Early Modern England: Illicit Sex and the Nobility* (Aldershot, 2008).

Rocke, Michael, *Forbidden Friendships: Homosexuality and Male Culture in Renaissance Florence* (Oxford and New York, 1996).

Roper, Lyndal, *The Holy Household: Women and Morals in Reformation Augsburg* (Oxford, 1989).

Ross, Richard J., 'Distinguishing Eternal from Transient Law: Natural Law and the Judicial Laws of Moses', *Past and Present*, 217 (November 2012), 79–115.

Rosser, Gervase, *Medieval Westminster, 1200–1540* (Oxford, 1989).

Rossiaud, Jacques, *Medieval Prostitution*, trans. Lydia G. Cochrane (Oxford, 1988).

Safley, Thomas Max, *Let No Man Put Asunder. The Control of Marriage in the German Southwest: A Comparative Study, 1550–1600* (Kirksville, MO, 1984).

Saint-Saëns, Alain, "'It Is Not a Sin!" Making Love According to the Spaniards in Early Modern Spain', in Alain Saint-Saëns (ed.), *Sex and Love in Golden Age Spain* (New Orleans, 1999), pp. 11–26.

Salkeld, Duncan, *Shakespeare among the Courtesans: Prostitution, Literature, and Drama, 1500–1650* (Farnham, 2012).

Schilling, Heinz, *Civic Calvinism in Northwestern Germany and the Netherlands: Sixteenth to Nineteenth Centuries* (Kirksville, MO, 1991).

Schmidt, Heinrich R., *Dorf und Religion: Reformierte Sittenzucht in Berner Landgemeinden der Frühen Neuzeit* (Stuttgart, 1995).

Schuster, Beate, *Die unendlichen Frauen. Prostitution und städtische Ordnung in Konstanz in 15. und 16. Jahrhundert* (Constance, 1996).

Seaver, Paul, 'Introduction' to 'Symposium: Controlling (Mis)Behavior', *Journal of British Studies*, 37 (1998), 231–45.

Sère, Bénédicte and Jörg Wettlaufer (eds.), *Shame between Punishment and Penance. La honte entre peine et pénitence* (Florence, 2013).

Sheehan, M. M., 'The Formation and Stability of Marriage in Fourteenth-Century England: Evidence of an Ely Register', *Medieval Studies*, 33 (1971), 228–63.

Sheils, W. J., 'Erecting the Discipline in Provincial England: The Order of Northampton, 1571', in James Kirk (ed.), *Humanism and Reform: The Church in Europe, England, and Scotland, 1400–1643. Essays in Honour of James K. Cameron* (Studies in Church History, Subsidia 8, Oxford, 1991), pp. 331–45.

Shepard, Alexandra, *Meanings of Manhood in Early Modern England* (Oxford, 2003).

Simons, Patricia, *The Sex of Men in Premodern Europe: A Cultural History* (Cambridge, 2011).

Slack, Paul, *From Reformation to Improvement: Public Welfare in Early Modern England* (Oxford, 1999).

Smith, Bruce R., *Homosexual Desire in Shakespeare's England: A Cultural Poetics* (Chicago and London, 1991).

Smith, Llinos Beverley, 'A View from an Ecclesiastical Court: Mobility and Marriage in a Border Society at the End of the Middle Ages', in R. R. Davies and Geraint H. Jenkins (eds.), *From Medieval to Modern Wales: Historical Essays in Honour of Kenneth O. Morgan and Ralph A. Griffiths* (Cardiff, 2004), pp. 64–80.

Smith, Richard Dean, *The Middling Sort and the Politics of Social Reformation: Colchester, 1570–1640* (New York, 2004).

Smith, Richard M., 'Marriage Processes in the English Past: Some Continuities', in Lloyd Bonfield, Richard M. Smith, and Keith Wrightson (eds.), *The World We Have Gained: Histories of Population and Social Structure. Essays Presented to Peter Laslett on His Seventieth Birthday* (Oxford, 1986), pp. 43–99.

Strasser, Ulrike, *State of Virginity: Gender, Religion and Politics in an Early Modern Catholic State* (Ann Arbor, MI, 2004).

Swanson, R. N., 'Angels Incarnate: Clergy and Masculinity from Gregorian Reform to Reformation', in D. M. Hadley (ed.), *Masculinity in Medieval Europe* (London, 1999), pp. 160–77.

Tarbin, Stephanie, 'Moral Regulation and Civic Identity in London 1400–1530', in Linda Rasmussen, Valerie Spear and Dianne Tillotson (eds.), *Our Medieval Heritage: Essays in Honour of John Tillotson for His 60th Birthday* (Cardiff, 2002), pp. 126–36.

Tarbin, Stephanie, 'Civic Manliness in London, c.1380–1550', in Susan Broomhall and Jacqueline Van Gent (eds.), *Governing Masculinities in the Early Modern Period: Regulating Selves and Others* (Farnham, 2011), pp. 23–45.

Tentler, Thomas N., *Sin and Confession on the Eve of the Reformation* (Princeton, NJ, 1977).

Thayer, Anne T., *Penitence, Preaching and the Coming of the Reformation* (Aldershot, 2002).

Thomas, Keith, 'The Double Standard', *Journal of the History of Ideas*, 20 (1959), 195–216.

Thomas, Keith, 'The Puritans and Adultery: The Act of 1650 Reconsidered', in Donald Pennington and Keith Thomas (eds.), *Puritans and Revolutionaries: Essays in Seventeenth-Century History Presented to Christopher Hill* (Oxford, 1978), pp. 257–82.

Todd, Margo, *The Culture of Protestantism in Early Modern Scotland* (New Haven and London, 2002).

Tucker, Penny, *Law Courts and Lawyers in the City of London, 1300–1550* (Cambridge, 2007).

Usher, Roland G., *The Rise and Fall of the High Commission*, 2nd edn., with introduction by Philip Tyler (Oxford, 1968).

Von Friedeburg, Robert, 'Reformation of Manners and the Social Composition of Offenders in an East Anglian Cloth Village: Earls Colne, Essex, 1531–1642', *Journal of British Studies*, 29 (1990), 347–85.

Walsham, Alexandra, *Providence in Early Modern England* (Oxford, 1999).

Watt, Jeffrey R., *The Making of Modern Marriage: Matrimonial Control and the Rise of Sentiment in Neuchâtel, 1550–1800* (Ithaca and London, 1992).

Watts, John, '"Common Weal" and "Commonwealth": England's Monarchical Republic in the Making, c.1450–1530', in Andrea Gamberini, Jean-Paul Genet and Andrea Zorzi (eds.), *The Languages of Political Society: Western Europe, 14th–17th Centuries* (Rome, 2011), pp. 147–63.

Werner, Janelle, 'Promiscuous Priests and Vicarage Children: Clerical Sexuality and Masculinity in Late Medieval England', in Jennifer D. Thibodeaux (ed.), *Negotiating Clerical Identities: Priests, Monks and Masculinity in the Middle Ages* (Basingstoke, 2010), pp. 159–81.

Wiesner-Hanks, Merry E., *Christianity and Sexuality in the Early Modern World: Regulating Desire, Reforming Practice* (London, 2000).

Woodcock, Brian L., *Medieval Ecclesiastical Courts in the Diocese of Canterbury* (London, 1952).

Wrightson, Keith, *English Society, 1580–1680* (London, 1982).

Wrightson, Keith, and David Levine, *Poverty and Piety in an English Village: Terling, 1525–1700*, 2nd edn. (Oxford, 1995).

Wunderli, Richard M., *London Church Courts and Society on the Eve of the Reformation* (Cambridge, MA, 1981).

Wunderli, Richard M., 'Pre-Reformation London Summoners and the Murder of Richard Hunne', *Journal of Ecclesiastical History*, 33 (1982), 209–24.

Index

abortion, 135, 384

absolution, 205, 250, *See* excommunication

Adair, Richard, 25

adultery, 1–2, 4, 7, 8, 29, 44, 65, 71, 86, 93–6, 100,
107, 109, 111, 115, 117, 120, 123, 125, 127, 130,
133, 134, 141, 160, 169, 170, 172, 173, 178, 179,
181, 185, 188, 189, 191–3, 194, 195, 196, 199,
203, 207, 210, 211, 218, 219, 221, 222, 223, 224,
226, 235, 254, 256, 257, 258, 260, 263, 264,
269, 271, 277, 278, 283, 294, 300, 306, 319,
324, 326, 327–8, 332, 333, 339, 340, 344, 345,
346, 348, 358, 369, 374, 376, 377, 379, 382,
387, 393, 395, 401, 403, 404, 405, 406, 422–3,
425, *See also* statutes

   as grounds for divorce, 279–80, 281, 421

   debates about punishment, 9, 273–4, 278–80,
310–12, 401

   double standard, 93

   salience in patterns of prosecution, 3, 95,
393, 403

aiding and abetting sexual offences, 103–4,
123, 130, 133, 170, 187–8, 201, 259, 327,
332, 375–6, 387, 414–15, *See also* bawds,
bawdry

Alcock, John, 257

alehouses and inns, 14, 72, 119, 125, 129, 139, 159,
192, 257, 289, 304, 353, 383, 394, 404, 426, *See
also* London inns and taverns; Southwark
inns

Allen, Sir John, 293n.76

Alley, William, 348, 349

Amersham (Bucks.), 107

Angmering, West (Sussex), 71

annulment. *See* marriage

antenuptial incontinence, 25, 28, 98, 330, 333, 334,
337, 339, 384, 403, 412, 415–17, 423

Antichrist, 269

anticlericalism, 23, 150, 239–43, 275

apparel. *See* sumptuary laws

apparitors. *See* summoners

apprentices, 15, 24, 26, 49, 129, 189, 234, 286, 299,
301, 307, 362, 364, 365, 368, 373, 374, 381,
386, 397, 404, 414, 418

arbitration, 62, 68

archdeacons, 79, 82, 394, *See also* Calfhill, James;
Louth, John

Archer, Ian, 21, 174, 271, 356, 357, 364

Aristotle, 75, 140

Armstrong, Clement, 275

Arthur, Thomas, 264

articles for ecclesiastical government (1563), 317,
318, 319

Arundel (Sussex), 250

   countess of. *See* Fitzalan, Anne

   earls of. *See* Fitzalan, Henry; Fitzalan, William

Ashby de la Zouch (Leics.), 112, 321

Ashleworth (Glos.), 51

Aston Flamville (Leics.), 102

astrology, 226

Atwater, William, 111

Augsburg, 291

Augustine, St, 140

Avenon, Sir Alexander, 365

Babylon, Whore of, 268

Bacon, Francis, 359

Baker, Matthew, 153

Bale, John, 37

banishment. *See* punishments

Barking (Essex)

   deanery, 176, 203

   monastery, 264

Barlow, William, 323

Barne, Sir George, 300, 303

Barnes, Margaret, alias Long Meg of
Westminster, 302, 388

Barons, William, 199

barrators, barratry, 216, 218

Barrow (Leics.), 99

Basille, Thomas. *See* Becon, Thomas

454

Index